GUIDE®

Thirty-fifth Edition

THE SANFORD GUIDE TO ANTIMICROBIAL THERAPY 2005

David N. Gilbert, M.D.
Director of Medical Education & Earl A. Chiles Research Institute
Providence Portland Medical Center
Professor of Medicine
Oregon Health Sciences University
Portland, Oregon

Robert C. Moellering, Jr., M.D.
Physician-in-Chief, Beth Israel Deaconess Medical Center
Herman L. Blumgart Professor of Medicine
Harvard Medical School
Boston, Massachusetts

George M. Eliopoulos, M.D.
Chief, James L. Tullis Firm, Beth Israel Deaconess Hospital
Professor of Medicine
Harvard Medical School
Boston, Massachusetts

Merle A. Sande, M.D.
Clarence M. & Ruth N. Birrer Professor of Medicine
University of Utah School of Medicine
Salt Lake City, Utah

THE SANFORD GUIDE TO ANTIMICROBIAL THERAPY 2005
35TH EDITION

Jay P. Sanford, M.D.
1928-1996

Editors

David N. Gilbert, M.D.
George M. Eliopoulos, M.D.

Robert C. Moellering, Jr., M.D.
Merle A. Sande, M.D.

The Sanford Guides are published annually by

ANTIMICROBIAL THERAPY, INC.
P.O. Box 70, 229 Main Street, Hyde Park, VT 05655 USA
Tel 802-888-2855 Fax 802-888-2874
Email: info@sanfordguide.com   www.sanfordguide.com

Printed in the United States of America
ISBN 978-1-930808-22-4
Pocket Edition (English)

PUBLISHER'S PREFACE

This edition marks the 35th revision of the SANFORD GUIDE TO ANTIMICROBIAL THERAPY. The genesis of the SANFORD GUIDE was a grand rounds lecture by Jay P. Sanford on new antibiotics (amoxicillin). The lecture handout was a table, organized by anatomic site, summarizing etiologies, suggested regimens and comments on therapy. This handout became, and remains, the core of the SANFORD GUIDE -- Table 1 --Initial Choice of Antimicrobial Therapy. As the issues in treatment of infectious diseases have grown in number and complexity, the SANFORD GUIDE has evolved and expanded. Yet it remains consistent with Jay P. Sanford's vision: to provide the professional with a handy, up-to-date reference tool to assist in making informed clinical decisions.

Though many readers of the SANFORD GUIDE receive their copy from a pharmaceutical company representative, please be assured that the SANFORD GUIDE has been, and continues to be, independently prepared and published since its inception in 1969. Decisions regarding the content of the SANFORD GUIDE are solely those of the editors and the publisher. We welcome your questions, comments and feedback concerning the SANFORD GUIDE. All of your feedback is reviewed and taken into account in preparing the next edition.

NOTE TO READER

Every effort is made to ensure the accuracy of the content of this guide. However, current full prescribing information available in the package insert of each drug should be consulted before prescribing any product. The editors and publisher are not responsible for errors or omissions or for any consequences from application of the information in this book and make no warranty, express or implied, with respect to the currency, accuracy, or completeness of the contents of the publication. Application of this information in a particular situation remains the professional responsibility of the practitioner.

—TABLE OF CONTENTS —

TABLE 1
CLINICAL APPROACH TO INITIAL CHOICE OF ANTIMICROBIAL THERAPY
Treatment based on presumed site or type of infection. In selected instances, treatment and prophylaxis based on identification of pathogens

ANATOMIC SITE/DIAGNOSIS/ MODIFYING CIRCUMSTANCES	ETIOLOGIES (usual)	SUGGESTED REGIMENS*		ADJUNCT DIAGNOSTIC OR THERAPEUTIC MEASURES AND COMMENTS
		PRIMARY	ALTERNATIVE†	
BONE: Osteomyelitis. Microbiologic diagnosis is essential. If blood culture negative, need culture of bone. Culture of sinus tract drainage not predictive of bone culture. Review: *Ln 364:369, 2004*				
ABDOMEN: See Peritonitis, page 31; Gallbladder, page 10; and Pelvic Inflammatory Disease, page 9				
Hematogenous Osteomyelitis				
Empiric therapy—Collect bone and blood cultures before empiric therapy				
Newborn (< 4 mos.) See Table 16 for dose	S. aureus, Gm-neg. bacilli, Group B strep	**MRSA possible: Vanco + P Ceph 3**	**MRSA unlikely: (Nacillin or oxacillin) + P Ceph 3**	Table 16 for dose. Severe allergy or toxicity: (Linezolid^NAI 10 mg/kg IV/po q8h + aztreonam). Could substitute clindamycin for linezolid
Children (>4 mos.)	S. aureus, Group A strep, Gm-neg. bacilli rare	**MRSA possible: Vanco 1 IV q12h**	**MRSA unlikely: Nacillin or oxacillin**	Severe allergy or toxicity: Clinda or TMP/SMX or linezolid^NAI. Dosages in Table 16.
		Add: **P Ceph 3** if Gm-neg. bacilli on Gram stain. Doses: Table 16.		
Adult (>21 yrs)	S. aureus most common but variety other organisms. **Blood & bone cultures essential.**	**MRSA possible: Vanco 1.0 IV q12h**	**MRSA unlikely: Nacillin or oxacillin 2.0 gm q4h**	Severe allergy or toxicity: TMP/SMX 8-10 mg/kg/d div. q12h (AnIM 138:135, 2003)^NAI
Vertebral osteo ± epidural abscess; other sites				**Dx: MRI early to look for epidural abscess.** Allergy or toxicity: TMP/SMX 8-10 mg/kg/d div. q12h (AnIM 138:135, 2003)^NAI
Specific therapy—Culture and in vitro susceptibility results known				
MSSA		**Nacillin or oxacillin 2.0 gm q4h IV or cefazolin 2.0 gm q8h IV**	Vanco 1.0 gm q12h IV	Severe allergy or toxicity. Clinda 600-900 mg IV q8h or TMP/SMX 8-10 mg/kg/d div. If no response to clinda, check for "inducible" resistance. If susceptible in vitro: CIP 750 mg po bid or Levo 750 mg po 1x/d) + Rif 300 mg po bid.
MRSA—See Table 4, page 51. Resistant bacteria		Vanco 1.0 gm q12h IV	Linezolid 600 mg q12h IV/po	Severe allergy or toxicity: Clinda 600-900 mg q8h IV (check for inducible constitutive resistance); daptomycin. No data for daptomycin. See Table 4, page 51. Resistant bacteria
Hemoglobinopathy: Sickle cell/thalassemia	Salmonella, other Gm-neg. bacilli	CIP 400 mg IV q12h	Levo 750 mg IV q24h	Thalassemia: transfusion and iron chelation risk factors.
Contiguous Osteomyelitis Without Vascular Insufficiency				
Empiric therapy: Get cultures!				
Foot bone osteo due to nail through tennis shoe	P. aeruginosa	CIP 750 mg bid po or Levo 750 mg bid po	**Ceftaz 2.0 gm q8h IV or CFP 2.0 gm q8h IV**	See Skin—Nail puncture, page 38. Need debridement to remove foreign body.
Long bone post-internal fixation of fracture	S. aureus, Gm-neg. bacilli, P. aeruginosa	Vanco 1.0 gm q12h IV + (ceftaz or CFP (see footnote^NAI)). See Comment	Linezolid 600 mg q12h IV/po bid^NAI + ceftaz or CFP. See Comment	Often necessary to remove hardware to allow bone union. May need revascularization. Regimens listed are empiric. Adjust after culture data available. If susceptible Gm-neg. bacilli, CIP 750 mg po bid or Levo 750 mg po 1x/d.
Prosthetic joint	See Prosthetic joint, page 22			
Sternum, post-op	S. aureus, S. epidermidis	Vanco 1.0 gm q12h IV	Linezolid 600 mg bid po/IV^NAI	Sternal debridement for cultures & removal of necrotic bone.
Contiguous Osteomyelitis With Vascular Insufficiency Ref. CID S115-22, 2004				
Most pts are diabetics with peripheral neuropathy & infected skin ulcers (see *Diabetic foot, page 10*)	Polymicrobic: Gm+ cocci (to include MRSA) (aerobic & anaerobic) and Gm-neg. bacilli (aerobic & anaerobic)	Ideally, debride overlying ulcer & submit bone for histology & culture. Revascularize if possible. Full contact cast. Specific antibiotic(s) x6 wks.		**Diagnosis of osteo:** Culture of biopsied bone gold standard. Marrow edema on MRI best image. Probe to bone has high predictive value. **Treatment:** (1) Revascularize if possible. (2) Specific antimicrobial(s) if possible. (3) Specific antimicrobial(s) (4) Full contact cast.

---

† Drug dosage: **IMP** 0.5 gm q6h IV, **MER** 1.0 gm q8h IV, **ERTA** 1.0 gm q24h, **TC/CL** 3.1 gm q6h IV, **PIP/TZ** 3.375 gm q6h or 4.5 gm q8h IV, **AM/SB** 3.0 gm IV q6h, **cefazolin** 2.0 gm q8h IV, **CFP** 2.0 gm q8h IV, **metro** 1.0 gm q12h IV, **aztreonam** 2.0 gm q6h or po or 1.0 gm q12h IV, **vanco** 1.0 gm q12h IV. **NAI** = Not FDA-approved indication
(Footnotes and abbreviations on page 45) NOTE: All dosage recommendations are for adults (unless otherwise indicated) and assume normal renal function.

3

TABLE 1 (2)

ANATOMIC SITE/DIAGNOSIS/ MODIFYING CIRCUMSTANCES	ETIOLOGIES (usual)	SUGGESTED REGIMENS* PRIMARY	ALTERNATIVE†	ADJUNCT DIAGNOSTIC OR THERAPEUTIC MEASURES AND COMMENTS
BONE (continued) **Chronic Osteomyelitis: Specific therapy** By definition, implies presence of dead bone. **Need valid cultures**	S. aureus, Enterobacteriaceae, P. aeruginosa	Empiric rx not indicated. Base systemic rx on results of culture, sensitivity testing. In acute exacerbation of chronic osteo, rx as acute hematogenous osteo.		Important adjuncts: removal of orthopedic hardware, surgical debridement, vascularized muscle flaps, distraction osteogenesis (Ilizarov) techniques. Antibiotic-impregnated cement & hyperbaric oxygen adjunctive. NOTE: RIF + (vanco or β-lactam) effective in animal model and in a clinical trial of S. aureus chronic osteo (SMJ 79:947, 1986).
BREAST: Mastitis—Obtain culture; need to know if MRSA present				
Postpartum mastitis Mastitis without abscess Ref.: JAMA 289:1609, 2003	S. aureus; less often S. pyogenes (Gp A or B), E. coli & rarely (< 5%) rabies; maybe Corynebacterium sp. & selected coagulase-neg. staphylococci	**NO MRSA:** Outpatient: **Dicloxacillin** 500 mg qid po or **cephalexin** 500 mg qid po. Inpatient: **Nafcillin/oxacillin** 2.0 gm q4h IV	**MRSA Possible:** Outpatient: **TMP/SMX-DS** bid po Inpatient: **Vanco** 1.0 gm q12h IV	If no abscess, increased frequency of nursing may hasten response; no risk to infant. Corynebacterium sp. assoc. with chronic granulomatous mastitis (CID 35:1434, 2002).
Mastitis with abscess				With abscess, d/c nursing; I&D standard; needle aspiration reported successful (Am J Surg 182:117, 2001). Resume breast feeding from affected breast as soon as pain allows.
Non-puerperal mastitis with abscess	S. aureus; less often Bacteroides sp., peptostreptococcus, & selected coagulase-neg. staphylococci	(Nafcillin or oxacillin) 2.0 gm q4h IV + **P Ceph 3**	**Vanco** 1.0 gm q12h IV + **P Ceph 3**	If subareolar & odoriferous, most likely anaerobes; need to **add metro 500 mg IV or po tid**. If not subareolar, staph. Need pretreatment aerobic/anaerobic cultures. Surgical drainage for abscess.
CENTRAL NERVOUS SYSTEM **Brain abscess** Primary or contiguous source Ref.: CID 25:763, 1997	Streptococci (60–70%), bacteroides (20–40%), Enterobacteriaceae (25–33%), S. aureus (10–15%). Rare: Nocardia (Table 11A, page 80)	**P Ceph 3** (cefotaxime 2.0 gm q4h IV or ceftriaxone 2.0 gm q12h IV) + metro 7.5 mg/kg q6h or 15 mg/kg q12h IV	**Pen G** 20–24 mU IV qd + metro 7.5 mg/kg q6h or 15 mg/kg q12h IV Duration rx unclear; rx until response by neuroimaging (CT/MRI)	If CT scan suggests cerebritis (< 2.5 cm and pt neurologically stable and conscious, start antibiotics and observe. Otherwise, surgical drainage usually mandates surgery. Experience with Pen G (HD) + metro without P Ceph 3 or nafcillin/oxacillin has been good. We use P Ceph 3 because of frequency of isolation of Enterobacteriaceae. S. aureus rare without positive blood culture; if S. aureus, include vanco until susceptibility known. Strep. milleri group susp. prone to produce abscess. **If MRSA a consideration, substitute vanco for nafcillin or oxacillin. P Ceph 3 dose as for brain abscess. primary.**
Post-surgical, post-traumatic	S. aureus, Enterobacteriaceae	(Nafcillin or oxacillin) 2.0 gm q4h IV + **P Ceph 3**		
HIV-1 infected (AIDS)	Toxoplasma gondii	See Table 13, page 97		
Subdural empyema. In adult 60–90% are extension of sinusitis or otitis media. Rx same as primary brain abscess.				Surgical emergency: must drain (CID 20:372, 1995)
Encephalitis/encephalopathy Ref.: Ln 359:507, 2002 (See Table 14, page 108, and for rabies, Table 20C, page 141)	Herpes simplex, arboviruses, rabies, West Nile virus, flavivirus, listeria, cat-scratch disease	Start IV **acyclovir** while awaiting results of CSF PCR for H. simplex.		Newly recognized strain of bat rabies. May not require a break in the skin. Eastern equine encephalitis causes focal MRI changes in basal ganglia and thalamus (NEJM 396:1867, 1997). Cat-scratch ref.: PIDJ 14:866, 1995). Ref. on West Nile & related viruses: NEJM 351:370, 2004.
Meningitis, "Aseptic": Pleocytosis of 100s of cells, CSF glucose normal, neg. culture for bacteria (see Table 14, page 104)	Enteroviruses, HSV-2, LCM, HIV, other viruses, drugs (NSAIDs, metronidazole, carbamazepine, TMP/SMX, IVIG), rarely leptospirosis	For all but leptospirosis, IV fluids and analgesics. D/C drugs that may be etiologic. For lepto (doxy 100 mg q12h IV or po) or (Pen G 5 mU q6h IV) or (AMP 0.5–1.0 gm q6h IV). Repeat LP if suspect partially-treated bacterial meningitis.		If available, PCR of CSF for enterovirus. HSV unusual without concomitant genital herpes. Drug-induced aseptic meningitis: AIM 759:1185, 1999. For lepto, positive epidemiological history and concomitant hepatitis, conjunctivitis, dermatitis, nephritis.

Footnotes and abbreviations on page 45.   NOTE: All dosage recommendations are for adults (unless otherwise indicated) and assume normal renal function.

TABLE 1 (3)

ANATOMIC SITE/DIAGNOSIS/MODIFYING CIRCUMSTANCES	ETIOLOGIES (usual)	SUGGESTED REGIMENS[1]		ADJUNCT DIAGNOSTIC OR THERAPEUTIC MEASURES AND COMMENTS
		PRIMARY	ALTERNATIVE[1]	
CENTRAL NERVOUS SYSTEM (continued) **Meningitis, Bacterial, Acute: Goal is empiric therapy, then CSF exam within 30 min. If focal neurologic deficit, give empiric rx, then do head CT, then do LP.** (CID 39:1267, 2004) NOTE: In children, treatment caused CSF cultures to turn neg. in 2 hrs with meningococci & partial response with pneumococcal in 4 hrs (Peds 108:1169, 2001) **Empiric Therapy—CSF stain is negative—Immunocompetent**				
Age: Preterm to <1 month	Group B strep 49%, E. coli 18%, listeria 7%, misc. Gm-neg. 10%, misc. Gm-pos. 10%	**AMP + cefotaxime** Intraventricular rx not recommended. Repeat CSF exam/culture 24–36 hrs after start of rx For dosage, see Table 16	**AMP + gentamicin**	Primary & alternative regimens active vs Group B strep, most coliforms, & listeria. If premature infant with long nursery stay, & resist. coliforms potential pathogens. Optional empiric regimens: (nafcillin + ceftazidime or cefotaxime), high risk of MRSA, use vanco + cefotaxime. (After empiric therapy, tailor to culture/sensitivity)
Age: 1 month – 50 yrs 1999–2000 respiratory disease season, 34.1% of S. pneumo in U.S. were either intermediate in susceptibility or resistant to Pen (CID 34 (Suppl 1):S4, 2002). See footnote[3] for empiric treatment rationale.	S. pneumo, meningococci, H. influenzae now very rare, listeria unlikely in young & immunocompetent	**[(Cefotaxime 2 gm q4-6h IV OR ceftriaxone 2 gm IV q12h) + (dexamethasone) + vanco** (see footnote[3]) Peds: see footnote[3]] **Dexamethasone:** 0.15 mg/kg IV q6h x2-4 d. **Give with or just before 1st dose of antibiotic to block TNF production (see Comment).** See footnote[3] for ped. dosage	**[MER 2.0 gm q8h IV]** [Peds: 40 mg/kg IV q8h] + **IV dexamethasone** + **vanco** (see footnote[3]) Peds: see footnote[3]	For pts with severe pen. allergy: Chloro 12.5-25 mg/kg IV q6h (max. 4 gm/d.) (for meningococcus) + TMP/SMX 15-20 mg/kg/d div. q6-8h (for listeria if immunocompromised) + vanco. Rare meningococcal isolates chloro-resistant (NEJM 339:868, 1998). The standard alternative for pts with severe pen. allergy was chloro. However, high failure rate in pts with DRSP (Ln 339: 405, 1992; Ln 342:240, 1993). **So far, no vanco-resistant S. pneumo.** Value of dexamethasone documented in children with H. influenzae & now confirmed in adults with S. pneumo & N. meningitidis (NEJM 347:1549 & 1613, 2002; LnID 4:139, 2004). **Give 1st dose 15-20 min. Prior to or concomitant with 1st dose of antibiotic. Dose:** 0.15 mg/kg IV q6h x2-4 d. For meningococcal immunization, see Table 20, pages 139–140.
Age: >50 yrs or alcoholism or other debilitating associated diseases or impaired cellular immunity	S. pneumo, listeria, Gm-neg. bacilli. Note absence of meningococcus	**(AMP 2.0 gm IV q4h) + (ceftriaxone 2.0 gm IV q12h or cefotaxime 2.0 gm IV q4-6h) + vanco + dexamethasone.** For vanco dose, see footnote[3]. **Dexamethasone** 0.15 mg/kg IV q6h x2-4 d. 1st dose before or concomitant with 1st dose of antibiotic.	**(AMP 2.0 gm q4h) + vanco + IV dexametha- sone.** For severe pen. Allergy, see Comment.	Severe penicillin allergy: Vanco 500-750 mg/kg/d. div. q6-8h pending culture results. Chloro has failed vs DRSP (Ln 342:240, 1993). MER active vs listeria in vitro (JAC 36(Suppl. A):1, 1995). CSF levels appear adequate (JAC 34:175, 1994) but no clinical data.
Post-neurosurgery, post-head trauma, or post-cochlear implant (NEJM 349:435, 2003)	S. pneumoniae most common, esp. if CSF leak. Other: S. aureus, coliforms, P. aeruginosa	**Vanco** (until known not MRSA) 500-750 mg q6h[2] IV + **(cefepime or cef- tazidime** 2.0 gm q8h IV) Vano see footnote[3]	**MER** 2.0 gm q8h IV + **vanco** 1.0 gm q6-12h IV	Vanco alone not optimal for S. pneumo. If/when suscept. S. pneumo identified, quickly switch to ceftriaxone or cefotaxime. If coliform or pseudomonas meningitis, some add intrathecal gentamicin (4 mg q12h intra lateral ventricles) or q12h lumbar) Cure of acinetobacter meningitis with intrathecal (AAC 42:1495, 1998).
Ventriculitis/meningitis due to infected ventriculo-peritoneal (atrial) shunt	S. epidermidis, S. aureus, coliforms, diphtheroids (rare), P. acnes	**Vanco** 500-750 mg q6h[2] IV + **(cefepime or cef- tazidime** 2.0 gm q8h IV) Vano see footnote[3]	**Vanco** 500-750 mg q6h IV + **MER** 2.0 gm q8h IV	Usual dose. [†] remove infected shunt & culture; external ventricular catheter for drainage/pressure control; antimicrobic x10-14 d. For timing of new shunt, see CID 39:1267, 2004

[1] **Rationale:** Hard to get adequate CSF concentrations of anti-infectives, hence MIC criteria for in vitro susceptibility are lower for CSF isolates (AHM 161:2538, 2001).

[2] Low and erratic penetration of vanco into the CSF (PIDJ 16:895, 1997). Recommended dosage in children is 15 mg/kg q6h IV (double the standard adult dose). **In adults,** a maximum dose of 2–3 gm/day is suggested: **500–750 mg q6h IV.**

[3] **Dosage of drugs used to rx children ≥1 mo. of age:** Cefotaxime 200 mg/kg/d IV div. q6-8h; ceftriaxone 100 mg/kg/d IV div. q12h; vanco 15 mg/kg IV q6h. NOTE: All dosage recommendations are for adults (unless otherwise indicated) and assume normal renal function.

(Footnotes and abbreviations on page 45)

TABLE 1 (4)

ANATOMIC SITE/DIAGNOSIS/ MODIFYING CIRCUMSTANCES	ETIOLOGIES (usual)	SUGGESTED REGIMENS*		ADJUNCT DIAGNOSTIC OR THERAPEUTIC MEASURES AND COMMENTS
		PRIMARY	ALTERNATIVE†	
CENTRAL NERVOUS SYSTEM*				
Meningitis, Bacterial, Acute (continued) CID 39:1267, 2004)				
Empiric Therapy—Positive CSF Gram stain				
Gram-positive diplococci	S. pneumoniae	Either **(ceftriaxone** 2.0 gm IV q12h or **cefotaxime** 2.0 gm IV q4-6h) + **vanco** 500-750 mg IV q6h + timed **dexamethasone** 0.15 mg/kg q6h IV x2-4 d.		**Alternatives: MER** 2.0 gm IV q8h or **Moxi** 400 mg IV once daily or **Gati/Moxi** 400 mg IV once daily. All + **dexamethasone**.
Gram-negative diplococci	N. meningitidis	**Cefotaxime** 2.0 gm IV q4-6h or **ceftriaxone** 2.0 gm IV q12h) + timed **dexamethasone** (dose above)		**Alternatives: Pen G** 4 mill. units IV q4h or **AMP** 2.0 gm IV q4h or **Gati/Moxi** 400 mg IV once daily or **chloro** 1.0 gm IV q6h
Gram-positive bacilli or coccobacilli	Listeria monocytogenes	**AMP** 2.0 gm IV q4h + **gentamicin** 2 mg/kg loading dose then 1.7 mg/kg q8h		Listeria ref.: CID 24:1, 1997. **If pen.-allergic, use** TMP/SMX 15-20 mg/kg/d. div. q6-8h or **MER 2.0 gm IV q8h**
Gram-negative bacilli	H. influenzae, coliforms, P. aeruginosa	(Ceftazidime 2.0 gm IV q8h) + gentamicin 2 mg/kg 1° dose then 1.7 mg/kg q8h		**Alternatives: CIP** 400 mg IV q8-12h; **MER** 2.0 gm IV q8h
Specific Therapy—Positive culture of CSF with in vitro susceptibility results available. Interest in monitoring/reducing intracranial pressure: CID 38:384, 2004				
H. influenzae	β-lactamase +	**Ceftriaxone** (peds): 100 mg/kg/d. IV div q12h		**Pen. allergic: Chloro** 50 mg/kg/d. IV div q6h (max. 4 gm/d.)
Listeria monocytogenes		**AMP** 2.0 gm IV q4h + **gentamicin** 2 mg/kg loading dose, then 1.7 mg/kg q8h.		**Pen. allergic:** TMP/SMX 20 mg/kg/d. div. q6-12h. One report of greater efficacy of AMP + TMP/SMX as compared to AMP + gentamicin (JID 3379, 1996). **Alternative: MER** 2.0 gm IV q8h.
N. meningitidis	MIC < 0.1 µg/ml	**Ceftriaxone** 2.0 gm IV q12h x 7 d. (see Comment). If pen. allergic, **chloro** 1.0 gm IV q6h (up to 1.0 gm IV q6h)		Rare isolates chloro-resistant (MEJM 339:868 & 917, 1998). **Alternative: MER** 2.0 gm IV q8h or **Gati/Moxi** 400 mg once daily.
	0.1-1.0 µg/ml			
S. pneumoniae	Pen G MIC	**Ceftriaxone** 2.0 gm IV q12h or **cefotaxime** 2.0 gm IV q4h		**Alternatives: Ceftriaxone** 2.0 gm IV q12h, **chloro** 1.0 gm IV q6h
	< 0.1 µg/ml	**Pen G** 4 mU IV q4h or **AMP** 2.0 gm IV q4h		
	0.1-1.0 µg/ml	**Ceftriaxone** 2.0 gm IV q12h or **cefotaxime** 2.0 gm IV q4-6h + **(ceftriaxone or cefotax-ime** as above)		**Alternatives: Cefepime** 2.0 gm IV q8h or **MER** 2.0 gm IV q8h
	≥2.0 µg/ml	Vanco 500-750 mg IV q6h + **(ceftriaxone or cefotax-ime** as above)		**Alternatives: Gati or Moxi** 400 mg IV once daily
	Ceftriaxone MIC ≥1.0 µg/ml	Vanco 500-750 mg IV q6h + **(ceftriaxone or cefotax-ime** as above)		**Alternatives: Gati or Moxi** 400 mg IV once daily
NOTES: 1. Assumes dexamethasone just prior to 1st dose & q6 x4 d. 2. If MIC ≥1.0, repeat CSF exam after 24-48h. 3. Treat for 10-14 days				
E. coli, other coliforms, or P. aeruginosa	Consultation advised—need susceptibility results	(Ceftazidime or cefepime 2.0 gm IV q8h) ± gentamicin		**Alternatives: Cefepime** 2.0 gm IV q8h; **MER** 2.0 gm IV q8h. For discussion of intraventricular therapy: CID 38:1261, 2004
Prophylaxis for H. influenzae and N. meningitidis				
Hemophilus influenzae type b Household and/or day care contact: residing with index case of ≥4 hrs. day care contact: same day care as index case for 5-7 days before onset		**RIF** 20 mg/kg po (not to exceed 600 mg) q4 x4 doses		**Household:** If there is one unvaccinated contact ≤4 yrs in the household. RIF recommended for all contacts except pregnant woman. **Child Care Facilities:** With 1 case, if attended by unvaccinated children >2 yrs, consider prophylaxis → vaccinate susceptibles. If all contacts >2 yrs: no prophylaxis. If ≥2 cases in 60 days & unvaccinated children attend, prophylaxis recommended for children & personnel (Am Acad Ped Red Book 1997, page 222).

Specific Therapy—Positive culture of CSF with in vitro susceptibility results available. Interest in monitoring/reducing intracranial pressure: CID 38:384, 2004

(Footnotes and abbreviations on page 45)   NOTE: All dosage recommendations are for adults (unless otherwise indicated) and assume normal renal function.

TABLE 1 (5)

ANATOMIC SITE/DIAGNOSIS/ MODIFYING CIRCUMSTANCES	ETIOLOGIES (usual)	SUGGESTED REGIMENS*		ADJUNCT DIAGNOSTIC OR THERAPEUTIC MEASURES AND COMMENTS
		PRIMARY	ALTERNATIVE†	
CENTRAL NERVOUS SYSTEM/Meningitis, Bacterial/Prophylaxis (continued)				
Neisseria meningitidis exposure (close contact) [MMWR 46/(RR-5)1, 1997] CDC recommends informing college freshmen living in dormitories & residence halls of available vaccine [MMWR 46(RR-7):1, 2000 & 50/23:487, 2001]		**[RIF** 600 mg po q12h x4 doses. (Children >1 mo. age 10 mg/kg po q12h x4 doses, <1 mo. age 5 mg/kg q12h x4 doses)] or **[CIP** (adults) 500 mg po single dose] or **[Ceftriaxone** 250 mg IM x1 dose (child <15 yrs 125 mg IM x1)].		N. meningitidis spread by respiratory droplets, not aerosols, hence close contact required. † risk if close contact for at least 4 hrs during week before illness onset (e.g., household members, day care contacts, cellmates) or exposure to pt's oral-pharyngeal secretions (e.g., via kissing, mouth-to-mouth resuscitation, intubation, nasotracheal suctioning). Azithro 500 mg x1 as effective as RIF 600 mg bid x2 d. [PIDJ 17:816, 1998]. Ceftriaxone equivalent to RIF [JAC 45:909, 2000].
		Spiramycin 500 mg po q6h x5 d. Children 10 mg/kg po q6h x5 d.		Primary prophylactic regimen in many European countries.
Meningitis, chronic Defined as symptoms + CSF pleocytosis for ≥4 wks	M. tbc 40%, cryptococcosis 7%, neoplastic 8%, Lyme, syphilis, Whipple's disease	Treatment depends on etiology. No urgent need for empiric therapy.		Long list of possibilities: bacteria, parasites, fungi, viruses, neoplasms, vasculitis, and other miscellaneous etiologies—see chapter on chronic meningitis in latest edition of Harrison's Textbook of Internal Medicine.
Meningitis, eosinophilic AJM 114:217, 2003 (See Table 13A, page 98)	Angiostrongyliasis, gnatho-stomiasis, rarely others	Corticosteroids	Not sure antihelminthic rx works	1/3 lack peripheral eosinophilia. Need serology to confirm dx. Steroid ref.: NEJM 346:668, 202. Recent outbreak: MMWR 31:660, 2001.
Meningitis, HIV-1 Infected (AIDS)	As in adults, >50 yrs: also consider cryptococcus, M. tuberculosis, syphilis, HIV aseptic meningitis, Listeria monocytogenes	If etiology not identified: rx as adult >50 yrs + obtain CSF/serum cryptococcal antigen (see Comments)	For crypto, see Table 11A, page 78	C. neoformans most common etiology in AIDS. Other possibilities: H. influenzae, pneumococci, Tbc, syphilis, viral, histoplasma & coccidioides also need to be considered. Obtain blood cultures. L. monocytogenes risk >60x 1, ¾ present as meningitis [CID 17:224, 1993].
EAR				
External otitis "Swimmer's ear" [CID 22:299, 2003]	Pseudomonas sp., Entero-bacteriaceae, Proteus sp. (Fungi rare.) Acute infection usually 2° S. aureus	Eardrops: **Oflox 0.3% soln** bid or **[(polymyxin B + neomycin + hydrocortisone)** qid] or **[CIP + hydrocortisone** bid] For acute disease: **dicloxacillin** 500 mg po 4x/d		Rx should include gentle cleaning. Recurrences prevented (or decreased) by drying ear with hydrogen peroxide (1.5%) or acetic acid/rubbing alcohol (2/3 rubbing alcohol) after swimming, then antibiotic drops or 2% acetic acid solution. Ointments should not be used in ear. Do not use neomycin if tympanic membrane punctured.
Chronic	Usually 2° to seborrhea	Eardrops: **[(polymyxin B + neomycin + hydrocortisone** qid) + **selenium sulfide]**		Control seborrhea with dandruff shampoo containing selenium sulfide (Selsun) or (ketoconazole shampoo) + (medium potency steroid solution, triamcinolone 0.1%)
"Malignant otitis externa" Risk groups: Diabetes mellitus, AIDS, chemotherapy	Pseudomonas aeruginosa >90%	**[IMP** 0.5 gm q6h IV, or **(MER** 1.0 gm q8h IV, or **[CIP** 400 mg IV q12h or 750 mg q12h po] or **ceftaz** 2.0 gm q8h IV) or **[CFP** 2 gm q12h] or **[PIP** 4-6 gm q4-6h IV + **tobra**] or **[TC** 3.0 gm q4h IV + **tobra**]		CIP po especially useful for outpatient rx with early disease. Surgical debridement usually required but removal of bone excision of osteomyelitis. Do MRI scan more sensitive than x-ray. If bone involved, rx for 4-6 wks. Ref.: LnID 4:34, 2004

(Footnotes and abbreviations on page 45)   NOTE: All dosage recommendations are for adults (unless otherwise indicated) and assume normal renal function.

TABLE 1 (6)

ANATOMIC SITE/DIAGNOSIS/ MODIFYING CIRCUMSTANCES	ETIOLOGIES (usual)	SUGGESTED REGIMENS*		ADJUNCT DIAGNOSTIC OR THERAPEUTIC MEASURES AND COMMENTS
		PRIMARY	ALTERNATIVE¹	
EAR (continued)				
Otitis media—infants, children, adults				
Acute (NEJM 347:1169, 2002; Pediatrics 113:1451, 2004). For correlation of bacterial eradication from middle ear & clinical outcome, see LnID 2:593, 2002.	Overall detection in middle ear fluid:	**If NO antibiotics in prior month:**	**Received antibiotics in prior month:**	If allergic to β-lactam drugs? If history unclear or rash, oral ceph OK: avoid ceph if IgE-mediated allergy, e.g., anaphylaxis. High failure rate with TMP/SMX if
Initial empiric therapy of acute otitis media (AOM)	No pathogen 25%	Amox po HD¹	Amox HD¹ or AM/CL HD¹ or cefdinir or cefpodoxime or	etiology is DRSP or H. influenzae (PIDJ 20:260, 2001); azithro x5 d. or clarithro x10 d. (both have ↓ activity vs DRSP). Up to 50% S. pneumo resistant to
NOTE: Pending new data, rx children <2 yrs old. If >2 yrs old, afebrile, no ear pain, may/question observation—consider analgesic	Virus 5–48%		cefprozil or cefuroxime axetil	macrolides (plus azithro not active vs DRSP). AM/CL superior to azithro in recent controlled trial (ICAAC Abst. 2224:2003).
exam. If worsening, treat without anti-microbials	Bacteria only 55%	**For dosage, see footnotes¹ and²**		Spontaneous resolution: 90% pts infected with M. catarrhalis, 50% with H. influenzae, and 10% with S. pneumoniae; overall 80% resolve when 2–14 d. (Ln
	Role of viruses: Clin Micro Rev 16:230, 2003	**All doses are pediatric**		363:465, 2004).
		Duration of rx: <2 yrs old x10 d; ≥2 yrs old x5–7 d. Appropriate duration unclear, 5 d. may be inadequate for severe disease (NEJM 347:1169, 2002)		Risk of DRSP ↑ with age <2 yrs, antibiotics last 3 mos., and/or daycare attendance.
				Selection of drug based on (1) effectiveness against β-lactamase producing H. influenzae & M. catarrhalis and (2) effectiveness against S. pneumo, including DRSP. Cefaclor, cefprozil, loracarbef, & ceftibuten less active vs other
		For adult dosages, see Sinusitis, page 33, and Table 10		agents listed. Variable acceptance of drug taste/smell by children 4–8 y.o. (PIDJ 19 (Suppl.):S174, 2000).
				Clindamycin not active vs H. influenzae or M. catarrhalis. S. pneumo resistant to macrolides may also be resistant to clinda.
				Definition of failure: no change in ear pain, fever, bulging TM or otorrhea after 3 days of rx. Tympanocentesis will allow culture.
				Newer FDA active vs DRSP, but not approved for use in children (PIDJ 19:1040, 2000). Ceftriaxone IM x3 d. superior to x1 d. treatment vs DRSP & S. pneumo AOM (PIDJ 20:829, 2001).
				AM/CL HD reported successful for pen-resistant S. pneumo AOM (NEJM 344:1188, 2001).
Treatment for clinical failure after 3 days rx	Drug-resistant S. pneumoniae main concern	**NO antibiotics in month prior to last 3 days:** AM/CL HD¹ or cefdinir or cefpodoxime or cefuroxime axetil x3 d.	**Antibiotics in month prior to last 3 days:** (IM ceftriaxone) and/or (clindamycin) and/or (tympanocentesis) See clindamycin Comments	
		For dosage, see footnotes¹ and² **All doses are pediatric**		
After >48 hrs of nasotracheal intubation.	Pseudomonas sp., Klebsiella, enterobacter	Cefazidime or CFP or IMP or MER or TC/CL or CIP (For dosages, see Ear, malignant otitis externa, page 6)		With nasotracheal intubation >48 hrs, about ½ pts will have otitis media with effusion.
Prophylaxis: acute otitis media NEJM 344:403, 2001; PIDJ 22:10, 2003	Pneumococci, H. influenzae, M. catarrhalis, Staph. aureus, Group A strep (see Comments)	Sulfisoxazole 50 mg/kg po at bedtime or amoxicillin 20 mg/kg po qd	Duration of rx as above. **Use of antibiotics to prevent otitis media is a major contributor to emergence of antibiotic-resistant S. pneumo!**	Pneumococcal protein conjugate vaccine decreases freq. AOM in general & due to vaccine serotypes (NEJM 344:403, 2003). ↓ need for future hospitalization for AOM (NEJM 344:1188, 2001). Adenoidectomy at time of tympanostomy tubes ↓ need for future rx (NEJM 344:1188, 2001).

---

¹ Amoxicillin UD or HD = aMoxicillin usual dose or high dose; **AM/CL HD** = aMoxicillin/clavulanate high dose. **Dosages in footnote 2. Drug and ped dosage (all po unless specified) for acute otitis media: Amoxicillin UD** = 40 mg/kg/d div q12h or q8h; **Amoxicillin HD** = 90 mg/kg/d div q12h or q8h; **AM/CL HD** = 90 mg/kg/d div of amox component. **Extra-strength AM/CL oral suspension** (Augmentin ES-600) available with 600 mg AM & 42.9 mg CL per 5 ml—dose: 90/6.4 mg/kg/d div bid. **Cefaclor** 40 mg/kg/d div q8h; **Cefdinir** 14 mg/kg/d div q12–24h; **cefixime** 8 mg/kg/d div q12–24h; **Cefixime axetil** 30 mg/kg/d div q12h.

² **Clindamycin** 30 mg/kg/d div q8h; **erythromycin-sulfisoxazole**—50 mg/kg/d of erythro div q6–8h. **Clarithro** 15 mg/kg/d div q12h; **Clindamycin-sensitive S. pneumo:** TMP/SMX 8 mg/kg/d div q12h; **Erythro-sulfisoxazole**—50 mg/kg/d of erythro div q6–8h. **Clarithro** 15 mg/kg/d div q12h; **azithro** 10 mg/kg x1 and then 5 mg/kg qd on days 2–5. Other FDA-approved regimens: 10 mg/kg qd x3 d. & 30 mg/kg x1; **cefpodoxime proxetil** 10 mg/kg/d div q12h; **Cefprozil** 30 mg/kg/d div q12h; **cefpodoxime proxetil** 10 mg/kg/d as single dose; **cefaclor** 40 mg/kg/d div q8h; **loracarbef** 30 mg/kg/d div q12h or 14 mg/kg q24h.

NOTE: All dosage recommendations are for adults (unless otherwise indicated) and assume normal renal function.

(Footnotes and abbreviations on page 45)

TABLE 1 (7)

ANATOMIC SITE/DIAGNOSIS/ MODIFYING CIRCUMSTANCES	ETIOLOGIES (usual)	SUGGESTED REGIMENS*		ADJUNCT DIAGNOSTIC OR THERAPEUTIC MEASURES AND COMMENTS
		PRIMARY	ALTERNATIVE†	
EAR *(continued)*				
Mastoiditis				
Acute				
Outpatient	Strep. pneumoniae 22%, S. pyogenes 16%, Staph. aureus 7%, H. influenzae 4%, P. aeruginosa 4% others	Empirically, same as Acute otitis media, above; need **vanco** or **nafcillin/oxacillin** if culture + for S. aureus.		Has become a rare entity, presumably as result of the aggressive rx of acute otitis media.
Hospitalized		**Cefotaxime** 1–2 gm IV q4–8h (depends on severity) or **ceftriaxone** 2 gm (q24h IV) + **nafcillin** 2 gm (q4h IV); age 60, 1 gm q24h IV; > age 60, 2 gm q24h IV; < age 60		Small ↑ in incidence in Netherlands where use of antibiotics limited to children with complicated course or high risk (*PIDJ 20:140, 2001*).
Chronic	Often polymicrobic: Staph. aureus, P. aeruginosa, Enterobacteriaceae, P. aeruginosa	Treatment for acute exacerbations or perioperatively. Ideally, culture and sensitivity obtained. Examples of empiric regimens: **IMP** 0.5 gm q6h IV, **TC/CL** 3.1 gm q6h IV, **PIP/TZ** 3.375 gm q4–6h or 4.5 gm q8h IV.		May or may not be associated with chronic otitis media with drainage via ruptured tympanic membrane. Antimicrobials given in association with surgery. Mastoidectomy indications: chronic drainage and evidence of osteomyelitis by MRI or CT, evidence of spread to CNS (epidural abscess, suppurative phlebitis, brain abscess).
EYE—General Reviews: *CID 21:479, 1995; IDCP 7:447, 1998*				
Eyelid				
Blepharitis	Etiol. unclear. Factors include Staph. aureus & Staph. epidermidis, seborrhea, rosacea, & dry eye	Lid care with baby shampoo & warm compresses qd. Artificial tears if assoc. dry eye (see Comment)		Usually topical ointments of no benefit. If associated rosacea, add doxy 100 mg po bid x2 wks and then qd.
Hordeolum (stye)				
External (gland of Zeis)	Staph. aureus	Hot packs only. Will drain spontaneously.		Infection of superficial sebaceous gland.
Internal (Meibomian glands)	Staph. aureus	Oral **nafcillin/oxacillin** + hot packs		Also called acute meibomianitis. Rarely drain spontaneously.
Conjunctiva: *NEJM 343:345, 2000*				
Conjunctivitis of the newborn (ophthalmia neonatorum): by day of onset post-delivery—all doses pediatric				
Onset 1st day	Chemical due to AgNO₃	None		Usual prophylaxis is erytho ointment; hence, AgNO₃ irritation rare.
Onset 2–4 days	N. gonorrhoeae	**Ceftriaxone** 25–50 mg/kg IV x1 dose (see Comment), not to exceed 125 mg		Mother and her sexual partners. **Hospitalize. Topical rx inadequate.** **Treat neonate for concomitant Chlamydia trachomatis.**
Onset 3–10 days	Chlamydia trachomatis	**Erythro syrup** 50 mg/kg/d (po in 4 div. doses x14 d) No topical rx needed.		Diagnosis by antigen detection. Azithro susp. 20 mg/kg po qd x3 d reported efficacious (*PIDJ 17:1049, 1998*). Treat mother & sexual partner.
Onset 2–16 days	Herpes simplex types 1, 2	See keratitis, next page		Consider IV acyclovir if concomitant systemic disease.
Ophthalmia neonatorum prophylaxis: **Silver nitrate 1%** x1 or **erythro** 0.5% ointment x1 or **tetra 1%** ointment x1 application				
Pink eye (viral conjunctivitis) Usually unilateral	Adenovirus (types 3 & 7 in children, 8, 11 & 19 in adults)	No treatment. If symptomatic, cold artificial tears may help.		Highly contagious. Onset of ocular pain and photophobia in an adult suggests associated keratitis—rare.
Inclusion conjunctivitis (adult) Usually unilateral	Chlamydia trachomatis	**Doxy** 100 mg po x1–3 weeks	**Erythro** 250 mg qid po x1–3 weeks	Oculogenital disease. Diagnosis by culture or antigen detection by PCR—availability varies by region and institution. Treat sexual partner.
Trachoma	Chlamydia trachomatis	**Azithro** 20 mg/kg po single dose—78% effective in children	**Doxy** 100 mg po bid x14 d or **tetracycline** 250 mg qid po x14 d	Starts in childhood and can persist for years with subsequent damage to cornea. Topical therapy of marginal benefit. Avoid doxy/tetracycline in young children. Ref.: *CID 24:363, 1997.* Mass treatment works (*JAMA 292:721, 2004*)
Suppurative conjunctivitis				
Non-gonococcal; non-chlamydial *Med Lett 46:25, 2004*	Staph. aureus, S. pneumoniae, H. influenzae, and in S. pneumoniae due to atypical S. pneumoniae *NEJM 348:1112, 2003*	Ophthalmic solution: Gati 0.3%, Levo 0.5%, or Moxi 0.5%, All 1 gtt qh q2h while awake for 2 days, then q4h (4–8) up to 7 d.	Polymyxin B + trimethoprim solution 1–2 gtts q3–6h x7–10 d.	FQs toxic for empiric therapy but expensive: $40–50 for 5 ml. High concentrations ↑ likelihood of activity vs S. aureus—even MRSA. TMP spectrum may include MRSA. Polymyxin B spectrum only Gm-neg. bacilli with partial prep of only TMP. Most S. pneumo resistant to pen & tobra.
Gonococcal (peds/adults)	N. gonorrhoeae	**Ceftriaxone** 125 mg IM or IV as one dose in children; 1 gm IM/IV as one dose in adults		High dose in adults

(Footnotes and abbreviations on page 45)   NOTE: All dosage recommendations are for adults (unless otherwise indicated) and assume normal renal function.

TABLE 1 (8)

ANATOMIC SITE/DIAGNOSIS/ MODIFYING CIRCUMSTANCES	ETIOLOGIES (usual)	SUGGESTED REGIMENS* PRIMARY	ALTERNATIVE†	ADJUNCT DIAGNOSTIC OR THERAPEUTIC MEASURES AND COMMENTS
EYE (continued)				
Cornea (keratitis):	**Usually serious and often sight-threatening. Prompt ophthalmologic consultation essential! Herpes simplex most common etiology in developed countries; bacterial and fungal infections more common in underdeveloped countries.**			
Viral				
H. simplex	H. simplex, types 1 & 2	**Trifluridine** one drop q2h, 9v/d, for up to 21 days	**Vidarabine** ointment—useful in children. Use 5x/d. for up to 21 days.	Fluorescein staining shows topical dendritic figures. 30–50% rate of recurrence within 2 years. 400 mg acyclovir po bid + recurrences, p 0.005 (*NEJM* 339:300, 1998). If child fails vidarabine, try trifluridine.
Varicella-zoster ophthalmicus	Varicella-zoster virus	**Famciclovir** 500 mg tid po or **valacyclovir** 1.0 gm po x10 days	**Acyclovir** 800 mg 5x/day x10 days	Clinical diagnosis most common—dendritic figures with fluorescein staining in patient with varicella-zoster of ophthalmic branch of trigeminal nerve.
Bacterial		*All rx listed for bacterial, fungal, & protozoan is topical*		
Contact lens users	P. aeruginosa	**Tobra** or **gentamicin** (14 mg/ml) + **piperacillin** or **ticarcillin** eye drops (6–12 mg/ml) q15-60 min. around clock x24–72 hrs, then slow reduction	**CIP** 0.3% or **Levo** 0.5% drops q15-60 min. around clock x24–72 hrs	Pain, photophobia, impaired vision. Recommend alginate swab for culture and sensitivity testing.
	Staph. aureus, S. epidermidis, S. pneumoniae, S. pyogenes, Enterobacteriaceae, listeria	**Cefazolin** (50 mg/ml) + **gentamicin** or **tobra** (14 mg/ml) q15-60 min. around clock x24–72 hrs, then slow reduction	**Vanco** (50 mg/ml) + **ceftazidime** (50 mg/ml) q15-60 min. around clock x24–72 hrs, then slow reduction. See Comment	Specific therapy guided by results of alginate swab culture and sensitivity. CIP 0.3% found clinically equivalent to cefazolin + tobra, only concern was efficacy of CIP against S. pneumoniae (*Ophthalmology* 163:1854, 1996).
Dry cornea, diabetes, immunosuppression				
Fungal	Aspergillus, fusarium, candida. No empiric therapy—see Comment	**Natamycin** (5%) drops q4–3 hrs with subsequent slow reduction	**Ampho B** (0.05–0.15%) q4-3 hrs with subsequent slow reduction	No empiric therapy. Wait for results of Gram stain or culture in Sabouraud's medium.
Protozoan Soft contact lens users (overnight use ↑ risk 10–15 fold)	Acanthamoeba, hartmannella	**Propamidine** 0.1% + **neomycin-gramicidin/ polymyxin** Eyedrops q waking hour x1 week and then slow taper	**Polyhexamethylene biguanide (PHMB)** 0.02% or **chlorhexidine** 0.02%	Uncommon. Trauma and soft contact lenses are risk factors. Corneal scrapings stained with calcofluor white show characteristic cysts with fluorescent microscopy. PHMB source: Leiter's Park Ave. Pharm. 800-292-6773. Ref.: *CID* 35:434, 2002
Lacrimal apparatus				
Canaliculitis	Actinomyces most common. Rarely, Arachnia, fusobacterium, nocardia, candida	Remove granules & irrigate with **pen G** (100,000 approx. 5 µg/ml)	If fungi, irrigate with **nystatin**	Digital pressure produces exudate at punctum; Gram stain confirms diagnosis. Hot packs to punctal area qid.
Dacryocystitis (lacrimal sac)	S. pneumo, S. aureus, H. influenzae, S. pyogenes, P. aeruginosa	**Child: AM/CL** or **O Ceph 2**	**immediate ophthal. consult.** If only light perception or worse, immediate vitrectomy + intravitreal steroid. May need to repeat intravitreal antibiotics in 2–3 days. Can usually leave lens in situ.	Often consequence of obstruction of lacrimal duct. Empiric rx based on Gram stain of aspirate—see Comment.
Endophthalmitis For post-op and endophthalmitis, see *CID* 38:542, 2004.				
Bacterial: Haziness of vitreous is key to diagnosis. Needle aspirate of both vitreous and aqueous humor for culture prior to therapy. Intravitreal administration of antimicrobials essential.				
Postocular surgery (cataracts) Early, acute onset (incidence 0.05%)	S. epidermidis 60%, Staph. aureus, streptococci & enterococci each 5–10%, Gm-neg. bacilli 6%	May require removal of lens material. Intraocular **vanco** ± vitrectomy.		Intravitreal **vanco** 1 mg & intravitreal **ceftaz** 2.25 mg. No clear data on intravitreal steroid.
Low grade, chronic	Propionibacterium acnes, S. epidermidis, S. aureus (rare)			Need ophthalmologic consultation. Can be acute or chronic. Culture to detect MRSA.

(Footnotes and abbreviations on page 45) NOTE: All dosage recommendations are for adults (unless otherwise indicated) and assume normal renal function.

TABLE 1 (9)

ANATOMIC SITE/DIAGNOSIS/ MODIFYING CIRCUMSTANCES	ETIOLOGIES (usual)	SUGGESTED REGIMENS		ADJUNCT DIAGNOSTIC OR THERAPEUTIC MEASURES AND COMMENTS
		PRIMARY	ALTERNATIVE[1]	
EYE/Endophthalmitis/Bacterial (continued)				
Post filtering blebs for glaucoma	Strep. species (viridans & others)	H. influenzae	Intravitreal rx as above + consider systemic **AM/CL, AM/SB** or **P Ceph 2**	
Post-penetrating trauma	Bacillus sp., S. epiderm.		Intravitreal agent as above + systemic **clinda** or **vanco**. Use topical antibiotics post-surgery (tobra & cefazolin drops).	
None, suspect hematogenous	S. pneumoniae, N. meningitidis, Staph. aureus		**P Ceph 3** (cefotaxime 2.0 gm q4h IV or ceftriaxone 2.0 gm q24h IV) + **vanco** 1.0 gm q12h IV pending cultures. Intravitreal antibiotics as with trauma.	
IV drug abuse	Bacillus cereus, Candida sp.			
Mycotic (fungal)	Candida sp.	Intravitreal agent + [systemic vanco]	Intravitreal **ampho B** 0.005-0.010 mg in 0.1 ml. Also systemic rx ± intravitreal vitrectomy ± intra-	
Broad-spectrum antibiotics, often corti- costeroids, indwelling venous catheters	Aspergillus sp.	Intravitreal **ampho B** & systemic therapy. See Comment.	vitreal ampho B (CID 27:1130 & 1134, 1998). Report of failure of ampho B lipid complex (CID 28:1177, 1999).	
Retinitis				
Acute retinal necrosis	Varicella zoster, Herpes simplex.	IV **acyclovir** 10-12 mg/kg IV q8h x5-7 d, then 800 mg po 5x/d x6 wks.		Strong association of VZ virus with atypical necrotizing herpetic retinopathy (CID 24:603, 1997).
HIV+ (AIDS) CD4 usually <100/mm³	Cytomegalovirus	See Table 14, page 107		Occurs in 5-10% of AIDS patients
Orbital cellulitis (see page 36 for erysipelas, facial)	S. pneumoniae, H. influenzae, M. catarrhalis, S. aureus, anaerobes, group A strep, occ. Gm-neg. bacilli post-trauma	**P Ceph 2/3** (**cefuroxime** 1.5 gm q8h IV, **cefotaxime** 2.0 gm q4-6h IV or **ceftizoxime** 2.0 gm q8-12h IV, or **AM/SB** 1.5 gm q6h IV	**TC/CL** (see foot-note[1] for dosages) or **cefotetan** 2.0 gm q4h IV or **ceftriaxone** 2.0 gm q24h IV	See mucor/rhizopus, Table 11, page 80. H. influenzae becoming a rare etiology.
FOOT				
"Diabetic." Reviews: NEJM 351:48, 2004; Ln 361:1545, 2003; CID 39-S73 & S104, 2004				
Ulcer without deep ulceration or suspected osteomyelitis	Colonizing skin flora	Glucose control, no antibiotic		2/3 of pts have peripheral vascular disease; assess early & revascularize if possible.
Mild; only skin, no inflam- mation, pulses present	Polymicrobic: S. aureus (including MRSA), Strep. species, coliforms, anaerobic bacteria	Glucose control, non-invasive vascular studies, superficial ulcer swabs not helpful.	**TC/CL** or **PIP/TZ** (see foot-note[1] for dosages) or **AM/CL-ER** 2000/(125 bid)	Treatment: (1) Peripheral neuropathy. Determine if osteomyelitis present (See Comp. osteo, page 2).
Severe—limb-threatening: skin, subcutaneous, maybe bone, inflammation, fever, neutrophilia		**Rx: TMP/SMX-DS** 1 tab po bid or **AM/CL-ER** 2000/(125 bid)	Gl.: 2 wks. Some add **RIF** 300 mg bid to TMP/SMX-DS.	Principles of treatment: (1) Revascularize if needed & possible. (2) Eradicate infection if present. (3) Remove pressure on ulcer. Best method is a non-removable total contact cast.
		Glucose control debridement with cultures. & then: (**IMP** or **MER** or **ERTA** or **PIP/TZ**)	Glucose control debridement with cultures, & then: (**IMP** or **MER** or **ERTA** or **PIP/TZ**)	Notes: (1) Charcot foot ref.: Ln 360:1776, 2002 (2) ERTA not active vs. P. aeruginosa (3) Linezolid superior to AM/SB in 1 study (CID 38:17, 2004).
Onychomycosis. See Table 11, page 78, fungal infections		Dosages in footnote[1] [4] [2]		
Puncture wound: Nail	P. aeruginosa	See page 2. 1-2% evolve to osteomyelitis.		
GALLBLADDER				
Cholecystitis, cholangitis, biliary sepsis, or common duct obstruc- tion (partial or 2° to tumor, stones, stricture)	Enterobacteriaceae 68%, enterococci 14%, bacteroi- des 10%, Clostridium sp. 7%, rarely candida	**PIP/TZ** or **AM/SB** or **TC/CL** or **ERTA** or **MER** If life-threatening: **IMP**	**P Ceph 3** + **metro** OR **Aztreonam** + **metro** OR **CIP** + **metro** Dosages in footnote[1]	For severely ill pts, antibiotic rx is complementary to adequate biliary drainage. 15-30% of pts will require decompression: surgical, percutaneous or ERCP-placed stent. Whether empirical rx should always cover pseudomonas & anaerobes is unclear (Ln 2:925, 1979). Gram stain of bile can be helpful in associating the biliary sludge (by ultrasound) with symptomatic infection (NEJM 320:1517, 1990), clinical relevance still unclear but has led to surgery (MMWR 42:39, 1993).

---

[1] **Cephalothin** 500 mg po qid, **cefotixin** 2.0 gm q8h IV, **CIP** 750 mg po bid or 400 mg IV q12h, **clinda** 300 mg q6h po or 450-900 mg po q6h IV, **IMP** 0.5 gm q6h IV, **MER** 1.0 gm q8h IV, **AM/CL** 875/125 mg q12h or 500/125 mg tid or 2000/125 bid po, **TC/CL** 3.1 gm q4h IV, **PIP/TZ** 3.75 gm q6h IV or 4.5 gm q8h IV, **azttreonam** 2.0 gm q6h IV, **FQ IV CIP** 400 mg q12h, **Gati** 400 mg q24h, **Oflox** 400 mg q12h. **Linezolid** 600 mg q12h.

[2] **AP Pen** (**ticarcillin** 4.0 gm q6h IV), **metro** 1.0 gm q6h IV, **TC/CL** 3.1 gm q4h IV, **PIP/TZ** 3.375 gm q6h or 4.5 gm q8h IV, **AM/SB** 3.0 gm q6h IV, **AM/CL** 875/125 mg q12h po, **MER** 1.0 gm q8h IV, **IMP** 0.5 gm q6h IV, **ERTA** 1.0 gm q24h IV, **clinda** 450-900 mg q8h IV (max. 4 gm/d.), **linezolid** 600 mg IV q12h.

Footnotes and abbreviations on page 45.

TABLE 1 (10)

ANATOMIC SITE/DIAGNOSIS/ MODIFYING CIRCUMSTANCES	ETIOLOGIES (usual)	SUGGESTED REGIMENS*		ADJUNCT DIAGNOSTIC OR THERAPEUTIC MEASURES AND COMMENTS
		PRIMARY	ALTERNATIVE†	
GASTROINTESTINAL				
Gastroenteritis—Empiric Therapy (laboratory studies not performed or culture, microscopy, toxin results NOT AVAILABLE) (Ref. *NEJM* 350:38, 2004)				
Premature infant with necrotizing enterocolitis	Associated with intestinal	Treatment (and rationale as for diverticulitis/peritonitis; page 14, bowel perforation, page 151) for anaerobic dosages		Pneumatosis intestinalis on x-ray confirms dx. Bacteremia-peritonitis in 30–50%. If bowel perforated, add coverage for anaerobes
Mild diarrhea (≤3 unformed stools/day, minimal associated symptomatology)	Bacterial (see *Severe*, below), Viral (usually causes mild to moderate disease. For traveler's diarrhea, see page 13	Fluids only + lactose-free diet, avoid caffeine		**Rehydration:** For fluid replacement, see *Cholera, page 12*. **Antimotility:** Loperamide (Imodium) 4 mg po, then 2 mg after each loose stool to max. of 16 mg/day. Bismuth subsalicylate (Pepto-Bismol) 2 tablets (262 mg) po qid.
Moderate diarrhea (≥4 unformed stools/day and/or systemic symptoms)	Shigella, salmonella, C. jejuni, E. coli 0157:H7, toxin-	Antimotility agents (see *Comments*) + fluids		Do not use if suspect hemolytic uremic syndrome **Hemolytic uremic syndrome (HUS):** Risk in **children** infected with E. coli 0157:H7 is 8–10%. Early treatment with TMP-SMX or FQs ↑ risk of HUS (*NEJM 342:1930 & 1990, 2000*). Controversial meta-analysis: *JAMA 288:996 & 3111, 2002*
Severe diarrhea (≥6 unformed stools/day, and/or temperature ≥101°F, tenesmus, blood, or fecal leukocytes)	positive E. coli, E. histo- lytica. For *typhoid fever*, see page 41	**TMP-SMX-DS** bid ×3–5 days. Campylobacter resist- ance to TMP/ SMX common in tropics.	**FQ** (CIP 500 mg q12h po or **Levo** 500 mg qd) ×3–5 days	**Other potential etiologies:** Cryptosporidia—no treatment in immuno- competent host (see *Table 13A & JID 170:272, 1994*). Cyclospora—usually chronic diarrhea, responds to TMP-SMX (see *Table 12A & NM 123:409, 1995*). **Severe diarrhea** treated with CIP 500 mg bid po decreases duration of diarrhea
NOTE: **Severe afebrile bloody diarrhea should ↑ suspicion of E. coli 0157:H7 infection**—Causes days of bloody diarrhea (≥4 days only 1–3% all causes diarrhea in U.S.—but causes up to 36% cases of bloody diarrhea (*CID 32:573, 2001*)		If recent antibiotic therapy possible) **add: Metro** 500 mg qid po ×10–14 days	**Vanco** 125 mg qid po ×10– 14 days	and other symptoms without changing duration of fecal carriage. 10% campy- lobacter resistant to FQs in Minn. resistant to FQs (*NEJM 340:1525, 1999*).
Gastroenteritis—Specific Therapy (results of culture, microscopy, toxin assay AVAILABLE). Ref. *NEJM 350:38, 2004*				
If culture negative, probably viral (norovirus), esp. if rarely in adults) **Rotavirus**—see *Table 14A, page 111*	Aeromonas/plesiomonas	**CIP** 500 mg bid ×3 d.	**TMP/SMX-DS** po bid ×3 d.	Although no absolute proof, increasing evidence as cause of diarrheal illness.
	Amebiasis *Entamoeba histolytica, Cyclospora, Cryptosporidia (Giardia),* see *Table 13A*			
	Campylobacter jejuni Fever in 53–83%, H/O¹ bloody stools 37%	**Azithro** 500 mg po qd ×3 (Thailand) OR CIP 500 mg po bid (See *Comment*)	**Erythro stearate** 500 mg po qid ×5 d	**Worldwide resistance to FQs** varies by region from 10% (USA) to 84% (Thailand). (*AAC 47:2358, 2003*). Erythro resistance rarely reported (*CID 37:131, 2003*).
	C. difficile toxin positive antibiotic-associated colitis (Ref. *NEJM 346:334, 2002*)	**Metro** 500 mg tid or 250 mg qid po ×10–14 d. Rare reports of in vitro resistance to metro (*AAC 46:1647, 2002*)	**Vanco** 125 mg (dil) po qid po ×10–14 d. **or (cholestyramine** 4 gm tid po) ×10–14 d.	Post-Campylobacter Guillain-Barré, assoc: 15% of cases (*CID 37:307, 2003*). Assoc. with small bowel lymphoproliferative disease, may respond to antimicro- bials (*NEJM 350:239, 2003*)
	Remember: contact isola- tion indicated Diagnosis: Tissue culture—detects toxin A&B, most sensitive. Takes 48 hrs. Rapid immunoassays— Less sens., detect toxin A, B, or both. 10–20% false- neg. rate.	If ileus or po rx not possible, **metro** 500 mg q6h IV (efficacy not established) or if ileus, add **vanco** by N-G or small bowel tube (see *Comment*) &/or retrograde colonic catheter &/or **vanco** enemas (see *Comment*)	**Teicoplanin** [4,6] 400 mg po bid ×10 d. For relapses: **metro** 500 mg tid po × [4,6] OR **RIF** 300 mg bid po ×10 d. (see *Comment*)	**DC antibiotic if possible; avoid antimotility agents; hydration; enteric isolation.** Relapse occurs in 10–20%. First, re-treat with **metro** ×10 d., then check again for clearance. **metro** OR **vanco**. See *Table 13A*. **Other relapse rx regimens: metro** po tid × 1 wk, then (**cholestyramine** 4 gm po tid + **vanco** po tid) × 1 wk or vanco po × 1 wk × 4 wks OR IV **vanco taper**: all doses 125 mg po: week 1—qid, week 2—bid, week 3—qd, week 4— qod, weeks 5 & 6 q 3 days. **When po rx not possible**, use IV metro + vanco, 500 mg/L saline via small bowel tube and/or via pigtail catheter in cecum (in severe typhlitis pts). Perfuse at ~3 ml/min to daily max. of 2.0 gm; see *Table 14A & CID 35:690, 2002*. **NOTE:** IV metro gets to colonic mucosa & colonic content; hence combination of IV metro & po (or via tube) vanco. **NOTE:** IV vanco not effective. Unclear how much IV metro gets to colonic vanco.

¹ H/O = history of

(Footnotes and abbreviations on page 45)

NOTE: All dosage recommendations are for adults (unless otherwise indicated) and assume normal renal function.

TABLE 1 (11)

ANATOMIC SITE/DIAGNOSIS/ MODIFYING CIRCUMSTANCES	ETIOLOGIES (usual)	SUGGESTED REGIMENS* PRIMARY	ALTERNATIVE†	ADJUNCT DIAGNOSTIC OR THERAPEUTIC MEASURES AND COMMENTS
Gastrointestinal/Gastroenteritis—Specific Therapy *(continued)*				
	E. coli 0157:H7 Fever in 16–45%, H/O† bloody stools 63%	**NO TREATMENT** with antimicrobials or anti-motility drugs, as may enhance toxin release and ↑ risk of hemolytic uremic syndrome (NEJM 342:1930 & 1990, 2000). Rehydration important.		NOTE: 5–10% of pts develop HUS (approx. 10% with HUS die or have permanent renal failure; 50% HUS pts have some degree of renal impairment) (CID 38:1298, 2004).
	Listeria monocytogenes	**AMP** 200 mg/kg/d IV div. q6h		Recently recognized cause of food poisoning; manifest as febrile gastroenteritis. Not detected in standard stool culture (NEJM 336:100 & 130, 1997).
	Salmonella, non-typhi— For typhoid fever, see page 41 Fever in 71–91%, H/O† bloody stools in 34%	If pt asymptomatic or illness mild, antimicrobial therapy not indicated. Treat if < 1 yr old or > 50 yrs old. If immunocompromised, if vascular graft(s) or prosthetic joints (see footnote, page 41). **CIP** 500 mg po bid X5–7 d. Resistance ↑ (Ln 353:1590, 1999)	**Azithro** 1.0 gm po x1, then 500 mg x4 d or **TMP/SMX-DS** bid po x3 d. See Comment for peds indose	↑ resistance to TMP/SMX and chloro. Ceftriaxone, cefotaxime usually active (see footnote, page 16, for dosage); ceftriaxone & FQ resistance in SE Asia (EID 9:255 & 323, 2003; Ln 363:1285, 2004). Primary treatment of enteritis is fluid and electrolyte replacement. No adverse effects from FQs in children (Ln 348:547, 1996). If immunocompromised, rx 14 d. **Peds doses:** TMP/SMX 5/25 mg/kg po x3 d. For severe disease, ceftriaxone 50–75 mg/kg q12–q-5 d. CIP suspension 10 mg/kg bid x5 d (Ln 352:522, 1998). CIP superior to ceftriaxone in children (JiD 3:337, 2003) **Immunocompromised children & adults: Treat for 7–10 d.**
	Shigella Fever in 58%, H/O† bloody stools 51%	**FQs** po: **CIP** 500 mg bid, or (**Levo** 500 mg qd)×3 d. See Comment for peds indose	**TMP/SMX-DS** bid po x3 d [TMP/SMX 5/25 mg/kg po] or (**azithro** 500 mg po once, then 250 mg qd x4)	Azithro superior to cefixime[NB] in trial in children (PIDJ 22:374, 2003).
	Vibrio cholerae Treatment decreases duration of disease, vol loss and duration of excretion. CID 37:272, 2003; Ln 363:223, 2004	**CIP** 1.0 gm po x1 + fluids. **Primary rx is hydration** (see Comment)	**Doxy** 300 mg po x1 + fluids (See Comment) (FQs & in pregnancy). Peds alternative **azithro** x1—see dose in Comment	Primary rx is fluid. IV use (per liter): 4 gm NaCl, 1 gm KCl, 5.4 gm Na lactate, 8 gm glucose. PO use (per liter potable water): 1 level teaspoon table salt + 4 heaping teaspoons sugar (JTMH 84:73, 1981). Add orange juice or 2 bananas for K+. Volume given = fluid loss. 7% body weight (Refs: CID 21:1485, 1995; TRSM 89:1103, 1995). Peds azithro: 20 mg/kg (to 1 gm max.) x1 (Ln 360:1722, 2002)
	Vibrio parahaemolyticus	Antimicrobial rx does not shorten course		Sensitive in vitro to FQ, doxy. Often history of seafood ingestion.
	Vibrio vulnificus	Usual presentation in skin lesions & bacteremia—see page 37		
	Yersinia enterocolitica Fever in 68%, bloody stools in 26%	No treatment unless severe. If severe, combine **doxy** 100 mg IV bid + **tobra** or **genta** 5 mg/kg IV once daily). **TMP/SMX** or **FQs** are alternatives.		Mesenteric adenitis pain can mimic acute appendicitis. Lab diagnosis difficult; requires "cold enrichment" and/or yersinia selective agar. Desferrioxamine rx ↑ severity; discontinue (if pt ill. Iron overload states predispose to yersinia (CID 21:1282 & 1:367, 1998).
Gastroenteritis—Specific Risk Groups—Empiric Therapy **Anorectal/proctocolitis intercourse**				
Proctitis (distal 15 cm only):	Herpes viruses, gonococci, chlamydia, syphilis. See Genital Tract, page 15			
Colitis:	Shigella, salmonella, campylobacter, E. histolytica (see Table 13A).	**FQ** [e.g. **CIP** 500 mg q12h po] x3 d.		See CID 28:701, 1999
HIV-1 infected (AIDS): > 10 days diarrhea	[G. lamblia]			See Table 13A
Acid-fast organisms:	Cryptosporidium parvum, Cyclospora cayetanensis			See Table 13A
Other:	Isospora belli, microsporidia [Enterocytozoon bieneusi, Septata intestinalis]			For influence of highly active antiretroviral therapy, see CID 28:701, 1999
Neutropenic enterocolitis or "typhlitis" (CID 27:695 & 700, 1998)	Mucosal invasion by **Clostridium** caused by C. Occasionally caused by C. sordelli or P. aeruginosa	As for periclostridial abscess. Ensure empiric regimen includes drug active vs Clostridia species; e.g., **pen G**, **AMP** or **clinda** (see Comment re: resistance) regimen should have penetrative active vs P. aeruginosa also.		Tender right lower quadrant. Surgical resection controversial but may be necessary. **NOTE:** Resistance of clostridia to clindamycin reported.

† H/O = history of
(Footnotes and abbreviations on page 45)   NOTE: All dosage recommendations are for adults (unless otherwise indicated) and assume normal renal function.

TABLE 1 (12)

ANATOMIC SITE/DIAGNOSIS/MODIFYING CIRCUMSTANCES	ETIOLOGIES (usual)	SUGGESTED REGIMENS* PRIMARY	ALTERNATIVE†	ADJUNCT DIAGNOSTIC OR THERAPEUTIC MEASURES AND COMMENTS
Gastrointestinal/Gastroenteritis—Specific Risk Groups—Empiric Therapy (continued)				
Traveler's diarrhea, self-medication. Patient usually afebrile (NEJM 342:1716, 2000)	**Acute**: 60% due to toxigenic E. coli, shigella, salmonella, C. difficile, amebiasis. (see Table 13). **If chronic**: cyclospora, cryptosporidia, giardia, isospora	**Azithro** 1.0 gm po x1 dose or **rifaximin** 200 mg po bid x3 d. **Imodium** optional: 4 mg x1, then 2 mg after each loose stool (see footnote)	**Levo** 500 mg po x1 dose. Alternative: **CIP** or **other FQ** bid x3 d. (see footnote)	Treatment based on randomized trial (CID 37:1165, 2003). Peds & pregnancy: **Azithro** 10 mg/kg/d x3 d. Rifaximin not approved for age 12 or older. Adverse effects similar to placebo
				No loperamide if fever or blood in stool.
Prevention	Not routinely indicated. Current recommendation is to take **FQ** + **Imodium** with 1st loose stool (NEJM 328:1821, 1993)		Alternative during 1st 3 weeks only if activities are essential: **Bismuth subsalicylate** (Pepto-Bismol) 2 tabs (262 mg) po qid or **FQ—CIP** 500 mg po qd		**Options: Bismuth subsalicylate** can cause black tongue and dark stool.
Gastrointestinal Infections by Anatomic Site				
Esophagitis	Candida albicans, HSV, CMV	See SANFORD GUIDE TO HIV/AIDS THERAPY		**Dx: Stool antigen**—>90% sens. & specific. Cheap & practical. Rare false-pos. due to other Helicobacter species (BMJ 320:148, 2000). Other tests: Urea breath test, if endoscoped, rapid urease &/or histology &/or culture.
Duodenal/Gastric ulcer; gastric cancer, MALT lymphomas (ind 2° NSAIDs) (NEJM 347:1175, 2002; Can J Gastro 17:25B, 2003)	**Helicobacter pylori** See Comment Prevalence of pre-treatment resistance increasing	**Rx 2x/day po for 14 days: Omeprazole or rabeprazole 20 mg³ + amox 1 gm + clarithro 500 mg**. Efficacy 80-95%	**Bismuth** (see footnote): bismuth subsalicylate 2 tabs 4x/d + **tetracycline** 500 mg 4x/d + **metronidazole 500** mg 3x/d + **omeprazole** 20 mg 2x/d. Efficacy 90-99%	**Antimicrobial resistance: Predicts rx failure** (AJM 139-463, 2003). Geographic differences but overall resistance: amox & tetra uncommon, clarithro 10%, metro 30-50%. **Treatment success:** Correlates with active drugs & pt compliance. Suggested **rx duration** varies between 7-14 d; we suggest bid regimen x14 d. For ↑ compliance & hopefully efficacy (7-9% ↑ cures with 14 d.) (Aliment Pharmacol Ther 14:603, 2000). **Test of cure:** Repeat stool antigen >8 wks post-treatment.
Whipple's disease (CID 32:457, 2001; Ln 363:654, 2004)	Tropheryma whippleii	**Initial 10-14 days** (**Pen G** 6-24 mill. U IV q4h OR ceftriaxone 2.0 gm IV qd) IM/IV q4h **Then, for approx. 1 year TMP/SMX-DS** 1 tab po bid	**TMP/SMX-DS** 1 tab po bid	Rx regimen based on empiricism and retrospective analyses. TMP/SMX relapses during TMP/SMX rx reported. Interesting in vitro susceptibility study: combination of doxy & hydroxychloroquine bactericidal (AAC 48:747, 2004).
See *Infective endocarditis, culture-negative, page 20*				
Inflammatory bowel disease: Ulcerative colitis, Crohn's disease	Unknown	**Sulfasalazine** 1.0 gm q6h po or **mesalamine (5ASA)** 1.0 gm q6h po	**Doxy** 100 mg po bid or (**Pen VK** 500 mg po bid or qid)	Check stool for E. histolytica. Try aminosalicylates 1° in mild/mod. disease. See review article for more aggressive therapy.
Mild to moderate Ref. Ln 359:331, 2002		**Coated mesalamine** (Asacol) 800 mg bid or qid equally effective.	**Corticosteroid enemas**	
		In randomized controlled trial, **CIP** + metro had no benefit (Gastro 123:33, 2002)	**Coated mesalamine**	Screen for latent TBc before blocking TNF (MMWR 53:683, 2004).
Severe Crohn's	Unknown	**Etanercept**	**Infliximab/adalimumab**	

---

¹ **FQ** dosage po for self-rx traveler's diarrhea—mild disease: **CIP** 750 mg x1; severe: 500 mg po bid x3 d. **Ofl ox** 300 mg po bid x3 d. probably would work but not FDA-approved indication.

² Can substitute other **proton pump inhibitors** for omeprazole or rabeprazole—all bid: esomeprazole 20 mg (FDA-approved), lansoprazole 30 mg (FDA-approved), pantoprazole 40 mg (not FDA-approved for this indication)

³ **bismuth preparations:** (1) In U.S., **bismuth subsalicylate** (Pepto-Bismol) 262 mg tabs; adult dose for helicobacter is 2 tabs (524 mg) 4x/day. (2) Outside U.S., colloidal bismuth subcitrate (De-Nol) 120 mg chewable tablets; dose is 1 tablet 4x/day. (3) Another interesting option: Ranitidine bismuth citrate 400 mg bid + amox 500 mg and clarithro 500 mg—all bid x14 d. Worked despite metro/clarithro resistance (Gastro 114:A23, 1998)

¹ **FQ** dosage po for self-rx traveler's diarrhea—mild disease: **CIP** 750 mg x1; severe: 500 mg po bid x3 d. **Ofl ox** 300 mg po bid x3 d. Once daily **Levo** 500 mg. **Gati** or **Moxi** 400 mg x3 d.

* Dosage recommendations are for adults (unless otherwise indicated) and assume normal/renal function.

NOTE: All dosage recommendations are for adults (unless otherwise indicated) and assume normal renal function.

(Footnotes and abbreviations on page 45)

TABLE 1 (13)

ANATOMIC SITE/DIAGNOSIS/ MODIFYING CIRCUMSTANCES	ETIOLOGIES (usual)	SUGGESTED REGIMENS*		ADJUNCT DIAGNOSTIC OR THERAPEUTIC MEASURES AND COMMENTS
		PRIMARY	ALTERNATIVE†	
GASTROINTESTINAL/Gastrointestinal infections by anatomic site (continued)				
Diverticulitis, perirectal abscess Also see *Peritonitis, page 31* CID (in press)	Enterobacteriaceae, occ. P. aeruginosa, Bacteroides sp., enterococci	**Outpatient rx—mild diverticulitis, drained perirectal abscess:** (TMP/SMX-DS bid) or (CIP 750 mg bid or **Levo** 750 mg 1x/d) + **metro** 500 mg q6h. All po x7–10 d.	**AM/CL-ER** 1000/62.5 mg 2 tabs po bid x7–10 d.	Must "cover" both Gm-neg. aerobic and Gm-neg. anaerobic bacteria. **Drugs active only vs anaerobic Gm-neg. bacilli:** clinda, metro. **Drugs active only vs aerobic Gm-neg. bacilli:** APAG, aztreonam, AP Pen, CIP, **Levo,** cefotaxim, TC/CL, PIP/TZ, AM/SB, ERTA, IMP, MER, Gati, & **Moxi.** Increasing resistance of Bacteroides species:
		Mild-moderate disease—Inpatient—Parenteral Rx: (e.g., focal peri-appendiceal perforation, peri-diverticular abscess, endomyometritis) PIP/TZ 3.375 gm IV q6h or 4.5 gm IV q8h or AM/SB 3 gm IV q6h, or TC/CL 3.1 gm IV q6h, or ERTA 1.0 gm IV qd	[(CIP 400 mg IV q12h) or (**Levo** 750 mg IV q24h)] + **metro** 500 mg IV q6h or 1.0 gm IV q12h	**% Resistant:** Cefoxitin Cefotetan Clindamycin 7–25 17–87 16–44 **Ertapenem** no resistance to metro, PIP/TZ [CID 35(Suppl.1):S126, 2002]. **Ertapenem** less active vs P. aeruginosa/Acinetobacter sp. than IMP or MER. **Concomitant surgical management important,** esp. with moderate-severe disease. **Role of enterococci remains debatable.** Probably pathogenic in infections of biliary tract. Probably need drugs active vs enterococci in pts with valvular heart disease.
		Severe life-threatening disease, ICU patient: IMP 500 mg IV q6h or MER 1 gm IV q8h	See Comment AMP + metro + (CIP 400 mg IV q12h or **Levo** 750 mg IV q24h) OR [AMP 2 gm IV q6h + **metro** 500 mg IV q6h + **APAG** (see Table 10C, page 72)	**Severe penicillin/cephalosporin allergy:** (aztreonam 2.0 gm IV q6h) + **metro** (500 mg IV q6h) or (1.0 gm IV q12h) OR [(CIP 400 mg IV q12h) or (**Levo** 750 mg IV qd) + **metro**].
GENITAL TRACT: Mixture of empiric & specific treatment. Divided by sex of the patient. For sexual assault (rape), see Table 15A, page 123. See Guidelines for Dx of Sexually Transmitted Diseases, *MMWR 51(RR-6), 2002 or CID 35(Suppl.2):S135, page 123.*				
Both Women & Men:				
Chancroid Ref. *CID 28(Suppl.1):S14, 1999*	H. ducreyi	**Ceftriaxone** 250 mg IM single dose **OR azithro** 1.0 gm po single dose	**CIP** 500 mg bid po x3 d. **OR erythro base** 500 mg qid po x7 d	In HIV+ pts, failures reported with single dose azithro *(CID 21:409, 1995).*
Chlamydia, et al. non-gonococcal or post-gonococcal urethritis, cervicitis NOTE: Assume concomitant **N. gonorrhoeae** Chlamydia conjunctivitis, see page 8	Chlamydia 50%, Mycoplasma hominis. Other known etiologies (10–15%): Ureaplasma, Trichomonas, herpes simplex virus, Mycoplasma genitalium. Chlamydia ref.: *NEJM 349:2424, 2003*	(**Doxy** 100 mg bid po x7 d) or (**azithro** 1.0 gm po as single dose). Evaluate & treat sex partner. **In pregnancy: erythro base** 500 mg po qid x7 d. OR **amox** 500 mg po tid x7 d	(**Erythro base** 500 mg po x7 d) or (**Ofloxe** 300 mg po x7 d) or (**Levo** 300 mg po x7 d). Evaluate & treat sex partner(s). **In pregnancy: azithro** 1.0 gm po x1. **Doxy & Oflox** contra-indicated	**Diagnosis:** Methods to detect C. trachomatis & N. gonorrhoeae summarized by CDC: *MMWR 51 (RR-15):1–39, 2002.* For C. trachomatis, a nucleic acid ampl. test on urine, urethral swab (men) or endocervical swab (women) suggested. **Treatment of non-pregnant disease:** either metro 2.0 gm po x1 + either erythro base 500 mg po qid x7 d. or erythro ethylsuccinate 800 mg po qid x7 d. **Evaluate & treat sex partners.**
Recurrent/persistent urethritis	Occult trichomonas, tetra-resistant U. urealyticum	**Metro** 2.0 gm po x1 + **erythro base** 500 mg po qid x7 d.	**Erythro ethylsuccinate** 800 mg po qid x7 d.	In men with NGU, 20% infected with trichomonas *(JID 188:465, 2003).*
Gonorrhoea *[MMWR 51(RR-6), 2002 or CID 35(Suppl.2):S135, 2002]*	N. gonorrhoeae			
Conjunctivitis (adult)		**Ceftriaxone** 1 gm IM or IV x one dose		Consider saline lavage of eye x1

¹ **APAG = antipseudomonal aminoglycoside, e.g., amikacin, gentamicin, tobramycin** (Footnotes and abbreviations on page 45)   NOTE: All dosage regimens are for adults (unless otherwise indicated) and assume normal renal function.

TABLE 1 (14)

ANATOMIC SITE/DIAGNOSIS/ MODIFYING CIRCUMSTANCES	ETIOLOGIES (usual)	SUGGESTED REGIMENS*		ADJUNCT DIAGNOSTIC OR THERAPEUTIC MEASURES AND COMMENTS
		PRIMARY	ALTERNATIVE†	
GENITAL TRACT/Both Women & Men/Gonorrhea *MMWR 51(RR-6), 2002 (continued)*				
Disseminated gonococcal infection (DGI, dermatitis-arthritis syndrome)	N. gonorrhoeae	(Ceftriaxone 1.0 gm IV qd) or (cefotaxime 1.0 gm q8h IV) or (ceftizoxime 1.0 gm q8h IV)—see Comment	Spectinomycin 2.0 gm q12h IM or Oflox 400 mg IV q12h or CIP 400 mg IV q12h or Levo 250 mg IV q24h—see Comment	Continue IM or IV regimen for 24 hrs after symptoms ↓; reliable pts may be discharged 24 hrs after sx resolve to complete 7 days rx with ceftime^AUS 400 mg po bid or CIP 500 mg po bid or Oflox 400 mg po bid or Levo 500 mg po qd. R/O meningitis/ endocarditis. Treat presumptively for concomitant C. trachomatis.
Endocarditis	N. gonorrhoeae	Ceftriaxone 1-2 gm IV q12h x ≥ 4 wks		If chlamydia not ruled out: Azithro 1 gm po x1 or doxy 100 mg po bid x 7 d
Pharyngitis	N. gonorrhoeae	Ceftriaxone 125 mg IM x1	CIP 500 mg po x1 or Levo 250 mg po x1	Some suggest test of cure culture after 1 week. Spectinomycin not effective
Urethritis, cervicitis, proctitis (uncomplicated) For prostatitis, see pages 17, 18 **Diagnosis:** Nucleic acid amplification test on urine or urethral swab—see *MMWR 51 (RR-15), 2002*	N. gonorrhoeae (50% of pts with urethritis, cervicitis have concomitant C. trachomatis —treat for both)	(Ceftriaxone 125 mg IM x1) or cefpodoxime 400 mg po x1) or (cefixime 400 mg po x1) or (CIP 500 mg po x1) or (Oflox 400 mg po x1) or Gati 400 mg po x1) PLUS [(Azithro 1 gm po x1) or (doxy 100 mg po 2x/d x7 days)] NOTE: Due to resistance of FQs to treat (1) men who have sex with men or (2) GC acquired in Hawaii, other Pacific areas, or England	(cefixime 400 mg po x1) or (CIP 500 mg po x1) or (Oflox 400 mg po x1) or (doxy 100 mg po 2x/d x7	Treat for both GC & C. trachomatis. Screen for syphilis. Other alternatives for GC: Spectinomycin 2 gm IM x1 Other single-dose cephalosporins: ceftizoxime 500 mg IM, cefoxitime 500 mg IM, cefotaxime 500 mg IM, cefotiam 1 gm IM + probenecid 1 gm po. Azithro 1 gm po x1 marginal for chlamydia but need 2 gm po for GC; not recommended for GC due to GI side-effects and expense. FQ resistance refs: *MMWR 53:335, 2004; CID 38:649, 2004*
Granuloma inguinale (Donovanosis)	Calymmatobacterium granulomatis	Doxy 100 mg bid po x3-4 wks OR TMP/SMX-DS 2x/d x3 wks	Erythro 500 mg qid po x3 wks OR CIP 750 mg po x3 wks OR Azithro 1.0 gm po 2x/d wk x3 wks	Clinical response usually seen in 1 week. Rx until all lesions healed, may take 4 weeks. Treatment failures & recurrence seen with doxy and TMP/SMX. Report of efficacy with FQ and chloro. Ref.: *CID 25:24, 1997*
Herpes simplex virus.		See Table 14, page 108		
Lymphogranuloma venereum	Chlamydia trachomatis, serovars, L1, L2, L3	Doxy 100 mg bid po x21 d.	Erythro 0.5 gm po x21 d.	Dx based on serology, biopsy contraindicated because sinus tracts develop. Nucleic acid ampli tests in development
Phthirus pubis (pubic lice, "crabs") & scabies	Phthirus pubis & Sarcoptes scabiei		See Table 13, page 100	
Syphilis *(JAMA 290:1510, 2003)*	T. pallidum			
Syphilis & HIV: *LnID 4:456, 2004*				
Early, primary, secondary, or latent <1 year	Benzathine pen G (Bicillin L-A) 2.4 mU IM x1	Doxy 100 mg bid po x14 d or tetracycline 500 mg po x14 d. Follow-up mandatory.		If early or congenital syphilis, quantitate VDRL at 0, 3, 6, 12 & 24 months after rx. If 1° or 2° syphilis, VDRL should ↓ 2 tubes at 6 months, 3 tubes 12 months, & 4 tubes 24 months. Early latent: 2 tubes ↓ at 12 months. With 1° 50% will be RPR seronegative at 12 months, 24% neg. at 24 months (*NEJM 351:122 & 154, 2004*).
More than 1 yr's duration (latent of indeterminate duration, cardiovascular, late benign)	Benzathine pen G (Bicillin L-A) 2.4 mU IM q week x3 = 7.2 mU total	Doxy 100 mg bid po x28 d or tetracycline 500 mg po qid x28 d		Azithro-resistant syphilis documented in California, Ireland, & elsewhere (*NEJM 351:122 & 154, 2004*). No published data on efficacy of alternatives. The value of routine lumbar puncture in asymptomatic late syphilis is being questioned in the U.S., i.e. no FQ, rx all patients as primary recommendation. *AIM 145:465, 1985.* Indications for LP (CDC): neurologic symptoms, treatment failure, serum non-treponemal antibody titer ≥1:32, other evidence of active syphilis (aortitis, gumma, iritis), non-penicillin rx. + HIV test.
Neurosyphilis—Very difficult to treat. Includes ocular (retrobulbar neuritis) syphilis		Pen G 3-4 mU q4h IV x10-14 d.	Procaine pen G 2.4 mU qd IM + probenecid 0.5 gm qid po) both x10-14 d —See Comment	Penicillin allergy: either desensitize to penicillin or obtain infectious diseases consultation. Ceftriaxone 2.0 gm qd (IV or IM) x14 d: 23% failure rate reported (*AJM 93:481, 1992*). For serologic criteria for response to rx: 4-fold or greater ↓ in VDRL titer over 6-12 mos. (*CID 28 (Suppl. 1):S21, 1999*)

(Footnotes on page 45)

NOTE: All dosage recommendations are for adults (unless otherwise indicated) and assume normal renal function.

TABLE 1 (15)

ANATOMIC SITE/DIAGNOSIS/ MODIFYING CIRCUMSTANCES	ETIOLOGIES (usual)	SUGGESTED REGIMENS¹ PRIMARY	ALTERNATIVE¹	ADJUNCT DIAGNOSTIC OR THERAPEUTIC MEASURES AND COMMENTS
GENITAL TRACT/Both Women & Men/Syphilis *(continued)*				
HIV infection (AIDS) (*See* Sanford Guide to HIV/AIDS Therapy *& refs. in Comments)*	T. pallidum	Add to 10 d. of **amox + probenecid** to **pen G** did not change efficacy in 1° & 2° syphilis (*NEJM* 337: 307, 1997).	For neurosyphilis, recommendations vary; some use **pen G** 24 mU qd IV for 14-21 d.	HIV+ plus RPR ≥1:32 plus CD4 count <350/µl increases risk of neurosyphilis nearly 19-fold—examine CSF (*JID* 189:369, 2004); also, CSF changes less likely to normalize (*CID* 38:1001, 2004). Review of syphilis & HIV: *LnID* 4:456, 2004.
Pregnancy and syphilis		Same as for non-pregnant, some recommend 2° dose (2.4 mU) **benzathine pen G** 1 wk after initial dose esp. in 3° trimester or with 2° syphilis		Monthly quantitative VDRL or equivalent. If 4-fold ↑, re-treat. Doxy, tetracycline contraindicated because of high risk of failure to cure fetus.
Congenital syphilis		**Aqueous crystalline pen G** 50,000 u/kg/dose IV q8-12h x10-14 d.	**Procaine pen G** 50,000 u/kg IM qd IM for 10 d.	Another alternative: Ceftriaxone ≤30 days old 75 mg/kg IV/IM qd or >30 days old 100 mg/kg IV/IM qd. Evaluate for penicillin allergy; ophthalmologic exam indicated. If more than 1 day of rx is missed, restart entire course. **Need serologic follow-up!**
Warts, anogenital	*See Table 14, page 111*			
Women:				
Amnionitis, septic abortion	Bacteroides, esp. Prevotella bivius; Group B, A streptococci; Enterobacteriaceae; C. trachomatis.	[(**Cefoxitin** or **TC/CL** or **IMP** or **MER** or **ERTA** or **PIP/TZ**) + **doxy**] **OR** [**Clinda** + (**APAG** or **Ceph 3**)] *Dosage: see footnote¹*		D&C of uterus. **In septic abortion**, Clostridium perfringens may cause fulminant intravascular hemolysis. **In postpartum patients** with enigmatic fever and/or pulmonary embol, **consider septic pelvic vein thrombophlebitis** (*see Vascular, septic pelvic vein thrombophlebitis, page 44*). After discharge, doxy or continue clinda. **NOTE:** IV clinda effective for C. trachomatis, no data on po clinda (*CID 19:720, 1994*).
Cervicitis, mucopurulent	N. gonorrhoeae; Chlamydia trachomatis.	Treat for gonorrhea, *page 15;* Treat for non-gonococcal urethritis, *page 14*		Criteria for dx: yellow or green pus on cervical swab.; >10 WBC/oil field. Gram stain for GC. If negative for GC, do nucleic acid amplification test and rx for both.
Endomyometritis/septic pelvic phlebitis Early postpartum (1ˢᵗ 48 hrs) (usually after C-section)	Bacteroides, esp. Prevotella bivius; Group B, A streptococci; Enterobacteriaceae; C. trachomatis	[(**Cefoxitin** or **TC/CL** or **ERTA** or **IMP** or **MER** or **AM/SB** or **PIP/TZ**) + **doxy**] **OR** [**Clinda** + (**APAG** or **Ceph 3**)] *Dosage: see footnote¹*		See Comments under *Amnionitis, septic abortion,* above
Late postpartum (48 hrs to 6 wks) (usually after vaginal delivery)	C. trachomatis, M. hominis	**Doxy** 100 mg q12h IV or po x14 d		Tetracyclines not recommended in nursing mothers, discontinue nursing. M. hominis sensitive to tetra, clinda, not erythro (*CID 17:S200, 1993*).
Fitz-Hugh-Curtis syndrome	C. trachomatis, N. gonorrhoeae	Treat as for pelvic inflammatory disease		Perihepatitis (violin-string adhesions)
Pelvic inflammatory disease (PID), salpingitis, tubo-ovarian abscess Outpatient rx, limit to pts with temp <38° C, WBC <11,000/mm³, minimal evidence of peritonitis, active bowel sounds & able to tolerate oral nourishment	N. gonorrhoeae, chlamydia, bacteroides, Enterobacteriaceae, streptococci	**Outpatient rx:** (**Oflox** 400 mg po bid or **Levo** 500 mg po qd) + **metro** 500 mg po bid) x14 d **OR** (**ceftriaxone** 250 mg IM or (Y x1) (± **metro** 500 mg po bid x14d) then **doxy** 100 mg po bid x 14 d].	**Inpatient regimens:** (**Cefotetan** 2 gm IV q12h or **cefoxitin** 2 gm IV q6h) + (**doxy** 100 mg IV/po q12h)]. [**Clinda** 900 mg IV q8h) + **gentamicin** 2 mg/kg loading dose, then 1.5 mg/kg q8h or 4.5 mg/kg 1x/d.), then **doxy** 100 mg po bid **Alternative parenteral regimens:** 1. (Oflox 400 mg IV q12h or Levo 500 mg IV qd) + metro 500 mg IV q8h 2. AM/SB 3 gm IV q6h + doxy 100 mg IV/po q12h + Levo Remember: Evaluate and treat sex partner.	

¹ **P Ceph 1** (cefazolin 2.0 gm q8h IV; cefotetan 2.0 gm q12h IV; cefoxitin 2.0 gm q6-8h IV; **TC/CL** 3.1 gm q6h IV; **AM/SB** 3.0 gm q6h IV; **PIP/TZ** 3.375 gm q6h or for nosocomial pneumonia: 4.5 gm q6h IV; **doxy** 100 mg IV q12h; **clinda** 450-900 mg q8h IV; **APAG gentamicin**. *see Table 10C, page 72;*) **P Ceph 3** (**cefotaxime** 2.0 gm q8h IV; **ceftriaxone** 2.0 gm q24h IV); **ertapenem** 1.0 gm qd IV; **IMP** 0.5 gm q6h IV; **MER** 1.0 gm q8h IV; **linezolid** 600 mg IV/po q12h; **vanco** 1.0 gm IV q12h. *(Footnotes and abbreviations on page 45)* NOTE: *All dosage recommendations are for adults (unless otherwise indicated) and assume normal renal function.*

TABLE 1 (16)

ANATOMIC SITE/DIAGNOSIS/ MODIFYING CIRCUMSTANCES	ETIOLOGIES (usual)	SUGGESTED REGIMENS*		ADJUNCT DIAGNOSTIC OR THERAPEUTIC MEASURES AND COMMENTS
		PRIMARY	ALTERNATIVE[1]	
GENITAL TRACT, Women				
Vaginitis—*MMWR 51(RR-6), 2002 or CID 35 (Suppl 2):S135, 2002 (continued)*				
Candidiasis Pruritus, thick cheesy discharge, pH <4.5 See Table 11A, page 76	Candida albicans 80-90%. C. glabrata, C. tropicalis may be increasing—they are less susceptible to azoles	**Oral azoles: Fluconazole** 150 mg po x1; **Itraconazole** 200 mg po bid x1 day	**Intravaginal azoles:** variety of strengths—from 1 dose to 7-14 d. Drugs available (all end in -azole): butocon-, clotrima-, micon-, terconazole (doses): *Table 11A, footnote page 76).*	Nystatin vag. tabs x14 d. less effective. Other rx for azole-resistant strains: gentian violet, boric acid. If recurrent candidiasis (4 or more episodes/yr): 6 mos. suppression with: fluconazole 150 mg po q week or itraconazole 100 mg po qd or clotrimazole vag. suppositories 500 mg q week.
Trichomoniasis Copious foamy discharge, pH >4.5 Treat sexual partners—see Comment	Trichomonas vaginalis	**Metro** 2.0 gm as single dose or 500 mg po bid x7 d. **OR Tinidazole** 2.0 gm po single dose **Pregnancy** *See Comment*	**For rx failure:** Re-treat with metro 500 mg po bid x7 d.; if 2nd failure: metro 2.0 gm po qd x3-5 d. If still failure, suggest ID consultation and/or contact CDC: 770-488-4115 or www.cdc.gov/std.	**Treat male sexual partners (2.0 gm metronidazole as single dose).** Nearly 20% men with NGU are infected with trichomonas (*JID 188:465, 2003*). Another option if metro-resistant: **Tinidazole** 500 mg po qid + intravaginal 500 mg po bid x14 d. Available from Panorama Pharm: 800-247-9767. Ref.: *CID 33:1341, 2001.* **Pregnancy:** No data indicating metro teratogenic or mutagenic [*MMWR 51(RR-6), 2002].*
Bacterial vaginosis Malodorous vaginal discharge, pH >4.5	Polymicrobic: associated with Gardnerella vaginalis, bacteroides non-fragilis, mobiluncus, peptococci, Mycoplasma hominis	**Metro** 0.5 gm po bid x7 d. or **metro vaginal gel** (1 applicator intravaginally) 1x/d x5 d.	**Clinda** 0.3 gm bid po x7 d. **Clinda** 2% vaginal cream 5 gm intravaginally hs x7 d. or **clinda ovules** 100 mg intravaginally hs x3 d.	**Rx** of male sex partner **not** indicated unless balanitis present. **Metro 2.0 gm po** is **not as effective as 5-7 day course** (*JAMA 268:92, 1992*). Metro extended-release tabs 750 mg po qd x7 d. available. No published data. **Pregnancy:** Rx same as non-pregnancy, except avoid clindamycin cream (↑ risk premature birth). Treatment of asymptomatic pts with oral clinda ↓ premature birth (*Ln 361:983, 2003).*
Men:				
Balanitis	Candida 40%, Group B strep, gardnerella	Oral **azoles** as for vaginitis		Occurs in ¼ of male sex partners of women infected with candida. Exclude circinate balanitis (Reiter's syndrome). Plasma cell balanitis (non-infectious) responds to hydrocortisone cream.
Epididymo-orchitis				
Age <35 years	N. gonorrhoeae, Chlamydia trachomatis	**Ceftriaxone** 250 mg IM x1 + **doxy** 100 mg po bid x10 d. or **Oflox** 300 mg bid po x10 d.		Also: bedrest, scrotal elevation, and analgesics.
Age >35 years or homosexual men (insertive partners in anal intercourse)	Enterobacteriaceae (coli-forms)	**FQ: (CIP-ER** 500 mg po 1x/d or **CIP** 400 mg IV bid/d or **Levo** 750 mg IV/po x10-14 d.)	**AM/SB, P Ceph 3, TC/CL, PIP/TZ:** see footnote page 16	Midstream pyuria and scrotal pain and edema. Also: bedrest, scrotal elevation, and analgesics.
Prostatitis—Review *AJM 106:327, 1999*				
Acute	N. gonorrhoeae, C. trachomatis	**Oflox** 400 mg po x1 then 300 mg po bid x10 d. or **doxy** 100 mg bid x10 d.		Oflox effective vs gonococci & C. trachomatis and penetrates prostate. In AIDS pts, prostate may be focus of Cryptococcus neoformans.
≤35 years of age		**Ceftriaxone** 250 mg IM x1 then **doxy** 100 mg bid x10 d.		
≥35 years of age	Enterobacteriaceae (coli-forms)	**FQ** (dosage: see *Epididymo-orch.*, >35 yrs, above) or **TMP/SMX** 1 DS tablet (160 mg TMP) po x10-14 d.		Treat as acute urinary infection, 14 days (not single dose regimen). Some authorities recommend 3-4 week rx (*IDCP 4:325, 1995).*
Chronic bacterial	Enterobacteriaceae 80%, enterococci 15%, P. aeruginosa	**FQ (CIP** 500 mg bid po x4 wks, **Levo** 500 mg q24h po x4 wks—See *Comment)*	**TMP/SMX-DS** 1 tab po bid x1-3 mos.	With rx failures consider infected prostatic calculi.

[1] 1 applicator contains 5.0 gm of gel with 37.5 mg metronidazole
(Footnotes and abbreviations on page 45)

NOTE: All dosage recommendations are for adults (unless otherwise indicated) and assume normal renal/renal function.

TABLE 1 (17)

ANATOMIC SITE/DIAGNOSIS/ MODIFYING CIRCUMSTANCES	ETIOLOGIES (usual)	SUGGESTED REGIMENS*		ADJUNCT DIAGNOSTIC OR THERAPEUTIC MEASURES AND COMMENTS
		PRIMARY	ALTERNATIVE†	
GENITAL TRACT, Men/Prostatitis (continued)				
Chronic prostatitis/chronic pelvic pain syndrome (New NIH classification, JAMA 282:236, 1999)	The most common prostatitis syndrome. Etiology is unknown, molecular probe data suggest infectious etiology (Clin Micro Rev 11: 604, 1998).	α-adrenergic blocking agents are controversial (AnIM 133:367, 2000).		Pt has rx of prostatitis but negative cultures and no cells in prostatic secretions. Rev.: JAC 46:157, 2000.
HAND [Bites: See Skin]				
Paronychia				
Nail biting, manicuring	Staph. aureus, anaerobes	Clinda 300 mg qid po	Erythro 500 mg qid po	Onset usually 2–5 days after trauma. No lymphangitis.
Contact with oral mucosa—dentists, anesthesiologists, wrestlers	Herpes simplex (Whitlow)	Acyclovir 400 mg tid po x10 days	Famciclovir or valacyclovir should work, see Comment	Gram stain and routine culture negative. Famciclovir/valacyclovir doses used for primary genital herpes see Table 14, page 108
Dishwasher (prolonged water immersion)	Candida sp.	Clotrimazole (topical)		Avoid immersion of hands in water as much as possible.
HEART				
Atherosclerotic coronary artery disease	Chlamydia pneumoniae—under study	New name: Chlamydophila pneumoniae. Ref. JAMA 290:1459 & 1515, 2003		
Infective endocarditis—Native valve—empirical rx awaiting cultures—No IV illicit drugs	NOTE: Diagnostic criteria include cases of continuous bacteremia (multiple positive blood cultures), new murmur (worsening of old murmur) of valvular insufficiency, definite emboli, and echocardiographic (transthoracic or transesophageal) evidence of valvular vegetations. Reviews: NEJM 345:1318, 2001; Ln 363:139, 2004			
Valvular or congenital heart disease including mitral valve prolapse but w/o modifying circumstances		[[Pen G 20 mU qd IV, continuous or div. q4h) or (AMP 12 gm qd IV continuous or div. q4h)] + **(nafcillin or oxacillin** 2.0 gm q4h)] + **gentamicin** 1.0 mg/kg q8h IM or IV (see **Comment**)	**Vanco** 15 mg/kg¹ q12h IV (not to exceed 1 gm unless serum levels monitored) + **gentamicin** 1.0 mg/kg¹ q8h IM or IV	If patient not acutely ill and not in heart failure, we prefer to wait for blood culture results. If initial 3 blood cultures neg. after 24–48 hrs, obtain 2–3 more blood cultures before empiric rx started. Nutritional variants may not be adequate coverage of enterococci, hence addition of penicillin G pending cultures. When blood cultures +, modify regimen from empiric to specific based on organism, in vitro susceptibilities, clinical experience.
See Table 15C, page 126 for prophylaxis				
Infective endocarditis—Native valve—IV illicit drug use ± infected prosthetic device—right-sided endocarditis—empiric rx.	S. aureus. Others rare	**Vanco** 1.0 gm q12h	**Dapto** 6 mg/kg q24h (not FDA-approved indication, 9/04)	Dapto clinical trials for bacteremia/endocarditis in progress. Quinupristin/dalfopristin cidal vs S. aureus if both constituents active.
Infective endocarditis—Native valve—culture positive (Consensus opinion on rx by organism: JAMA 274:1706, 1995/Review: NEJM 345:1318, 2001/Combination rx: CID 36:615, 2003)				
Viridans strep, S. bovis with penicillin G MIC ≤0.1 µg/ml	Viridans strep, S. bovis	[[Pen G 12–18 mU/d IV, continuous or q4h) x2 wks) PLUS (gentamicin IV 1 mg/kg q8h IV x2 wks)] **OR** (Pen G 12–18 mU/d IV continuous or q4h x4 wks) OR (ceftriaxone 2.0 gm qd IV x4 wks)	[[Ceftriaxone 2.0 gm qd IV + (netilmicin⁴³ 4 mg/kg qd) x2 wks (CID 21: 1406, 1995)]. Target dose: peak 3 µg/ml, trough <1 µg/ml. If very obese pt, recommend consultation for dosage adjustment.	Also effective: (ceftriaxone 2.0 gm qd) + (netilmicin⁴³ 4 mg/kg qd) x2 wks (CID 21: 1406, 1995). Target dose: peak 3 µg/ml, trough <1 µg/ml. If very obese pt, recommend consultation for dosage adjustment. Infuse vanco over ≥1 hr to avoid "red man" syndrome.
Viridans strep, S. bovis, nutritionally variant streptococci,¹ tolerant strep²	Viridans strep, S. bovis, nutritionally variant streptococci,² tolerant strep²	(Pen G 18 mU/d IV (continuous or q4h) x4 wks PLUS gentamicin 1 mg/kg q8h IV x2 wks	**Vanco** 30 mg/kg/d IV in 2 div. doses not to exceed 2 gm/d max unless serum levels measured x4 wks	Since relapse rate may be greater in pts III for >3 mos, prior to start of rx, the penicillin-gentamicin synergism theoretically may be advantageous in this group.
Viridans strep, S. bovis with penicillin G MIC >0.1 to <0.5 µg/ml	Viridans strep, S. bovis, nutritionally variant streptococci,² tolerant strep²	(Pen G 18 mU/d IV (continuous or q4h) x4 wks PLUS gentamicin 1 mg/kg q8h IV x2 wks NOTE: Low dose of gentamicin	**Vanco** 30 mg/kg/d IV in 2 div. doses not to exceed 2 gm/d max unless serum levels documented x4 wks	Can use cefazolin for pen G in pt with allergy that is not IgE-mediated (e.g., anaphylaxis). Alternatively, can use vanco. (See **Comment** above on gent and vanco)

¹ Assumes estimated creatinine clearance ≥80 ml/min, see Table 17.   NOTE: All dosage recommendations are for adults (unless otherwise indicated) and assume normal renal function.
² Tolerant streptococci² = MBC 32-fold greater than MIC

(Footnotes and abbreviations on page 45)

TABLE 1 (18)

ANATOMIC SITE/DIAGNOSIS/ MODIFYING CIRCUMSTANCES	ETIOLOGIES (usual)	SUGGESTED REGIMENS* PRIMARY	ALTERNATIVE†	ADJUNCT DIAGNOSTIC OR THERAPEUTIC MEASURES AND COMMENTS
HEART/Infective endocarditis—Native valve—culture positive *(continued)*				
For viridans strep or S. bovis with **pen G MIC ≤0.5** and enterococci susceptible to AMP. **NOTE:** Inf. Dis. consultation suggested	**"Susceptible" entero-cocci, viridans strep, S. bovis, nutritionally variant streptococci** (new names are: Abiotrophia sp. & Granulicatella sp.)	(Pen G 18–30 mu/24h IV, continuous or q4h x4–6 wks) **PLUS** (gentamicin 1–1.5 mg/kg q8h IV x4–6 wks) **OR** (AMP 12 gm/24 IV, continuous or q4h + gent as above x4–6 wks)	Vanco 30 mg/kg/24h IV in 2 div doses to max. of 2 gm/d unless serum levels meas-ured x4–6 wks **PLUS** gentamicin 1.5 mg/kg q8h IV x4–6 wks. **NOTE: Low dose of gent.**	4 wks of rx if symptoms <3 mos.; 6 wks of rx if symptoms >3 mos. Vanco for pen-allergic pts. **Do not give gent once-daily for enterococcal endocarditis.** Target gent levels: peak 3 µg/ml, trough <1 µg/ml. Vanco target serum levels: peak 20–50 µg/ml, trough 5–12 µg/ml. **NOTE:** Because of ↑ frequency of resistance (see below), all enterococci causing endocarditis should be tested in vitro for susceptibility to penicillin, β-lactamase production, gent. susceptibility and vanco. susceptibility.
Enterococci, high-level aminoglycoside resistance MIC streptomycin >2000, MIC gentamicin >500–2000, no resistance to penicillin	Enterococci, high-level aminoglycoside resistance	Pen G or AMP IV as above x4–6 wks (approx. 50% cure).	If prolonged pen G/AMP cure, surgical removal of infected valve. See Comment.	10–25% E. faecalis and 45–50% E. faecium resistant to high gent levels. May be gent or strepto resistant but not both. See footnote. Cases report of success with combination of AMP, IMP, and vanco (*Scand J Inf Dis 29:628, 1997*).
Enterococci, penicillin resistance β-lactamase production test is positive and resistance	Enterococci, penicillin resistance	**AM/SB** 3.0 gm IV q6h **PLUS gentamicin 1–1.5 mg/kg q8h IV x4–6 wks.** **Low dose of gent.**	**AM/SB** 3.0 gm IV q6h **PLUS Vanco** 30 mg/kg/24h IV in 2 div doses (check levels) x4–6 wks	β-lactamase **not** detected by MIC tests with standard inocula. Detection requires testing with the chromogenic cephalosporin nitrocefin. **Once-daily gentamicin rx not efficacious** in animal model of E. faecalis endocarditis (*JAC 39:437, 2002*).
Enterococci, intrinsic pen G/AMP resistance β-lactamase test neg., pen G/AMP MIC >16 µg/ml; no gentami-cin resistance. **Consultation suggested**	Enterococci, intrinsic pen G/AMP resistance	**Vanco** 30 mg/kg/24h IV q12h (>2 gm) **PLUS gent** 1–1.5 mg/kg q8h IV x4–6 wks (see Comment)	Teicoplanin active against a subset of vanco-resistant enterococci, but teicoplanin not available in U.S.	Desired vanco serum levels: peak 20–50 µg/ml, trough 5–12 µg/ml. **Gentamicin** used for synergy; peak levels need not exceed 4 µg/ml.
Enterococci, vanco-resistant Pen/AMP resistant + high-level gent/strep resistance, i.e., vancomycin-susceptible VRE. **Consultation suggested**	Enterococci, vanco-resistant, usually E. faecium	No reliable effective rx. Can try quinupristin/ dalfopristin (Synercid) or linezolid—see *Comment, footnote*[1] *and Table 5.*		Synercid activity limited to E. faecium and is usually bacteriostatic; therefore expect high relapse rate. Dose: 7.5 mg/kg IV (via central line) q8h. **Linezolid** active most enterococci, but bacteriostatic: 600 mg po/IV q12h. Linezolid failed in U.S. PMA (*CID 37:e29, 2003*).
Staphylococcal endocarditis. Aortic and/or mitral valve infection—MSSA	Staph. aureus, methicillin sensitive	Nafcillin (oxacillin) 2 gm q4h IV x4–6 wks **PLUS gentamicin** 1.0 mg/kg q8h IV x3–5 d. **NOTE: Low dose of gent for only 3–5.**	(Cefazolin 2.0 gm q8h IV x4–6 wks **PLUS** gentami-cin 1.0 mg/kg q8h IV x3–5 d)	If IgE-mediated penicillin allergy, 10% cross-reactivity to cephalosporins (*AnJM 141:16, 2004*). Cefazolin failure reported (*CID 37:1194, 2003*). No definitive data, pro or con, on once-daily gentamicin for S. aureus endocar-ditis. At present, favor q8h dosing x3–5 d. † recognition of IV catheter-associated S. aureus endocarditis. May need TEE to detect endocarditis. 23% of S. aureus bacteremia in association with IV catheter had endocarditis (*CID 115:106 & 115, 1999*). If TEE neg., may only need 2 wks of therapy.
Aortic and/or mitral valve infection—MRSA	Staph. aureus, methicillin resistant	**Vanco** 1.0 gm IV q12h x4–6 wks	Vanco 30 mg/kg/24h IV in 2 div doses (check levels if >2 gm/d) x4–6 wks	Quinupristin/dalfopristin cidal if both components active (both active if S. aureus sensitive to erythro in vitro). Other alternatives less desirable because bacteriostatic; e.g., TMP-SMX, clinda, linezolid.
Tricuspid valve infection (usually IVDUs): MSSA (MRSA next page)	Staph. aureus, methicillin sensitive	Nafcillin (oxacillin) 2 gm q4h IV **PLUS gentami-cin** 1 mg/kg q8h IV x2 wks. **NOTE: low dose of gent**	If penicillin allergy: not clear. Half failure rate with 2 gm/d of Vanco + gentamicin (*CID 33:120, 2001*). Can try **RIF.** (If sensitive) Dapto 6 mg/kg IV q24h[d][e]	**2-week regimen not recommended if metastatic infection (e.g., osteo) or left-sided endocarditis.** 2 reports of success with **4-week oral** regimen: CIP 750 mg bid + RIF 300 mg bid. Less than 10% pts had MRSA (*Ln 2:1071, 1989; AJM 101:68, 1996*).

[1] Three interesting recent reports: (1) Successful rx of vanco-resistant E. faecium prosthetic valve endocarditis with Synercid without change in MIC (*CID 25:163, 1997*); (2) resistance to Synercid emerged during therapy of E. faecium bacteremia (*CID 24:90, 1997*); and (3) super-infection with E. faecalis occurred during Synercid rx of E. faecium (*CID 24:91, 1997*). **NAI** = Not FDA-approved indication
(Footnotes and abbreviations on page 45) **NOTE: All dosage recommendations are for adults (unless otherwise indicated) and assume normal renal function.**

TABLE 1 (19)

ANATOMIC SITE/DIAGNOSIS/ MODIFYING CIRCUMSTANCES	ETIOLOGIES (usual)	SUGGESTED REGIMENS* PRIMARY	ALTERNATIVE†	ADJUNCT DIAGNOSTIC OR THERAPEUTIC MEASURES AND COMMENTS
HEART, Infective endocarditis/Staphylococcal endocarditis/Tricuspid valve infection *(continued)*				
Methicillin resistance (MRSA)	Staph. aureus, methicillin resistant	Vanco 30 mg/kg/d IV in 2 div doses (check levels if >2 gm/d) x4-6 wks	Fails/intolerant to vanco, can try **daptomycin** or **linezolid**	For MRSA, no difference in duration of bacteremia or fever between pts rx with vanco or daptomycin (AnIM 5.074, 1991). **Daptomycin:** Endocarditis studies in progress. **Linezolid:** Bacteriostatic.
Slow-growing fastidious Gm-neg. bacilli	HACEK group (see Comments) (Mayo Clin Proc 72: 532, 1997). Change to HABCEK for H add Bartonella	Ceftriaxone 2.0 gm qd IV x4 wks	AMP 12 gm (continuous or div. q4h) x4 wks + genta 1.0 mg/kg q8h IV or IM x4 wks	HACEK (acronym for Hemophilus parainfluenzae, H. aphrophilus, Actinobacillus, Cardiobacterium, Eikenella, Kingella). H. aphrophilus resistant to vanco, clinda and methicillin. Penicillinase-positive HACEK organisms should be susceptible to AM/SB + gentamicin. For hemophilus, see CID 24:1087, 1997.
Bartonella species (for bacteremia, see page 40 – Urinary tract see p 28 AAC 48:1921, 2004	B. henselae, B. quintana	Optimal rx evolving. Retrospective & open prospective trials support **gentamicin** 3 mg/kg IV once daily x14 days + **doxy** 100 mg po bid x4-6 wks		**Dx:** Immunofluorescent antibody titer ≥1:800; blood cultures only occ. positive, or PCR of tissue from surgery. **Surgery:** Over 1/2 require valve surgery; relation to cure unclear. B. quintana transmitted by body lice among homeless; asymptomatic colonization of RBCs described (Ln 360:226, 2002).
Infective endocarditis—culture negative				
Fever, valvular disease, and ECHO vegetations ± emboli and neg. cultures	T. whipplei, Q fever (see below), psittacosis, brucellosis, bartonella (see above), fungi	Emphasis on dx on diagnosis. See specific organism for treatment regimens.		For Q fever, see CID 33:1347, 2001. 4 pts with afebrile culture-neg. endocarditis had T. whipplei identified by PCR of resected heart valves (AnIM 131:112 & 144, 1999). Whipple's endocarditis (CID 33:1309, 2001); TMP/SMX or (tobra + β-lactam)
Infective endocarditis—Prosthetic valve—empiric therapy (cultures pending)				
Early (<2 months post-op)	S. epidermidis, S. aureus. Rarely, Enterobacteriaceae, diphtheroids, fungi	Vanco 15 mg/kg q12h IV + RIF 600 mg po daily		Early surgical consultation advised. Watch for evidence of heart failure.
Late (>2 months post-op)	S. epidermidis, viridans strep, enterococci, S. aureus			
Infective endocarditis—Prosthetic valve—positive blood cultures				
	Staph. epidermidis	(Vanco 15 mg/kg q12h IV + RIF 300 mg q8h po) x6 wks + gentamicin 1.0 mg/kg IV x14 d.		If S. epidermidis is susceptible to nafcillin/oxacillin (not common), then substitute nafcillin (or oxacillin) for vanco.
	Staph. aureus	Methicillin sensitive: (Nafcillin 2.0 gm q4h IV + RIF 300 mg q8h po) x6 wks + gentamicin 1.0 mg/kg IV x14 d.		
	Viridans strep, enterococci	See infective endocarditis, native valve, culture positive, pages 18-20		
	Enterobacteriaceae or P. aeruginosa	Aminoglycoside (tobra if P. aeruginosa) + (AP Pen or Ceph 3 AP or P Ceph 4)		In theory, could substitute CIP for APAG, but no clinical data.
	Candida, aspergillus	Ampho B ± an azole, e.g. fluconazole (Table 11, page 75)		High mortality. Valve replacement plus antifungal therapy standard therapy but some success with antifungal therapy alone (CID 22:262, 1996).
Infective endocarditis—Q fever LnID 3:709, 2003	Coxiella burnetii	Doxy 100 mg po bid + hydroxychloroquine 600 mg/d, x1.5-3 yrs		**Dx:** Complement-fixing IgG antibody of 1:40 is diagnostic of acute Q fever; IgG C-F antibody of 1:200 to phase I antigen diagnostic of chronic Q fever (LnID 3:709, 2003). Want doxy serum conc. >5 µg/ml (JID 188:1322, 2003).
Intracardiac-device related infections: Pacemaker/defibrillator, left ventricular assist device	S. aureus, S. epidermidis, rarely others	Device removal + vanco 1.0 gm IV q12h + RIF 300 mg IV bid	Device removal + dapto 6 mg/kg IV q24h‡ ± RIF (no data) 300 mg q12h	Duration of rx after device removal: 2 wks if "pocket" or subcutaneous infection, 10-14 d. if lead-assoc. endocarditis, 4-6 wks depending on organism. Refs: Circulation 108:2015, 2003; NEJM 350:1422, 2004

* **Daptomycin** 6 mg/kg/d IV. **Quinupristin/dalfopristin** (Synercid) 7.5 mg/kg IV (via central venous line) q8h. **Linezolid** 600 mg IV or po q12h.
NOTE: All dosage recommendations are for adults (unless otherwise indicated) and assume normal renal function. **NAI** = Not FDA-approved indication

† *(Footnotes and abbreviations on page 45)*

TABLE 1 (20)

ANATOMIC SITE/DIAGNOSIS/MODIFYING CIRCUMSTANCES	ETIOLOGIES (usual)	SUGGESTED REGIMENS*		ADJUNCT DIAGNOSTIC OR THERAPEUTIC MEASURES AND COMMENTS
		PRIMARY	ALTERNATIVE† (see footnote†)	
HEART (continued)				
Pericarditis, purulent—empiric rx _Rev: Medicine 82:385, 2003_	Staph. aureus, Strep. pneumoniae, Strep. A strep, N. meningitidis—see below	**Vanco + CIP** (_Dosage, see footnote‡_)	**Vanco + CFP** (see footnote‡)	Drainage required if signs of tamponade. Forced to use empiric vanco due to high prevalence of MRSA.
Rheumatic fever with carditis Ref: _CID 33:806, 2001_ For acute rheumatic fever, see page 41, reactive arthritis, below		Diuretics, ASA, and usually prednisone 2 mg/kg/d po		Clinical features: Carditis, polyarthritis, chorea, subcutaneous nodules, erythema marginatum. For Jones criteria: _Circulation 87:302, 1993._ Prophylaxis: _see page 41_
JOINT—Also see Lyme Disease, _page 39_				
Reactive arthritis				
Reiter's syndrome (See Comment for definition)	Occurs wks after infection with C. trachomatis, Campylobacter jejuni, Yersinia enterocolitica, Shigella, Salmonella sp.	Only treatment is non-steroidal anti-inflammatory drugs		Definition: Treatment is non-steroidal anti-inflammatory drugs Arthritis: asymmetrical oligoarthritis of ankles, knees, feet, sacroiliitis. Rash: palms and soles—keratoderma blennorrhagica, circinate balanitis of glans penis. HLA-B27 positive predisposes to Reiter's.
Poststreptococcal reactive arthritis (See Rheumatic fever, above)	Immunologic reaction after strep pharyngitis: (1) arthritis onset in <10 d (2) lasts months, (3) unresponsive to ASA	Treat strep pharyngitis and then NSAIDs (prednisone needed in some pts)	See Comment	A reactive arthritis after a β-hemolytic strep infection in absence of sufficient Jones criteria for acute rheumatic fever. Ref: _Mayo Clin Proc 75:144, 2000._
Septic arthritis: Treatment requires both adequate drainage of purulent joint fluid and appropriate antimicrobial therapy. Empiric therapy after collection of blood and joint fluid for culture; review Gram stain of joint fluid. For full differential, see LN 351:197, 1998.				There is no need to inject antimicrobials into joints.
Infants <3 months (neonate)	Staph. aureus, Enterobacteriaceae, Group B strep, N. gonorrhoeae	**(Nafcillin** or **oxacillin)** + **Ceph 3** (_Dosage, see Table 16, page 131_)	**(Nafcillin** or **oxacillin)** + **APAG** See Comment	Blood cultures frequently positive. Adjacent bone involved in 2/3 pts. Group B strep and gonococci most common community-acquired etiologies. **If MRSA a concern, use vanco in place of nafcillin/oxacillin.**
Children (3 months–14 years)	Staph. aureus 27%, S. pyogenes & S. pneumo 14%, H. influenzae 3%, Gm-neg. bacilli 6%, other (GC, N. meningitidis) 14%, unknown 36%	**Vanco + P Ceph 3** until culture results available	If Gram stain shows Gm+ cocci in clusters: **vanco** 1.0 gm q12h IV See Comment	Marked ↓ in H. influenzae since use of conjugate vaccine. NOTE: Septic arthritis due to salmonella has no association with sickle cell disease, unlike salmonella osteomyelitis. Duration of therapy varies with specific microbial etiology. Short-course steroid: Benefit reported (PIDJ 22:883, 2003).
Adults (review Gram stain); See page 39 for Lyme Disease				
Acute monoarticular				
At risk for sexually transmitted disease	**N. gonorrhoeae** (see page 15), S. aureus, streptococci, rarely aerobic Gm-neg.	Gram stain negative: **Ceftriaxone** 1.0 gm qd IV or **cefotaxime** 1.0 gm q8h IV or **ceftizoxime** 1.0 gm q8h IV	All empiric choices guided by Gram stain	For GC comments, see _Disseminated GC, page 15_
Not at risk for sexually-transmitted disease	S. aureus, streptococci, Gm-neg. bacilli	**Vanco + P Ceph 3** For dosage, see footnote page 23 See Tables 2, 11, & 12	Gm+ cocci in clusters: **Vanco** 1.0 gm q12h IV (or **Levo**) For treatment duration, see Table 3	Differential includes gout and chondrocalcinosis (pseudogout). **Look for crystals in joint fluid.** Levo has appropriate in vitro spectra and should work, but no clinical data. NOTE: Substitute vanco for nafcillin/oxacillin if MRSA suspected or proven.
Chronic monoarticular	Brucella, nocardia, mycobacteria, fungi			
Polyarticular, usually acute	**Gonococci**, B. burgdorferi, acute rheumatic fever, viruses, i.e., hepatitis B, rubella vaccine, parvo B19	Gram stain usually negative for GC. If sexually active, culture urethra, cervix, anal canal, throat, blood, joint fluid, and then: **ceftriaxone** 1.0 gm qd daily	If GC, usually negative for GC. If sexually active, culture urethra, cervix, anal canal, throat, blood, joint fluid, and then: **ceftriaxone** 1.0 gm qd daily	If GC, usually associated petechiae and/or pustular skin lesions and tenosynovitis. Consider Lyme disease if exposure areas known to harbor infected ticks. See page 39. Expanded differential includes gout, pseudogout, reactive arthritis (HLA-B27 pos).

*APAG (see Table 10C, page 72), **IMP** 0.5 gm q6h IV, **MER** 1.0 gm q8h IV, **TC/CL** 3.1 gm q6h IV, **PIP/TZ** 3.375 gm q6h or 4.5 gm q8h IV, **AM/SB** 3.0 gm q6h IV, **P Ceph 1 (cephalothin** 2.0 gm q4h IV or **cefazolin** 2.0 gm q8h IV or q6h IV), **Ceph 3** (see footnote‡), **CIP** 750 mg bid po or 400 mg q12h IV, **vanco** 1.0 gm q12h IV, **RIF** 600 mg/d po or IV, **aztreonam** 2.0 gm q8h IV, **CFP** 2.0 gm q12h (Footnotes and abbreviations on page 45) NOTE: All dosage recommendations are for adults (unless otherwise indicated) and assume normal renal function.

TABLE 1 (21)

ANATOMIC SITE/DIAGNOSIS/ MODIFYING CIRCUMSTANCES	ETIOLOGIES (usual)	SUGGESTED REGIMENS*		ADJUNCT DIAGNOSTIC OR THERAPEUTIC MEASURES AND COMMENTS
		PRIMARY	ALTERNATIVE†	
JOINT (continued)				
Septic arthritis, post intra-articular injection	MSSE/MRSE 40%, MSSA/ MRSA 20%, P. aeruginosa, Propionibacteria	**NO empiric therapy.** Arthroscopy for culture/sensitivity, crystals, washout		Treat based on culture results x14 days (assumes no foreign body present).
Infected prosthetic joint CID 36:1157, 2003; JAC 53:127, 2004	See below	**No empiric therapy.** Need culture & sens. results. Surgical options in Comment.		**Surgical options: 1. 2-stage:** Remove infected prosthesis & leave spacer, anti-microbics, then new prosthesis. Highest cure rate. **2. 1-stage:** Remove prosthesis, then new prosthesis, then antimicrobics. **3. Extensive debride-ment & leave prosthesis in place.** Antimicrobial therapy.
	S. pyogenes; Gps A, B, or G, viridans strep	Debridement & prosthesis retention; **Pen G or ceftriax) IV x4 wks.** Cured 17/19 pts CID 36:847, 2003)		
See surgical options in Comments	MSSE/MSSA	**(Naficillin/oxacillin** IV + **RIF** po) x6 wks	**(Vanco** IV + **RIF** po) x6 wks	Other: Remove prosthesis & treat ± bone fusion of joint. Last: Chronic antimicrobial suppression.
	MRSE/MRSA	**(Vanco** IV + **RIF** po) x6 wks	**CIP or Levo**—if suscepti-ble—po) x6 wks	Value of RIF: JAMA 279:1537 & 1575, 1998.
	P. aeruginosa	**Ceftaz** IV + (**CIP** or **Levo po)		
Rheumatoid arthritis	TNF inhibitors (adalimumab, etanercept, infliximab) ↑ risk of TBc, fungal infection CID 38:1261, 2004). Treat latent TBc first (MMWR 53:683, 2004). See TNF, page 41.			AAC 39:2423, 1995
Septic bursitis; Olecranon bursitis; prepatellar bursitis	Staph. aureus >80%, M. tuberculosis (rare), M. marinum (rare)	**(Naficillin** or **oxacillin** 2 gm, IV q4h or **dicloxa-cillin** 500 mg po qid) if MSSA	**(Vanco** 1 gm IV q12h or linezolid **600 mg po bid)** if MRSA	**Initially aspirate daily and treat for a minimum of 2-3 weeks.** If recurrence, surgical excision of bursa—should not be necessary often if treated for 3 weeks +. Ref.: Semin Arth & Rheum 24:391, 1995.
KIDNEY, BLADDER AND PROSTATE [For review, see AJM 113(Suppl.1A):1S, 2002 & NEJM 349:259, 2003]				Other doses, see footnote page 23
Acute uncomplicated urinary tract infection (cystitis–urethritis) [NOTE: Routine use of TMP/SMX not necessary; self-works works (CID 39:75, 2004)				
NOTE: Resistance of E. coli to TMP/SMX approx. 15–20% (CID 36:183, 2003) & corre-lates with microbiologic) clinical failure (CID 34:1061 & 1165, 2002). Recent reports of E. coli resistant to CIP & Levo as well	Enterobacteriaceae (E. coli), Staph. saprophyticus, enterococci	Local E. coli resistant to TMP/SMX <20% & no allergy: **TMP/SMX-DS** bid x3 d. If E. coli resistant ≥20% or sulfa allergy: **NF** x 7 d. or **fosfomycin** single dose	Local E. coli resistant >20% or TMP/SMX allergy; then 3 days of **CIP** 250 mg bid, **CIP-ER** 500 mg qd, **Gati** 200 or 400 mg qd, **Levo** 250 mg qd. **Do not use Moxi or Gemi.**	Try to spare FQs (CID 39:75, 2004) 7-day Rx recommended in pregnancy (discontinue or do not use sulfonamides (TMP/SMX) near term (2 weeks before EDC) because of potential ↑ in kernicterus). If failure on 3-day course, culture and x 2 weeks. **Fosfomycin** 3.0 gm po x1 less effective vs E. coli than multi-dose TMP/SMX or FQ (Med Lett 39:66, 1997). Fosfo active vs E. faecalis; poor activity vs other coliforms **Moxifloxacin & gemifloxacin:** Neither approved for UTI. Do not use; inadequate urine concentration **Phenazopyridine (Pyridium)**—non-prescription—may relieve dysuria: 200 mg po tid x2 d. Hemolysis if G6PD deficient.
Risk factors for STD. Dipstick-positive leukocyte esterase or hemoglobin, neg. Gram stain	C. trachomatis	**Azithro** 1.0 gm single dose po	**Doxy** 100 mg po x7 d.	Pelvic exam for vaginitis & herpes simplex; urine LCR/PCR for GC and C. trachomatis.
Recurrence (3 or more episodes/ year) in young women	Any of the above bacteria	Eradicate infection, then TMP/SMX 1 single-strength tab qd po long term		A cost-effective alternative to continuous prophylaxis is self-administered single dose rx [TMP/SMX DS, 2 tabs, 320/1600 mg] at symptom onset. Another alternative: 1 TMP/SMX tablet TMP/SMX post-coitus.
Child ≤5 yrs old and grade 3–4 reflux	Coliforms	Treat as for uncomplicated UTI. Evaluate for potentially correctable urologic factors—see Comment.		Treat as for uncomplicated UTI. Evaluate for potentially correctable urologic factors—see Comment.
Recurrent UTI in postmenopausal women See CID 30:152, 2000	E. coli & other Enterobac-teriaceae, enterococci, S. saprophyticus	**TMP/SMX** (2 mg TMP/10 mg SMX/kg po qd) or **nitrofurantoin** 2 mg/kg po qd)		NF more effective than vaginal cream in decreasing frequency, but authors worry about prolonged pulmonary fibrosis with long-term NF Rx (CID 36:1362, 2003). Definition: ≥3 culture + symptomatic UTIs in 1 year or 2 UTIs in 6 months. Urologic factors: (1) cystocele, (2) incontinence, (3) ↑ residual urine volume (≥50 ml).

(Footnotes and abbreviations on page 45)   NOTE: All dosage recommendations are for adults (unless otherwise indicated) and assume normal renal function.

TABLE 1 (22)

ANATOMIC SITE/DIAGNOSIS/ MODIFYING CIRCUMSTANCES	ETIOLOGIES (usual)	SUGGESTED REGIMENS*		ADJUNCT DIAGNOSTIC OR THERAPEUTIC MEASURES AND COMMENTS
		PRIMARY	ALTERNATIVE†	
KIDNEY, BLADDER AND PROSTATE *(continued)*				
Acute uncomplicated pyelonephritis (usually women 18–40 y)	Enterobacteriaceae (most likely E. coli), enterococci			UTI *(NEJM 335:635, 1996)*: temperature >102°F; definite costovertebral tenderness) [NOTE: Culture of urine and blood indicated prior to therapy. Report of hemolytic uremic syndrome as result of toxin-producing E. coli.
Moderately ill (outpatient)	(Gm stain of uncentrifuged urine may allow identification of Gm-neg. bacilli vs Gm+ cocci)	An oral FQ, e.g. CIP-ER 1000 mg po qd **or** CIP 500 mg bid **or** CIP-ER 1000 mg, Gati 400 mg qd, Levo 250 mg qd, Oflox 400 mg	AM/CL,¹ O Ceph, or TMP/SMX-DS. Treat for 14 days.	In randomized double-blind trial, bacteriologic and clinical success higher for **7 days of CIP than for 14 days of TMP/SMX**: failures correlated with TMP/SMX in vitro resistance *(JAMA 283:1583, 2000)*. Since CIP worked with 7-d rx, suspect other FQs effective with 7 d. of rx. Do not use Moxi or Gemi due to low urine concentrations.
Hospitalized	E. coli most common, enterococci 2°¹ in frequency	FQ (IV) or (AMP + gent- amicin **or** AM/SB or PIP/TZ or AP Pen. Treat for 14 d. *Dosages in footnotes* Do not use FQ or TMP/SMX when possible enterococcal infection	TC/CL or AM/SB or PIP/TZ **or** ERTA. Treat for 14 d.	Treat until pt afebrile 24–48 hrs, then complete 2-wk course with oral drugs (as "Moderately ill" above). If no clinical improvement in 3 days, we recommend imaging. On CT if single focal mass-like lesion avg, response requires 6 d, if lesions diffuse avg, response 13 d. *(AJM 93:289, 1992)*. **If pt hypotensive, prompt imaging (Echo or CT) is recommended to ensure absence of obstructive uropathy.** NOTE: **O Ceph 3 & ertapenem not active vs enterococci.**
Complicated UTI/catheters Obstruction, reflux, azotemia, transplant, Foley catheter-related	Enterobacteriaceae, P. aeruginosa, enterococci	**(AMP + gent)** or PIP/TZ or TC/CL or IMP or MER x2–3 wks	IV FQ CIP, Gati, Levo, x2– 3 wks	Rule out obstruction. Watch for enterococci and P. aeruginosa—not all listed drugs have predictable activity. **CIP-ER** oral dose: 1000 mg qd
Asymptomatic bacteriuria **Preschool children**		Base regimen on C&S, not empirical		Diagnosis requires ≥10⁵ CFU/ml urine of same bacterial species in 2 specimens obtained 3–7 days apart.
Pregnancy	Aerobic Gm-neg. bacilli & Staph. hemolyticus	Screen 1ˢᵗ trimester. If (+), rx 3 d. with **amox, NF,** O Ceph, TMP/SMX, or TMP alone		Screen monthly for recurrence. Some authorities treat continuously until delivery (stop, TMP/SMX 2 wks before EDC). ↑ resistance of E. coli to TMP/SMX.
Before and after invasive urologic intervention, e.g., Foley catheter	Aerobic Gm-neg. bacilli	Obtain urine culture and treat rx 3 d. with TMP/SMX-DS,		In one study, single dose ≥TMP/SMX-DS 80% effective *(AHM 114:713, 1991)*. Use of silver-alloy Foley catheter may ↓ risk of clinically significant bacteriuria *(AJM 105:236, 1998; AHM 160:3294, 2000)*.
Neurogenic bladder		No rx if asymptomatic; intermittent catheterization if possible		Ref. *AJM 113(7A):67S, 2002*
Asymptomatic, advanced age, male or female		No rx indicated unless in conjunction with surgery to correct obstructive uropathy; measure residual urine vol. in females; prostate exam/PSA in males		Chronic, pyelo with abnormal inflammatory response. See *CID 29:444, 1999*
Malacoplakia	E. coli	Bethanechol chloride + (CIP or TMP/SMX)	Vanco if MRSA	
Perinephric abscess Associated with staphylococcal bacteremia	Staph. aureus	**Nafcillin/oxacillin or P Ceph 1** *(Dosage, see footnote page 17)*	Vanco if MRSA	Drainage, surgical or image-guided aspiration
Associated with pyelonephritis	Enterobacteriaceae	See pyelonephritis, above		Drainage, surgical or image-guided aspiration
Prostatitis		See prostatitis, pages 17–18		

NOTE: qd = once daily; bid = twice daily; tid = 3 times a day; qid = 4 times a day

¹ **AM/CL** 875/125 mg q12h or 500/125 mg tid po, **aztreonam** 2.0 gm IV q8h, **CIP** 400 mg IV q12h, **Gati** 400 mg IV qd, **Levo** (250 mg po qd for mild uncomplicated disease, 500 mg IV qd for hospital pt]), **cefoxitin** 2.0 gm q8h IV, **P Ceph 3 [cefotaxime** 2.0 gm q8h IV or q4h IV for life-threatening infections; **ceftriaxone** 1.0–2.0 gm qd IV (use 2.0 gm q4h IV for nosocomial pneumonia (see *Table 10C, page 72*) & meningitis; **ceftazidime** 2.0 gm q8h IV], **gentamicin** 4.5 gm q8h IV or **oxacillin** 2.0 gm q4h IV, **P Ceph 4 [cefepime** 2.0 gm q12h IV], **ERTA** 1.0 gm qd IV, **IMP** 0.5 gm q6h IV, **MER** 1.0 gm q8h IV, **Nafcillin** or **oxacillin** 2.0 gm q4h IV, **Vanco** 1.0 gm IV q12h; **TMP/SMX** 2.0 mg/kg (TMP) q6h IV, **P Ceph 1 [cefazolin** 2.0 gm q8h IV]. **P Ceph 2 [cefuroxime** 1.5 gm q8h IV], **TC/CL** 3.1 gm q4h IV, **PIP/TZ** 3.375 gm q6h IV or for nosocomial pneumonia 4.5 gm q6h IV, **AM/SB** 3.0 gm q6h IV. For oral cephalosporin dosages, see *Table 10B, page 67.* **Dicloxacillin** 500 mg po qid, **Metronidazole** 500 mg po qid.
gm (all IV) or oral (oral) 600 mg IV/po q12h NOTE: All dosage recommendations are for adults (unless otherwise indicated) and assume normal renal function.
(Footnotes and abbreviations on page 45)

TABLE 1 (23)

ANATOMIC SITE/DIAGNOSIS/ MODIFYING CIRCUMSTANCES	ETIOLOGIES (usual)	SUGGESTED REGIMENS*		ADJUNCT DIAGNOSTIC OR THERAPEUTIC MEASURES AND COMMENTS
		PRIMARY	ALTERNATIVE†	
LIVER (for spontaneous bacterial peritonitis, see page 31)				
Cholangitis		See Gallbladder, page 10		
Hepatic abscess	Enterobacteriaceae, bacteroides, enterococci, Entamoeba histolytica, Yersinia enterocolitica (rare) *For echinococcus, see Table 13, page 99. For cat-scratch disease (CSD), see pages 30 & 38.*	**Metro** + (**P Ceph 3** or **cefoxitin** or **TC/CL** or **PIP/TZ** or **AM/SB** or **FQ**) **AMP + APAG + metro** traditional & effective but AMP-resistant Gm-neg. bacilli increasing.	**Metro** (for amoeba) + either **IMP** or **MER** (dosage, see footnote page 23)	Serological tests for amebiasis should be done on all patients; if neg, ½ have surgical drainage or percutaneous aspiration. In pyogenic abscess, if identified G surgically. If amoebic serology positive, treat with metro alone without surgery. Metro inclusively for both E. histolytica & bacteroides. **Hemochromatosis** associated with Yersinia enterocolitica liver abscess (*CID 18:938, 1994*); regimens listed are effective for yersinia.
Leptospirosis	Leptospirosis, see page 40			
Peliosis hepatis in AIDS pts	Bartonella henselae and B. quintana	*See page 38*		
Post-transplant biloma (*CID 39:517, 2004*)	Enterococci (incl. VRE), Candida, Gm-neg bacilli (P. aeruginosa 8%), anaerobes 5%	**Linezolid** 600 mg IV bid + **CIP** 400 mg IV q12h + **fluconazole** 400 mg IV qd	**Dapto** 6 mg/kg/d + **Levo** 750 mg IV qd + **fluconazole** 400 mg IV qd	Suspect if fever & abdominal pain post-transplant. Exclude hepatic artery thrombosis. Presence of candida and/or VRE bad prognosticators.
Viral hepatitis	Hepatitis A, B, C, D, E, G	See Table 14		
LUNG/Bronchi				
Bronchiolitis/wheezy bronchitis Infants/children (≤ age 5)	**Respiratory syncytial virus** (RSV) 50%, parainfluenza 25%, other viruses 20% (expiratory wheezing)	Antibiotics not useful, mainstay of rx is oxygen. Ribavirin of no benefit (*AJRCCM 160:829, 1999*). 2 products available for prevention. RSV-immune globulin and a humanized mouse monoclonal antibody, **palivizumab** See Table 14, page 112		RSV most important. Rapid dx with antigen detection methods. Ribavirin: No data on IV ribavirin but little enthusiasm. Emphasis now on vaccine development and preventive modulation with immunoglobulins. Reviews: *PIDJ 19:773, 2000; Red Book of Peds 2003, 26th Ed.*
Bronchitis				
Infants/children (≤ age 5)	< Age 2: Adenovirus; 3 virus parainfluenza; 3 virus	Respiratory syncytial	Antibiotics indicated only with associated sinusitis or heavy growth for S. pneumo, Group A strep, H. influenzae or no improvement in 1 week. Otherwise rx is symptomatic.	
Adolescents and adults with acute tracheobronchitis (Acute bronchitis) **Acute bronchitis with cough)**	Usually viral. M. pneumoniae 5%, C. pneumoniae 5%. See Persistent cough, below	**Antibiotics not indicated.** Antitussive ± inhaled bronchodilators		Purulent sputum alone not an indication for antibiotic rx. Azithro was no better than low-dose vitamin C in a controlled trial (*Ln 359:1648, 2002*). Expect cough to last 2 weeks. If fever/rigors, get chest x-ray. M. pneumoniae ref. (*LnID 1:334, 2001*). Rare (if with true C. pneumo infection may require 6 wks of clarithro to clear organism (*J Med Micro 52:265, 2003*).
Persistent cough (>14 d.), afebrile **during community outbreak:** **Pertussis (whooping cough)** 10–20% adults with prolonged cough have pertussis (*CID 32:1691, 2001*). Rev. *LnID 2:744, 2002*	Bordetella pertussis & parapertussis occ. Bordetella parapertussis. Also consider asthma, gastro-esophageal reflux, post-nasal drip	**Peds doses: Azithro** or **clarithro** (dose in footnote[1]) OR **erythro** 40 mg/kg/d div q6-12h x14 d OR **erythro base** po 40 mg/kg/d div q6h x14 d.	**Adult doses: Azithro** 500 mg po day 1, 250 mg qd days 2–5 OR **clarithro** 500 mg po bid x7 d OR TMP/SMX-DS 1 tab po bid x14 d. OR take 500 mg bid or 1.0 gm ER qd x7 d.)	**3 stages of illness:** catarrhal (1–2 wks), paroxysmal coughing (2–4 wks), and convalescence (1–2 wks). Treatment may abort or eliminate pertussis in catarrhal stage, but does not shorten paroxysmal stage. **Diagnosis:** PCR on nasopharyngeal secretions or † pertussis-toxin antibody. **Rx aimed at eradication** of NP carriage. Azithro works fastest (*PIDJ 22:847, 2003*). Hypertrophic pyloric stenosis reported in infants under 6 wks of age given erythro (*MMWR 48:1117, 1999*).
Prophylaxis of household contacts.		**Erythromycin—Children:** 50 mg/kg/d po div in 4 doses. **Adults:** 500 mg qid po. x 14 d. **Alternative:** *azithro* or *clarithro* 7.5 mg/kg po bid x 4 d. See footnote[1]		Recommended by Am. Acad. Ped., *Red Book 2003* for all household or close contacts, community-wide prophylaxis not recommended

---

1 Peds doses: azithro 10 mg/kg/d day 1, then 5 mg/kg 1x/d. x4 d. (*PIDJ 22:847, 2003*) or clarithro 7.5 mg/kg po twice a day x5–7 d.
2 Compliance with ↓ days w/ poor adherence due to nausea/vomiting; clarithro costs more but compliance may be better.
(*Footnotes and abbreviations on page 45*)   NOTE: All dosage recommendations are for adults (unless otherwise indicated) and assume normal renal function.

TABLE 1 (24)

ANATOMIC SITE/DIAGNOSIS/ MODIFYING CIRCUMSTANCES	ETIOLOGIES (usual)	SUGGESTED REGIMENS*		ADJUNCT DIAGNOSTIC OR THERAPEUTIC MEASURES AND COMMENTS
		PRIMARY	ALTERNATIVE†	
LUNG/Bronchi/Bronchus *(continued)* Acute bacterial exacerbation of chronic bronchitis (ABECB), adults (almost always smokers with COPD) Refs.: *AnIM 134:595,6,6, 2001; NEJM 346:988, 2002; 2001; AnIM 162:256, 2002*	Viruses 20–50%, C. pneumoniae (<1%, inhaled antichallenge bronchodilator; (3) oral corticosteroid; (4) antimicrobial treatment or maybe influenzae & M. catarrhalis controversial. Tobacco use, air pollution contribute.	**Severe ABECB =** ↑ dyspnea, ↑ sputum viscosity/purulence. For severe ABECB: (1) consider chest x-ray, esp. if febrile and/or HIV (+), sat., (2) inhaled anticholinergic bronchodilator; (3) oral corticosteroid; (4) D/C tobacco use; (5) non-invasive positive pressure ventilation. **Role of antimicrobial rx debated even for severe disease. For mild or moderate disease, no antimicrobial treatment or maybe amox, doxy, TMP/SMX, or cefaclor/cefprozil. For severe disease, AM/CL, azithro/ clarithro, or O Ceph or telithro or FQs with enhanced activity vs drug-resistant S. pneumo (Gati, Gemi, Levo, or Moxi)**		
Pneumonia Neonatal: Birth to 1 month	Viruses: CMV, rubella, H. simplex **Bacteria:** Group B strep, listeria, coliforms, S. aureus, P. aeruginosa **Other:** Chlamydia trachomatis, syphilis	**AMP + gentamicin ± cefotaxime** Add **vanco** if MRSA a concern. For chlamydia rx, **erythro** 12.5 mg/kg po or IV qid x14 d.		Blood cultures indicated. Consider C. trachomatis if afebrile pneumonia, staccato cough, IgM ↑ + 1.8; in infant with erythro and sulfisoxazole. If MRSA documented, **vanco**, **TMP/SMX**, & **linezolid** alternatives. **Linezolid** dosage birth to age 11 yrs is **10 mg/kg q8h**. Ref.: *PIDJ 22(Suppl.):S158, 2003.*

CONSIDER TUBERCULOSIS IN ALL PATIENTS. ISOLATE ALL SUSPECT PATIENTS

Age 1–3 months *(Adapted from NEJM 346:429, 2002)* Pneumonitis syndrome. Usually afebrile	C. trachomatis, RSV, paraflu virus 3, Bordetella, S. pneumoniae, S. aureus (rare)	**Outpatient: po erythro** 10 mg/kg q6h or po **azithro** 10 mg/kg x1, then 5 mg/kg x4 d.	**Inpatient: If afebrile erythro** 10 mg/kg IV q6h or **azithro** 2.5 mg/kg IV q12h. **If febrile**, add **cefotaxime** 200 mg/kg/d div q8h	Pneumonitis syndrome: cough, tachypnea, dyspnea, diffuse infiltrates, afebrile. Usually requires hospital care. Reports of hypertrophic pyloric stenosis after erythro under age 6 wks; not sure about azithro. If lobar pneumonia, give AMP 200–300 mg/kg/d to cover S pneumoniae. No empiric coverage for S. aureus.
		For RSV, see bronchiolitis, page 24		
Age 4 months–5 years For RSV, see bronchiolitis, pages 24 & Table 14 Ref.: *NEJM 346:429, 2002*	RSV, other resp. viruses, S. pneumo, H. flu, myco-plasma, S. aureus (rare), M. tbc	**Outpatient: po erythro** 10 mg/kg q6h or po **azithro** 10 mg/kg x1, then 5 mg/kg x4 d. (Peds susp 7.5 mg/kg q12h) **OR AMP** 200 mg/kg/d div q8h	**Inpatient (ICU): Cefotaxime** 200 mg/kg/d div q8h **or ceftriaxone** 50–75 mg/kg/d IV 1x/d.	Common "other" viruses: rhinovirus, influenza, parainfluenza, adenovirus *(PIDJ 19: 293, 2000)*. Often of mild to moderate severity. S. pneumo, non-type B H. flu in 4-6 wks. NOTE: High frequency of resistance of DRSP to ceftriaxone. *See footnote†, footnote 1 page 24, footnote 4 page 26, and Table 5, page 54, for rx of drug-resistant S. pneumo.*
Age 5 years–15 years, Non-hospitalized immunocompetent *NEJM 346:429, 2002; PIDJ 21:592, 2002*	Mycoplasma, Chlamydia pneumoniae, S. pneumoniae, Mycobacterium tuberculosis e.g., influenza Bacterial/viral infection in 23% *(Ped 113:701, 2004)*	**Outpatient: po erythro** 10 mg/kg q6h (po azithro 0.5 gm on day 1, then 0.25 gm/d. Peds dose: 10 mg/kg x1 d. then 5 mg/kg/d, max of 500 mg then, 250 mg).	**Inpatient (ICU): Amox** 100 mg/kg/d + (**Clarithro** 500 mg po bid or **azithro** 500 mg IV qd) **OR azithro** 10 mg/kg IV q8h	If otherwise healthy and if not concomitant with (or post-) influenza, S. pneumonia & S. aureus uncommon in this subset, suspect S. pneumo if sudden onset and large amount of purulent sputum. **Macrolide-resistant S. pneumo** an issue. Higher prevalence of macrolide-resistant S. pneumo in pts <5 yrs old *(JAMA 286:1857, 2001)*.
			See Comment regarding macrolide resistance	**Mycoplasma** PCR/viral culture usually not done for outpatients. **Mycoplasma requires 2–3 wks of rx.** C. pneumoniae up to 6 wks. *(LnID 1:334, 2001; J Med Micro 52:265, 2003)*. †Linezolid approved for peds use for pen-susceptible S. pneumo (including bacteremia) & methicillin-sensitive S. aureus.

NOTE: qd = once daily; bid = twice daily; tid = 3 times a day, qid = 4 times a day.

TMP/SMX 1 double-strength tab (160 mg TMP) bid po, **doxy** 100 mg bid po, **amox** 500 mg tid po, **cefaclor** 500 mg bid or 500 mg tid po, **amox/clav (AM/CL)** 875/125 mg bid po, 500/125 mg tid po, **O Ceph [cefaclor** 500 mg q8h or 500 mg CD (extended release) q12h po, **cefdinir** 300 mg q12h po, **cefditoren** 400 mg q12h po, **cefpodoxime proxetil** 200 mg q12h po, **cefprozil** 500 mg q12h po, **cefuroxime axetil** 250 or 500 mg q12h po, **cefditoren** 400 mg q12h po, **cefprozil** 500 mg q12h po, **cefuroxime axetil** 250 or 500 mg q12h po, **cefixime** 400 mg q24h, **azithro** 500 mg initial dose then 250 mg qd x4 or 500 mg qd x3 d., **clarithro** 500 mg q12h po **or ER** 1000 mg q24h po, **erythro** 500 mg q6h, **Levo** 500 mg qd po, **Gati** 400 mg qd po, **Gemi** 320 mg qd po x5 d, **Moxi** 400 mg qd po. **Ketolide: Telithromycin** 800 mg po qd x5 d. **NOTE:** CIP and ofloxacin have relatively poor activity vs S. pneumo.

(Footnotes after abbreviations on page 45) *NOTE: All dosage recommendations are for adults (unless otherwise indicated) and assume normal renal function.*

TABLE 1 (25)

ANATOMIC SITE/DIAGNOSIS/ MODIFYING CIRCUMSTANCES	ETIOLOGIES (usual)	SUGGESTED REGIMENS* PRIMARY	ALTERNATIVE†	ADJUNCT DIAGNOSTIC OR THERAPEUTIC MEASURES AND COMMENTS
LUNG/Pneumonia (continued) **Children, hospitalized, immunocompetent—2–18 yrs**	S. pneumoniae, viruses, mycoplasma, consider abscesses or necrotizing	**Ceftriaxone** 50 mg/kg IV (to max. 2 gm/d) + **azithro** 10 mg/kg up to 500 mg IV div q12h. Add anti-staph drug if evidence of lung necrosis	**Alternatives are a problem in children:** If proven S. pneumo resistant to azithro & ceftriaxone (or severe ceftriaxone allergy) IV vanco, linezolid, or off-label respiratory FQ. No doxy under age 8, **telithro** not approved efficacious in children (PIDJ 22:677, 2003). Ceftriaxone failures vs DRSP (CID 29:462, 1999).	
Adults (over age 18)—See IDSA Guidelines (CID 37:1405, 2003; Thorax 2001 & 1913, 2004; AJM 117:39(S), 2004) **Community-acquired, not hospitalized** **Empiric therapy** **Microbiologic diagno-sis:** (1) Outpts: No stud-ies; (2) Inpts: (a) cultures of sputum & blood, (b) urine Legionella antigen, esp. II in ICU, (c) pneumo-coccal urine antigen (JCM 41:2810, 2003) **Focus of therapy is S. pneumo, % resistant:** Gati/Levo/Moxi <1; doxy 12–23, telithro <1; peni-cillin 17, amox 4, azithro 28, TMP/SMX 24 In vitro resistance refs.: Trust 7—2003; DMID 49:147, 2004	Varies with clinical setting. **No co-morbidity:** Pneumococci, Mycoplasma pneumo, et al., S. pneumo, viral **Co-morbidity:** Alcoholism: S. pneumo, anaerobes, coliforms Bronchiectasis: see Cystic fibrosis, page COPD: H. influenzae, M. catarrhalis, S. pneumo (V.) methanogenic(?)/ S. aureus Post-CVA aspiration: Oral flora, incl. S. pneumo Post-obstruction of bronchus Post-viral: e.g., influenza	**No co-morbidity:** **Azithro** 0.5 gm po x1, then 0.25 gm/d OR **clarithro** 500 mg po bid OR **clarithro-ER** 1.0 gm po qd OR **doxy** 100 mg po bid OR (**azithro** or **clarithro**) If antibiotic within 3 months: (**azithro** or **clarithro**) + (**amox** 1.0 gm po tid or **AM/CL**)	**Co-morbidity present:** Respiratory FQ (see footnote³) OR (**azithro** or **clarithro**) + (high dose **amox**, high dose **AM/CL**, **cefdinir, cefpodox-ime, cefprozil,** or **telithromycin**) Doses in footnote³ **Duration of therapy:** S. pneumo—Not bacteremic: until afebrile 3 days reasonable C. pneumoniae—Unclear. Some reports suggest 21 days. Some bronchitis pts required 5–6 wks of clarithro (J Med Micro 52:265, 2003) Legionella—10–21 days Necrotizing pneumonia 2° to coliforms, S. aureus, anaerobes: ≥2 weeks —Bacteremic: 10–14 days	**Azithro/clarithro:** Pro: appropriate spectrum of action, more in vitro resistance than clinical failure (CID 34:1008, 2002; LnID 3:483, 2003). If proven S. pneumo resistant to azithro, go to alternative FQ (see footnote³). If pen G resist, S. pneumo, up to 50%+ resistance. Breakthrough infections reported (NEJM 346:630, 2002; CID 35:556, 2002) **Amoxicillin:** Pro: Active 90–95% S. pneumo at 3–4 gm/d Con: No activity atypicals or β-lactamase + bacteria. Need 3–4 gm/day **AM/CL:** Pro: spectrum includes β-lactamase + H. influenzae, M. catarrhalis, MSSA, & Bacteroides sp. Con: No activity atypicals **Cephalosporins:** Pro: cefdinir, cefpodoxime, cefprozil, cefuroxime & others—see footnote³ Con: Cefuroxime least active & higher mortality rate when S. pneumo & H. influenzae. Cefuroxime resistant (CID 37:230, 2003). **Doxycycline:** Pro: Active vs S. pneumo (DMID 49:147, 2004) but resistance may be increasing. Active vs H. influenzae, atypicals, & bioterrorism agents (anthrax, plague, tularemia). Con: Resistance of S. pneumo 18–20% (CID 35:633, 2002). Sparse clinical data (AJM 159:266, 1999; CID 37:870, 2003). **FQs—Respiratory FQs:** Gemi Pro: Active vs S. pneumo & pen-sensitive & pen-resistant S. pneumo. **NOTE: dose of Levo is 750 mg qd.** QD dosing. Gemi only available po. Con: Geographic pockets of resistance with clinical failure (NEJM 346:747, 2002). Drug-drug interactions (see Table 22A, page 144). Unique reversible rash in young females given **Telithromycin:** Pro: Virtually no resistant S. pneumo. Active vs atypical pathogens. Con: Rarely reversible blurry vision due to paralysis of lens accommo-dation; avoid in myasthenia gravis pts.
Community-acquired, hos-pitalized—NOT in the ICU **Empiric therapy**	Etiology by co-morbidity & risk factors as above	**Ceftriaxone** 2.0 gm IV qd (1.0 gm IV qd if ≤65) + **azithro** 500 mg IV qd	**Gati** 400 mg IV qd or **Levo** 750 mg IV qd or **Moxi** 400 mg IV qd	**Ceftriaxone/cefotaxime:** Pro: Drugs of choice for pen-sens. S. pneumo, active H. influenzae, M. catarrhalis, & MSSA Con: Not active atypicals or pneumonia due to bioterrorism organisms. Add macrolide for atypicals. **Telithromycin:** Pro: Virtually no resistant S. pneumo. Active vs atypical pathogens. Linezolid not recommended.

NOTE: qd = once daily; bid = twice daily; tid = 3 times a day; qid = 4 times a day.

¹ Atypical pathogens: Chlamydophila pneumoniae, C. psittaci, Legionella sp., M. pneumoniae, C. burnetii (Q fever)

² Respiratory FQs with enhanced activity vs S. pneumo with HLR to penicillin: **Gati** 400 mg IV/po qd, **Gemi** 320 mg po qd, **Levo** 750 mg IV/po qd, **Moxi** 400 mg IV/po qd. Ketolide: **telithro** 800 mg po qd.

³ AM/CL—use **AM/CL-ER** 1000/62.5 mg 2 tabs po bid, **cefpodoxime proxetil** 200 mg q12h, **cefprozil** 500 mg po q12h, high dose **amox** 1.0 gm po tid, high dose **amox/clav** 2000/125 mg po bid.

(Footnotes and abbreviations on page 45)   NOTE: All dosage recommendations are for adults (unless otherwise indicated) and assume normal renal function.

TABLE 1 (26)

ANATOMIC SITE/DIAGNOSIS/ MODIFYING CIRCUMSTANCES	ETIOLOGIES (usual)	SUGGESTED REGIMENS*		ADJUNCT DIAGNOSTIC OR THERAPEUTIC MEASURES AND COMMENTS
		PRIMARY	**ALTERNATIVE†**	
LUNG/Pneumonia/Adults (continued)				
Community-acquired, hospitalized—IN ICU Empiric therapy	Severe COPD: S. pneumo, H. influ, M. catarrhalis Legionella Post-influenza: S. aureus Coliforms & P. aeruginosa rare unless bronchiectasis (see below)	**Aggressive attempts at micro. diagnosis justified:** Culture sputum, blood, maybe pleural fluid. Urine antigen tests for both legionella & pneumococcus. Empiric therapy must be active vs S. pneumo & legionella. **Gati** 400 mg IV qd or **Levo** 750 mg IV qd or **Moxi** 400 mg IV qd	**Ceftriaxone** 2.0 gm IV qd (1.0 gm IV qd > age 65) + **azithro** 500 mg IV qd or **ERTA** 1.0 gm IV qd + **azithro** 500 mg IV qd (see Comment)	Various studies indicate improved outcome when azithro added to a β-lactam (CID 36:389 & 1239, 2003). A/M 163:1837, 2001 & 159:2562, 1999. Empiric choice depends on whether critically ill pts with pneumococcal bacteremia (AJRCCM 170:440, 2004). **Ertapenem** can substitute for ceftriaxone but limited clinical experience. Need azithro for atypical pathogens. Do not use if suspect P. aeruginosa.
Hospital-acquired— usually with mechanical ventilation (empiric therapy) Diagnosis confirmed by quantitative cultures (see Comment)	Highly variable depending on clinical setting: S. pneumo, S. aureus, Legionella, coliforms, P. aeruginosa, acinetobacter anaerobes all possible	(**IMP** 0.5 gm IV q6h or **MER** 1.0 gm IV q8h) plus **FQ (Gati, Levo or Moxi)** NOTE: Regimen not active vs MRSA—see specific rx below See Comment regarding dosages. Dosages: See footnotes pages 16, 23, 25, & 26	(**Cefepime** or **high-dose PIP/TZ**) + **tobra**. Add if suspect legion- ella or bioterrorism, **respiratory FQ** if suspect legion- ella or bioterrorism.	**Dx of ventilator-associated pneumonia:** Fever & lung infiltrates often not pneu- monia (Chest 106:221, 1994). Quantitative cultures helpful: bronchoalveolar lavage (>10³ ml pos.) or protect. spec. brush (>10³ ml pos.). Ref. AJRCCM 165:867, 2002. **Microbial etiology:** No empiric regimen covers all possibilities. Regimens listed active vs MRSA, Stenotrophomonas is. **most coliforms; see below. Specific rx when culture results known. Ventilator-associated pneumonia—Prevention:** If possible, keep head of bed elevated 30° or more. Remove N-G, endotracheal tubes as soon as possible. If available, continuous subglottic suctioning. Limit stress ulcer prophylaxis. Refs.: NEJM 340:627, 1999; CCM 32:1396, 2004.
Hospital- or community- acquired, neutropenic pt (<500 neutrophils/mm³)	Any of organisms listed under community- & hospital- acquired + fungi (aspergillus, Candida sp.)	See Hospital-acquired, immediately above. Vanco not included in initial rx unless high suspicion of infected IV access or drug-resistant S. pneumo not suspected or unless still febrile after 3 days or high clinical likelihood. See Comment		See consensus document of management of febrile neutropenic pt: CID 34:730, 2002.
Adults—Selected specific rx (sputum, blood, pleural fluid, etc.) available. Also see Table 2, page 47				
Burkholderia (Pseudo- monas) pseudomallei (etiology of melioidosis) Ref: Ln 361:1715, 2003	Gram-negative	**Initial parenteral rx: Ceftazidime** 40 mg/kg IV q8h or **IMP** 20 mg/kg IV q8h. Rx minimum 10 days & improving, then po therapy →	**Post-parenteral po rx: Adults** (see Comment for children) **Chloro** 10 mg/kg q6h x8 wks: **Doxy** 2 mg/kg bid x20 wks: **TMP/SMX** 5 mg/kg (TMP component) bid x20 wks	**Children ≤8 yrs old & pregnancy:** For oral regimen, use **AM/CL-ER** 1000/62.5, 2 tabs po bid x20 wks. Even with compliance, relapse rate is 10%.
Haemophilus influenzae	β-lactamase negative	**AMP** IV, **amox** po, **TMP/SMX, azithro/clarithro, doxy**		25–35% strains β-lactamase positive. † resistance to both TMP/SMX and doxy. See Table 10B, page 65 for dosages.
	β-lactamase positive	**AM/CL, O Ceph 2/3, P Ceph 3, FQ, azithro/clarithro**		
Legionella species	Hospitalized/immunocom promised	**Azithro** IV or **Levo** IV or **Gati** or **Moxi** See Table 10B, page 65 for dosages. Treat for 10–21 days.		Ref: JAC 51:1119, 2003. Best Legionella website: www.legionella.org. Urine antigen detects serogroup 1, 80–90% of clinical isolates, Legionella, 87% sens. CAP, & 46% from travel-associated Legionella (JCM 41:838, 2003).
Moraxella catarrhalis	95% β-lactamase positive	**AM/CL, O Ceph 2/3, P Ceph 3, macrolide ‡ telithro†, FQ, TMP/SMX**. **Doxy** another option. See Table 10B, page 65 for dosages.		

¹ **PIP/TZ** dose: 4.5 gm IV q6h
² **Telithro** = telithromycin 800 mg po qd
³ **Macrolide** = azithromycin, clarithromycin, dirithromycin, and erythromycin. Dirithromycin serum levels inadequate for bacteremic S. pneumo.

(Footnotes and abbreviations on page 45)

NOTE: All dosage recommendations are for adults (unless otherwise indicated) and assume normal renal function.

TABLE 1 (27)

ANATOMIC SITE/DIAGNOSIS/ MODIFYING CIRCUMSTANCES	ETIOLOGIES (usual)	SUGGESTED REGIMENS*		ADJUNCT DIAGNOSTIC OR THERAPEUTIC MEASURES AND COMMENTS
		PRIMARY	ALTERNATIVE†	
LUNG/Pneumonia/Adults, when culture results available *(continued)*				
Pseudomonas aeruginosa	Often ventilator-associated	PIP/TAZ 4.5 gm IV q6h + tobra 5 mg/kg IV once daily (see Table 10C, page 72)		
Staphylococcus aureus	Nafcillin/oxacillin susceptible	Nafcillin/oxacillin 2.0 gm IV q4h	Vanco 1.0 gm IV q6h + linezolid 600 mg IV q12h	Retrospective analysis of 2 prospective randomized double-blind studies of linezolid vs vanco: for hospital-acquired MRSA, linezolid showed enhanced survival with linezolid, p 0.03 (Chest 124:1632, 2003): efficacy perhaps related to superb linezolid lung concentrations.
	MRSA	Vanco 1.0 gm IV q12h	linezolid 600 mg IV q12h	Concern of possible misinterpretation of post hoc subgroup analysis expressed with responses of authors: Chest 126:314, 2004.
Stenotrophomonas maltophilia		TMP/SMX		In vitro synergy (refs.: AAC 39:2220, 1995; CMR 11:57, 1998
Streptococcus pneumoniae	Penicillin-susceptible	AMP 2.0 gm IV q6h, amox 1.0 gm po tid, macrolide (see footnote 2 page 27), pen G IV;¹ doxy. O Ceph 2 & 3, telithro 800 mg po qd. See Table 10B, pages 65 for other dosages	TC/CL ± aztreonam	
	Penicillin-resistant, high level	FQs with enhanced activity: Gatt, Gemi, Levo, Moxi (IV)—see Table 5, page 54 for more data. If all options not possible (e.g., allergy), linezolid active: 600 mg IV or po q12h. Telithro 800 mg po qd		
LUNG—Other				
Anthrax Inhalation (applies to oro-pharyngeal & gastrointestinal forms): Treatment (Cutaneous: See page 34)	Bacillus anthracis **To report possible bioterrorism event: 770-488-7100**	**Adults (including preg-nancy):** CIP 400 mg IV (q12h) or doxy 100 mg IV (q12h) **plus** (clindamycin 900 mg IV q8h and/or RIF 300 mg IV q12h) Switch to po when able & lower CIP to 500 mg po bid or doxy 100 mg po q8h, & RIF 300 mg po bid. Treat x60 days. (Other alternatives: Table 2, page 47). For oral dosage.	**Children:** CIP 10 mg/kg IV q12h or 15 mg/kg po (q12h) or (Doxy >8 y/o & >45 kg: 100 mg IV q12h; >8 y/o & ≤45 kg: 2.2 mg/kg IV (q12h); ≤8 y/o: 2.2 mg/kg IV q12h) **plus clindamycin** 7.5 mg/kg IV q8h **and/or RIF** 20 mg/kg (max. 600 mg) IV qd.	1. Clinda may block toxin production 2. Rifampin penetrates CSF & intracellular sites. 3. If isolate shows penicillin-susceptible: a. **Adults: Pen G** 4 mU IV q4h b. **Children: Pen G** <12 y/o: 50,000 U/kg IV q6h; >12 y/o: 4 mU IV q4h c. Constitutive & inducible β-lactamases—do not use pen or amp alone. 4. Do not use cephalosporins or TMP/SMX. 5. Erythro, azithro activity borderline; clarithro active. 6. No person-to-person spread.
Refs.: JAMA 287:2236, 2002 & MMWR 50:909, 2001. Clinical experience: JAMA 286:2549, 2001. FDA rationale: CID 39:303, 2004	Chest x-ray, mediastinal widening & pleural effusion (AnnIM 139:337, 2003; Ln 364:449, 2004)			
Post-exposure prophylaxis	Info: www.bt.cdc.gov	**Adults (including preg-nancy):** CIP 500 mg po bid x60 d. **Children:** CIP 20-30 mg/kg/d div q12h x60 d.	**Adults (including pregnancy): Doxy** 100 mg po bid x60 d. **Children** (>8 y/o & ≤45 kg: 100 mg po bid; & >8 y/o & >45 kg: 2.2 mg/kg po bid; ≤8 y/o: 2.2 mg/kg po bid. All for 60 days.	Once organism shows suscept. to penicillin, switch to amoxicillin 80 mg/kg/div. q8h (max. 500 mg q8h), pregnant pt to amoxicillin 500 mg po tid. Do **not** use cephalosporins or TMP/SMX. Other FQs (Gatt, Levo, Moxi) & clarithro should work but no clinical experience.
Aspiration pneumonia ± lung abscess (CJM 88:409, 1995)	Bacteroides sp. (~15% B. fragilis), peptostreptococci, Fusobacterium sp., S. milleri group, nocardia (pts taking steroids)	**Clinda** 450–900 mg q8h IV [For nocardia, see Table 11, page 80]	**TC/CL** 3.1 gm q6h (IV) or **PIP/TAZ** 3.375 gm q6h or 4.5 gm q8h (IV) [Historically **pen gm** q8h IV] has been effective]	Bronchoscopy to R/O neoplasm if pt fails to clear or recurs. Metro not as effective as clinda. Occasionally Type 3 pneumococci, Staph. aureus, Klebsiella pneumoniae are etiologic. A recent review questioned the etiologic role of anaerobic bacteria; the editors respectfully disagree (NEJM 344:665, 2001)
Chronic pneumonia with fever, night sweats and weight loss	M. tuberculosis, coccidioidomycosis, histoplasmosis	See Tables 11, 12		HIV+, foreign-born, alcoholism, contact with TB, travel into developing countries

---

¹ **IV Pen G dosage:** Blood cultures neg., 1 mU IV q4h; blood cultures pos. & no meningitis, 2 mU IV q4h. Another option is continuous infusion (CI) 3 mU loading dose & then CI of 10–12 mU over 12 hrs (Chest 112:1657, 1997).

(Footnotes and abbreviations on page 45)   *NOTE: All dosage recommendations are for adults (unless otherwise indicated) and assume normal renal function.*

TABLE 1 (28)

ANATOMIC SITE/DIAGNOSIS/MODIFYING CIRCUMSTANCES	ETIOLOGIES (usual)	SUGGESTED REGIMENS* PRIMARY	ALTERNATIVE†	ADJUNCT DIAGNOSTIC OR THERAPEUTIC MEASURES AND COMMENTS
LUNG/Other (continued) **Cystic fibrosis** Refs.: *Ln 361:681, 2003; AJRCCM 168:918, 2003*	S. aureus & H. influenzae early in disease; P. aeruginosa later in disease	**For P. aeruginosa: Tobra** 3.3 mg/kg q8h or 10 mg/kg IV qd. Combine tobra with **PIP** or **ticarcillin** 100 mg/kg q6h or with **ceftaz** 50 mg/kg q8h IV. Also see footnote[1] & Comment	**For S. aureus: (1) MSSA—oxacillin/nafcillin** 2.0 gm IV q4h (Peds dose, Table 16) **(2) MRSA—vanco** 1.0 gm q12h. See Comment	Additional therapy: Clarithro synergistic with tobra vs P. aeruginosa *(AAC 46: 1105, 2002)* + anti-inflammatory azithromycin *(Pharmacotherapy 22:227, 2002)*. Azithro modestly improved FEV₁ pts chronically infected with P. aeruginosa *(JAMA 290: 1749, 2003)*. For pharmacokinetics of aminoglycosides in CF, see *JAC 50:553, 2002*
	Burkholderia (Pseudomonas) cepacia	**TMP/SMX** 5.0 mg/kg (TMP) q6h	**Chloro** 15–20 mg/kg IV or po & check serum levels.	For chronic suppression of P. aeruginosa, tobramycin soln for inhal 300 mg bid x28 d, then no rx x28 d, then repeat cycle *(AJRCCM 167:841, 2003; NEJM 340:23, 1999)*. B. cepacia has become a major pathogen. Patients develop progressive respiratory failure, 62% mortality at 1 year. **Fail to respond to APAG**, piperacillin, & ceftazidime. Patients with B. cepacia should be isolated from other CF patients *(AAC 43:213, 1999)*
Empyema Ref.: *CID 22:747, 1996;* Neonatal	Pleural effusion review: *NEJM 346:1971, 1996.*	See Pneumonia, neonatal, page 25		NOTE: 3- & 4-drug combinations under study in refractory pts *(AAC 43:213, 1999)*
Infants/children (1 month–5 yrs)	Staph. aureus; Strep. pneumoniae, H. influenzae	See Pneumonia, age 1 month–5 years, page 25		Drainage indicated.
Child >5 yrs to ADULT—Diagnostic/therapeutic thoracentesis; chest tube for empyemas				Drainage indicated.
Acute, usually parapneumonic	Strep. pneumoniae, Group A strep	**Cefotaxime** or **Ceftriaxone** (Dosage, see footnote[1] page 23)	**Vanco**	Randomized trial showed benefit of intrapleural streptokinase (250,000 units in 100 mL) in adults with 2-hr dwell after q.d. for up to 3 days *(AJRCCM 170:49, 2004)*. Urokinase 100,000 IU/d. x3 d. effective in double-blind study *(AJRCCM 159:37, 1999)*.
Subacute/chronic	Staph. aureus: Check for MRSA	**Nafcillin** or **oxacillin**	**Vanco**	Gram-pos. cocci in clusters
	H. influenzae	**P Ceph 3**	**TMP/SMX** or **AM/SB**	Pleomorphic Gm-neg. bacilli. † resistance to TMP/SMX.
	Anaerobic strep, Strep. milleri, Bacteroides sp., Enterobacteriaceae, M. tuberculosis	**Clinda** 450–900 mg q8h IV + **P Ceph 3**	**Cefoxitin** or **IMP** or **TC/CL** or **PIP/TZ**, or **AM/SB** (Dosage, see footnote[1] page 23)	If organisms not seen, treat as subacute. Drainage R/O tuberculosis or tumor. Pleural biopsy with culture for mycobacteria and histology if TBc suspected *(CID 22:747, 1996)*.
Human immunodeficiency virus infection (HIV+) CD4 T-lymphocytes <200/mm³ or clinical AIDS Dry cough, progressive dyspnea, & diffuse infiltrate	Pneumocystis carinii most likely; also M. tbc, fungi, Kaposi's sarcoma, & lymphoma. NOTE: AIDS pts may develop drug-induced fever due to DRSP or other pathogens (see next box below)	**Prednisone 1st** (see Comment), then: **TMP/SMX** (IV: 15 mg/kg/d div q8h) (po-component 2 DS tabs q8h) total of 21 days	Rx listed here is **for severe** pneumocystis; see Table 13, page 96 for po regimens **for mild disease.** **Prednisone 40 mg bid x5 d, then 40 mg qd po x5 d, then 20 mg qd po x11 d, is indicated with PCP (pO₂ <70 mmHg), should be given at initiation of anti-PCP rx; don't wait until pt condition deteriorates** *(Table 13, page 96)*. **Clinda** 600 mg q8h IV + **primaquine** 30 mg/d po qd (if G6PD screen negative, consider alternative) *(pentamidine 4 mg/kg IV) x21 d*	Diagnostic procedure of choice is sputum induction; if negative, bronchoscopy. Pts with PCP or <200 CD4 cells/mm³ should be on anti-PCP prophylaxis for life. **Pentamidine not active vs bacterial pathogens.** If Gram stain of sputum shows Gm-neg. bacilli, options include P Ceph 3 AP, TC/CL, PIP/TZ, IMP or MER. FQs: Levo 500 mg po/IV qd; Gati 400 mg po/IV qd; Moxi 400 mg po/IV qd. **NOTE: Pneumocystis resistant to TMP/SMX, albeit rare, does exist.**
CD4 T-lymphocytes normal Acute onset, purulent sputum & pulmonary infiltrate ± pleuritic pain. **Isolate pt until TBc excluded: Adults**	Strep. pneumoniae, H. influenzae, aerobic Gm-neg. bacilli (including P. aeruginosa), S. aureus, Legionella rare. M. tbc.	**P Ceph 3** (Dosages in footnotes on pages 16 & 23) ± **azithro**. Could use **Gatl**, **Levo**, or **Moxi** IV as alternative		In children with AIDS, LIP responsible for 1/3 of pulmonary complications, usually >1 yr of age vs PCP, which is seen at <1 yr of age. Clinically: clubbing, hepatosplenomegaly, salivary glands enlarged (take up gallium), lymphocytosis.
As above: Children	Same as adult plus lymphoid interstitial pneumonia (LIP)	As for HIV+ adults with pneumonia. If diagnosis is LIP, rx with steroids.		

---

* Other options: (Tobra + aztreonam 50 mg/kg q8h IV); (IMP 15–25 mg/kg q6h IV + tobra); (IMP 15–25 mg/kg q6h IV + tobra). ** CIP commonly used in children**, e.g., CIP IV/po + ceftaz IV/po qd (page 45)

(Footnotes and abbreviations on page 45)   NOTE: All dosage recommendations are for adults (unless otherwise indicated) and assume normal renal function.

TABLE 1 (29)

ANATOMIC SITE/DIAGNOSIS/MODIFYING CIRCUMSTANCES	ETIOLOGIES (usual)	SUGGESTED REGIMENS* PRIMARY	ALTERNATIVE†	ADJUNCT DIAGNOSTIC OR THERAPEUTIC MEASURES AND COMMENTS
LUNG/Other (continued) **Viral (interstitial) pneumonia suspected** (See Table 14, page 104)	Consider: Adenovirus, coronavirus (SARS), hantavirus, influenza, metapneumovirus, parainfluenza virus, respiratory syncytial virus	**For influenza A or B:** oseltamivir 75 mg po bid x5 d or zanamivir 10 mg (2 inhalations) bid. Start within 48 hrs of symptom onset	**For influenza A:** rimantadine 100 mg po x2/d. or amantadine 100 mg po 2x/d.	No known efficacious drugs for adenovirus (SARS), hantavirus, metapneumovirus, parainfluenza or RSV. Need travel (SARS) & exposure (Hanta) history.
LYMPH NODES (approaches below apply to lymphadenitis without an obvious primary source)				
Lymphadenitis, acute Generalized	Etiologies: EBV, early HIV infection, syphilis, toxoplasma, tularemia, Lyme disease, sarcoid, lymphoma, systemic lupus erythematosus, and Kikuchi-Fujimoto disease (CID 39:138, 2004). Complete history and physical examination followed by appropriate serological tests. Treat specific agent(s).			
Regional **Cervical—see cat-scratch disease (CSD), below**	CSD (B. henselae), Grp A strep, Staph. aureus, anaerobes, M. TBc (scrofula), M. scrofulaceum, M. malmoense, toxo, tularemia	History & physical exam directs evaluation. In nodes fluctuant, aspirate and base rx on Gram & acid-fast stains. Review of mycobacterial etiology: CID 20:954, 1995. Kikuchi-Fujimoto disease causes fever and benign self-limited adenopathy, the etiology is unknown (AJM 171:401, 1996; CID 39:138, 2004).		
Inguinal Sexually transmitted	HSV, chancroid, syphilis, LGV			
Not sexually transmitted	GAS, SA, tularemia, Y. pestis, sporotrichosis.			
Axillary	GAS, SA, CSD, tularemia, sporotrichosis, Nocardia brasiliensis.	Treatment varies with specific etiology		
Extremity, with associated nodular lymphangitis (For full description: AnIM 118:883, 1993)	Sporotrichosis, leishmania, Mycobacterium marinum, Mycobacterium chelonae, tularemia			A distinctive form of lymphangitis characterized by subcutaneous swellings along inflamed lymphatic channels. Primary site of skin invasion usually present; regional adenopathy variable.
Cat-scratch disease—immunocompetent patient Axillary/epitrochlear nodes 46%, neck 26%, inguinal 17%	Bartonella henselae Reviews: IDC Ns Amer 12: 137, 1998; AAC 48:1921, 2004	**Azithro dosage—Adults** (>45.5 kg): 500 mg po x1, then 250 mg/d 6 mos. **Children** (<45.5 kg): liquid azithro 10 mg/kg x1, then 5 mg/kg/d x4 d. Rx is controversial — see Comment		**Clinical:** Approx. 10% nodes suppurate. Atypical presentation in <5% pts, i.e., lung nodules, liver/spleen lesions, Parinaud's oculoglandular syndrome, CNS manifestations in 2% of pts (encephalitis, peripheral neuropathy, retinitis). **Dx:** Cat exposure. Positive IFA serology. Rarely need biopsy. **Rx:** Only 1 prospective randomized blinded study, used azithro with ↑ rapidity of resolution of enlarged lymph nodes (PID 17:447, 1998).
MOUTH				
Odontogenic infection, including Ludwig's angina Can result in more serious parapharyngeal space infection (see page 33)	Oral microflora, infection polymicrobial	**Clinda** 300–450 mg q6h po or 600 mg IV q6–8h	**AM/CL** 875/125 mg bid po or 500/125 mg bid po; liquid **cefotetan** 2 gm IV q12h	Surgical drainage and removal of necrotic tissue essential. β-lactamase producing organisms are ↑ in frequency. Ref.: Carad Dental Assn J 64:508, 1998 Other parenteral alternatives: AM/SB, PIP/TZ, or TC/CL.
Buccal cellulitis Children <5 yrs	H. influenzae	**Cefuroxime** or **P Ceph 3** Dosage: see Table 16, page 131	**AM/CL** or **TMP/SMX** Dosage: see Table 16, page 131	With Hib immunization, invasive H. influenzae infections have ↓ by 95%. Now occurring in infants prior to immunization.
Herpetic stomatitis	Herpes simplex virus 1 & 2	See Table 14		
Aphthous stomatitis ("canker sore")	Etiology unknown	Topical steroids (Kenalog in Orabase) may ↓ pain and swelling. If AIDS, see SANFORD GUIDE TO HIV/AIDS THERAPY.		
MUSCLE				
"Gas gangrene" Can be spontaneous, traumatic wound or post-surgical. Can be spontaneous without trauma (CID 28:159, 1999)	Cl. perfringens, other histotoxic Clostridium sp.	**(Clinda** 900 mg q8h IV) + (**Pen G** 24 million U/d div. q4–6h IV)	**Ceftriaxone** 2.0 gm q12h IV or **Ertapenem** 1.0 gm IV (not by bolus)	Surgical debridement primary rx. Hyperbaric oxygen adjunctive, efficacy debated, CNS toxicity of debridement not complete or possible (NEJM 334:1642, 1996). Clinda ↓ toxin production.
Buccal cellulitis Children <5 yrs		**(Nafcillin** or **oxacillin** 2.0 gm q4h IV) or **(P Ceph 1** or **cefazolin** 2.0 gm q8h IV)	**Vanco** 1.0 gm q12h IV if MRSA	
Pyomyositis	Staph. aureus, Group A strep, (rarely Gm-neg. bacilli, variety of anaerobic bacteria)	**(Nafcillin** or **oxacillin** 2.0 gm q4h IV) or **(P Ceph 1** or **cefazolin** 2.0 gm q8h IV)	**Vanco** 1.0 gm q12h IV if MRSA	Has been common in tropics, rare but occurs in temperate zones (IDCP 7:265, 1998). Follows exercise or muscle injury, see Necrotizing fasciitis. Now seen in HIV/AIDS (AJM 91:129, 1991). Add clinda or Pen G if anaerobes suspected/proven (IDCP 8:252, 1999).

Footnotes and abbreviations on page 45)   NOTE: All dosage recommendations are for adults (unless otherwise indicated) and assume normal renal function.

TABLE 1 (30)

ANATOMIC SITE/DIAGNOSIS/ MODIFYING CIRCUMSTANCES	ETIOLOGIES (usual)	SUGGESTED REGIMENS*		ADJUNCT DIAGNOSTIC OR THERAPEUTIC MEASURES AND COMMENTS
		PRIMARY	**ALTERNATIVE†**	
PANCREAS: Review—*Ln 361:1447, 2003; JAMA 291:2865, 2004*				
Acute alcoholic (without necrosis) (idiopathic) pancreatitis	Not bacterial	None CT-diagnosed	1–9% become infected but prospective studies show no advantage of prophylactic antimicrobials (*Ln 346;652, 1995*). Observe for pancreatic abscesses or those which require rx.
Pancreatic abscess, infected pseudocyst, post-necrotizing pancreatitis	Enterobacteriaceae, enterococci, S. aureus, S. epidermidis, anaerobes, candida	Need culture of abscess/infected pseudocyst to direct therapy		Can often get specimen by fine-needle aspiration.
Antimicrobic prophylaxis, necrotizing pancreatitis	As above	Use of antimicrobial prophylaxis remains unclear—see *Comment*. If used, suggest IMP		Meta-analysis of 4 random-controlled trials supportive (*Cochrane Database, 2004 (2): CD002941*), prospective random double-blind trial—**no benefit** (*Gastro 126:997, 2004*).
PAROTID GLAND				
"Hot" tender parotid swelling	S. aureus, oral flora & aerobic Gm-bacilli (rare), mumps, rarely enteroviruses/ influenza. **Nafcillin OR oxacillin** 2.0 gm IV q4h			Predisposing factors: stone(s) in Stensen's duct, dehydration. Rx depends on ID of specific etiologic organism.
"Cold" non-tender parotid swelling	Granulomatous disease (e.g., mycobacteria, fungi, sarcoidosis, Sjögren's syndrome), drugs (iodides, et al.), diabetes, cirrhosis, tumors			History/lab results may narrow differential; may need biopsy for dx.
PERITONEUM/PERITONITIS: *Reference—CID 31:997, 2003*				
Primary (spontaneous bacterial peritonitis, SBP) Rev.: *CID 27:669, 1998* ESBL ref.: *CID 28:683, 1999* Microbiology: *CID 33:1513, 2001*	Enterobacteriaceae 63%, S. pneumo 15%, enterococci 6–10%, anaerobes <1%.	**[Cefotaxime** 2.0 gm q8h IV (if life-threatening), q4h)] or **TC/CL** or **PIP/TZ** or **AM/SB**] OR **(ceftriaxone** 2.0 gm q24h IV)] or **(ERTA** 1.0 gm IV q24)] **If resistant E. coli/ Klebsiella species (ESBL+), then: [IMP or MER] or FQ: Cipro, Levo, Gati, Moxi]** (*Dosage in* footnote‡)	**TMP/SMX** ↓ peritonitis or spontaneous bacteremia from 27% to 3% (*AntM 122:595, 1995*). Ref. for CIP: *Hepatol 22:1171, 1995*. One-year **risk of SBP** in pts with ascites and cirrhosis as high as 29% (*Gastro 104: 1133, 1993*). 30–40% of pts have neg. cultures of blood and ascitic fluid. % pos. cultures ↑ if 10 ml of pt's ascitic fluid added to blood culture bottles. **Value of rx unclear**. Suggest 2 wks if blood culture pos. One report suggests repeat paracentesis after 48 hrs of cefotaxime. If PMNs <250/mm³ and ascitic fluid sterile, success with 5 days of rx (*AJM 97:169, 1994; Hepatol 5:457, 1995*). IV albumin (1.5 gm/kg at day 1, 1 gm/kg on day 3) may ↑ frequency of renal impairment (p 0.002) & ↓ hospital mortality (p 0.01) (*NEJM 341:403, 1999*).
Prevention of SBP				
Cirrhosis & ascites		**TMP/SMX-DS** 1 tab po 5 d/ wk or **CIP** 750 mg once a wk		
Cirrhosis & UGI bleeding		**CIP** 500 mg IV q12h x 7 d.		
Secondary (bowel perforation, ruptured appendix, ruptured diverticula) Refs.: *NEJM 338:1521, 1998 & CID 37:997, 2003*	Enterobacteriaceae. Bacteroides sp., enterococci, P. aeruginosa (3–15%)	**Mild–moderate disease—Inpatient—parenteral rx:** (e.g., focal periappendiceal/peridiverticular abscess, endomyometritis)	**Cautious approach (from recent meta-analysis:** *Cochrane Database 2002 (2): CD002907*) **Must "cover" both Gm-neg. aerobic & Gm-neg. anaerobic bacteria. Drugs active only vs anaerobic Gm-neg. bacilli:** clinda, metro. **Drugs active only vs aerobic Gm-neg. bacilli:** APAG, P Ceph 2/3/4, aztreonam, AP Pen, CIP, Levo. **Drugs active vs both aerobic/anaerobic Gm-neg. bacilli:** cefoxitin, cefotetan, TC/CL, PIP/TZ, AM/SB, IMP, MER, Gati, Moxi.	
		PIP/TZ 3.375 gm IV q6h or 4.5 gm IV q8h, **OR** **TC/CL** 3.1 gm IV q6h **OR** **ERTA** 1 gm IV qd	**(CIP** 400 mg IV q12h or **Levo** 750 mg IV q24h) + **(metro** 1.0 gm IV q12h) or **FQ:** Gati/Moxi **(CFP** 2.0 gm IV q12h) + **metro**	Increasing resistance. TC/CL, PIP/TZ, AM/SB, IMP, MER, Gati, Moxi.
		Severe life-threatening disease—ICU patient: **IMP** 500 mg IV q6h or **MER** 1 gm IV q8h	**See Comment** (**AMP + metro**) + **(CIP** 400 mg IV q12h **OR Levo** 750 mg IV q24h) or **metro** 500 mg IV q6h + **APAG** (see *Table 10C, page 72*)	**% R** Cefoxitin Cefotetan Clindamycin Erta-penem less active vs P. aeruginosa/Acinetobacter species than IMP or MER. Based on in vitro activity, could sub **Gati/Moxi/ CIP/Levo**, but insufficient clinical data. If absence of ongoing fecal contamination, aerobic/anaerobic culture of peritoneal exudate/ abscess of help in guiding specific therapy. Less need for aminoglycosides. **With severe pen allergy** can "cover" Gm-neg. aerobes with CIP or aztreonam. **Remember IMP/MER are β-lactams.**
		Concomitant surgical management important.		Essentially no resistance: metro, PIP/TZ (*CID 35(Suppl 1):S126, 2000*)

‡ Parenteral **IV therapy** for peritonitis: **TC/CL** 3.1 gm q6h, **PIP/TZ** 3.375 gm q6h, **AM/SB** 3.0 gm q6h, **IMP** 0.5 gm q6h, **MER** 1.0 gm q8h, **FQ [CIP** 400 mg q12h, **Oflox** 400 mg q12h, **Levo** 500 mg qd, **Gati** 400 mg qd], **Moxi** 400 mg qd], **APAG** (see *Table 10C, page 72*) q8h, **P Ceph 4** [cefepime 2.0 gm q8h], **P Ceph 3** [cefotaxime 2.0 gm q4–8h, ceftriaxone 1–2 gm qd, ceftazidime 2.0 gm q8h], **P Ceph 2** [cefoxitin 2.0 gm q8h, cefotetan 2.0 gm q12h], **cefpirome**‡§ 2.0 gm q12h], **ceftizoxime**‡§ 2.0 gm q12h], **ceftriaxone** 1.0 gm loading then 0.5 gm q6h or 1.0 gm q8h, **clinda** 450–900 mg q8h. 500 mg q6h, **Gati** 400 mg qd, **Moxi** 400 mg qd, **aztreonam** 2.0 gm q6–8h], **PIP** 4.0 gm q6h, **aztreonam** 2.0 gm q8h. *NOTE: All dosage recommendations are for adults (unless otherwise indicated) and assume normal renal function.*

TABLE 1 (31)

ANATOMIC SITE/DIAGNOSIS/ MODIFYING CIRCUMSTANCES	ETIOLOGIES (usual)	SUGGESTED REGIMENS*		ADJUNCT DIAGNOSTIC OR THERAPEUTIC MEASURES AND COMMENTS
		PRIMARY	ALTERNATIVE†	
PERITONEUM/PERITONITIS (continued)				
Associated with chronic ambulatory peritoneal dialysis (defined as >100 WBC/μL, >50% PMNs)	Staph. aureus (most common), Staph. epidermidis, P. aeruginosa 7%, Gm-neg. bacilli 11%, sterile 20%, M. fortuitum (rare)	It of moderate severity, can rx by adding drug to dialysis fluid—see Table 17 for dosage. Reasonable empiric combinations: **vanco + P Ceph 3 AP** or **vanco + APAG**. If severely ill, rx with same drugs IV (adjust dose for renal failure, see Table 17) & wait culture. If multiple Gm-neg. bacilli cultured, consider bowel perforation and catheter removal.		For diagnosis, concentrate several hundred ml of removed dialysis fluid by centrifugation. Gram stain concentrate and then inject into aerobic/anaerobic blood culture bottles. A positive Gram stain will guide initial therapy. If culture shows Staph. epidermidis, good chance of "saving" dialysis catheter. If multiple Gm-neg. bacilli cultured, consider bowel perforation and catheter removal. Excellent ref.: Perit Dialysis Int 13:14, 1993
PHARYNX				
Pharyngitis/Tonsillitis—Reviews: NEJM 344:205, 2001; AnIM 139:113, 2003. Guideline for Group A strep: CID 35:113, 2002				
Exudative or diffuse erythema *For relationship to acute rheumatic fever, see footnote*[1] Rheumatic fever ref.: Ln 349:935, 1997	Group A,C,G strep, "viral," infectious mononucleosis (NEJM 329:156, 1993), C. diphtheriae, A. haemolyticum, Mycoplasma pneumoniae In adults, only 10% pharyngitis due to Group A strep	**Pen V** po x10 d. or if compliance unlikely: **benzathine pen** IM x1	**Erythro** x10 d. or **O Ceph 2** x4-6 d. (CID 38:1526 & 1535, 2004) or **clarithro** x10 d. or **azithro** x5 d. or **clarithro** x10 d. or **dirithro** x10 d. See footnote[2] for adult and pediatric dosages	**Dx:** In children & adults—Rapid strep test or culture. (Some debate: JAMA 291:1587, 2004; & 292:167, 2004) **Pen allergy & macrolide resistance:** No penicillin or oxphalosporin-resistant S. pyogenes, but now **macrolide-resist.** S. pyogenes. Need culture & in vitro susceptibility testing. **If clinical failure with empiric azithro/clarithro,** clarithro, clinda resistant to erythro, azithro. **S. pyogenes Groups C & G cause pharyngitis but not a risk for post-strep rheumatic fever.**
			Acetaminophen effective for pain relief (Br J Gen Pract 50:817, 2000) If macrolide-resistant & pen-allergy: Children—Linezolid should work; Adults—FQ of telithro	To prevent rheumatic fever, eradicate Group A strep. Requires 10 d. of pen V po; 4-6 d. of O Ceph 2; 5 d. of po azithro; 10 d. of clarithro. In controlled trial, better eradication rate with 10 d. azithro (82%) than 5 d. azithro (54%) (CID 35:1798, 2001)
	Gonococci	**Ceftriaxone** 125 mg IM x1 + **(azithro** or **doxy)** (see Comment)	**[Cip** 500 mg (po x1) or **Gati** 400 mg po x1) or **Ofox** 400 mg po x1) or **(Oflox** 400 mg po 2x/d x7 d.) + **(azithro** or **doxy)** (see Comment)	Because of risk of concomitant genital C. trachomatis, add either (azithro 1.0 gm po x1) or (doxy 100 mg po 2x/d x7 d.) See pages 15 for more options
Asymptomatic post-rx carrier Group A strep Multiple repeated culture-positive episodes (CID 25:574, 1997)	Group A strep	No rx required		Routine post-rx throat culture not advised. Small % of pts have recurrent culture-pos. Group A strep with symptomatic pharyngitis "It difficult to tell if true Group A strep carrier or new infection or carrier of RiF may help. 20 mg/kg/d x4 d. to max. of 300 mg/d (J Ped 106:481 & 876, 1985).
		Clinda or **AM/CL**, see footnote[2]	**Parenteral benzathine pen G** + **RIF** (footnote) Dosages in footnote[2]	
Whitish plaques, HIV+: (thrush)	Candida albicans (see Table 11, page 76)	Antibacterial agents not indicated, but for HSV:		
Vesicular, ulcerative	Coxsackie A9, B1-5, ECHO (multiple types); Enterovirus 71; Herpes simplex 1,2		[1,2] **acyclovir** 400 mg po x10 d.	May be caused by F. necrophorum bacteremia, see Jugular vein phlebitis (Lemierre's), page 33
Membranous—Diphtheria or Vincent's angina	C. diphtheriae	[**Antitoxin** + **erythro** 20–25 mg/kg q12h IV x7-14 d. (JAC 35:717, 1995) or (**benzyl pen G** 50,000 U/kg/d x5 d. then po **pen VK** 50 mg/kg q6h)]		Diphtheria occurs in immunized individuals. Antibiotics may ↓ toxin production, ↓ spread of organisms. Penicillin superior to erythro in randomized trial (CID 27:845, 2004).
Vincent's angina	Vincent's angina (anaerobes/spirochetes)	**Pen G** 4 mU q4h IV	**Clinda** 600 mg q8h IV	

---

[1] Primary rationale for rx is eradication of Group A strep (GAS) from pharynx because it was associated with clearance of GAS on pharyngeal cultures (CID 19:1110, 1994). Subsequent studies have been based on cultures, not actual prevention of ARF. Treatment ↓ duration of symptoms.

[2] **Treatment of Group A strep: All po unless otherwise indicated. PEDIATRIC DOSAGE: Benzathine penicillin** 25,000 u/kg IM to max. 1.2 mU). **Pen V** 25–50 mg/kg/div. q6h x10 d.; **erythro estolate** 20-40 mg/kg/div. bid x10 d.; **cefuroxime axetil** 20 mg/kg/d div. bid x10 d. or x5 d.; **cefpodoxime proxetil** 10 mg/kg/div. q12h x10 d.; **erythro succinate** 40 mg/kg/div. bid x10 d.; **azithro** 12 mg/kg/d x5 d. or 10 mg/kg/d x1 d. then 5 mg/kg x4 d.; **clinda** 20-30 mg/kg/d div. tid x10 d.; **dirithromycin** not approved; **clarithro** 15 mg/kg/d div. q12h x10 d. **ADULT DOSAGE: Benzathine penicillin** 1.2 mU IM x1; **pen V** 500 mg po bid or tid x10 d.; **erythro** estolate or base 500 mg bid or 250 mg qid x10 d.; **erythro estolate** 500 mg po bid x10 d.; **cefpodoxime proxetil** 100 mg po q12h x5 d.; **azithro** 500 mg x1 d. then 250 mg qd x4 d.; **cefuroxime axetil** 250 mg bid x4 d.; **cefdinir** 300 mg q12h x5–10 d. or 600 mg qd x10 d.; **cefprozil** 500 mg bid x10 d.; **cefditoren** 200 mg bid x10 d.; **cefpodoxime** proxetil 200 mg q12h x5 d.; **clarithro** 250 mg po bid x10 d.; **dirithromycin** 500 mg qd x10 d.

NOTE: All **O Ceph 2** drugs approved for 10 d. rx of strep. pharyngitis; increasing number of studies show efficacy of 4-6 d.; **clarithro** 250 mg q12h x10 d. or 500 mg q×3 d. **dirithromycin** 500 mg qd x10 d. **NOTE:** All dosage recommendations for adults (unless otherwise indicated) and assume normal renal function.

(Footnotes and abbreviations on page 45)

TABLE 1 (32)

ANATOMIC SITE/DIAGNOSIS/ MODIFYING CIRCUMSTANCES	ETIOLOGIES (usual)	SUGGESTED REGIMENS*		ADJUNCT DIAGNOSTIC OR THERAPEUTIC MEASURES AND COMMENTS
		PRIMARY	ALTERNATIVE†	
PHARYNX (continued)				
Epiglottitis				
Children	H. influenzae (rare), S. pyogenes, S. pneumoniae, S. aureus	**Peds dosage: Cefotaxime** 50 mg/kg q8h IV or **ceftriaxone** 50 mg/kg q12h	**Peds dosage: AM/SB** 100–200 mg/kg/d div q6h or **TMP/SMX** 8–12 mg TMP comp./kg/d div q12h	Have tracheostomy set "at bedside." Chloro is effective, but potentially less toxic alternative agents available. Review (adults): JAMA 272:1358, 1994)
Adults	Group A strep, H. influenzae (rare)	**Cefotaxime** 2.0 gm IV q8h or **ceftriaxone** 2.0 gm IV q12h		
Parapharyngeal space infection Poor dental hygiene, dental extractions, foreign bodies (e.g., toothpicks, fish bones)	Spaces include: sublingual, submaxillary, submandibular (Ludwig's angina, used loosely for these) lateral pharyngeal, retropharyngeal, pretracheal Polymicrobic: Strep sp., anaerobes, Eikenella corrodens	See footnote for epiglottitis.		
		(Clinda 600–900 mg IV q8h) or (**pen G** 24 mU by cont. infusion or div. q4–6h IV + **metro** 1.0 gm load and then 0.5 gm q6h IV) (Dosage, see footnote 21 page 31)	**Cefoxitin** 2.0 gm q8h IV or **Clinda** 600–900 mg q8h IV	Usual rx includes external drainage of lateral pharyngeal space. Emboli, pulmonary and systemic common. Erosion into carotid artery can occur.
		Penicillin allergy:	or	
		Clinda 600–900 mg q8h IV		
Jugular vein septic phlebitis (Lemierre's disease) (PIDJ 21:921, 2003; CID 31:524, 2000)	Fusobacterium necrophorum in vast majority.	**Pen G** 24 mU IV by cont. infusion or div. q4–6h		
Laryngitis (hoarseness)/tracheitis	Viral (90%)	Not indicated		
SINUSES, PARANASAL				
Sinusitis, acute: current terminology:				
Obstruction of sinus ostia, viral infection, allergens Refs.: Otolaryn-Head & Neck Surg. 130:1, 2004; AHM 134:498 & 498, 2001. For rhinovirus infections (common cold), see Table 14, page 112 Pediatric Guidelines: Pediatrics 108:798, 2001	Strep. pneumoniae 31%, H. influenzae 21%, M. catarrhalis 2%, Group A strep 2%, anaerobes 6%, viruses 15%, Staph. aureus 4%. By CT scans, sinus mucosa inflamed in 87% of viral URIs; only 2% develop bacterial rhinosinusitis	Reserve antibiotic rx for 7 d. who have (1) maxillary/facial pain & (2) purulent nasal discharge; if severe illness or pain, treat sooner—usually requires hospitalization. For mild/mod. disease: Ask if antibiotics in prior month and/or DRSP prevalence >30% ??		Rx goals: (1) Resolve infection, (2) prevent complications of bacterial disease, e.g., bacteremia, meningitis, brain abscess, (3) avoid chronic sinus disease, (4) avoid unnecessary antibiotic rx. High rate of spontaneous resolution. For pts with cephalosporin or penicillin allergy/intolerance, or severe IgE-mediated allergy, e.g., hives, anaphylaxis, treatment options: clarithro, azithro, telithro, TMP/SMX, doxy or FQs. FQs if under age 18. Dosages in footnote 2 page 32. If allergy just skin rash, no cephalosporin OK. Usual rx 10 days. In 1 study, results of 3 & 10 d. of TMP/SMX the same (JAMA 273:1015, 1995).
		NO:	**YES:**	
		Amox-HD or AM/CLER or **cefdinir** or **cefpodoxime** or **cefprozil**	**AM/CL-ER** (adults) or resp. **FQ** (adults). For pen. allergy, see Comment	Watch for pts with fever & facial erythema: ↑ risk of S. aureus infection. In areas with prevalence of DRSP >30% and recent prior antibiotic use, consider increasing amoxicillin dose to 3.0–3.5 gm/d: use extra amox, do not increase AM/CL beyond standard dosage.
		In general, treat ≤10 days; exceptions in prior allergy and pediatric doses, footnote 2 page 7	Use AM/CL susp. in peds.	Pts aged 1–18 yrs with clinical diagnosis of sinusitis randomized to placebo, amox, or AM/CL for 14 d. No difference in multiple measures of efficacy (Pediatrics 107:619, 2001). Similar study in adults: AIM 163:1793, 2003. Hence, without bacteriologic endpoints, data are hard to interpret. AM/CL-ER ref.: AJM 117(Suppl 3A):23S, 2004.
			Mild/Mod. Disease: AM/CL-ER OR (**cefpodoxime, cefuroxime, or cefdinir**)	
			Severe Disease: Gati, Gemi, Levo, Moxi	
			Treat 10 days. Adult doses in footnote 2 page 32 & Comment.	
Clinical failure after 3 days	As above; consider diagnostic tap/aspirate			

Footnotes:

¹ **Ceftriaxone** 2.0 gm IV qd; **cefotaxime** 2.0 gm q4–8h IV; **AM/SB** 3.0 gm IV q6h; **PIP/TZ** 3.375 gm IV q6h; **TC/CL** 3.1 gm IV q4–6h; **TMP/SMX** 8–10 mg/kg/d (based on TMP component) div q6h, q8h, or q12h.

² **Penicillin** may be given in divided doses q4–6h or by continuous infusion.

³ **Pediatric doses for sinusitis (all oral): Amoxicillin** high dose 90 mg/kg/d div. q8h or q12h, **AM/CL-ES** (extra strength) pediatric susp.: 90 mg amox component/kg/d div, **azithro** 10 mg/kg x1, then 5 mg/kg x4; **clarithro** 15 mg/kg/d div q12h; **cefpodoxime** 10 mg/kg/d div. q12–24h; **cefuroxime axetil** 30 mg/kg/d div q12h, **cefdinir** 14 mg/kg/d once daily or divided bid, **TMP/SMX** 8–12 mg TMP/40–60 mg q12h.
Adult doses for sinusitis (all oral): AM/CL-ER (Augmentin XR) 2000/125 mg bid; **amox high-dose (HD)** 1.0 gm tid, **clarithro** 500 mg bid or **clarithro ext. release** 1.0 gm qd; **doxy** 100 mg bid, **respiratory FQs (Gati)** 400 mg qd, **Gemi** 320 mg qd (not FDA indication but should work), **Levo** 750 mg qd, **Moxi** 400 mg qd; **O Ceph** (**cefdinir** 300 mg q12h or 600 mg qd) or **cefpodoxime** 200 mg bid, **cefprozil** 250–500 mg bid; **cefuroxime** 250 mg bid; **TMP/SMX** 1 double-strength (TMP 160 mg) bid (results after 3 & 10 d. Ax similar), **telithro** 800 mg qd
(Footnotes and abbreviations on page 45) NOTE: All dosage recommendations are for adults (unless otherwise indicated) and assume normal renal function.

TABLE 1 (33)

ANATOMIC SITE/DIAGNOSIS/ MODIFYING CIRCUMSTANCES	ETIOLOGIES (usual)	SUGGESTED REGIMENS* PRIMARY	ALTERNATIVE†	ADJUNCT DIAGNOSTIC OR THERAPEUTIC MEASURES AND COMMENTS
SINUSES, PARANASAL/Sinusitis. Acute (continued)				
Diabetes mellitus with acute ketoacidosis; neutropenia; deferoxamine rx	Rhizopus sp. (mucor), aspergillus	See Table 11, pages 73 & 80. Ref.: NEJM 337:254, 1997		See above
Hospitalized + nasotracheal or nasogastric intubation	Gm-neg. bacilli 47% (pseudomonas, acinetobacter, E. coli common), Gm+ (S. aureus) 35%, yeasts 18%. Polymicrobial in 80%	Remove nasotracheal tube and if fever persists, recommend sinus aspiration for Gm+ & C/S. Rx to empiric rx. **(IP or PIP) + CIP** 0.5 gm q8h IV, or **MER** 1.0 gm q8h IV	**CFP** or **ceftaz** or **vanco** 1.0 gm IV or **CFP** 2.0 gm q12h IV	After 7 d. of nasotracheal or gastric tubes, 95% have x-ray "sinusitis" (fluid in sinuses), but only 38% have infection when fluid sampled (Am J Resp Crit Care Med 150:776, 1994). For pts requiring mechanical ventilation for ≥1 wk, bacterial sinusitis occurs in <10% (CID 27:851, 1998). May need fluconazole if yeast on Gram stain of aspirate. Review: CID 27:463, 1998
Sinusitis, chronic Adults	Prevotella, anaerobic strep, & fusobacterium—anaerobes, no inflammation. Strep sp., hemophilus, P. aeruginosa, S. aureus & moraxella—aerobes. (CID 35:428, 2002)	Antibiotics usually not effective	Otolaryngology consultation. If acute exacerbation, rx as acute	Pathogenesis unclear and may be polyfactorial: damage to ostiomeatal complex during acute bacterial disease, allergy ± polyps, occult immunodeficiency, and/or odontogenic disease (periodontitis in maxillary teeth).
SKIN				
Acne vulgaris (Med Lett 44:52, 2002; Ped Drugs 5:301, 2003; Dermatol 206:29, 2003; JAMA 292:726, 2004)				
Comedones (noninflammatory): "blackheads," "whiteheads," earliest form, no inflammation	↑ excess sebum production & gland obstruction. No active infection. Propionibacterium acnes	Topical **tretinoin** (cream 0.025 or 0.05%) or (gel 0.01 or 0.025%)	All once-daily: Topical **adapalene** 0.1% gel OR topical **azelaic acid** 20% cream OR **tazarotene** 0.1% cream	Goal is prevention. ↓ number of new comedones and create an environment unfavorable to P. acnes. Adapalene causes less irritation than tretinoin. Azelaic acid less potent but less irritating than retinoids. Expect 40-70% ↓ in comedones in 12 weeks.
Mild inflammatory acne: small papules or pustules	Proliferation of P. acnes + abnormal desquamation of follicular cells	Topical **erythro 3% + benzoyl peroxide 5%** bid	Can substitute **clinda 1%** gel for erythro	Topical metro has anti-inflammatory activity but P. acnes not susceptible. If tolerable to rx, combine topical antimicrobial with a topical retinoid.
Inflammatory acne: comedones, papules & pustules. Less common: deep nodules (cysts)	Progression of above events	Topical **erythro 3% + benzoyl peroxide 5%** bid) + oral antibiotic	Oral rx: **doxy** 100 mg bid) or **minocycline** 50 mg bid). Others: **tetracycline, erythro, TMP/SMX, clinda**	Systemic **isotretinoin** reserved for pts with severe widespread nodular cystic lesions that fail oral antibiotic rx. 4-5 mo. course of 0.1-1.0 mg/kg/day. Aggressive/violent behavior reported. Tetracyclines stain developing teeth. Doxy can cause photosensitivity. Minocycline stain-side-effects: urticaria, vertigo, pigment deposition in skin or oral mucosa.
Acne rosacea	? skin mite: Demodex	Metro topical cream bid	Metro topical cream bid	More pt satisfaction with azelaic acid [J Am Acad Derm 40(6, Pt 1):961, 1998].
Anthrax, cutaneous, inhalation (pulmonary, mediastinal) **To report bioterrorism event:** 770-488-7100; **For info: www.bt.cdc.gov** Refs.: JAMA 281:1735, 1999; & MMWR 50:909, 2001	B. anthracis See Lung, page 28, and Table 1B, page 46	**Adults (including pregnancy):** CIP 500 mg po bid x60 d. **Children:** CIP 20-30 mg/kg/d div q12h (max. 500 mg q8h) to max. 1 gm/d) x60 d. All for 60 days.	Azelaic acid gel bid, topical **Adults (including pregnancy):** CIP 500 mg po bid x60 d. **Children:** CIP 20-30 mg/kg/d div q12h (max. 500 mg q8h) to max. 1 gm/d) x60 d. All for 60 days.	1. If penicillin susceptible, then: **Adults: Amox** 500 mg po q8h x60 d. **Children: Amox** 80 mg/kg/d div. q8h (max. 500 mg q8h) 2. Usual treatment of cutaneous anthrax is 7-10 d.; 60 d. in setting of bioterrorism with presumed aerosol exposure 3. Other **FQs** (Gati, Levo, Moxi) should work based on in vitro susceptibility data
Bacillary angiomatosis: For other Bartonella infections, see Cat-scratch disease lymphadenitis, page 30, and Bartonella, page 38	Bartonella henselae and quintana	**Adults (including pregnancy): Clarithro** 500 mg po bid or **azithro** 250 mg po or **doxy** 100 mg po bid	**Adults (including pregnancy): Erythro** 500 mg po qid or **doxy** 100 mg po bid	Usual treatment of cutaneous anthrax is 7-10 d.; 60 d. in setting of bioterrorism with presumed aerosol exposure
In immunocompromised (HIV-1, bone marrow transplant) patients. Also see SANFORD GUIDE TO HIV/AIDS THERAPY				In immunocompromised pts with severe disease, doxy 100 mg/IV bid + RIF 300 mg po bid reported effective (IDC In Amer 12:37, 1998; Adv PID 11:1, 1996).

All dosage recommendations are for adults (unless otherwise indicated) and assume normal renal function.

NOTE: All dosage recommendations are for adults (unless otherwise indicated) and assume normal renal function.

(Footnotes and abbreviations on page 45)

TABLE 1 (34)

ANATOMIC SITE/DIAGNOSIS/MODIFYING CIRCUMSTANCES	ETIOLOGIES (usual)	SUGGESTED REGIMENS*		ADJUNCT DIAGNOSTIC OR THERAPEUTIC MEASURES AND COMMENTS
		PRIMARY	ALTERNATIVE†	
SKIN (continued)				
Bite: Remember tetanus prophylaxis—see Table 20. See Table 20C for rabies prophylaxis				
Bat, raccoon, skunk	Strep & staph from skin; rabies	**AM/CL** 875/125 mg bid or 500/125 mg tid po	**Doxy** 100 mg bid po	In Americas, **antirabies rx indicated**; rabies immune globulin + vaccine. (See Table 20C, pages 141–142)
Cat (Ref.: NEJM 340:85 & 138, 1999). Cat-scratch disease, page 30	**Pasteurella multocida,** Staph. aureus	**AM/CL** 875/125 mg bid or 500/125 mg tid po	**Cefuroxime axetil** 0.5 gm q12h po or **doxy** 100 mg bid po. **Do not use cephalexin**	80% cat bites become infected. **P. multocida resistant to dicloxacillin, cephalexin, clinda; many strains resistant to erythro** (most sensitive to azithro but no clinical data with azithro). If Clostridium tetani develops osteomyelitis, 24 hr. Observe for osteomyelitis. If culture +, for only P. multocida, can switch to pen G IV or pen VK po.
Catfish sting	Toxins	See Comments		Presents as immediate pain, erythema and edema. Resembles strep cellulitis. May become secondarily infected; AM/CL is reasonable choice for prophylaxis.
Dog (Ref.: NEJM 340:85 & 138, 1999)	**P. multocida,** S. aureus, Bacteroides sp., Fusobacterium sp., EF-4, Capnocytophaga	**AM/CL** 875/125 mg bid or 500/125 mg tid po	**Clinda** 300 mg qid po + FQ (adults) or **clinda** + **TMP/SMX** (children)	Only 5% dog bites become infected. Prophylaxis may be worthwhile (AnEM 23:535, 1994). Consider antirabies rx; rabies immune globulin + vaccine (Table 20C). May transmit blastomycosis. Capnocytophaga in splenectomized pts may cause local eschar, sepsis with DIC. **P. multocida resistant to dicloxacillin, cephalexin, clinda and erythro;** sensitive to FQs in vitro (AAC 43:1475, 1999).
Human For bacteriology, see CID 37:1481, 2003	Viridans strep 100%, Staph epidermidis 53%, corynebacterium 41%, **Staph. aureus 29%, eikenella 15%, bacteroides 82%, pep-tostrep 26%**	**Early** (not yet infected): **AM/CL** 875/125 mg bid po ×5 d. **Later:** Signs of infection (usually in 3–24 hrs): **(AM/SB** 1.5 gm q6h IV or **cefoxitin** 2.0 gm q8h IV) or **[PIP/TZ** 3.375 gm q6h IV] or **TC/CL** 3.1 gm q6h IV. Pen allergy: **Clinda** ± (either **CIP** or **TMP/SMX)**	**Cephalexin, clinda and erythro,** all **P. multocida resistant to clinda, naficillin/oxacillin, metro, P Ceph 1, and erythro.** For in vitro susceptibility to FQs and macrolides: JAC 41:391, 1998
Pig (swine)	Polymicrobic: Gm+ cocci, Gm-neg. bacilli, anaerobes, Pasteurella sp.	**AM/CL** 875/125 mg bid po	**P Ceph 3** or **TC/CL** or **AM/SB** or **IMP**	Information limited but infection is common and serious (Ln 348:888, 1996).
Prairie dog	Monkeypox	See Table 14A, page 111.	No rx recommended	CID 20:421, 1995
Primate, non-human	Herpesvirus simiae	**Acyclovir** See Table 14B, page 113		
Rat	Spirillum minus & Streptobacillus moniliformis	**AM/CL** 875/125 mg bid po	**Doxy**	Antirabies rx is not indicated.
Seal	Marine mycoplasma	**Tetracycline** ×4 wks		
Snake: pit viper (Ref.: NEJM 347:347, 2002)	Pseudomonas sp., Enterobacteriaceae, Staph. epidermidis, Clostridium sp.			Can take weeks to appear after bite (Ln 349:649, 2004). Primary therapy is antivenom. Ceftriaxone should be more effective. Tetanus prophylaxis indicated.
Spider bite: Most necrotic ulcers attributed to spiders are probably due to another cause. Remember cutaneous anthrax. (Ln 349:549, 2004)				
Widow (Latrodectus)	Not infectious	None		May be confused with "acute abdomen." Diazepam or calcium gluconate helpful to control pain, muscle spasm. Tetanus prophylaxis.
Brown recluse (Loxosceles) (not west of Nebraska)	Not infectious Ref.: CID 32:636, 2001	**Dapsone** 50 mg qid po (see Comment)		Most pts do well without systemic rx. Dapsone followed by excision at 6 weeks (AnSurg 202:659, 1985) reported effective. Screen for G6PD deficiency, if positive dapsone contraindicated. Dapsone inhibits PMNs.
Boils—Furunculosis—Subcutaneous abscesses in drug addicts ("skin poppers")	Carbuncles = multiple connecting furuncles			
Active lesions	Staph, both MSSA & MRSA	Hot packs, incision, & drainage	Systemic antibiotics do not shorten course; theoretically could lower risk of bacteremia	Epidemic of **community-acquired MRSA,** currently susceptible to TMP/SMX, clinda, minocycline. If erythro-resistant, probably clinda-resistant. Seems reasonable in pts with large and/or multiple abscesses and/or fever to: (1) do culture & sens. & (2) start empiric TMP/SMX-DS, 1 tab

(Footnotes and abbreviations on page 45)   NOTE: All dosage recommendations are for adults (unless otherwise indicated) and assume normal/renal function.

TABLE 1 (35)

ANATOMIC SITE/DIAGNOSIS/ MODIFYING CIRCUMSTANCES	ETIOLOGIES (usual)	SUGGESTED REGIMENS*		ADJUNCT DIAGNOSTIC OR THERAPEUTIC MEASURES AND COMMENTS
		PRIMARY	ALTERNATIVE†	
SKIN/Boils—Furunculosis—Subcutaneous abscesses in drug addicts				
To lessen number of recurrences	MSSA & MRSA	Guided by in vitro susceptibilities: (**Diclox 500 mg** po qid or **TMP/SMX-DS** 1 tab po bid) + **RIF** 600 mg po qd, all x10 d	Plus Nasal & under fingernail fragment with either **bacitracin ointment** or **mupirocin ointment** bid	Plus Shower with Hibiclens daily x3 d, then 3x/week. Others have tried 5% povidone-iodine cream intranasal 4x/d, x5 d. Reports of S. aureus resistant to bacitracin & mupirocin. Mupirocin resistant to bacitracin had no effect on S. aureus infection in placebo-controlled study (AVIM 140:419 & 484, 2004).
Hidradenitis suppurativa	Lesions secondarily infected: S. aureus, Enterobacteriaceae, pseudomonas, anaerobes	Aspirate, base rx on culture	Many pts ultimately require surgical excision.	Caused by keratinous plugging of apocrine glands of axillary and/or inguinal areas.
Burns. For overall management: NEJM 350:810, 2004				
Initial burn wound care (CID 37:543, 2003)	Not infected	Early excision & wound closure; shower hydrotherapy. Role of topical antimicrobics unsettled	**Silver sulfadiazine** cream, 1%, apply 1–2x/ day or 0.5% **silver nitrate** solution or **mafenide acetate** cream. Apply 2x/day	Marrow-induced neutropenia that resolves even if use is continued. Silver nitrate leaches electrolytes from wounds & stains everything. Mafenide inhibits carbonic anhydrase and can cause metabolic acidosis.
Burn wound sepsis	Strep. pyogenes, Enterobacter sp., S. aureus, S. epidermidis, E. faecalis, E. coli, P. aeruginosa, Fungi rare. Herpesvirus rare	**Vanco** 1.0 gm q12h IV) + (**amikacin** 10 mg/kg loading dose then 7.5 mg/kg q12h IV) + **RIF** 4.0 gm q4h IV (give ½ daily dose of **piperacillin** into subeschar tissues with surgical eschar removal q12 hours))		Monitor serum levels. ½ of most antibiotics ↓ Staph. aureus tend to remain localized to burn wound. If patient more toxic than expected, consider toxic shock syndrome. Candida sp. colonize but seldom invade. Pneumonia has become the major infectious complication, most often staph. Other alternatives: clinda, Gati, Levo, Moxi.
Cellulitis, erysipelas: Be wary of macrolide-resistant (myc-resistant) Group A strep. Review: NEJM 350:904, 2004				
Extremities, not associated with venous catheter (see Comments): non-diabetic. For diabetes, see below	Group A strep, occ. Group B, C; Staph. aureus (uncommon but difficult to exclude)	**Pen G** 1–2 mU IV q6h or (**Nafcillin** or **oxacillin** 2.0 or **diclox**acillin 500 mg q6h po or **cefazolin** 1.0 gm q8h IV). See Comment	**AM/CL** or **azithro** or **clarithro** or **dirithro** (Dosage, see footnote page 25)	**"Spontaneous" erysipelas of leg in non-diabetic is usually due to strep. Gps A,B,C or G.** Hence OK to **start with IV pen G 1–2 mU q6h** & observe for localized S. aureus infection. Look for tinea pedis with fissures, a common portal of entry; can often culture strep from between toes (CID 23:1162, 1996). For rx of pts with lymphedema & recurrent erysipelas, see prophylaxis, Table 15.
Facial, adult (erysipelas)	Group A strep, Staph. aureus (to include MRSA), S. pneumo	**Vanco** 1.0 gm IV q12h	**Dapto** 4 mg/kg/d	**Choice of empiric therapy must have activity vs S. aureus** since facial erysipelas or S. pyogenes erysipelas of an extremity. Forced to treat empirically for MRSA until in vitro susceptibilities available.
Diabetes mellitus and erysipelas (See Foot, Diabetic, page 10)	Group A strep, Staph. aureus, Enterobacteriaceae, clostridia (rare)	**Early mild: TMP/SMX-DS** bid po + **RIF** 300 mg po. **For severe disease:** IMP or **ERTA** IV + (**linezolid** 600 mg IV/po or **vanco** IV) (Dosage, see footnote)		Prompt surgical debridement indicated to rule out necrotizing fasciitis and to obtain cultures. If septic, consider x-ray of extremity to demonstrate gas. **Prognosis dependent on blood supply; assess arteries.** See diabetic foot, page 10.
Erysipelas 2° to lymphedema (congenital = Milroy's disease); post-breast surgery with lymph node dissection	S. pyogenes, Groups A, C, G	**Benzathine pen G** 1.2 mU IM once to prevent recurrences (See footnote)		Indicated only if pt is having frequent episodes of cellulitis. Pen V 250 mg po bid should be effective but not aware of clinical trials. In pen-allergic pts: erythro 500 mg po qd, azithro 250 mg po qd, or clarithro 500 mg po qd.
Dandruff (seborrheic dermatitis)	Malassezia species	Ketoconazole shampoo 2% or selenium sulfide 2.5% (see page 6, chronic external otitis)		
Decubitus or venous stasis or arterial insufficiency ulcers: with exudate	Polymicrobic: S. pyogenes (Gps A,C,G), enterococci, anaerobes (GI/GU), Enterobacteriaceae, Pseudomonas sp., Bacteroides sp., Staph. aureus	IMP or MER or TC/CL or (CIP Gati, Levo, or Moxi) (+ clinda + metro) Dosages, see pages 10, 16, 21, 42		Without sepsis or extensive cellulitis local care may be adequate. Debride as needed. Topical mafenide or silver sulfadiazine adjunctive. R/O underlying osteomyelitis. May need wound coverage with skin graft or skin substitute (JAMA 283:716, 2000).
Erythema multiforme	H. simplex type 1, mycoplasma, Strep. pyogenes, drugs (sulfonamides, phenytoin, penicillins)			**Rx: Acyclovir** if due to H. simplex

(Footnotes and abbreviations on page 45)   NOTE: All dosage recommendations are for adults (unless otherwise indicated) and assume normal renal function.

TABLE 1 (36)

ANATOMIC SITE/DIAGNOSIS/ MODIFYING CIRCUMSTANCES	ETIOLOGIES (usual)	SUGGESTED REGIMENS*		ADJUNCT DIAGNOSTIC OR THERAPEUTIC MEASURES AND COMMENTS
		PRIMARY	ALTERNATIVE†	
SKIN (continued)				
Erythema nodosum	Sarcoidosis, inflammatory bowel disease, M. tbc, coccidioidomycosis, yersinia, sulfonamides			**Rx: NSAIDs; glucocorticoids** (if refractory).
Erythrasma	Corynebacterium minutissimum	**Erythro** 250 mg q6h po x14 d.		Coral red fluorescence with Wood's lamp. Alt: 2% aqueous clinda topically.
Folliculitis	Many etiologies: S. aureus, candida, P. aeruginosa, malassezia, demodex	See individual entities. See Whirlpool follicles, page 36		
Furunculosis	Staph. aureus	See Boils, page 36		
Hemorrhagic bullous lesions				
Hx of sea water-contaminated abrasion or eating raw seafood, shock	Vibrio vulnificus, V. damsela (CID 37:272, 2003)	**Ceftazidime** 2.0 gm q8h IV + **doxy** 100 mg bid (IV or po)	Either **cefotaxime** 2.0 gm q8h IV or (**CIP** 750 mg bid po or 400 mg bid IV)	¼ pts have chronic liver disease with mortality in 50% (NEJM 312:343, 1985). In Taiwan, where a number of cases are seen, the impression exists that ceftazidime is superior to tetracyclines (CID 15:271, 1992), hence both.
Impetigo, ecthyma—usually children				
"Honey-crust" lesions (non-bullous)	**Group A strep impetigo,** crusted lesions can be Staph. aureus + streptococci	Mupirocin ointment 2% tid x3–5 d. For dosages, see Table 10B for adults and Table 16, page 131 for children	**Azithro or clarithro** or **erythro** or **O Ceph 2**	In meta-analysis that combined strep & staph impetigo, mupirocin had higher cure rates than placebo. Mupirocin superior to oral erythro. Penicillin inferior to erythro. Few placebo-controlled trials. Ref.: Cochrane Database Systemic Reviews, 2004 (2).
Bullous (if ruptured), thin "varnish-like" crust)	**Staph. aureus impetigo**	**Dicloxacillin** po or **oxacillin** po or **O Ceph 1** For dosages, see Table 10B	**Mupirocin** ointment or **AM/CL** po or **azithro** or **clarithro** For dosages, see Table 10B	
Infected wound, extremity—Post-trauma (for bites, see page 45; for post-operative, see below)—**Gram stain negative**				
Mild to moderate; uncomplicated	Polymicrobic; Staph. aureus (MSSA & MRSA), Group A Strep, Enterobacteriaceae, Cl. perfringens, Cl. tetani; if water exposure, Pseudomonas sp., Aeromonas sp.	**TMP/SMX-DS** po bid & **clinda** 300–450 mg po bid (see Comment)	**Minocycline** 100 mg po bid or **linezolid** 600 mg po bid (see Comment)	Culture & sensitivity, check Gram stain. **Tetanus toxoid if indicated. Mild infection:** Suggested drugs focus on S. aureus & Strep species. If suspect Gm-neg. bacilli, add **AM/CL-ER** 1000/62.5 two tabs po bid. If MRSA erythro-resistant, may have inducible resistance to clinda.
Febrile with sepsis— hospitalized		**AM/SB** or **TC/CL** or **PIP/TZ** or **IMP** or **MER** or **ERTA** (Dosage, page 16) + **vanco** 1.0 gm IV q12h	**Vanco** 1.0 gm IV q12h (see Comment) + **CIP** or **Levo** IV	**Fever—sepsis:** Alternative to vanco is **linezolid** 600 mg IV/po q12h. If Gm-neg bacilli & severe pen allergy, CIP 400 mg IV q12h or Levo 750 mg IV qd.
Infected wound, post-operative—Gram stain negative				
Surgery not involving GI or female genital tract				
Without sepsis (mild)	Staph. aureus, Group A, B, C or G strep	**TMP/SMX-DS** po bid	**Clinda** 300–450 mg po tid	Check Gram stain of exudate. If Gm-neg. bacilli, **add** β-lactam/β-lactamase inhibitor: AM/CL-ER po or (ERTA or PIP/TZ or TC/CL) IV. Dosage on page 16.
With sepsis (severe)	MSSA/MRSA, coliforms, bacteroides & other anaerobes	**Vanco** 1.0 gm IV q12h	**Dapto** 6 mg/kg IV qd or daptomycin 4 mg/kg IV qd or 6 mg/kg qd if septic	For all treatment options, see Peritonitis, page 31.
Surgery involving GI tract (includes oropharynx, esophagus) or female genital tract		**PIP/TZ** or (**P Ceph 3** + **metro**) or **ERTA** or **IMP** or **MER** + **vanco** 1.0 gm IV q12h **Mild infection: AM/CL-ER** 2 tabs po bid	**Dapto** 6 mg/kg IV qd + **metro** 1.0 gm IV q12h (see Comment)	Most important: Drain wound & get cultures. Can sub linezolid for vanco. Can sub CIP or Levo for β-lactams.
Meleney's synergistic gangrene	See Necrotizing fasciitis, page 38			
Infected wound, febrile patient—Gram stain: Gram-positive cocci in clusters	S. aureus, possibly MRSA	**Do culture & sensitivity** Oral: **TMP/SMX-DS** 1 tab po bid or **clinda** 300–450 mg po tid (see Comment)	**IV: Vanco** 1.0 gm IV q12h	↑ in community-acquired MRSA (CA-MRSA). Need culture & sensitivity to verify. Other po options for CA-MRSA include minocycline 100 mg po q12h (inexpensive) & linezolid 600 mg po q12h (expensive). If MRSA clinda-sensitive but erythro-resistant, watch for inducible clinda resistance.

(Footnotes and abbreviations on page 45)   NOTE: All dosage recommendations are for adults (unless otherwise indicated) and assume normal renal function.

TABLE 1 (37)

ANATOMIC SITE/DIAGNOSIS/ MODIFYING CIRCUMSTANCES	ETIOLOGIES (usual)	SUGGESTED REGIMENS* PRIMARY	ALTERNATIVE†	ADJUNCT DIAGNOSTIC OR THERAPEUTIC MEASURES AND COMMENTS
SKIN (continued)				
Necrotizing fasciitis ("flesh-eating bacteria") Post-surgery, trauma, strepto-coccal skin infections *See Gas gangrene, page 30, & Toxic shock (gangrene)*	**3 types: (1)** Streptococ, Grp A, C, G; **(2)** Clostridia; **(3)** polymicrobic: aerobic + anaerobic (If S. aureus alone, see Staph scalded skin/synergistic gangrene)	For treatment of clostridia, see *Muscle, gas gangrene, page 30*. Meleney's synergistic gangrene, Fournier's gangrene, necrotizing fasciitis have a common pathophysiology. **All require prompt surgical debridement** as well as antibiotics. Dx of necrotizing fasciitis requires incision and probing. If no resistance to probing subcutaneously (fascial plane), dx necrotizing fasciitis. **Med Grd stain/culture** to determine etiology is strep, clostridia + gas gangrene, add clinda (*SMJ 96:968, 2003*). **IMP or MER or ER** —... **Treatment: If strep**, reasonable to treat with penicillin & clinda. If polymicrobial, clostridia ± gas gangrene, add clinda. NOTE: If strep necrotizing fasciitis, reasonable to treat with penicillin & clinda *(see page 30).*		The terminology of **polymicrobic** wound infections is not precise.
Puncture wound—nail	Through tennis shoe: P. aeruginosa	Local debridement to remove foreign body & tetanus prophylaxis		Osteomyelitis evolves in only 1-2% of plantar puncture wounds.
Staphylococcal scalded skin syndrome *Ref.: Ln I 354:819, 2000*	Toxin-producing S. aureus	**Nafcillin** or **oxacillin** 2.0 gm IV q4h (children: 150 mg/kg/d div. q6h) x5-7 days		Toxin causes **intraepidermal split** and positive Nikolsky sign. Drugs cause epidermal split, called **toxic epidermal necrolysis**—more serious (*Ln 351:1417, 1998*). Biopsy differentiates.
Ulcerated skin lesions	Consider anthrax, tularemia, P. aeruginosa (ecthyma gangrenosum), plague, blastomycosis, spider (rarely), mucormycosis, mycobacteria, leishmania, arterial insufficiency, venous stasis, and others.			
Whirlpool (Hot Tub) folliculitis *See Folliculitis, page 37*	Pseudomonas aeruginosa	Usually self-limited, treatment not indicated		Decontaminate hot tub: drain and chlorinate. Also associated with exfoliative beauty aids (loofah sponges) (*J Clin Micro 31:480, 1993*)
SPLEEN. For post-splenectomy prophylaxis, see Table 15A, page 123				
Splenic abscess Endocarditis, bacteremia Contiguous from intra-abdominal site Immunocompromised	Staph. aureus, streptococci Polymicrobic Candida sp.	**Nafcillin** or **oxacillin** 2.0 gm q4h IV Treat as *Peritonitis, secondary, page 31.* **Amphotericin B** *(Dosage: see Table 11, page 74)*	**Vanco** 1.0 gm q12h IV **Fluconazole, caspofungin**	Burkholderia (Pseudomonas) pseudomallei is common cause of splenic abscess in SE Asia.
SYSTEMIC FEBRILE SYNDROMES Spread by infected TICK, FLEA, or LICE (*CID 29:888, 1999*): Epidemiologic history crucial. Babesiosis, Lyme disease, & granulocytic Ehrlichiosis have same reservoir & tick vector (*CID 33:676, 2001*).				
Babesiosis: *see NEJM 343:*	Etiol: B. microti et al. Vector: Usually Ixodes ticks. Host: White-footed mouse & others	[**Atovaquone** 750 mg po q12h + **azithro** 500 mg po q24h, then 250 mg po q24h ‖ OR **clinda** 1.2 gm bid IV or 600 mg tid po x7 d + **quinine** 650 mg po x7 d. **Ped. dosage: Clinda** 20-40 mg/kg/d + **quinine** 25 mg/kg/d] plus **exchange transfusion**		Exposure endemic areas May to Sept. Can result from blood transfusion (*JAMA 281: 927, 1999*). Usually subclinical illness likely in asplenic pts, pts with concomitant Lyme disease, older pts, pts with HIV. **Dx:** Giemsa-stained blood smear; antibody test available. PCR under study. **Rx:** Exchange transfusions successful **adjunct, used early, in severe disease.**
Bartonella infections: *NEJM 340:184, 1999; CID 35:684, 2002*				
Asymptomatic bacteremia	B. quintana	**Doxy** 100 mg po/IV x15 d		Can lead to endocarditis &/or trench fever: found in homeless, esp. if lice/leg
Cat-scratch disease	B. henselae	**Azithro** (or symptomatic only--see page 30, usually lymphadenitis, can involve CNS, liver in immunocompetent pts.		**Immunocompetent Patient:** Bacteremia/endocarditis/FUO Cat scratch disease
Bacillary angiomatosis; Peliosis hepatis—pts with AIDS	B. henselae, B. quintana	**Azithro** 500 mg po q24h or **clarithro** 500 mg bid po or **clarithro** ER 1.0 gm po q24h po or **azithro** 250 mg po bid, or **CIP** 500-750 mg bid x8 wks	[**Erythro** 500 mg qid po or **doxy** 100 mg bid po] x8 wks or if severe, combination of **doxy** 100 mg bid po + **RIF** 300 mg bid po] x4-6 wks	**HIV/AIDS Patient:** Manifestations of Bartonella infections: Bacillary angiomatosis Bacillary peliosis Bacteremia/endocarditis/FUO Trench Fever
Endocarditis (see page 20) (*AAC 47:2204, 2003*)	B. henselae, B. quintana	**Gentamicin** 3 mg/kg IV q24h x14 d, minimum 14 d + **doxy** 200 mg po once daily x4-6 wks		Hard to detect with conventional blood culture systems. Need lysis-centrifugation and/or blind subculture onto chocolate agar at 7 & 14 days. Diagnosis often by antibody titer ≥1:800.
Trench fever (FUO)	B. quintana	**Doxy** 100 mg po (doxy alone if no endocarditis)		Same as Urban Trench Fever (page 40)

NOTE: All dosage recommendations are for adults (unless otherwise indicated) and assume normal renal function.

TABLE 1 (38)

ANATOMIC SITE/DIAGNOSIS/ MODIFYING CIRCUMSTANCES	ETIOLOGIES (usual)	SUGGESTED REGIMENS*		ADJUNCT DIAGNOSTIC OR THERAPEUTIC MEASURES AND COMMENTS
		PRIMARY	ALTERNATIVE†	
SYSTEMIC FEBRILE SYNDROMES				
TICK, FLEA or LICE (continued)				
Ehrlichiosis*. CDC def. of confirmed case as one of: (1) 4x↑ IFA antibody, (2) detection of Ehrlichia DNA by PCR, (3) visible morulae in WBC and IFA ≥1:64 (MMWR 46(RR-10):1–55, 1997)	Spread from concomitant tick-borne disease—babesiosis (JAMA 275:1657, 1996) or ehrlichiosis			
Human monocytic ehrlichiosis (HEM) (IDCP 7:252, 1998)	Ehrlichia chaffeensis (Lone Star tick is vector)	**Doxy** 100 mg bid po or IV x7–14 d.	**Tetracycline** 500 mg qid po x7– 14 d. No current recommendation for children or pregnancy	30 states; mostly SE of line from NJ to Ill. to Missouri to Oklahoma to Texas. History of outdoor activity and tick exposure. April-Sept. Fever, rash (36%), leukopenia and thrombocytopenia. Blood smears: no help. PCR for early dx
Human granulocytic ehrlichiosis (HGE) (CID 31:554, 2000)	Anaplasma (Ehrlichia) phagocytophilum (Ixodes sp. ticks are vector). Dog variant is Ehrlichia ewingii (NEJM 341:148 & 195, 1999)	**Doxy** 100 mg bid po or IV x7–14 d.	**Tetracycline** 500 mg 4/d po x7–14 d. Not in children (ref. See Comment)	Upper Midwest, NE, West Coast & Europe. April-Sept. Fever, febrile flu-like illness after outdoor activity. No rash. Leukopenia/thrombocytopenia common. **Dx:** Up to 80% have positive blood smear. Antibody test for confirmation. **Rx:** RIF successful in pregnancy (CID 27:213, 1998) but worry about resistance developing. Based on in vitro studies, no clear alternative rx—Levo activity marginal (AAC 47:413, 2003)
Lyme Disease NOTE: Think about co-infection with both HGE and B. burgdorferi.	Borrelia burgdorferi			Reviews: LnID 3:489 & 761, 2003; Ln 362:1639, 2003
Tick bite, possible Ixodes acquired in endemic area		Urine antigen test reported unreliable (AJM 110:217 & 236, 2001).	**If endemic area**, if engorged, not deer tick: No treatment	Prophylaxis study in endemic area: erythema migrans developed in 3% of the control group and 0.4% doxy group (NEJM 345:79 & 133, 2001)
Early (erythema migrans) See Comment		**If not endemic area**, not lymphal partially engorged deer tick: **doxy** 200 mg po x1 with food		Terminology ref. AnIM 136:413, 2002
		Doxy 100 mg bid po or **amoxicillin** 500 mg tid or **cefuroxime axetil** 500 mg bid or **erythro** 250 mg qid. All regimens for 14–21 d. (10 d. as good as AnIM 138:697, 2003) See Comment for peds doses	**Doxy** 100 mg bid po or **amoxicillin** 500 mg tid or **erythro** 250 mg po qid x14–21 d.	High rate of clinical failure with azithro & erythro (Drugs 57:157, 1999). **Peds** (all for 14–21 d.): Amox 50 mg/kg/d in 3 div. doses or cefuroxime axetil 30 mg/kg/d in 2 div. doses or erythro 30 mg/kg/d in 3 div. doses. Lesions usually homogeneous—not target-like (AnIM 136:423, 2002)
Lyme Disease National Surveillance Case Definition available at either NEJM				
Carditis See Comment		**(Ceftriaxone** 2.0 gm q24h IV) or **(pen G** 24 mU q4h IV) or **(pen G** 20 mU/d IV) x14–21 d.	**Doxy** (see Comments) 100 mg bid x14–21 d. or **amoxicillin** 250–500 mg po x14–21 d.	First degree AV block. Oral regimen. High degree AV block (PR >0.3 sec.): IV therapy—permanent pacemaker not necessary.
Facial nerve paralysis (isolated finding, early)		**Doxy** 100 mg bid po or **amoxicillin** 500 mg tid po	**Ceftriaxone** 2.0 gm q24h IV x14–21 d.	**DF** suggested to exclude neurological disease. If LP neg. oral regimen OK. If abnormal or not done, suggest parenteral regimen.
Meningitis, encephalitis For encephalopathy, see Comment		**Ceftriaxone** 2.0 gm q24h IV x14–28 d.	**(Pen G** 20 mU/d IV in div. dose IV) or **(cefotaxime** 2.0 gm q8h IV) x14–28 d.	Encephalopathy: memory difficulty, depression, somnolence, or headache. CSF abnormalities. 89% had objective CSF abnormalities. 18/18 pts improved with ceftriaxone 2 gm/d, x30 d. (JID 180:377, 1999).
Arthritis		**Doxy** 100 mg bid po or **amoxicillin** 500 mg qid po, both x30–60 d.	**(Ceftriaxone** 2 gm (aIV) or **(cefotaxime** 2 gm q8h IV) or **(Pen G** 20–24 mU/d IV) x14–28 d.	
Pregnant women		**[**Choice should not include doxy. **amoxicillin** 500 mg po tid x21 d. If **pen. allergic: (azithro** 500 mg po x7–10 d.) or **(erythro** 500 mg qid po x14–21 d.)**]**		
Asymptomatic seropositivity and symptoms post-rx		None indicated		No benefit from rx (NEJM 345:85, 2001).
Plague **As biological weapon:** JAMA 283:2281, 2000 and Table 1B, page 46	Yersinia pestis Reservoir: rat Vector: rat flea	**Gentamicin** 2.0 mg/kg IV loading dose then 1.7 mg/kg q8h IV or **streptomycin** 1.0 gm IV or IM q12h	**Doxy** 100 mg bid po or IV or **chloro** 500 mg qid po or IV	Reference IV streptomycin: CID 19:1150, 1994. Septicemic form can occur without buboes. **CIP** effective in vitro + in animal models (JAC 41:301, 1998); success in 1 pt (CID 36:521, 2003).
Relapsing fever Tick-borne or louse-borne (Lancet 52:909, 2003)	Borrelia recurrentis, B. hermsii, & other borrelia sp.	**Doxy** 100 mg bid po	**Erythro** 500 mg qid po	Jarisch-Herxheimer (fever, ↑ pulse, ↑ resp., ↓ blood pressure) occurs in ~2 hrs). Not prevented by prior steroids. Can relapse up to 10 times. **Dx:** Examine peripheral blood smear during fever for spirochetes.

* In endemic area (New York), high % of both adult ticks and nymphs were jointly infected with both HGE and B. burgdorferi (NEJM 337:49, 1997)
† NOTE: All dosage recommendations are for adults (unless otherwise indicated) and assume normal renal function.
(Footnotes and abbreviations on page 45)

TABLE 1 (39)

ANATOMIC SITE/DIAGNOSIS/ MODIFYING CIRCUMSTANCES	ETIOLOGIES (usual)	SUGGESTED REGIMENS* PRIMARY	SUGGESTED REGIMENS* ALTERNATIVE†	ADJUNCT DIAGNOSTIC OR THERAPEUTIC MEASURES AND COMMENTS
SYSTEMIC FEBRILE SYNDROMES. Spread by vector TICK, FLEA or LICE *(continued)*				
Rickettsial diseases				
Spotted fevers (NOTE: Rickettsial pox not included)				
Rocky Mountain spotted fever (RMSF) *(AJTMH 63:21, 2000; AJM 163:769, 2000)* NOTE: Can mimic monocytic ehrlichiosis. Pattern of rash important—see Comment	R. rickettsii *(Dermacentor ticks)*	**Doxy** 100 mg bid po or IV x7 d. or for 2 days until temp. normal	**Chloro** use found as risk factor for fatal RMSF *(JID 184:1437, 2001)*	Fever, rash (95%), petechiae 40–50%. **Rash spreads from distal extremities to trunk.** Dx: Immunohistology on skin biopsy; confirmation with antibody titers. Highest incidence in Mid-Atlantic states; also seen in Oklahoma, S. Dakota, Montana. **NOTE: Only 3–18% of pts present with fever, rash, and hx of tick exposure; esp. in children many early deaths and empiric doxy reasonable** *(MMWR 49: 888, 2000)*
Other spotted fevers, e.g.: R. conorii et al. (multiple below) in sub-Saharan Africa, R. africae. R. africae review: *NEJM 344:1504, 2001*	6 species: R. conorii et al. (multiple below) in sub-Saharan Africa, R. africae	**Doxy** 100 mg bid po x7 d.	**Chloro** 500 mg qid po/IV x7 d. Children <8 y.o.: **azithro** or **clarithro** *(see Comment)*	Clarithro 15 mg/kg/d in 2 div doses & azithro 10 mg/kg/d x1 for 3 days equally efficacious in children with Mediterranean spotted fever *(CID 34:154, 2002)*. R. africae reviews: *LnID 3:557, 2003; CID 36:1411, 2003. R. parkeri in U.S.: CID 38:805, 2004*
Typhus group—Consider in returning travelers with fever				
Louse-borne	R. prowazeki (body louse)	**Doxy** 100 mg IV/po bid x7 d.	**Chloro** 500 mg IV/po qid x7 d	**Brill-Zinsser disease** *(Ln 357:1198, 2001)* is a relapse of remote past infection, e.g. WW II. Truncal rash spreads centrifugally—opposite of RMSF. A winter disease.
Murine typhus (cat flea typhus similar)	R. typhi (rat reservoir and flea vector)	**Doxy** 100 mg IV/po bid x7 d	**Chloro** 500 mg IV/po qid x7 d	Most U.S. cases south Texas and southern Calif. Flu-like illness. Rash in <50%. Dx based on suspicion; confirmed serologically.
Scrub typhus	O. tsutsugamushi (rodent reservoir, vector is larval stage of mites (chiggers))	**Doxy** 100 mg IV/po bid x7 d NOTE: **RIF** alone 450 mg bid po x7 d. effective *(Ln 356:1057, 2000)*	**Chloro** 500 mg IV/po qid x7 d. NOTE: Reports of doxy and chloro resistance from northern Thailand *(Ln 348:86, 1996)*. **RIF** alone 450 mg bid po x7 d. reported effective *(Ln 356:1057, 2000)*	Limited to Far East (Asia, India). Cases imported into U.S. Evidence of chigger bite, flu-like illness.
Tularemia, typhoidal type Ref. bioterrorism: see Table 1B, page 46, & JAMA 285:2763, 2001	Francisella tularensis. (Vector reservoir dep. on geography, ticks, biting flies, mosquitoes identified)	**Gentamicin** or **tobra** 5 mg/kg/d div. q8h IV x7–14 d.	Add **chloro** if evidence of meningitis. **CIP** reported effective in 12 children *(PIDJ 19:449, 2000)*.	Typhoidal form in 5–30% pts. No lymphadenopathy. Diarrhea, pneumonia common. Dx: blood cultures. Antibody confirmation. Rx: Jarisch-Herxheimer reaction may occur. Clinical failures with rx with P Ceph 3 *(CID 17:976, 1993)*.
Urban trench fever (endocarditis) *(AAC 47:2204, 2003)*	Bartonella quintana. Vector: louse	**Gentamicin** 3 mg/kg IV once daily x min. of 14 d. + **doxy** 200 mg po single daily dose x6 d		One of many Bartonella syndromes; see pages 20 & 38
Other Zoonotic Systemic Bacterial Febrile illnesses: Obtain careful epidemiologic history				
Brucellosis Reviews: *CID 21:283, 1995; EID 3:213, 1997*				
Adult or child >8 years	Brucella sp. B. abortus—cattle B. suis—pigs B. melitensis—goats B. canis—dogs	[**Doxy** 100 mg bid po x6 wks + **gentamicin** x2–3 wks (see Table 10C, page 220)] or [**doxy** 100 mg bid po x6 wks + **streptomycin** 1.0 gm qd IM x2–3 wks] See Comment	[**Doxy** + **RIF** 600–900 mg qd po, both x6 wks] or [**TMP/SMX** 1 DS tab (160 mg TMP) po bid x6 wks + **gentamicin** x2 wks]	**Relapses:** Doxy 100 mg po x6 wks + strep 1.0 gm IM x2 wks, relapse rate 6%. With doxy + RIF relapse rate 14%. Doxy + RIF may be less effective than doxy + SM in pts with spondylitis *(AJM 117:25, 1992)*. CIP alone initially effective but relapse in 25% *(AAC 36:150, 1992)*; however Ofox + RIF reported effective. **Duration of rx unclear:** For B. melitensis, gent for 7 d. + doxy for 45 d.—fewer relapses than gent x7 d. + doxy for 30 d. *(AAC 41:80, 1997)*. Usual recommendation is 6 wks rx.
Child <8 years		[**Doxy** 2 mg/kg q8h IV or po or **cefotaxime** 1.0 gm q8h IV or **AMP** 0.5–1.0 gm q8h IV Duration: 7 days]	[**TMP/SMX** 5 mg/kg TMP q12h IV or po x2 wks + **gentamicin** 2 mg/kg q8h IV or IM x2 wks]	Longer rx for spondylitis—see CID 29:1440, 1999
Leptospirosis *(CID 36:1507 & 1514, 2003; LnID 3:757, 2003)*	Leptospira—in urine of domestic livestock, dogs, small rodents	**Pen G** 1.5 mU IV q6h or **AMP** 0.5–1.0 gm qd IV	**Doxy** 100 mg IV/po q12h or **ceftriaxone** 1.0 gm qd IV	**Severity varies.** Two-stage mild anicteric illness to severe icteric disease (Weil's disease) with renal failure, myocarditis and death. Sensitivity/specificity of rapid screening tests poor *(J Clin Micro 40:1464, 2002)*

NOTE: All dosage recommendations are for adults (unless otherwise indicated) and assume normal renal/renal function.

(Footnotes and abbreviations on page 45)

TABLE 1 (40)

ANATOMIC SITE/DIAGNOSIS/ MODIFYING CIRCUMSTANCES	ETIOLOGIES (usual)	SUGGESTED REGIMENS* PRIMARY	SUGGESTED REGIMENS* ALTERNATIVE†	ADJUNCT DIAGNOSTIC OR THERAPEUTIC MEASURES AND COMMENTS
SYSTEMIC FEBRILE SYNDROMES/Other Zoonotic Systemic Bacterial Illnesses (continued)				
Salmonella bacteremia (enteric fever most often caused by *S. typhi*)	Salmonella enteritidis—a variety of serotypes	**CIP** 400 mg q12h IV x14 d. (switch to po 750 mg bid when clinically possible)	**Ceftriaxone** 2.0 gm q12h IV x14 d. (switch to po **CIP** when possible)	Usual exposure is contaminated poultry and eggs. Many others. Myriad of complications to consider, e.g. mycotic aneurysm (10% of adults over age 50, *AJM 110:60, 2001*), septic shock. Sporadic reports of resistance to CIP.
Miscellaneous Systemic Febrile Syndromes				
Kawasaki syndrome 6 weeks to 12 yrs of age, peak at 1 yr of age; 85% below age 5. (*Ln 364:533, 2004*)	Acute self-limited vasculitis with ↑ temp, rash, conjunctivitis, stomatitis, cervical adenitis, red hands/feet & coronary artery aneurysms (25% if untreated)	**IVIG** 2 gm/kg over 12 hrs + **ASA** 80-100 mg/kg/d po div in 4 doses **THEN** **ASA** 3-5 mg/kg/d po 1x/d, x6-8 wks	If still febrile after 1st dose of IVIG, give 2nd dose (*PID 17:1144, 1998*)	IV gamma globulin (2.0 gm/kg over 10 hrs) in pts before 10th day of illness ↓ coronary artery lesions (*AJM 347:1128, 1994*) See Table 14B, page 115 for IVIG adverse effects and expense.
Rheumatic Fever, acute Ref: *CID 33:806, 2001*	Post–Group A strep, pharyngitis (not Group B, C, or G)	(1) Symptom relief: **ASA** 80-100 mg/kg/d in children; 4-8 gm/d in adults. (2) Eradicate Group A strep: **Pen** x10 d. (*see Pharyngitis, page 32*) (3) Start prophylaxis; see below		**Pen**icillin to eradicate Group A strep even if culture negative. *See Pharyngitis, page*
Prophylaxis Primary prophylaxis		**Benzathine pen G** 1.2 mU IM		**Pen** prophylaxis for 10 days, prevents rheumatic fever even when started 7-9 days after onset of illness
Secondary prophylaxis (previous documented rheumatic fever)		**Benzathine pen G** 1.2 mU IM q3-4 wks	**Penicillin V** 250 mg po bid or **sulfadiazine** (**sulfisoxazole**) 1.0 gm/d, po or **erythro** 250 mg po bid. Duration of 2° prophylaxis varies: with carditis continue 10 yrs or until age 25, without carditis continue 5 yrs or until age 18 (*AnIM 118:401, 1993*)	
Tumor necrosis factor (TNF) blockade for Crohn's disease, rheumatoid arthritis, or other	Drugs used: Etanercept (Enbrel), infliximab (Remicade), adalimumab (Humira)	Suggest: TBc history, PPD ± chest x-ray prior to initiating TNF blockade. Ref: *CID 39:295 & 300, 2004.* Also ↑ risk of histoplasmosis, listeria, pneumocystis, neutropenia, pericardial effusion, cutaneous/systemic vasculitis, & even myositis from mosquito microsporidium (*NEJM 351:42, 2004*)		Pts at increased risk of reactivation of latent tuberculosis (Tbc). Ideally, pts with latent Tbc would start INH ≥1 month prior to anti-Tbc drugs & risk of Tbc blockade completed. (*MMWR 53:683, 2004*)
Typhoid syndrome (typhoid fever, enteric fever) (*NEJM 347:1770, 2002*)	Salmonella typhi, S. paratyphi NOTE: 14% relapse rate with 5 d. of **ciprofloxacin** (*AAC 44:450, 2000*)	(**CIP** 500 mg bid po x10 d.) or (**ceftriaxone** 2.0 gm IV/d x14 d.). If associated shock, give **dexamethasone** a few minutes before antibiotic. In children, CIP superior to ceftriaxone (*LnID 3:537, 2003*)	**Azithro** 1 gm po, 1st day, then 500 mg po x6 d. (*AAC 43:1441, 1999*) or 1 gm po daily x5 d. (*AAC 46:1855, 2000*) ------ (See Comment)	**Dexamethasone dose:** 3 mg/kg then 1 mg/kg q6h x8 doses ↓ mortality (*NEJM 310:82, 1984*). **Complications:** perforation of terminal ileum &/or cecum, osteo, septic arthritis, **mycotic aneurysm** (approx. 10% over age 50, *AJM 110:62, 2001*); meningitis. **Other rx options:** Controlled trial of CIP vs chloro. Efficacy equivalent. After 5 days, blood culture positive: CIP 18%, chloro 36% (*AAC 47:1727, 2003*) **Children & adolescents: Ceftriaxone** (75 mg/kg/d) and **azithro** (20 mg/kg/d, to 1.0 gm max.) equal efficacy with ceftriaxone (*CID 38:951, 2004*). More relapses with ceftriaxone.
Sepsis: Following suggested **empiric** therapy assumes pt is bacteremic; mimicked by viral, fungal, rickettsial infections and pancreatitis. Blood cultures are key but only 5-10% +. Discontinue antibiotics after 72 hrs if cultures and course do not support diagnosis. In Spain, listeria predominates; in S. America, salmonella.				
Neonatal—early onset <1 week old	Group B strep, E. coli, klebsiella, enterobacter, Staph. aureus (uncommon), listeria (rare in U.S.)	**AMP** 25 mg/kg q8h IV + **cefotaxime** 50 mg/kg q12h	**AMP** + **APAG** 2.5 mg/kg q12h IV or IM or (**AMP** + **cefotaxime** 50 mg/kg q12h)	
Neonatal—late onset 1-4 weeks old	As above + H. influenzae & S. epidermidis	**AMP** 25 mg/kg q6h IV + **cefotaxime** 50 mg/kg q8h IV (or **AMP** + **ceftriaxone** 75 mg/kg q24h IV)	**AMP** + **APAG** 2.5 mg/kg q8h IV or IM	If MSSA/MRSA a concern
Child; not neutropenic	Strep. pneumoniae, meningococci, Staph. aureus (MSSA & MRSA), H. influenzae now rare.	**Cefotaxime** 50 mg/kg q6h IV or **ceftriaxone** 100 mg/kg q24h IV	**Aztreonam** 7.5 mg/kg IV q6h + **linezolid** (see Table 16, page 131 for dose) or **vanco** 15 mg/kg IV q6h.	Major concerns are S. pneumoniae & community-acquired MRSA. Coverage for Gm-neg. bacilli essential. MRSA infection now rare. Meningococcemia mortality remains high (*Ln 356:961, 2000*).

(Footnotes and abbreviations on page 45)   NOTE: All dosage recommendations are for adults (unless otherwise indicated) and assume normal renal function.

TABLE 1 (41)

ANATOMIC SITE/DIAGNOSIS/ MODIFYING CIRCUMSTANCES	ETIOLOGIES (usual)	SUGGESTED REGIMENS*		ADJUNCT DIAGNOSTIC OR THERAPEUTIC MEASURES AND COMMENTS
		PRIMARY	ALTERNATIVE†	
SYSTEMIC FEBRILE SYNDROMES (continued)				
Adult; not neutropenic; NO HYPOTENSION—For Septic Shock, see page 43				Systemic inflammatory response syndrome (SIRS): 2 or more of the following:
Source unclear	Aerobic Gm-neg. bacilli; S. aureus; streptococci; others	**Dapto** (IV 6 mg/kg q24h) **+ vanco**	**P Ceph 3/4** or **PIP/TZ** or **TC/CL**	1. Temperature >38°C or <36°C. 2. Heart rate >90 beats/min. 3. Respiratory rate >20 breaths/min. 4. WBC >12,000/µl or <4000/µl, or >10% bands.
		Could sub linezolid for vanco or dapto vs S. aureus. *Dosages in footnote*		Sepsis: SIRS + a documented infection (+ culture) Severe sepsis: Sepsis + organ dysfunction: hypotension or hypoperfusion abnormalities (lactic acidosis, oliguria, ↓ mental status)
				Septic shock: Sepsis-induced hypotension (systolic BP <90 mmHg or responsive to 500 ml IV fluid challenge) + peripheral hypoperfusion.
If suspect biliary source (see p. 17)	Enterococci + aerobic Gm-neg. bacilli	**TAM/SB, PIP/TZ**, or **TC/CL**	**P Ceph 3** + **metro**	
If illicit use IV drugs	S. aureus	**Vanco** (high prevalence of MRSA). Some empirically use vanco + oxacillin pending susceptibility results.		
If suspect intra-abdominal source	Mixture aerobic & anaerobic bacilli	*See secondary peritonitis, page 31*		
If petechial rash	Meningococcemia	**Ceftriaxone** 2.0 gm IV q12h (until sure no meningitis); consider Rocky Mountain spotted fever—*see page 40*		
If suspect urinary source	Aerobic Gm-neg. bacilli & enterococci	*See pyelonephritis, page 23.*		
Prophylaxis—afebrile				
Neutropenic: Child or adult (absolute PMN count <500/mm³)				
Post-chemotherapy	Aerobic Gm-neg. bacilli, pneumococcus (PCP)	TMP/SMX-DS po bid–adults; 10 mg/kg/d div bid po –children	**Guideline: CID 34:730, 2002**	TMP/SMX ↓ number of febrile episodes and prevents PCP. CIP, Oflox also reported effective but no activity vs PCP. Problem is TMP/SMX- & FQ-resistant Gm-neg. bacilli.
Post-chemotherapy in AIDS patient	↑ risk pneumocystis (PCP)	**TMP/SMX** as above + (either **acyclovir** or **ganci-clovir**) + **fluconazole**		**Paradox:** TMP/SMX or FQ works; not recommended²' to ↑ bacterial resistance. Need TMP/SMX to prevent PCP. Hard to predict which leukemia/lymphoma/solid tumor pt at ↑ risk of PCP.
Allogeneic hematopoietic stem-cell transplant	↑ risk pneumocystis, herpes viruses, candida	As above		Combined regimen justified by combined effect of neutropenia and immuno-suppression.
Empiric therapy–febrile (≥38.3°C x 1 or ≥38°C for ≥1 hr)				
Low-risk adults *(Def. low risk in Comment)*	Aerobic Gm-neg. bacilli, ceph-resistant viridans strep, MRSA	**CIP** 750 mg po bid + **AM/CL 875** mg po bid	**Treat as outpatients with 24/7 access to inpatient care if: no focal findings, no hypotension, no COPD, no fungal infection, age <60 & >16.** Neutropenic children with neg. blood cultures, safely switched to po cefixime^6,8 4 mg/kg q12h (CID 32:36, 2001).	Peds data pending *(Footnote¹ and Table 10)*
High-risk adults and children		**Monotherapy:** **CFP** or **ceftaz** or **IMP** or **MER**	**Combination therapy:** (Gent or tobra) + (either **TC/CL** or **PIP/TZ**)	Increasing resistance of viridans streptococcus to penicillins, cephalosporins & FQs (CID 34:1469 & 1524, 2002; CID 31:1126, 2000; JAC 47:87, 2001). **What if severe IgE-mediated β-lactam allergy?** No formal trials, but [APAG (or CIP) + aztreonam] ± vanco should work.
		Dosages: Footnote¹ and Table 10		
		Include empiric vanco if: suspect IV access infected; colonized with DRSP or MRSA blood culture pos. for Gm-pos. cocci; pt hypotensive		
Persistent fever and neutropenia after 5 days of empiric antibacterial therapy—see CID 34:730, 2002	Candida species, aspergillus	Add either **ampho B** or **voriconazole** *CID 34:730, 2002*		Empirically adding vanco of **no benefit** (CID 37:382, 2003)

P Ceph 3 (cefotaxime 2.0 gm q8h IV, use q4h if life-threatening; **cefotaxime** 2.0 gm q8h IV, **ceftriaxone** 2.0 gm q12h IV, **ticarcillin** 3.0 gm q4h IV), **TC/CL** 3.1 gm q4h IV, **PIP/TZ** 3.375 gm q4h IV, **AM/SB** 3.0 gm q6h IV, **APAG** 3.0 gm q6h IV, (see Table 10C, page 72). **AMP** 2.0 gm q4h IV, **IMP** 0.5 gm q6h IV, **MER** 1.0 gm q8h IV, **Naficillin** or **oxacillin** 2.0 gm q4h IV, **aztreonam** 2.0 gm q8h IV, **metro** 1.0 gm loading dose then 0.5 gm q6h IV, **vanco** 1.0 gm q12h IV, **ceftazidime** 2.0 gm q8h IV, **P Ceph 4 (CFP** 2.0 gm q12h IV, **cefepime** 2.0 gm q12h IV), **ofloxacin (oflox** 400 mg q12h IV), **levo** 750 mg q24 IV, **linezolid** 600 mg q12h IV. If neutropenic, q12h IV. *(Footnotes and abbreviations on page 45) NOTE: All dosage recommendations are for adults (unless otherwise indicated) and assume normal renal function.*

TABLE 1 (42)

ANATOMIC SITE/DIAGNOSIS/ MODIFYING CIRCUMSTANCES	ETIOLOGIES (usual)	SUGGESTED REGIMENS* PRIMARY	ALTERNATIVE†	ADJUNCT DIAGNOSTIC OR THERAPEUTIC MEASURES AND COMMENTS
SYSTEMIC FEBRILE SYNDROMES (continued)				
Shock syndromes				
Septic shock: Fever & hypo-tension	Bacteremia with aerobic Gm-neg. bacteria or Gm + cocci	**Proven therapy: (1)** Replete intravascular volume, **(2)** correct, if possible, disease that allowed bloodstream invasion, **(3)** appropriate empiric antimicrobial rx: see suggestions under life-threatening illness, above. **(4)** For recombinant activated protein C (drotrecogin alfa) see Comment for criteria. **(5)** Investigational: low-dose steroids if document relative adrenal insufficiency (see Comment for criteria). (Hydrocortisone 50 mg IV q6h + fludrocortisone (Florinef) 50 µg via NG q day x 7 d. **(6)** Low-dose vasopressin reported effective for catecholamine-resistant septic shock (Ln 359:1209, 2002)		**Activ. Protein C: Drotrecogin (Xigris).** In a prospective randomized double-blind study (NEJM 344:699, 2001), 28-d. mortality ↓ from 31 to 25% in sickest pts. Study in less ill pts showed no benefit. Speculation: benefit in pts with low or decreasing levels of activ. protein C (protein C levels not routinely available). **Hemodynamics:** at 3.5%, drotrecogin alfa. Stop 2 hrs before & restart 12 hrs after surgery. Approx. **cost** of drug for 4-day course: $8000. **Low-dose steroids** in controlled random double-blind trial, rx if low baseline cortisol ≤9 µg/dl response to 250 mg IV cosyntropin. 28-day mortality 63% placebo, 53% steroid group (JAMA 288:862 & 886, 2002). Results in question because 'total' & not 'free' plasma cortisol was measured (NEJM 350:1601 & 1629, 2004). **Low-dose vasopressin:** Dose should not exceed 0.04 units/min.
Septic shock: post-splenectomy (asplenia)	S. pneumoniae, N. meningitidis, H. influenzae. Capnocytophaga (DF-2)	Ceftriaxone 2.0 gm q12h (↑ to 2.0 gm q12h if meningitis) IV	**Gati** 400 mg or **Levo** 750 mg or **Moxi** 400 mg all once daily IV	Howell-Jolly bodies in peripheral blood smear confirm absence of functional spleen. Often results in **symmetrical peripheral gangrene of digits** due to severe DIC. For prophylaxis, see Table 15A, page 123
Toxic shock syndrome, staphylococcal. Superantigen review (IJID 2:156, 2002)	Staph. aureus (toxic shock toxin-mediated)	**Colonization** by toxin-producing Staph. aureus of: vagina (tampon-assoc.), surgical/traumatic wounds, endometrium, burns	Naf (or clox) **Naf**cillin or **oxa**cillin 2.0 gm q4h IV, or (if MRSA, **vanco** 1.0 gm q12h) + **IVIG**	**Cefazolin** 1–2 gm q8h IV or (if MRSA, **vanco** 1.0 gm q 12h) + **IVIG**	Nafcillin/oxacillin/cefazolin have no effect on toxic syndrome, but ↓ recurrences. Seek occult abscess. TSS may occur with "clean" colonized post-op wounds. Case fatality, 5–15%. **IVIG reasonable** (see Streptococcal TSS)—dose 1.0 gm/kg day 1, then 0.5 gm/kg days 2 & 3.
Toxic shock syndrome, streptococcal [Ref.: cIID 179(Suppl 2):S366–374, 1999]. NOTE: For necrotizing fasciitis without toxic shock, see page 38	Group A, B, C, & G Strep.	Associated with invasive disease, i.e., erysipelas, necrotizing fasciitis; secondary strep infection of varicella. Secondary cases TSS reported (NEJM 335:547 & 590, 1996; CID 27:150, 1998).	(**Pen** G 24 mU/d) x 4h IV for 1st doses) + **clinda** (900 mg) IV q8h IV. **IVIG** associated with ↓ in sepsis-related organ failure	**Pen** G 2.0 gm q24h IV + **clinda** 900 mg q8h IV	**Definition:** Isolation of Group A strep, hypotension and ≥2 of: renal impairment, coagulopathy, liver involvement, ARDS, generalized rash, soft tissue necrosis (JAMA 269:390, 1993). Associated with invasive disease. **Surgery usually required.** Mortality with fasciitis 30–50%, myositis 80% even with early rx (CID 14:2, 1992). Clinda ↓ toxin production. Use of NSAIDs may predispose to TSS. For discussion of possible reasons pen G may fail in fulminant S. pyogenes infections, see cIID 167:1401, 1993.
Other Toxin-Mediated Syndromes—no fever unless complicated				
Botulism (AnIM 129:221, 1998; CID 31:1018, 2000. **As biologic weapon:** JAMA 285:1059, 2001; Table 1B, page 46; www.bt.cdc.gov)	C. botulinum	For all types: Trivalent (types A, B, E) equine serum antitoxin from State Health Dept. or CDC (see Comment)		**Equine antitoxin:** Obtain from State Health Depts. or CDC (404-639-2206 M-F OR 404-639-2888 evenings/weekends). Skin test first & desensitize if necessary. One vial (10 mL) IV and one vial IM. Untested in wound botulism.
Food-borne		Dyspnea at presentation bad sign (CID 39:357 & 363, 2004).	If no ileus, purge GI tract	**Antimicrobials:** May induce infant botulism worse. Untested in wound botulism. When used, pen G 10–20 MU/d used dose. If complications (pneumonia, UTI) occur, avoid antimicrobials with assoc. neuromuscular blockade, i.e. aminoglycosides, tetracycline. **Differential dx:** myasthenia gravis, tick paralysis, organophosphate toxicity, West Nile virus.
Infant		Human botulinum immunoglobulin (BIG) IV, single dose. Call 510-540-2646. Do not use equine antitoxin.	No antibiotics; may lyse C. botulinum in gut and ↑ load of toxin	**Differential dx:** Guillain-Barre, myasthenia gravis, tick paralysis, organophosphate toxicity, West Nile virus.

NOTE: All dosage recommendations are for adults (unless otherwise indicated) and assume normal renal function.

(Footnotes and abbreviations on page 45)

TABLE 1 (43)

ANATOMIC SITE/DIAGNOSIS/ MODIFYING CIRCUMSTANCES	ETIOLOGIES (usual)	SUGGESTED REGIMENS* PRIMARY	ALTERNATIVE†	ADJUNCT DIAGNOSTIC OR THERAPEUTIC MEASURES AND COMMENTS
SYSTEMIC FEBRILE SYNDROMES/Other Toxin-Mediated Syndromes/Botulism (continued)				
Wound		Debridement & anaerobic cultures. No proven value of local antitoxin. Role of antibiotics untested		Can result from spore contamination of tar heroin.
Tetanus	C. tetani	Pen G 24 mU IV div. dose or **doxy** 100 mg q12h IV x7–10 d.	**Metro** 500 mg q6h po or 1.0 gm q12h IV x7–10 d. (See Comment)	Multifaceted treatment: Wound debridement, tetanus immunoglobulin (250–500 IU IM), antimicrobics, & tetanus toxoid (tetanus does not confer immunity). Options for control of muscle spasms, continuous IV administration of midazolam, IV propofol, and/or intrathecal baclofen (CID 38:321, 2004).
			Trivalent equine antitoxin (see Comment)	
VASCULAR				
Cavernous sinus thrombosis	Staph. aureus, Group A strep, H. influenzae, aspergillus/mucor/rhizopus	**Vanco** 1.0 gm IV q12h + **ceftriaxone** 2.0 gm IV qd	(**Dapto** 6 mg/kg IV qd^{NAI} or **linezolid** 600 mg IV q12h) + **ceftriaxone** 2.0 gm IV qd	CT or MRI scan for diagnosis. Heparin indicated (Ln 338:597, 1991). If patient diabetic consider ketoconazole rx or post-desferrioxamine rx or neutropenic, consider fungal etiology: aspergillus, mucor, rhizopus, see Table 11A, pages 73 & 80)
IV line infection (see IDSA Guidelines: CID 32:1249, 2001): **Treatment**				
Heparin lock, midline catheter, non-tunneled central venous catheter (subclavian, internal jugular), peripherally inserted central catheter (PICC). Avoid antecubital vein if possible: risk of loss of arm if thrombophlebitis. (JAMA 296:700, 2001)	Staph. epidermidis, Staph. aureus (MSSA/MRSA)	**Vanco** 1.0 gm IV q12h. **Comment.** Other rx and duration: (1) If **S. aureus**, remove catheter. Can use TEE result to determine if 2 or 4 wks of rx. (2) If **S. epidermidis**, can try to "save" catheter. 80% cure rate if >10 d. of rx. Catheter removal: Infections may respond to "antibiotic lock" rx & allow salvage of catheter (JAC 48: 597, 2001). Drug (**vanco, gent, CIP**) at 1–5 mg/ml mixed with 50–100 units heparin (or saline) in 2–5 ml volume; fill catheter when not in use. Continue 2 wks. If candida, need full course of therapy. If candida, see Hyperalimentation below and Table 11A, pages 74–75.	**Linezolid alternative—see Comment**	**Linezolid has predictable bacteriostatic activity vs both S. aureus and S. epidermidis isolates—including MRSA/MRSE. Authors prefer vanco in order to ? longevity of linezolid activity. If MRSA/MRSE and either renal failure or vanco rx or vanco allergy, linezolid dose 600 mg IV/po q12h.** Culture removed catheter. With "roll" method, >15 colonies (NEJM 312:1142, 1985) suggests infection. Can do "roll" method or require "routine" changing when not infected. When infected, do not insert new catheter over a wire.
Tunnel type indwelling venous catheters and ports (Broviac, Hickman, Groshong, Quinton), dual lumen hemodialysis catheters (Perma-cath)	Staph. epidermidis, Staph. aureus, (Candida sp.), Rarely: leuconostoc or lactobacillus—resistant to vanco (see Table 2)	**Vanco** 1.0 gm IV q12h Linezolid alternative—see **Comment**		If **S. epidermidis & catheter left in**, vanco can cure 80% of infections limited to exit site but only 25% cure if infection in subcutaneous tunnel between skin and subclavian vein. If **S. aureus & catheter left in**, vanco cure rate 10% at exit site & 3% with tunnel infection (CID 29: 1102, 1999). Similar statistics for infected "ports" (CID 29: 1102, 1999). Infected hemodialysis access catheters should be removed (AJM 127: 275, 1997).
Impaired host (burn, neutropenic)	As above + Pseudomonas sp., Enterobacteriaceae, Corynebacterium jeikeium, aspergillus, rhizopus	(**Vanco + P Ceph 3 AP**) or (**P Ceph 3 + APAG**)‖ (Dosage, see page 42)	(**Vanco + AP Pen**) or **IMP** or **MER** or **ERTA** or (**aztreonam + APAG**)‖	Usually have associated septic thrombophlebitis. Biopsy of vein to rule out fungi. If fungal, surgical excision + amphotericin B. Surgical drainage, ligation or removal often indicated.
Hyperalimentation	As with tunnel (see Table 11, resistant Candida species)	If candida, **amphotericin B** 0.5–0.6 mg/kg qd IV total dose 5.0 mg/kg or **voriconazole** 3 mg/kg bid IV or **caspofungin** 70 mg IV day 1, then 50 mg IV qd		Remove venous catheter and discontinue antimicrobial agents if possible. Ophthalmologic consultation recommended. **Rx all patients with + blood cultures.** See Table 11A, Candidiasis.
Intravenous lipid emulsion	Staph. epidermidis, Malassezia furfur	**Vanco** 1.0 gm q12h IV		Discontinue intralipid AJM 90:129, 1991
		Amphotericin B		
IV line infection: Prevention (CID 35:1281, 2002; NEJM 348:1123, 2003) To minimize the risk of infection:		1. Maximal sterile barrier precautions during catheter insertion 2. Use 2% chlorhexidine for skin antisepsis 3. If infection rate high despite #1 & 2, use either silver sulfadiazine or minocycline/rifampin-impregnated catheters		Tunneled hemodialysis catheters: Small study, ↓ infection rate when catheter locked with gentamicin (5 mg/ml) + heparin 5000 IU/ml), p < 0.02 (Kidney Int 66:801, 2004)
Septic pelvic vein thrombophlebitis (with or without septic pulmonary embol) postpartum or postabortion or postpelvic surgery	Streptococci, bacteroides, Enterobacteriaceae	**Metro + P Ceph 3, cefoxitin, TC/CL, PIP/TZ,** or **AM/SB**	**IMP** or **MER** or **ERTA** or **clinda + (aztreonam** or **APAG)**‖	Heparin during antibiotic regimen. Continued oral anticoagulation not recommended. Cefotetan less active than cefoxitin vs non-fragilis bacteroides. Cefotetan and cefmetazole have methyltetrazole side-chain which is associated with hypoprothrombinemia (prevent with vitamin K).

NOTE: All dosage recommendations are for adults (unless otherwise indicated) and assume normal renal function. NAI = Not FDA-approved indication.

(Footnotes and abbreviations on page 45)

TABLE 1 (44): FOOTNOTES AND ABBREVIATIONS

* **Dosages suggested are for adults** (unless otherwise indicated) with clinically severe (often life-threatening) infections. Dosages also assume normal renal function, and not severe hepatic dysfunction. See *Table 16, page 131,* for pediatric dosages.

§ **Alternative therapy** includes these considerations: allergy, pharmacology/pharmacokinetics, compliance, costs, local resistance profiles.

AHA = American Heart Association
AM/SB = ampicillin/sulbactam (Unasyn)
Amox = amoxicillin
AMP = ampicillin
APAG = antipseudomonal aminoglycosidic antibiotics
AP Pen = antipseudomonal β-lactamase susceptible penicillins, e.g. piperacillin. See *Table 4, page 52* for details.
ARDS = adult respiratory distress syndrome
ARF = acute rheumatic fever
ASA = acetylsalicylic acid (aspirin)
Azithro = azithromycin O
Ceftaz = ceftazidime
CFP = cefepime
Chloro = chloramphenicol
CIP = ciprofloxacin; **CIP-ER** = ciprofloxacin extended release
Clarithro = clarithromycin; **clarithro ER** = clarithromycin extended release
Clinda = clindamycin
C&S = culture and sensitivities
Dapto = daptomycin
DIC = disseminated intravascular coagulation
Doxy = doxycycline
DRSP = drug-resistant Streptococcus pneumoniae
EBV = Epstein-Barr virus
EDC = expected date of confinement
EES = erythromycin ethyl succinate
ERTA = ertapenem

Erythro = erythromycin
ETB = ethambutol
FQ = fluoroquinolone
Gati = gatifloxacin
GAS = Group A streptococci
GC = gonorrhea (N. gonorrhoeae)
GNB = Gram-negative bacilli
HHV-2 = human herpesvirus 2
HIV-1 = human immunodeficiency virus type 1
HLR = high-level resistance
I = investigational
IMP = imipenem cilastatin (Primaxin)
INH = isoniazid
IVDU = intravenous drug users
IVIG = intravenous immune globulin
LCM = lymphocytic choriomeningitis virus
LCR = ligase chain reaction
Levo = levofloxacin
Macrolides = erythro, azithro, clarithro, dirithro
MER = meropenem
Metro = metronidazole
Moxi = moxifloxacin
MRI = magnetic resonance imaging
MSSA/MRSA = methicillin-sensitive/methicillin-resistant Staph. aureus
MSSE/MRSE = methicillin-sensitive/methicillin-resistant Staph. epidermidis
MTBc = Mycobacterium tuberculosis
NAI = FDA-approved indication

RIF = rifampin
NSAIDs = nonsteroidal anti-inflammatory drugs
NUS = not available in the United States
O Ceph 1, 2, 3 = oral cephalosporins—see *Table 9B, page 65*
Oflox = Ofloxacin
P Ceph 1, 2, 3 = parenteral cephalosporins—see *Table 9B, pages 64, 65*
P Ceph 3 AP = third generation with enhanced antipseudomonal activity
P Ceph 4 = third generation with antistaphylococcal and antipseudomonal activity
PCR = polymerase chain reaction
PIP/TZ = piperacillin/tazobactam
Q/D = quinupristin/dalfopristin
R/O = rule out
RIF = rifampin
Rick = rickettsia (spotted fever, Q fever)
SA = Staph. aureus
SM = streptomycin
STD = sexually transmitted diseases
TBc = tuberculosis
TC/CL = ticarcillin/clavulanate (Timentin)
TEE = transesophageal echocardiography
Telithro = telithromycin
TMP/SMX = trimethoprim/sulfamethoxazole
Tobra = tobramycin
Toxo = toxoplasmosis
UTI = urinary tract infection
Vanco = vancomycin

ABBREVIATIONS OF JOURNAL AND TEXT TITLES

AAC: Antimicrobial Agents & Chemotherapy
Adv PID: Advances in Pediatric Infectious Diseases
AIDS: AIDS
AJM: American Journal of Medicine
AJRCCM American Journal of Respiratory Critical Care Medicine
AJTMH American Journal of Tropical Medicine & Hygiene
AnEM Annals of Emergency Medicine
AnIM Annals of Internal Medicine
AnSurg Annals of Surgery
ARIM Archives of Internal Medicine
ARRD American Review of Respiratory Disease
CCM Critical Care Medicine
CID Clinical Infectious Diseases

COID: Current Opinion in Infectious Disease
CTID: Current Topics in Infectious Disease
DMID: Diagnostic Microbiology and Infectious Disease
EID: Emerging Infectious Diseases
EJCMID: European Journal of Clin. Micro. & Infectious Disease
Gastro: Gastroenterology
ICHE: Infection Control and Hospital Epidemiology
IDC No. Amer: Infectious Disease Clinics of North America
IDCP: Infectious Diseases in Clinical Practice
J Clin Micro: Journal of Clinical Microbiology
JAC: Journal of Antimicrobial Chemotherapy
JAMA: Journal of the American Medical Association
JAVMA: Journal of the American Veterinary Medical Association

JID: Journal of Infectious Diseases
JNS: Journal of Neurosurgery
JTMH: Journal of Tropical Medicine and Hygiene
Ln Lancet
LnID: Lancet Infectious Disease
Med Lett: Medical Letter
MMWR: Morbidity & Mortality Weekly Report
NEJM: New England Journal of Medicine
Peds Pediatrics
PIDJ: Pediatric Infectious Disease Journal
QJM: Quarterly Journal of Medicine
SMJ: Southern Medical Journal
TRSM: Transactions of the Royal Society of Medicine

TABLE 1B: PROPHYLAXIS AND TREATMENT OF ORGANISMS OF POTENTIAL USE AS BIOLOGICAL WEAPONS

DISEASE	ETIOLOGY	SUGGESTED EMPIRIC TREATMENT REGIMENS		SPECIFIC THERAPY AND COMMENTS
		PRIMARY	ALTERNATIVE	
Anthrax **Cutaneous, inhalational, gastrointestinal** Refs: JAMA 286: 2549, 2554 & 2595, 2001; NEJM 345:1607 & 1621, 2001; MMWR 50:909, 2001; CID 35:851, 2002 www.bt.cdc.gov Also see Table 1, pages 28 & 34 To report bioterrorism event: 770-488-7100 Rationale for CIP: CID 39:303, 2004	Bacillus anthracis **Post-exposure prophylaxis** **Treatment—** **Cutaneous anthrax** NEJM 345:1611, 2001	**Adults (including pregnancy): CIP 500 mg po bid x60 d.** **Children: CIP 20–30 mg/kg/d div q12h x60 d.**	**Adults (including pregnancy): Doxy 100 mg po bid x60 d.** **Children (see Comment): Doxy >8 y/o & >45 kg: 100 mg po bid; >8 y/o & ≤45 kg: 2.2 mg/kg po bid; ≤8 y/o: 2.2 mg/kg po bid.** All for 60 days.	1. Once organism shows susceptibility to penicillin, switch children to **amoxicillin** 80 mg/kg/d div. q8h (max. 500 mg q8h); switch pregnant pt to **amoxicillin** 500 mg po tid. 2. Other **FQs** (Gati, Levo, Moxi) should work but no clinical experience. 3. If penicillin susceptible, then: **Adults: Amox 500 mg q8h x60 d.** **Children: Amox 80 mg/kg/d div. q8h (max. 500 mg q8h)** Usual treatment of cutaneous anthrax is 7–10 d. 60 d. in setting of bioterrorism with presumed aerosol exposure Other **FQs** (Gati, Levo, Moxi) should work based on in vitro susceptibility data

	Treatment—Inhalational, gastrointestinal, or oropharyngeal
	Characteristic signs & symptoms—**Present**
	Dyspnea, Rhinorrhea
	Absent: Rhinorrhea, sore throat
	(AnM 139:337, 2003)
		Adults (including pregnancy): CIP 400 mg IV q12h) or (doxy 100 mg IV q12h) + clinda 900 mg IV q8h + RiF 300 mg IV q12h. Switch to po when able & ↓ CIP to 500 mg po bid; clinda to 450 mg po q8h; & RiF 300 mg po q12h. Treat x60 d. See Table 2, page 47 for other alternatives	**Children: (CIP 10 mg/kg IV q12h or 15 mg/kg po q12h) or (Doxy >8 y/o & >45 kg: 100 mg IV q12h; >8 y/o & ≤45 kg: 2.2 mg/kg IV q12h; ≤8 y/o: 2.2 mg/kg IV q12h) plus clindamycin 7.5 mg/kg IV q6h plus RiF 20 mg/kg IV qd. Treat x60 d. See Table 16, page 131 for dosage**	1. Clinda may block toxin production.
				2. Rifampin penetrates CSF & intracellular sites.
				3. If isolate shown penicillin-susceptible:
				  a. **Adult: Pen G 4 mU IV q4h**
				  b. **Child: Pen G <12 y/o: 50,000 U/kg IV q6h; >12 y/o: 4 mU IV q4h**
				  c. Constitutive & inducible β-lactamases—do not use pen or AMP alone.
				4. Do not use cephalosporins or TMP/SMX.
				5. erythro, azithro active; clarithro active.
				6. No person-to-person spread.

Botulism Ref: JAMA 285:1059, 2001 Food-borne See Table 1, pages 43–44	Clostridium botulinum	Purge GI tract if no ileus. **Trivalent antitoxin** (types A, B, & E): single 10 ml vial/pt, diluted in saline (slowly).	Antibiotics have no effect on toxin	Supportive care for all types. Follow vital capacity. Submit suspect food for toxin testing. Ref: CID 39:357 & 363, 2004
Hemorrhagic fever virus Ref: JAMA 287:2391, 2002	Ebola, Lassa, Hanta, yellow fever, & others	Fluid/electrolyte balance. Optimize circulatory volume.	For Lassa & Hanta: **Ribavirin** dose same as Adults. Pregnancy. Children: LD 30 mg/kg IV x1, then 16 mg/kg IV (max. 2 gm) q6h x4 d, then 8 mg/kg IV (max. 500 mg) q8h x6 d	**Ribavirin** active in vitro, not FDA-approved for this indication. NOTE: Ribavirin contraindicated in pregnancy. However, in this setting, the benefits outweigh the risks.
Plague Ref: JAMA 283:2281, 2000 Inhalation pneumonic plague[1] See Table 1, page 39	Yersinia pestis **Treatment**	**Gentamicin 5 mg/kg IV qd or streptomycin 15 mg/kg IV bid. Tobramycin should work.**	**(Doxy 200 mg IV x1, & then 100 mg po or IV q12h) or CiP 500 mg po bid or 400 mg IV q12h)**	Chloro also active: 25 mg/kg IV qid. In mass casualty situation, may have to treat po. Pediatric doses: see Table 16, page 131. Pediatric doses, as for non-pregnant adults
	Post-exposure prophylaxis	Doxy 100 mg po bid x7 d.	CiP 500 mg po bid x7 d.	Isolate during first 48 hrs of treatment. For community with pneumonic plague epidemic. Pediatric doses, see Table 16, page 131.
Smallpox Ref: NEJM 346:1300, 2002 See Comment	Variola virus	Smallpox vaccine to be given within 4 days after exposure; isolation; gloves, gown, & N&S respirator	Cidofovir protected mice against aerosol cowpox (JID 181:10, 2000)	**Immediately notify State Health Dept.** & State notifies CDC (770-488-7100). Vaccinia immune globulin (IV) for complications, see JAMA 288:1901, 2002.
Tularemia Inhalational tularemia[1] Ref: JAMA 285:2763, 2001 See Table 1, page 40	Francisella tularensis **Treatment**	**Streptomycin 15 mg/kg IV bid or gentamicin 5 mg/kg IV qd**	**Doxy 100 mg IV bid x14–21 d, or CiP 400 mg IV bid (or 750 mg po) bid x14–21 d.**	For pediatric doses, see Table 131. Pregnancy: As for non-pregnant adults
	Post-exposure prophylaxis	Doxy 100 mg po bid x14 d.	Children: Doxy 100 mg po bid x14 d. / CiP 500 mg po bid x14 d.	For pediatric doses, see Table 16, page 131. Pregnancy: As for non-pregnant adults

[1] There are other clinical forms of botulism, plague, and tularemia, but the inhalation form seems most probable in bioterrorism.

TABLE 2: RECOMMENDED ANTIMICROBIAL AGENTS AGAINST SELECTED BACTERIA

BACTERIAL SPECIES	ANTIMICROBIAL AGENT (See footnote[2] for abbreviations)		
	RECOMMENDED	ALTERNATIVE	ALSO EFFECTIVE[1] (COMMENTS)
Alcaligenes xylosoxidans (Achromobacter xylosoxidans)	IMP, MER, AP Pen	TMP/SMX. Some strains susc. to ceftaz (AAC 32: 276, 1988)	Resistant to APAG; P Ceph 1, 2, 3, 4; aztreonam; FQ (AAC 40:772, 1996)
Acinetobacter calcoaceticus–baumannii complex	IMP or MER or [FQ + (amikacin or ceftaz)]	AM/SB (CID 24:932, 1997). Sulbactam[4,5] also effective (JAC 42: 793, 1998);colistin (CID 36: 1111, 2003)	Polymyxin B; up to 5% isolates resistant to IMP; resistance to FQs, amikacin increasing. Doxy + amikacin effective in animal model (AAC 45: 493, 2000). (See Table 5, page 55)
Actinomyces israelii	AMP or Pen G	Doxy, ceftriaxone	Clindamycin, erythro
Aeromonas hydrophila	FQ	TMP/SMX or (P Ceph 3, 4)	APAG; ERTA; IMP; MER; tetracycline (some resistant to carbapenems)
Arcanobacterium (C.) haemolyticum	Erythro	Benzathine Pen G	Sensitive to most drugs, resistant to TMP/SMX (AAC 38:142, 1994)
Bacillus anthracis (anthrax): inhalation	See Table 1B, page 46		
Bacillus cereus, B. subtilis	Vancomycin, clindamycin	FQ, IMP	
Bacteroides fragilis (ssp. fragilis) "DOT" group of bacteroides[3]	Metronidazole	Clindamycin	Cefoxitin, ERTA, IMP, MER, TC/CL, PIP/TZ, AM/SB, cefotetan, AM/CL (not cefotetan)
Bartonella (Rochalimaea) henselae, quintana See Table 1, pages 30, 34, 38	Azithro or clarithro or CIP (bacillary angiomatosis) or azithro (cat-scratch) (PIDJ 17:447, 1998; AAC 48:1921, 2004)	Erythro or doxy	Other drugs: TMP/SMX (IDC No. Amer 12:137, 1998). Consider doxy + RIF for severe bacillary angiomatosis (IDC No Amer 12:137, 1998); doxy + gentamicin optimal for endocarditis (AAC 47:2204, 2003)
Bordetella pertussis	Erythro	TMP/SMX	An erythro-resistant strain reported in Arizona (MMWR 43:807, 1994)
Borrelia burgdorferi, B. afzelii, B. garini (See Comments)	Ceftriaxone, cefuroxime axetil, doxy, amox	Penicillin G (HD), cefotaxime	Clarithro. Choice depends on stage of disease, Table 1, page 39
Borrelia sp.	Doxy	Erythro	Penicillin G
Brucella sp.	Doxy + either gentamicin or streptomycin (IDCP 7, 2004)	(Doxy + RIF) or (TMP/SMX + gentamicin)	FQ + RIF (AAC 41:80, 1997; Emerg ID 3:213, 1997; CID 21:283, 1995). Minocycline + RIF (J Chemother 15:248, 2003)
Burkholderia (Pseudomonas) cepacia	TMP/SMX or MER or CIP	Minocycline or chloramphenicol	(Usually resistant to APAG, AG, polymyxins) (AAC 37: 123, 1993 & 43:213, 1999; Inf in Med 18:49, 2001) (Some resistant to carbapenems). Combination rx may be necessary (AJRCCM 161:1206, 2000).
Burkholderia (Pseudomonas) pseudomallei See Table 1, page 27, & Ln 361:1715, 2003	Initially, IV ceftaz or IMP (CID 29:381, 1999)	Then, combination of po chloro, doxy, & TMP/SMX	(In Thailand, 12–80% strains resistant to TMP/SMX). FQ active in vitro. Combination of chloro, TMP/SMX, doxy more effective than doxy alone for maintenance rx (CID 29:375, 1999). MER also effective (AAC 48: 1763,2004)
Campylobacter jejuni	Erythro	FQ (↑ resistance, NEJM 340:1525,1999)	Clindamycin, doxy, azithro, clarithro (see Table 5, page 55)
Campylobacter fetus	IMP	Gentamicin	AMP, chloramphenicol, erythro
Capnocytophaga ochracea (DF-1) and canimorsus (DF-2)	Clindamycin or AM/CL / AM/CL	CIP, Pen G	P Ceph 3, IMP, cefoxitin, FQ, (resistant to APAG, TMP/SMX). C. hemolytica & C. granulosa are often resistant to β-lactams & aminoglycosides [CID 3 5(Suppl.1):S17, 2002].
Chlamydophila pneumoniae	Doxy	Erythro, FQ	Azithro, clarithro, telithro
Chlamydia trachomatis	Doxy or azithro	Erythro or oflox	Levofloxacin
Chryseobacterium (Flavobacterium) meningosepticum	Vancomycin ± RIF (CID 26:1169, 1998)	CIP, levofloxacin	In vitro susceptibilities may not correlate with clinical efficacy (AAC 41:1301, 1997; CID 26:1169, 1998)
Citrobacter diversus (koseri), C. freundii	CARB	FQ	APAG
Clostridium difficile	Metronidazole (po)	Vancomycin (po)	Bacitracin (po)
Clostridium perfringens	Pen G ± clindamycin	Doxy	Erythro, chloramphenicol, cefazolin, cefoxitin, AP Pen, CARB
Clostridium tetani	Metronidazole or Pen G	Doxy	CARB
Corynebacterium jeikeium	Vancomycin	Pen G + APAG	
C. diphtheriae	Erythro	Clindamycin	RIF. Penicillin reported effective (CID 27:845, 1998)
Coxiella burnetii (Q fever) acute disease	Doxy (see Table 1, page 20)	Erythro	In meningitis consider FQ (CID 20:489, 1995). Endocarditis: doxy + hydroxychloroquine (JID 188:1322, 2003; LnID 3:709, 2003).
chronic disease	(CIP or doxy) + RIF	FQ + doxy x3 yrs (CID 20:495, 1995)]	Chloroquine + doxy (AAC 37:1773, 1993). ? gamma interferon (Ln 20:546, 2001)

TABLE 2 (2)

BACTERIAL SPECIES	ANTIMICROBIAL AGENT (See footnote² for abbreviations)		
	RECOMMENDED	ALTERNATIVE	ALSO EFFECTIVE¹ (COMMENTS)
Ehrlichia chaffeensis, Ehrlichia ewubguum Anaplasma (Ehrlichia) phagocytophilium	Doxy	Tetracycline, RIF *(CID 27:213, 1998)*	CIP, oflox, chloramphenicol also active in vitro. Resistant to clinda, TMP/SMX, IMP, AMP, erythro, & azithro *(AAC 41:76, 1997)*
Eikenella corrodens	Penicillin G or AMP or AM/CL	TMP/SMX, FQ	Doxy, cefoxitin, cefotaxime, IMP (Resistant to clindamycin, cephalexin, erythromycin, and metronidazole)
Enterococcus faecalis	*See Table 5, page 54*		
Enterococcus faecium, β-lactamase +, high-level aminoglycoside resist., vancomycin resist.: *See Table 5, page 54*			
Erysipelothrix rhusiopathiae	Penicillin G or AMP	P Ceph 3, FQ	IMP, AP Pen (vancomycin, APAG, TMP/SMX resistant)
Francisella tularensis (tularemia) *See Table 1B, page 46*	Gentamicin, tobramycin, or streptomycin	Doxy or CIP	Chloramphenicol, RIF. Doxy/chloro bacteriostatic → relapses
Gardnerella vaginalis (bacterial vaginosis)	Metronidazole	Clindamycin	*See Table 1, page 17 for dosage*
Hafnia alvei	*Same as Enterobacter spp.*		
Helicobacter pylori	*See Table 1, page 13*		
Hemophilus aphrophilus	[(Penicillin or AMP) + gentamicin] or [AM/ SB ± gentamicin]	P Ceph 2, 3 ± gentamicin	(Resistant to vancomycin, clindamycin, methicillin)
Hemophilus ducreyi (chancroid)	Azithro or ceftriaxone	Erythro, CIP	Most strains resistant to tetracycline, amox, TMP/SMX
Hemophilus influenzae Meningitis, epiglottitis & other life-threatening illness	Cefotaxime, ceftriaxone	TMP/SMX, CARB, FQs (AMP if β-lactamase negative) (U.S. 25–30% AMP resistance, Japan 35%)	Chloramphenicol (downgraded from 1st choice because of hematotoxicity). 9% of U.S. strains resistant to TMP/SMX *(AAC 41:292, 1997)*
non-life threatening illness	AM/CL, O Ceph 2/3, TMP/SMX, AM/SB		Azithro, clarithro, telithro
Klebsiella ozaenae/rhino-scleromatis	FQ	RIF + TMP/SMX	*(Lancet 342:122, 1993)*
Lactobacillus sp.	(Pen G or AMP) ± gentamicin	Clindamycin, erythro	**May be resistant to vancomycin**
Legionella sp. *(42 species & 60 serotypes recognized) (Sem Resp Inf 13:90, 1998)*	FQ, or azithro, or (erythro ± RIF)	Clarithro, telithro	TMP/SMX, doxy. Most active FQs in vitro: Gemi, Gati, Levo, Moxi. *See AnIM 129:*
Leptospira interrogans	Penicillin G	Doxy	Ceftriaxone *(CID 36:1507, 2003)*
Leuconostoc	Pen G or AMP	Clindamycin, erythro, minocycline	APAG **NOTE: Resistant to vancomycin**
Listeria monocytogenes	AMP	TMP/SMX	Erythro, penicillin G (high dose), APAG may be synergistic with β-lactams. **Cephalosporin-resistant!**
Moraxella (Branhamella) catarrhalis	AM/CL or O Ceph 2/3, TMP/SMX	Azithro, clarithro, dirithromycin, telithro	Erythro, doxy, FQs
Mycoplasma pneumoniae	Erythro, azithro, clarithro, dirithro, or FQ	Doxy	(Clindamycin and β lactams NOT effective)
Neisseria gonorrhoeae (gonococcus)	Ceftriaxone, cefixime^NUS, cefpodoxime	Ofloxacin & other FQs *(Table 1, page 15)*, spectinomycin	Kanamycin (used in Asia). FQ resistance in Asia; rare in U.S. *(MMWR 47:405, 1998)*
Neisseria meningitidis (meningococcus)	Penicillin G	Ceftriaxone, cefuroxime, cefotaxime	Sulfonamide (some strains), chloramphenicol. Penicillin-resistant strains found in SE Asia *(NEJM 339:868, 1998)* (Prophylaxis: *page 6*)
Nocardia asteroides	TMP/SMX, sulfonamides (high dose)	Minocycline	Amikacin + (IMP or ceftriaxone or cefuroxime) for brain abscess
Nocardia brasiliensis	TMP/SMX, sulfonamides (high dose)	AM/CL	Amikacin + ceftriaxone
Pasteurella multocida	Pen G, AMP, amox	Doxy, AM/CL, P Ceph 2, TMP/SMX	Ceftriaxone, cefpodoxime, FQ (active in vitro), azithro (active in vitro) *(DMID 30:99, 1998; AAC 43:1475, 1999)*
Plesiomonas shigelloides	CIP	TMP/SMX	AM/CL, P Ceph 1,2,3,4, IMP, MER, tetracycline, aztreonam
Proteus mirabilis (indole–)	AMP	TMP/SMX	Most agents except nafcillin/oxacillin. β-lactamase (including ESBL) production now being described in P. mirabilis *(JCM 40:1549, 2002)*
vulgaris (indole +)	P Ceph 3 or FQ	APAG	CARB, aztreonam, BL/BLI
Providencia sp.	Amikacin or P Ceph 3 or FQ	TMP/SMX	AP Pen + amikacin, IMP
Pseudomonas aeruginosa	AP Pen, AP Ceph 3, IMP, MER, tobramycin, CIP, aztreonam. For serious inf., use AP β-lactam + tobramycin or CIP	For UTI, single drugs usually effective: AP Pen, AP Ceph 3. cefepime, IMP, APAG, CIP, aztreonam	Resistance to β-lactams (IMP, ceftaz) may emerge during rx. β-lactam inhibitor adds nothing to activity of TC or PIP against P. aeruginosa. Clavulanic acid has been shown to antagonize TC in vitro *(AAC 43:882, 1999)*. *(See also Table 5)*

TABLE 2 (3)

BACTERIAL SPECIES	ANTIMICROBIAL AGENT (See footnote[2] for abbreviations)		
	RECOMMENDED	ALTERNATIVE	ALSO EFFECTIVE[1] (COMMENTS)
Rhodococcus (C.) equi	IMP, APAG, erythro, vancomycin, or RIF (consider 2 agents)	CIP (variable) [resistant strains SE Asia (CID 27: 370, 1998)], TMP/SMX, tetracycline, or clindamycin	Vancomycin active in vitro but intra-cellular location of R. equi may impair efficacy (Sem Resp Inf 12:57, 1997; CID 34:1379, 2002)
Rickettsiae species	Doxy	Chloramphenicol	FQ; clari, azithro effective for Mediter-ranean spotted fever in children (CID 34:154, 2002)
Salmonella typhi	FQ, ceftriaxone	Chloramphenicol, amox, TMP/SMX, azithro (for uncompli-cated disease: AAC 43:1441, 1999)	Multi drug resistant strains (chloram-phenicol, AMP, TMP/SMX) common in many developing countries, seen in immigrants. FQ resistance now being reported (AJTMH 61:163, 1999).
Serratia marcescens	P Ceph 3, ERTA, IMP, MER, FQ	Aztreonam, gentamicin	TC/CL, PIP/TZ
Shigella sp.	FQ or azithro	TMP/SMX and AMP (resistance common in Middle East, Latin America). Azithro ref.: AnIM 126:697, 1997	
Staph. aureus, methicillin-susceptible	Oxacillin/nafcillin	P Ceph 1, vancomycin, clindamycin	Erta, IMP, MER, BL/BLI, FQ, erythro, clarithro, dirithromycin, azithro, quinu/dalfo, linezolid
Staph. aureus, methicillin-resistant	Vancomycin	Teicoplanin[NUS] TMP/SMX (some strains resistant), quinu/dalfo, linezolid, daptomycin	Fusidic acid[NUS]: >60% CIP-resistant in U.S. (+RIF). TMP/SMX (+ RIF), novobiocin. Partially vancomycin-resistant strains isolated (MMWR 27:624, 1997).
Staph. aureus, methicillin-resistant [community-acquired (CA-MRSA)]			CA-MRSA usually not multiply-resistant (Ln 359: 1819, 2002; JAMA 286: 1201, 2001). Often resist. to erythro & variably to FQ. Vanco, teico[NUS], or daptomycin can be used in pts requiring hospitalization.
Mild-moderate infection	(TMP/SMX or doxy) ± RIF	Clinda (if susceptible to erythro & clinda)	
Severe infection	Vanco or teico[NUS]	Linezolid or daptomycin	
Staph. epidermidis	Vancomycin ± RIF	RIF + (TMP/SMX or FQ)	Cephalothin or nafcillin/oxacillin if sensitive to nafcillin/oxacillin but 75% are resistant. FQs. (See Table 5)
Staph. haemolyticus	TMP/SMX, FQ, nitro-furantoin	Oral cephalosporin	Recommendations apply to UTI only.
Staph. lugdunensis	Oxacillin/nafcillin or penicillin G (if β-lactamase neg.) (Inf Dis Alert 22:193, 2003)	P Ceph 1 or vancomycin or teico[NUS]	Approx. 75% are penicillin-susceptible. Usually susceptible to gentamicin, RIF (AAC 32:2434, 1990).
Staph. saprophyticus (UTI)	Oral cephalosporin or AM/CL	FQ	Susceptible to most agents used for UTI; occ. failure of sulfonamides, nitro-furantoin reported (JID 155:170, 1987). Resistant to fosfomycin.
Stenotrophomonas (Xanthomonas, Pseudo-monas) maltophilia	TMP/SMX	TC/CL or (aztreonam + TC/CL) (AAC 41:2612, 1997)	Minocycline, doxy, ceftaz. [In vitro synergy (TC/CL + TMP/SMX) and (TC/CL + CIP), AAC 39:2220, 1995; CMR 11:57, 1998]
Streptobacillus moniliformis	Penicillin G or doxy	Erythro, clindamycin	
Streptococcus, anaerobic (Peptostreptococcus)	Penicillin G	Clindamycin	Erythro, doxy, vancomycin
Streptococcus pneumoniae penicillin-susceptible	Penicillin G	Multiple agents effect-ive, e.g., amox	See footnote, page 4
penicillin-resistant (MIC ≥2.0)	(Vancomycin ± RIF) or (Gati, Levo, or Moxi) See footnote page 4 and Table 5, page 54		For non-meningeal infections: P Ceph 3/4, CARB, quinu/dalfo, linezolid
Streptococcus pyogenes, Groups A, B, C, G, F, Strep. milleri (constellatus, intermedius, anginosus)	Penicillin G or V (some add gentamicin for serious Group B strep infections & some add clinda for serious inva-sive Group A strep infec-tions) (S Med J 96: 968,2003)	All β lactams, erythro, azithro, dirithromycin, clarithro, telithro	Macrolide resistance increasing.
Vibrio cholerae	Doxy, FQ	TMP/SMX	Strain 0139 is resistant to TMP/SMX
Vibrio parahaemolyticus	Antibiotic rx does not ↓ course		Sensitive in vitro to FQ, doxy
Vibrio vulnificus, alginolyticus, damsela	Doxy + ceftaz	Cefotaxime, FQ (e.g., levo, AAC 46:3580, 2002)	APAG often used in combination with ceftaz
Yersinia enterocolitica	TMP/SMX or FQ	P Ceph 3 or APAG	CID 19:655, 1994
Yersinia pestis (plague)	See Table 1B, page 46		

[1] These agents are more variable in effectiveness than the "Recommended" or "Alternative". Selection of "Alternative" or "Also Effective" agents is based on in vitro susceptibility tests, pharmacokinetics, host factors such as auditory, renal, hepatic function, and cost.

[2] **AM/CL**: amoxicillin clavulanate; **Amox**: amoxicillin; **AMP**: ampicillin; **AM/SB**: ampicillin sulbactam; **APAG**: anti-pseudomonal aminoglycosides (see page 51); **AP Pen**: antipseudomonal penicillin (see page 51); **Azithro**: azithromycin; **BL/BLI**: β-lactam/β-lactamase inhibitor (AM/CL, TC/CL, AM/SB, or PIP/TZ); **CARB**: carbapenems (ertapenem, imipenem, or meropenem); **Ceftaz**: ceftazidime; **CIP**: ciprofloxacin; **Clarithro**: clarithromycin; **Clinda**: clindamycin; **Dirithro**: dirithromycin; **DOT group**: B. distasonis, B. ovatus, B. thetaiotaomicron; **Doxy**: doxycycline; **ERTA**: ertapenem; **Erythro**: erythromycin; **FQ**: fluoroquinolones (ciprofloxacin, ofloxacin, lomefloxacin, enoxacin, pefloxacin, levofloxa-cin); **Gati**: gatifloxacin; **IMP**: imipenem + cilastatin; **Levo**: levofloxacin; **MER**: meropenem; **Moxi**: moxifloxacin; **NUS**: not available in the U.S.; **P Ceph**: parenteral cephalosporins; **PIP/TZ**: piperacillin/tazobactam; **Quinu/dalfo**: quinupristin/dalfopristin; **R**: resistant; **RIF**: rifampin; **TC/CL**: ticarcillin clavulanate; **Teico**: teicoplanin **Telithro**: telithromycin; **TMP/SMX**: trimethoprim/sulfamethoxazole; **Vanco**: vancomycin

TABLE 3: SUGGESTED DURATION OF ANTIBIOTIC THERAPY IN IMMUNOCOMPETENT PATIENTS[1,2]

	CLINICAL SITUATION	DURATION OF THERAPY
SITE	**CLINICAL DIAGNOSIS**	**(Days)**
Bacteremia	Bacteremia with removable focus (no endocarditis)	10–14 (Clin Inf Dis 14:75, 1992) (See Table 1)
Bone	Osteomyelitis, adult; acute	42
	adult; chronic	Until ESR[6] normal (often > 3 months)
	child; acute; staph. and enterobacteriaceae[3]	21
	child; acute; strep., meningococci, hemophilus[3]	14
Ear	Otitis media with effusion	<2 yrs: 10 (or 1 dose ceftriaxone).; ≥2 yrs: 5–7
	Recent meta-analysis suggests 3 days of azithro (JAC 52: 469, 2003). or 5 days of "short-acting" antibiotics effective for uncomplicated otitis media (JAMA 279:1736, 1998), but may be inadequate for severe disease (NEJM 347:1169, 2002).	
Endocardium	Infective endocarditis, native valve	
	Viridans strep	14 or 28 (See Table 1, pages 18–19)
	Enterococci	28 or 42 (See Table 1, page 19)
	Staph. aureus	14 (R-sided only) or 28 (See Table 1, pages 19–20)
Gastrointestinal	Bacillary dysentery (shigellosis)/traveler's diarrhea	3
Also see Table 1	Typhoid fever (S. typhi): Azithro	5 (children/adolescents)
	Ceftriaxone	14*
	FQ[6]	5–7
	Chloramphenicol	14
		*[Short courses less effective (AAC 44:450, 2000)]
	Helicobacter pylori	10–14
	Pseudomembranous enterocolitis (C. difficile)	10
Genital	Non-gonococcal urethritis or mucopurulent cervicitis	7 days doxy[6] or single dose azithro[6]
	Pelvic inflammatory disease	14
Heart	Pericarditis (purulent)	28
Joint	Septic arthritis (non-gonococcal) Adult	14–28 (Ln 351:197, 1998)
	Infant/child	Rx as osteomyelitis above
	Gonococcal arthritis/disseminated GC infection	7 (See Table 1, page 15)
Kidney	Cystitis (bladder bacteriuria)	3
	Pyelonephritis	14 (7 days if CIP effective)
	Recurrent (failure after 14 days rx)	42
Lung	Pneumonia, pneumococcal	Until afebrile 3–5 days (minimum 5 days)
	Pneumonia, enterobacteriaceae or pseudomonal	21, often up to 42
	Pneumonia, staphylococcal	21–28
	Pneumocystis carinii, in AIDS;	21
	other immunocompromised	14
	Legionella, mycoplasma, chlamydia	14–21
	Lung abscess	Usually 28–42[4]
Meninges[5]	N. meningitidis	7
(CID 39:1267,	H. influenzae	7
2004)	S. pneumoniae	10–14
	Listeria meningoencephalitis, gp B strep, coliforms	21 (longer in immunocompromised)
Multiple systems	Brucellosis (See Table 1, page 40)	42 (add SM[6] or GM[6] for 1st 7–14 days)
	Tularemia (See Table 1, pages 30, 40)	7–14
Muscle	Gas gangrene (clostridial)	10
Pharynx	Group A strep pharyngitis	10 (O Ceph 2/3; azithromycin effective at 5 d.)
Also see Pha-		(JAC 45, Topic TI 23, 2000). 3 d. less effective
ryngitis, Table 1,		(Inf Med 18:515, 2001)
page 32	Diphtheria (membranous)	7–14
	Carrier	7
Prostate	Chronic prostatitis (TMP/SMX)[6]	30–90
	(FQ)	28–42
Sinuses	Acute sinusitis	10–14[7]
Skin	Cellulitis	Until 3 d. after acute inflammation disappears
Systemic	Lyme disease	See Table 1, page 39
	Rocky Mountain spotted fever (See Table 1, page 39)	Until afebrile 2 days

---

[1] It has been shown that early change from parenteral to oral regimens (about 72 hours) is cost-effective with many infections, i.e., intra-abdominal (AJM 91:462, 1991)

[2] The recommended duration is a minimum or average time and should not be construed as absolute

[3] These times are with proviso: sx & signs resolve within 7 days and ESR[6] is normalized (J.D. Nelson, APID 6:59, 1991)

[4] After patient afebrile 4-5 days, change to oral therapy

[5] In children relapses seldom occur until 3 days or more after termination of rx. Practice of observing in hospital for 1 or 2 days after rx is expensive and non-productive. For meningitis in children, see Table 1, page 4.

[6] **Azithro** = azithromycin; **CIP** = ciprofloxacin; **Doxy** = doxycycline; **ESR** = erythrocyte sedimentation rate; **FQ** = fluoroquinolones; **GM** = gentamicin; **rx** = treatment; **SM** = streptomycin; **TMP/SMX** = trimethoprim/sulfamethoxazole

[7] If pt not sx-free at 10 d., sinus puncture and/or rx for 7 more days (NEJM 326:319, 1992). One study reports 3 days of TMP/SMX effective (JAMA 273:1015, 1995). Therapy with azithro for 3 & 6 days as effective as 10 days of AM/CL (AAC 47:2770, 2003).

TABLE 4
COMPARISON OF ANTIMICROBIAL SPECTRA*
(These are generalizations; there are major differences between countries, areas and hospitals depending upon antibiotic usage patterns—verify for individual location. See Table 5 for resistant bacteria)

PENICILLINS, CARBAPENEMS, AZTREONAM, FLUOROQUINOLONES

Organisms	Penicillin G	Penicillin V	Methicillin	Nafcillin/Oxacillin	Cloxacillin/Dicloxacillin	Amp/Amox	Amox/Clav	Amp/Sulb	Ticarcillin	Ticar/Clav	Pip/Tazo	Piperacillin	Ertapenem	Imipenem	Meropenem	Aztreonam	Ciprofloxacin	Ofloxacin	Lomefloxacin	Pefloxacin	Levofloxacin	Moxifloxacin	Gemifloxacin	Gatifloxacin
GRAM-POSITIVE:																								
Strep, Group A,B,C,G	+	+	+	+	+	+	+	+	+	+	+	+	+	+	+	0	±	±	0	0	+	+	+	+
Strep. pneumoniae	+	+	+	+	+	+	+	+	+	+	+	+	+	+	+	0	±	±	0	0	+	+	+	+
Viridans strep	±	±	±	±	±	±	±	±	±	±	±	±	+	+	+	0	0	0			+	+	+	+
Strep. milleri	+	+	+	+	+	+	+	+	+	+	+	+	+	+	+	0	0	0			+	+	+	+
Enterococcus faecalis	+	+	0	0	0	+	+	+	±	±	±	±	0	+	+	0	**	**			0	+	+	±
Enterococcus faecium	±	±	0	0	0	+	+	+	±	±	±	±	0	±	0	0	0	0			0	0	±	±
Staph. aureus (MSSA)	0	0	+	+	+	0	+	+	0	+	+	0	+	+	+	0	+	+	+	+	+	+	+	+
Staph. aureus (MRSA)	0	0	0	0	0	0	0	0	0	0	0	0	0	0	0	0	0	0	0	0	0	0	±	±
Staph. epidermidis	0	0	±	±	±	±	±	±	±	±	±	±	±	±	±	0	±	±	±	±	±	±	±	±
C. jeikeium	0	0	0	0	0	0	0	0	0	0	0	0	0	0	0	0	0	0			0	0	±	±
L. monocytogenes	+	0	0	0	0	+						+	±	+	+	0	+							
GRAM-NEGATIVE:																								
N. gonorrhoeae	0	0	0	0	0	+	+	+	+	+	+	+	+	+	+	+	+	+	+	+	+	+	+	+
N. meningitidis	+	0	0	0	0	+	+	+	+	+	+	+	+	+	+	+	+	+	+	+	+	+	+	+
M. catarrhalis	0	0	0	0	0	0	+	+	0	+	0	±	+	+	+	+	+	+	+	+	+	+	+	+
H. influenzae	0	0	0	0	0	±	+	+	±	+	±	+	+	+	+	+	+	+	+	+	+	+	+	+
E. coli	0	0	0	0	0	±	+	+	±	+	+	+	+	+	+	+	+	+	+	+	+	+	+	+
Klebsiella sp.	0	0	0	0	0	0	+	+	0	+	+	+	+	+	+	+	+	+	+	+	+	+	+	+
Enterobacter sp.	0	0	0	0	0	0	0	0	0	±	+	+	0	+	+	+	+	+	+	+	+	+	+	+
Serratia sp.	0	0	0	0	0	0	0	0	0	±	±	+	+	+	+	+	+	+	+	+	+	+	+	+
Salmonella sp.	0	0	0	0	0	±	+	±	+	+	+	+	+	+	+	+	+	+	+	+	+	+	+	+
Shigella sp.	0	0	0	0	0	±	±	+	+	+	+	+	+	+	+	+	+	+	+	+	+	+	+	+
Proteus mirabilis	0	0	0	0	0	+	+	+	+	+	+	+	+	+	+	+	+	+	+	+	+	+	+	+
Proteus vulgaris	0	0	0	0	0	0	±	+	0	+	+	+	+	+	+	+	+	+	+	+	+	+	+	+
Providencia sp.	0	0	0	0	0	0	+	+	+	+	+	+	+	+	+	+	+	+	+	+	+	+	+	+
Morganella sp.	0	0	0	0	0	0	±	+	±	+	+	+	+	+	+	+	+	+	+	+	+	+	+	+
Citrobacter sp.	0	0	0	0	0	0	0	±	0	+	+	+	+	+	+	+	+	+	+	+	+	+	+	+
Aeromonas sp.	0	0	0	0	0	0	±	+	+	+	+	+	+	+	+	+	+	+	+	+	+	+	+	+
Acinetobacter sp.	0	0	0	0	0	0	0	+	0	+	+	+	0	+	+	0	±	+	±	±	±	±	±	±
Ps. aeruginosa	0	0	0	0	0	0	0	0	+	+	+	+	0	+	+	+	+	±	±	±	+	±	0	±
B. (S.) cepacia§	0	0	0	0	0	0	0	0	0	0	±	+	0	0	±	0	0	0			0			0
S. (X.) maltophilia§	0	0	0	0	0	0	0	0	0	±	+	+	0	0	0	0	0	0	0	0	0	±	+	±
Y. enterocolitica	0	0	0	0	0	0	±	+	±	+	+	+	+	+	+	+	+	+	+	+	+	+	+	+
Legionella sp.	0	0	0	0	0	0	0	0	0	0	0	0	0	0	0	0	+	+	+	+	+	+	+	+
P. multocida	+	+	0	0	0	+	+	+	±	+	±	+	+	+	+	+	+	+	+	+	+	+	+	+
H. ducreyi	+					0	+	+	±	+	±	+					+							
MISC.:																								
Chlamydia sp.	0	0	0	0	0	0	0	0	0	0	0	0	0	0	0	0	+	+	+	+	+	+	+	+
M. pneumoniae	0	0	0	0	0	0	0	0	0	0	0	0	0	0	0	0	+	+			+	+	+	+
ANAEROBES:																								
Actinomyces	+	±	0	0	0	+	+		+		+		+	+	+	0	±						+	±
Bacteroides fragilis	0	±	0	0	0	0	+	+	0	+	+	0	+	+	+	0	0	0	0	0	0	±	+	±
P. melaninogenica§	+	0	0	0	0	+	+	+	+	+	+	+	+	+	+	0	±	0			±	+	+	+
Clostridium difficile	+[1]							+[1]				+[1]	+[1]	+[1]	+[1]	0	0	0			0	±	±[1]	±[1]
Clostridium (not difficile)	+	+				+	+	+	+	+	+	+	+	+	+	0	±	±	0		+	+	+	+
Peptostreptococcus sp.	+	+				+	+	+	+	+	+	+	+	+	+	0	±	±	0		+	+	+	+

+ = usually effective clinically or >60% susceptible; ± = clinical trials lacking or 30–60% susceptible; 0 = not effective clinically or <30% susceptible; blank = data not available

§ B. melaninogenicus → Prevotella melaninogenica, Pseudomonas cepacia → Burkholderia cepacia, Xanthomonas → Stenotrophomonas

** Most strains ±, can be used in UTI, not in systemic infection

Ticar/Clav = ticarcillin clavulanate; **Amp/Sulb** = ampicillin sulbactam; **Amox/Clav** = amoxicillin clavulanate; **MSSA** = methicillin-sensitive Staph. aureus; **MRSA** = methicillin-resistant Staph. aureus; **Pip/Tazo** = piperacillin/tazobactam

[1] No clinical evidence that penicillins or fluoroquinolones are effective for C. difficile enterocolitis (but they may cover this organism in mixed intra-abdominal and pelvic infections)

TABLE 4 (2)

| | CEPHALOSPORINS | | | | | | | | | | | | | | | | |
| | 1st Generation | 2nd Generation | | | 3rd/4th Generation | | | | | 1st Generation | | 2nd Generation | | | 3rd Generation | | |
Organisms	Cefazolin	Cefotetan	Cefoxitin	Cefuroxime	Cefotaxime	Ceftizoxime	Ceftriaxone	Ceftazidime	Cefepime	Cefadroxil	Cephalexin	Cefaclor/Loracarbef*	Cefprozil	Cefuroxime axetil	Cefixime[AUS]	Ceftibuten	Cefpodox[3]/Cefdinir/Cefditoren
GRAM-POSITIVE:																	
Strep, Group A,B,C,G	+	+	+	+	+	+	+	+[1]	+	+	+	+	+	+	+	+	+
Strep. pneumoniae[1]	+	+	+	+	+	+	+	+[1]	+	+	+	+	+	+	+	±	+
Viridans strep	+	+	+	+	+	+	+	±[1]	+	+	+	+	0	+		0	+
Enterococcus faecalis	0	0	0	0	0	0	0	0	0	0	0	0	0	0	0	0	0
Staph. aureus (MSSA)	+	+	+	+	+	+	+	±	+	+	+	+	+	+	0	0	0
Staph. aureus (MRSA)	0	0	0	0	0	0	0	0	0	0	0	0	0	0	0	0	0
Staph. epidermidis	±	±	±	±	±	±	±	±	±	±	±	±	±	±	0	0	0
C. jeikeium	0	0	0	0	0	0	0	0	0	0	0	0	0	0	0	0	0
L. monocytogenes	0	0	0	0	0	0	0	0	0	0	0	0	0	0	0	0	0
GRAM-NEGATIVE:																	
N. gonorrhoeae	+	±	±	±	±	±	±	+	±	0	0	±	±	±	±	±	+
N. meningitidis	0	±	±	±	+	+	+	±	+	0	0	±	±	±	±	±	+
M. catarrhalis	±	+	+	+	+	+	+	+	+	0	0	±	±	+	+	+	+
H. influenzae	+	+	+	+	+	+	+	+	+	0	0	+	+	+	+	+	+
E. coli	+	+	+	+	+	+	+	+	+	+	+	+	+	+	+	+	+
Klebsiella sp.	+	+	+	+	+	+	+	+	+	+	+	+	+	+	+	+	+
Enterobacter sp.	0	±	0	±	+	+	+	+	+	0	0	0	0	0	0	±	0
Serratia sp.	0	+	0	0	+	+	+	+	+	0	0	0	0	0	0	±	0
Salmonella sp.					+	+		0									
Shigella sp.								0									
Proteus mirabilis	+	+	+	+	+	+	+	+	+	+	+	0	0	+	+	+	+
Proteus vulgaris	0	+	+	+	+	+	+	+	+	0	0	0	0	0	+	+	±
Providencia sp.	0	+	0	+	+	+	+	+	+	0	0	0	0	0	+	+	
Morganella sp.	0	+	+	+	+	+	+	+	+	0	0	0	0	±	0	0	0
C. freundii	0	0	0	0	0	0	0	0	+	0	0	0	0	0	0	0	0
C. diversus	0	±	±	+	+	+	+	+	+	0	0	0	0			+	
Citrobacter sp.	0	±	±	±	+	+	+	+	+	0	±	0	0	+	+	+	
Aeromonas sp.	0	+	±	+	+	+	+	+	+						+	+	+
Acinetobacter sp.	0	0	0	0	+	+	+	+	±	0	0	0	0	0	0	0	0
Ps. aeruginosa	0	0	0	0	±	±	±	+	+	0	0	0	0	0	0	0	0
B. (Ps.) cepacia[3]	0	0	0	0	±	±	0	±	0	0	0	0	0	0	0	0	0
S. (X.) maltophilia[§]	0	0	0	0	0	0	0	±	0	0	0	0	0	0	+	+	
Y. enterocolitica	0	±	±	+	+	+	+	+							+	+	
Legionella sp.	0	0	0	0	0	0	0	0	0	0	0	0	0	0	0	0	0
P. multocida					+	+		0							+		+
H. ducreyi			+		+	+	+	+	+							+	
ANAEROBES:																	
Actinomyces					+	+											
Bacteroides fragilis	0	±[2]	+	0	0	0	±	0	0	0	0	0	0	0	0	0	0
P. melaninogenica[§]		+	+	+	+	+	±	+	0			+	+	+	+		
Clostridium difficile			0		0	0		0									
Clostridium (not difficile)	+	+	+	+	+	+	+	+					+	+	0		
Peptostreptococcus sp.		+	+	+	+	+	+	+				+	+		+	+	

+ = usually effective clinically or >60% susceptible; **±** = clinical trials lacking or 30–60% susceptible; **0** = not effective clinically or <30% susceptible; blank = data not available.

[§] B. melaninogenicus → Prevotella melaninogenica, P. cepacia → Burkholderia cepacia, Xanthomonas → Stenotrophomonas

* A 1-carbacephem best classified as a cephalosporin

[1] Ceftaz 8–16x less active than cefotax/ceftriax, effective only vs Pen-sens. strains *(AAC 39:2193, 1995)*. Oral cefuroxime, cefprozil, cefpodoxime most active in vitro vs resistant S. pneumo *(PIDJ 14:1037, 1995)*.

[2] Cefotetan is less active against B. ovatus, B. distasonis, B. thetaiotamicron

[3] **Cefpodox** = Cefpodoxime proxetil

MSSA = methicillin-sensitive Staph. aureus; **MRSA** = methicillin-resistant Staph. aureus

TABLE 4 (3)

Organisms	Gentamicin	Tobramycin	Amikacin	Netilmicin^AUS	Chloramphenicol	Clindamycin	Erythro/Dirithro	Azithromycin	Clarithromycin	Telithromycin	Doxycycline	Minocycline	Vancomycin	Teicoplanin	Fusidic Acid^AUS	Trimethoprim	TMP/SMX	Fosfomycin	Nitrofurantoin	Rifampin	Metronidazole	Quinupristin/dalfopristin	Linezolid	Daptomycin	Colistimethate (Colistin)
GRAM-POSITIVE:																									
Strep Group A,B,C,G	0	0	0	0	+	+	+	+	+	+	±	±	+	+	±	±	+[2]	+		+	0	+	+	+	0
Strep. pneumoniae	0	0	0	0	+	+	+	+	+	+	+	+	+	+	+	±	±	+		+	0	+	+	+	0
Enterococcus faecalis	S	S	S	S	±	0	0	0	0	±	0	0	+	+	+	+	+[2]	+	+	±	0	0	+	+	0
Enterococcus faecium	S	0	0	0	±	0	0	0	0	0	±	±	+	±		0	0	+	±	±	0	+	+	+	0
Staph.aureus (MSSA)	+	+	+	+	±	+	±	+	+	+	±	±	+	+	+	+	+	+	+	+	0	+	+	+	0
Staph.aureus (MRSA)	0	0	0	0	0	0	0	0	0	0	±	±	+	+	+	±	±	0		+	0	+	+	+	0
Staph. epidermidis	±	±	±	±	0	0	0	0	0	0	±	±	+	+	+	+	+		+	+	0	+	+	+	0
C. jeikeium	0	0	0	0	0	0	0	0	0	0	0	0	+	+	+	+	0	0		+	0	+	+	+	0
L. monocytogenes	S	S	S	S	+		+	+	+	+	+	+	+	+		+	+			+	0	+	+	+	0
GRAM-NEGATIVE:																									
N. gonorrhoeae	0	0	0	0	+	0	±	±	±		±	±	0			+	0	±	+	+	0	+	0		0
N. meningitidis	0	0	0	0	+	0	+	+	+		+	+	0	0		+	±	+		+	0	0	0	0	0
M. catarrhalis§	+	+	+	+	+	0	+	+	+	+	+	+	0			±	+			+	0	±	±		
H. influenzae	+	+	+	+	+	0	0	+	+	+	+	+	0			±	+			+	0	±			
Aeromonas	+	+	+		+	0					+	+		0			+		+	0	0				
E. coli	+	+	+	+	+	0	0	0	0	0	0	0	0	0		+	+	+	+	0	0	0	0	0	+
Klebsiella sp.	+	+	+	+	+	0	0	0	0	0	±	0	0	0		±	±	±	±	0	0	0	0	0	+
Enterobacter sp.	+	+	+	+	+	0	0	0	0	0	0	0	0	0		±	±	±	+	0	0	0	0	0	+
Salmonella sp.	+	+	+	+	+	0	0	0	0	0	0	0	0	0		±	+	+		0	0	0	0	0	
Shigella sp.	+	+	+	+	+	0	0	±	0	0	±	±	0	0		±	±	+		0	0	0	0	0	
Serratia marcescens	+	+	+	+	+	0	0	0	0	0	0	0	0	0		±	±	±	0	0	0	0	0	0	
Proteus vulgaris	+	+	+	+	±	0	0	0	0	0	0	0	0	0		±	±	±	0	0	0	0	0	0	
Acinetobacter sp.	0	±	+	0	0	0	0	0	0	0	±	±	0	0		0	±	0		0	0	0	0	0	+
Ps. aeruginosa	+	+	+	+	0	0	0	0	0	0	0	±	0	0		0	0	0	0	0	0	0	0	0	+
B. (Ps.) cepacia§	0	0	0	0	+	0	0	0	0	0	0	±	0	0		0	+			0	0	0	0	0	0
S. (X.) maltophilia§	0	0	0	0	+	0	0	0	0	0	±	+	0	0		0	+			0	0	0	0	0	±
Y. enterocolitica	+	+	+		+	0	0	0	0	0	±			0			+	0		0	0	0			+
F. tularensis	+				+						+						+			0	0				
Brucella sp.	+				+	0	0	0	0	0	+		0	0			+			+	0	0			
Legionella sp.					+	+	+	+	+	+	+	+		0		±	±	+		+	0				
H. ducreyi					+	+	+	+	+					0			±			0	0				
V. vulnificus	±	±	±		+						+	+					±			+	0	0			
MISC.:																									
Chlamydophila sp.	0	0	0	0	+	±	+	+	+	+	+	+				0	0			+	0	+	0		
M. pneumoniae	0	0	0	0	+	0	+	+	+	+	+	+					0			0	0	+	0		
Rickettsia sp.	0	0	0	0	+		±		+	+	+	+		0		0	0			0	0				
Mycobacterium avium			+					+	+											0	0	0			
ANAEROBES:																									
Actinomyces	0	0	0	0	+	+	+	+	+		+	+	+		+			+		0			0		
Bacteroides fragilis	0	0	0	0	+	+	0	0	0		±	±	0		+		+	0		+	+			±	
P. melaninogenica§	0	0	0	0	+	+	+		+		+	+	0		+					+	+				
Clostridium difficile	0	0	0	0	±								+	+						+	+	±			
Clostridium (not difficile)**					+	±	±	+	+		+	+	+		+			+		+	+	+	+		
Peptostreptococcus sp.	0	0	0	0	+	+	±	±	±		+	+	+		+			+		+	+				

+ = usually effective clinically or >60% susceptible; ± = clinical trials lacking or 30–60% susceptible; 0 = not effective clinically or <30% susceptible; S = synergistic with penicillins (ampicillin); blank = data not available. Antimicrobials such as azithromycin have high tissue penetration and some such as clarithromycin are metabolized to more active compounds, hence in vivo activity may exceed in vitro activity.

[1] In vitro results discrepant, + in one study, 0 in another [JAC 31(Suppl. C):39, 1993]

[2] Although active in vitro, TMP/SMX is not clinically effective for Group A strep pharyngitis or for infections due to E. faecalis.

§ B. melaninogenicus → Prevotella melaninogenica, P. cepacia → Burkholderia cepacia, Xanthomonas → Stenotrophomonas

** Vancomycin, metronidazole given po active vs C. difficile; IV vancomycin not effective

Dirithro = dirithromycin; **Erythro** = erythromycin; **TMP/SMX** = trimethoprim/sulfamethoxazole; **MSSA** = methicillin-sensitive Staph. aureus; **MRSA** = methicillin-resistant Staph. aureus; **S** = potential synergy in combination with penicillin, ampicillin, vancomycin, or teicoplanin

TABLE 5: TREATMENT OPTIONS FOR SELECTED HIGHLY RESISTANT BACTERIA[1]

ORGANISM/RESISTANCE	THERAPEUTIC OPTIONS	COMMENT[1]
E. faecalis. Resistant to:		
Vanco + strep/gentamicin (MIC >500 µg/ml), β-lactamase neg. (JAC 40:161, 1997)	Penicillin G or AMP (systemic infections); Nitrofurantoin, fosfomycin (UTI only). Usually resistant to Synercid	Non BL+ strains of E. faecalis resistant to penicillin and AMP recently described in Spain, but so far rare in the U.S. and elsewhere (AAC 42:2420, 1996). Linezolid also effective in 60–70% of cases (AnlM 138:135, 2003). Daptomycin active in vitro.
Penicillin (β-lactamase producers)	Vanco, AM/SB	Appear susceptible to AMP and penicillin by standard in vitro methods. Must use direct test for β-lactamase with chromogenic cephalosporin (nitrocefin) to identify in lab (JCM 31:1905, 1993). Rarely seen since early 1990s.
E. faecium. Resistant to:		
Vanco and high levels (MIC >500 µg/ml) of streptomycin and gentamicin	Penicillin G or AMP (systemic infections); fosfomycin, nitrofurantoin (UTI only)	For strains with pen/AMP MICs of >8 ≤64 µg/ml there is anecdotal evidence that high-dose (300 mg/kg/day) AMP rx may be effective. Daptomycin active in vitro (JAC 52:123, 2003).
Penicillin, AMP, vanco, & high-level resist. to streptomycin and gentamicin (NEJM 342:710, 2000)	Linezolid 600 mg po or IV q12h and quinu/ dalfo 7.5 mg/ kg IV q8h are bacteriostatic against most strains of E. faecium. Can try combinations of cell wall-active antibiotics with other agents (including FQ, chloramphenicol, RIF, or doxy). Chloramphenicol alone effective in some cases of bacteremia (CMI 7:17, 2001). Nitrofurantoin or fosfomycin may work for UTI.	For strains with Van B phenotype (vanco R, teico S), teicoplanin[1], preferably in combination with streptomycin or gentamicin if not highly AG resistant (NEJM 342:710, 2000 & 33:1816, 2001). Linezolid shows similar efficacy. Comparable but somewhat lower (58% linezolid, 43% QD) response rates in cancer pts (AAC 53:646, 2004). Emergence of resistance with therapeutic failure has occurred during mono-therapy with either quinu/dalfo or linezolid (CID 30:790, 2000; Ln 357:1179, 2001). Nosocomial spread of linezolid-resistant E. faecium possible (NEJM 346:867, 2002). Daptomycin active in vitro against most strains (JAC 52:123, 2003). **Infectious disease consultation imperative!**
S. aureus. Resistant to:		
Methicillin (Ln 349:1901, 1997; Clin Micro Rev 10:781, 1997; CID 32:108, 2001)	Vanco	Other alternatives include teicoplanin[1,8], linezolid (Chest 124:1789, 2003), TMP/SMX (test susceptibility first), minocycline & doxy (some strains), daptomycin, or quinu/dalfo (CID 34:1481, 2002). Fusidic acid[4], fostomycin, RIF, novobiocin, FQ may be active but resistance may appear during therapy. Staphylococci (incl. CA-MRSA) with inducible MLS$_B$ resistance may appear susceptible to clindamycin in vitro. Candida failure of clindamycin in this infection may result. Negative "D" test (done in lab with double-disc "D" test) before treating with clindamycin (Clin Micro 42:2777, 2004). **Investigational drugs with activity against MRSA include oritavancin (LY333328), and dalbavancin.**
Vanco, methicillin (VRMRSA) (NEJM 339:520, 1998; CID 32:108, 2001; MMWR 51:902, 2002; NEJM 348:1342, 2003)	Unknown, but even high-dose vanco may fail. Linezolid, quinu/ dalfo, daptomycin active in vitro	Most clinical isolates of VRMRSA have had only low levels (MIC ≤16 µg/ml) of vanco resistance (MMWR 27:624, 1997; JAC 40:135, 1997). Some call these strains VISA or GISA. Only anecdotal data on therapeutic regimens. Most susceptible to TMP/SMX, minocycline, doxycycline, RIF and AGs (CID 32:108, 2001). RIF should always be combined with a 2nd therapeutic agent to prevent emergence of RIF resistance during therapy. 3 clinical isolates of truly vancomycin-resistant (MIC >64) MRSA described. Organisms still susceptible to TMP/SMX, chloro, linezolid, minocycline, quinu/dalfo (MMWR 51:902, 2002; NEJM 348:1342, 2003)
S. epidermidis. Resistant to:		
Methicillin	Vanco ± RIF and gentamicin for prosthetic valve endocarditis	
Methicillin, glycopeptides	Quinu/dalfo (see comments on E. faecium) generally active in vitro also see linezolid & daptomycin.	
S. pneumoniae. Resistant to:		
Penicillin G (MIC >1 ≤1.0)	Ceftriaxone or cefotaxime. High-dose penicillin (≥10 million units/day) or other β-lactams likely effective for nonmeningeal sites of infection (e.g. pneumonia)	IMP, ERTA, cefepime, cefpodoxime, cefuroxime also active (DCP 3:75, 1994). MER less active than IMP (AAC 38:898, 1994). Gati, gemi, levo, moxi also have activity (AAC 38:989, 1994; DMID 31:45, 1998; Exp Opin Invest Drugs 8:123, 1999).
Penicillin G (MIC ≥2.0)	(Vanco ± RIF) Alternatives if non-meningeal infection: ceftriax/cefotax, high-dose AMP, ERTA, IMP, MER, or an active FQ: Gati, Gemi, Levo, Moxi.	High-dose cefotaxime (300 mg/kg/day, max 24 gm/day) effective in meningitis due to strains with cefotaxime MICs as high as 2 µg/ml (AAC 40:218, 1996). Review: IDCP 6(Suppl 2):S21, 1997.
Penicillin, erythro, tetracycline, chloram-phenicol, TMP/SMX	Vanco ± RIF	60–65% of strains susceptible to clindamycin (Diag Microbiol Inf Dis 25:201, 1996). Levo, Gemi, Gati, Moxi active in vitro (AAC 40:2431, 1996).

* Footnotes on next page

TABLE 5 (2)

ORGANISM/RESISTANCE	THERAPEUTIC OPTIONS	COMMENT[1]
Acinetobacter baumannii. Resistant to: IMP, AP Pen 3, AP APAG, FQ	AM/SB (sulbactam alone is active against some A. baumannii, *JAC 42:793, 1998*)	6/8 patients with A. baumannii meningitis (7 organisms resistant to IMP) cured with AM/SB (*CID 24: 932, 1997*). Various combinations of FQs and AGs, IMP and AGs, or AP Pens or AP Ceph 3s with AGs may show activity against **some** multiresistant strains (*AAC 41:881, 1997; AAC 41:1073, 1997; CID 36:1268, 2003*). IV colistin also effective (*CID 28:1008, 1999; CID 36:1111, 2003*). MER + sulbactam active in vitro & in vivo (*JAC 53:393, 2004*) & triple drug combinations of polymyxin B, IMP, & RIF active in vitro (*AAC 48:753, 2004*).
Campylobacter jejuni. Resistant to: FQs	Erythro, azithro, clarithro, doxy, clindamycin	Strains resistant to FQs & macrolides have been reported from Thailand (*CID 22:868, 1996*) & elsewhere (*EID 7:24, 2002; AAC 47:2358, 2003*).
Klebsiella pneumoniae (producing ESBL) Resistant to: Ceftazidime, P Ceph 3, aztreonam	IMP, MER, ERTA (*CID 39:31, 2004*) (See Comment)	P Ceph 4, TC/CL, PIP/TZ, show in vitro activity, but have not been proven entirely effective in animal models (*LIAA 8:37, 1997*) and some strains which hyperproduce ESBLs are primarily resistant to TC/CL and PIP/TZ (*JCM 34:358, 1996*). Note that there are strains of ESBL-producing Klebsiella for which in vitro tests suggest susceptibility to P Ceph 2, 3 but resistance to ceftazidime. Infections due to such strains do not respond to P Ceph 2 or 3 (*JCM 39:2206, 2001*). FQ may be effective if susceptible. Note emergence of Klebsiella sp. with carbapenem resistance due to class A carbapenemase. Some of these organisms resistant to all antimicrobials except colistin (*AAC 48:55, 2004*).
Pseudomonas aeruginosa. Resistant to: IMP, MER	CIP (check susceptibility), APAG (check susceptibility)	Many strains remain susceptible to aztreonam & ceftazidime or AP Pens (check susceptibility). Combinations of AP Pen & APAG or (AP Ceph 3 + APAG) may show in vitro activity (*AAC 39:2411, 1995*). IV colistin may have some utility (*CID 28:1008, 1999*).

[1] Guideline on prevention of resistance *CID 25:584, 1997*. **Abbreviations: AGs** = aminoglycosides, **Amox** = amoxicillin, **AMP** = ampicillin, **AM/SB** = ampicillin/sulbactam, **AP Ceph 3** = third generation parenteral cephalosporin with enhanced antipseudomonal activity, **AP Pen** = antipseudomonal β-lactam penicillins, **APAG** = antipseudomonal aminoglycoside antibiotics, **Azithro** = azithromycin, **BL** = beta-lactamases, **Clarithro** = clarithromycin, **CIP** = ciprofloxacin, **Doxy** = doxycycline, **ERTA** = ertapenem, **Erythro** = erythromycin, **ESBLs** = extended spectrum β-lactamases, **FQ** = fluoroquinolone, **Gemi** = gemifloxacin, **Gati** = gatifloxacin, **IMP** = imipenem cilastatin, **Levo** = levofloxacin, **MER** = meropenem, **Moxi** = moxifloxacin, **P Ceph** = parenteral cephalosporin, **PIP/TZ** = piperacillin/tazobactam, **Quinu/dalfo** = quinupristin/dalfopristin, **R** = resistant, **RIF** = rifampin, **S** = sensitive, **TC/CL** = ticarcillin/clavulanate, **Vanco** = vancomycin, **VISA** = vancomycin intermediately-resistant Staph. aureus, **VRMRSA** = vancomycin-resistant Staph. aureus, methicillin-resistant Staph. aureus.

TABLE 6A: METHODS FOR PENICILLIN DESENSITIZATION

[Penicillin Allergy Reviews: *Curr Clin Topics Int Dis 13:131, 1993*]

Oral Route: If oral prep available and pt has functional GI tract, oral route is preferred. 1/3 pts will develop transient reaction during desensitization or treatment, usually mild.

Step*	1	2	3	4	5	6	7	8	9	10	11	12	13	14
Drug (mg/ml)	0.5	0.5	0.5	0.5	0.5	0.5	0.5	5.0	5.0	5.0	50	50	50	50
Amount (ml)	0.1	0.2	0.4	0.8	1.6	3.2	6.4	1.2	2.4	4.8	1.0	2.0	4.0	8.0

* Interval between doses: 15 min. After Step 14, observe for 30 minutes.

Parenteral Route:

Step**	1	2	3	4	5	6	7	8	9	10	11	12	13	14
Drug (mg/ml)	0.1	0.1	0.1	0.1	1.0	1.0	1.0	1.0	10	10	10	100	100	100
Amount (ml)	0.1	0.2	0.4	0.8	0.16	0.32	0.64	1.2	0.24	0.48	1.0	0.2	0.4	0.8

** Interval between doses: 15 min after Step 17, observe for 30 minutes, then 1.0 gm IV
[Penicillin Allergy Reviews: *CID 35:26, 2002 & MMWR 51(RR-6):28–30, 2002*]

Perform in ICU setting. Discontinue all β-adrenergic antagonists. Have IV line, ECG and spirometer *(Curr Clin Topics Int Dis 13:131, 1993)*. Once desensitized, rx must not lapse or risk of allergic reactions ↑. A history of Stevens-Johnson syndrome, exfoliative dermatitis, erythroderma are nearly absolute contraindications to desensitization (use only as an approach to IgE sensitivity).

TABLE 6B: RAPID ORAL TMP/SMX DESENSITIZATION*

Hour	Dose TMP/SMX (mg)	Comment
0	0.004/0.02	Perform in hospital or clinic. Use oral suspension [40 mg TMP/200 mg SMX/5 ml (tsp)]. Take 6 oz water after each dose. Corticosteroids, antihistamines NOT used. Refs.: *CID 20:849, 1995; AIDS 5:311, 1991*
1	0.04/0.2	
2	0.4/2	
3	4/20	
4	40/200	
5	160/800	

[Adapted from Sullivan, T.J. in Allergy: Principles and Practice, Middleton, E. et al. Eds. C.V. Mosby, 1993, p. 1726, with permission]

TABLE 7: RISK CATEGORIES OF ANTIMICROBICS IN PREGNANCY

DRUG	FDA PREGNANCY RISK CATEGORIES*
Antibacterial Agents	
Aminoglycosides:	
Amikacin, gentamicin, isepamicin[N4]	
netilmicin[N4], streptomycin & tobramycin	D
Beta Lactams: (CPh 27:49, 1994)	
Penicillins; pens + BLI; cephalosporins; aztreonam	B
Imipenem/cilastatin	C
Meropenem, ertapenem	B
Chloramphenicol	C
Clindamycin	B
Ciprofloxacin, oflox, levoflox, gatiflox, gemiflox, moxiflox	C
Colistin	C
Daptomycin	B
Fosfomycin	B
Linezolid	C
Macrolides:	
Erythromycin/azithromycin	B
Clarithromycin	C
Metronidazole	B
Nitrofurantoin	B
Rifaximin	C
Sulfonamides/trimethoprim	C
Telithromycin	C
Tetracyclines	D
Tinidazole	C
Vancomycin	C
Antifungal Agents: (CID 27:1151, 1998)	
Amphotericin B preparations	B
Caspofungin	C
Fluconazole, itraconazole, ketoconazole,	C

DRUG	FDA PREGNANCY RISK CATEGORIES*
Antifungal Agents: (continued)	
Terbinafine	B
Voriconazole	D
Antiparasitic Agents:	
Albendazole/mebendazole	C
Atovaquone/proguanil	C
Chloroquine, eflornithine	C
Ivermectin	C
Mefloquine	C
Miltefosine	X
Nitazoxanide	B
Pentamidine	C
Praziquantel	B
Pyrimethamine/pyrisulfadoxine	C
Quinidine	C
Quinine	X
Antimycobacterial Agents:	
Capreomycin	C
Clofazimine/cycloserine	"avoid"[1]
Dapsone	C
Ethambutol	"safe"[1]
Ethionamide	C
INH, pyrazinamide, rifampin	"do not use"[1]
Rifabutin	B
Rifapentin	C
Thalidomide	X
Antiviral Agents:	
Abacavir	C
Acyclovir	B
Adefovir	C
Amantadine	C

DRUG	FDA PREGNANCY RISK CATEGORIES*
Antiviral Agents: (continued)	
Amprenavir	C
Atazanavir	B
Cidofovir	C
Delavirdine	C
Didanosine (ddI)	B
Efavirenz	C
Emtricitabine	B
Entecavir	C
Famciclovir	B
Fosamprenavir	C
Foscarnet	C
Ganciclovir	C
Indinavir	C
Interferons	C
Lamivudine	C
Lopinavir/ritonavir	C
Nelfinavir	B
Nevirapine	C
Oseltamivir	C
Ribavirin	X
Rimantadine	C
Ritonavir	B
Saquinavir	B
Stavudine	C
Tenofovir	B
Valacyclovir	B
Valganciclovir	C
Zalcitabine	C
Zanamivir	B
Zidovudine	C

* **FDA Pregnancy Categories:** (CID 27:1151, 1998): **A**—studies in pregnant women, no risk; **B**—animal studies no risk, but human not adequate or animal toxicity but human studies no risk; **C**—animal studies show toxicity, human studies inadequate but benefit of use may exceed risk; **D**—evidence of human risk, but benefits may outweigh; **X**—fetal abnormalities in humans, risk > benefit.
Abbreviations: **BLI** = β-lactamase inhibitor; **FQ** = fluoroquinolones

[1] From CDC: TB Core Curriculum, 3rd Ed., 1994

TABLE 8: ANTIMICROBIAL AGENTS ASSOCIATED WITH PHOTOSENSITIVITY

The following drugs are known to cause photosensitivity in some individuals. There is no intent to indicate relative frequency or severity of reactions.

Source: 2004 Drug Topics Red Book, Medical Economics, Montvale, NJ. Listed in alphabetical order.

Amantadine, azithromycin, benznidazole, ciprofloxacin, clofazimine, dapsone, doxycycline, erythromycin ethyl succinate, flucytosine, ganciclovir, griseofulvin, interferons, levofloxacin, lomefloxacin, ofloxacin, pefloxacin, pyrazinamide, saquinavir, sulfonamides, tetracyclines, tretinoins, trimethoprim

TABLE 9. SELECTED PHARMACOLOGIC FEATURES OF ANTIMICROBIAL AGENTS

DRUG	DOSE, ROUTE OF ADMINIS-TRATION	FOR PO DOSING—Take Drug[b]			% AB[1]	PEAK SERUM LEVEL µg/ml[6]	PROTEIN BINDING, %	SERUM T½, HOURS[2]	BILIARY EXCRETION, %[3]	CSF[4]/BLOOD, %	CSF LEVEL POTENTIALLY THERAPEUTIC[5]
		WITH FOOD	WITHOUT FOOD[b]	WITH OR WITHOUT FOOD							
PENICILLINS: Natural											
Benzathine Pen G	1.2 MU IM					0.15					
Penicillin G	2 MU IV					20	65		500	5-10	Yes for Pen-sens. S. pneumo
Penicillin V	500 mg po		X		60-73	5-6	65	0.5			
PEN'ASE-RESISTANT PENICILLINS											
Clox/Diclox	500 mg po		X		50	10-15	95-98	0.5			
Nafcillin/Oxacillin	500 mg po		X		Erratic	10-15	90-94	0.5	>100/25	9-20	Yes-high-dose IV therapy
AMINOPENICILLINS											
Amoxicillin	250 mg po			X	75	4-5	17	1.2	100-3000	13-14	Yes
AM/CL	875/125 mg po			X		11.6/2.2	20/30	1.4/1.1	100-3000	13-14	
AM/CL-ER		X				17/2.1	18/25	1.3/1.0			
Ampicillin	2.0 gm IV					47	18-22	1.2	100-3000	13-14	Yes
AM/SB	3 gm IV					109-150	28/38	1.2			
ANTIPSEUDOMONAL PENICILLINS											
Indanyl carb.	382 mg po			X	35	6.5	50	1.0			
Piperacillin	4 gm po					400	16-48	1.0	100-6000	30	Not for P. aeruginosa; marginal for coliforms
PIP/TZ	3/375 gm IV					209	16-48	1.0	>100	40	Not for P. aeruginosa; marginal for coliforms
Ticarcillin	3.0 gm IV					260	45	1.2	>100	40	
TC/CL	3.1 gm IV					324	45/30	1.2			
CEPHALOSPORINS—1ˢᵗ Generation											
Cefadroxil	500 mg po		X		90	16	20	1.5	22	1-4	No
Cefazolin	1.0 gm IV					188	73-87	1.9	29-300		
Cephalexin	500 mg po		X		90	18-38	5-15	1.0	216	1-4	
CEPHALOSPORINS—2ⁿᵈ Generation											
Cefaclor	500 mg po		X		93	9.3	22-25	0.8	≥60		
Cefaclor-CD	500 mg po		X			8.4	22-25	0.8	≥60		
Cefotetan	1.0 gm IV					124	78-91	4.2	2-21		
Cefoxitin	1.0 gm IV					110	65-79	0.8	280	3	
Cefprozil	500 mg po			X	95	10.5	36	1.5			±
Cefuroxime	1.5 gm IV					100	33-50	1.5	35-80	17-88	Yes
Cefuroxime axetil	250 mg po			X	52	4.1	50	1.5			
Loracarbef	250 mg po		X		90	8	25	1.2			

See page 61 for all footnotes.

TABLE 9 (2)

Columns under "FOR PO DOSING—Take Drug[7]": WITH FOOD[6], WITHOUT FOOD[6], WITH OR WITHOUT FOOD.

DRUG	DOSE, ROUTE OF ADMINISTRATION	WITH FOOD[6]	WITHOUT FOOD[6]	WITH OR WITHOUT FOOD	% AB[1]	PEAK SERUM LEVEL μg/ml[6]	PROTEIN BINDING, %	SERUM T½, HOURS[2]	BILIARY EXCRETION, %[3]	CSF[4]/BLOOD, %	CSF LEVEL POTENTIALLY THERAPEUTIC[5]
CEPHALOSPORINS—3rd Generation											
Cefdinir pivoxil	300 mg po				25	1.6	60-70	1.7			
Cefditoren	400 mg po	X			16	4	88	1.6			
Cefixime[NUS]	400 mg po				50	3-5	65	3.1	800		
Cefotaxime	1.0 gm					100	30-51	1.5	15-75	10	Yes
Cefpodoxime proxetil	200 mg po	X			46	2.9	40	2.3	115		
Ceftazidime	1.0 gm					60	<10	1.8	13-54	20-40	Yes
Ceftibuten	400 mg po		X		80	15	65	2.4			
Cefuroxime	1.0 gm					132	30	1.7	34-82	10	
Ceftriaxone	1.0 gm IV					150	85-95	8	200-500	8-16	Yes
CEPHALOSPORIN—4th Generation											
Cefepime	2.0 gm IV					193	20	2.0	∝ 5	10	Yes
CARBAPENEMS											
Ertapenem	1.0 gm IV					154	95	4	10	21	Yes
Imipenem	500 mg IV					40	15-25	1	minimal	8.5	+[9]
Meropenem	1.0 gm IV					49	2	1	3-300	Approx. 2	±
MONOBACTAM											
Aztreonam	1.0 gm IV					125	56	2	115-405	3-52	+
AMINOGLYCOSIDES											
Amikacin, gentamicin, kanamycin, tobramycin—see Table 10C, page 72, for dose & serum levels											
Neomycin	po				<3	0	0-10	2.5	10-60	0-30	No; intrathecal: 5-10 mg
FLUOROQUINOLONES[10]											
Ciprofloxacin	750 mg po			X	70	1.8-2.8	20-40	4	2800-4500	26	1 μg/ml: Inadequate for Strep. species (CID 31:1131, 2000).
	400 mg IV			X		4.6	20-40	4	2800-4500		
	500 mg ER po			X		1.6	20-40	6.6			
	1000 mg ER po			X		3.1	20-40	6.3			
Gatifloxacin	400 mg po/IV			X	96	4.2-4.6	20	7-8		36	
Gemifloxacin	320 mg po			X	71	0.7-2.6	55-73	7			
Levofloxacin	500 mg po/IV			X	98	5.7	24-38	7		30-50	
	750 mg po/IV			X	98	8.6	24-38	7			
Moxifloxacin	400 mg po/IV			X	89	4.5	50	10-14			
Ofloxacin	400 mg po/IV			X	98	4.6/6.2	24-38	7			

See page 61 for all footnotes.

TABLE 9 (3)

DRUG	DOSE, ROUTE OF ADMINISTRATION	FOR PO DOSING—Take Drug WITH FOOD	WITHOUT FOOD?	WITH OR WITHOUT FOOD	% AB[1]	PEAK SERUM LEVEL μg/ml[6]	PROTEIN BINDING, %	SERUM T½, HOURS[2]	BILIARY EXCRETION, %	CSF[7]/BLOOD, %	CSF LEVEL POTENTIALLY THERAPEUTIC[5]
MACROLIDES, AZALIDES, LINCOSAMIDES, KETOLIDES											
Azithromycin	500 mg po / 500 mg IV			X	37	0.4 / 3.6		68 / 12/68	High		
Clarithromycin	500 mg po / ER–500 mg po	X / X			50 / ≈ 50	3-4 / 2-3	65-70 / 66-70	5-7	7000		
Dirithromycin	500 mg po			X	10	0.4	15-30	8			
Erythromycin Oral (various) / Lacto/gluco	500 mg po / 500 mg IV		X		18-45	0.1-2 / 3-4	70-74 / 70-74	2-4 / 2-4			
Telithromycin	400 mg po			X	57	2.3	60-70	10	250-300	2-13	No
Clindamycin	150 mg po / 600 mg IV			X / X	90	2.5 / 10	85-94 / 85-94	2.4 / 2.4	250-300		
MISCELLANEOUS ANTIBACTERIALS											
Chloramphenicol	1.0 gm IV			X	High	11-18	25-50	4.1	0		No
Colistin	150 mg IV					5-7.5		2-3			
Daptomycin	6 mg/kg IV					99	92	9	0		
Doxycycline	100 mg po			X		1.5-2.1	93	18	200-3200		
Fosfomycin	3.0 gm po		X			26	<10	5.7			
Linezolid	600 mg po/IV			X	100	15-20	31	5			60-70
Metronidazole	500 mg po/IV			X		20-25	20	6-14	100		
Minocycline	200 mg po			X		2.0-3.5	76	16	200-3200		No
Polymyxin B	20,000 U/kg IV					1-8		4.3-6			
Quinu/Dalfo	7.5 mg/kg IV					5		1.5			
Rifampin	600 mg po		X			4-32	80	2-5	10,000		
Rifaximin	200 mg po			X	<0.4	0.004-0.01		7-12			
Sulfamethoxazole (SMX)	2 gm po				70-90	50-120		8-15			
Trimethoprim (TMP)	100 mg po				80	1					
TMP/SMX-DS	160/800 mg po / 160/800 mg IV			X	85	1-2/40-60 / 9/105			100-200 / 40-70	50/40	Most meningococci resistant. Static vs coliforms.
Tetracycline	250 mg po		X			1.5-2.2		7-12		7-14	No
Vancomycin	1.0 gm IV					20-50		4-6	50		Need high doses. See Meningitis, Table 1, page 4
ANTIFUNGALS											
Amphotericin B											
Standard: 0.4-0.7 mg/kg IV						0.5-3.5		24		0	
Ampho B lipid complex (ABLC): 5 mg/kg IV						1-2.5		24			
Ampho B cholesteryl complex: 4 mg/kg IV						2.9		39			
Liposomal ampho B: 5.0 mg/kg IV						58 ± 21		7-10/100			

See page 61 for all footnotes

TABLE 9 (4)

DRUG	DOSE, ROUTE OF ADMINISTRATION	FOR PO DOSING—Take Drug WITH FOOD	WITHOUT FOOD	WITH OR WITHOUT FOOD	% AB	PEAK SERUM LEVEL µg/ml	PROTEIN BINDING, %	SERUM T½, HOURS	BILIARY EXCRETION, %	CSF/BLOOD, %	CSF LEVEL POTENTIALLY THERAPEUTIC
ANTIFUNGALS (continued)											
Caspofungin	70 mg IV x1, then 50 mg IV qd						97	9-11			
Flucytosine	2.5 gm po		X		78-90	30-40		3-6		60-100	Yes
Azoles											
Fluconazole	400 mg po/IV			X	90	6.7		20-50		50-94	Yes
	800 mg po/IV							20-50			
Itraconazole	Oral soln 200 mg po		X		90	Approx. 1.4	99.8	20-50		0	No Intrathecal
	200 mg po			X	Low	0.3-0.7		30-50			
Voriconazole	200 mg po		X		96	3	58	35		22-100	Yes (CID 37:728, 2003)
ANTIMYCOBACTERIALS											
Ethambutol	25 mg/kg po	X			80	2-6	10-30	4		25-50	No
Isoniazid	300 mg po		X		100	3-5		0.7-4		20-90	Yes
Pyrazinamide	20-25 mg/kg po	X			95	30-50	5-10	10-16		100	Yes
Rifampin	600 mg po		X		70-90	4-32	80	1.5-5	10,000	7-56	Yes
Streptomycin	1.0 gm IV (see Table 10C, page 72)					25-50	0-10	2.5	10-60	0-30	No Intrathecal: 5-10 mg
ANTIPARASITICS											
Albendazole	400 mg po	X				0.5-1.6	70				
Atovaquone suspension	750 mg po				47	15	99.9	67		<1	No
Dapsone	100 mg po	X			100	1.1		10-50			
Ivermectin	12 mg po					0.05-0.08	98				
Mefloquine	1.25 gm po	X				0.5-1.2	98	13-24 days			
Nitazoxanide	200 mg po	X				3	99				
Proguanil	200 mg po						75				
Pyrimethamine	25 mg po			X	"High"	0.1-0.3	87	96			
Praziquantel	20 mg/kg po	X			80	0.2-2.0		0.8-1.5			
Tinidazole	2 gm po	X			48		12	13	Chemically similar to metronidazole		
ANTIVIRAL DRUGS—NOT HIV											
Acyclovir	400 mg po			X	10-20	1.21	9-33	2.5-3.5			
Adefovir	10 mg po			X		0.02				<1	No
Famciclovir	500 mg po			X	77	3-4	<20	2-3			
Foscarnet	60 mg/kg IV					155		4			
Ganciclovir	5 mg/kg IV					8.3	1-2	3.5			
Oseltamivir	75 mg po			X	75	0.65/3.5[12]	3	1-3			
Ribavirin	600 mg po	X			64	0.8		44			
Rimantadine	100 mg po			X		0.1-0.4	40	25			
Valacyclovir	1000 mg po			X	55	5.6	13-18	3			
Valganciclovir	900 mg po	X			59	5.6	1-2	4			

See page 61 for all footnotes.

TABLE 9 (5)

DRUG	DOSE, ROUTE OF ADMINISTRATION	FOR PO DOSING—Take Drug			PEAK SERUM LEVEL μg/ml[6]	% AB[1]	PROTEIN BINDING, %	INTRACELLULAR T½, HOURS[2]	SERUM T½, HOURS[6]	CYTOCHROME P450
		WITH FOOD	WITHOUT FOOD[3]	WITH OR WITHOUT FOOD[3]						
ANTI-HIV VIRAL DRUGS										
Abacavir	300 mg po			X	3.0	83	50	20.6	1.5	
Amprenavir	1200 mg po			X	6-9	No data	90		7-11	Inhibitor
Atazanavir	400 mg po	X			2.5	"Good"	86		7	
Delavirdine	400 mg po			X	19 ± 11	85	98		5.8	Inhibitor
Didanosine	400 mg EC[13] po		X		?	30-40	<5	25-40	1.4	
Efavirenz	600 mg po		X		13 μM	42	99		52-76	Inducer/inhibitor
Emtricitabine	200 mg po			X	1.8	93	<4	10	10	
Enfuvirtide	90 mg sc				5	84	92		4	
Fosamprenavir	700 mg + 100 ritonavir po			X	6	No data	90	No data	7.7	
Indinavir	800 mg po		X		12.6 μM	65	60		1.2-2	Inhibitor
Lamivudine	300 mg po			X	2.6	86	<36	16	5-7	
Lopinavir	400 mg po	X			9.6	No data	98-99		5-6	Inhibitor
Nelfinavir	750 mg po	X			3-4	20-60	98		3.5-5	Inhibitor
Nevirapine	625 mg po			X	2	>90	60		25-30	Inducer
Ritonavir	300 mg po	X			7.8	65	98-99		3-5	Potent inhibitor
Saquinavir (gel)	400 mg po (with ritonavir)	X			?	?	97		1-2	Inhibitor
Stavudine	100 mg XR[14] po			X	1.4	86	"Low"	3.5	1.0	
Tenofovir	300 mg po	X			0.12	39	<7	10-50	17	
Zalcitabine	0.75 mg po			X	0.03	85		3	1.2	
Zidovudine	300 mg po			X	1-2	60	<38	3	1.1	

FOOTNOTES:

1 % absorbed under optimal conditions
2 Assumes CrCl >80 ml/min
3 Relative concentration in bile/peak concentration in serum x 100. If blank, no data.
4 CSF levels with inflammation
5 Judgment based on drug dose & organ susceptibility. CSF concentration ideally ≥10 above MIC
6 Total drug; adjust for protein binding to determine free drug concentration.
7 For adult oral preps; not applicable for peds suspensions.

8 Food decreases rate and/or extent of absorption
9 Concern over seizure potential; see Table 10
10 Take all po FQs 2-4 hours before sucralfate or any multivalent cations: Ca++, Fe++, Zn++
11 Given with atovaquone as Malarone for malaria prophylaxis.
12 Oseltamivir/oseltamivir carboxylate
13 EC = enteric coated
14 XR = extended release

TABLE 9B: PHARMACODYNAMICS OF ANTIBACTERIALS*

BACTERIAL KILLING/PERSISTENT EFFECT	DRUGS	THERAPY GOAL	PK/PD MEASUREMENT
Concentration-dependent/Prolonged persistent effect	Aminoglycosides; daptomycin; ketolides; quinolones	High peak serum concentration	24-hr AUC/MIC
Time-dependent/No persistent effect	Penicillins; cephalosporins; carbapenems	Long duration of exposure	Time above MIC
Time-dependent/Moderate to long persistent effect	Clindamycin; erythro/azithro/clarithro; linezolid; tetracyclines; vancomycin	Long duration of exposure	24-hr AUC/MIC

AUC = area under drug concentration curve

* Adapted from Craig, IDC No. Amer 17:479, 2003

TABLE 10A
SELECTED ANTIBACTERIAL AGENTS—ADVERSE REACTIONS—OVERVIEW

Adverse reactions in individual patients represent all-or-none occurrences, even if rare. After selection of an agent, the physician should read the manufacturer's package insert [statements in the product labeling (package insert) must be approved by the FDA].

Numbers = frequency of occurrence (%); + = occurs, incidence not available; ++ = significant adverse reaction; 0 = not reported; R = rare, defined as <1%. NOTE: Important reactions in bold print.

Table header group: PENICILLINS, CARBAPENEMS, MONOBACTAMS, AMINOGLYCOSIDES

The Aminoglycosides column represents: Amikacin, Gentamicin, Kanamycin, Netilmicin[NUS], Tobramycin. The Misc. columns are Linezolid and Telithromycin.

Adverse Reactions	Penicillin G,V	Cloxacillin	Dicloxacillin	Nafcillin	Oxacillin	Amoxicillin	Amox/Clav	Ampicillin	Amp/Sulb	Piperacillin	Pip/Tazo	Ticarcillin	Ticar/Clav	Ertapenem	Imipenem	Meropenem	Aztreonam	Aminoglycosides	Linezolid	Telithromycin
Local, phlebitis	+			++	+				3	4	1	3		4	3	1	4			
Hypersensitivity	+														3	3				
Fever	+	+	+	+	+	+	+	+	+	+	2	+	+				2	+		+
Rash	**3**	4	4	4	4	5	3	5	2	1	4	3	2	+	+	+	2			
Photosensitivity	0	0	0	0	0	0	0	0	0	0	0	0	0		0		+			
Anaphylaxis	R	0	0	R	R	0	R	R		0	0	+	+				+	+		
Serum sickness	4									+	+	+	+					+		
Hematologic																				
+ Coombs	3	0	0	0	0	+	0	+	0	+	+	0	+		2	+		R		
Neutropenia	R	0	0	+	R	+	+	+	0	6	+	0	+		+		+		1.1	
Eosinophilia	+	+	+	22	22	2	+	22	22	+	+	+	5	1	+		8			
Thrombocytopenia	R	0	0	R	R	R	R	R		+	+	R	R		+	+	+		3–10 (see 10B)	
↑ PT/PTT	0						+		0		+		0			R				
GI																				
Nausea/vomiting		+	+	0	0	2	3	2	+	+	7	+	1	3	2	4	R		3/1	6/2
Diarrhea		+	+	0	0	**5**	**9**	**10**	**2**	2	11	3	1	6	2	5	R		4	8
C. difficile colitis		R	R	R	R	R	+	+	+	+	+	+	+		+		+		+	+
Hepatic, LFTs	R	R	R	0	+	R	+	R	6	+	+	0	+	6	4	4	2		1.3	
Hepatic failure	0	0	0	0	0	0	0	0	0	0	0	0	0		0					
Renal: ↑ BUN, Cr	R	0	0	0	0	R	0	R	R	+	+	0	0		+	0		5–25[1]		
CNS																				
Headache	R	0	0	R	R	0	+	R	R	R	8	R	R	2	+	3	+		2	1.5
Confusion	R	0	0	R	R	0	0	R	R	R	R	R			+	+	+			
Seizures	R	0	0	0	+	0	R	R	0	0	R	R	+	See footnote[2]			+			
Special Senses																				
Ototoxicity	0	0	0	0	0	0	0	0	0	0	0	0	0		0	0	R	3–14[1]		
Vestibular	0	0	0	0	0	0	0	0	0	0	0	0	0		0	0	0	4–6[1]		
Cardiac																				
Dysrhythmias	R	0	0		0		0		0	0	0	0					+			
Miscellaneous, Unique (Table 10B)	+		+	+	+	+	+	+	+		+				+	+			+	
Drug/drug interactions, common (Table 22)	0	0	0	0	0	0	0	0	0	0	0	0	0	0	0	0	0	+	+	+

[1] Varies with criteria used

[2] **All β-lactams in high concentration can cause seizures** (*JAC 45:5, 2000*). In rabbit, IMP 10x more neurotoxic than benzylpenicillin (*JAC 22:687, 1988*). In clinical trial of IMP for pediatric meningitis, trial stopped due to seizures in 7/25 IMP recipients; hard to interpret as purulent meningitis causes seizures (*PIDJ 10:122, 1991*). Risk with IMP less with careful attention to dosage (*Epilepsia 42:1590, 2001*).

   Postulated mechanism: Drug binding to GABA$_A$ receptor. IMP binds with greater affinity than MER.

   Package insert, percent seizures: ertapenem 0.5, IMP 0.4, MER 0.7. However, in 3 clinical trials of MER for bacterial meningitis, no drug-related seizures (*Scand J Inf Dis 31:3, 1999; Drug Safety 22:191, 2000*). In febrile neutropenic cancer pts, IMP-related seizures reported at 2% (*CID 32:381, 2001; Peds Hem Onc 17:585, 2000*).

TABLE 10A (2)

ADVERSE REACTIONS	CEPHALOSPORINS/CEPHAMYCINS																			
	Cefazolin	Cefotetan	Cefoxitin	Cefuroxime	Cefotaxime	Ceftazidime	Ceftizoxime	Ceftriaxone	Cefepime	Cefpirome[NUS]	Cefaclor/CefER[1]/Loracarb	Cefadroxil	Cefdinir	Cefixime[NUS]	Cefpodoxime	Cefprozil	Ceftibuten	Cefditoren pivoxil	Cefuroxime axetil	Cephalexin
Local, phlebitis	+	R	R	2	5	1	4	2	1											
Hypersensitivity																				
Fever	+	+	+			R	+	R		+			R	+					R	R
Rash	+		2	R	2	2	2	2	2	1	1	+	R	1	1	1	R	R	R	1
Photosensitivity	0	0	0	0	0	R	0	0												
Anaphylaxis	R	+			R						R				R				R	
Serum sickness											≤0.5[2]	+								+
Hematologic																				
Anemia				10	R						+							2	R	
+ Coombs	3	+	2	R	6	8			14	3	+							R	R	+
Neutropenia	+		2	R	+	1	+	2	1		+	+	R	R	R	R				3
Eosinophilia		+	3	7	1	8	4	6	1				R	R	3	2	5	R	1	9
Thrombocytopenia	+					+	+		+		2				R	R	+	R		
↑ PT/PTT		+ +	+		+	+	+	+	+											
GI																				
Nausea/vomiting		1	2	R	R			R	1	+	3		13	7	4	4	2	6/1	3	2
Diarrhea		4		R	1	1		3	1	+	1-4		15	16	7	3	3	1.4	4	
AAC	+		4	+	+	+	+	+	+	+	+	+	+	+	+	+	+	+	+	+
Hepatic, ↑ LFTs	+	1	3	4	1	6	4	3	+	+	3	+	1	R	4	2	R	R	2	+
Hepatic failure	0	0	0	0	0	0	0	0	0	0										
Renal: ↑ BUN, Cr	+		3			R		1	+		+		R	+	4	R	R	R		+
CNS																				
Headache	0				2			R	2		3		2		1	R	R	2	R	+
Confusion	0										+						R			+
Seizures	0																			
Special Senses																				
Ototoxicity	0	0	0		0	0	0	0			0	0	0	0	0	0	0		0	0
Vestibular	0	0	0		0	0	0	0			0	0	0	0	0	0	0		0	0
Cardiac																				
Dysrhythmias	0	0	0		0	0	0	0			0	0	0	0	0	0	0		0	0
Miscellaneous, Unique (Table 10B)								+			+[2]							+		
Drug/drug interactions, common (Table 22)	0	0	0	0	0	0	0	0			0	0							0	0

[1] Cefaclor extended release tablets

[2] Serum sickness requires biotransformation of parent drug plus inherited defect in metabolism of reactive intermediates (*Ped Pharm & Therap 125:805, 1994*)

* See note at head of table, page 62

TABLE 10A (3)

ADVERSE REACTIONS (AE)	Azithromycin	Clarithromycin, Reg. & ER[4]	Erythromycin	Ciprofloxacin/Cipro XR	Gatifloxacin	Gemifloxacin	Levofloxacin	Moxifloxacin	Ofloxacin	Chloramphenicol	Clindamycin	Colistimethate (Colistin)	Daptomycin	Metronidazole	Minocycline	Quinupristin/dalfopristin[2]	Rifampin	Tetracycline/Doxycycline	TMP/SMX	Vancomycin
	MACROLIDES			QUINOLONES[1]						OTHER AGENTS										
Rx stopped due to AE	1	3		3.5	2.9	2.2	4	3.8	4					2.8						
Local, phlebitis						5				+			6			++			+	13
Hypersensitivity																				
Fever				R	R		R			+	+		2							
Rash	R		+	3	R	1-22[6]	1.7		2	+	+	+	4	+	+	R		+	3	
Photosensitivity	R			R	R	R	R	R	R									+	+	0
Anaphylaxis			+	R			R		R											
Serum sickness										+										
Hematologic																				
Anemia				R						++			2				R			+
Neutropenia	R	1		R	R				1	+	+				+			+	+	2
Eosinophilia				R					1		+				+			+	+	+
Thrombocytopenia	R	R		R						+	+				R		+	+	+	+
↑ PT/PTT		1																		0
GI			++																	
Nausea/vomiting	3	3[5]	25	5	8/2	2.7	7/2	7/2	7	+	+			6.3	12			+	+	3
Diarrhea	5	3-6	8	2	4	3.6	1.2	6	4	+	7		5	+				+		3
AAC				**R**	**R**		**R**	**R**	**R**	++	+						R	+		+
Hepatic, LFTs	R	R	+	2	R		1.5	+	2	+					2			+	+	+
Hepatic failure	0	0																+	+	0
Renal																				
↑ BUN, Cr	+	4		1					R	0		R						+	+	5
CNS																				
Dizziness, lightheadedness				R	3	0.8	**2.5**	3	3					++						
Headache	R	2		1	4	1.2	5.4	2						5				+	+	
Confusion			+	+				+	2	+				+	+				+	
Seizures			+	+				+	R					+					+	
Special senses																				
Ototoxicity	+		+	0																R
Vestibular															21					
Cardiac																				
Dysrhythmias		+	+	R	+[3]	+[3]	+[3]	+[3]	+[3]	R										0
Miscellaneous, Unique (Table 10B)	+		+	+	+	+	+	+	+	+	+	+	+	+	+	+	+	+	+	
Drug/drug interactions, common (Table 22)	+	+	+	+	+	+	+	+	+					+			++	+	+	+

[1] Concern expressed that quinolones may be associated with episodes of tendonitis.

[2] Quinupristin/dalfopristin = Synercid

[3] Fluoroquinolones as class assoc. with QT_c **prolongation**; ↑ QT_c can cause torsades de pointes which can lead to ventricular fibrillation. ↑ risk with concomitant ↓K^+, ↓Mg^{++}, or concomitant class Ia or IIIa antiarrhythmic agents. Ref.: CID 34:861, 2002.

[4] Regular and extended-release formulations

[5] Less GI upset/abnormal taste with ER formulation

[6] **Highest frequency:** females <40 years of age after 14 d. of rx

* See note at head of table, page 62

65

TABLE 10B: SUMMARY OF CURRENT ANTIBIOTIC DOSAGE,* SIDE-EFFECTS, AND COST†

CLASS, AGENT, GENERIC NAME (TRADE NAME)	USUAL ADULT DOSAGE† (Cost*)	ADVERSE REACTIONS, COMMENTS (See Table 10A for Summary)
NATURAL PENICILLINS		**Most common adverse reactions are hypersensitivity.** Anaphylaxis in up to 0.05%, 1–5% milder. Commercially available skin test antigen (penicilloyl) does not predict anaphylactic reactions. Hematologic, renal, CNS (seizures) reactions usually seen with high dose (>20 million units/day) and renal failure. With procaine pen G and benzathine pen G, an immediate but transient (5–30 min. after injection) toxic reaction with bizarre behavior and neurologic reactions can occur (Hoignes syndrome). Coombs test positive hemolytic anemias are rare but typically severe; in contrast to Coombs test (+) without hemolysis seen with cephalosporin therapy, but clinically significant hemolysis is rare.
Benzathine penicillin G (Bicillin)	600,000–1.2 million u IM q2–4 wks Cost: 1.2 mU/$66	
Penicillin G	Low: 600,000–1.2 million u/d IM High: >20 million u/d IV (=12 gm) Cost: 20 mU $5.66	
Penicillin V	0.25–0.5 gm tid, qid before meals & hs Cost: 500 mg G $0.39	Penicillin allergy ref.: JAMA 278:1895, 1997
PENICILLINASE-RESISTANT PENICILLINS		
Cloxacillin (Cloxapen)	0.25–0.5 gm q6h ac, po. Cost: 250 mg G $0.70	Blood levels ~2x greater than cloxacillin. Acute hemorrhagic cystitis reported. Acute abdominal pain with GI bleeding without antibiotic-associated colitis also reported.
Dicloxacillin (Dynapen)	0.125–0.5 gm q6h ac, po. Cost: 500 mg G $1.20	In Australia, cholestatic hepatitis (women predominate, age >65, rx mean 2 weeks, onset 3 weeks from starting rx (Ln 339:679, 1992)). 16 deaths since 1980, recommendation, use only in severe infection (Ln 344:676, 1994).
Flucloxacillin[×8] (Floxapen, Lutropin, Staphcil)	0.25–0.5 gm q6h po 1.0–2.0 gm q4h IV	Extravasation can result in tissue necrosis. With dosages of 200–300 mg/kg/d hypokalemia may occur. **Reversible neutropenia (over 10% with ≥21-day rx, occasionally WBC <1000/mm³).**
Nafcillin (Unipen, Nafcil)	1.0–2.0 gm q4h IV, IM. Cost: 1.0 gm $5.63	
Oxacillin (Prostaphlin)	1.0–2.0 gm q4h IV, IM. Cost: 2.0 gm IV $6.53	† SGOT >10x with 9/11 HIV+ pts reversible. † LFTs usually † 2–24 days after start of rx, reversible. **Hepatic dysfunction with ≥12 gm/d** (AnIM 120:1048, 1994). In children, more rash and liver toxicity with oxacillin as compared to nafcillin (CID 34:50, 2002).
AMINOPENICILLINS		
Amoxicillin (Amoxil, Polymox)	250 mg–1.0 gm tid po Cost: 500 mg G $0.58; NB $0.55	IV available in UK, Europe. IV amoxicillin rapidly converted to ampicillin. Rash with infectious mono—see Ampicillin. 500–875 mg po if listed in past; may be inadequate due to † resistance.
Amoxicillin/clavulanate (Augmentin)	See Comment for products/cost	With bid regimen, less clavulanate & less diarrhea. Clavulanate assoc. with rare reversible cholestatic hepatitis, esp. men >60 yrs, on rx >2 weeks (AnIM 156:1327, 1996). 2 cases anaphylactic reaction to clavulanic acid (J All Clin Immun 95:748, 1995). **Comparison Augmentin product dosage regimens:**
AM/CL extra-strength peds suspension	Peds susp.: 600/42.9 per 5 mL. Dose: 90/6.4 mg/kg div bid.	
AM/CL—extended release adult tabs		Cost for 10 days rx: Augmentin 500/125 1 tab po tid $124 Augmentin 875/125 1 tab po bid $110 Augmentin-XR 1000/62.5 2 tabs po bid $117
Ampicillin (Principen)	0.25–0.5 gm q6h po. Cost: 500 mg G $0.34 150–200 mg/kg/d IV. Cost: 1.0 gm IV G $2.80	A maculopapular rash occurs (not urticarial), **not true penicillin allergy** in 65–100% pts with infectious mono, 90% with chronic lymphocytic leukemia, and 15–20% with allopurinol therapy.
Ampicillin/sulbactam (Unasyn)	1.5–3.0 gm q6h IV. Cost: 3.0 gm NB $24.39 (see Comment)	Supplied in vials: ampicillin 1.0 gm, sulbactam 0.5 gm or amp 2.0 gm, sulbactam 1.0 gm. Antibiotic is not active vs pseudomonas. Total daily dose sulbactam ≤4 gm
ANTIPSEUDOMONAL PENICILLINS NOTE: Platelet dysfunction may occur with any of the antipseudomonal penicillins, esp. in renal failure patients.		
Piperacillin (Pipracil)	3.0–4.0 gm q4–6h IV (200–300 mg/kg/d) up to 500 mg/kg/d). **For urinary tract infection: 2.0 gm IV.** Cost: 3.0 gm NB $12.92	1.85 mEq Na+/gm
Piperacillin/tazobactam (Zosyn)	3.375 gm q6h IV. Cost: 3.375 gm NB $16.52 3.375 gm NB $16.58 4.5 gm NB $20.83	Supplied as: piperacillin 3.0 gm + tazobactam (TZ) 0.375 gm. TZ similar to clavulanate, more active than sulbactam as β-lactamase inhibitor. Has † activity over pip alone vs gram-negatives and anaerobes. PIP/TZ 3.375 gm q6h as monotherapy **not adequate for serious pseudomonas infections.** For empiric or specific treatment of P. aeruginosa dose is 4.5 gm IV q6h + tobramycin. Rx longer than 10 d. may † risk of neutropenia (CID 37:1568, 2003). Piperacillin can cause false-pos. test for galactomannan—a test for invasive aspergillosis.

(See page 71 for abbreviations)

* NOTE: all dosage recommendations are for adults (unless otherwise indicated) & assume normal renal function.   § Cost = average wholesale price from 2004 Drug Topics Red Book, Medical Economics

TABLE 10B (2)

CLASS, AGENT, GENERIC NAME (TRADE NAME)	USUAL ADULT DOSAGE* (Cost§)	ADVERSE REACTIONS, COMMENTS (See Table 10A for Summary)
ANTIPSEUDOMONAL PENICILLINS (continued)		
Ticarcillin disodium (Ticar)	3.0 gm q4-6h IV. Cost: 3.0 gm NB $13.43	Coagulation abnormalities common with large doses, interferes with platelet function, ↑ bleeding times; may be clinically significant in pts with renal failure. (4.5 mEq Na⁺/gm)
Ticarcillin/clavulanate (Timentin)	3.1 gm q4-6h IV. Cost: 3.1 gm NB $15.37	Supplied in vials: ticarcillin 3.0 gm, clavulanate 0.1 gm/vial. 4.5–5.0 mEq Na⁺/gm. Diarrhea due to clavulanate. Rare reversible cholestatic hepatitis secondary to clavulanate (AIM 156:1327, 1996).
CARBAPENEMS. NOTE: In pts with pen allergy, 11% had allergic reaction after imipenem or meropenem (CID 38:1102, 2004).		
Ertapenem (Invanz)	1.0 gm qd IV/IM. Cost: 1.0 gm NB $49.97.	Lidocaine diluent for IM use; ask about lidocaine allergy.
Imipenem + cilastatin (Primaxin)	0.5 gm q6h IV. Cost: 500 mg NB $33.10	For seizure comment, see footnote 2, Table 10A, page 62. In pts with history of pen allergy & pos. pen skin tests, ½ had pos. IMP skin tests (J All Clin Imm 82:213, 1988). Resistance of P. aeruginosa reported (see Table 5).
Meropenem (Merrem)	0.5–1.0 gm q8h IV. Up to 2.0 gm q8h IV for menin- gitis. Cost: 1.0 gm NB $54.94	For seizure incidence see footnote 2, Table 10A, page 62. Comments: Does not require a dehydropeptidase inhibitor (cilastatin). Activity vs aerobic gm-neg. slightly ↑ over IMP, activity vs staph & strep slightly ↓, anaerobes = to IMP. B. ovatus, B. distasonis more resistant to meropenem.
MONOBACTAMS		
Aztreonam (Azactam)	1.0 gm q8h–2.0 gm q6h IV. Cost: 1.0 gm NB $21.61	Can be used in pts with allergy to penicillins/cephalosporins. Animal data and a letter raise concern about cross-reactivity with ceftazidime (Rev Inf Dis 7:613, 1985), side-chains of aztreonam and ceftazidime are identical.
CEPHALOSPORINS (1st parenteral, then oral drugs).		**NOTE:** Prospective data demonstrate correlation between use of cephalosporins (esp. 3rd generation) and ↑ risk of C. difficile toxin-induced diarrhea. May also ↑ risk of colonization with vancomycin-resistant enterococci. **For cross-allergenicity, see Oral, next page.**
1st Generation, Parenteral		
Cefazolin (Ancef, Kefzol)	0.25 gm q8h–1.5 gm q6h IV, IM. Cost: 1.0 gm G $2.74, NB $5.60	Do not give into lateral ventricles—seizures
2nd Generation, Parenteral		
Cefotetan (Cefotan)	1–3 gm q12h IV, IM. (Max. dose not >6 gm qd). Cost: 1.0 gm NB $11.90	Increasing resistance of B. fragilis, Prevotella bivius, Prevotella disiens (most common in pelvic infections). Ref: CID 35(Suppl 1):S126, 2002. Methylthiotetrazole (MTT) side chain can inhibit vitamin K activation.
Cefoxitin (Mefoxin)	1.0 gm q8h–2.0 gm q4h IV, IM. Cost: 1.0 gm G $11.23, NB $15.29	In vitro induce ↑ β-lactamase, esp. in Enterobacter sp.; clinical significance ?
Cefuroxime (Kefurox, Ceftin, Zinacef)	0.75–1.5 gm q8h IV/IM. Cost: 1.5 gm IV G $23.90	More stable vs staphylococcal β-lactamase than cefazolin.
3rd Generation, Parenteral—Use of P. ceph 3 drugs correlates with incidence of C. difficile (CID 38:646, 2004).		
Cefotaxime (Claforan)	1.0 gm q8–12h to 2.0 gm q4h IV. Cost: 2.0 gm G $22, NB $26.38 [Maximum daily dose: 12 gm]	↑ incidence of C. difficile—assoc. diarrhea, perhaps due to cephalosporin resistance of C. difficile (CID 38:646, 2004).
Ceftazidime (Fortaz, Tazicef)	1.0–2.0 gm q8–12h IV, IM. Cost: 2.0 gm NB $28.93–43.30	Excessive use may result in ↑ incidence of C. difficile-assoc. diarrhea and/or selection of vancomycin-resistant E. faecium. Ceftaz is susceptible to extended-spectrum cephalosporinases (CID 27:76 & 81, 1998).
Ceftizoxime (Cefizox)	1.0 gm q8–12h to 4.0 gm q8h IV. Cost: 1.0 gm NB $24.64	Maximum daily dose: 12 gm

(See page 71 for abbreviations)
* NOTE: all dosage recommendations are for adults (unless otherwise indicated) & assume normal renal function.   **§ Cost** = average wholesale price from 2004 DRUG TOPICS RED BOOK, Medical Economics

TABLE 10B (3)

CLASS, AGENT, GENERIC NAME (TRADE NAME)	USUAL ADULT DOSAGE* (Cost†)	ADVERSE REACTIONS, COMMENTS (See Table 10A for Summary)
CEPHALOSPORINS, 3rd Generation, Parenteral *(continued)*		
Ceftriaxone (Rocephin)	**Commonly used IV doses in adults:** **Age 65: 2.0 gm once daily** **> Age 65: 1.0 gm once daily** **Purulent meningitis: 2.0 gm q12h. Can give** IM in 1% lidocaine. Cost: 1.0 gm NB $56.16	Dosage: 2.0 gm IV qd gives better tissue levels than 1.0 gm q12h (overcomes protein binding) (see footnote†). "Pseudocholelithiasis" 2° to sludge in gallbladder by ultrasound (50%), symptomatic (9%) (NEJM 322:1821, 1990). More likely with ≥2 gm/d with pt on total parenteral nutrition and not eating (AnIM 115:712, 1991). Clinical significance still unclear but has led to cholecystectomy (JID 17:356, 1995) and gallstone pancreatitis (Ln 17:662, 1998).
4th Generation, Parenteral		
Cefepime (Maxipime)	1.0–2.0 gm q12h IV. Cost: 2.0 gm NB $35.86	Active vs P. aeruginosa and many strains of Enterobacter, serratia, C. freundii resistant to ceftazidime, cefotaxime, aztreonam (CID 20:56, 1995). More active vs S. aureus than 3rd generation cephalosporins.
Cefpirome[ace] (HR 810)	1.0–2.0 gm q12h IV	Similar to cefepime; ↑ activity vs enterobacteriaceae, P. aeruginosa, Gm + organisms. Anaerobes: less active than cefoxitin, more active than cefotax or ceftaz.
Oral Cephalosporins		
1st Generation, Oral		
Cefadroxil (Duricef)	0.5–1.0 gm q12h po. Cost: 0.5 gm G $2.48, NB $6.32	The oral cephalosporins are generally safe. **Patients with a history of IgE-mediated allergic reactions to a penicillin (e.g., anaphylaxis, angioneurotic edema, immediate urticaria) should not receive a cephalosporin.** If the history is a "measles-like" rash to a penicillin, available data suggest a 5–10% risk of rash in such patients; there is no enhanced risk of anaphylaxis. Cephalosporin skin tests, if available, predictive of reaction (AnIM 141:16, 2004).
Cephalexin (Keflex, Keftab, generic)	0.25–0.5 gm q6h po. Cost: 0.5 gm G $0.44, NB $1.64–4.95.	Any of the cephalosporins can result in **C. difficile toxin-**mediated diarrhea/enterocolitis. The reported frequency of nausea/vomiting and non-C. difficile toxin diarrhea is summarized in Table 10A.
2nd Generation, Oral		
Cefaclor (Ceclor)	0.25–0.5 gm q8h po. Cost: 0.25 gm G $0.66, NB $2.46	There are few drug-specific adverse effects, e.g.,
Cefaclor-ER (Ceclor CD)	0.375–0.5 gm q12h po. Cost: 0.5 gm $3.50	**Cefaclor** - Serum sickness-like reaction 0.1–0.5%—arthralgia, rash, erythema multiforme but not adenopathy, proteinuria or demonstrable immune complexes. Anecdotal reports of similar reaction to loracarbef. Appear due to mixture of drug
Cefprozil (Cefzil)	0.25–0.5 gm q12h po. Cost: 0.5 gm NB $9.10	biotransformation and genetic susceptibility (Ped Pharm & Therap 125:805, 1994).
Cefuroxime axetil po (Ceftin)	0.125–0.5 gm q12h po. Cost: 0.5 gm NB $10.30	**Cefditoren pivoxil:** Hydrolysis yields pivalate. Pivalate absorbed (70%) & becomes pivaloylcarnitine which is renally excreted; 39–63% ↓ **in serum carnitine concentrations.** Carnitine involved in fatty acid (FA) metabolism & FA transport into mitochondria. Effect transient & reversible. No clinical events documented to date (Med Lett 44:5, 2002).
Loracarbef (Lorabid)	0.4 gm q12h po. Cost: 0.4 gm NB $6.37	Also contains casein (milk protein); **avoid if milk allergy** (not same as lactose intolerance). Need gastric acid for optimal absorption.
3rd Generation, Oral		
Cefdinir (Omnicef)	300 mg q12h or 600 mg qd po. Cost: 300 mg $4.45	**Cefpodoxime:** There are rare reports of acute liver injury, bloody diarrhea, pulmonary infiltrates with eosinophilia.
Cefditoren pivoxil (Spectracef)	200–400 mg bid po. Cost: 200 mg $1.88	
Cefixime[ace] (Suprax)	0.2–0.4 gm q12–24h po. Cost: 0.4 gm NB $10.18, G $1.00	
Cefpodoxime proxetil (Vantin)	0.1–0.2 gm q12h po. Cost: 0.2 gm NB $7.80	
Ceftibuten (Cedax)	0.4 gm qd po. Cost: 0.4 gm NB $9.10	
AMINOGLYCOSIDES AND RELATED ANTIBIOTICS—See Table 10C, page 72, and Table 17, page 132		

† The age-related dosing of ceftriaxone is based on unpublished pharmacokinetic data that show an age-related reduction in hepatic clearance of ceftriaxone; hence, there is possible underdosing in younger pts, therefore the suggested 2 gm/day dose. (See page 71 for abbreviations)

* NOTE: all dosage recommendations are for adults (unless otherwise indicated) & assume normal renal function.

$ Cost = average wholesale price from 2004 DRUG TOPICS RED BOOK, Medical Economics

TABLE 10B (4)

CLASS, AGENT, GENERIC NAME (TRADE NAME)	USUAL ADULT DOSAGE* (Cost†)		ADVERSE REACTIONS, COMMENTS (See Table 10A for Summary)
GLYCOPEPTIDES			
Teicoplanin^NUS (Targocid)	**For septic arthritis—maintenance dose 12 mg/kg d; S. aureus endocarditis—trough serum levels >20 μg/ml required (12 mg/kg q12h x3 loading dose, then 12 mg/kg qd)**		Hypersensitivity: fever (at 3 mg/kg 2.2%, at 24 mg/kg 8.2%), skin reactions 2.4%. Marked ↓ platelets (high dose ≥15 mg/kg/d). Red neck syndrome less common than with vancomycin (JAC 32:792, 1993).
Vancomycin (Vancocin)	15 mg/kg q12h IV; 125 mg po, q6h; intrathecal 5-10 mg q48-72h. Oral: *Pulvule* 125 mg, Cost $7.70 Cost: 1.0 gm (V G $6.00, NB $16.00. For severe overwhelming infection: One report of safety & efficacy of once-daily vanco, 30 mg/kg (JAC 49:155, 2002).		Measure serum levels if: planned dose ≥2.0 gm/d, rapidly changing renal function, chronic renal failure, or on hemodialysis Target levels: peak 20-50 μg/ml, trough 5-10 μg/ml. Rapid infusion (over <1 hr) can cause non-specific histamine release manifest as angioedema, flushed skin ("red neck syndrome") or hypotension. Can continue vanco but slow infusion rate over 1-2 hrs. **Once daily dose** with an aminoglycoside: aminoglycoside amplifies the risk of nephrotoxicity. Neutropenia, rash occur. Rarely, association with linear IgA bullous dermatosis (CID 38:442, 2004). **Intrathecal vanco** occ. used for meningitis and/or ventriculitis/shunt infections. **Initial** dosing ranges from 5-10 μg/ml (infants) to 10-20 mg/d (children/adults) adjusted to achieve trough CSF conc. of 10-20 μg/ml (AnPharmacotherapy 27:912, 1993) to 10-20 mg/d (children/adults) adjusted to give loading dose of 25 mg/kg in high pts (JAC 47:246, 2001). **Critically ill pts:** Safe & reasonable to give loading dose of 25 mg/kg in high pts (JAC 47:246, 2001).
CHLORAMPHENICOL, CLINDAMYCIN(S), ERYTHROMYCIN GROUP, KETOLIDES, OXAZOLIDINONES, QUINUPRISTIN/DALFOPRISTIN (SYNERCID)			
Chloramphenicol (Chloromycetin)	0.25-1 gm po/IV q6h to max. of 4 gm/day Cost: 1.0 gm IV $7.60; po $2.40		No oral drug interactions with azithromycin/clarithromycin (↓ RBC ~1/3 pts, aplastic anemia 1:21,600 courses). Gray baby syndrome in premature infants, anaphylactoid reactions, optic atrophy or neuropathy (very rare), digital paresthesias, minor disulfiram-like reactions.
Clindamycin (Cleocin)	0.15-0.45 gm q6h po; 600-900 mg q8h IV, IM. Cost: 300 mg po NB $5.43, G $3.76, 600 mg IV NB $7.92, G $8.44	Lincomycin (Lincocin)	0.6 gm q8h IV, IM. Cost: 600 mg IV $10.51	Based on number of exposed pts, these drugs are the most frequent cause of **C. difficile toxin-mediated diarrhea** in most severe form can cause pseudomembranous colitis/toxic megacolon.
Erythromycin Group (Review drug interactions before use) Ref.: Mayo Clin Proc 74:613, 1999			**Motilin** is gastric hormone that activates duodenal/jejunal receptors with resultant peristalsis. Eryo (E) and E esters, both po and IV, activate motilin receptors and cause uncoordinated peristalsis with resultant 20-25% incidence of anorexia, nausea or vomiting (Gut 33:397, 1992). Less binding and GI distress with azithromycin/clarithromycin.
Azithromycin (Zithromax)	**po:** 0.5 gm on day 1, then 0.25 gm qd on days 2-5 po or 0.5 gm po qd x3 d Cost: 250 mg IV $7.85, Z-Pak $47.00, 600 mg $10.00 **IV:** 0.5 gm/d Cost: $27.38		Systemic erytho in 1st 2 wks of life associated with **infantile hypertrophic pyloric stenosis** (J Peds 139:380, 2001). Major concern is prolonged QT, interval on EKG. **Prolonged QTc:** Mutations in 6 genes (LQT 1-6) alter abnormal cardiac K+/Na+ channels. Variable penetrance: no symptoms, repeated syncope, to sudden death. **↑ risk if female & QTc >500 msec! Risk amplified by drugs** [macrolides, antiarrhythmics, & many drug interactions (see FDx page 7 for list)]. Can result in torsades de pointes (ventricular tachycardia) and/or cardiac arrest. Refs.: NEJM 348:1837 & 1866, 2003; 351:1053 & 1089, 2004; www.qtdrugs.org.
Base and esters (Erythromn, Ilosone) IV later: E. lactobionate	0.25-0.5 gm q6h-q12h po, IV: 15-20 mg/kg up to 4.0 gm qd. Infuse over 30 or more minutes Cost: po 250 mg base $0.18, stearate $0.18, estolate $0.31, ESS 400 $0.23. IV 1.0 gm NB $6.50		**Transient reversible tinnitus or deafness** with ≥4 gm/d of erytho IV in pts with renal or hepatic impairment. Reported with ≥600 mg/d of azithro (CID 24:76, 1997). Cholestatic hepatitis in approx. 1:1000 adults (not children) given E estolate.
Clarithromycin (Biaxin) or clarithro extended release (Biaxin XL)	0.5 gm q12h po. Cost: 500 mg 14.55 **Extended release: Two 0.5 gm tabs po/d.** Cost: 500 mg ER $4.66		Dosages of oral preparations expressed as base equivalents. With differences in absorption/biotransformation, variable amounts of erytho esters required to achieve same free erytho serum level. e.g. 400 mg E ethyl succinate = 250 mg E base.
Dirithromycin (Dynabac)	0.5 gm po qd. Cost: 250 mg $4.36		Macrolide-induced Churg-Strauss syndrome reported in an atopic pt (Ln 350:563, 1997). Dirithromycin available as once-daily macrolide. **Very low serum levels; do not use if potential for bacteremic disease.**
Ketolide Telithromycin (Ketek)	**Two 400 mg tabs po qd—anticipated dose.** Cost: 400 mg tabs $5.36		1st ketolide (similar to erythro). **Common:** diarrhea 10%, nausea 7%, vomiting 2%, **Uncommon: blurred vision** 2% slow accommodation, occurs in 1% (women <40 y/o 2%), may cause exacerbation of **myasthenia gravis**. Potential QTc prolongation. Several drug-drug interactions (Table 22, page 147).

(See page 71 for abbreviations)
* All dosage recommendations are for adults (unless otherwise indicated) & assume normal renal function. § Cost = average wholesale price from 2004 DRUG TOPICS RED BOOK, Medical Economics

TABLE 10B (5)

CLASS, AGENT, GENERIC NAME (TRADE NAME)	USUAL ADULT DOSAGE* (Cost†)	ADVERSE REACTIONS, COMMENTS (See Table 10A for Summary)
CHLORAMPHENICOL, CLINDAMYCIN(S), ERYTHROMYCIN GROUP, KETOLIDES, OXAZOLIDINONES, QUINUPRISTIN/DALFOPRISTIN (SYNERCID) (continued)		
Linezolid (Zyvox)	**PO or IV dose: 600 mg q12h for all indications except 400 mg q12h for uncomplicated skin infections.** Available as 400 & 600 mg tabs, oral suspension (100 mg/5 ml), & IV solution. 600 mg po $62; 600 mg IV $82.	**Reversible myelosuppression:** Thrombocytopenia, anemia, & neutropenia reported. Most often after >2 wks of therapy. Not sure of incidence of thrombocytopenia after 2 wks of rx: 7/20 osteomyelitic pts; 5/7 pts treated with vanco & then linezolid. Refs: CID 37:1609, 2003 & 38:1058 & 1065, 2004. **Other reported serious adverse effects:** Lactic acidosis (N/V, low HCO₃), toxic neuropathy reported after prolonged therapy (peripheral neuropathy) (AAC 47:4528, 2004 & optic neuropathy (JAC 53:1114, 2004). **Inhibition of takes with drugs** containing pseudoephedrine, phenylpropanolamine or if taking SSRIs.* **Serotonin syndrome** (fever, agitation, mental status changes, tremors) reported (CID 36:1197, 2003 & 37:1274, 2003).
Quinupristin + dalfopristin (Synercid)	7.5 mg/kg q8h IV via central line. Cost: 350 mg–150 mg $122	Venous irritation (5%): none with central venous line. Asymptomatic ↑ in unconjugated bilirubin. **Arthralgia 2%–50%** (CID 36:476, 2003). **Drug-drug Interactions:** Cyclosporine, nifedipine, midazolam, many more—see Table 22
TETRACYCLINES (Mayo Clin Proc 74:727, 1999)		Similar to other tetracyclines. ↑ nausea on empty stomach. Erosive esophagitis, esp. if taken hs. Phototoxicity + but less than with tetracycline. Deposition in teeth less. Can be used in patients with renal failure.
Doxycycline (Vibramycin, Doryx, Monodox, Adoxa)	0.1 gm po or IV q12h. Cost: 100 mg po G $0.08–0.11, NB $4.86, 100 mg IV NB $14.16	**Comments:** Effective in treatment and prophylaxis for malaria, leptospirosis, typhus fevers.
Minocycline (Minocin, Dynacin)	0.1 gm q12h po. Cost: 100 mg G $1.80, NB $3.88	Similar to other tetracyclines. **Vestibular symptoms** (30-90% in some groups, none in others): vertigo 33%, ataxia 43%, nausea 50%, vomiting 3%, women more frequently than men. Hypersensitivity pneumonitis, reversible. ~34 cases reported (BMJ 310:1520, 1995). **Comments:** More effective than other tetracyclines vs staph and in prophylaxis of meningococcal disease. P. acnes: many resistant to other tetracyclines. **Minocycline a cause of lupus.** (Ann IM 132:81, 2000).
Tetracycline, Oxytetracycline (Sumycin)	0.25–0.5 gm q6h po, 0.5–1.0 gm q12h IV. Cost: 250 mg IV $0.06	GI (oxy 19%, tetra 4%), esophagitis (rare), deposition in teeth, negative N balance, hepatotoxicity, enamel hypoplasia, pseudotumor cerebri/encephalopathy. Outdated drug: Fanconi syndrome. See drug-drug interactions, Table 22 **Contraindicated in pregnancy, hepatotoxicity in mother, transplacental to fetus.** Comments: IV dosage over 2.0 gm/d may be associated with fatal hepatotoxicity.
FLUOROQUINOLONES (FQs)		
Ciprofloxacin (Cipro) and Ciprofloxacin-extended release (Cipro XR)	**500-750 mg bid po. Urinary tract infection: 250 mg q12h po or Cipro XR 500 mg qd. Parenteral** rx 200–400 mg q12h IV. Cost: 500 mg po $5.86; Cipro XR 500 mg $9.30; Cipro XR 1000 mg $6.66, 400 mg IV $30.00.	**Children:** No FQ approved for use under age 16 based on joint cartilage injury in immature animals. Articular SEs in children est. at 2–3% (Ln ID 3:537, 2003). **CNS toxicity:** Poorly understood. Varies from mild (lightheadedness) to moderate (confusion) to severe (seizures). May be aggravated by NSAIDs. **Gemi skin rash:** Macular rash after 8–10 d. of rx. Frequency highest females, < age 40, treated 14 d. (22.6%). In men, < age 40, treated 14 d. frequency 7.7%. Mechanism unclear. Indication to DC therapy. **Hypoglycemia/hyperglycemia** (Med Lett 45:64, 2003): Data based on case reports. Various FQs ↑ insulin release in rats. Less known drug-drug interactions; most pts reported have type 2 diabetes; no interaction with oral hypoglycemic drugs found. No data to allow comparative frequency between FQs.
Gatifloxacin (Tequin)	200–400 mg IV/po qd. Cost: 400 mg po po $9.56, 400 mg/d $38.20.	**Opiate screen false-positives:** FQs can cause **false-positive urine assay for opiates** (JAMA 286:3115, 2001).
Gemifloxacin (Factive)	320 mg po qd. Cost: 320 mg/d $18.78	**GI:** See Table 8, page 56
		(Continued on next page—QTc interval prolongation & Tendinopathy)
Levofloxacin (Levaquin)	250–750 mg po or IV Cost: 750 mg po $20; 750 mg/d $58	**Photosensitivity.**

¹ **SSRI** = selective serotonin reuptake inhibitors, e.g., fluoxetine (Prozac).

(See pages 71 for abbreviations)
* NOTE: all dosage recommendations are for adults (unless otherwise indicated) & assume normal renal function.
§ SSRI = selective serotonin reuptake inhibitors, e.g., fluoxetine (Prozac).
§ Cost = average wholesale price from 2004 DRUG TOPICS RED BOOK, Medical Economics

TABLE 10B (6)

CLASS, AGENT, GENERIC NAME (TRADE NAME)	USUAL ADULT DOSAGE* (Cost§)	ADVERSE REACTIONS, COMMENTS (See Table 10A for Summary)

FLUOROQUINOLONES (continued)

	(Continued from previous page)	
Moxifloxacin (Avelox)	400 mg po or IV qd. Cost: 400 mg po or IV $10.00.	**QT₂, (corrected QT) interval prolongation:** ↑ QTc (>500 msec or >60 msec from baseline) with any FQ. ↑QTc can lead to torsades de pointes and ventricular tachycardia (with current marketed drugs). Risk ↑ in women, ↓ K⁺, ↓ Mg⁺⁺; bradycardia. (Refs.: *NEJM 348:*
	U.S. $44.00.	
Ofloxacin (Floxin)	200–400 mg bid po. Cost: 400 mg po $6	*1837 & 1866, 2003*). Major problem in pts with concomitant drugs.

Avoid concomitant drugs with potential to prolong QT₂:

Antiarrhythmics:	Anti-infectives:	Misc.
Amiodarone	Clarithro	Salmeterol
Disopyramide	Erythro	Naratriptan
Dofetilide	Foscarnet	Sumatriptan
Flecainide	Mefloquine	Dolasetron
Ibutilide	Pentamidine	Droperidol
Procainamide	**CNS Drugs**	Fosphenytoin
Quinidine	Fluoxetine	Indapamide
Risperidone	Sertraline	Tamoxifen
Sotalol	Tricyclics	Tizanidine
	Venlafaxine	
Anti-Hypertensives:	Haloperidol	
Bepridil	Phenothiazines	
Isradipine	Pimozide	
Nicardipine	Quetiapine	
Moexipril	Ziprasidone	

Updates online: www.qtdrugs.org; www.torsades.org.

Tendinopathy: Over age 60, approx. 2–6% of all Achilles tendon ruptures attributable to use of FQ (*AJM 163:1801, 2003*). ↑ risk with concomitant steroid or renal disease (*CID 36:1404, 2003*).

POLYMYXINS (*CID, in press*)

Polymyxin B (Poly-Rx)	Rarely used parenterally in U.S. Use colistin for parenteral therapy	Used as/for: bladder irrigation, intrathecal, ophthalmic. Source: Bedford Labs, Bedford, OH
Polymyxin E = colistin	1 mg colistin = 12,500 IU	inhalation dose: 80 mg q12h. intrathecal: not standardized. Reports range from 1.6 mg to 20 mg intraventricularly.
Colistin sulfate used po or topical; IV form is **colistimethate** (Coly-Mycin M)	U.S.: 2.5–5.0 mg/kg/d in 2–4 equal doses U.K., >60 kg: 80–160 mg q8h	usually 10 mg. **Neurotoxicity** (frequency?): Vertigo, facial paresthesia, abnormal vision, confusion, ataxia, & neuromuscular blockade → respiratory failure. Dose-dependent.

MISCELLANEOUS AGENTS

Daptomycin (Cubicin) (*Med Lett 46:11, 2004; CID 38:994, 2004*)	Skin/soft tissue: **4 mg/kg qd IV** Bacteremia/endocarditis: **6 mg/kg qd IV** (see Comment). Cost 500 mg $161	FDA approved skin/soft tissue infections. Bacteremia/endocarditis trials ongoing. **Potential muscle toxicity:** At 4 mg/kg/d, ↑ CPK in 2.8% dapto pts & 1.8% comparator-treated pts. In very small study, no CPK ↑ in pts taking a statin drug given daptomycin (manufacturer suggests stopping statins during dapto rx).
Fosfomycin (Monurol)	3.0 gm with water po x1 dose. Cost $35.00	Diarrhea in 9% compared to 6% of pts given nitrofurantoin and 2.3% given TMP/SMX.
Fusidic acid⁴ᵁ (Fucidin) (*Leo Laboratories, Denmark*)	500 mg tid po, IV (NUS)	(Mild GI, occ. skin rash, jaundice (17% with IV, 6% with po). (None in CSF; <1% in urine).
Immune globulin IV therapy	Dosage, frequency vary with the indication. Cost for 10–12 gm ranges from $500–$1100.	At least 7 manufacturers. Fever, headache, myalgia, N/V relate to rate of infusion, mild, & self-limited. **More serious:** anaphylactoid reactions, thromboemboli, aseptic meningitis, & renal injury in 6.7% (*QJM 93:751, 2000*).
Methenamine hippurate (Hiprex, Urex)	1.0 gm q6h po. Cost: 1.0 gm $1.49 1.0 gm = 480 mg methenamine	Nausea and vomiting, skin rash or dysuria. Overall ~3%. Methenamine requires (pH <5) urine to liberate formaldehyde. Useful in chronic suppression of bacteriuria after urologic surgery. Do not use for acute pyelonephritis. **Comment:** Do not force fluids; may dilute formaldehyde. No value in pts with chronic Foley. If urine pH >5.0, co-administer ascorbic acid (1–2
Methenamine mandelate (Mandelamine)	1.0 gm q6h po (480 mg methenamine) Cost: 1.0 gm NB $0.69	gm q4h) to acidify the urine; cranberry juice (1200–4000 mU/day) has been used, results ±.

(See page 71 for abbreviations)
* NOTE: all dosage recommendations are for adults (unless otherwise indicated) & assume normal renal function.
§ Cost = average wholesale price from 2004 Drug Topics RED BOOK, Medical Economics

TABLE 10B (7)

CLASS, AGENT, GENERIC (G) TRADE NAMES (T)	USUAL ADULT DOSAGE* (Cost†)	ADVERSE REACTIONS, COMMENTS (See Table 10A for Summary)
MISCELLANEOUS AGENTS (continued)		
Metronidazole (Flagyl) Ref.: *Mayo Clin Proc.* 74:825, 1999	**Anaerobic infections:** usually IV, 7.5 mg/kg (~500 mg) q6h (not to exceed 4.0 gm qd). With long T½, can use IV at 15 mg/kg q12h. **If life-threatening, use loading dose of 15 mg/kg IV. Oral dose: 500 mg qid.** Cost: 500 mg tab G \$0.21, NB \$4.56; 500 mg IV G \$2.80, NB \$26.16; 70 gm vaginal gel \$57.48	Can be given rectally (enema or suppository). In pts with **decompensated liver disease** (manifest by ≥2 L of ascites, encephalopathy, ↑ prothrombin time, ↓ serum albumin) **↓ dose ↓ by approx. ½**, **side-effects**. **Neural:** headache, rare paresthesias or peripheral neuropathy, ataxia, seizures, aseptic meningitis; report of reversible metro-induced cerebellar lesions (*NEJM* 346:68, 2002). **Avoid alcohol during & 48 hrs after (disulfiram-like reaction).** Very dark urine (common but harmless). Skin: urticaria. Mutagenic in Ames test. Tumorigenic in animals (high dose over lifetime). No evidence of risk in man. No teratogenicity.
Mupirocin (Bactroban)	Skin cream or ointment 2%: Apply tid x10 d. ointment 2%: apply bid x5 d. 22 gm NB \$74.50, G \$42.70	Headache 1.7%, rash & nausea 1.1%
Nitrofurantoin macrocrystals (Macrodantin, Furadantin))	100 mg q6h po. Cost: 100 mg G \$1.21, NB \$2.15. **Dose for long-term UTI suppression: 50–100 mg at bedtime**	Absorption ↑ with meals. Increased activity in acid urine, much reduced at pH 8 or over. Not effective in endstage renal disease (*JAC* 33(Suppl A):121, 1994). Nausea & vomiting, hypersensitivity, peripheral neuropathy. Pulmonary reactions (with chronic rx): **acute ARDS type, chronic desquamative interstitial pneumonia with fibrosis**. Intrahepatic cholestasis & hepatitis similar to chronic active hepatitis. Hemolytic anemia in G6PD deficiency.
monohydrate/macrocrystals (Macrobid)	100 mg bid po. Cost: 100 mg \$2.26	Contraindicated in renal failure. Should not be used in infants <1 month of age. Efficacy of Macrobid 100 mg bid = Macrodantin 50 mg qid, less nausea than with Macrodantin.
Rifaximin (Xifaxan)	One 200 mg tab po tid x3 d. Cost: 200 mg \$3.66	For traveler's diarrhea. In general, adverse events equal to or less than placebo.
Sulfonamides [e.g., sulfisoxazole (Gantrisin) sulfamethoxazole (Gantanol)]	Sulfisoxazole (Gantrisin) peds suspension: Cost 500 mg/5 ml: 480 ml \$46.02	**Short-acting ones are best:** high urine concentration and good solubility at acid pH. More active in alkaline urine. **Allergic reactions**: skin rash, drug fever, pruritus, photosensitization. Periarteritis nodosa & SJE, Stevens-Johnson syndrome, serum sickness syndrome, myocarditis. Neurotoxicity (psychosis, neuritis). Hepatic toxicity. Blood dyscrasias, usually agranulocytosis. Crystalluria. Nausea & vomiting, headache, dizziness, lassitude, mental depression, acidosis, sulfhemoglobin. Hemolytic anemia in G6PD deficient & unstable hemoglobins (Hb Zurich). Do not use in newborn infants or in women near term; ↑ frequency of kernicterus (binds to albumin, blocking binding of bilirubin to albumin).
Tinidazole (Tindamax)	2 gm po x1 with food. Cost: 2 gm \$18.24	**Adverse reactions:** metallic taste 3.7%, nausea 3.2%, anorexia/vomiting 1.5%. All higher with multi-day dosing.
Trimethoprim (Trimpex), Proloprim, and others)	100 mg tab po q12h or 200 mg (2 tabs) po q24h. Cost: 100 mg NB \$0.90, G \$0.15	Frequent side-effects are rash and pruritus. Stevens-Johnson syndrome, toxic epidermal necrosis, and aseptic meningitis (*CID* 19:431, 1994). Check drug interaction with phenytoin. Increases serum K⁺ (see *TMP/SMX Comments*). TMP can ↑ homocysteine blood levels (*Ln* 352:1827, 1998).
Trimethoprim (TMP) Sulfamethoxazole (SMX) (Bactrim, Septra) Single-strength (SS) is 80 TMP/400 SMX, double- strength (DS) 160/800 TMP/800 SMX Ref.: *AnM* 163:402, 2003	**Standard dx (UTI, otitis media): 1 DS tablet bid, P. carinii: see Table 13, page 96. IV rx (base on mg TMP component): standard 8–10 mg/kg/d divided q6h, q8h, or q12h. For shigellosis: 2.5 mg/kg IV q6h.** Cost: 160/800 po G \$0.15, NB \$2; 160/800 IV \$11.21	Adverse reactions in 10% or more of pts. GI: nausea, vomiting, anorexia. Skin: Rash, urticaria, photosensitivity. Less often but more serious (1–10%), Stevens-Johnson syndrome and toxic epidermal necrosis: Skin adverse reactions may represent toxic metabolites of SMX, and ↓ glutathione (ratio) that allow it (*An J Pharm* 32:381, 1998). Daily ascorbic acid (0.5–1 gm) may promote toxic metabolite detoxification (*AIDS* 36:1041, 2004). TMP competes with creatinine for tubular secretion and serum creatinine can ↑. TMP also blocks distal renal tubule reabsorption of Na⁺ and secretion of K⁺. ↑ serum K⁺ in 21% of pts (*AnIM* 124:316, 1996). TMP/SMX suspected etiology of aseptic meningitis, esp. TMP component (*CID* 19:431, 1994). TMP/SMX contains sulfites and may trigger asthma in sulfite-sensitive pts. One of most frequent drugs to cause thrombocytopenia (*AnIM* 129:886, 1998)

Abbreviations: **G** = generic, **NB** = name brand, **MRSA** = methicillin-resistant Staph. aureus, **APAG** = antipseudomonal aminoglycoside, **NUS** = not available in the U.S.

§ Cost = average wholesale price from 2004 *DRUG TOPICS RED BOOK*, *Medical Economics*

* NOTE: all dosage recommendations are for adults (unless otherwise indicated) & assume normal renal function.

TABLE 10C
AMINOGLYCOSIDE ONCE-DAILY AND MULTIPLE DAILY DOSING REGIMENS
(See *Table 17, page 132*, if estimated creatinine clearance <90 ml/min.)

General: Dosage given as both once-daily (OD) and multiple daily dose (MDD) regimens.
Pertinent formulae: (1) Estimated creatinine clearance (CrCl): $\frac{[140-age](ideal\ body\ weight\ in\ kg)}{(72)(serum\ creatinine)}$ = CrCl for men in ml/min; multiply answer x 0.85 for CrCl of women

(2) Ideal body weight (IBW)—Females: 45.5 kg + 2.3 kg per inch over 5' = weight in kg
Males: 50.0 kg + 2.3 kg per inch over 5' = weight in kg

(3) Obesity adjustment: use if actual body weight (ABW) is ≥30% above IBW. To calculate adjusted dosing weight in kg: IBW + 0.4(ABW–IBW) = adjusted weight in kg

DRUG	MDD AND OD IV REGIMENS/ TARGETED PEAK (P) AND TROUGH (T) SERUM LEVELS	COST§ Name Brand (NB), Generic (G)	COMMENTS For more data on once-daily dosing, see *AJM 105:182, 1998, and Table 17, page 132*
Gentamicin (Garamycin), **Tobramycin** (Nebcin)	MDD: 2 mg/kg load, then 1.7 mg/kg q8h P 4–10 µg/ml, T 1–2 µg/ml OD: 5.1 (7 if critically ill) mg/kg q24h P 16–24 µg/ml, T <1 µg/ml	Gentamicin: 80 mg $5.75 Tobramycin: 80 mg NB $7.28, G $11.96	**All aminoglycosides have potential to cause tubular necrosis and renal failure, deafness due to cochlear toxicity, vertigo due to damage to vestibular organs, and rarely neuromuscular blockade.** Risk minimal with oral or topical application due to small % absorption unless tissues altered by disease.
Kanamycin (Kantrex), **Amikacin** (Amikin), Streptomycin	MDD: 7.5 mg/kg q12h P 15–30 µg/ml, T 5–10 µg/ml OD: 15 mg/kg q24h P 56–64 µg/ml, T <1 µg/ml	Kanamycin: 1.0 gm $6.92 Amikacin: 500 mg NB $34.26, G $7.80 Streptomycin: 1.0 gm $9.75	Risk of nephrotoxicity ↑ with concomitant administration of cyclosporine, vancomycin, ampho B, radiocontrast. Risk of nephrotoxicity ↓ by concomitant AP Pen and perhaps by once-daily dosing method (especially if baseline renal function normal).
Netilmicin[AUS]	MDD: 2.0 mg/kg q8h P 4–10 µg/ml, T 1–2 µg/ml OD: 6.5 mg/kg q24h P 22–30 µg/ml, T <1 µg/ml		In general, same factors influence risk of ototoxicity. **NOTE: There is no known method to eliminate risk of aminoglycoside nephro/ototoxicity. Proper rx attempts to ↓ the % risk.** The clinical trial data of OD aminoglycosides have been reviewed and analyzed extensively (*CID 24:816, 1997*). Serum levels: Collect blood for a peak serum level (PSL) exactly 1 hr after the start of the infusion of the 3rd dose. In critically ill pts, it is reasonable to measure the PSL after the 1st dose as well as later doses as volume of distribution and renal function may change rapidly. Other dosing methods and references: For once-daily 7 mg/kg/d of gentamicin—Hartford Hospital method, see *AAC 39:650, 1995*.
Isepamicin[AUS]	Only OD: Severe infections 15 mg/kg q24h, less severe 8 mg/kg q24h		
Spectinomycin (Trobicin)	2.0 gm IM x1—gonococcal infections	2 gm NB $29.76	
Neomycin—oral	Prophylaxis GI surgery: 1.0 gm po x3 with erythro, see *Table 15B, page 124* For hepatic coma: 4–12 gm/d po	500 mg $1.24	

Tobramycin—inhaled (Tobi): See *Cystic fibrosis, Table 1, page 29.* Adverse effects few: transient voice alteration (13%) and transient tinnitus (3%). Cost: 300 mg $54.46

Paromomycin—oral: See *Entamoeba and Cryptosporidia, Table 13, page 93.* Cost: 250 mg $1.90

---

[1] Estimated CrCl invalid if serum creatinine <0.6 mg/dl. Consultation suggested.
§ Cost = average wholesale price from *2004 Drug Topics Red Book, Medical Economics*.

TABLE 11A: TREATMENT OF FUNGAL, ACTINOMYCOTIC, AND NOCARDIAL INFECTIONS—ANTIMICROBIAL AGENTS OF CHOICE*
(See Table 11B for Amphotericin B Preparations and Adverse Effects)

TYPE OF INFECTION/ORGANISM/ SITE OF INFECTION	ANTIMICROBIAL AGENTS OF CHOICE		COMMENTS
	PRIMARY	**ALTERNATIVE**	
Actinomycosis (CID 26:1255, 1998) (A. israelii most common, also A. naeslundii, A. viscosus, A. odontolyticus, A. meyeri, A. gerencseriae) Cervicofacial, pulmonary, abdominal, cerebral & rarely pericarditis (ID Clin Pract 12:233, 2004)	**Ampicillin** 50 mg/kg/d IV x 4-6 wks, then 0.5 gm **amoxicillin** tid po **OR Penicillin G** 10-20 million u/d IV x 4-6 wks, then **penicillin V** 2-4 gm/d po. Duration can likely be individualized, e.g. with uncomplicated cervicofacial, only 3 mos with surgery; total duration of high-dose IV & po with po usually adequate for thoracic & abdominal & 3-6 wks for cervicofacial (AJ to 2004)	**Doxycycline** or **ceftriaxone** or **clindamycin** or **erythromycin** 12.5-15 mg/kg IV/po q8h has been used for CNS infection in pen-allergic pts	Tuboovarian abscesses may complicate IUDs. Removal of IUD is primary rx. With abscesses or fistulas, surgery often required. While penicillin G and ampicillin IV have been effective in some, other agents may allow rx to be individualized, are more practical (CID 19:161, 1994). **Surgery may be necessary for hemoptysis** (An Thor Surg 74:185, 2002).
Aspergillosis (A. fumigatus most common, also A. flavus and others) (CID 30:696, 2000)			
Allergic bronchopulmonary aspergillosis (ABPA) ABPA found in 1-2% of pts with asthma & 1-15% with cystic fibrosis (CID 37:S225, 2003). Marked by episodic obstruction (asthma), fever, malaise, expectoration of brownish mucus plugs, transient pulmonary infiltrates, bronchiectasis. Airway colonization assoc. with ↑ blood eosinophils, ↑ serum IgE & specific serum IgE & IgG antibodies.	Rx controversial: systemic corticosteroids + surgical debridement (80% respond but 2/3 relapse) **Corticosteroids**	Rx of ABPA: **itracona-zole** 200 mg po qd x16 wks or longer	In 2 PRCTs, ↓↑, itra ↓ number of exacerbations requiring corticosteroids (p <0.05), ↓ IgE levels, improvement of immunological markers (eosinophils in sputum) & ↓ serum IgE levels in 1 study improved lung function & exercise tolerance (NEJM 342:756, 2000; Cochrane Database Syst Rev 3:CD001108, 2004). Itra improved 21 cystic fibrosis pts with ABPA (Allergy 57:723, 2002). [For rx of ABPA in CF see CID 37(Suppl 3): 225, 2003].
Allergic fungal sinusitis: relapsing chronic sinusitis, nasal polyps without bony invasion; asthma, eczema or allergic rhinitis; ↑ IgE levels and isolation of Aspergillus sp. or other fungi. Assoc. with dematiaceous sp. (Alternaria, Cladosporium, etc.)	For failures might try **itra** 200 mg po bid x12 mos. (CID 37:S203, 2000)		In 1 report, fungal elements identified by histopathology in up to 93% of cases of "chronic sinusitis" & in a randomized double-blind placebo-controlled trial in 24 pts, intranasal ampho was assoc. with a ↓ in mucosal thickening (8.8% by CT scan vs ↑ of 2.5% in placebo. Nasal inflammation score ↓ by 70% vs placebo (JAID 4:257, 2004). Controversial area, need more data.
Aspergilloma (fungus ball) (J Resp Dis 23:300, 2002)	Efficacy of antimicrobial agents not proven. Itraconazole has been reported (in small series) to have responded to itra 200 mg/d x3 mos. (JAMA Derm 23:607, 1990). Another case responded to itra 200 mg/d x3 mos.		**Surgery if hemoptysis becomes massive** (post-op complications 25%)
Invasive, pulmonary (IPA) or extrapulmonary*[2] (CID 31:1155, 2000) Occurs post-transplantation and post-chemotherapy in neutropenic pts (PMN <500/mm³). Appears particularly common in lung transplant recipients with graft vs host disease (CID 35:659, 2002). Usually a late (≥100 days) complication in allogeneic bone marrow & liver transplantation; median survival 36 days, but **overall mortality rates vary, 78-84%** (LnID 2:479, 2003).

Typical chest/CT lung lesions (halo sign, cavitation, or mycotic lung abscesses) have 90% positive predictive value for invasive aspergillosis in pts with hematologic malignancies (CID 31:859, 2000).

The platelia aspergillus sandwich ELISA test that detects circulating galactomannan has been very useful to diagnose invasive aspergillosis. The test has a high specificity (85%) but variable sensitivity (30-100%) (see LnID 4:349, 2004). Detection at an early stage of the disease makes prospective monitoring of high risk for oral **vori** after 2-3 wks.
(continued on next page) | **Voriconazole** 6 mg/kg IV q12h on day 1; then either (4 mg/kg IV q12h) or (200 mg po q12h for body weight ≥40 kg, but 100 mg po q12h for body weight <40 kg) **OR**
Lipid-based ampho B may be as effective and less nephrotoxic than standard ampho B **but much more expensive** (see footnote page 75 for dosages). Some authorities now prefer lipid-based ampho B over standard ampho B as initial rx (CID 32: 415, 2000). **OR**
Ampho B (see footnote[4] page 74); Rapid increase by ↑ dose (1-1.25 mg/kg maximum total dose of 2-2.5 gm; iv & voripenic) ad IV infusion (see footnote[4]) is 0.1-1.5 mg/kg (IV in above dosages)[3] **Combination rx: Vori** (in above dosages) + **caspo** (dosage below) are currently preferred in many bone marrow transplant units, esp. in pts receiving high doses of corticosteroids.

Alternative: Caspofungin 70 mg IV on day 1, then 50 mg IV qd (reduce to 35 mg/d with moderate hepatic insufficiency). For all stages of Aspergillus rx, see Table 11B, page 83). | **Voriconazole** more effective than ampho B in one large randomized trial of 277 immunosuppressed pts: survival 71% with vori vs 58% with ampho (better 12-wk: 71%/58%) (NEJM 347:408, 2002). Overall survival better (70.8%/57.9%) (CID 39:192, 2004). Use vori as primary rx for invasive & advantageous in cerebral aspergillosis (Eur J Haematol 83(Suppl 1):542, 2004) & as salvage in those with refractory infection (Eur J Haematol 73:50, 2004; PJD 23:584, 2004). However, 12/139 when not successfully treated breakthrough fungal infections (6 zygomyces) with more resistant (MIC >1 μg/ml to vori (LnID 4:257, 2004).

Ampho B: overall success rate 34-42% (CID 26:781, 1998; 32:358, 2001) in pulmonary aspergillosis in those pts rx ≥14 days. Success dependent on underlying disease: 83% heart/kidney transplants, 54% neutropenic leukemia pts, 33% bone marrow transplant, 20% liver transplant (CID 23: 608, 1996). **A. terreus infections particularly resistant to ampho B** (AAC 48:373, 2004) in 83 cases, **73.4% mortality with ampho B** (CID 39:192, 2004). **Use vori** in those receiving >7 days of caspofungin as salvage rx (CAAC 2002, Abst. M-856). 42% with hematological malignancies had favorable response but 45% but was 56% in those receiving >7 days of caspofungin as salvage rx (CAAC 2002, Abst. M-856). Minimal toxicity reported (Transpl Inf Dis 1:25, 1999). 4% with allogeneic stem cell transplants. Minimal toxicity reported (Transpl Inf Dis 1:25, 1999). **Combination antifungal rx** (CID 38:1445, 2003). While new drugs may ↑ response & survival, IPA remains one of the most refractory fungal infections. This has led clinicians to combination rx albeit to date **no controlled clinical trials have been reported to support this approach.** Antagonism between the 3 classes of drugs (azoles, ampho, & echinocandins) (ind. lipid-based) + caspo (AAC 46:245, 2002) is demonstrated in vitro & in neutropenic animal models (AAC 46:2564, 2002; JID 187:1834, 2003). Case reports & small uncontrolled series reported in pts who (continued on next page) |

---

[1] Oral solution preferred to tablets because of ↑ absorption (see Table 11B, page 83).
[2] **PRCTs** = Prospective randomized controlled trials
See page 81 for abbreviations. All dosage recommendations are for adults (unless otherwise indicated) and assume normal renal function

TABLE 11A (2)

TYPE OF INFECTION/ORGANISM/ SITE OF INFECTION	ANTIMICROBIAL AGENTS OF CHOICE		COMMENTS
	PRIMARY	ALTERNATIVE	
Aspergillosis/Invasive, pulmonary (IPA) or extrapulmonary: (continued)	(See previous page)	*(continued from previous page)*	*(continued from previous page)* have failed conventional ampho B rx: >100 pts have either had caspo added to ampho B-based rx or caspo substituted for ampho B rx with an overall response rate of approx. 50% (Clin Inf Dis 97:1025, 2003; AnHematol 83:390, 2004). In a retrospective series of bone marrow transplant pts who failed short-course ampho B, caspo was superior to vori alone (CID 39:797, 2004). Randomized trials needed (CID 39:903, 2004). Toxicity of the vori & caspo is low, high cost is the major obstacle to combination rx. Unfortunately, already variants of A. fumigatus isolated from 7 stem cell transplant pts who received itra showed ↓ susceptibility to itra, vori, caspo, & vort ampho (AAC 48:1197, 2004).
(continued from previous page) (A attractive (IJID 190:441, 2004; CID 39:199, 2004). **False-pos. tests consistently found in serum from pts receiving PIP/TZ** (CID 38:913 & 917, 2004; NEJM 349:24, 2003). Test not available at Miravista, 1-866-647-2847.			
Blastomycosis (CID 30:679, 2000) (Blastomyces dermatitidis) Cutaneous, pulmonary or extrapulmonary	**Itraconazole** oral solution 200–400 mg/d po for 6 mos. **OR Ampho B[3]** 0.7–1 mg/kg/d to a total dose of ≥1.5 gm for very sick pts	**Itraconazole** 200–400 mg/d for at least 6 mos. 85% effective in non life-threatening disease (CID 25:200, 1997).	**Itra:** in patients treated for ≥2 months, 95% cure (AJM 93: 489, 1992). Itra successful in >90% when ≥1.5 gm total dose used (CID 22:S102, 1996). For blood/urine antigen, call 1-866-647-2847.

Candidiasis: A decrease in C. albicans and increase in non-albicans species show ↓ susceptibility to antifungal agents (esp. fluconazole). These changes have predominantly affected immuno-compromised pts in environments where antifungal prophylaxis is widely used [JAC 49 (Suppl 1):3, 2002; PIDJ 23:635 & 687, 2004]. In vitro susceptibility testing for antifungal drugs to date has not undergone rigorous in vivo validation studies, and clinical outcomes are more dependent on host factors (Am J Med 112:380, 2002). Yet it seems prudent to use susceptibility profiles to help select empiric antifungal therapy. The table summarizes current published reports of frequency of candida isolates, and interpretation as to whether a drug is likely to be clinically effective (**S = susceptible**), may require dose escalation), or is likely to be ineffective (**R = resistant**) (Ln 359:1135, 2002). **S-I = less active in vitro but clinically effective**, only rare failures reported (IDSA Guidelines, 2004; CID 38:161, 2004). In vitro testing for caspo not standardized.

	% of Candida Isolates	Risk Factors	% Sensitive In Vitro					Rx if species known
			Fluconazole	Itraconazole	Voriconazole	Ampho B	Caspofungin	
C. albicans	41–65	HIV/AIDS, surgery	97% (S)	93% (S-D)	99% (S)	>95% (S)	(S)	Flu,++ caspo, ampho B, or vori
C. glabrata	10–15	Heme malignancies, azole prophylaxis	85–90% (S)	50% (S-D)	92% (S)	>95% (S-I)	(S-I)	Flu, caspo, or ampho B
C. parapsilosis	15–24	Azole prophylaxis, neonates, foreign bodies	99% (S)	4% (R)	99% (S)	>95% (S-I)	(S-I)	Flu, caspo, or ampho B
C. tropicalis	5–10	Neutropenia	98% (S)	58% (S-D)	99% (S)	>95% (S)	(S)	Flu, caspo, ampho B
C. krusei	2–10	Heme malignancies, azole prophylaxis	5% (R)	69% (R)	>95% (R)	>95% (S-I)	(S)	Caspo, ampho B, or vori
C. guilliermondi	1	Azole prophylaxis, previous ampho rx	>95% (S)	?	>95% (S)	?	(R)	Flu, caspo, or vori
C. lusitaniae	1	Previous ampho rx	>95% (S)	?	>95% (S)	(R)	(S)	Flu, caspo, or vori

++ If patient had prior heavy basal exposure, use ampho B or caspo (IDSA Guidelines, 2004; CID 38:161, 2004)

Bloodstream: clinically stable with or without venous catheter (IDSA Guidelines, 2002; 36:1497, 2003)

- **All positive blood cultures require therapy!**
  - **Fluconazole** ≥6 mg/kg/d IV or 400 mg/d IV or po[4] (I dunno?) followed by 50 mg IV or po for 14 d after last + blood culture **OR Caspofungin** 70 mg IV on day 1 followed by 50 mg/d IV maintenance rx. Would use in place of flu in those heavily pretreated with azoles, i.e. flu or itra prophylaxis) **OR Ampho B** 0.6 mg/kg/d IV, total dose 5–7 mg/kg IV for candidemia | In pts who fail to respond or deteriorate, higher doses of either drug may be used (**ampho B** 0.8–1 mg/kg/d or **fluconazole** 800 mg/d IV or po) (CID 25:43, 1997). **Be sure catheter is removed.** | **Voriconazole^MRA-1, loading dose 6 mg/kg q12h x1 d, IV, then maintenance dose 3 mg/kg q12h IV** for serious candidal infections.
- Remove & replace venous catheter ("not over a wire")[1] if possible (CID 34:591 & 600, 2002; 36:1221, 2003) esp. in non-neutropenic; mortality 21% vs 41% in randomized for all pts with candidemia. Ophthalmologic exam recommended for all pts with candidemia.
- Treat for 2 wks after last last pos. blood culture and resolution of infection.

Observational studies suggest flu & ampho B are similarly effective in neutropenic pts (IDSA Guidelines, 2003). A randomized study (277 pts, 10% were neutropenic) found caspofungin equivalent to ampho B (0.6–1 mg/kg/d) for invasive candidiasis. For candidemia 71.7% vs caspo vs 62.8% with ampho B had favorable outcomes but caspo had significantly less toxicity (NEJM 347:2020, 2002).

---

1 **Dosages: ABLC** 5 mg/kg/d IV over 2 hrs. **Ampho B cholesteryl complex** 3–4 mg/kg/d IV given via 1 mg/kg/hr. **liposomal Ampho B** 3–5 mg/kg/d IV given over 1–2 hrs.

2 Hydration before and after infusion with 500 ml saline has been shown to reduce renal toxicity.

3 ABLC or liposomal ampho B preferred over ampho B because of ↓ nephrotoxicity (see Table 11B, page 83).

4 From 2004 Drug Topics Red Book, Medical Economics Data and Hospital Formulary Pricing Guide. **Price is average wholesale price (AWP).**

* See page 81 for abbreviations. All dosage recommendations are for adults (unless otherwise indicated) and assume normal renal function.

TABLE 11A (3)

TYPE OF INFECTION/ORGANISM/ SITE OF INFECTION	ANTIMICROBIAL AGENTS OF CHOICE		COMMENTS
	PRIMARY	ALTERNATIVE	
Candidiasis (continued) **Bloodstream: unstable, deteriorating ± neutropenia OR stable disseminated (pulmonary, eye, hepatosplenic)** (IDSA Guidelines: CID 38:161, 2004) For endophthalmitis, see below	**Ampho B** 0.8–1 mg/kg IV ± 5FC 37.5¹ mg/kg po q6h or **lipid-based ampho B** (ABLC) 5 mg/kg/d IV **OR Fluconazole** 400–800 mg (or >6 mg/kg mg po qd IV x1d, after last positive blood culture/resolution of neutropenia & disappearance of signs/ symptoms of candidal infection **OR Combination of fluconazole** 800 mg/d + **ampho B** 0.7 mg/kg/d for first 5–6 days, then switch to flu 400 mg/d po	**Voriconazole** loading dose 6 mg/kg q12h x1 d IV, then maintenance dose 3 mg/kg q12h IV for serious candida infections Cap 50 mg/10 mg on day 1 followed by 50 mg/d IV (reduction of hepatic insufficiency with moderate hepatic insufficiency)	In a randomized trial of 219 pts with non-neutropenic candidemia, fluconazole (800 mg/d) + ampho B (0.7 mg/kg/d for the 1ˢᵗ 5 days) was slightly better than flu alone: Primary analysis, overall success rate 69% vs 56% (p = .08) respectively. Excluded were 9% vs 65% (p = .045) and clearance of candida 94% vs 85% (p = .02). The flu alone group were slightly sicker (APACHE 15.0 vs 16.8, p = .039) and with toxicity in combination greater (23% vs 3%, p <.001) (CID 36:1221, 2003). Given difficulty with interpretation of this study, the editors would reserve combination of flu + ampho B for only the sickest candidemic patient. (Eur Con Clin Micro & Inf Dis 2002, Abst. 237; IDSA 2002, Abst. 352.)
Chronic mucocutaneous	**Ketoconazole** 400 mg/d po (as single daily dose with food) for 3–9 months	Usually children: Peds dose of **fluconazole** 3–6 mg/kg/d as single daily dose	Respond to ampho B but relapse is usual. Fluconazole used and may be less toxic but experience limited.
Cutaneous (including paronychia, Table 1, page 18)	Apply topical **ampho B, clotrimazole, econazole, miconazole,** or **nystatin** 3–4x daily for 7–14 days or **ketoconazole** 400 mg po once daily x1d. **Ciclopirox olamine** 1% cream/lotion. Apply topically bid x7–14 d.		Cost (30 gm tube cream): AB $29, Clo $13, Eco $19, MIC $21, Nys $6, Keto $31. Clo: $16.20.
Endocarditis (IDSA Guidelines: CID 38:161, 2004) Causes: C. albicans 24%, non-albicans Candida sp. 24%, Aspergillus sp. 24%, others 27% (CID 32:50, 2001)	(**Ampho B** 0.6–1 mg/kg/d IV + **lipid-based ampho B** 3–5 mg/kg/d. Continue 6–8 weeks after surgery) **+ flucytosine** 25–37.5 mg/kg po qid) + surgical resection	**Caspofungin** 50 mg/d (70 mg load x1) or **voriconazole** 4 mg/kg q12h IV or po used when valve cannot be replaced (Chest 122:302, 2002) **+ Surgical resection**	**Adjust flucyt dose and interval to produce serum levels: peak 70–80 mg/L, trough 30–40 mg/L** With nephrotoxicity, dosage of flucyt needs to be ↓. Surgery may not always be required (CID 22:262, 1996; Scand J Inf Dis 32:86, 2000). Caspofungin ocidal vs candida & may be of value: no data. Candida endocarditis has propensity to relapse; requires careful follow-up for at least a year (Chest 99:1531, 1991).
Endophthalmitis (IDSA Guidelines: CID 38:161, 2004) Occurs in 10% of candidemia (PIDJ 23:635, 2004), thus ophthalmologic consult for all pts Diagnosis: typical white exudates on retinal exam and/or isolation from vitrectomy	[**Ampho B** or **lipid-based ampho B** (ABLC 4.5 mg/kg/d] **OR fluconazole** 400 mg/d IV or po either as initial rx or follow-up after ampho B. Role of intravitreal ampho B not well defined but commonly used in pts with substantial vision loss (CID 27:1130, 1998). Treat x6–12 weeks.		Treatment results mixed in several small series: Fluconazole (CID 20:657, 1995), ABLC (J Inf 40:92, 2000), and vitrectomy (CID 27:1130, 1998)
Oral (thrush) not AIDS patient (See below for vaginitis)	**Fluconazole** 200 mg single dose or 100 mg/d x14 days or **Itraconazole** oral solution 200 mg (20 ml) qd without food x7 days.	**Nystatin pastilles** (200,000 u) lozenge qid, **Nystatin** (500,000 u (swish & swallow) qid or 2 (500,000 u) tabs tid for 14 d. **OR Clotrimazole** 1 troche (10 mg) 5x/d x1-d.	Maintenance not required in non-AIDS pts. Usually improves in 3–4 days, longer if ↓ relapse. Fluconazole-resistant C. krusei fungemia reported in flucon-rx pts (NEJM 325:1315, 1991).

serum Cr (to > 2.5 mg/dl for adults or 1.5 mg/dl for children) or severe acute administration-related toxicity (CID 26:1383, 1998). Since efficacy similar and toxicity less, some now recommend lipid-based preps in place of ampho B as initial rx. (CID 32:415, 2003).
¹ Some experts reduce dose of 5FC to 25 mg/kg q6h
* From 2004 Drug Topics Red Book, Medical Economics Data and Hospital Formulary Pricing Guide. **Price is average wholesale price (AWP).**
See page 81 for abbreviations. All dosage recommendations are for adults (unless otherwise indicated) and assume normal renal function

TABLE 11A (4)

TYPE OF INFECTION/ORGANISM/ SITE OF INFECTION	ANTIMICROBIAL AGENTS OF CHOICE		COMMENTS
	PRIMARY	**ALTERNATIVE**	

Candidiasis/Oral (thrush) *(continued)*

AIDS patient **Stomatitis, esophagitis, vaginitis** Oral colonization with candida correlates with HIV RNA levels in plasma, less so with CD4 counts (*JID 180:534, 1999*). Protease inhibitors appear to ↓ recurrent oral candidiasis themselves vs rx with other antiretroviral agents (*AIDS 13:1147; AIDS 21:20, 1999*). May be due to direct effect on candida aspartic protease (*J AIDS 22:106, 1999*).	**Fluconazole** 200 mg po 1st day then 100 mg qd x14 d. [21 d. or 2 wks following resolution of symptoms for esophagitis] or **Itraconazole** oral solution 200 mg po qd or 100 mg po bid x14 d. Some recommend oral topical agents¹ for oral withhold esophageal involvement with CD4 > 50 & receiving (or will receive) HAART.	**For fluconazole-refractory disease:** Options include: 1. **Fluconazole** 400–800 mg po qd or 2. **Itraconazole** solution 100 mg po bid or 3. **Ampho B** 0.3–0.5 mg/kg IV qd or 4. **Ampho B oral suspension** (see Table 11B, page 83 for dose) or 5. **Caspofungin** 50 mg IV qd	**Fluconazole-refractory disease remains low** (4% in ACTG 816). Risk is with low CD4 counts (<50). **Flu** superior to oral suspension of **nystatin** (*CID 24:1204, 1997*). **Itra** 100 mg po bid x14 d. achieved clinical response in 11/14 (55%) pts unresponsive to flu (*AIDS Res Hum Retrovir 15:1413, 1999*). **Ampho B oral suspension** gave 42.6% response rate in 54 pts refractory to flu, but 70% of those relapsed (*AIDS 14:845, 2000*). For esophagitis, **caspofungin** as effective as **fluconazole** for esophagitis (*CID 33:1529, 2001; AAC 46:451, 2002; J AIDS 31:183, 2002*). **Voriconazole,** **anidulafungin & micafungin** as effective as fluconazole for esophagitis (*CID 33:1447, 2001; CID 39:770 & 842, 2004*).
Post-treatment chronic suppression (secondary prophylaxis) for recurrent oral, esophageal infection	**Current recommendation is to avoid chronic suppressive rx** & only rx acute episode (*AIDS Res Hum Retroviruses 10:1619, 1999*). However, some use **fluconazole** 100 mg to 100–150 mg po q week.		**Fluconazole** 200 mg qd does reduce risk of candida esophagitis & cryptococcosis (*NEJM 332:700, 1995*). Disadvantages: Concern of enhanced risk of emergence of fluconazole (azole)-resistant Candida species.
Peritonitis (Chronic Ambulatory Peritoneal Dialysis) *See Table 19, page 137*	**Ampho B** 400 mg po qd x2–3 wks	**Ampho B**, continuous IP dosing at 1.5 mg/L of dialysis fluid x4–6 weeks	Remove cath immediately & rx no clinical improvement in 4–7 d.
Urinary. Candiduria • Usually colonization of urinary catheter, a foreign body. • Rarely may be source of dissemination if pt has obstructive uropathy or marker of acute hematogenous dissemination Persistent candiduria in immunocompromised pt warrants ultrasound or CT of kidneys	**Remove urinary catheter or stent:** 40% will clear (may ↑ replaced (*CID 30:14, 2000*) Antifungal rx not indicated unless pt has symptoms of UTI, neutropenia, low-birthweight infant, renal allograft or is undergoing urologic manipulation. Then, **fluconazole** 200 mg po or IV x7–14 d. OR **ampho B** 0.5 mg/kg IV x7–14 d.	**Ampho B,** continuous IP dosing at 1.5 mg/L of dialysis fluid x4–6 weeks. In a placebo-controlled trial, candiduria was cleared rapidly in pts treated with **fluconazole** 200 mg x14 d. or placebo (*CID 30:19, 2000*). Yes day after antifungal rx, 50% of flu group, 60% of placebo group (*CID 30:15, 2000*). **Bladder washout** with ampho B not recommended; will not treat upper tract infection. 5FC may be of value in non-albicans UTI but resistance develops rapidly in 12 pts (most with candidemia) but urine levels low (*IDSA 2003, Abst. 135*). **NOTE:** 5FC not in urine in active form.	
Vaginitis—Non-AIDS patients. Review article: *MMWR 51(RR-6), 2002.* (Candida vaginitis see Stomatitis, vaginitis above). *(See Table 1, page 17)*			
Sporadic/infrequent	**Fluconazole** 150 mg po x1 OR **Itraconazole** 200 mg po bid x1 d.	**Intravaginal:** Multiple imidazoles with 85–95% cure rates. See doses in footnote² ** for over-the-counter preparations, see footnote**	**In general, oral & vaginal rx are similarly effective.** Rx aided by avoiding tight clothing, e.g., pantyhose. Oral drugs ↓ rectal candida & may ↓ relapses. Fluconazole resistance in both HIV+ & HIV-neg pts (*CID 22:726, 1996*). Incidence of flu-refractory disease remains low (*CID 26:557, 1998*). Boric acid solution intravaginally has also been used (*CID 26:1240, 1999*).
Chronic recurrent (5–8%) ≥4 episodes/yr Ref.: *NEJM 351:876, 2004*	**Fluconazole** 150 mg po x3 & then 150 mg po q wk		After 6 mos.: >90% of 170 women free of disease vs 36% of 173 receiving fluconazole maintenance. By 6 mos. off rx, 42.9% free of disease vs 21.9% who received placebo (*p <0.001*).

---

¹ **Oral agents:** Nystatin, clotrimazole troche 10 mg 5v/d.

² **Butaconazole** 2% cream (5 gm) qd hs x3 d** or **clotrimazole** 100 mg vaginal tabs (2 qd hs x3 d. or 1% cream (5 gm) qd hs x7 d** or **miconazole** 200 mg vaginal supp qd hs x3 d. or 100 mg vaginal tab qd hs x7 d** or 100 mg vaginal tab (1 qd hs x7 d. or 0.4% cream (5 gm) qd hs x7 d** or **terconazole** 80 mg vaginal supp qd hs x3 d. or **tioconazole** 6.5% intravaginal oint x1 d. or **tioconazole** 2% cream (5 gm) qd hs x7 d** or 0.8% cream 5 gm intravaginal qd hs x3 d. 100 mg vaginal tab qd hs x7 d. x3 d.

* From 2004 Drug Topics Red Book, Medical Economics Data and Hospital Formulary Pricing Guide. **Price is average wholesale price (AWP).**

** for over-the-counter product

TABLE 11A (5)

TYPE OF INFECTION/ORGANISM/ SITE OF INFECTION	ANTIMICROBIAL AGENTS OF CHOICE		COMMENTS
	PRIMARY	ALTERNATIVE	
"Candida syndrome"	In a double-blind study, nystatin did not reduce systemic or psychological symptoms vs placebo (NEJM 323:1717, 1990)		
Chromomycosis (J Am Acad Derm 44:585, 2001) (Cladosporium or Fonsecaea). Cutaneous (usually feet, legs)	If lesions small and few, surgical excision or **cryosurgery with liquid nitrogen** (Int J Dermatol 42:408, 2003). If lesions extensive, burrowing, treatment disappointing		In a double-blind study, 2 relapses (18, 24 mos.) (CID 5:553, 1988). Itraconazole effective in a small number of pts (Eur J Clin Pharm Ther 5:247, 2004). In 4 pts resistance to itra developed on rx with 2 clinical failures (Mycosis 47:216, 2004)
Coccidioidomycosis (Coccidioides immitis) (see AnIM 130:293, 1999; DCP 9:21, 1999; CID 30:658, 2000; IDCP N.A. 17:41, 2003; NEJM 83:149, 2004)			
Primary infection (San Joaquin or Valley Fever): Pts low risk persistence/complication	Antifungal rx not generally recommended but pt should experience periodically and if fever, wt loss and/or fatigue do not resolve within several wks to 2 months (see below)		Uncomplicated pulmonary in normal host. Influenza-like illness of 1– 2 wks duration.
Primary pulmonary in pts with ↑ risk for complications or disseminated: Rx indicated	**Mild to moderate severity:** Itraconazole solution 200 mg po or IV bid OR Fluconazole 400 mg po q24 hr		**Relapse rate 50–70%. Responses to azoles are similar** Itra may have slight advantage esp. in soft tissue infection. Relapse rates after rx 40%. Relapse rate ↑ if ↑ CF titer ≥1:256 (RR=4.7) or neg. coccidioidin skin test (RR=4.8) (CID 25:1205, 1997). Following administration of rx important, rising titers warrant re-administration of rx (CID 25:1211, 1997). In an RDBS* of 198 pts
• Immunosuppressive Rx (steroids, TNF-α antagonists) therapies (steroids, TNF-α antagonists) • Pregnancy in 3rd trimester. • Diabetes • ↑ F antibody >1:16 • Risk pulmonary infiltrates • Dissemination (identification of spherules or culture of organism from ulcer, joint effusion, pus from abscess or bone bx, etc.)	**Locally severe or disseminated disease:** **Ampho B** 0.6–1 mg/kg/d×7 d, then 0.8 mg/kg/qod. Total dose 2.5 gm or more, followed by **itra** or **flu** **Consultation with specialist recommended:** surgery may be required		with progressive non-meningeal cocci, 57% responded to flu vs 72% to itra (p=0.05). (AnIM 133:676, 2000). Those with skeletal infections responded twice as frequently to itra than flu. Relapse after dc rx: 28% after flu, 18% after itra. Lifetime suppression in HIV+ patients: flu 200 mg qd or itra 200 mg bid (Mycosis 46:42, 2003). Targeted fluconazole prophy-laxis for pt with hx of cocci or sero+cos. may reduce reactivation post-transplant (Transpl Inf Dis 5:3, 2003). Caspofungin also used in a renal transplant pt (CID 39:879, 2004).
Meningitis: occurs in 1/3 to 1/2 of pts with disseminated coccidioidomycosis			
Adult	**Fluconazole** 400–800 mg qd po indefinitely	**Ampho B** IV as for pulmonary (above) & intrathecal daily intra-ventricular/intrathecal via reservoir device. **OR itra** 400–800 mg po qd **OR voriconazole** (see Comment) **OR caspo** (see Comment)	80% relapse rate, continue flucon indefinitely (AnIM 124: 305, 1996). Voriconazole successful in high doses (6 mg/kg q12h IV) followed by oral suppression (400 mg q12h po) (CID 36:1619, 2003). In a pt with relapsed flu: intrathecal ampho B (AJC 54:292, 2004)
Child	**Fluconazole** (po) (Pediatric dose not estab-lished, 6 mg/kg qd used)		
Cryptococcosis (CID 30:710, 2000)			
Non-meningeal (non-AIDS) Immunocompetent or organ transplant (Transpl Inf Dis 4:183, 2002)	**Fluconazole** 400 mg/d IV or po for 8 wks to 6 mos For more severe disease: **Ampho B** 0.5–0.8 mg/kg/d IV till response then change to **fluconazole** 400 mg po for 8–10 wk course	**Itraconazole** 200–400 mg solution qd for 6–12 mos OR **Ampho B** 0.3 mg/kg/d IV + **flucyto-sine** 37.5 mg/kg qid po x6 wks.	Adjust flucyt dose & interval to produce serum levels of peak 70–80 mg/L, trough 30–40 mg/L. **Flucon alone 90% effective for meningeal and non-meningeal forms** (74% on steroid Rx). Studies suggest fluconazole as effective as ampho B (CID 22:S154, 1996; CID 36:E145, 2003). Addition of voriconazole (NEJM HB 50 mg/kg/d×6 wks) to liposomal ampho B associated with response in pt failing antifungal rx (CID 38: 910, 2004).
Meningitis (non-AIDS)	**Ampho B** 0.7–0.8 mg/kg/d IV + **flucytosine** 37.5 mg/kg qid po until pt afebrile and cultures negative (~6 weeks) (NEJM 301:126, 1979), then stop ampho B/flucyt, start **fluconazole** 200 mg po qd x8–10 wks (less severely ill patient). Some recommend **Fluconazole** 200 mg po qd po×8–10 wks to reduce relapse rate (no controlled data available) (CID 28:297, 1999).		**Flucytosine levels must be measured:** adjust dose and interval to give serum levels: peak 70–80 mg/L, trough 30–40 mg/L. **Fluconazole alone used successfully,** comparative clinical trials lacking (NEJM 326:83, 1992). Hydrocephalus develops in 9% pts and may require VP shunt, ↑ VP shunting with 1P shunting (CID 28:629, 1999), poor response (6 pts in coma) (CID 37:673, 2003).

[1] Same experts would reduce to 25 mg/kg q6h
[2] Intraventricular injection of AB, VA = ventricular
* From 2004 Drug Topics Red Book, Medical Economics Data and Hospital Formulary Pricing Guide. **Price is average wholesale price (AWP).**
See page 81 for abbreviations. All dosage recommendations are for adults (unless otherwise indicated) and assume normal renal function

TABLE 11A (6)

TYPE OF INFECTION/ORGANISM/ SITE OF INFECTION	ANTIMICROBIAL AGENTS OF CHOICE		COMMENTS
	PRIMARY	**ALTERNATIVE**	
Cryptococcosis (continued)			
Treatment (see CID 30:710, 2000) ↓ in era of HAART (Neurol 56:257, 2001; CID 36:789, 2003) but still common when pts present with AIDS & HIV status unknown (AIDS 18:555, 2004).	**Ampho B** 0.7–1 mg/kg/d. IV + **flucytosine**[1] **25 mg/kg po q6h x2 wks** or until clinically stable **followed by flu 400 mg/d. for minimum of 10 wks,** then switch to flucon qd (suppression) rx (see Comments below).	**Fluconazole** 400 mg po qd x6–10 wks, then suppressive rx (see Comments) or **Fluconazole** 400 mg po qd + flucytosine 37.5 mg/kg po q6h x10 wks (↑ toxicity)	If normal mental status >20 cells/mm³ CSF and CSF crypto antigen <1:1024, flucon alone is reasonable (CID 22:322, 1996). ↑ CSF pressure, lower with CSF removal. Must monitor 5-FC levels: peak 70–80 mg/L, trough 30–40 mg/L. Higher doses of ampho with bone marrow transplant patients. Itraconazole does not penetrate CSF (CID 22:329, 1996). In 64 pts ampho + 5FC ↓ crypto CFU in CSF more rapidly than ampho + fluconazole or combination of all 3 drugs (p <0.001) (Ln 363:1764, 2004).
Cryptococcosis HIV+/AIDS: Cryptococcemia and/or Meningitis			
Cryptococcus in blood may be manifest by positive blood culture or positive test of serum for cryptococcal antigen	**Ampho B** alone: 0.7–1.0 mg/kg/d IV x2 wks or until afebrile, headache, nausea and vomiting gone. Then dc ampho B, start **flucon** 400 mg po qd x8–10 week course. Then maintain on flucon 200 mg po qd.	or **Liposomal amphotericin B** 4 mg/kg/d x2 wks followed by fluconazole as above (Mycoses 46:24, 2003)	Even with rx (ampho B + 5FC regimen) 29/236 pts died within 1st 2 wks & 62 (26%) by 10 wks; only 129 (55%) were alive & culture-neg. at 10 wks ↑ rate of sterilization of CSF at 2 wks (36%) vs antifungal rx (ampho B + 5FC) alone (13%) (NEJM 189; 2185, 2004). Also, addition of INF–γ–1b 100 μg SC twice wkly ↑ rate of sterilization.
With HAART, symptoms of acute meningitis may return; immune reconstitution (AIDS 12:1491, 1999). If failure to respond to initial rx, think dual infection with tbc, neurosyphilis, toxo, etc. (Neurol 51:1213, 1998).	Start Highly Active Antiretroviral Therapy (HAART) if possible.	or **Ampho B lipid complex** IV 5 mg/kg/d x2 wks, then 3x/wk x4 to complete CRAG might predict relapse (CID 38:565, 2004).	In 163 pts (15 on HAART) survival was 85%, 6 months after discharge from hospital & receiving flucon suppression in Uganda. (IDSA 2003, Abst 630).
Suppression	**Fluconazole** 200 mg/d po. [If CD4 count rises to >100/mm³ with effective antiretroviral rx, most authorities recommend dc suppressive rx. See www.hivatis.org.]	**Ampho B** 1.0 mg/kg IV 1x/week or **Itraconazole** 200 mg po bid if flu intolerant or failure	Itraconazole should be used as fluconazole. Not recommended. No recurrences of crypto meningitis in 22 pts who dc flu suppression with >100 CD4 x3 mos. in Thailand (CID 36:1329, 2003). Only 4/100 with >100 CD4 relapsed with 2-year follow-up + serum CRAG might predict relapse (CID 38:565, 2004).
Dermatophytosis			
Erythrasma (Corynebacterium minutissimum)	**Erythromycin** 250 mg po qid x14 d	**2% aqueous clindamycin** topically	Diff. dx with Tinea versicolor, Tinea cruris. Erythrasma gives coral red fluorescence with Woods light.
Onychomycosis (Tinea unguium) (Brit J Derm 146:402, 2003; Am J Clin Derm 5:225, 2004; Cutis 74:516, 2004) Serious but rare cases of hepatitis failure have been reported in pts receiving terbinafine & should not be used in those with chronic or active liver disease (Am J Health Sys Pharm 58:1076, 2001). A topical nail lacquer (ciclopirox) approved but cure in only 5–9% after 48 wks (Med Lett 42:51, 2000) but ↑ to 50% cure in another study (J Am Acad Derm 44:479, 2001; Cutis 73:81, 2004). May enhance oral rx (Cutis 74:55, Terbinafine: ↑ cure rate & ↓ relapse vs itra at 5 yrs (JAm Acad Derm 42:97, 2000); appears to be most cost-effective rx (Manag Care 12:47, 2003).	**Fingernail Rx Options: Terbinafine**[3] 250 mg po qd (children <20 kg, 67.5 mg/d, 20–40 kg, 125 mg/d, >40 kg 250 mg/d) x6 wks (79% effective) or **Itraconazole** 200 mg po bid x3 mos.[NFDA] or **Fluconazole** 150–300 mg po q wk x3–6 mos.[NFDA]	**Toenail Rx Options: Terbinafine**[3] 250 mg po qd (children <20 kg, 67.5 mg/d, 20–40 kg, 125 mg/d, >40 kg, 250 mg/d) x12 wks (76% effective) or **Itraconazole** 200 mg po qd x3 mos (59% effective) or **Fluconazole** 200 mg bid x1 wk/mo. x3–4 mos (63% effective)[NFDA]
			Itraconazole 200 mg po bid x1 wk/mo. x6–12 mos (48% effective)[NFDA] [Data reflect cure rate from meta-analysis of all randomized controlled trials (Brit J Derm 150:537, 2004).]

NOTE: For side-effects, see footnotes 2, 3

---

[1] Flucytosine = 5-FC.

[2] **Serious but rare cases of hepatic failure** have been reported in pts receiving terbinafine & should not be used in those with chronic or active liver disease (see Table 11B, page 83). ALT & AST before prescribing.

[3] Use of itraconazole has been associated with myocardial dysfunction and with onset of congestive heart failure (see Ln 357:1766, 2001).

* From 2004 Drug Topics Red Book, Medical Economics Data and Hospital Formulary Pricing Guide. **Price** is assume wholesale price **(AWP)**.

See page 81 for abbreviations. All dosage recommendations are for adults (unless otherwise indicated) and assume normal renal function.

TABLE 11A (7)

TYPE OF INFECTION/ORGANISM/ SITE OF INFECTION	ANTIMICROBIAL AGENTS OF CHOICE		COMMENTS
	PRIMARY	ALTERNATIVE	
Dermatophytosis *(continued)*			
Tinea capitis ("ringworm") (Trichophyton tonsurans, Microsporum canis. In America, other sp. elsewhere) (PIDJ 18:191, 1999)	**Terbinafine** (see footnote 2 page 78) 250 mg po qd x4 wks (for *T. tonsurans*, 4-8 wks for *Microsporum*). Children ≤20 kg: 62.5 mg/d; (for 6-10 yrs) 125 mg/d for adults (JID 17:97, 2004; Expert Opin Pharmacother 5:219, 2004; J Eur Acad Dermatol Venereol 18:155, 2004)	**Itraconazole** (see footnote 2 page 78) 250 mg po qd 5 mg/kg/d for 30 d/sup^PUA^ **Fluconazole** 6 mg/kg/d qwk x8-12 wks. ^PUA^ Cap at 150 mg/d x6 mos for adults **Griseofulvin** adults 500 mg po qd x4-6 wks, children 10-20 mg/kg/d until hair regrows, usually 6-8 wks	All agents with similar cure rates (60-100%) in clinical studies (Ped Derm 17:304, 2000). Griseofulvin considered drug of choice by some although concerns for resistance. Keto po often effective in severe recalcitrant infection. Addition of topical ketoconazole or selenium sulfate shampoo reduces transmissibility (J Invest Derm 39:261, 2000)
Tinea corporis, cruris, or pedis (Trichophyton rubrum, T. mentagrophytes, Epidermophyton floccosum) "Athlete's foot, jock itch," and ringworm	**Topical rx:** Generally applied 2x/d. Available as creams, ointments, sprays, by prescription and "over the counter." Apply 2x/d for 2-3 wks. See footnote for names and prices. Recommend Lotrimin Ultra & Lamisil AT; contain butenafine & terbinafine—both are fungicidal	**Terbinafine** 250 mg po qd x2 wks^PUA^ OR **Itraconazole** 200 mg po qd x4 wks^PUA^ OR **Fluconazole** 150 mg po qwk x4 wks^PUA^ **Griseofulvin** adults 500 mg po qd x4-6 wks, children 10-20 mg/kg/d. Duration: 2-4 wks for pedis	Keto po effective in severe recalcitrant infection. Follow for hepatotoxicity. Terbinafine: 87% achieved mycological cure in double-blind study (x2 wks) (United Asian Thai 76:388, 1993; Brit J Derm 130(S4):9,22, 1994) and fluconazole 78% (J Am Acad Derm 40:S31, 1999)
Tinea versicolor (Malassezia furfur or Pityrosporum orbiculare)	**Ketoconazole** (400 mg po single dose)^PUA^ or (200 mg qd x7 days) or (2% cream applied 1x qd x2 wks)	**Fluconazole** (400 mg po single dose of **Itraconazole** (400 mg/d po x3-7 days	Keto 1 97% effective in 1 study. Another alternative: Selen sum sulfide (Selsun), 2.5% lotion, apply as lather, leave on 10 min then wash off, 1x/d x7d or 3-5x/wk x2-4 weeks
Fusariosis Infections in eye, skin, sinus & disseminated diseases—↑ in transplant pts (CID 34:909, 2001; Clin Micro Inf 10:567, 2004)	**Voriconazole** 6 mg/kg IV q12h on day 1, then either (4 mg/kg q12h) or (200 mg po q12h for body weight ≥40 kg, 100 mg q12h for body weight <40 kg)	**Ampho B** 1–1.2 mg/kg or **lipid-associated ampho B**	Voriconazole successful in 9/21 x4 eye, 2 blood stream, 2 sinus & 1 skin (CID 35:909, 2002; 36:1122, 2003; 37:311, 2003)
Histoplasmosis (Histoplasma capsulatum): See CID 30:688, 2000; IDC N.A. 17:1, 2003. Best diagnostic test is urinary antigen (ELISA) (CID 22:S102, 1996), MiraVista Diagnostics (1-866-647-2847).			
Immunocompetent:			
Pulmonary, acute diffuse	**Itraconazole:** 200 mg/d solution po x 6-9 months. If life-threatening 200 mg po tid x3 d, then 200 mg po bid until response	**With >2 months rx, 86% success in chronic pulmonary disease** (AJM 93:489, 1992). Antifungal rx not useful for histo fibrosclerosis mediastinitis. Clinical response in acute diffuse <39.5°C, Karnofsky <40, albumin <3 gm/dl meaningful
Pulmonary, localized, disseminated	**Moderate: Itraconazole** 200 mg/d solution po x6 mo		
Severe, including meningitis: Ampho B 0.5–1 mg/kg/d IV x7 d, followed by 0.8 mg/kg/d x3 d then 200 mg po bid if positive clinical response / If iv necessary: Dose 200 mg IV bid x4 d followed by 200 mg IV qd x14 d. **Itra is not recommended for meningitis** (South Med J 96:410, 2003)			>5x normal, WBC <500, platelets <50,000, creatinine ≥6 mg/dl (10^9/supl/1);S19, 1994). Flu less effective than itra (CID 2:3, 1996)
Immunocompromised patient (AIDS) (CID 24:1195, 1997; & 32:1215, 2001)	**For moderate to severe disease:** Lipid-based Ampho B: **Liposomal Ampho B** 3 mg/kg/d IV x14 d, then suppressive therapy with itraconazole 200 mg po qd (AIM 137:435, 2002) OR **Ampho B** 0.5–1 mg/kg/d IV x7 d, followed by 0.8 mg/kg qd or suppressive therapy (see page 78) **Itra is not recommended for meningitis**	**For less severe disease: Itraconazole** (300 mg bid po x3 d, then 200 mg bid po x12 wks) / or (400 mg po qd x12 wks) (85-90% response) then suppression (see page 78). **Not recommended for meningitis.** IV if unable to take po.	Suspension of Ampho B (88% vs 64% clinical success) in 81 patients with a decrease in nephrotoxicity (97% vs 37%). No difference in mortality (AIM 137: 105, 2002) **Itra (ACTG 120) 50/59 (85%) pts responded,** cleared fungemia with only 5% toxicity, 1 pt with meningitis failed, 2 failed because of low serum levels. Avoid with rifampin, reduce dose and follow for hepatic toxicity (J AIDS **Itra best drug for suppression at 200 mg qd** but 3/46 had probable hepatic toxicity Human Retro 16:100, 1997). Flu less effective & induces flu resistance
	None, unless Nocardia (see below)	**Suppression:** Fluconazole ≥800 mg/d or itraconazole after 12 wks. Can be safely dc after 12 mos. of antifungal rx & 6 mos. of HAART if CD4 count >150, 6 relapses after 2-yr follow-up in 32 pts (CID 38:1485, 2004)
Madura foot (See footnote, Nocardia, Pseudallescheria boydii, below)	None, unless Nocardia	In U.S. usually Pseudallescheria boydii, usually Nocardia brasiliensis. In Mexico, usually Nocardia brasiliensis. Pseudallescheria (Scedosporium spp.), N. asteroides	Itraconazole IV agent of choice. In Mexico, Amikacin IV most preferred for Nocardia, N. asteroides

---

¹ Drug name (trade name) & wholesale price for 15 gm. All are applied to affected area twice daily: butenafine (Mentax) $27, ciclopirox (Loprox) $12, clotrimazole (Lotrimin) $13, Myodex $10, econazole (Spectazole) $13, ketoconazole (Nizoral) $15, miconazole (Micatin, Monistat-Derm) $18, naftifine (Naftin) $17, oxiconazole (Oxistat) $14, sulconazole (Exelderm) $10, terconazole (Terazol) $9, sertaconazole (Ertaczo) $45.24. Non-prescription (over-the-counter): Tolnaftate (Tinactin $5, Ting or Tolnate $2), undecylenic acid (Cruex $5, Desenex $5), Lotrimin 1% 12 gm $6.17, Lamisil AT 1%, 12 gm $6.79.

² Oral antifungals and altered absorption of ↑ tablets because of ↑ absorption (see Table 11B, page 83)

* From 2004 Drug Topics Red Book, Medical Economics Data and Pharmaceutical Pricing Guide. Price is average wholesale price (AWP).

See page 81 for abbreviations. All dosage recommendations are for adults (unless otherwise indicated) and assume normal renal/hepatic function.

TABLE 11A (B)

TYPE OF INFECTION/ORGANISM/SITE OF INFECTION	ANTIMICROBIAL AGENTS OF CHOICE		COMMENTS
	PRIMARY	ALTERNATIVE	
Mucormycosis (Zygomycosis—Rhizopus, Rhizomucor, Absidia) Rhinocerebral, pulmonary (AJM 159:1301, 1999)	**Ampho B.** Increase rapidly to 0.8 - 1.5 mg/kg/d IV, when improving, then ped. Total dose usually 2.5–3 gm. or **Lipid-based Ampho B.** **Azoles and caspofungin usually inactive.**		Treatment requires control of underlying condition, esp. diabetic ketoacidosis, neutropenia. Surgical debridement usually required and discontinue deferoxamine if applicable. Deferoxamine ↑ risk of mucormycosis, use hydroxypyridinone chelators, nonazone (J Infect Dis 78:1743, 1998). Deferasirox, a new iron chelator may help (J Clin Invest July 2, 2007). With pulmonary disease, 40–15 mg/kg/d IV) lipo-some amphotericin B in some series successful in 2 cases (J Int 41:265, 2000). 1 pt who failed ampho B responded to posaconazole, a new triazole under development (CID 36:1488,2003)
Nocardiosis (N. asteroides & N. brasiliensis). Culture & sensitivities may be valuable in refractory cases. Reference Labs, R.J. Wallace (903) 877-7680 or CDC (404) 639-3158 (IDCP 8:27, 1999)			
Cutaneous and lymphocutaneous (sporotrichoid)	**TMP/SMX** 5–10 mg/kg/d of TMP & 25–50 mg/kg/d of SMX in 2–4 div. doses/d, po or IV.	**Sulfisoxazole** 2 gm po qid or **minocycline** 100–200 mg po bid	Linezolid 300–600 mg po bid x3–24 mos. successful in 6/6 pts, 4 with disseminated disease of whom 2 had brain abscesses (CID 36:313, 2006). In vitro most active & cidal. Synergy with IMP + amikacin in vitro & in vivo (AAC 40:832, 2004).
Pulmonary, disseminated, brain abscess. Duration of rx is generally 3 mos. for immunocompetent host (38%) & 6 mos. for immuno-compromised (62% organ transplant, malignancy, chronic lung disease, diabetes, ETOH use, steroid rx, & AIDS).	**TMP/SMX:** Initially 15 mg/kg/d of TMP & 75 mg/kg/d of SMX IV or po div. in 2–4 doses. After 3–4 wks, ↓ dose to 10 mg/kg/d TMP in 2–4 doses po. Do serum level (see Comment)	(**IMP** 500 mg IV q6h) + (**amikacin** 7.5 mg/kg IV q12h) x3–4 wks & then po regimen	Survival may be improved when sulfa-containing regimen used (Medicine 88:38, 1999). Prosthetic valve endocarditis with N. asteroides cured with IMP + amikacin x2 mos. followed by TMP/SMX x4 mos. (Am J Med 115:330, 2003). Measure sulfonamide blood levels early to ensure absorption of po rx. Desire peak level of 100–150 μg/ml 2 hrs post-po dose.
Paracoccidioidomycosis (South American blastomycosis)/P. brasiliensis	**Itraconazole** 200 mg/d po x 6 months or **Ketoconazole** 400 mg/d po for 6–18 months	**Ampho B** 0.4–0.5 mg/kg/d IV to total dose of 1.5–2.5 gm or **sulfonamides** (dose: see Comment)	Improvement in >90% pts on itra or keto. NEJM Sulfa: 4–6 gm/d for several weeks, then 500 mg/d for 3–5 yrs also used (CID 14 (Suppl.):S-68, 1992). Low-dose itra (50–100 mg/d), keto (200–400 mg/d) & sulfadiazine (up to 6 gm/d) showed similar clinical responses in 4–6 mos. in a randomized study (AAC 44:14, 14:14:14, 13/14, respectively (Med Mycol 40: 411, 2002). HIV + TMP/SMX suppressive & indefinitely (CID 21:1275, 1995). Terbinafine has good in vitro activity (JCM 40:2828, 2002).
Lobomycosis (keloidal blastomycosis)/P. loboi	**Surgical excision, clofazimine** or **ampho B**		
Penicilliosis (Penicillium marneffei). Common disseminated fungal infection in AIDS pts in SE Asia (esp. Thailand & Vietnam) (CID 24:1080, 1997; Int J Inf Dis 3:48, 1998)	**Ampho B** 0.5–1 mg/kg/d x2 wks followed by **itraconazole** 400 mg/d po x10 wks followed by 200 mg/d indefinitely for HIV-infected pts (NEJM 339:1739, 1998). See Comment	**Itra** 200 mg po tid x3, then 200 mg bid x12 wks. (IV if unable to take po)	3rd most common OI in AIDS following TB; and cryptococcal meningitis. May resemble histoplasmosis or TB; skin nodules are umbilicated (molluscum contagiosum). In AIDS long-term suppression with itra was as effective in **preventing relapses in 36/36 pts** whereas 20/35 pts receiving placebo relapsed within 6 mos. (NEJM 339:1739, 1998).
Phaeohyphomycosis (black molds) dematiaceous fungi) (See CID 34:467, 2002) encasement, skin, brain abscess Species: Cladosporium, Bipolaris, Wangiella, Curvularia, Exophiala, Phialemonium, Scytalidium, Alternaria, & others	**Surgery** + **itraconazole**, UNKN duration not defined, probably 6 months	**Voriconazole** has some in vitro activity but clinical experience limited to date w/S. prolificans (AAC 45:2151, 2001). **Itraconazole + terbinafine** synergistic against S. prolificans (AAC 44:470, 2000). No clinical data but combination could show ↑ response (see Table 11B, page 83).	Notoriously resistant to antifungal rx including amphotericin & azoles (CID 34:909, 2002). Mortality >80%. Cause of disseminated disease in immunosuppressed pts (3/4), esp. neutropenia (accounted for 10% of mycelial infections post-transplant (CID 37:221, 2003)) & fungal endocarditis, esp. porcine valve. Blood cultures pos. in >5% bostoconi/dal in some cases.
Scedosporium apiospermum (Pseudallescheria boydii)—for rx of disseminated mold by infection, caused by the dematiaceous mold) (IM 1333, 2002). Skin, subcutaneous (Madura foot), brain abscess, recurrent meningitis	**Voriconazole** 6 mg/kg IV q12h on day 1, then either q4 mg IV q12h (IV) or 200 mg po bid (oral) for body weight ≥40 kg, but 100 mg po q12h for body weight <40 kg	**Itraconazole** 400 mg/d po, some now resistant or refractory to itra) or **Miconazole**NUS 600 mg IV q8h	Refractory to antifungals including amphotericin, esp. in vitro voriconazole more active than itra (J Clin Micro 39: 954, 2001). Case reports of successful rx of disseminated CNS disease with voriconazole (CID 31:1499 & 673, 2000; Clin Microbiol Infect 9:750, 2003) EJCHID 22:408, 2003).

* **Oral solution preferred to tablets because of ↑ absorption** (see Table 11B, page 83).
* From 2004 Drug Topics Red Book, Medical Economics Data and Hospital Formulary Pricing Guide. **Price is average wholesale price (AWP).**
See pages for abbreviations. All dosage recommendations are for adults (unless otherwise indicated) and assume normal renal function

TABLE 11A (9)
ANTIMICROBIAL AGENTS OF CHOICE

TYPE OF INFECTION/ORGANISM/ SITE OF INFECTION	PRIMARY	ALTERNATIVE	COMMENTS
Sporotrichosis (CID 29:231, 1999; CID 36:684, 2000; CID 36:1403, 2003; ID Clin N A. 17:59, 2003) Cutaneous/Lymphonodular	**Itraconazole** 200-200 mg po qid x3-6 mos. (then 200 mg po bid long-term) for HIV-infected pts[alt6a]	**Fluconazole** 400 mg po qd x6 mos or until lesions resolve. Amphotericin B resistant (SSKI) 10 gm of K in 1 ml of H₂O). Start with 5-10 drops tid, gradually ↑ to 40-50 drops tid for 3-6 mos. Take after meals.	Itra: CID 17:210, 1993. Some authorities use ampho B as primary rx. Amphotericin B suppression reported (AJM 95:279, 1993). Itra rx for up to 24 months effective in multifocal osteoarticular infection (CID 23: 394, 1996). SSKI side-effects: nausea, rash, fever, metallic taste, salivary gland swelling.
Extraarticular: Osteoarticular pulmonary, disseminated, meningeal	**Osteoarticular, pulmonary: Itraconazole** 300 mg po bid x6-12 mos., then 200 mg po bid (long-term) for HIV-infected pts[alt6a]	**Disseminated, meningeal: Ampho B** 0.5 mg/kg to total of 1-2 gm, followed by **itra** 200 mg bid or **flu** 800 mg qid	

Abbreviations: AM/CL = amoxicillin clavulanate; **dc** = discontinue; **Clot** = clotrimazole; **Flu** = fluconazole; **G** = generic; **Griseo** = griseofulvin, **I** = investigational; **IMP** = imipenem; **IT** = intrathecal or intraventricular; **Itra** = itraconazole; **IUD** = intrauterine contraceptive device; **Keto** = ketoconazole; **NB** = name brand; **NFDA-I** = not FDA-approved indication; **NUS** = not available in the U.S.; **PSL** = peak ser level; **R/O** = rule out; **TMP/SMX** = trimethoprim/sulfamethoxazole; **vag. oint.** = vaginal ointment

TABLE 11B: ANTIFUNGAL DRUGS: ADVERSE EFFECTS, COMMENTS, COST

DRUG NAME, GENERIC (TRADE) USUAL DOSAGE/COST*	ADVERSE EFFECTS, COMMENTS, COST
Non-lipid Amphotericin B deoxycholate (Fungizone): 0.3-1 mg/kg/d as single infusion 50 mg $28 Mixing ampho B with lipid emulsion results in precipitation and is discouraged (Am J Hlth Pharm 52:1463, 1995)	**Admin.** Ampho B is a colloidal suspension that must be prepared in electrolyte-free D5W at 0.1 mg/ml to avoid precipitation. No need to protect drug suspensions from light. Ampho B infusions cause chills/fever, myalgia, anorexia, nausea, rarely hemodynamic collapse/hypotension. Postulated due to proinflammatory cytokines but does not appear to be related to speed of infusion usually 4 or more hrs. No difference found in 1- vs 4-hr infusions (AAC 34:1402, 1992) except chills/fever occurred sooner with 1-hr infusion. Febrile reactions decrease with repeated doses. Rare pulmonary reactions (severe dyspnea and focal infiltrates suggesting pulmonary edema) associated with rapid infusion (CID 33:75, 2001). Severe rigors respond to meperidine (25-50 mg IV). Premedication with acetaminophen, diphenhydramine, hydrocortisone (25-50 mg) and heparin (1000 units) had no influence on rigors/fever (CID 70:755, 1995). If cytokine postulate correct, NSAIDs or high-dose steroids may prove efficacious but their use may risk worsening infection under rx or increased risk of nephrotoxicity (i.e. NSAIDs). Clinical side effects ↓ with ↑ age (CID 26:334, 1996). **Toxicity:** Major concern is nephrotoxicity (15% of 102 pts in one survey, CID 26:334, 1996). Manifest initially by kaliuresis and hypokalemia, then fall in serum bicarbonate (may proceed to renal tubular acidosis), ↓ in renal erythropoietin and anemia, and rising BUN/serum creatinine. Hypomagnesemia may occur. Can reduce risk of renal injury by **(a) pre- and post-infusion hydration with 500 ml saline (if clinical status will allow salt load)**, (b) avoidance of other nephrotoxins, e.g. radiocontrast, aminoglycosides, cis-platinum. (c) Use of lipid prep of ampho B. Use of low-dose dopamine did not significantly reduce renal toxicity (AAC 42:3103, 1998). In a single randomized controlled trial of 80 neutropenic pts with refractory fever & suspected or proven invasive fungal infection, 0.97 mg/kg/d amphotericin **continuously infused over a 24-hr period** was compared to the classic 4x infusion over 4 hrs. Continuous infusion produced less nephrotoxicity (26% vs 46%, serum Cr (p <0.005), a reduction in fever, chills & vomiting (BMJ 322:1, 2001). Continuous infusion also allows effective as rapid infusion in very few proven fungal infections (7 & 3, respectively) (CID 36:943, 2003). It is disturbing that these escalating observations have not led to controlled trials examining efficacy in administered dosage without sig. toxicity (CID 36:952, 2003). Await trials of continuous infusion in larger number of proven fungal infections!

(continued on next page) *(continued on next page)*

* From 2004 Drug Topics Red Book, Medical Economics Data and Hospital Formulary Pricing Guide. Price is **a**verage **w**holesale **p**rice (AWP).
See page 81 for abbreviations. All dosage recommendations are for adults (unless otherwise indicated) and assume normal renal function.

TABLE 11B (2)

DRUG NAME, GENERIC (TRADE)/ USUAL DOSAGE/COST*	ADVERSE EFFECTS/COMMENTS
(continued from previous page)	*(continued from previous page)*
Lipid-based ampho B products¹ **Amphotericin B lipid complex (ABLC) (Abelcet)** 5 mg/kg/d as single infusion 100 mg IV $255 ($890/350 mg)	**Admin.:** Consists of ampho B complexed with 2 lipid bilayer ribbons. Compared to standard ampho B, larger volume of distribution, rapid blood clearance and high tissue concentrations (liver, spleen, lung). Do NOT use an in-line filter. **Dosage: 5 mg/kg once daily:** infuse at 2.5 mg/kg/hr; adult and ped. dose the same. Do NOT use an in-line filter. **Toxicity:** Fever and chills in 14-18%, nausea 9%, vomiting 8%, serum creatinine ↑ in 11%, renal failure 5%, anemia 4%, ↓ K 5%; rash 4%.
Liposomal amphotericin B (L-AmB, AmBisome) 3-5 mg/kg/d as single infusion. 50 mg $196 ($172/350 mg)	**Admin.:** Consists of vesicular bilayer liposome with ampho B intercalated within the membrane. **Dosage: 3-5 mg/kg IV as single dose** infused over a period of approx. 120 min (1 mg/min). In cats & rats in vivo infusion can be reduced to 60 min.² ↑ 1 mg/kg/d was as effective as 4 mg/kg/d (6 mos. survival rates 43% vs 37%). In studies with invasive aspergillosis, response bone marrow &/or neutropenia from malignancy (*CID 27:1406, 1998*). **Major toxicity:** Generally less than ampho B. Nephrotoxicity 18.7% vs 33.7% for ampho B, chills 47% vs 75%, nausea 39.7% vs 38.7%, vomiting 31.8% vs 43.9%, rash 24% for both, ↓ K 20.4% vs 25.6%, ↓ Mg 20.4% vs 25.6%. Acute infusion-related reactions are common with liposomal ampho B, 20-40%. 86% occurred within 5 min. of infusion, including chest pain, dyspnea & hypoxia or severe abdominal, flank or leg pain; 14% developed flushing & urticaria near the end of 4-hr infusion. All responded to diphenhydramine 1 mg/kg) & interruption of L-AmB infusion. These reactions may be due to complement activation by the liposome (*Curr Med Res Opin 33:211, 2003*).
Amphotericin B cholesteryl complex (amphotericin B colloidal dispersion, ABCD, Amphotec) 3-4 mg/kg/d as single infusion. 100 mg $160	**Admin.:** Consists of ampho B deoxycholate stabilized with cholesteryl sulfate resulting in a disc-shaped colloidal complex. Compared to standard ampho B, larger volume of distribution, rapid blood clearance, high tissue concentrations. **Dosage:** Initial dose for adults & children: **3-4 mg/kg/day.** If necessary, can ↑ to 6 mg/kg/day. Dilute in D5W & infuse at 1 mg/kg/hr. Do NOT use in-line filter. **Toxicity:** Chills, fever 33%,* serum creatinine 12-20%, ↓ K 6%,* ↓ K 17%.
Caspofungin (Cancidas) 70 mg IV on day 1 followed by 50 mg IV qd (reduce to 35 mg IV qd with moderate hepatic impairment) 70 mg $515; 50 mg $449. Ref.: *Ln 362:1142, 2003*	An echinocandin which inhibits synthesis of β-(1,3)-D-glucan, a critical component of fungal cell walls. Fungicidal against candida (MIC < 2 μg/ml) including those resistant to other antifungals & active against aspergillus (MIC 0.4-2.7 μg/ml). Serum levels on dosages: peak 12, trough 1.3 (24 hrs) μg/ml. Approved for rx of aspergillosis & other candida infections in severely impaired hosts who had failed other antifungals. For invasive aspergillus in 48 pts, successful in 41/57 pts with invasive aspergillosis (*Transpl Inf Dis 1:25, 2002*). 14% had ↑ transaminases (similar to triazoles). Only 2% of 263 pts in double-blind trial dc drug due to drug-related adverse event (*Transpl Inf Dis 1:25, 2002*). 14% had ↑ transaminases (similar to triazoles). Most common adverse effect: pruritus at infusion site & headache, fever, chills, vomiting, & diarrhea associated with infusion. Drug metabolized in liver, not nephrotoxic. Drug interactions (similar to triazoles): Class C for pregnancy (embryotoxic in rats & rabbits), so only use if potential benefits outweigh risks. See Table 22, page 143 for drug interactions, esp. cyclosporine (hepatic toxicity) & tacrolimus (↓ drug level monitoring recommended) (*Curr Med Res Opin 21:469-889, 2003*).
Fluconazole (Diflucan) (available generically) 100 mg tabs $8.54 150 mg tabs $13.60 200 mg tabs $14 400 mg tabs $135 Oral suspension: 40 mg/mL, $130/35 mL bottle	IV and oral. Example of excellent bioavailability. **Pharmacology:** absorbed po, water solubility enables IV. Peak serum levels (see Table 9, page 60) T½: 30 hrs (range 20-50 hrs). 12% protein bind. CSF levels 50-90% of serum in normals.* No effect on mammalian steroid metabolism. **Drug-drug interactions common, see Table 22.** Side-effects overall 16% [more common in HIV+ pts (21%)]. Headache 1.9%, skin rash 1.8%, abdominal pain 1.7%, vomiting 1.7%, diarrhea 1.5%, ↑ SGOT 20%. Alopecia (scalp, pubic crest) in 12-20% pts on >400 mg po qd after median of 3 months (reversible in approx. 6 mos.) (*AnIM 123:354, 1995*). Rare: severe hepatotoxicity, exfoliative dermatitis. Anaphylaxis (*CID 13:61, 1993*), thrombocytopenia, leukopenia. Good reference: *NEJM 330:263, 1994*
Flucytosine (Ancobon) 500 mg cap $9	**AEs:** Overall 30%. GI 6% (diarrhea, nausea, vomiting); hematologic 22% [leukopenia, thrombocytopenia, when serum level > 100 μg/ml (esp. in azotemic pts)]; hepatotoxicity (asymptomatic ↑ SGOT, reversible); skin rash 7%; aplastic anemia (rare--2 or 3 cases). False ↑ in serum creatinine on EKTACHEM analyzer (*JAC 26:171, 2000*).
Griseofulvin (Fulvicin, Grifulvin, Grisactin) 500 mg $1.66, susp 125 mg/ml: 120 ml $36	Photosensitivity, urticaria, GI upset, fatigue, leukopenia (rare). Interferes with warfarin drugs. Increases blood and urine porphyrins, should not be used in patients with porphyria. Minor disulfiram-like reactions. Exacerbation of systemic lupus erythematosus.

¹ Published data from patients intolerant of or refractory to conventional ampho B (Amp B d). **None of the lipid ampho B preps has shown superior efficacy compared to ampho B in prospective trials (except liposomal ampho B was more effective vs ampho B in rx of disseminated histoplasmosis at 2 wks** (*AnIM 137:105, 2002; CID 27:415, 2003*). **Dosage equivalency has not been established** (*CID 36:1500, 2003*). Nephrotoxicity ↑ with all lipid ampho B preps (*IDCP 7:516, 1998; CID 27:603, 1998; NEJM 340:764, 1999*).

² Comparisons between Abelcet & AmBisome suggest higher infusion-assoc. toxicity (rigors) & febrile episodes with Abelcet (70% vs 36%) but a higher frequency of mild hepatic toxicity with AmBisome (69% vs 38%, p=0.05). Mild elevations in serum creatinine were observed in 1/3 of both (*Bone Marrow Tx 20:39, 1997; CID 26:1383, 1998*). Acute infusion-assoc. toxicity is average with both (*Bone Marrow Tx 20:39, 1997*).

* From 2004 Drug Topics Red Book, Medical Economics Data and Hospital formulary at UCSF Medical Center. Price is average wholesale price **(AWP)**.

See page 81 for abbreviations. All dosage recommendations are for adults (unless otherwise indicated) and assume normal renal function.

TABLE 11B (3)

DRUG NAME, GENERIC (TRADE)/ USUAL DOSAGE/COST*	ADVERSE EFFECTS/COMMENTS
Imidazoles, topical For vaginal and/or skin use	Not recommended in 1st trimester of pregnancy. Local reactions: 0.5-1.5% dyspareunia, mild vaginal or vulvar erythema, burning, pruritus, urticaria, rash. Rarely similar symptoms in sexual partner.
Itraconazole (Sporanox) 100 mg tab $9.50 10 mg/ml oral solution (fasting state) (150 ml: $147) (AAC 42:1862, 1998) IV usual dose 200 mg bid x4 doses followed by 200 mg qd for a maximum of 14 days ($222/250 mg)	Itraconazole tablet and solution forms are not interchangeable; solution preferred. Many authorities recommend measuring drug serum concentration after 2 wks on prolonged rx to ensured satisfactory absorption. To obtain the highest plasma concentration, the tablet is given with food and acidic drinks (e.g., Coca-Cola) and the solution is taken in the fasted state; under these conditions, the peak conc. of the capsule is approx. 3 µg/ml and of the solution 5.4 µg/ml. Peak levels are reached faster (2.2 vs 5 hrs) with the solution. **Peak plasma concentrations after IV injection (200 mg) compared to oral capsule (200 mg); 2.8 µg/ml (IV) vs 2 µg/ml (po) on day 36 of rx).** Protein-binding is over 99%, which explains the virtual absence of penetration into the CSF **(do not use to treat meningitis)**. Most common adverse effects are dose-related nausea 10%, diarrhea 8%, vomiting 6%, abdominal discomfort 5.7%. Allergic rash 8.6%,[*] bilirubin 6%, edema 3.5%, and hepatitis 2.7% reported.[*] doses may produce hypokalemia 6% and[*] blood pressure 3.2%. Thrombocytopenia and leukopenia reported (AnIM 125:157, 1996). Delirium reported (Psychosomatics 44:260, 2003). **Reported to produce inotropic effect—other concern, as with fluconazole and terbinafine, is drug-drug interactions; see Table 22**
Ketoconazole (Nizoral) 200 mg tab $3.50	Gastric acid required for absorption—cimetidine, omeprazole, antacids block absorption. In achlorhydria, dissolve tablet in 4 ml 0.2N HCl, drink with a straw. **Drug-drug interactions important, see Table 22. Some interactions can be life-threatening. Dose-dependent nausea and vomiting.** Liver toxicity of hepatotoxic-type reported in about 1:10,000 exposed pts—usually after several days to weeks of exposure. At doses of 2800 mg/d serum testosterone and plasma cortisol levels fall. With high doses, adrenal (Addisonian) crisis reported.
Miconazole (Monistat IV) 200 mg—not available in U.S.	IV miconazole indicated in patient critically ill with Pseudallescheria boydii. Very toxic due to vehicle needed to get drug into solution.
Nystatin (Mycostatin) 30 gm cream $6 500,000 u oral tab $0.36	Topical: virtually no adverse effects. Less effective than imidazoles and triazoles. PO: large doses give occasional GI distress and diarrhea.
Terbinafine (Lamisil) 250 mg tab $10.50	Rare cases (8) of idiosyncratic & symptomatic hepatic injury and more rarely liver failure leading to death or liver transplantation reported in pts receiving terbinafine for onychomycosis. Therefore, the drug is **not recommended** for pts with **chronic or active liver disease** although hepatotoxicity may occur in pts without pre-existing disease. Pretreatment & monitoring of serum transaminases (ALT & AST) is advised & alternate rx used for those with abnormal levels. Pts started on terbinafine should be warned and advised to report promptly persistent nausea, anorexia, fatigue, vomiting, RUQ pain, jaundice, dark urine or pale stools). If symptoms develop, drug should be discontinued & liver function immediately evaluated. In controlled trials, changes in ocular lens and retina reported—clinical significance unknown. Major drug-drug interaction is 100%[*] in rate of clearance by rifampin. AEs: usually mild, transient and rarely caused discontinuation of rx, % with AE, terbinafine vs placebo: nausea/diarrhea 2.6-5.6 vs 2.9; rash 5.6 vs 2.2; taste abnormality 2.8 vs 0.7. Inhibits CYP2D6 enzymes (see Table 22).
Voriconazole (Vfend) **IV: Loading dose 6 mg/kg q12h x1 d., then** **4 mg/kg q12h IV** for invasive aspergillus & serious mold infections; **3 mg/kg q12h IV** for serious Candida infections **Oral: >40 kg body weight:** 400 mg po q12h x1 d., then 200 mg po q12h. **<40 kg body weight:** 200 mg po q12h x1 d., then 100 mg po q12h **Take oral dose 1 hour before or 1 hour after eating.** Oral suspension (40 mg) $36.49/200 mg dose. Oral suspension dosing: Same as for oral tabs. Reduce to ½ maintenance dose for moderate hepatic insufficiency.	A triazole with activity against Aspergillus sp., including Ampho resistant strains of A. terreus (JCM 37:2343, 1999). Active vs Candida sp. (including krusei), Fusarium sp., & various molds. Steady state serum levels reach 12.5-4 µg/ml. Toxicity similar to other azoles/triazoles including uncommon serious hepatic toxicity (hepatitis, cholestasis & fulminant hepatic failure). Liver function tests should be monitored during rx & drug d/c if abnormalities develop. Rash reported in 26.648, 2001). 1 case of QT prolongation with ventricular tachycardia in a 15 y/o pt with ALL reported (CID 39:884, 2004). **Approx. 30% experience transient visual disturbance** following IV or po ("altered/enhanced visual perception" blurred or colored visual change or photophobia) within 30-60 minutes. Visual changes resolve within 30-60 minutes after administration. AEs are attenuated with repeated doses (**do not drive at night for outpatient rx**). No persistence of effect reported. Cause unknown. Potential for drug-drug interactions high—see Table 22 (CID 36:630, 1087, 1122, 2003). **NOTE:** Not in urine in active form. Cost: Oral susp $9; 200 mg IV $35; 200 mg IV $109

* From 2004 Drug Topics Red Book, Medical Economics Data and Hospital Formulary Pricing Guide. **Price is average wholesale price (AWP).**
See page 81 for abbreviations. All dosage recommendations are for adults (unless otherwise indicated) and assume normal renal function.

TABLE 12A: TREATMENT OF MYCOBACTERIAL INFECTIONS*

Tuberculin skin test (TST). Same as PPD [MMWR 52(RR-2):15, 2003]

Criteria for positive TST after 5 tuberculin units (intermediate PPD) read at 48–72 hours:
- ≥5 mm induration: + HIV, immunosuppressed, <15 mg prednisone/day, healed TBc on chest x-ray, recent close contact
- ≥10 mm induration: foreign-born, countries with high prevalence, IVDUsers, low income, NH residents; chronic illness, silicosis
- ≥15 mm induration: otherwise healthy

Two-stage testing: If select wrong (negative) initially. If 1st PPD is <10 mm induration, & from country with TBc, should be attributed to M. tuberculosis. Prior BCG may result in false positive result [AIM 1611:1760, 2001].

BCG vaccine as child: If ≥10 mm induration, & from country with TBc, should be attributed to M. tuberculosis. Prior BCG may result in false positive result [AIM 1611:1760, 2001].

Routine energy testing no longer recommended in HIV+ or HIV-negative patients [JAMA 283:2003, 2000].

Whole blood interferon-gamma release assay [QuantiFERON-TB (QFT)] approved by U.S. FDA as diagnostic test for TB [JAMA 286:1740, 2001; CID 34:1449 & 1457, 2002]. CDC recommends TST for tuberculosis suspects & pts at risk for progression to active TB & suggests either QFT or TST for individuals at low risk but are deemed at low risk for LTBI [MMWR 52(RR-2):15, 2003]. An extremely sensitive enzyme-linked immunospot method (ELISpot) using antigens specific for MTB (do not cross-react with BCG) is under evaluation & looks promising [Thorax 58:916, 2003; Ln 361:1168, 2003; AIM 140:709, 2004].

I. Mycobacterium tuberculosis — TST negative (household members & other close contacts of potentially infectious cases)

CAUSATIVE AGENT/DISEASE	MODIFYING CIRCUMSTANCES	INITIAL THERAPY	SUGGESTED REGIMENS / CONTINUATION PHASE OF THERAPY
I. Mycobacterium tuberculosis — TST negative (household members & other close contacts of potentially infectious cases)	Neonate—Rx essential	INH (10 mg/kg/day for 3 months)	Repeat tuberculin skin test (TST) in 3 mos. If mother's smear negative & infant's TST negative & chest x-ray (CXR) normal, stop INH. In UK, BCG is then given [Ln 2:1479, 1990], unless mother HIV+. If infant's repeat TST positive &/or CXR abnormal (hilar adenopathy &/or infiltrate), treat for 6 months. Total rx 6 months. If mother is being rx, separation of infant from mother not indicated. If INH not given initially, repeat TST at 3 mos. If positive rx with INH for 9 mos. (see Category II below).
	Children <5 years of age—Rx indicated	As for neonate for 1st 3 months	repeat TST at 3 months. If negative, stop. If repeat TST positive, continue INH for total of 9 months.
	Older children & adults—Risk 2–4% 1st year	No rx	repeat TST at 3 months. If positive rx with INH for 9 mos.

II. Treatment of latent infection with M. tuberculosis (formerly known as "prophylaxis")
[AIDS CLIN CARE 11:61; S221, 2000; NEJM 347:1860, 2002; NEJM 350:2060, 2004]

A. INH indicated due to high-risk
Assumes INH-susceptibility. INH 54–88% effective in preventing active TB for ≥20 years.

MODIFYING CIRCUMSTANCES
(1) + tuberculin reactor & HIV+ (risk of active disease HIV+ 170x ↑, HIV+ & 113x ↑). Development of active TBc in HIV+ pts after INH usually due to reinfection, not INH failure [CID 34:386, 2002]
(2) Newly infected persons (TST conversion in past 2 yrs — risk 3.3%, 1st yr)
(3) Past tuberculosis, not rx with adequate chemotherapy [INH, RIF, or alternative]
(4) + tuberculin reactors with non-granulomatous tuberculous disease (risk 0.5–5.0%/yr)
(5) + tuberculin reactors with specific predisposing conditions: illicit injection drug use [MMWR 98:236, 1989]; silicosis; diabetes mellitus; prolonged adrenocortico-steroid rx (>15 mg prednisone/day), immunosuppressive rx, hematologic diseases (Hodgkin's, leukemia), endstage renal disease, clinical condition with substantial rapid weight loss or chronic under-nutrition, previous gastrectomy [AARD 134:355, 1986]
* NOTE: For HIV+, see SANFORD GUIDE TO HIV/AIDS THERAPY and/or MMWR 48:(RR)-1, 1999

INITIAL THERAPY
INH (5 mg/kg/d, maximum 300 mg/d for adults; 10 mg/kg/d for child—not to exceed 300 mg/d for children). May use twice-weekly with ↓DOT† (MMWR 52:735, 2003). Optimal duration 9 mos. (includes children, HIV+, and those with fibrotic lesions on chest x-ray). In some cases, 6 mos. may be given for cost-effectiveness [AJRCCM 161: S221, 2000]. Do not use 6 mo. regimen in HIV+ persons <18 yrs old, or those with fibrotic lesions on chest film [NEJM 345:189, 2001].

SUGGESTED REGIMENS — ALTERNATIVE
If compliance problem: INH by DOT† 15 mg/kg 2xwk x9 mos. 2-month RIF + PZA regimen effective in HIV+ and HIV− [AJRCCM 157:1735, 1998; MMWR 52:735, 2003]. However, there are recent descriptions of severe & fatal hepatitis in pts on RIF + PZA. This regimen is no longer recommended for LTBI (MMWR 52:735, 2003).
RIF 600 mg po for 4 mos. (HIV− and HIV+).

COMMENTS
Reanalysis of earlier studies favors INH prophylaxis (if INH related, hepatitis case fatality rate <1% and TB case fatality ≥6.7%, which appears to be the case) [AIM 150:2517, 1990]. Recent data suggest INH prophylaxis has positive risk-benefit ratio in pts ≥35 if monitored for hepatotoxicity [AIM 127: 1051, 1997]. Overall risk of hepatotoxicity 0.1–0.15% [JAMA 281:1014, 1999].

B. TST positive (or more likely to be INH-susceptible)

CAUSATIVE AGENT/DISEASE	MODIFYING CIRCUMSTANCES	SUGGESTED REGIMENS — INITIAL THERAPY	ALTERNATIVE	COMMENTS
B. TST positive (or more likely to be INH-susceptible)	Age no longer considered a modifying factor (see Comments)	INH (5 mg/kg/d, max 300 mg/d for adults; 10 mg/kg/d for children; should not exceed 300 mg/d for children). Results with 6 mos. rx not quite as effective as (65% vs 75% twofold) as 9 mos. is current recommendation. See IIA above for details and alternate rx.		

*Dosages are for adults (unless otherwise indicated) and assume normal renal/renal function   † DOT = directly observed therapy

See pages 90 & 92 for footnotes

TABLE 12A (2)

CAUSATIVE AGENT/DISEASE	MODIFYING CIRCUMSTANCES	SUGGESTED REGIMENS — INITIAL THERAPY	SUGGESTED REGIMENS — ALTERNATIVE	COMMENTS
II. Treatment of latent infection with M. tuberculosis ("prophylaxis") TST positive (organisms likely to be susceptible) (continued)				
	Pregnancy—Any risk factors (III.A above)	Treat with INH as below. Rx for women w/ risk factors for progression of latent to active tuberculosis, esp. those who are HIV+ or who have been recently infected, rx should not be delayed even during the first trimester.		Risk of INH hepatitis may be ↑ (Ln 346:199, 1995)
	Pregnancy—No risk factors	No initial rx (see Comment)		Delay rx until after delivery (AJRCCM 149:1359, 1994)
C. TST positive & drug resistance likely (For data on worldwide prevalence of drug resistance, see NEJM 344:1294, JID 185:1197, 2002)	INH-resistant (or adverse reaction to INH), RIF-sensitive organisms likely	RIF 600 mg/d po for 4 mos. (HIV+ or HIV–)		IDSA guideline lists rifabutin in 600 mg/d dose as another alternative; however, current recommended max. dose of rifabutin is 300 mg/d. Estimate rifabutin alone has no protective effect of 56%, 26% of pts reported adverse effects; only 21/157 did not complete 6 mos. rx.) (AJRCCM 155:1735, 1997)
	INH- and RIF-resistant organisms likely	Efficacy of all regimens unproven: (**PZA 25-30 mg/kg/d** to max. of 2 gm/d + **ETB 15-25 mg/kg/d po**) x6-12 mos.	[(**PZA 25 mg/kg/d** to max. of 2.0 gm/d) + (**levofloxacin 500 mg/d** or **ofloxacin 400 mg bid**)], all po x6-12 mos.	PZA + ofloxacin has been associated with asymptomatic hepatitis (CID 21:1264, 1997)

SUGGESTED REGIMENS — INITIAL PHASE* (DIRECTLY OBSERVED THERAPY (DOT) REGIMENS) and CONTINUATION PHASE OF THERAPY* (in vitro susceptibility known). SEE COMMENTS FOR DOSAGE AND SCHEDULE.

CAUSATIVE AGENT/DISEASE	MODIFYING CIRCUMSTANCES	INITIAL PHASE — Regimen; in order of preference	INITIAL PHASE — Drugs	INITIAL PHASE — Interval/Doses (min. duration)	CONTINUATION PHASE — Regimen	CONTINUATION PHASE — Drugs	CONTINUATION PHASE — Interval/Doses (min. duration)	Range of Total Doses (min. duration)
III. Mycobacterium tuberculosis **A. Pulmonary TB** (General reference on rx of adults & children: Ln 362:887, 2003; MMWR 52(RR-11):1, 2003) Isolation essential: Pts with active TB should be isolated in single rooms, not cohorted. Older observations on infectivity of suscepti-ble & resistant M. tbc suggest isolation before and after rx (ARRD 85:511, 1962) and may be applicable to MDR M. tbc or to the HIV+ individual. Extended isolation may be appropriate. See footnotes, page 88 (continued on next page)	Rate of INH resistance known to be <4% (drug-susceptible organisms) (recs. from MMWR 52:(RR-11):1, 2003)	1 (See Fig. 1, page 87)	INH RIF PZA ETB	7 d/wk x56 doses (8 wk) or 5 d/wk x40 doses (8 wk)[3]	1a / 1b / 1c[1]	INH/RIF[4] / INH/RIF / INH/RIF	7 d/wk x126 doses (18 wk) or 5 d/wk x90 doses (18 wk)[3] ; 2x/wk x36 doses (18 wk) ; 1x/wk x18 doses (18 wk)	182-130 (26 wk) ; 92-76 (26 wk) ; 74-58 (26 wk)
		2 (See Fig. 1, page 87)	INH RIF PZA ETB	7 d/wk x14 doses (2 wk), then 2x/wk x12 doses (6 wk) or 5 d/wk x10 doses (2 wk), then 2x/wk x12 doses (6 wk)[3]	2a / 2b[3]	INH/RIF / INH/RIF	2x/wk x36 doses (18 wk) ; 1x/wk x18 doses (18 wk)	62-58 (26 wk) ; 44-40 (26 wk)
		3 (See Fig. 1, page 87)	INH RIF PZA ETB	3x/wk x24 doses (8 wk)	3a	INH/RIF	3x/wk x54 doses (18 wk)	78 (26 wk)
		4 (See Fig. 1, page 87)	INH RIF ETB	7 d/wk x56 doses (8 wk) or 5 d/wk x40 doses (8 wk)[3]	4a / 4b	INH/RIF[4] / INH/RIF	7 d/wk x217 doses (31 wk) or 5 d/wk x155 doses (31 wk)[3] ; 2x/wk x62 doses (31 wk)	273-195 (39 wk) ; 118-102 (39 wk)

COMMENTS — Dose in mg/kg (max. daily dose)

Regimen*	INH	RIF	PZA	ETB	SM	RFB
Daily						
Child	10-20 (300)	10-20 (600)	15-30 (2000)	15-25	20-40 (1000)	10-20 (300)
Adult	5 (300)	10 (600)	15-30 (2000)	15-25	15 (1000)	5 (300)
2x/wk (DOT)						
Child	20-40 (900)	10-20 (600)	50-70 (4000)	50	25-30 (1500)	10-20 (300)
Adult	15 (900)	10 (600)	50-70 (4000)	50	25-30 (1500)	5 (300)
3x/wk (DOT)						
Child	20-40 (900)	10-20 (600)	50-70 (3000)	25-30	25-30 (1500)	NA
Adult	15 (900)	10 (600)	50-70 (3000)	25-30	25-30 (1500)	NA

Second-line anti-TB agents can be dosed as follows to facilitate DOT: Cycloserine 500-750 mg qd (5x/wk) po. Ethionamide 500-750 mg qd (5x/wk) po. Kanamycin or capreomycin 15 mg/kg qd (3-5x/wk) IM/IV. Ciprofloxacin 750 mg qd (5x/wk) po. Ofloxacin 600-800 mg qd (5x/wk) po. Levofloxacin 750 mg qd (5x/wk) po (CID 21:1245, 1995)

Risk factors for drug-resistant TB: Recent immigration from Latin America or Asia or living in area of ↑ resistance (≥4%) or previous rx without RIF; exposure to known MDR TB. Incidence of MDR TB in U.S. appears to have stabilized and may be slightly decreasing in early 1990s (JAMA 278:833, 1997). Incidence of primary drug resistance is increasing in parts of Europe, N. Africa, Thailand, Russia, Estonia & Latvia (NEJM 344:1294, 2001; NEJM 347:1850, 2002). (continued on next page)

SEE DOT REGIMENS IF POSSIBLE

* Dosages are for adults (unless otherwise indicated) and assume normal renal function † DOT = directly observed therapy

See pages 90 & 92 for abbreviations, page 88 for footnotes

TABLE 12A (3)

CAUSATIVE AGENT/DISEASE; MODIFYING CIRCUMSTANCES	MODIFYING CIRCUM-STANCES	SUGGESTED REGIMEN[a]	DURATION OF TREATMENT (mo.)	SPECIFIC COMMENTS[b]	COMMENTS
III. Mycobacterium tuberculosis A. Pulmonary TB (continued from previous page) REFERENCE: CID 22:683, 1996	INH (± SM) resistance	RIF, PZA, ETB (an FQ may strengthen the regimen for pts with extensive disease). Emergence of FQ resistance a concern (LnID 3:432, 2003)	6	In British Medical Research Council trials, 6-mo. regimens without >90% success rates despite resistance to INH if 4 drugs were used in the initial phase & RIF + ETB or SM was used throughout (ARRD 133: 423, 1986). Additional studies suggest that results were best if PZA was also used throughout the 6 mos (ARRD 136:1339, 1987). FQs were not employed in BMRC studies, but may strengthen the regimen for pts with extensive disease. Resect. surgery for pts w/ localized disease in cases of INH resistance [see MMWR 52(RR-11):1, 2003 for additional discussion].	(continued from previous page) For MDR-TB, consider rifabutin (~30% RIF-resistant strains are rifabutin-susceptible). Note that CIP not as effective as PZA + ETB in multidrug regimen for TB in HIV+ pts (LnID 22:287, 1996). Moxifloxacin, gatifloxacin and levofloxacin have enhanced activity compared with CIP against M. tuberculosis (AAC 46: 1022, 2002; AAC 47:2242, 2002; AAC 47:3117, 2003; JAC 53:441, 2004; AAC 48:780, 2004). FQ resistant M. tuberculosis in pts previously treated with FQ (CID 37:1448, 2003). Linezolid has excellent in vitro activity, including MDR strains (AAC 47: 416, 2003). Mortality reviewed: Ln 349:71, 1997. Rapid (24-hr) diagnostic tests for M. tuberculosis: (1) the Amplified Mycobacterium tuberculosis Direct Test amplifies and detects M. tuberculosis ribosomal RNA; (2) the AMPLICOR Mycobacterium tuberculosis Test amplifies and detects M. tuberculosis DNA. Both tests have sensitivities & specificities >95% in sputum samples that are AFB-positive. In negative smears, specificity remains >95% but sensitivity is 40-77% (AJCCM 155:1497, 1997). Note that MTB may grow in < 2 wks; blood agar plates in 1-2 wks (JCM 41: 1770,2003).
Multidrug-Resistant Tuberculosis (MDR TB: Defined as resistant to at least 2 drugs, TB clusters with high mortality (AJM 118: 17, 1993; EJCMID 23: 174, 2004)) See footnotes, page 88	Resistance to INH & RIF (± SM)	FQ, PZA, ETB, IA ± alternative agent†	18-24	In such cases, extended rx is needed to ↓ the risk of relapse. In cases with extensive disease, the use of an additional agent (alternative agents) may be prudent to ↓ the risk of failure & additional acquired drug resistance. Resectional surgery may be appropriate. Use the first-line agents to which there is susceptibility. Add 2 or more alternative agents in case of extensive disease. Surgery should be considered. Survival ↑ in pts receiving active FQ + surgical intervention (AJRCCM 169:1103, 2004).	
	Resistance to INH, RIF (± SM), & ETB (± PZA)	FQ (ETB or PZA if active), IA, & 2 alternative agents†	24		
	Resistance to RIF	INH, ETB, PZA supplemented with PZA for the first 2 mos. (an IA may be included for the first 2-3 mos. with extensive disease)	12-18	Daily & 3x/wk regimens of INH, PZA, & SM given for 9 months were effective in a BMRC trial (ARRD 115:727, 1977). However, extended use of an IA may not be feasible. It is not known if ETB would be as effective as SM in these regimens. An alt-oral regimen for rx options with extensive disease. It may be prudent to shorten the duration (e.g., to 12 mos.); an IA may be added in the initial 2 mos. of rx.	

SUGGESTED REGIMENS

CAUSATIVE AGENT/DISEASE; MODIFYING CIRCUMSTANCES	INITIAL THERAPY	CONTINUATION PHASE OF THERAPY (in vitro susceptibility known)	COMMENTS
B. Extrapulmonary TB	INH + RIF (or RFB) + PZA daily x2 months Authors are agreed that include INH.	INH + RIF (or RFB) that include INH.	6-month regimens probably effective. Most experience with 6 mos. rx for pulmonary tuberculosis. Am Acad Ped (1984) recommends 6 mos. rx for isolated cervical adenitis, renal and 12 mos. for meningitis. IDSA recommends 6 mos. for lymph node, pleura, pericarditis, disseminated disease, genitourinary & peritoneal TB; 6-9 mos. for bone & joint; 9-12 mos. for CNS (including meningitis). Longer duration if slow response or meningeal involvement [MMWR 52(RR-11):1, 2003].
C. Tuberculous meningitis For severe rx with adjunctive steroids: CID 25:872, 1997	INH + RIF + ETB + PZA	May omit ETB when susceptibility to INH and RIF established. See Table 9, page 60, for CSF drug penetration.	3 drugs often recommended for initial rx, we prefer 4. May substitute ethionamide for ETB. Infection with MDR TB ↑ mortality & morbidity (CID 38:851, 2004). Dexamethasone (for 1st month) has been shown to ↓ complications (Pediatrics 99:226, 1997). PCR of CSF markedly increases diagnostic sensitivity and provides rapid dx (Neurol 45:2228, 1995; Arch Neurol 52:511, 1996) but considerable variability in sensitivity depending on methods used.
D. Tuberculosis during pregnancy	INH + RIF + ETB for 9 months		PZA not recommended because no teratogenicity data on fetus throughout pregnant women (16%). SM should not be used due to ototoxicity to fetus. Add pyridoxine 25 mg/kg/d for pregnant women on INH. Pzn-isoniazid should not be discouraged in pts on first-time drugs [MMWR 52(RR-11):1, 2003]
E. Treatment failure or relapse: Usually due to poor compliance or resistant organisms (AJM 102:164, 1997)	Directly observed therapy (DOT). Check susceptibilities. (See section III.A, page 85 & above)		Patients whose sputum has not converted after 5-6 mos = treatment failures. Failures may be due to non-compliance or resistant organisms. Check susceptibilities of original isolates and obtain susceptibility on current isolates. Non-compliance common, therefore modify regimen. Don't add single drug to failing regimen; add at least 2 drugs. If cerebral or less to which patient has not received. Surgery may be necessary in HIV+ patients; reinfection is a possible explanation for "failure".

See pages 90 & 92 for abbreviations, page 88 for footnotes

* Dosages are for adults (unless otherwise indicated) and assume normal renal function   † DOT = directly observed therapy

TABLE 12A (4)

FIGURE 1: TREATMENT ALGORITHM FOR TUBERCULOSIS [Modified from MMWR 52(RR:11):1, 2003]

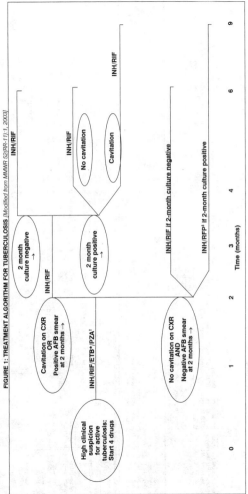

If the pt has HIV infection & the CD4 cell count is <100/μl, the continuation phase should consist of daily or 3x/wk INH & RIF for 4-7 months.

* ETB may be discontinued in <2 months if drug susceptibility testing indicate no drug resistance. † PZA may be discontinued after 2 months (56 doses). ‡ RFP should not be used in HIV patients with tuberculosis or in patients with extrapulmonary tuberculosis.

See pages 90 & 92 for abbreviations, page 88 for footnotes   * Dosages are for adults (unless otherwise indicated) and assume normal renal/renal function   † DOT = directly observed therapy

TABLE 12A (5)

CAUSATIVE AGENT/DISEASE	MODIFYING CIRCUMSTANCES	SUGGESTED REGIMENS PRIMARY/ALTERNATIVE	COMMENTS
III. **Mycobacterium tuberculosis** (continued)			
F. **HIV infection or AIDS—pulmonary or extrapulmonary**	INH + RIF (or RFB) + PZA months (x3 months). May treat up to 9 mos. in pts with delayed response. (Authors add **pyridoxine** 25–50 mg daily to regimens that include INH.)		1. Because of the possibility of developing resistance to RIF in pts with low CD4 cell counts who receive weekly or biweekly doses of RFB, it is recom. that such pts receive daily (or weekly 3x/ weekly) doses of RFB for initiation & continuation phase of rx (MMWR 51:214, 2002). 2. Clinical and microbiologic response same as in HIV-negative patient although there is considerable evidence for malabsorption in some (CID 32:561, 2001). 3. Post-treatment suppression not necessary for drug-susceptible strains. 4. Rate of INH resistance known to be <4% (for ↑ rates of resistance, see Section III.A). 5. For more information, see MMWR 47(RR-20):1, 1998; CID 28:139, 1999; MMWR 52(RR-11):1, 2003 6. May use partially intermittent therapy, 1 dose/day for 2 weeks followed by 2–3 doses/week for 24 weeks (CID 10:21B, 1998).
	Concomitant protease inhibitor (PI) therapy (Modified from MMWR 49:185, 2000; AJRCCM 162:7, 2001)	**Initial & cont. therapy:** INH 300 mg + RFB (see below for dose) + PZA 25 mg/kg + ETB 15 mg/kg daily x2 mos.; then INH + RFB daily x4 mos. (up to 7 mos.) **PI Regimen** / **RFB Dose** Nelfinavir 1200 mg q12h or indinavir 1000 mg q8h or amprenavir 1200 mg q12h: 150 (U) mg qd or 300 mg intermittently Lopinavir/ritonavir—standard dose: 150 U mg 2x/wk	**Comments:** Rifamycins induce cytochrome CYP450 enzymes (RIF > RFB > RFB) & reduce serum levels of concomitantly administered PIs. Conversely, PIs (ritonavir > amprenavir > indinavir = nelfinavir > saquinavir) inhibit CYP450 & cause ↑ serum levels of RIF, RFP & RFB. **Do not use RIF + PI**. RFB+PI combinations are therapeutically effective (CID 30:779, 2000). RFB has no effect on nelfinavir levels at dose of 1250 mg bid (Can JID 10:21B, 1999).
		Alternative regimen: INH + SM + PZA + ETB x2 mos.; then INH + SM + PZA 2–3 times/wk for 7 mos. May be used with any PI regimen. May be prolonged up to 12 mos. in pts with delayed response.	

FOOTNOTES: [1] When DOT is used, drugs may be given 5 d/wk & the necessary number of doses adjusted accordingly. Although there are no studies that compare 5 with 7 daily doses, extensive experience indicates this would be an effective practice. [2] Patients with cavitation on initial chest x-ray & a positive culture at completion of 2 months of rx should receive a 7-month (31 wk; either 217 doses [daily] or 62 doses [2x/wk] continuation phase. [3] 5-day a wk administration is always given by DOT. [4] Not recommended for HIV-infected patients with CD4 cell counts <100 cells/ul. [5] Options 1c & 2c should be used only in HIV-neg. pts who have neg. sputum smears at the time of completion of 2 months of rx & who do not have cavitation on initial chest x-ray. For pts started on this regimen & found to have a pos. culture from the 2-month specimen, rx should be extended an extra 3 months. [6] Options 4a & 4b should be considered only when options 1–3 cannot be given. [7] Alternative agents = ethionamide, cycloserine, p-aminosalicylic acid, clarithromycin, AM/CL, linezolid. Modified from MMWR 52(RR-11):1, 2003. See also IDCP 11:329, 2002.

CAUSATIVE AGENT/DISEASE	MODIFYING CIRCUMSTANCES	SUGGESTED REGIMENS PRIMARY/ALTERNATIVE	COMMENTS
IV. **Other Mycobacterial Disease ("Atypical")** (See ATS Consensus: AJRCCM 152:51, 1997; IDC No. Amer. March 2002; CMR 15:716, 2002)			
A. **M. tuberculosis**		INH + RIF + ETB	The M. tuberculosis complex includes M. bovis. All isolates resistant to PZA. 9–12 months of rx used by some authorities. Isolation not required.
B. **Bacillus Calmette-Guerin (BCG)** (derived from M. bovis)	Only fever (>38.5°C) for 12–24 hrs. Systemic illness or sepsis	INH 300 mg x3 months INH + RIF + ETB	Intravesical BCG effective for bladder tumors and carcinoma in situ. Adverse effects: fever 2.9%, granulomatous pneumonitis, hepatitis 0.7%, sepsis 0.4% (J Urol 147:596, 1992). With sepsis, consider adjunctive prednisolone. Resistant to PZA.
C. **M. avium-intracellulare complex** (MAC, MAI, or Battery bacillus) ATS Consensus Statement: AJRCCM 156:51, 1997 Clin Chest Med 23:633, 2002	**Immunocompetent patients** with chronic pulmonary, disseminated disease (subcutaneous, bone)	**Clarithro** 500 mg po bid (or **azithro** 500 mg po qd) + **ETB** 25 mg/kg po x2 mos, then 15 mg/kg po qd + **RFB** 300 mg po qd). May add **SM** or **AMK** 15 mg/kg tiw for 2–6 mos. for severe disease. May add **CLO** 100–200 mg po qd (until "tan"; then 50 mg po qd or 100 mg 3x/wk). Rx until culture neg. x1 yr. Alternative: **azithro** 600 mg po bid + **RFB** 300 mg po bid + po qd to 24 (15–25 mg/kg) po qd **RFB** 300 mg po qd (CID 27:1278, 1998; CID 30:288, 2000). Regimens (CID 27:1278, 1998; CID 30:288, 2000). Late ↑re-lapses" (following completion of therapy) share with clarithro or azithro in pts with nodular bronchiectasis usually represent reinfection, not failure of rx (JID 186:266, 2002).	**"Classic" pulmonary MAC:** Men 50–75, smokers, COPD. May be associated with hot tub use (Clin Chest Med 23:633, 2002). **"Nodular bronchiectasis"**: Women 30–70, scoliosis, mitral valve prolapse, (bronchiectasis), pectus excavatum ("Lady Windermere syndrome"). May be associated with interferon gamma deficiency (AJM 113:756, 2002). Susceptibility testing of MAC not recommended except clarithro testing of isolates from pts who have failed prior clarithro rx. RFB (600 mg po) & initial 2x/wk SM may be effective in immunocompetent patients (JID 178:121, 1998; CID 30:288, 2000). Late ↑re-lapses" (following completion of therapy)

See pages 90 & 92 for footnotes	* Dosages are for adults (unless otherwise indicated) and assume normal renal function	** DOT = directly observed therapy

TABLE 12A (6)

CAUSATIVE AGENT/DISEASE; MODIFYING CIRCUMSTANCES	SUGGESTED REGIMENS		COMMENTS
	PRIMARY	ALTERNATIVE	
IV. Other Mycobacterial Disease ("Atypical") *(continued)*			
C. M. avium-intra-cellulare complex *(continued)*			**COMMENTS**
Immunocompromised pts:	**PRIMARY**	**ALTERNATIVE**	
Primary prophylaxis—Pt's CD4 count <50–100/mm³ Discontinue when CD4 count >100/mm³ in response to HAART (NEJM 342:1085, 2000; CID 34: 662, 2002). Guideline: AnIM 137:435, 2002	**Azithro** 1200 mg po weekly OR **Clarithro** 500 mg po bid	**RFB** 300 mg po qd OR **Azithro** 1200 mg po weekly + **RFB** 300 mg qd	RFB reduces MAC infection rate by 55% (no survival benefit); clarithro by 68% (30% survival benefit); azithro by 59% (no survival benefit) (NEJM 335:392, 1996). **Many drug-drug interactions**, Azithro + RFB more effective than either alone but not as well tolerated (CID 26:611, 1998). Azithro + RFB more effective than either alone but not as well tolerated while taking azithro (NEJM 335:384 & 392, 1996). If disease seen in 29–58% of pts in whom disease develops while taking MAI prophylaxis—but not too late to begin. Clarithro prophylaxis & in 11% of those on azithro prophylaxis (NEJM 335:384 & 392, 1996). Clarithro resistance more likely in pts with extremely low CD4 counts at initiation (CID 27:807, 1998). Need to be sure no active M. tbc. RFB used for prophylaxis may promote selection of rifamycin-resistant M. tbc (NEJM 335:384 & 428, 1996).
Treatment Either presumptive dx or after positive culture of blood, bone marrow, or other usually sterile body fluids, e.g., liver	**Clarithro** 500 mg* po bid or **azithro** 600 mg po qd + **ETB** 15–25 mg/kg/d + *Higher doses of clari (1000 mg po bid) may be associated with ↑ mortality (CID 29:125, 1999)*	**Clarithro** or **azithro** + **ETB** + **RFB** + one or more of: **CIP** 750 mg po bid + **Ofloxacin** 400 mg po bid + **Amikacin** 7.5–15 mg/kg IV qd In pts receiving protease inhibitors can use **clarithro** 500 mg bid (or 1 gm bid if pt has not had previous exposure to a macrolide or rifabutin) (Med Letter 39:125; Hopkins AIDS Report 9:2, 1997)	Median time to neg. blood culture: clarithro + ETB 4.4 wks vs azithro + ETB >16 wks. At 16 wks, clearance of bacteremia seen in 37.5% of clarithro- & 85.7% of clarithro-treated pts (CID 27:1278, 1998). More recent study suggests similar clearance rates by clarithro (56%) vs clarithro (46%) at 24 wks when combined with ETB (CID 37:1245, 2000). Azithro 250 mg po qd not effective, but azithro 600 mg po qd as effective as 1200 mg & yields fewer adverse effects (AAC 43:2869, 1999). Addition of RFB to clarithro + ETB ↓ emergence of resistance to clari & improves survival (CID 37:1234, 2003). Data on clofazimine difficult to assess. Earlier study suggested adding CLO of no value (CID 25:621, 1997). More recent study suggests it may be as effective as RFB at preventing clari resistance (CID 28:136, 1999). Thus, pending more data, we still do not recommend CLO for MAI in HIV+ pts.
	RFB 300 mg po qd		Treatment failure rate is high. Reasons: drug toxicity, development of drug resistance, & inadequate serum levels of clarithro + in pts also given RIF or RFB (JID 171:747, 1995). If clari tolerated + no clinical or microbiol. improvement (relapse) on initial regimen when drug doses are optimal, may add one or two drugs, e.g., amikacin 7.5–15 mg/kg IV qd & CIP 750 mg po bid (AAC 38:2215, 1994; CID 26:682, 1998). Several anecdotal reports of pts not responding to usual primary regimen who gained weight and became afebrile with dexamethasone 2–4 mg/d po (AAC 38:2276, 1994; result is reduction in max. dose of RFB to 300 mg.
Chronic post-treatment suppression—secondary prophylaxis	Always necessary. **Clarithro** or **azithro** (at dosage above)	**Clarithro** or **azithro** + **ETB** (lower dose to 15 mg/kg/d) (dosage above)	Recurrences common. Usually without chronic suppression. However, in patients on HAART with robust CD4 cell response, it may be possible to discontinue chronic suppression (JID 178:1446; NEJM 340:1301, 1999)
D. Mycobacterium celatum	Treatment, optimal regimen not defined		Isolated from pulmonary lesions and blood in AIDS patients (CID 24:144, 1997). Easily confused with M. xenopi (not MAC). Clarithro-resistant strains now described (CID 24:140, 1997).
E. Mycobacterium chelonae abscessus / **Mycobacterium chelonae chelonae**	Treatment; Surgical excision may facilitate clarithro rx in subcutaneous and disseminated infections is important adjunct to rx (CID 24:1147, 1997)	May be susceptible to **clarithro**, **FQ** (Clin Microbiol Inf 3:582, 1997), Suggest: like MAI, but often takes 3–6 mos. Most reported cases received 3 or 4 drugs, usually clarithro + ETB + CIP + RIF (EID 9:399, 2003)	M. abscessus susceptible to AMK (70%), cefoxitin (70%), CLO, cefmetazole. Single isolates of M. abscessus often not associated with disease. Clarithro-resistant strains now described (JCM 39:2745, 2001). M. chelonae susceptible to AMK (80%), clarithro, azithro, tobramycin (100%), IMP (60%), moxifloxacin (AAC 46:3283, 2002). Resistant to cefoxitin, FQ (CID 24:1147, 1997; AJRCCM 156:S1, 1997).
F. Mycobacterium fortuitum	Treatment; optimal regimen not defined. Surgical excision of infected areas.	**AMK** + **cefoxitin** + **probenecid** 2–6 weeks, then po **TMP/SMX**, or **doxycycline** 2–6 mos. Usually require surgical excision.	M. abscessus susceptible to AMK (100%), clarithro (80%), cefoxitin (50%), imipenem (50%), IMP, clofazimine. Based on susceptibility: **clarithro** 500 mg po bid x6 mos. (AnIM 119:482, 1993; CID 24:1147, 1997; EJCMID 19:43, 2000). Azithro may also be effective. For serious disseminated infections add **AMK** or **IMP** for 1 wk 2–6 wks (CMR 15:716, 2002). M. chelonae susceptible to AMK (80%), clarithro, azithro, tobramycin (100%), IMP, **doxycycline** 2–6 mos. (to which it is susceptible (AAC 46: 3283, 2002; CMR 15: 716, 2002). Nail salon-acquired infections respond to 4–6 mos. of minocycline or doxy or CIP (CID 38:38, 2004). Sensitive in vitro to doxycycline, minocycline, cefoxitin, IMP, TMP/SMX, CIP, oflox, azithro, clarithro, gatifloxacin, moxifloxacin, linezolid (CMR 15:716, 2002). May be resistant to azithromycin, rifabutin (JAC 39:567, 1997). **Resistant to all standard anti-TBc drugs**

* *Dosages are for adults (unless otherwise indicated) and assume normal renal function*   **DOT** = directly observed therapy

See pages 90 & 92 for footnotes

See pages 90 & 92 for abbreviations, page 88 for footnotes

TABLE 12A (7)

CAUSATIVE AGENT/DISEASE; MODIFYING CIRCUMSTANCES	SUGGESTED REGIMENS		COMMENTS
	PRIMARY	**ALTERNATIVE**	
IV. Other Mycobacterial Disease ("Atypical") (continued)			
G. Mycobacterium haemophilum	Regimen(s) not defined. In animal model, **clarithro**, **RFB** ± **rifabutin** effective (AAC 2:2316, 1995). Combination of **CIP** + **RFB** + **clarithro** reported effective but clinical relevance limited (CMR 9:435, 1996). Surgical debridement may be necessary (IDCP 20:505, 1998).	Clinical: Ulcerating skin lesions, synovitis, osteomyelitis. Lab: Requires supplemented media to isolate. Sensitive in vitro to: CIP, cycloserine, rifabutin. Over ½ resistant to: INH, RIF, EMB, PZA (AnIM 117:1, 1994).	
H. Mycobacterium genavense	Regimens used include ≥2 or more of the following: **RFB**, **clofaz**, **clarithro**. In animal model, **clarithro** & **RFB** (& to lesser extent amikacin & **ETB**) shown effective in reducing bacterial counts. CIP not effective (JAC 42:483, 1998).	Clinical: CD4 <50. Symptoms of: fever, weight loss, diarrhea. Lab: Growth in BACTEC vials slow (mean 42 days). Subcultures grow only on Middlebrook 7H11 agar containing 2 μg/ml mycobactin J—growth still insufficient for in vitro sensitivity testing (Ln 340:76, 1992; AnIM 117:586, 1992). Survival ↑ from 81 to 263 days in pts rx for at least 1 month with ≥2 drugs (Arch Int Med 155:400, 1995).	
I. Mycobacterium gordonae	Regimen(s) not defined, but consider **RIF** + **clarithro** + **ETB** + **KM** or **CIP** (J Inf 38:157, 1999).	In vitro, sensitive to ETB, RIF, AMK, CIP, clarithro, linezolid (AAC 47:1736, 2003). Resistant to INH (JCM 43:1293, 2005).	
J. Mycobacterium kansasii	Daily dose: **INH** (300 mg) + **RIF** (600 mg) + **ETB** (25 mg/kg x2 mos, then 15 mg/kg). Rx for 18–24 mos. (until culture-neg sputum x12 mos). (See Comment)	If RIF-resistant, daily **INH** (900 mg) + **pyridoxine** (50 mg) + **ETB** (25 mg/kg) + **sulfamethoxazole** (1.0 gm tid). Rx until culture-neg. x12–15 mos. (See Comment). **Clarithro** + **ETB** + **RIF** also effective in small study (CID 37:1178, 2003).	Susceptible to PZA. Rifampin-line, azithro, ETB effective alone or in combination in athymic mice (AAC 42:417, 2001). Highly susceptible to linezolid in vitro (AAC 47:1736, 2003). If HIV+ pt taking protease inhibitor, substitute either clarithro (500 mg bid) or RFB (150 mg/d) for RIF (AJRCCM 156:S1, 1997). Because of variable susceptibility to INH, some substitute clarithro or clofaz for INH, however, resistance to clarithro reported (DMID 31:369, 1998). Prognosis related to level of immunosuppression (CID 37:584, 2003).	
K. Mycobacterium marinum	(**Clarithro** 500 mg bid) or (**minocycline** 100–200 mg qd) or (**doxycycline** 100–200 mg qd), or (**TMP/SMX** 160/800 mg po bid), or (**RIF** + **ETB**) for 3 mos. (AJRCCM 156:S1, 1997). Surgical excision.	Resistant to INH & PZA (AJRCCM 156:S1, 1997). Also susceptible in vitro to linezolid (AAC 47:1736, 2003); CIP, gatifloxacin, moxifloxacin also show moderate in vitro activity (AAC 46:1114, 2002).	
L. Mycobacterium scrofulaceum	Surgical excision. Chemotherapy seldom indicated. Although regimens not well defined, **CLO** with or without **ETB**, **INH**, **RIF**, **strep** + **cycloserine** have also been used.	Susceptible to INH, RIF, ETB, PZA, AMK, CIP (CID 20: 549, 1995). Susceptible to clarithro, strep, erythromycin.	
M. Mycobacterium simiae	Regimen(s) not defined. Start 4 drugs as for MAI.	Most isolates resistant to all 1st-line anti-TB drugs. Isolates often not clinically significant (CID 26: 625, 1998).	
N. Mycobacterium ulcerans (Buruli ulcer)	**RIF** + **AMK** (7.5 mg/kg IM bid) or **RIF** + **ETB** or **RIF** + **SM** (AJRCCM 156:S1, 1997) or **RIF** + **INH** + **ETB** (Resp Med 97:439, 2003) but recent study suggests no need to treat in small study with MAI (CID 37:1250, 2003).	Surgical excision is standard rx for M. ulcerans. **RIF** + **AMK** for 4–6 weeks.	Susceptible in vitro to: RIF, strep, CLO, clarithro, CIP, amikacin (chemo not effective). RIF + streptomycin x8 wks reduced mutants in mice (AAC 48:3193, 2004); also effective x4 wks to all isolates of M. ulcerans in mice (AAC 47:1228, 2003). Treatment generally disappointing—see review, (Ln 354:1013, 1999. RIF + dapsone only slightly better (82% improved) than placebo (75%) in small study (Ln 381 6:60, 2002).
O. Mycobacterium xenopi	Regimen(s) not defined (CID 24:226 & 233, 1997). Some recommend a **macrolide** + **RIF** or **rifabutin** (1997) or **RIF** + **INH** + **ETB** (AJRCCM 156:S1, 1997).		In vitro, sensitive to clarithro, minocycline, RIF, moxifloxacin, and/or ofloxacin and many standard antimycobacterial drugs. Clarithro-containing regimens more effective than RIF/INH/ETB regimens in mice (AAC 45:3229, 2001). FQs, linezolid also active in vitro.
Mycobacterium leprae (leprosy) Paucibacillary (tuberculoid or indeterminate) Multibacillary (lepromatous or borderline) **See Comment for erythema nodosum leprosum**	Paucibacillary: daily **dapsone** 100 mg/d + **RIF** 600 mg po 1x/month, supervised for 6 months. Multibacillary: daily **dapsone** 100 mg + **CLO** 50 mg daily unsupervised] + (**RIF** 600 mg + **CLO** 300 mg) 1x/month supervised, all x 12 months (WHO Tech Rpt 874:1, 1998). Recent studies suggest 12 mos. rx effective (Ln 353:655, 1999).	Side-effects overall 0.4%. Single lesion paucibacillary disease may be treated with single-dose rx (**RIF** 600 mg + **ofloxacin** 400 mg + **minocycline** 100 mg) (Ln 353:655, 1999). For erythema nodosum leprosum: prednisone 60–80 mg/d or thalidomide 300 mg/d (BMJ 44:775, 1988; AJM 108:487, 2000). CLO available from Ciba-Geigy (908) 277-3572). **Ofloxacin** 800 mg qd po, ofloxacin 400 mg qd po, sparfloxacin 200 mg qd po bactericidal for M. leprae + ↓ log + in organisms in small trials (Int J Leprosy 58:281, 1990; AAC 38:662, 1994; Hand **RIF** (960 mg) daily rapidly bactericidal, other drugs (CLO, ETB, INH, dapsone) slower (AAC 45:12, 2001). **Ethionamide** (250 mg/d) or **prothionamide** (375 mg) may be substituted for CLO.	1 recent study suggests dapsone monotherapy as effective as combination therapy for multibacillary leprosy (AAC 38:2249, 1994). Regimens incorporating clarithro, minocycline, RIF, moxifloxacin, and/or oflox also show promise (AAC 41:1618, 1997; AAC 44:2919, 2000). High relapse rate in pts treated with daily dapsone + oflox for 4 wks (AAC 41:1953, 1997). Resistance to dapsone, RIF & oflox reported (Ln 349:103, 1997). Dapsone (or acedapsone*) effective for prophylaxis (J Inf 41:137, 2000).

Rev.: Lancet 363:1209, 2004

* Dosages are for adults (unless otherwise indicated) and assume normal renal function   † **DOT** = directly observed therapy

Abbreviations: AMK = amikacin; **ATS** = American Thoracic Society; **Azithro** = azithromycin; **BL/BLI** = β-lactam/β-lactamase inhibitors; **CIP** = ciprofloxacin; **CLO** = clotazimine, clarithromycin and kanamycin or the polypeptide capreomycin; **IDSA** = Infectious Diseases Society of America; **IMP** = imipenem/cilastatin; **INH** = isoniazid; **INH-CR** = complete INH resistance; **KM** = tycin, amikacin, or kanamycin or the polypeptide capreomycin; **IDSA** = Infectious Diseases Society of America; **IMP** = imipenem/cilastatin; **INH** = isoniazid; **INH-CR** = complete INH resistance; **KM** = kanamycin; **Neomacrolides** = azithromycin, clarithromycin, roxithromycin; **NUS** = not available in the U.S.; **Oflox** = ofloxacin; **pts** = patients; **PZA** = pyrazinamide; **RFB** = rifabutin; **RFP** = rifapentine; **RIF** = rifampin; **rx** = treatment; **sens** = sensitive; **SM** = streptomycin; **TBc** = tuberculosis; **TMP/SMX** = trimethoprim/sulfamethoxazole

TABLE 12A (8)

TABLE 12B: DOSAGE, PRICE AND SELECTED ADVERSE EFFECTS OF ANTIMYCOBACTERIAL DRUGS[1]

AGENT (TRADE NAME)	USUAL DOSAGE	ROUTE/% DRUG RESIST./AIDS[2] (RES)	PRICE US/\$/COST	SIDE-EFFECTS, TOXICITY AND PRECAUTIONS	SURVEILLANCE
FIRST LINE DRUGS					
Ethambutol (Myambutol)	25 mg/kg/day for 2 months & then 15 mg/kg/day qd as 1 dose (Bacteriostatic to both extracellular & intracellular organisms)	po RES:* 0.3% (0–0.7%) 400 mg tab \$2.00		**Optic neuritis** with decreased visual acuity & red/green and red perception, peripheral neuropathy and headache (~1%, rare). arthralgia (rare), hyperuricemia (rare). Anaphylactoid reaction (rare). *Comment:* Primarily used to inhibit resistance. Disrupts outer cell membrane in M. avium with ↑ activity to other drugs	Monthly visual acuity & red/green with dose >15 mg/kg/day. ≥10% loss considered significant. Usually reversible if drug discontinued.
Isoniazid (INH) (Nydrazid, Laniazid Teebaconin)	Daily dose: 5–10 mg/kg/day up to 300 mg/day as 1 dose. twice weekly dose: 15 mg/kg (900 mg maximum dose) (< 10% protein binding) (Bactericidal to both extracellular and intracellular organisms) Add pyridoxine in alcoholic, pregnant, or malnourished pts.	po RES: 4.1% (2, 6–8.5%) 300 mg tab \$0.02 IM (IV route not FDA-approved but has been used, esp. in AIDS) 100 mg/ml in 10 ml vials \$16.64		Overall ~1%. Liver: **Hepatitis** (children 10% mild ↑ SGOT, normalizes with continued rx, age <20 yrs rare, 20–34 yrs 1.2%, ≥35 yrs 2.3% [also,↑ with daily alcohol & previous exposure to hepatitis C (usually asymptomatic) —*CID 36:293, 2003*]). May be fatal. With prodromal sx, discontinue if SGOT >3–5x normal. **Peripheral neuropathy** (17% on 6 mg/kg/day, less on 300 mg, incidence ↑ in slow acetylators). **pyridoxine 10 mg daily will ↓ incidence** of neuropathy, psychosis, muscle twitching, dizziness, ataxia, paresthesias (rare). Other neurologic sequelae: convulsions, optic neuritis, toxic encephalopathy, psychosis, muscle twitching, dizziness, coma (all rare); allergic skin rashes, fever, hepatic dysfunction and blood dyscrasias (rare), + malaise (20%). **Drug-drug interactions** common, see *Table 22.*	Pre-rx liver functions. Repeat if symptoms (fatigue, weakness, malaise, anorexia, nausea or vomiting) >3 days (*AJRCCM 152: 1705, 1995*). Some recommend SGOT at 2, 4, 6 months esp. if age >50 years. Clinical evaluation every month.
Pyrazinamide	25 mg/kg/day (maximum 2.5 gm/d) qd as 1 dose [Bactericidal for intracellular organisms]	po RES: 0.3% (0–0.3%) 500 mg tab \$1.04		**Arthralgia; hyperuricemia** (with or without symptoms). Hepatitis (not over 2% if recommended dose not exceeded); gastric irritation; photosensitivity (rare)	Pre-rx liver functions. Monthly SGOT, uric acid. Measure serum uric acid if symptomatic gouty attack occurs.
Rifamate®— combination tablet	2 tablets single dose qd	po 1 tab \$5.58		1 tablet contains 150 mg INH, 300 mg RIF	As with individual drugs
Rifampin (Rifadin, Rimactane, Rifocin)	10.0 mg/kg/day up to 600 mg/day as 1 dose (60–90% protein binding) [Bactericidal to all populations of organisms]	po (1 hr before meal) RES: 0.2% (0–0.3%) 300 mg cap \$3.54 (IV available, Merrell Dow. Cost 600 mg \$90.28)		INH/RIF dec'd in ~3% for toxicity, gastrointestinal irritation, antibiotic-associated colitis, drug fever (1%), pruritus with or without skin rash (1%), anaphylactoid reactions in HIV+ pts, mental confusion, thrombocytopenia (1%), leukopenia (1%), hemolytic anemia, transient abnormalities in liver function. **"Flu syndrome"** (fever, chills, headache, bone pain, shortness of breath) seen if RIF taken irregularly or interval of no rx. **Discolors urine, tears, sweat, contact lens** an orange-brownish color. May cause drug-induced lupus erythematosus (*Ln 349: 1521, 1977*).	Pre-rx liver function. Repeat if symptoms. **Multiple significant drug-drug interactions, see Table 22.**
Rifater®— combination tablet (See Side-Effects)	Wt ≥55 kg, 6 tablets single dose qd	po (1 hr before meal) 1 tab \$1.91		1 tablet contains INH 120 mg RIF, 300 mg PZA. Used in 1st 2 months of rx (PZA 25 mg/kg). Purpose is convenience in dosing, ↑ compliance (*AnIM 122: 951, 1995*) but cost 1.58 more. Side-effects = individual drugs.	As with individual drugs, PZA 25 mg/kg
Streptomycin	15 mg/kg IM qd, 0.75–1.0 gm/day initially (0.50 gm/day in >60 yrs); then 1.0 gm 2–3 times/week (15 mg/kg/day) qd as 1 dose	IM (or IV) RES: 3.9% (2.7–7.6%) 1.0 gm \$6.45		Overall 8%. **Ototoxicity**: vestibular dysfunction (vertigo), paresthesias, dizziness, nausea and vomiting in 75% (with doses 1.8 gm/day) and high frequency hearing loss (1%); nephrotoxicity (rare); peripheral neuropathy (rare); allergic skin rashes (4–5%); drug fever, anaphylactoid reaction (rare). Available from X-Gen Pharmaceuticals, 607-732-4411. Ref: *In—CID 19:1150, 1994.* Toxicity similar with qd vs tid dosing (*CID 38:1538, 2004*)	Monthly audiogram. In older pts, serum creatinine or BUN at start of rx and weekly if pt stable

[1] Note: Metabolism of antimycobacterial drugs may occur in patients with AIDS enteropathy. For review of adverse effects, see *AJRCCM 167:1472, 2003.*   **DOT** = directly observed therapy

[2] **RES** = % resistance of M. tuberculosis

* *Dosages are for adults (unless otherwise indicated) and assume normal renal function*

See pages 90 & 92 for abbreviations, page 88 for footnotes

See pages 90 & 92 for abbreviations, page 88 for footnotes

TABLE 12B (2)

AGENT (TRADE NAME)	USUAL DOSAGE	ROUTE/1° DRUG RESISTANCE (RES) US$/COST	SIDE-EFFECTS, TOXICITY AND PRECAUTIONS	SURVEILLANCE
SECOND LINE DRUGS (more difficult to use and/or less effective than first line drugs)				
Amikacin (Amikin)	7.5–10.0 mg/kg qd [Bactericidal for extracellular organisms]	IV or IM RES: (est) 0.1% 500 mg NB $33, G $18.70	See Table 10, pages 62 & 72. Toxicity similar with qd vs tid dosing (CID 38:1538, 2004).	Monthly audiogram. Serum creatinine or BUN weekly if pt stable
Capreomycin sulfate (Capastat sulfate)	1 gm/day (15 mg/kg/day) qd as 1 dose	IM or IV RES: 0.1% (0–0.9%) 1 gm $26.90	Nephrotoxicity (36%), ototoxicity (11%), eosinophilia, leukopenia, skin rash, fever, hypokalemia, neuromuscular blockade.	Monthly audiogram, biweekly serum creatinine or BUN
Ciprofloxacin (Cipro)	750 mg bid	po, IV RES: 0.1% (0–0.9%) 750 mg $4.80	TB is an FDA-approved indication for CIP. Desired CIP serum levels 4–6 µg/ml, requires median dose 800 mg (AJRCCM 151:2006, 1995). Discontinuation rates 6–7%. CIP well tolerated (Med QJM 151:2006). CIP-resistant M. Tb identified in New York (Ln 345:1148, 1995). See Table 10, pages 64 & 69 for adverse effects.	None
Clofazimine (Lamprene)	50 mg/d (unsupervised) + 300 mg 1x/month supervised or 100 mg/d	po (with meals) 50 mg $0.20	Skin: pigmentation (pink-brownish black) 75–100%, dryness 20%, pruritus 5%, GI: abdominal pain 50% (rarely severe leading to exploratory laparoscopy), splenic infarction (VR), bowel obstruction (VR), GI bleeding (VR). Eye: conjunctival irritation, retinal crystal deposits.	None
Cycloserine (Seromycin)	750–1000 mg/day (15 mg/kg/day) 2–4 doses/day [Bacteriostatic for both extracellular & intracellular organisms]	po RES: 0.1% (0–0.3%) 250 mg cap $4.19	Convulsions, psychoses (5–10% of those receiving 1.0 gm/day), headache, somnolence, hyperreflexia, increased CSF protein and pressure, peripheral neuropathy. 100 mg pyridoxine (or more) daily should be given concomitantly. Contraindicated in epileptics.	None
Dapsone	100 mg/day	po 100 mg $0.20	Blood: ↓ hemoglobin (1–2 gm) & 1 retics (2–12%) in most pts. Hemolysis in G6PD deficiency. Methemoglobinemia. CNS: peripheral neuropathy (rare). GI: nausea, vomiting. Renal: albuminuria, nephrotic syndrome. Erythema nodosum leprosum in pts rx for leprosy (½ pts 1st year)	None
Ethionamide (Trecator-SC)	500–1000 mg/day (10–15 mg/kg/d) 1–3 doses/day [Bacteriostatic for extracellular organisms only]	po RES: 0.8% (0–1.5%) 250 mg tab $3.09	Gastrointestinal irritation (up to 50% in large dose); golter, peripheral neuropathy (rare); convulsions (rare); CNS effects (rare); difficulty in diabetes control; rashes; hepatitis; purpura; stomatitis; gynecomastia; menstrual irregularity. Give drug with meals or antacids; 50–100 mg pyridoxine per day concomitantly. SGOT monthly. Possibly teratogenic.	None
Ofloxacin (Floxin)	400 mg bid	po, IV 400 mg (po) $6.67	Not FDA-approved indication. Overall adverse effects 11%, 4% discontinued drug due to side-effects. GI nausea 3%, diarrhea 1%. CNS insomnia 3%, headache 1%, dizziness 1%.	None
Para-aminosalicylic acid (PAS, Paser) (Na⁺ or K⁺ salt)	4–6 gm bid (200 mg/kg/day) [Bacteriostatic for extracellular organisms only]	po RES: 0.8% (0–1.5%) 450 mg (po) $0.08 (see Comment)	Gastrointestinal irritation (10–15%), goitrogenic action (rare); depressed prothrombin activity (rare); G6PD-mediated hemolytic anemia (rare), drug fever, rashes, hepatitis, myalgia, joint pain. Inhibits enzyme induction (may ↑ INH hepatotoxicity). Available from CDC, (404) 639-3670, Jacobus Pharm. Co. (609) 921-7447.	None
Rifabutin (Mycobutin)	300 mg/day (prophylaxis or treatment)	po 150 mg $6.84	Polymyalgia, polyarthralgia, leukopenia, granulocytopenia. Anterior uveitis when given with concomitant clarithromycin; avoid 600 mg dose (NEJM 330:438, 1994). Uveitis reported with 300 mg/d (AnIM 12:510, 1994). Reddish urine, orange skin (pseudojaundice).	None
Rifapentine (Priftin)	600 mg twice weekly for 1st 2 mos., then 600 mg q week	po 150 mg $3.00	Similar to other rifabutins. (See RIF, RFB.) Hyperuricemia seen in 21%. Causes reddish-orange discoloration of body fluids. Note ↑ prevalence of RIF resistance with rx (CID 159:1545, 1999).	None
Thalidomide (Thalomid)	100–300 mg/day (may use up to 400 mg po qd for severe erythema nodosum leprosum)	po 50 mg $27.90	**Contraindicated in pregnancy. Causes severe life-threatening birth defects. Both male and female patients must use barrier contraceptive methods (Pregnancy Category X). Frequently causes drowsiness or somnolence. May cause peripheral neuropathy** (AJM 108:487, 2000). For review, see Lancet 363:1803, 2004.	Available only through pharmacists participating in System for Thalidomide Education and Prescribing Safety (S.T.E.P.S.)

* Adult dosage only.   ** Mean (range) (higher in Hispanics, Asians, and patients < 10 years old).   *** Average wholesale price according to 2004 DRUG TOPICS RED BOOK, Medical Economics
Abbreviations: VR = very rare, **esp** = especially, **dc** = discontinue,   **RES** = % resistance to M. tuberculosis   † **DOT** = directly observed therapy

* Dosages are for adults (unless otherwise indicated) and assume normal renal function

See pages 90 & 92 for abbreviations, page 88 for footnotes

TABLE 13A: TREATMENT OF PARASITIC INFECTIONS

Many of the drugs suggested are not licensed in the United States. The following are helpful resources available through the Center for Disease Control and Prevention (CDC) in Atlanta. Website is www.cdc.gov. General advice for parasitic diseases other than malaria: (770) 488-7760 or (770) 488-7775.
For CDC Drug Service: 8:00 a.m.–4:30 p.m. EST, (404) 639-3670 (or –2888), emergency after hours: (404) 639-2888; fax: (404) 639-3717.
For malaria: Prophylaxis advice: (770) 488-7788 or (877) 394-8747; treatment: (770) 488-7788; website: www.cdc.gov/travel, fax (888) 232-3299

NOTE: All dosage regimens are for adults with normal renal function unless otherwise stated.

For licensed drugs, suggest checking package inserts to verify dosage and side-effects. Occasionally, post-licensure data may alter dosage as package inserts.
For abbreviations of journal titles, see *Table 1, page 45*. **Reference with pediatric dosages: *Medical Letter on-line version: www.medletter.com (August 2004)***

INFECTING ORGANISM	PRIMARY	SUGGESTED REGIMENS ALTERNATIVE	COMMENTS
PROTOZOA—INTESTINAL (non-pathogenic: E. hartmanni, E. dispar, E. coli, Iodamoeba butschlii, Endolimax nana, Chilomastix mesnili)			
Balantidium coli	**Tetracycline** 500 mg po qid x10 d.	**Metronidazole** 750 mg po tid x5 d	*See Table 10B for side-effects.*
Blastocystis hominis	Role as pathogen supported random. trial: metro vs placebo	**Metronidazole** 750 mg po tid x10 d. **High dose** increases risk of adverse side-effects. **Alternatives: Iodoquinol** 650 mg po tid x20 d. or **TMP/SMX-DS**, one tid x7 d.	
Cryptosporidium parvum and hominis Treatment is unsatisfactory. Ref: *CID 39:504, 2004.*	**Immunocompetent—No HIV:** **Nitazoxanide** 500 mg po bid x3 d.	**Immunodeficiency:** **Nitazoxanide** 500 mg po bid x14 d. in adults (60% response). No response in HIV+ children.	**Nitazoxanide:** Approved in a liquid formulation for rx of children & 500 mg tabs for adults. Ref: *Med Lett 45:29, 2003.* C. hominis assoc. with 1 in post-infection eye & joint pain, recurrent headache, & dizzy spells (*CID 39:504, 2004*)
Cyclospora cayetanensis	Immunocompetent pts: **TMP/SMX-DS** tab 1 po bid x7-10 d.	AIDS pts: **TMP/SMX-DS** tab 1 po qid x10 d. then tab 1 po 3x/week	Ref: *CID 23:429, 1996.* If sulfa-allergic: **CIP** 500 mg po bid x7 d. & then 1 tab po 3x/wk x2 wks.
Dientamoeba fragilis	**Iodoquinol** 650 mg po x20 d.	**Tetracycline** 500 mg po qid x10 d. OR **Metronidazole** 500–750 mg po tid x10 d	Other alternatives: doxy 100 mg po bid x10 d; paromomycin 500 mg po tid x7 d.
Entamoeba histolytica; amebiasis Reviews: *Ln 361:1025, 2003; NEJM 348:1563, 2003.*			
Asymptomatic cyst passer	**Paromomycin** (aminosidine in U.K.) 500 mg po tid x7 d. OR **Iodoquinol** 650 mg po tid x20 d.	**Diloxanide furoate***[NUS]* (Furamide) 500 mg po tid x10 d. (Source: Panorama Compound. Pharm., 800-247-9767).	Metronidazole not effective vs cysts.
Patient with diarrhea/dysentery; mild/moderate disease. Oral rx possible	**Metronidazole** 500–750 mg po tid x10 d. or **tinidazole** 2 gm once daily x3 d. followed by: Either [**paromomycin** 500 mg po tid x7 d.] or [**iodoquinol** 650 mg po tid x20 d.]	**Tinidazole***[NUS]* 600 mg po q12h x3 d. or **Ornidazole***[NUS]* 500 mg po q12h x5 d.]	**Dx:** antigen detection & PCR better than O&P & serology. Watch out for non-pathogenic E. dispar (*Ln 351:1672, 1998*).
Severe or extraintestinal infection, e.g. hepatic abscess	**Metronidazole** 750 mg **IV** to **PO** tid x10 d. OR **paromomycin** 500 mg po tid x7 d.	**Metronidazole** 750 mg po tid x5 d. (high frequency of GI side-effects). See Comment. Rx if pregnant: **Paromomycin** 500 mg 4x/d. x7 d.	**Serology positive** (antibody present) with extraintestinal disease.
Giardia lamblia; giardiasis	**Tinidazole** 2.0 gm po x1) OR (**nitazoxanide** 500 mg po bid x3 d.)	**Metronidazole** 500–750 mg po tid x5 d. (high frequency of GI side-effects) See Comment. **Paromomycin** 500 mg 4x/d. x7 d.—87% response (*AnIM 132:885, 2000*).	Chronic suppression in AIDS pts; either 1 **TMP/SMX-DS** tab 3x/wk OR (pyrimethamine 25 mg/d po + folinic acid 5 mg/d po)
Isospora belli	**TMP/SMX-DS** tab 1 po bid x10 d. If AIDS pt.: TMP/SMX-DS qid x10 d. & then bid x3 wks.	(**Pyrimethamine** 75 mg/d po + **folinic acid** 10 mg/d po) x14 d. **CIP** 500 mg po bid x7 d.—87% response	

[superscript 1] **Drugs available from CDC Drug Service: 404-639-2888 or –3670 or www.cdc.gov/ncidod/srp/drugs/formulary.html: Bithionol, dehydroemetine, diethylcarbamazine (DEC), melarsoprol, nifurtimox, stibogluconate (Pentostam), suramin.**

[superscript 2] Quinacrine available from Panorama Compounding Pharmacy, (800) 247-9767; (818) 988-7979.

* *All doses are for adults(unless otherwise indicated) and assume normal renal function. See page 103 for abbreviations.*

TABLE 13A (2)

INFECTING ORGANISM	SUGGESTED REGIMENS		COMMENTS
	PRIMARY	ALTERNATIVE	
PROTOZOA—INTESTINAL (continued)			
Microsporidiosis (Ref.: CID 27:1, 1998)			
Ocular: Encephalitozoon hellum or cuniculi, Vittaforma corneae (Nosema sp.)	Albendazole 400 mg po bid x3 weeks	In HIV+ pts, reports of response of E. hellum to **fumagillin** eyedrops (not available in US). For V. corneae, may need keratoplasty	To obtain fumagillin: 800-292-6773 or www.leiterrx.com. Neutropenia & thrombocytopenia serious adverse events. Dx: Most labs use modified trichrome stain. Need electron micrographs for species identification. FA and PCR methods in development
Intestinal (diarrhea): Enterocytozoon bieneusi, Encephalitozoon (Septata) intestinalis	Albendazole 400 mg po bid x3 weeks	Oral **fumagillin 20 mg po tid** reported effective for E. bieneusi (NEJM 346:1963, 2002)—see Comment	For Trachipleistophora sp., try itraconazole + albendazole (NEJM 351:42, 2004).
Disseminated: E. hellum, cuniculi, or intestinalis; Pleistophora sp., others in Comment	Albendazole 400 mg po bid x3 weeks	No established rx for Pleistophora sp.	Other pathogens: Brachiola vesicularum & algerae (NEJM 351:42, 2004).
PROTOZOA—EXTRAINTESTINAL			
Amebic meningoencephalitis			
Acanthamoeba sp.— no proven rx. Rev.: Clin Micro Rev 16:273, 2003	Success with IV **pentamidine**, topical **chlorhexidine** & 2% **ketoconazole** cream & then po **itra** (NEJM 331:85, 1994), 2 children responded to po rx: **TMP/SMX + rifampin- keto** (PIDJ 20:623, 2001).		For treatment of keratitis, see Table 1, page 9
Balamuthia mandrillaris	A cause of chronic granulomatous meningitis		Case report: Ampho, miconazole, & RIf (NEJM 306:346, 1982)
Naegleria fowleri: >95% mortality. Sappinia diploidea	**Ampho B** 1.5 mg/kg/d in 2 div. doses & then 1 mg/kg/d x6 d. **Azithro** + **pentamidine** + **itra** + **flucytosine** (JAMA 285:2450, 2001)		
Babesia microti; babesiosis (CID 22:1117, 2001)	**Atovaquone** 750 mg bid po x7–10 d. + **azithro** 600 mg po daily x7–10 d. (NEJM 343:1454, 2000)	(**Clindamycin** 600 mg po tid) + (**quinine** 650 mg po bid) x7–10 d. For adults, can give **clinda** IV as 1.2 gm bid	Can cause overwhelming infection in asplenic patients. Reported in Washington State (EIN 10:622, 2004).
Ehrlichiosis—See Table 1, page 39			
Leishmaniasis. NOTE: Responses of various species differ—see references			
Visceral—Kala-azar	**Lipid formulations of ampho B** effective in short-course regimens but impractical due to expense: **Children:** Liposomal ampho B → 98% success (CID 36:560, 2003) in dose of 10 mg/kg/d x2 days. **Adults:** Liposomal Ampho B 2 mg/kg x5 d. (CID 38:377, 2004).	Antimony resistance is a problem in India (JID 180:564, 1999). **Antimony (stibogluconate** or **meglumine antimonate)** 20 mg/kg/d of antimony (Sb) (in 2 div. doses) IM or IV x28 d. Not marketed in U.S. Contact CDC Drug Service: (404) 639-3670. **Miltefosine:** Available from Zentaris, Frankfurt, Germany: Impavido@zentaris.de.	
L. donovani: India/Africa L. infantum: Mediterranean L. chagasi: New World **WARNING: Avoid combined antimony & ampho B** (Ln 351:1928, 1998)	**Miltefosine**[NB] drug of choice—see Comment. **Adults:** 2.5 mg/kg. po either as once or twice daily x28 d. **Children** (<12 yrs old): 2.5 mg/kg/d. in 3 div. doses after meals x28 d. Refs.: NEJM 347:1737, 1739, & 1794, 2002; PIDJ 22:434, 2003		
Mucosal—L. braziliensis	**Antimony,** as for Visceral		Approx. cure rates: antimony 60%, AmB ~75% or miltefosine, contact Zentaris: Impavido@zentaris.de
Cutaneous:			
Most resolve spontaneously; Rx goal: ↓ time, extent, & prevention of mucocutaneous spread	Fluconazole 200 mg po once daily x6 wks. Effective vs L. major (NEJM 346:891, 2002). Miltefosine[NB] 2.5 mg/kg po 1x/d. x28 d. 91% success (CID 38:1266, 2004).	Other options all IV: Antimony, as for visceral, or Pentamidine 2–4 mg/kg IV qd x20–30 doses	Treatment is species-specific. Good review (does not include miltefosine), JAC 53:158, 2004.
New World: Multiple species	**Ampho B**[1] 1 mg/kg IV daily x20-30 doses		
Old World: L. tropica & L. major			

NOTE: All dosage recommendations are for adults (unless otherwise indicated) and assume normal renal function. See page 103 for abbreviations.

TABLE 13A (3)

INFECTING ORGANISM	SUGGESTED REGIMENS		COMMENTS
	PRIMARY	ALTERNATIVE	

PROTOZOA—EXTRAINTESTINAL (continued)

Malaria (Plasmodium species)—NOTE: CDC Malaria info—prophylaxis (877) 394-8747; treatment (770) 488-7788. Websites: www.cdc.gov/ncidod/dpd/parasites/malaria/default.htm; www.who.int/health-topics/malaria.htm.

INFECTING ORGANISM	PRIMARY	ALTERNATIVE	COMMENTS
Prophylaxis—Drugs plus personal protection: screens, nets, etc. 30–35% DEET skin repellent (avoid 95% products in children), permethrin spray on clothing and nets. www.cdc.gov/ncidod/dpd/parasites/malaria/default.htm; www.who.int/health-topics/malaria.htm.			
For areas with no chloroquine (CQ)-resistance: Central American north of Panama Canal, Haiti, Dominican Republic, Central America west and north of the Panama Canal, and parts of the Middle East. For areas with **CQ-resistant P. falciparum** Mefloquine info on prophylaxis at (888) 232-3228 or website: www.cdc.gov Ref.: JAMA 278:1767, 1997	**CQ** 500 mg (300 mg base) po per week starting 1-2 wks prior to travel, during, & 4 wks post-travel or **AP**[1] 1 adult tab/day. **Atovaquone** 250 mg-**proguanil** 100 mg (Malarone): comb. tab. 1/day with food [1-2 prior to, during, & 7 days post-travel. Peds dose in footnote[4] Cost2 wks: $125.	**AP** by weight (peds tabs): 11-20 kg, 1 tab; 21-30 kg, 2 tabs; 31-40 kg, 3 tabs; >40 kg, 1 adult tab/day. **Doxycycline** 100 mg po daily for adults & children >12 years of age (2228 mg) can be used po per week, 1 wk before, during, and for 4 wks after travel. Cost2 wks: $80 Peds dose in footnote[4] Another option for adults: **primaquine (PQ)** 30 mg base po daily in non-pregnant G6PD-neg. travelers 88% protective vs P. falciparum & >92% vs P. vivax (CID 33:1990, 2001).	CQ site during pregnancy. **The areas free of CQ-resistant P. vivax** are the area north of the Panama Canal, Haiti, and parts of Middle East. CQ-resistant falciparum malaria reported from Saudi Arabia, Yemen, Oman, & Iran. **Pregnancy: MQ current best option.** Insufficient data with **Malarone. Avoid doxycycline and primaquine.** **Primaquine.** Use only if prolonged exposure to endemic area (e.g., Peace Corps). **Can cause hemolytic anemia if G6PD deficiency present.** **MQ not recommended** if cardiac conduction abnormalities, seizures, or psychiatric disorders, e.g., depression, psychosis. MQ outside U.S.: 275 mg tab, contains 250 mg of base. Malarone resistance: CID 37:450, 2003.
Treatment (NEJM 335:800, 1996) (P. falciparum, P. vivax, P. malariae, P. ovale) Blood smear consistent with **P. vivax and/or P. ovale** CDC: Malaria treatment— (770) 488-7788 or website: www.cdc.gov Blood smear consistent with **P. falciparum or P. malariae CQ-sensitive** Blood smear shows **P. falciparum assumed CQ-resistant** PO therapy in footnote[3]. Ref.: NEJM 335:800, 1996 Rx same for CQ-resistant P. vivax	For **chloroquine (CQ)-sensitive plasmodia:** CQ phosphate (1.0 gm (=600 mg base) po, 0.5 gm in 6 hrs, then 0.5 gm daily x2 d] **Primaquine (PQ)** 26.3 mg (15 mg base) po daily x14 d. Check for severe G6PD def. before rx. (CID 39:1336, 2004) For **chloroquine (CQ)-sensitive** primaquine (PQ) as for CQ-sensitive P. vivax (see above). Quinine sulfate (GS) 325-650 mg po tid x 3-7 d + **doxycycline** 100 mg bid x7 d, **OR** (2) **Atovaquone/proguanil 1 gm/400 mg** (4 adult tabs) po 1X/day for 3 days, with food.	[Quinine prolonged time to clear parasitemia (Ln 350:704, 1997). CG-resistant P. vivax (see Comment) **Quinine sulfate (GS)** 650 mg po q8h x3-7 d, + **doxycycline** 100 mg bid x7 d, then 500 mg 12 hrs later **OR halofantrine** 500 mg po q6h x3 doses. To prevent relapses, give PQ 26.3 mg (15 mg base) 1 tab po daily x14 d, screen for G6PD def. to avoid hemolysis. Assumes P. falciparum CQ-sensitive, i.e., acquired in Central America (west of Panama Canal), Haiti, and most of Middle East. **Other rx alternatives:** (1) **MQ**[6] 750 mg, then 500 mg 12 hrs later (peds & adults). Repeat regimen in 1 wk. (2) **Halofantrine** 500 mg q6h x3 doses.	No CQ-resistant P. vivax reported from Oceania and South America. For CQ-resistant P. falciparum: No PO in pregnancy or to newborns—risk of hemolysis. Peds rx doses: For CQ 10 mg of base per kg po, then 5 mg base/kg at 12, 24, 36 hrs. For PQ use 0.3 mg base/kg x14 d. Areas of drug resistance[4,5]: (1) NNV Thailand: **(Artesunate**[6,d] 4 mg/kg po x3 d + **mefloquine** 750 mg x2 d (peds & adults). Artesunate ref.: AAC 47:901, 2003 **Pregnancy:** High morbidity/mortality. Despite concerns of potential fetal toxicity, use **quinine** or **quinidine** followed by **Fansidar** (pyrimethamine), 3 tabs (500 mg) or 1500 mg **sulfadoxine** + 75 mg **pyrimethamine** single dose. Alternatives: (Quinine + doxycycline [despite fetal concerns]) OR (quinine + clindamycin (AAC 46:2315, 2002)). **Do not use AP during pregnancy.**

[1] **AP** = atovaquone proguanil; **CQ** = chloroquine phosphate; **CO** = chloroquine; **MQ** = mefloquine; **PQ** = primaquine; **GS** = quinine sulfate

[2] **prophylaxis dosages** (Ref.: CID 34:493, 2002): **Mefloquine** weekly dose by **weight** in kg: <15 = 5 mg/kg; 15-19 = ¼ adult dose; 20-30 = ½ adult dose; 31-45 = ¾ adult dose; >45 = adult dose. **atovaquone/proguanil** by **weight** in kg: 11-20 kg, 62.5/25 mg; 21-30 kg, 125/50 mg; 31-40 kg, 187.5/75 mg; >40 kg, 250/100 mg. **Doxycycline**, ages >8-12 yrs: 2 mg/kg/d up to 100 mg

[3] **Pediatric treatment dosage** (Ref.: CID 37:1340, 2003): **CQ** 25 mg/kg/d (max. 2 gm/d) po div. q8h x3 d. + a single po dose of **Fansidar** (pyrimethamine sulfadoxine) given on last day of quinine. Fansidar single dose by age (yr) of pt: <1 = ¼ tab; 1-3 = ½ tab; 4-8 yrs = 1 tab; 9-14 = 2 tabs; >14 = 3 tabs. **Atovaquone/proguanil** single daily dose by weight: 5-8 kg, 125/50 mg; 9-10 kg, 187.5/75 mg; 11-20 kg, 250/100 mg; 21-30 kg, 500/200 mg; 31-40 kg, 750/300 mg; >40 kg, adult dose. **Mefloquine** <45 kg, 15 mg/kg, then 10 mg/kg 12 hrs later. **Halofantrine** <40 kg, 8 mg/kg, repeat if same dose 6 hrs later x3 doses, all x3 days.

NOTE: All dosage recommendations are for adults (unless otherwise indicated) and assume normal renal function. See page 103 for abbreviations.

TABLE 13A (4)

INFECTING ORGANISM	SUGGESTED REGIMENS		COMMENTS
	PRIMARY	ALTERNATIVE	

PROTOZOA—EXTRAINTESTINAL/Malaria/Treatment *(continued)*

INFECTING ORGANISM	PRIMARY	ALTERNATIVE	COMMENTS
P. falciparum **Pt. able to take po therapy** **NOTE:** Steroids are harmful in cerebral malaria. Drug resistance ref.: *Ln Inf Dis 2:209, 2002*	In U.S.: **Quinidine gluconate** in normal saline (10 mg/kg IV over 1 hr, then 0.02 mg/kg/min x 72 hrs) OR EKG [2 mg/kg (15 mg/kg) IV over 4 hrs, then 7.5 mg/kg IV over 4 hrs q8h x72 hrs] OR until patient can take po meds. **NOTE:** No loading dose if mefloquine or quinine in past 24 hrs.	In U.S.: **Quinine dihydrochloride**[IV,IS in 5% dextrose 20 mg/kg IV over 4 hrs, then 10 mg/kg q8h (max. 1800 mg/d)] OR **Artemether**[IM,IS 3.2 mg/kg IM, then 1.6 mg/kg IM, daily] For both, switch to po regimen when possible to finish 7 days of rx.	May be manifest as cerebral malaria, renal failure, or ARDS. **Monitor parasitemia!** If rx effective, expect ≥75% ↓ parasite count after 48 hrs of rx. If parasitemia exceeds 15%, consider **exchange transfusion**: efficacy unclear. CDC: Malaria info (770) 488-7788 **Pregnancy:** See Comment, bottom of page 95
Malaria—self-initiated treatment: Only for emergency situation where medical care not available	**Atovaquone-proguanil** 4 adult tabs (1 gm/400 mg) po daily x3 d.	**Fansidar** (25 mg/tab pyrimethamine + 500 mg sulfadoxine) 3 tabs po x1 dose	

Microsporidia—systemic—see page 94 /Intestinal Protozoa

INFECTING ORGANISM	PRIMARY	ALTERNATIVE	COMMENTS
Pneumocystis carinii Pneumonia (PCP) New name is **Pneumocystis jiroveci** (yee-row-vek-ee). **Not acutely ill,** able to take po meds. PaO₂ >70 mmHg	**TMP/SMX-DS**, 2 tabs po q8h x21 d.) OR (**Dapsone** 100 mg po qd + **trimethoprim** 5 mg/kg po tid x21 d.) NOTE: Concomitant use of corticosteroids	Mutations encoding resistance to sulfamethoxazole identified (*JID 188:1017, 2003*). (**Clindamycin** 300-450 mg po q6h x21 d. OR 15 mg/kg with clinda/prim x21 d.) OR **Atovaquone** suspension 750 mg po bid with food x21 d.	DAP/TMP, TMP/SMX, clinda/prima regimens equally effective. Ref.: Rash/fever 10% with DAP/TMP, 19% with TMP/SMX, 21% with clindamycin. Ref.: clinda/prim vs TMP/SMX: *CID 27:524, 1998.* Dapsone ref.: *CID 27:191, 1998* **After 21 days, chronic suppression in AIDS pts (see below).**
Acutely ill, po rx not possible: PaO₂ <70 mmHg	**Prednisone** (15-30 min before TMP/SMX) 40 mg po bid x5 d., then 40 mg qd x5 d., then 20 mg po qd x11 d.) + **TMP/SMX** (15 mg of TMP component/kg/d IV div. q6-8h x21 d.)	usually reserved for sicker pts with PaO₂ <70 (see below). **TMP/SMX** as in primary rx. PLUS [(**Clinda** 600 mg IV q8h) + (**primaquine** 30 mg base po qd)] x21 d. OR **Pentamidine** 4 mg/kg/d IV x21 d.	**After 21 days, chronic suppression in AIDS pts (see below).** **PCP can occur in absence of HIV infection and steroids (CID 25:215 & 219, 1997).**
	Can substitute IV prednisone for po prednisone		
Primary prophylaxis and post-treatment suppression Refs.: *MMWR 51(RR-8), 6/14/2002;* *AnIM 137:435, 2002*	(**TMP/SMX-DS** or **SS**, 1 tab po qd or 1 DS 3x/wk) OR (**dapsone** 100 mg po qd). OR when CD4 >200 x3 mos. (*NEJM 344:159, 2001*)	**Pentamidine** 300 mg in 6 ml sterile water by aerosol q4 wks) OR (**dapsone** 200 mg po + **pyrimethamine** 75 mg po + **folinic acid** 25 mg po q wk) or **atovaquone** 1500 mg po qd with food	TMP/SMX-DS regimen provides cross-protection vs toxo and other bacterial infections. Dapsone + pyrimethamine protects vs toxo. Atovaquone suspension 1500 mg once daily as effective as daily dapsone (*NEJM 339:1889, 1998*) & inhaled pentamidine (*JID 180:369, 1999*).

Toxoplasma gondii (Reference: *Ln 363:1965, 2004*)

INFECTING ORGANISM	PRIMARY	ALTERNATIVE	COMMENTS
Immunologically normal patients (For pediatric doses, see reference) Acute illness with lymphadenopathy	No specific rx unless severe/persistent symptoms or evidence of vital organ damage		
Acquired via transfusion (lab accident)	Treat any for active chorioretinitis.		
Active chorioretinitis: meningitis; lowered resistance due to steroids or cytotoxic drugs	[**Pyrimethamine** (pyri) 200 mg po loa on 1st day, then 50-75 mg qd] + [**leucovorin (folinic acid)** 5-20 mg 3x/week] + (**sulfadiazine** (see Comment) [footnote[1]] 1-1.5 gm po qid) + **leucovorin (folinic acid)** (5-20 mg 3x/week) — **see Comment**. Treat 1-2 wks beyond resolution of signs/symptoms, continue leucovorin 1 wk after stopping pyri.		For congenital toxo, toxo meningitis in adults, and chorioretinitis, **add prednisone (1 mg/kg qd) div. doses** until CSF protein concentration falls or vision-threatening inflammation has subsided. Adjust folinic acid dose by following CBC results.
Acute in pregnant women	**Spiramycin** [From FDA, call (301) 827-2335] 1.0 gm (no q8h (without food) until term or until fetal infection. NOTE: Use caution in interpretation of commercial tests for toxoplasma IgM antibody, for help, FDA Advisory (301) 594-3060 or Toxoplasma Serology Lab of Palo Alto Med. Found: (650) 853-4828.		IgG avidity test of help in 1st trimester (*J Clin Micro 42:941, 2004*).
Fetal/congenital	[Management complex. Combination rx with pyrimethamine + sulfadiazine + leucovorin—see Comment		Details in *Ln 363:1965, 2004.* **Consultation advisable.**

[1] Sulfuramides now commercially available. Sulfisoxazole much less effective.

NOTE: All dosage recommendations are for adults (unless otherwise indicated) and assume normal renal/renal function. See page 103 for abbreviations.

TABLE 13A (5)

INFECTING ORGANISM	SUGGESTED REGIMENS		COMMENTS
	PRIMARY	ALTERNATIVE	
PROTOZOA—EXTRAINTESTINAL/Toxoplasma gondii *(continued)*			
Acquired immunodeficiency syndrome (AIDS)			
Cerebral toxoplasmosis	(Pyrimethamine (pyri) 200 mg x1 po, then 75 mg/d po) + (sulfadiazine 1–1.5 gm po q6h) + folinic acid 10–20 mg/d po) for 4–6 wks after resolution of signs/symptoms, and then suppression.	[Pyri + folinic acid (as in primary regimen)] + 1 of the following: (1) Clinda 600 mg po/IV q6h or (2) clarithro 1 gm po bid or (3) azithro 1.2–1.5 gm po qd or (4) atovaquone 750 mg po q6h or (5) atovaquone 750 mg po q6h + (pyri 75 mg po qd + folinic acid 10–25 mg po qd)	Use alternative regimen for pts with severe sulfa allergy. If multiple ring-enhancing brain lesions (CT or MRI), >85% of pts respond to 7–10 days of empiric rx; if no response, suggest brain biopsy.
Ref.: *Ln 363:1965, 2004*	TMP/SMX 10/50 mg/kg/d po or IV div q12h x30 d. (*AAC 42:1346, 1998*)	Treat 4–6 wks after resolution of signs/symptoms.	
Primary prophylaxis AIDS pts—IgG toxo antibody + CD4 count <100/μl	TMP/SMX-DS, 1 tab po qd or (TMP/SMX-SS, 1 tab po qd)	(Dapsone 50 mg po qd) + pyri 50 mg po a week) OR + (folinic acid 25 mg po qd) OR atovaquone 1500 mg po qd	Prophylaxis for pneumocystis also effective vs toxo. Refs.: *MMWR 51(RR-8), 6/14/2002; AnIM 137:435, 2002*
Suppression after rx of cerebral toxo	(Sulfadiazine 500–1000 mg po qid) + (pyri 25–50 mg po qd) + (folinic acid 10–25 mg po qd). SC if CD4 count >200 x3 months.	[(Clinda 300–450 mg po q6–8h) + (pyri 25–50 mg po qd) + (folinic acid 10–25 mg po qd)] OR atovaquone 750 mg po q6–12h	(Pyri + sulfa) prevents PCP and toxo; (clinda + pyri) prevents toxo only.
Trichomonas vaginalis	See Vaginitis, Table 1, page 17		
Trypanosomiasis. Ref.: *Ln 362:1469, 2003*			
West African sleeping sickness (T. brucei gambiense)			
Early: Blood/lymphatic	Pentamidine 4 mg/kg IM daily x10 d.	Suramin[CDC] 100 mg IV (test dose), then 1 gm IV on days 1, 3, 7, 14, & 21	
Late: Encephalitis	Melarsoprol[CDC] 2.2 mg/kg/d IV x10 d.	Eflornithine 100 mg/kg q6h IV x14 d.	
Prophylaxis	Pentamidine 3 mg/kg IM q6 mos.	Not for casual visitor.	
East African sleeping sickness (T. brucei rhodesiense)			
Early: Blood/lymphatic	Suramin[CDC] 100 mg IV (test dose), then 1 gm IV on days 1, 3, 7, 14, & 21	None	
Late: Encephalitis	Melarsoprol[CDC] 2–3.6 mg/kg/d IV x3 d.; repeat after 7 d. & for 3rd time 7 d. after 2nd course	Prednisone may prevent/attenuate encephalopathy	
T. cruzi—**Chagas disease** or acute American trypanosomiasis	Nifurtimox[CDC] 8–10 mg/kg/d po div. 4x/d. after meals x120 d. Ages 11–16 yrs: 12.5–15 mg/kg/d po qid x90 d. Children <11 yrs: 15–20 mg/kg/d div. qid po x90 d.	Benznidazole[MUS] 5–7 mg/kg/d po div. 2x/d x30–90 d. (*MMWR 63:111, 2000*) NOTE: Avoid tetracycline and steroids.	Treatment of no benefit in chronic late disease. Nifurtimox reported 70–95% effective. Immunosuppression for heart transplant can reactivate chronic Chagas disease.
Ref.: *Ln 357:797, 2001*			
NEMATODES—INTESTINAL (Roundworms). For significance of eosinophilia, see *CID 34:407, 2002*			
Ascaris lumbricoides (**ascariasis**)	Albendazole 400 mg po x1 dose or mebendazole 100 mg po bid x3 d. or 500 mg po x1 dose	Ivermectin 150–200 μg/kg po x1 dose or nitazoxanide 500 mg po bid x3 d	Can present with intestinal obstruction.
Capillaria philippinensis (**capillariasis**)	Mebendazole 200 mg po x20 d.	Albendazole 200 mg po x10 d.	
Enterobius vermicularis (**pinworm**)	Albendazole 400 mg po x1, repeat in 2 wks or mebendazole 100 mg po x1, repeat in 2 wks	Pyrantel pamoate 11 mg/kg (to max. dose of 1.0 gm) po x1 dose; repeat every 2 wks x2.	Side-effects in Table 13B, pages 101, 103
Hookworm (Necator americanus and Ancylostoma duodenale)	Albendazole 400 mg po x1 or mebendazole 100 mg po bid x3 d.	Pyrantel pamoate 11 mg/kg (to max. dose of 1.0 gm) po daily x3 d.	NOTE: Ivermectin not effective. Eosinophilia may not be present but eggs detectable in stool.

[1] **CDC** = available from CDC Drug Service
NOTE: All dosage recommendations are for adults (unless otherwise indicated) and assume normal renal function. See page 103 for abbreviations.

TABLE 13A (6)

INFECTING ORGANISM	SUGGESTED REGIMENS		COMMENTS
	PRIMARY	**ALTERNATIVE**	
NEMATODES—INTESTINAL (Roundworms) *(continued)*			
Strongyloides stercoralis (**strongyloidiasis**)	Ivermectin 200 µg/kg/d po x2 d	Albendazole 400 mg po bid x2 d. (7–10 d for hyperinfection syndrome)	Case report of ivermectin failure in pt with hypogamma-globulinemia (*Am J Med Sci* 311:178, 1996)
Trichostrongylus orientalis		Pyrantel pamoate 11 mg/kg (max. 1.0 gm) po x1	Mebendazole 100 mg bid x3 d
Trichuris trichura (**whipworm**)	Albendazole 400 mg po x1 dose	Mebendazole 100 mg po bid x3 d. or 500 mg once	Ivermectin 200 µg/kg daily po x3 d.
NEMATODES—EXTRAINTESTINAL (Roundworms)			
Angiostrongylus cantonensis—a cause of eosinophilic meningitis	Supportive care. Serial LPs to ↓ intracranial pressure.	Antihelminth therapy may worsen meningitis (*NEJM* 346:668, 2002). Prednisone may help	Mortality rate <1%. Ref: *AJM* 114:217, 2003.
Anisakis simplex (**anisakiasis**)	Physical removal: endoscope or surgery	Questionable response to albendazole (*Ln* 360:54, 2002)	Anisakiasis acquired by eating raw fish: herring, salmon, mackerel, cod, squid. Similar illness due to Pseudoterranova species acquired from cod, halibut, red snapper.
Ancylostoma braziliense & caninum: causes **cutaneous larva migrans**	Ivermectin 200 µg/kg x1 dose/d. x1–2 d	Albendazole 200 mg po bid x3 d	Also called "creeping eruption", dog and cat hookworm. Ivermectin cure rate 77% (1 dose) to 97% (2–3 doses) (*CID* 31:493, 2000).
Baylisascariasis (Raccoon ascaris)	No drug proven efficacious. Try albendazole 25 mg/kg/d x20 d		Usually pediatric problem (*PIDJ* 22:651, 2003)
Dracunculus medinensis: **Guinea worm**	Slow extraction of pre-emergent worm	Metronidazole 250 mg po tid x10 d. used to ↓ inflammation response and facilitate removal. Immersion in water induces worm emergence. Mebendazole 400–800 mg/d x6 d. may kill worm.	
Filariasis. Wolbachia bacteria needed for filarial development. Rx with doxy 100–200 mg x4–6 wks + ivermectin &/or albendazole & number of microfilaria (*BMJ* 326:207, 2003)			
Lymphatic (**Elephantiasis**). Wuchereria bancrofti or Brugia malayi or B. timori	Diethylcarbamazine[2] 6 mg/kg po once—similar effect as multiple dosages[1,2]	Diethylcarbamazine[2] (DEC) po over 14 days: Day 1, 50 mg; day 2, 50 mg tid; day 3, 100 mg tid; days 4–14, 2 mg/kg tid.	DEC 300 mg/wk po effective prophylaxis
Cutaneous			
Loiasis, **Loa loa**, eyeworm disease	Diethylcarbamazine (DEC)[1,2] 6 mg/kg po x1 dose		
Onchocerca volvulus (**onchocerciasis**)—river blindness (*Ln* 360:203, 2002)	Ivermectin 150 µg/kg po x1, repeat q6 months to suppress dermal and ocular microfilariae. If eye involved, start prednisone 1 mg/kg/d po several days before ivermectin. NOTE: Worm survival requires symbiotic bacteria Wolbachia (*Science* 295/365, 2002)		Ivermectin ↓ number of microfilariae in skin and impairs female worm fertility, does not kill adult worms (nothing does). Ivermectin CK in pregnancy.
Body cavity			
Mansonella perstans (dipetalonemiasis)	Diethylcarbamazine[2] as above for Wuchereria OR ivermectin 150 µg/kg x1	Usually no or vague allergic symptoms + eosinophilia. Ivermectin has no activity against this species.	
Mansonella streptocerca	Mebendazole[2] 100 mg bid x30 d. or albendazole 400 mg po bid x10 d.	Chronic pruritic hypopigmented lesions that may be confused with leprosy. Can be asymptomatic.	
Mansonella ozzardi	Ivermectin 200 µg/kg x1 dose may be effective	Usually asymptomatic. Articular pain, pruritus, lymphadenopathy reported. May have allergic reaction from dying organisms.	
Dirofilariasis: **Heartworms**			
D. immitis, dog heartworm	No effective drugs; surgical removal only option	Can lodge in pulmonary artery → coin lesion. Eosinophilia rare.	
D. tenius (raccoon), D. ursi (bear), D. repens (dogs, cats)	No effective drugs	Worms migrate to conjunctivae, subcutaneous tissue, scrotum, breasts, extremities	
Gnathostoma spinigerum: eosinophilic myeloencephalitis	Albendazole 400 mg po qd or bid x21 d.	Ivermectin 200 µg/kg x2 d.	

[1] May need antihistamine or corticosteroid for allergic reaction from disintegrating organisms

[2] Diethylcarbamazine available from Wyeth-Ayerst (610) 971-5509

NOTE: *All dosage recommendations are for adults (unless otherwise indicated) and assume normal renal function. See page 103 for abbreviations.*

TABLE 13A (7)

INFECTING ORGANISM	SUGGESTED REGIMENS		COMMENTS
	PRIMARY	ALTERNATIVE	
NEMATODES—Extraintestinal (Roundworms) *(continued)*	Rx directed at relief of symptoms as infection self-limited, e.g., steroids & antihistamines; use of anthelminthics controversial.		
Toxocariasis: *Clin Micro Rev 16:265, 2003*			
Visceral larval migrans	**Albendazole** 400 mg po bid x5 d.	**Mebendazole** 100–200 mg po bid x5 days	Severe lung, heart of CNS disease may warrant steroids. Differential dx of larval migrans syndromes: Toxocara canis and catis, Ancylostoma spp, Gnathostoma spp, Spirometra spp.
Ocular larval migrans	First 4 wks of illness: (Oral **prednisone** 30–60 mg po qd + subtenon **triamcinolone** 40 mg weekly) x2 weeks		No added benefit of anthelminthic drugs. Rx of little effect after 4 wks.
Trichinella spiralis (**trichinosis**)—muscle infection	**Albendazole** 400 mg po bid x8–14 d.	**Mebendazole** 200–400 mg po tid x3 d, then 400–500 mg tid x10 d.	Use albendazole/mebendazole with caution during pregnancy.
	Concomitant **prednisone** 40–60 mg po qd		
TREMATODES (Flukes)			
Clonorchis sinensis (liver fluke)	**Praziquantel** 25 mg/kg po tid x1 day or **albendazole** 10 mg/kg/d po x7 d		Same dose in children
Fasciola buski (intestinal fluke)	**Praziquantel** 25 mg/kg po tid x1 day		Same dose in children
Fasciola hepatica (sheep liver fluke)	**Triclabendazole**[NUS] (Fasinex; Novartis Agribusiness) 10 mg/kg po x1 dose. Ref: *CID 32:1, 2001*	**Bithionol**[CDC] Adults and children: 30–50 mg/kg (max. dose 2 gm/d) qod x10–15 doses	
Heterophyes heterophyes (intestinal fluke); Metagonimus yokogawai (intestinal fluke); Opisthorchis viverrini (liver fluke)	**Praziquantel** 25 mg/kg po tid x1 day		Same dose in children. Same regimen for **Metorchis conjunctus (North American liver fluke)** **Nanophyetus salmincola:** Praziquantel 20 mg/kg po tid x1 d
Paragonimus westermani (lung fluke)	**Praziquantel** 25 mg/kg po tid x2 days or **bithionol**[CDC] 30–50 mg/kg qod x10 d		Same dose in children
Schistosoma haematobium: GU bilharziasis *(NEJM 346:1212, 2002)*	**Praziquantel** 20 mg/kg po bid x1 day (2 doses)	**Oxamniquine**[NUS] single dose of 15 mg/kg po once; in North and East Africa 20 mg/kg po daily x3 d. Do not use during pregnancy.	Same dose in children. Alternative: metrifonate 10 mg/kg/dose po q2 wks for 3 doses.
Schistosoma intercalatum:	**Praziquantel** 20 mg/kg po bid x1 day (2 doses)		Same dose in children.
Schistosoma japonicum: Oriental schisto. *(NEJM 346:1212, 2002)*	**Praziquantel** 20 mg/kg po **tid x1 day (3 doses)**		Same dose in children. Cures 60–90% pts.
Schistosoma mansoni (intestinal bilharziasis) **Possible praziquantel resistance** *(JID 176:304, 1997)* *(NEJM 346:1212, 2002)*	**Praziquantel** 20 mg/kg po bid x1 day (2 doses)	**Praziquantel** 20 mg/kg po bid x1 day (2 doses)	Same dose for children. Cures 60–90% pts.
Schistosoma mekongi	**Praziquantel** 20 mg/kg po **tid x1 day (3 doses)**		Same dose for children
Toxemic schisto, Katayama fever	**Praziquantel** 25 mg/kg po q4h with food x3 doses		Massive infection with either S. japonicum or S. mansoni
CESTODES (Tapeworms)			
Echinococcus granulosus (hydatid disease) *(CID 37:1073, 2003; Ln 362:1295, 2003)*	Meta-analysis supports percutaneous aspiration-injection-reaspiration (PAIR) + albendazole. Before and after drainage. **Albendazole** >60 kg, 400 mg po bid or <60 kg, 15 mg/kg div. bid, with meals. Then: Puncture (P) & needle aspirate (A) cyst content. Instill (I) hypertonic saline (15–30%) or absolute alcohol & wait 20–30 min., then re-aspirate (R) with final irrigation. **Continue albendazole x28 d.** In 96% as compared to 90% pts with surgical resection.		
Echinococcus multilocularis (alveolar cyst disease) *(COID 16:437, 2003)*	**Albendazole** efficacy not clearly demonstrated; can try in dosages used for hydatid disease. Wide surgical resection only reliable rx; technique evolving *(Radiology 198:259, 1996)*		
Intestinal tapeworms			
Diphyllobothrium latum (fish), Dipylidium caninum (dog), Taenia saginata (beef), and	**Praziquantel** 5–10 mg/kg po x1 dose for children and adults. **Alternative: Niclosamide** 2 gm po x1.		
Taenia solium (pork)	**Praziquantel** 25 mg/kg po x1 dose for children and adults		
Hymenolepis diminuta (rats) and H. nana (humans)	**Praziquantel** 25 mg/kg po x1 dose for children and adults. **Alternative: Niclosamide** 500 mg po x3 d.		

[1] **CDC** = Available from CDC Drug Service
NOTE: All dosage recommendations are for adults (unless otherwise indicated) and assume normal renal function. See page 103 for abbreviations.

TABLE 13A (8)

INFECTING ORGANISM	SUGGESTED REGIMENS		COMMENTS
	PRIMARY	ALTERNATIVE	
CESTODES (Tapeworms) (continued)			
Cerebral (neuro) cysticercosis Larval stage of *T. solium*—see *Comment* Management refs.: *Ln 361:547, 2003 & Ln ID 2:751, 2002*	Cysticercosis outside CNS—benign—no treatment. Inside CNS—no unanimity. Expert panel: (1) If growing &/or many &/or giant cysts &/or subarachnoid disease: **Treat**. (2) Calcified cysticercosis: **no treatment** (3) **Disagreement**: Few viable cysts, degenerating cysts (see *Comment*)	Albendazole cheaper & more effective than praziquantel. **Albendazole** 15 mg/kg/d (max. 800 mg) in 2 div. doses x8 d. **OR** **Praziquantel** 50–100 mg/kg/d in 3 div. doses x30 Anti-seizure meds for inflamed degenerating cysts.	**Dexamethasone (6 mg/d) ± seizure meds may be needed to control rx-induced inflammation from cyst death.** Viable cyst = hypodense vesicle on CT or hyperintense on MRI T₂-signal. If viable cysts, 10 d. of albendazole + dexamethasone ↓ number of viable cysts & number of generalized seizures (*NEJM 350:249, 2004*).
Sparganosis (Spirometra mansonoides) Larval cysts; source—frogs/snakes	Surgical resection or ethanol injection of subcutaneous masses (*NEJM 330:1887, 1994*).		
ECTOPARASITES Ref.: *CID 36:1355, 2003; NEJM 346:1645, 2002; Ln 363:689, 2004.* **NOTE: Due to potential neurotoxicity, lindane products should only be used as last resort.**			
Pediculus humanus corporis (body lice). *P. humanus* var. *capitis* (**head louse**, nits)	Treat the clothing. Organism lives in, deposits eggs in seams of clothing. Discard clothing, if not possible, treat clothing with 1% malathion powder or 10% DDT powder.	Body louse leaves clothing only for blood meal. Nits in clothing viable for 1 month. Ref. *Med Lett 38:6, 1997*. Benefit of residual permethrin on hair reduced by shampoos or vinegar. No residual effect with lindane or pyrethrin products.	
Phthirus pubis (crabs)	**Permethrin**, 5% prescription strength (ELIMITE) or 1% non-prescription (Nix). Wash hair, apply lotion for 10 min., then rinse off, comb; 2nd treatment 7–10 days after 1st to kill newly hatched lice (all products); **OR iver-mectin** 200 μg/kg single-dose po in 2 doses 10 days apart; **does not affect nits. OR Malathion 0.5% lotion** (not in neonates/infants) (Ovide). Apply for 8–12 hrs. No need to comb for lice after malathion.	Nit removal important adjunct. Use nit comb ± enzymatic egg remover (CLEAR is one example). Treat sex partners if body or pubic lice. Cost: Permethrin 60 gm $9.20; malathion $31.25; ivermectin $9.97. For failures with 1% permethrin, repeat permethrin → po TMP/SMX 10 mg/kg/d. in 2 div. doses x10 days (*Ped 107:E30, 2001*).	
Sarcoptes scabiei (scabies) (mites) (*CID 27:646, 1998*)			
Immunocompetent patients	**Primary: Permethrin** 5% cream (ELIMITE). Apply entire skin from chin to toes. Leave on 8–10 hrs. Repeat in 1 week. Safe for children >2 mos. old. **Alternative: Ivermectin** 200 μg/kg po x1 (*NEJM 333:26, 1995*) **or** 10% crotamiton topically 1.x/d x2-5.	Trim fingernails. Reapply to hands after handwashing. Pruritus may persist x2 wks after mites gone.	
AIDS patients, CD4 <150/mm³ (Norwegian scabies—see *Comments*)	**Crusted scabies: Permethrin** as above on day 1, then 6% sulfur in petrolatum daily on days 2–7, then repeat x several weeks. **Ivermectin** 200 μg/kg po x1 reported effective.	Norwegian scabies in AIDS pts.: Extensive, crusted. Can mimic psoriasis. Not pruritic. ELIMITE: 60 gm $18.10; lindane 60 ml $2.60–10.50. Highly contagious—isolate!	

NOTE: All dosage recommendations are for adults (unless otherwise indicated) and assume normal renal/renal function. See page 103 for abbreviations.

TABLE 13B: DOSAGE, PRICE, AND SELECTED ADVERSE EFFECTS OF ANTIPARASITIC DRUGS

NOTE: Drugs available from CDC Drug Service indicated by "CDC." Call (404) 639-3670 (or -2888).
Doses vary with indication. For convenience, drugs divided by type of parasite; some drugs used for multiple types of parasites, e.g., albendazole.
COMMENT: Cost data represent average wholesale prices as listed in 2004 Drug Topics Red Book, Medical Economics.

CLASS, AGENT, GENERIC NAME (TRADE NAME)	USUAL ADULT DOSAGE (Cost)	ADVERSE REACTIONS/COMMENTS
Antiprotozoan Drugs		
Intestinal Parasites		
Albendazole (Albenza)*	Doses vary with indication, 200–400 mg bid po 200 mg tab $1.50	Teratogenic, Pregnancy Cat. C; give after negative pregnancy test. Abdominal pain, nausea/vomiting, alopecia, ↑ serum transaminase. Rare leukopenia.
Dehydroemetine (CDC)*	1.5 mg/kg/d to max. of 90 mg IM	Local pain, ECG changes, cardiac arrhythmias, precordial pain, paresthesias, weakness, peripheral neuropathy. GI: nausea/vomiting, diarrhea. Avoid strenuous exercise for 4 wks after rx.
Diloxanide furoate (CDC)*	500 mg po tid	GI: flatulence, abdominal distention, nausea/vomiting. Pruritus, urticaria.
Furazolidone (Furoxone)	Peds: 6 mg/kg/d div. qid. Not for infants <1 mo. old. Liquid: 50 mg/15 ml 473 ml $100	Only liquid antigiardiasis rx in U.S. Disulfiram-like reaction with alcohol. Occasional side-effects: Fever, urticaria, arthralgia, nausea/vomiting, headache. Hemolysis if G6PD deficient. May turn urine brown.
Iodoquinol (Yodoxin) (650 mg $0.93)	Adults: 650 mg po tid, children: 40 mg/kg/d div. tid	Rarely causes nausea, abdominal cramps, rash, acne. Contraindicated if iodine intolerance.
Metronidazole/Ornidazole[NUS] (Tiberal)	Side-effects similar for all. See metronidazole in Table 10A, page 64, & 10B, page 71	
Paromomycin (Humatin) Aminosidine in U.K.	Up to 750 mg tid 250 mg caps $1.90	Drug is aminoglycoside similar to neomycin; if absorbed due to concomitant inflammatory bowel disease can result in oto/nephrotoxicity. Doses >3 gm assoc. with nausea, abdominal cramps, abd. pain.
Quinacrine (Atabrine, Mepacrine)	100 mg tid. No longer available in U.S.; 2 pharmacies will prepare as a service: (1) Connecticut 203-785-6818; (2) California 800-247-9767	Contraindicated for pts with history of psoriasis or psoriasis. Yellow staining of skin. Dizziness, headache, vomiting, toxic psychosis (1.5%), hemolytic anemia, leukopenia, thrombocytopenia, urticaria, rash, fever, minor disulfiram-like reactions.
Tinidazole (Tindamax)	500 mg tabs, with food. Regimen varies with indication. Cost: 2 gm $18.24	Chemical structure similar to metronidazole but better tolerated. Seizures/peripheral neuropathy reported. **Adverse effects:** Metallic taste 4–6%, nausea 3–5%, anorexia 2–3%.
Extraintestinal Parasites		
Antimony compounds[NUS] Stibogluconate sodium (Pentostam, Triostam) (CDC) Meglumine antimonate (Glucantime), Glucantim—French tradenames	Solution containing 30–34% pentavalent antimony	Cough/vomiting IV infusion too fast. Arthralgia 50%. Others: myalgia, bradycardia, cramps/diarrhea, pruritus/rash, renal toxicity, ↑ amylase. **Coombs'(+), abnormalities occur. Combination rx with, or sequential rx with, ampho B may trigger fatal arrhythmias (Ln 351:1928, 1998).**
Artesunate[NUS]	Adults: 4 mg/kg/d po x3 d.; can give IM	Drug fever, abdominal pain, diarrhea, primary heart block. Refs: CID 33:2009, 2001; Ln 359:1365, 2002, AAC 46:778, 2002
Atovaquone (Mepron) Ref: AAC 46:1163, 2002	Suspension: 1 tsp (750 mg) po bid 750 mg/5 ml. Cost 210 ml $744.00	No. pts reporting rx due to side-effects was 9%; rash 22%, GI 20%, headache 16%, insomnia 10%, fever 14%
Atovaquone and proguanil (Malarone)* For prophylaxis of P. falciparum; little data on P. vivax	Prophylaxis: 1 tab po (250 mg + 100 mg) qd with food Treatment: 4 tabs po (1000 mg + 400 mg) once daily with food x3 days Tabs: Either 250/100 mg or 62.5/25 mg. Peds dosage: footnote 2 page 95. Cost 250/100 mg tab $5.15	Adverse effects in rx trials: Adults—abd pain 17%, N/V 12%, headache 10%, dizziness 5%. Rx stopped in 1%. Asymptomatic mild (↑ in ALT/AST). Children—cough, headache, anorexia, vomiting, abd. pain. See drug interactions, Table 22. Safe in G6PD-deficient pts. Can crush tabs for children and give with milk or other liquid nutrients.
Benznidazole[NUS] (Rochagan, Roche), Brazil	7.5 mg/kg/d po	Photosensitivity in 50% of pts. GI abdominal pain, nausea/vomiting/ anorexia. CNS: disorientation, insomnia, twitch/seizures, paresthesias, polyneuritis.
Chloroquine phosphate (Aralen)*	Dose varies—see Malaria prophylaxis and rx, pages 95, 96 500 mg tabs $5.16	Minor: nausea/vomiting, headache, dizziness, blurred vision, pruritus in dark-skinned pts. Major: protracted rx in rheumatoid arthritis can lead to retinopathy. Can exacerbate psoriasis. Can block response to rabies vaccine.

NOTE: All dosage recommendations are for adults (unless otherwise indicated) and assume normal renal/renal function. See page 103 for abbreviations.

TABLE 13B (2)

CLASS, AGENT, GENERIC NAME (TRADE NAME)	USUAL ADULT DOSAGE (Cost)	ADVERSE REACTIONS/COMMENTS
Antiprotozoan Drugs/Extraintestinal Parasites (continued)		
Dapsone Ref.: CID 27:191, 1998	100 mg bid 100 mg tabs $0.20	Usually tolerated by pts with rash after TMP/SMX. Adverse effects: nausea/vomiting, rash, oral lesions (CID 18:630, 1994). Methemoglobinemia (usually asymptomatic if > 0–15%: stop drug. Hemolytic anemia if G6PD deficient). Sulfone syndrome: fever, rash, hemolytic anemia, and liver injury (West J Med 156:303, 1992).
Eflornithine[AUS] (Ornidyl)	Approved in U.S. for trypanosome infections but not marketed. Contact Hoechst Marion Roussel, (800) 552-3656.	
Fumagillin	Eyedrops + po. 20 mg po bid Call 800-547-1392.	Adverse events: Neutropenia & thrombocytopenia
Halofantrine (Halfan)	Adults: 500 mg po q6h x3 doses Children: 8 mg/kg po q6h x3 doses 250 mg tab $9.88	Poor oral bioavailability ↑ with fatty meal. Causes delay in A-V conduction; **do not use if long QT interval or pt taking drugs known to ↑ QT interval (e.g., quinine/quinidine, astemizole, chloroquine, antidepressants, neuroleptic drugs).** Other side-effects: nausea, abdominal pain, diarrhea. Do not use in pregnancy.
Mefloquine (Lariam)	One 250 mg tab/week for malaria prophylaxis; for rx, 1250 mg x1 or 750 mg & then 500 mg in 6–8 hrs. 250 mg tab $11.83. In U.S. 250 mg tab = 228 mg base; outside U.S. 275 mg tab = 250 mg base	Side-effects in roughly 3%. Minor: headache, irritability, insomnia, weakness, diarrhea. Toxic psychosis, seizures can occur. Teratogenic—do not use in pregnancy. Do not use with quinine, quinidine, or halofantrine. Rare: Prolonged QT interval and toxic epidermal necrolysis (Ln 349:101, 1997). Not used for rx if due to neuropsychiatric side-effects.
Melarsoprol (CDC) (Mel B, Arsobal) (Manufactured in France)	See Trypanosomiasis in adult dose Peds dose: 0.36 mg/kg IV, then gradual ↑ to 3.6 mg/kg q1–5 days for total of 9–10 doses.	Post-rx encephalopathy (10%) with 5% mortality; risk of death 2° to rx 4–8%. Prednisolone 1 mg/kg/d po may ↓ encephalopathy. Other: Heart damage, albuminuria, abdominal pain, vomiting, peripheral neuropathy, Horxheimer-like reaction, pruritus.
Miltefosine[AUS] (Zentaris, Impavido)	100–150 mg (approx. 2.25 mg/(kg-d)) po x28 d Cutaneous leishmaniasis 2.25 mg/kg po od x6 wks	Contact Astra Medica. Ger. **Pregnancy—No**, teratogenic. Side-effects vary, kala-azar pts, vomiting in up to 40%, diarrhea in 1/3, mild to moderate in severity—may resolve in < 1 day.
Nifurtimox (Lampit) (CDC) (Manufactured in Germany by Bayer)	8–10 mg/kg/d po div. 4v/day	Side-effects in 40–70% of pts. GI: abdominal pain, nausea/vomiting. CNS: polyneuritis (1/3), disorientation, insomnia, twitching, seizures. Skin rash. Hemolysis with G6PD deficiency.
Nitazoxanide (Alinia)	Oral suspension with 100 mg/ml. Take with food.	Abdominal pain 7.8%, diarrhea 2.1%, vomiting/headache 1%.
Pentamidine (NebuPent)	300 mg via aerosol q1 month. Also used IM. 300 mg $98.75 + admin. costs	Hypotension, hypocalcemia, hypoglycemia followed by hyperglycemia, pancreatitis. Neutropenia (15%), thrombocytopenia. Nephrotoxicity. Others: nausea/vomiting, liver tests, rash.
Primaquine phosphate	26.3 mg (=15 mg base) $0.77	In G6PD def. pts, can cause hemolytic anemia with hemoglobinuria, esp. African, Asian peoples. Methemoglobinemia. Nausea/abdominal pain if pt. fasting. (CID 39:1336, 2004)
Pyrimethamine (Daraprim, Malocide) Also combined with sulfadoxine as **Fansidar**	100 mg first day, then 25 mg qd. 25 mg $0.43. Cost of folinic acid (leucovorin) 5 mg $2.00	Major problem is hematologic: megaloblastic anemia ↓ WBC, ↓ platelets. Can give 5 mg folinic acid/day to ↓ bone marrow depression and not interfere with antitoxoplasmosis effect. If high-doses pyrimethamine, ↑ folinic acid to 10–50 mg/d. Other: Rash, vomiting
Quinacrine[AUS]		Compounded by Med. Center Pharm., New Haven, CT, (203) 688-6816 or Panorama Compound. Pharm., Van Nuys, CA, (800) 247-9767.
Quinidine gluconate	Loading dose of 10 mg (equivalent to 6.2 mg of quinidine base)/kg IV over 1–2 hrs, and then constant infusion of 0.02 mg of quinidine gluconate/kg/minute.	Adverse reactions of quinidine/quinine similar. (1) IV bolus injection can cause fatal hypotension, (2) hyperinsulinemic hypoglycemia, esp. in pregnancy, (3) ↓ rate of infusion if QT interval ↑ > 25% of baseline, (4) reduce dose 30–50% after day 3 due to ↓ renal clearance and vol. of distribution.
Quinine sulfate (300 mg salt = 250 mg base)	325 and 650 mg tabs. No IV prep. in U.S. Oral rx of chloroquine-resistant falciparum malaria: 650 mg po tid x3d, then tetracycline 250 mg po qid x7 d. 325 mg $0.16	Cinchonism: tinnitus, headache, nausea, abdominal pain, blurred vision. Rarely: blood dyscrasias, drug fever, asthma, hypoglycemia. Transient blindness in < 1% of 500 pts (AnIM 136:339, 2002).
Spiramycin[AUS] (JAC 42:572, 1998)	Up to 3–4 gm/d	GI and allergic reactions have occurred. Not available in U.S.

[1] Available from FDA: (301) 443-5680
NOTE: All dosage recommendations are for adults (unless otherwise indicated) and assume normal renal/renal function. See page 103 for abbreviations.

TABLE 13B (3)

CLASS, AGENT, GENERIC NAME (TRADE NAME)	USUAL ADULT DOSAGE (Cost)	ADVERSE REACTIONS/COMMENTS
Antiprotozoan Drugs/Extraintestinal Parasites *(continued)*		
Sulfadiazine	1.0–1.5 gm po q6h 500 mg $0.34	See *Table 10B, page 71, for sulfonamide side-effects.*
Sulfadoxine and pyrimethamine combination (Fansidar)	Contains 500 mg of sulfadoxine and 25 mg of pyrimethamine One tab $3.77	Very long mean half-life of both drugs: Sulfadoxine 169 hrs, pyrimethamine 111 hrs allows weekly dosage. Fatalities reported due to Stevens-Johnson syndrome and toxic epidermal necrolysis. Renal excretion—use with caution in pts with renal impairment.
DRUGS USED TO TREAT NEMATODES, TREMATODES, AND CESTODES		
Bithionol *(CDC)*	Adults & children: 30–40 mg/kg (to max. of 2 gm/d) po qod x10–15 doses	Photosensitivity, skin reactions, urticaria, GI upset
Diethylcarbamazine (Hetrazan) *(CDC)*	Used to treat filariasis. Licensed (Lederle) but not available in U.S.	Headache, dizziness, nausea, fever. Host may experience inflammatory reaction to death of adult worms: fever, urticaria, asthma, GI upset (Mazzotti reaction).
Ivermectin (Stromectol, Mectizan)	Strongyloidiasis dose: 200 µg/kg x1 dose po Onchocerciasis: 150 µg/kg x1 po Scabies: 200 µg/kg po x1 3 mg tabs $5.45	Mild side-effects: fever, pruritus, rash. In rx of onchocerciasis, can see tender lymphadenopathy, headache, bone/joint pain. Can cause Mazzotti reaction (see above).
Mebendazole (Vermox)	Doses vary with indication. 100 mg tab $5.91	Rarely causes abdominal pain, nausea, diarrhea. Contraindicated in pregnancy and children <2 yrs old.
Oxamniquine (Vansil)^NUS	For S. mansoni. Some experts suggest 40–60 mg/kg over 2–3 days in all of Africa.	Rarely: dizziness, drowsiness, neuropsychiatric symptoms. GI upset. EKG/EEG changes. Orange/red urine.
Praziquantel (Biltricide)	Doses vary with parasite; see *Table 13A*. 600 mg $11.90	Mild: dizziness/drowsiness, N/V, rash, fever. Only contraindication is ocular cysticercosis. Metabolism induced by anticonvulsants and steroids; can negate effect with cimetidine 400 mg po tid.
Pyrantel pamoate (over-the-counter as Reese's Pinworm Medicine)	Oral suspension. Dose for all ages: 11 mg/kg (to max. of 1 gm) x1 dose	Rare GI upset, headache, dizziness, rash
Suramin (Germanin) *(CDC)*	For early trypanosomiasis. Drug powder mixed to 10% solution with 5 ml water and used within 30 minutes.	Does not cross blood-brain barrier; "no effect on CNS infection. Side-effects: vomiting, pruritus, urticaria, fever, paresthesias, albuminuria (discontinue drug if casts appear). Do not use if renal/liver disease present. Deaths from vascular collapse reported.
Thiabendazole (Mintezol)	Take after meals. Dose varies with parasite; see *Table 12A* 500 mg $1.25	Nausea/vomiting, headache, dizziness. Rarely: liver damage, ↓ BP, angioneurotic edema, Stevens-Johnson syndrome. May ↓ mental alertness.

Abbreviations **Clinda** = clindamycin, (610) 971-5509   **CQ** = chloroquine phosphate; **MQ** = mefloquine; **NUS** = not available in the U.S.; **PQ** = primaquine; **Pyri** = pyrimethamine; **QS** = quinine sulfate;
TMP/SMX = trimethoprim/sulfamethoxazole

[1] Available from Wyeth-Ayerst, (610) 971-5509
NOTE: All dosage recommendations are for adults (unless otherwise indicated) and assume normal renal function. See page 103 for abbreviations.

TABLE 14A: ANTIVIRAL THERAPY (Non-HIV)

VIRUS/DISEASE	DRUG/DOSAGE	SIDE EFFECTS/COMMENTS
Adenovirus. Cause of RTIs including fatal pneumonia in children & young adults (*CID* 35:808, 2002). **Findings include:** fever, ↓ liver enzymes, leukopenia, thrombocytopenia, diarrhea, pneumonia, or hemorrhagic cystitis.	**No proven rx.** Cidofovir 5 mg/kg q wk x2 wks, then q2 wks + probenecid 1.25 gm/M² given 3 hrs before cidofovir and 3 & 9 hrs after each infusion (*Ln* 38:45, 2004). Successful in 3/8 immunosuppressed children.	PCR⁴ for adenovirus DNA [+ in 72% of children with 1° infection (*JID* 187:311, 2003)]. ↑ viral load assoc. with fatal outcome in (*Ln* 38:45, 2004); stem cell transplant (*CID* 35:526, 2002). ↓ in virus load predicted response to cidofovir (*CID* 38:45, 2004).
Coronavirus—SARS-CoV (Severe Acute Respiratory Distress Syn.) (see *CID* 36:1420, 2004) A new coronavirus, labeled SARS-CoV, appeared in Nov. 2002 (Guandong, China) and became widespread rapidly from Hong Kong to 32 countries. Healthcare workers account for >50% of cases (>90% in Taiwan) (*Ln* 361: 1319, 2003). Effective adherence to infection control guidelines was finally responsible for finally controlling the epidemic (*Ln* 361: 1519, 2003; *NEJM* 350:2352, 2004). Only 4 mini-outbreaks in 2004, 3/4 from research labs testing live virus (*Science* 304:1097, 2004)	Therapy tried or under evaluation (see *Comments*): Interferon alfa ± steroids—small case series (animal reservoir may account for >50% of cases). Pegylated interferon-α effective in monkeys. Lopinavir/ritonavir benefit in uncontrolled studies	**Therapy remains predominantly supportive care.**
Enterovirus—Meningitis: most common cause of aseptic meningitis. PCR on CSF valuable for early dx (*Scand J Inf Dis* 34:359, 2002)	**No rx currently recommended;** however, **pleconaril** (VP 63843) still under investigation. [For compassionate use call 63843) 4587-7300, ext. 6297 (Donna Kolbuh, RN)]	No clinical benefit demonstrated in double-blind placebo-controlled study in 21 infants with enteroviral aseptic meningitis (*PIDJ* 22:335, 2003)
Hemorrhagic Fever Virus Infections **Congo-Crimean Hemorrhagic Fever (HF)** (*CID* 38:1731, 2004	Oral **ribavirin** 30 mg/kg as initial loading dose & 15 mg/kg q6h x4 days & then 7.5 mg/kg x6 days (WHO recommendation) (see *Comment*)	3/3 healthcare workers in Pakistan had complete recovery (*Ln* 346:472, 1995) & 61/69 (89%) with confirmed CCHF rx with ribavirin survived in Iran (*CID* 36:1613, 2003).
Ebola/Marburg HF (Central Africa) Epidemic continues in Africa (*JAMA* 290: 317, 2003)	**No effective antiviral rx** (*J Virol* 77:9733, 2003)	An intense inflammatory response within 4 d. after infection may control viral proliferation & result in asymptomatic infection (*Science* 303:387, 2004)
With pulmonary syndrome: Hantavirus "hemorrhagic fever with renal syndrome"—others now found around the world (*EID* 18:768, 2002)	**No benefit from ribavirin has been shown;** none expected (see discussion in progress). Refs. *JID* 173:1297, 1996; *Emerg Inf Dis* 3:95, 1997; *Curr Inf Dis Rep* 3:258, 2001.	Acute onset of fever, headache, myalgias, non-productive cough, thrombocytopenia and non-cardiogenic pulmonary edema. Dx: exposure to rodents (deer mice), diarrhea, dramatic: ↓ shift in blood smear, ↓ platelets, & ↑ PCO₂ predicted Hanta pulmonary syndrome (*HPS* 34:293, 2002). Can infect gorillas & chimps that in turn infect and result with the dead animal carcasses
With renal syndrome: Lassa, Venezuelan, Korean, HF, Sabia, Argentinian HF, Bolivian HF, Junin, Machupo	**Ribavirin** IV 2 gm loading dose, then 1 gm q6h x4 days, then 0.5 gm q8h x6 d. (see *Comment: Congo-Crimean HF*)	Toxicity low, hemolysis reported but recovery when treatment stopped. No significant changes in WBC, platelets. Hepatic or renal function. Effective in Lassa and in 2 cases of Bolivian HF (*CID* 24:718, 1997). No data on others. See *CID* 36:1254, 2003, for management of contacts.
Dengue and dengue hemorrhagic fever (DHF)— Dengue: aseptic meningitis (*JID* 176:313, 1997). Death rate high in young children & adults (*Int J Inf Dis* 6:118, 2002; *CID* 35:277, 2002).	**No data on antiviral rx.** Fluid replacement for **DHF** with colloids may be more effective than crystalloids in pts with low pulse pressures (*CID* 32:204, 2001; *J Ped* 140:629, 2002). 5 pts with severe **DHF** rx with dengue antibody-neg. gamma globulin 500 mg/kg qd IV x3–5 d. had rapid ↑ in platelet counts (*CID* 36:1623, 2003).	Resurgence in Southeast Asia, Central & South America and Caribbean. No specific test; prevention is to limit mosquito contact (*AnIM* 128: 931, 1998) gene specifics. *BMJ* 324:1563, 2002)
West Nile virus (see *AnIM* 104:545, 2004) A flavivirus introduced in the U.S. (NYC) in 1999, transmitted by mosquitoes, blood transfusions, transplanted organs (*NEJM* 348:2196, 2003), & breast-feeding (*MMWR* 51:877, 2002). Birds (*MMWR* 51:1107, 2002) (>200 species) are main host with man & horses incidental hosts. In 2003, >7000 cases in U.S. with 220 deaths with epidemic concentrated in Midwest & mountain states. In 2004 ↑ activity in west. Usually produces nonspecific febrile disease but 1/150 cases develops meningoencephalitis, aseptic meningitis or polio-like paralysis (*AnIM* 104:545, 2004; *JCI* 113:1102, 2004)	**No proven rx to date,** 2 clinical trials in progress: (1) Interferon alfa-N3, 4 wks (for information, see www.clinicaltrials.gov) (2) WNV from Israel with high titer antibody West Nile (*JID* 188:5, 2003; *Transpl Inf Dis* 4:160, 2003). Contact www.clinicaltrials.gov/show/NCT00068055.	Dx by IgM in serum & CSF or CSF PCR (contact State Health Dept./CDC). Blood supply now tested in U.S. & in June–Dec. 2003, 818 viremic donors identified (*MMWR* 53:281, 2004).
Yellow fever	**No therapy recommended**	For vaccine recommendations, see *Table 20* (*MMWR* 48:RR-1, 1999). 40% of pts with chronic Hep C who developed superinfection with Hep A developed fulminant hepatic failure in 1 study (*NEJM* 338:286, 1998)
Hepatitis Viral Infections **Hepatitis A** (*JID* 161:7,643, 1998)	**No therapy recommended** if within 2 wks of exposure, IgamMA globulin 0.02 ml/kg IM protects x1 is protective	Most common cause of death from acute hepatitis in Italy (*Dig Liver Dis* 35:404, 2003)
Hepatitis B **Acute**	**No therapy recommended**	For vaccine recommendations, see *Table 20B*

¹ RTIs = respiratory tract infections.   ⁴ PCR = polymerase chain reaction

TABLE 14A (2)

VIRUS/DISEASE	DRUG/DOSAGE	SIDE EFFECTS/COMMENTS
Hepatitis Viral Infections/Hepatitis B (continued)		**Goal of rx:** ↓ liver inflammation, stop progression of cirrhosis, & prevent hepatocellular carcinoma. INF, lamivudine (LAV), & adefovir (ADF) work: ↓ of HBV DNA levels to ~20,000 copies/mL (41–774). This usually followed by appearance of HBs Ag, &, & appearance of HBs antibody, loss of HBe Ag, & appearance of HBe antibody. Histological improvement seen in 50–60%. Sustained viral response (SVR: lack of reappearance of HBV DNA in pts with loss of both the Ag & Ab) occurs in >80% with seroconversion predicts viral relapse. **The drugs work best when baseline HBV DNA ↓ & ALT high** (J Virol Hep 9:208, 2002) *esp.* **in pts with HBeAg (+).**
Chronic: For HBeAg+, 3 goals currently FDA-approved: Lamivudine, or until 6 mos. after HBeAg sero-conversion **or**	1st line: rx. well-tolerated & non-toxic but drug-resistant YMDD mutations emerge: after 1 year rx. 15%, 2 year 38%, 3 year 56%, 4 year 67%. Mutants less virulent than wild type virus, breakthrough associated with flare of hepatitis & occ. hepatic decomposition. But long-term continuous rx (yrs) improves effectiveness: sustained viral response (SVR), delays progression &, ↓ incidence of hepatic decompensation & HCC (NEJM 351:1521, 2004). ($260 for 30-day rx.)	adefovir (ADF) or lamivudine (LAV), & **adefovir (ADF) work:** ↓ of HBV DNA levels to ~20,000 copies/mL (41–774). This usually followed by appearance of HBs Ag. In general, consider rx. in pts with persistent↑ of aminotransferase; detectable levels of HBsAg in serum; HBV DNA levels of >10⁵ copies/ml, don't rx unless known histological disease. Monitor all HBeAg(+) pts q6–12 months.
		LAV rx. normal 26%, ~5x normal 64% (Hepatol 36:186, 2002). **tenofovir** (JID 189:1183, 2004; antiviral (AAC 46: 2525, 2002; emtricitabine).
In general, **consider rx** in pts with persistent↑ of aminotransferase; detectable levels of HBsAg in serum; HBV DNA levels of >10⁵ copies/ml, don't rx unless known histological disease. & rx if hepatitis present. If consider↑ of ALT normal	Adefovir (ADF) 10 mg po qd x12 mos. **or**	Recommended if either compensated or uncompensated disease & effective against YMDD mutants (for LAV failures). Well tolerated but must adjust dose for renal impairment (CrCl <50%). May show exacerbation of hepatitis after discontinuation & up to 25% show exacerbation of hepatitis after discontinuation. No resistance reported to date. (Hep J Hepatol 2003).
Monitor all HBeAg(+) pts q6–12 months.	**PEG INF alfa-2a** 180 μg sq q week (not FDA-approved) Repeat dose but once-weekly dosing makes it very attractive	PEG INF alfa-2a at 90, 180 & 270 μg/wk (x24) more effective than standard INF 4.5 million units 3x/wk (24% combined response vs 12%, p=.036) & will likely replace INF alfa-2b (J Virol Hepat 10:298, 2003). For HBeAg-, PEG INF for 48 wks, more effective than LAV alone (NEJM 351:1206, 2004).
	or **Interferon alfa-2b 10 MU 3x/wk or 5 MU daily x16–24 wk.** Repeat dose but HBV DNA titers (<10 pg/ml) at end of initial 16 wks.	Recommended only for compensated liver disease. Do not use if↑ bilirubin or pro time, ↑ albumin, history of ascites, encephalopathy, or variceal bleeding. ≥x of other drugs, best response with ↑ HBV DNA. Best HBeAg response rates of the 3 drugs & shorter duration of rx but multiple side-effects (myalgias, bone marrow suppression, depression (severe), etc.), subcutaneous administration & ↑ cost ($1420 for 30-d course).
Prevention Re-infection after transplantation for hepatitis B-induced cirrhosis (See Table 15D, page 127 for post-exposure prophylaxis recommendations)	**Lamivudine** 100 mg qd. Start at least 4 wks pre-transplant and continue for at least 12 months post-transplant (Hgt 30: 1222A, 1999; Tnpt 62:1456, 1996; Ln 348: 1212, 1996).	Recommended for compensated or uncompensated liver disease. Best HBeAg seroconversion rates. When combined with HBIG (Hpt 28:585, 1999) but HBeAg (+) has been used alone in low-risk (J Hpt 34:888, 2007). Optimal dose unknown.
Hepatitis C (up to 3% of world infected, 4 million in U.S.) See AnIM 136:747, 2002; www.va.gov/hepatitis **Acute:** Most pts asymptomatic (~75%), occasionally non-specific complaints such as fatigue. Anti-HCV antibody may remain undetectable for several months after infection while HCV RNA is positive early; mean time to detection 12.6 days in inoculation-acquired HCV (JID 189:3, 2004).	**Ref: www.va.gov/hepatitis** Rx recommended for persistent elevations ALT, HCV RNA, & finding of fibrosis & at least moderate inflammation by liver bx.	[Based on 3 uncontrolled studies, data suggest that early rx of HBV reinfection/post-transplant. Most pts were clinically stable at 1 yr. Post-transplant 43/44 pts in Germany with hepatitis C with INF alfa-2b rx 24 wks after start to start of rx after exposure (mean 89 days to start of rx)] 5/6 of hepatitis and mean alfa-2b rx (Wk14 days to sign/symptoms) (NEJM 345:1452, 2001). 5/6 jaundiced pts in Portugal in with INF alfa-2b for 6 mos. had SVR (neg. HCV RNA for 1 year) (hepatogastroenterol. 50:1057, 2003). A review of published trials (206 pts) concluded that SVR following rx of acute HCV (Cochrane Database Sys & Rev:CD000369, 2002). However, 2b was ~30% vs 4% with placebo reported in 24/51 (92%) with symptomatic disease (Gastroenterol 125:80, 2003). spontaneous clearance reported in 24/51 (92%) with symptomatic disease.
Chronic: see 2002 NIH consensus statement; http://consensus.nih.gov/cons/116/116cons.htm; http://www.va.gov/hepatitisc. Intro. & Postgrad Med 114:48, 57, 62, 2003. Genotype 1 is most common in U.S. (>90%), & least important to rx. Once infected only 15% spontaneously clear virus. *(continued on next page)*	*(continued on next page)*	Obtain baseline CBC and at wks 2 & 4 of rx (See Table 14B, pages 114) & HCV RNA at 24 wks. Sustained viral response (SVR) [neg. HCV RNA <50 IU/ml] at least 24 wks after end of rx assoc. with resolution of liver injury & reduction in risk. hepatic fibrosis (Dig Dis Sci 48:1425, 2003) & **low likelihood** of liver relapse. Rx assoc. with ↓ hepatocellular carcinoma (AnIM 131:174, 1999) & at 8 yrs past INF rx: ↓ in liver-related death (RR 0.21 (.09–.5)) esp. in those with SVR (RR .03 (.033–.2)) (Hepatol 38:493, 2003). *(continued on next page)*

NOTE: All dosage recommendations are for adults (unless otherwise indicated) and assume normal renal/renal function. **NB** = name brand, **G** = generic

* From 2004 DRUG TOPICS RED BOOK, Medical Economics. Price is average wholesale price (AWP).

TABLE 14A (3)

VIRUS/DISEASE	DRUG/DOSAGE	SIDE EFFECTS/COMMENTS

Hepatitis Viral Infections/Chronic C/Chronic (continued)

(continued from previous page)

85% who have chronic infection. 15–30% progress to cirrhosis (med. time 28–32 yrs), 4% hepatocellular (HCCA) carcinoma. 5–10,000 deaths in U.S./yr. Co-infection with HIV extremely common.

Consider in high-risk pts (see Prevention, below) with ↑ ALT. Dx made by EIA for HCV antibody, sensitivity & specificity >99% in at-risk populations & those with liver disease. Qualitative HCV PCR used for confirmation and as adjunct when infection with out obvious risk factors or no evidence of liver disease. Immunoblot assay used as confirmatory test for pos. EIA in non-disease setting or neg. HCV RNA. HCV RNA pos. 1–3 wks after initial exposure, EIA Ab (+) ~90% by 3 mos.). **Persistent infection dx by +HCV PCR for >6 mos.** Progressive liver disease associated with older age, immunosuppressed state (HIV), concurrent Hep B, & alcohol use (30 gm/d). 50% pts for serum aminotransferase levels with clinical manifestations uncommon.

Prevention of acute and chronic infection (see review. *CID* 26:541, 1998)

— DRUG/DOSAGE column:

When genotype 1:

Pegylated INF:
Alfa-2a (Pegasys)
180 µg sc q wk
or
Alfa-2b (PEG-Intron)
>75kg 1.5 µg/kg sc q wk

	Ribavirin Wt
	(400 mg a.m., 600 mg p.m. = ~75 kg)
	or 600 mg bid

Duration of rx:

Genotype 1: check quantitative HCV RNA after 12 wks. If not ↓ by 2 log₁₀, stop (unlikely to respond). If ↓ by ≥2 log₁₀ or if HCV RNA neg., continue to 48 wks (up to 51% SVR reported). If pos. or ↓2 log, ↓: dc rx (unlikely to respond & consider rx failure). (*Hepatol* 38:645, 2003; *J Hepatol* 39:106, 2003)

When genotype 2 or 3 (non-1), alternatives for 24 wks:

Standard INF alfa
3 mU sc 3x/wk
or
PEG INF alfa similar to PEG-INF above for genotypes 2&3

	Ribavirin as with Genotype 1
	or Ribavirin 400 mg po bid
	(since SVR similar to PEG-INF)

— SIDE EFFECTS/COMMENTS column:

(continued from previous page)

3 large clinical trials have demonstrated superiority of pegylated interferon + ribavirin over standard interferon-ribavirin combination or PEG INF alone. (Sustained viral response (SVR) = similar with both forms of PEG INF.) For genotypes 2 & 3 after 24 weeks). Rates 42–51% PEG INF + ribavirin similar to INF-Rib (76–82% for genotypes 2 & 3 where PEG INF + ribavirin similar to INF-Rib (78–82% after 24 wks). Factors that ↓ success: genotype 1, other than 1, lower dose, wt. & duration of rx. (*NEJM 347:975, 2002; Hepatol 38:639, 2003*). Certain genetic markers (HLA class, B44) may predict ↑ response (*Am J Gastro 98:1621, 2003*). The rate of SVR in 100 black pts was strikingly lower than in 100 non-Hispanic whites (19% vs 52%, p <0.001); 98% had genotype 1 (*NEJM 350:2265, 2004*).

Alcohol consumption (>5 oz/d) accelerates hepatic fibrosis from HCV (*Lancet 349:825, 1997*). Occult HBV or HIV infection might account for lack of response to rx in some pts (*NEJM 341:22, 1999; CID 33:562, 2001*). In HIV-HCV co-infected pts, SVR substantively better with PEG-INF + ribavirin than with non-PEG INF + ribavirin (*NEJM 351:438, 2004*).

Decisions regarding re-treatment of prior non-responders or relapses complex. Only 15–20% of non-responders will respond to retreatment with PEG INF-Rib combination. However, 61% of those with viral relapse with 1 yr of INF-Rib had SVR 21% for INF alone (*Liver Int 23:255, 2003*). Response is independent of ribavirin dose (*J Virol Hepat 10:215, 2003*). Pts with advanced fibrosis/cirrhosis have ↑ risk of hepatic decompensation & should be monitored closely. *See drug section, Table 14B*. **Ribavirin is teratogenic & must not be used** currently being studied in non-responders with PEG INF + Rib may improve SVR for Genotype 1 (*UID 189:964, 2004*).

Herpesvirus Infections (see review. *CID 26:541, 1998*)

Cytomegalovirus (CMV)

Normal host — No rx for acute mononucleosis-like syndrome and not established for congenital CMV (see Comment)

SIDE EFFECTS: A study of newborns with symptomatic congenital CMV infection rx'd w/ IV ganciclovir has limited efficacy but ↓ hearing loss. (*J Peds 143:16, 2003*)

Immunocompromised host — Treatment of AIDS patients with highly active antiretroviral therapy (HAART) is effective in reducing mortality in pts with CMV infection by 81% (*CID 37: 1365, 2003*) and by decreasing CMV viremia. 16/16 pts became CMV DNA (−) by PCR without specific CMV therapy and none developed retinitis (*AIDS 13:1203, 1999*). Monitoring CMV DNA of value in organ transplant pts; CMV level >19 pg/ml correlated with active infection (*JID 186:829, 2002*).

Ganciclovir as with retinitis except induction period extended for 3–6 wks. No agreement on value of maintenance rx than for retinitis (*AJM 98:169, 1995*).

Colitis/esophagitis — Ganciclovir as with retinitis. Consider combination of ganciclovir and Foscarnet if prior CMV rx used. Switch to valganciclovir when possible.

SIDE EFFECTS: Side effects significant: 10–14% receiving PEG INF-Rib dc rx⁰⁹ to side effects (flu-like symptoms, hemetologic & neuropsychiatric). Similar to INF-α but with ↑ bone marrow suppression and aggravation of life-threatening neuropsychiatric, autoimmune, ischemic & ischemic disorders. See drug section, Table 14B. Ribavirin also teratogenic. **If pregnancy possible in pt or partner.** Because of toxicity, ribavirin inflammation by liver tox or low to normal ALT is usually not recommended.

Foscarnet 90 mg/kg q12h IV. Valganciclovir also likely effective. Switch to oral.

Chlv of the nervous system — Ganciclovir as with retinitis. Foscarnet if prior CMV rx used. Switch to valganciclovir when possible.

Lumbosacral polyradiculopathy / Mononucleitis multiplex — Due to vasculitis and may not be responsive to antiviral rx (*Arch Neurol 29:139, 1991*).

NOTE: *All dosage recommendations are for adults (unless otherwise indicated) and assume normal renal function.*

* From 2004 DRUG TOPICS RED BOOK, Medical Economics. Price is average wholesale price (AWP). NB = not available. G = generic

TABLE 14A (4)

VIRUS/DISEASE	DRUG/DOSAGE	SIDE EFFECTS/COMMENTS
Herpesvirus Infections/Cytomegalovirus *(continued)*		
Cytomegalovirus (CMV) pneumonia—seen predominantly in HIV pts	**Ganciclovir** 5 mg/kg IV q12h x3 wks followed by ganciclovir 5 mg/kg IV qd or ganciclovir 900 mg po qd or ganciclovir 5 mg/kg IV qd	11/15 pts showed initial improvement with either ganciclovir or foscarnet but disease progressed despite continued rx *(J Clin Invest 20:413, 1996)*. In BMT pts CMV antigen was useful in establishing early dx of CMV interstitial pneumonia with good results if GCV initiated within 6 days of antigen positivity *(Bone Marrow Transplant 26:413, 2000)*. For preventive therapy, see *Table 15E, page 129*.
Retinitis (most common in AIDS) Differential dx: HIV retinopathy, herpes simplex retinitis, varicella-zoster retinitis, syphilis (esp if diag-nosis) *(Ophthal 111:1326, 2004)* 33–63% with inactive CMV retinitis who respond to HAART (rash of ≥60 CD4 cells/ml) devel. immune recovery vitreitis (vision ↓ & floaters—with posterior segment inflammation—vitreitis, papillitis & macular changes) an avg. of 43 wks after rx started *(JID 179:697, 1999; AIDS 14:1163, 2000; CID 38:1063, 2003)*. Continued oph-thalmologic follow-up needed. Corticosteroid rx ↓ Inflammatory reaction of immune recovery vitre-itis without reactivation of CMV retinitis *(5th CRV, Abst.751)*. See *Guidelines (Int Antiviral Panel (AIM 158: 957, 1998)*	**Induction therapy, primary**: **Valganciclovir 900 mg po bid** with food x 21 days **OR ganciclovir (GCV)** 5 mg/kg IV q12h (adjust for renal function) x14–21 days **OR foscarnet (FOS)** 90 mg/kg IV q12h (adjust for renal function) IV at constant rate (requires infusion pump) over minimum of 1 hr x14–21 days **OR cidofovir** 5 mg/kg IV once weekly x 2 doses (adjust for renal function) (NOTE: concomitant IV hydration & probenecid required to prevent renal failure) **OR oral valganciclovir** 900 mg po bid with food

Induction therapy, alternative: **Cidofovir** 5 mg/kg IV q week x2 wks then q2 wks + (either concomitant **IV GCV** 5 mg/kg IV qd or **oral valganciclovir** 900 mg po qd with food)

Induction therapy, alternative: **Cidofovir** 5 mg/kg IV q week x2 wks then q2 wks. Each dose requires probenecid (2 gm po 3 hrs before cidofovir dose, 1 gm 2 hrs immediately afer dose, and 1 gm 8 hrs after dose) and 1 liter of normal saline (IV 1 hr before cidofovir infusion *(AIDSHIV 17:339, 1996; Blood 107:388, 2001)* **OR fomivirsen** 330 mg by direct intravitreal injection q2wk x2, then q month in combination with valganciclovir as above **OR** for pts who fail monotherapy, consider combination rx with both: (1) **GCV** 5 mg/kg IV qd or FOS, q12h up to total of 125 mg/kg q12h up to q12h (see www.actshinfo.nih.gov for guidelines) and retinitis

Suppression (maintenance therapy): After induction rx, suppressive rx may be dc if CD4 response to HAART. USPHS/IDSA guidelines recommend suppressive rx of minimal even >100/mm³ after 6 mos of HAART (see www.actshinfo.nih.gov for guidelines) inactive.

Primary suppression/prophylaxis: **Valganciclovir** 900 mg po qd **OR GCV** 5 mg/kg IV qd or 6 mg/kg IV qd 5 days/week **OR FOS** 90–120 mg/kg/day IV with hydration and dose adjust-ment for renal function. (NOTE: oral and IV hydration required) **OR cidofovir** 5 mg/kg IV q week x1, then q2wk with probenecid and hydration (as above under induction rx)

Alternative: Combination of **GCV intraocular implant** q6 mos. + **valganciclovir** 900 mg po qd **OR cidofovir** 5 mg/kg IV q2 wks + probenecid & hydration (see www.actshinfo.nih.gov for guidelines & rx) | Cannot use GCV ocular implant alone as approx. 50% risk of CMV retinitis in other eye at 6 mos. & 31% risk visceral disease. Risk x with systemic rx *(NEJM 337:83, 1997)*. Intravitreal injection of fomivirsen x hastens rx to prevent contralateral eye or systemic/visceral disease. *(Am J Ophth 133:467, 475, 484, 552, 2002)*. **Concurrent systemic rx recommended! Fomivirsen** may have a role in rx.

Watch for retinal detachments; 50–60% within 1 yr of dx of retinitis.

Equal efficacy of IV GCV and FOS. GCV avoids nephro-toxicity of FOS; FOS avoids bone marrow suppression of GCV. **Oral valganciclovir should replace both.** Emerg-ence of resistance to both GCV & valganciclovir minimal even with prophylactic use *(JID 189:1615, 2004)*.

Reports indicate success of combination rx with GCV and 5 mg/kg q24h & FOS up to 125 mg/kg/d for GCV-resistant isolates in solid organ transplants *(CID 34:1337, 2002)*. Hypomagnesemia common complication. Valganciclovir 900 mg po qd is as effective as IV ganciclovir. Valaciclovir response is IV ganciclovir but with fewer IV-related events *(J AIDS 30: 392, 2002)*.

become resistant to other therapies. |
EBV—Mononucleosis *(NEJM 343:481, 2000; Ln ID 3:131, 2003)*	**No treatment**. Corticosteroids for tonsillar obstruction of airway or CNS complications.	Acyclovir and prednisolone inhibited oropharyngeal EBV replication but did not affect duration of symptoms *(Curr Inf Dis Rept 6:200, 2004)*. Valacyclovir terminated EBV replication & resolved one case of hairy leukoplakia. In 16/18 cases but recurrence with termination of rx in 1/3 of cases *(JID 188:883, 2003; JID 190:387, 2004)*.
HHV-6 (see excellent review *PIDJ 21:563, 2002*) **HHV-6** (see excellent review *PIDJ 21:563, 2002*) yrs.) Fever & rash documented in transplant pts *(JID 179:311, 1999)*. 38% of 82 HHV-6 seropositive BMT pts developed HHV-6 viremia 2–4 wks after transplant. ½ had fever *(JID 185:847, 2002)*. A single immunocompetent pt with HHV-6 associated encephalomyelitis responded to cidofovir followed by ganciclovir *(EID 10:729, 2004)*. Foscarnet rx improved thrombotic microangiopathy due to HHV-6 *(Am J Hematol 76:156, 2004)*		HHV-6 ubiquitous virus (>90% of the population is infected by age 3 yrs). No relationship to human disease. Infects CD4 lymphocytes via CD4 receptor; transmitted via saliva.
HHV-7 ubiquitous virus (>90% of the population is infected by age 3 yrs). No relationship to human disease. Infects CD4 lymphocytes via CD4 receptor; transmitted via saliva. **HHV-8**—The agent of Kaposi's sarcoma, Castleman's disease, & body cavity lymphoma (primary effusion lymphoma). Transmission sexually within families & heterosexual partners, probably via saliva *(CID 37:82, 2003)*.	**No additional treatment** Currently recommended. Effective anti-HIV rx may help.	Localized lesions: radiotherapy, laser surgery or intralesional chemotherapy. Systemic: chemo-therapy. Remission in 5 pts given foscarnet 60 mg/kg/d. *(Scand J Inf Dis 26: 749, 1994)*. Castleman's disease has responded to ganciclovir *(Blood 103:1632, 2004)*.
Herpes simplex virus (HSV Types 1 & 2) *(See Ln 357:1513, 2001)*		
Bell's palsy (May also be caused by H. zoster, Lyme disease, HHV-6) *(CID 30:529, 2000)*	**Either [Acyclovir** (400 mg po 5x/d for 10 days)] with or without **prednisone** (mg po qd) for 1 mg/kg daily dose given 5x d., then taper to 5 mg bid and dc after total of 10 days) **or no rx.**	HSV-1 genomes in facial nerves of 11/14 pts by PCR *(AnM 124:27, 1996)*. 99 pts with symptoms <3 days had better recovery and less neural degeneration when rx with acyclovir + prednisone compared to prednisone alone *(Ann Oto/Rhino/Laryngo 105:371, 1996)*, but another study was underpowered to detect a clear difference. No data to support use of antivirals *(Cochrane Database Syst Rev CD001869, 2004)*. If caused by VZV (Ramsay Hunt syndrome), acyclovir may help *(PIDJ 21:615, 2002)*.

NOTE: All dosage recommendations are for adults (unless otherwise indicated) and assume normal renal function.
* From 2004 DRUG TOPICS RED BOOK, Medical Economics. Price is average wholesale price (AWP). **NB** = name brand. **G** = generic

TABLE 14A (5)

VIRUS/DISEASE	DRUG/DOSAGE	SIDE EFFECTS/COMMENTS
Herpesvirus infections/Herpes simplex virus (HSV Types 1 & 2) (continued)		
Encephalitis (Excellent reviews: CID 35: 254, 2002; EID 9:234, 2003)	**Acyclovir** IV 10 mg/kg (infuse over 1 hr) q8h x14–21 days	HSV-1 is most common cause of sporadic encephalitis. Survival & recovery from neurological sequelae are related to mental status at time of initiation of rx. **Early dx and rx imperative.** Mortality reduced from >70% to 19% with acyclovir. PCR analysis of CSF for HSV-1 DNA is 100% specific & 75–98% sensitive. 8/33 (25%) CSF samples drawn before day 3 were neg. by PCR; rep. PCR assoc. with ↓ protein & <10 WBC/mm³ in CSF (CID 36:1335, 2003). All were + after 3 days. CSF PCR (gG Ab usually appears late (>1st week). Dose: up to 20 mg/kg q8h in neonates (CID 36:1335, 2003). Relapse described in children after 1st treatment, successful rx of relapse with 2nd course acyclovir (CID 30:185, 2000). CSF glucose reported (CID 38:1506, 2004).
Genital, immunocompetent **Primary (initial episode)** See excellent reviews: NEJM 350:1970, 2004 & AnIM 137:257, 2002 or CDC 2002 Guidelines	**Acyclovir** (Zovirax or generic) 400 mg po tid x7–10 days (FDA-approved dosage is 200 mg 5x/d po x10 days). (NB $60/course; $20/course). OR **Valacyclovir** (Valtrex) 1000 mg po bid x10 days ($134/course) or **Famciclovir** (Famvir) 250 mg po tid x7–10 days (not FDA-approved for this indication) ($96–99/course)	↓ by 2 days time to resolution of signs & symptoms, ↓ by 4 d. time to healing & ↓ duration of viral shedding. Does not prevent recurrences. For severe cases: acyclovir. 5 mg/kg IV q8h x5–7 days. An ester of acyclovir, which is well absorbed, bioavailability 3–5x greater than acyclovir. Found to be **equal to acyclovir** (Sex Trans Dis 24:481, 1997). Metabolized to penciclovir, which is active component. Side effects and activity similar to acyclovir.
Episodic recurrences	**Acyclovir** 400 mg po tid x5 days or 800 mg po bid **x5 days** or **famciclovir** 125 mg po bid **x5 days** or **valacyclovir** 500 mg po bid **x3 days**	Famciclovir 125 mg po bid found to be **equal to acyclovir** 200 mg po 5x/d for ease & convenience. Trend is to ↓ duration of rx. The 2-day course of acyclovir + duration of episode & lesions from 6 to 4 days vs placebo, & viral shedding from 58 to 25 hrs (CID 34:944, 2002). The 3-day course of valacyclovir was equivalent to 5 days; duration of episode & lesions 4.4 days (CID 34:958, 2002).
Chronic suppression (JAMA 280:928, 1998; JID 178:603, 1998) Decision to rx arbitrary, but rx sig. improves quality of life over 1 yr (Sex Trans Infect 75:398, 1999).	**Suppressive rx reduces the frequency of genital herpes recurrences by 70–80% among pts who have frequent recurrences** (i.e., >6 recurrences/yr) & many report no symptomatic outbreaks (MMWR 51 RR-6, 2002). **Acyclovir** 400 mg po bid (cost/yr $1511), or **famciclovir** 250 mg po bid (cost/yr $2686); or **valacyclovir** 1 gm po qd ($2249/yr); for pts with <9 recurrences/yr, use 500 mg po qd ($1650/yr). May use 1 gm po qd if breakthrough at lower dose.	All suppress subclinical HSV-2 shedding between episodes of active disease (80–94% ↓ in number of days with subclinical shedding), ↓ risk of transmission by ↓ symptomatic recurrences. Vala ↓ risk of transmission to susceptible partner (NEJM 350:11 & 67, 2004). Drug resistance unlikely to develop with ↑ use, e.g., 6–7% HSV are resistant (Clin Micro Rev 16:114, 2003). Since in a large natural hx study 2/3 of pts demonstrated ↓ in recurrences between yrs 1 & 5 (approx. median 6 to 3 episodes/yr), daily suppressive rx should be reassessed periodically and after 3–5 yrs episodic rx may become more practical (AnIM 131:14, 1999).
Gingivostomatitis, primary (children)	**Acyclovir** 15 mg/kg po 5x/d x 7 d	Efficacy demonstrated in randomized double-blind placebo-controlled trial (BMJ 314:1800, 1997).
Kerato-conjunctivitis and recurrent epithelial keratitis	**Trifluridine** (Viroptic), 1 drop 1% solution q2h (max. 9 drops/d)	In controlled trials, response 1% acyclovir reduced duration of virus shedding. Suppressive rx with oral acyclovir (400 mg bid) reduced recurrences of HSV from 1 yr & incl. ocular dis. (EJCMID 23:560, 2004).
Mollaret's recurrent "aseptic" meningitis (usually HSV-2) (Ln 363:1772, 2004)	**Acyclovir** 5 mg/kg IV q8h or famciclovir reasonable. No controlled trials of antiviral but no clinical trials.	Pos. PCR for HSV in CSF confirms dx.
Mucocutaneous **Oral labial, primary** **Oral labial, recurrent "fever blisters"**: See Ann Pharm Ther 38:705, 2004; J Anti-micro & Chemo Ther 3:703, 2004	Start rx with prodrome symptoms (tingling or burning) before lesions appear **Oral:** Valacyclovir, Famciclovir[A,DA], Acyclovir[A,DA] **Topical:** Penciclovir 1% cream, Docosanol 1% cream[A], Acyclovir 5% cream[A]	Penciclovir (J Derm Treat 13:67, 2002; JAMA 277:1374, 1997; AAC 46:2848, 2002). Docosanol (J Am Acad Derm 45:222, 2001). Oral acyclovir (J Infect Dis 179:303, 1999). Topical fluoroconucleosides (0.05% Lidex gel) q8h x5 d. in combination with famciclovir ↓ lesion size and pain when compared to famciclovir alone (JID 181:1906, 2000).

Dosage table:

Drug	Dose	Cost	Duration Sx
Oral: Valacyclovir	2 gm po q12h x1 d	$36	↓ 1 day
Famciclovir[A,DA]	500 mg po bid x7 d	$112	↓ 2 days
Acyclovir[A,DA]	400 mg po 5x/d	$18 (generic)	↓ ½ day
Topical: Penciclovir 1% cream	q2h during days x4 d.	$23	↓ 1 day
Docosanol 1% cream[A]	5 x/d. until healed	$13.3 gm	↓ ½ day
Acyclovir 5% cream[A]	6 x/d. (q3h) x7 d.	$78/5 gm	↓ ½ day

[1] FDA approved only with HIV
[A] Approved for immunocompromised

NOTE: All dosage recommendations are for adults (unless otherwise indicated) and assume normal renal function.
* From 2004 DRUG TOPICS RED BOOK, Medical Economics. Price is average wholesale price (AWP). **NB** = name brand, **G** = generic

TABLE 14A (6)

VIRUS/DISEASE	DRUG/DOSAGE	SIDE EFFECTS/COMMENTS
Herpesvirus Infections/Herpes Simplex Virus (HSV Types 1 & 2)/Mucocutaneous/Oral labial, "fever blisters" *(continued)*		
Herpes Whitlow	*See Table 1, page 18*	
Oral labial or genital: Immunocompromised (includes pts with AIDS) and HSV in pts in ICU setting *(See Comment)*	**Acyclovir** 5 mg/kg IV (infused over 1 hr) q8h x 7 d. (250 mg/M²) **OR Acyclovir** 400 mg po 5x/d x14 d. (see *Comment*) **Suppressive rx with Acyclovir** 400 mg po bid or ganciclovir 500 mg po bid for 7 d. for recurrent episodes of genital herpes **OR valacyclovir:** In HIV-infected, 500 mg po bid for 5–10 d. for recurrent episodes of genital herpes or 500 mg po bid for chronic suppressive rx.	Acyclovir-resistant HSV occurs, esp. in large ulcers. Most will respond to **IV foscarnet**, but recur after drug discontinued [median duration 8 weeks] *(NEJM 325:551, 1991)*. Suppressive rx with famciclovir 500 mg po bid reduced (both) subclinical and clinical restoration [total days with lesions 5% vs 5%) in HIV-infected pts *(AnIM 128:21, 1998)*. similar to findings with acyclovir & valacyclovir 500 mg po bid (at 6 mos. 65% of vala-rx were recurrence-free vs 26% of placebo-rx *(JID 188:1009, 2003)*.
Perinatal (genital in pregnancy) at delivery	Acyclovir useful in dose of 10 mg/kg (20 mg/kg in infected infants), IV q8h x 10-21 d (or longer)	Cidofovir (topical) has been used with moderate success *(JID 176:892, 1997)*. In 25% HSV reactivated in last month of pregnancy. Infant exposure to primary lesion 4%, 50% mortality in infected neonates. If visible genital lesion, deliver by **C-section**, regardless of duration of membrane rupture. If no lesions or symptoms, vaginal delivery. Routine HSV cultures no longer recommended *(Ln 364:1507, 2004)*; useful during active recurrence *(Ln 364:1569, 1997)*.
Herpes simiae—Monkey bite (Herpes B virus) *CID 35:1191, 2002*	Postexposure prophylaxis: Valacyclovir 1 gm po q8h x14 d or acyclovir 800 mg po 5x/d x14 d. Treatment of disease: (1) CNS symptoms absent: Acyclovir 12.5–15 mg/kg IV q8h or ganciclovir 5 mg/kg IV q12h; (2) CNS symptoms present: Ganciclovir 5 mg/kg IV q12h	Fatal human cases of myelitis and hemorrhagic encephalitis have been reported following bites, scratches, or even inoculation of saliva from monkeys. Initial sx include fever, headache, myalgias and diffuse adenopathy, incubation period of 2–14 days *(EID 9:246, 2003)*.
Herpes Varicella-Zoster Virus (VZV)		
Varicella		
Normal host (chickenpox) Child (2-12 years)	Rx not recommended by American Academy of Pediatrics. Oral acyclovir recommended for healthy persons at ↑ risk for moderate to severe varicella, i.e., >12 yrs of age, chronic cutaneous or pulmonary diseases; chronic salicylate rx (↑ risk of Reye syndrome), use **acyclovir 20 mg/kg** po qid x5 days (start within 24 hrs of rash).	Modest response to acyclovir. Slowed development and ↓ number of new lesions; duration of disease ↓ in children receiving acyclovir in Europe: 7.6 vs 9.0 days *(PIDJ 21:739, 2002)*. Analgesic requirements decreased *(NEJM 325:1539, 1991)*. Oral dose of acyclovir in children should not exceed 80 mg/kg/d or 3200 mg/d.
Adolescents, young adults	**Acyclovir** 800 mg po 5x/d x5–7 days (start within 24 hrs of rash) **or valacyclovir**[FDA] 1000 mg po 3x/d x 5 d. **Famciclovir**[FDA] 500 mg po 3x/d; also probably effective for rx	↓ duration of fever, time to healing, and symptoms *(AnIM 117:358, 1992)*.
Pneumonia or chickenpox in 3rd trimester of pregnancy	**Acyclovir** 800 mg po 5x/d or 10 mg/kg IV q8h x5 days. Risks and benefits to fetus and mother still unknown. Many experts recommend rx, especially in 3rd trimester. Some would add VZIG (varicella-zoster immune globulin).	Varicella pneumonia severe in pregnancy (41% mortality, *Ob Gyn 25:734, 1965*) and acyclovir ↓ incidence and severity *(JID 165:422, 1992)*. If varicella-susceptible mother exposed and respiratory symptoms develop within 10 days after exposure, start acyclovir *(CCTID 13:123, 1993)*. Acyclovir is pregnancy category B; no evidence of ↑ birth defects *(MMWR 42:806, 1993)*.
Immunocompromised host	**Acyclovir** 10–12 mg/kg IV (infused over 1 hr) q8h x7 days (500 mg/M²)	Continuous infusion of high-dose acyclovir (2 mg/kg/hr) successful in 1 pt with severe hemorrhagic varicella *(NEJM 336:732, 1997)*. Mortality high (43%) in AIDS pts *(Int J Inf Dis)*.
Prevention Varicella is the leading cause of vaccine-preventable deaths in children in the U.S. *(MMWR 47:365, 1998)*	**CDC Recommendations for Prevention:** Since <5% of cases of varicella occur in adults >20 yrs of age, the CDC recommends a more aggressive approach in this age group: **1st, varicella-zoster immune globulin** (VZIG) (125 U/10 kg (22 lbs) body weight IM up to a max. of 625 U; minimum dose is 125 U) is recommended for post-exposure prophylaxis in susceptible persons at greater risk for complications (immunocompromised such as HIV, malignancies, pregnancy, and steroid rx) as soon as possible after exposure (<96 hrs). If varicella develops, initiate rx quickly (<24 hrs of rash) with acyclovir. **2nd,** acyclovir prophylaxis in susceptible high-risk pts. **3rd,** susceptible children should receive vaccination. Check antibody in adults with negative or uncertain hx of varicella (10–30% will be Ab-neg.) and vaccinate those who are Ab-neg. Age 12–18 mos. but OK at any age.

NOTE: All dosage recommendations are for adults (unless otherwise indicated) and assume normal renal function.
* From 2004 Drug Topics Red Book, Medical Economics. Price is average wholesale price (AWP).   **NB** = name brand, **G** = generic

TABLE 14A (7)

VIRUS/DISEASE	DRUG/DOSAGE	SIDE EFFECTS/COMMENTS
Herpesvirus Infections/Herpes Varicella-Zoster Virus (VZV) (continued)		
Herpes zoster (shingles) (See NEJM 347:340, 2002)	Valaciclovir ↓ post-herpetic neuralgia more rapidly than acyclovir in pts >50 yrs of age; median duration of zoster-associated pain was 38 days with valacyclovir and 51 days with acyclovir (AAC 39:1546, 1995).	
Normal host	**NOTE: Trials show greatest benefit of rx only in pts treated within 3 days of onset of rash)**	
Effective rx most evident in pts >50 yrs	Valacyclovir 1000 mg po tid x7 days (adjust dose for renal failure). **OR**	Toxicity of both drugs similar (Arch Fam Med 9:863, 2000).
(For rx of post-herpetic neuralgia, see CID 36:877, 2003)	Famciclovir 750 mg po q8h or 500 mg q8h or 250 mg 3x/d x7 d, equal efficacy (J Clin Virol 29:248, 2004). Adjust for renal failure (NEJM 347:340, 2002). **OR**	Time to healing more rapid. Reduced duration of PHN with famciclovir 63 days, placebo 163 days. Famciclovir similar to acyclovir in reduction of duration of PHN (Clin Ther 16:1077, 1994).
25-fold ↑ in zoster after immunization (MMWR 48:7–6, 1999)	Acyclovir 800 mg po 5x/d x7–10 days	A meta-analysis of 4 placebo-controlled trials (691 pts) demonstrated that acyclovir accelerated by approx. 2-fold pain resolution by all measures employed and reduced post-herpetic neuralgia at 3 & 6 mos (CID 22:341, 1996); also, med. time to resolution of pain 41 days vs 101 days in those >50 yrs.
	[Prednisone po 30 mg bid days 1–7, 15 mg bid days 8–14 and 7.5 mg bid days 15–21 also recommended by some authorities in pts >50 yrs of age (NEJM 335:32, 1996) and especially when pt has large number of lesions (≥21) and/or severe pain at presentation (JID 179:9, 1999).	In post-herpetic neuralgia, controlled trials demonstrated effectiveness of gabapentin, the lidocaine patch (5%), & opioid analgesic in controlling pain (Drugs 64:937, 2004); J Clin Virol 29:248, 2004). Nortriptyline & amitriptyline are equally effective but nortriptyline is better tolerated (AJM 175:19, 1991).
Immunocompromised host		
Not severe	Acyclovir 800 mg po 5x/d x7 d. **Options: Famciclovir** 500 mg po tid x7 d, **OR valacyclovir** 1000 mg po tid x7 d, though both are not FDA-approved for this indication)	If progression, switch to IV
Severe: >1 dermatome, trigeminal nerve or disseminated	Acyclovir 10–12 mg/kg IV (infusion over 1 hr) q8h x7–14 days. If ≥50 kg, 500 mg/m², q8h. If nephrotoxicity and pt improving, ↓ to 5 mg/kg q8h.	A common manifestation of immune reconstitution following HAART. Prednisone added to acyclovir improved quality of life measurements (↓ acute pain, sleep, and return to normal activity) (AIM 125:376, 1996). Foscarnet (40 mg/kg IV q8h for 14–26 days) successful in 4/5 pts but 2 relapsed in 7 and 14 days (AIM 115:19, 1991). Acyclovir-resistant VZV occurs in HIV+ pts previously treated with acyclovir. Foscarnet (40 mg/kg IV q8h).
Influenza (A & B); known community influenza activity; and 1st 48 hrs of illness, consider:	**Options:**	
Rapid diagnostic tests available (J Clin Virol 25: 15, 2002); antiviral rx cost-effective without viral testing in febrile pts with typical symptoms during flu season (Am J Med 113:180, 2002).	**For influenza A & B; also For influenza A (H5N1) or avian (H5N1):**	Pts with COPD or asthma, **potential risk of bronchospasm with zanamivir.** If using inhaled bronchodilator, use before dose of zanamivir. Amantadine & rimantadine equally effective, but rimantadine ↓ side effects (Cochrane Database Sys Rev CD1169, 2004).
Highly pathogenic avian influenza (H5N1) now in poultry (chickens & ducks) in East & Southeast Asia; >100 million chickens died or were slaughtered & 23 of the 34 human cases died (Ln340:1261, 2004). Little evidence for human-to-human transmission, most have had direct contact with poultry (medical <3 days) (NEJM 350: 1179, 2004). Human isolates demonstrate resistance to a mantadine/rimantadine. Oseltamivir rx recommended if avian H5N1 suspected (MMWR 53:97, 2004).	**Oseltamivir** 75 mg po bid x5 d. (also approved for rx of influenza age 1–12 yrs, dose 2 mg/kg up to a total of 75 mg bid x5 d.) OR **Zanamivir** 2 inhalations (2x5 mg) bid x5 d.	For avian (H5N1): 36 hrs after onset of symptoms. Benefit influenced by duration of sx before rx, initiation of oseltamivir within 1st 12 hrs after fever onset (3.1 days; 41%) more than if given after 48 hrs of fever onset (JAC 51:123, 2003). **Disturbing report** of oseltamivir-resistant virus, 1° detected after 4 days of rx, & continued to shed potentially infectious virus (Ln 364:733 & 759, 2004). Whether these resistant viruses are transmissible is unknown. In another study of 298 rx cases of adults & children, no oseltamivir-resistant viruses found (JID 189:440, 2004).
		Rapid diagnostic tests available (J Clin Virol 25: 15, 2002); antiviral rx
Prevention: See MMWR 52:RR-8, 2003 & RR-6:1, 2004.	**Prevention of influenza A & B:** give vaccine; **For influenza A only:** **amantadine** (dosages as above)	Immunization contraindicated if hypersensitivity to eggs. Both amantadine and rimantadine are
Suspect or proven acute infection		
If fever & cough; known community influenza activity; and 1st 48 hrs of illness, consider: **For influenza (H5N1) or avian (H5N1):** **For influenza A only:** **amantadine or amantadine** 1–9 yrs, 5 mg/kg/d to max. of 75 mg po bid; 10–65 yrs, 100 mg po bid (adults, 100 mg/day if adverse or renal function) **or 3–5 d. or 1–2 d after the disappearance of symptoms.**	**amantadine** 75 mg po tid or for duration of peak influenza A activity in community for outbreak control in high-risk populations (CID 39:459, 2004). (Consider for similar populations as immunization recommendations.)	>65 yrs age, residents of nursing homes or chronic care facilities that house persons with chronic medical conditions, chronic metabolic diseases (diabetes), renal failure, etc., immunosuppression, and children on chronic ASA therapy. Household or persons who can transmit flu to above (HCWs, etc.)
	Prevention of influenza A & B: oseltamivir 75 mg po qd for duration of peak influenza in community in high-risk populations (CID 39:459, 2004). (Consider for similar populations as immunization recommendations.)	about 70–90% effective against influenza A. Both oseltamivir and zanamivir reported efficacious (82 & 84% respectively) in children (JAMA 285: 748, 2001; JID 186:1582, 2002). In families, rx of index case as well as prophylaxis more effective than rx of index case alone (p<0.01) (JID 189:440, 2004).

NOTE: All dosage recommendations are for adults (unless otherwise indicated) and assume normal renal function. Price is average wholesale price (AWP). **NB** = name brand, **G** = generic

From 2004 DRUG TOPICS Red Book, Medical Economics.

TABLE 14A (B)

VIRUS/DISEASE	DRUG/DOSAGE		SIDE EFFECTS/COMMENTS
Measles			
Children	No therapy or **vitamin A** 200,000 u po x2 days	Vitamin A ↓ severity of measles in one study *(NEJM 323:160, 1990)*, not in others.	
Adults	No rx or **ribavirin** IV (i) 20–35 mg/kg/d x7 d	↓ severity of illness in adults *(CID 20:454, 1994)*	
Metapneumovirus [HMPV] A paramyxovirus *(PIDJ 22:923, 2003)* isolated from pts of all ages, with illnesses ranging from mild bronchiolitis/bronchospasm to pneumonia. All persons in the Netherlands had antibody to HMPV by age 5 yrs.	**No proven anti-viral therapy**		HMPV accounted for 2.3% of all respiratory viral isolates in Canada over the winter of 2000–2001. Similar to parainfluenza 2.3%, adenovirus 3.4%, RSV 4.8%, while influenza A & B was 20% *(JID 186:1330, 2002)*. Human metapneumovirus isolated from 6.2% of children with respiratory infections in Massachusetts *(JID 190:20, 2004)*, 12% in children with lower respiratory tract infections *(NEJM 350:443, 2004)* & 21% of hospitalized children with URI in Norway *(PIDJ 23:436, 2004, JID 190:27, 2004)*.
Monkey pox (orthopox virus) *(see LnID 4:17, 2004)* In 2003, 72 pts contracted monkey pox from contact with ill prairie dogs. Source likely imported Gambian giant rats *(MMWR 42:642, 2003)*			Incubation period of 12 days, then fever, headache, cough, adenopathy, & a vesicular papular rash that pustulates, umbilicates, & crusts on the head, trunk, & extremities.
Norovirus (Norwalk-like virus, or NLV) Caused 93% of outbreaks of non-bacterial gastroenteritis reported to CDC between 1997 & 2000. 23 million cases of norovirus AGE annually in the U.S. *(JID 186:1, 2002)*, & account for 2/3 of all food-borne illnesses *(CID 38:748, 2002)*. Transmission is by contaminated food, fecal-oral contact with contaminated surfaces, or fomites. Commonly causes outbreaks on cruise ships. A new norovirus variant may account for ↑ number of cases in Europe *(Ln 363:682, 2004)*.	**No proven antiviral therapy.** Cidofovir is active in vitro & in mouse model *(AAC 46:1329, 2002; Antiviral Res 57:13, 2003)*		Incubation period 12–48 hrs, followed by sudden onset of nausea, vomiting, & watery diarrhea lasting 12–60 hours.
Papillomavirus. Therapies generally unsatisfactory with limited efficacy, high recurrence rates & ↑ side-effects *(JAC 53:137, 2004)*.			
Anogenital Warts: Condyloma acuminatum *[See CID 28(Suppl.1):S37, 1999]* [NOTE: Results of 2 Pap smears likely to fall to identify cervical cancer & its precursors with high rate of false-negatives. Therapy is directed at obvious lesions, but none of the methods eradicate HPV.]	See *CID 27:796, 1998*, for consensus statement: **[Podofilox** (Condylox) 2x daily application with cotton swab for 3 days followed by 4 days without rx; repeat cycle 4–6x as necessary] **OR** [25% **podophyllin** in tincture of benzoin (Podocon-25): apply only weekly for up to 6 wks, wash after 4 hrs] **OR** [80–90% **trichloroacetic acid** or **bichloroacetic acid**].		Podofilox: Local reactions—pain, burning, inflammation in 50%. No systemic effects. Efficacy in genital warts 74% vs placebo 8%. Recurrences 55% vs 100% with placebo. (Podocon-25 15 ml $32.40. Condylox 3.5 ml $56.64.) Warts recur in 1/3 with either agent within 1st month after rx.
avoid rx in pregnant women NOTE: Recurrences common after all treatments	**interferon alfa-2b** (Intron A) or **alfa-n3** (Alferon N): 1 million units (0.1 ml) into lesion 3x/week x3 weeks		Painful: dilute to 10 million units/1 ml. Other concentrations are hypertonic *(CID 28:S37, 1999)*. Use with caution IV rx fails, esp. in AIDS.
	imiquimod [5% cream]: Apply 3x/week prior to sleep; remove 6–10 hrs later when awake. Continue until cleared or max. 16 wks.		When applied 3x/wk overnight for up to 16 wks of warts completely cured, produced clearance rates of 52% vs 14% for controls *(AAC 42:789, 1998)*. Cost of 1–4 wks rx: $108–432. Imiquimod: Local reactions—local erythema 60%, erosion 30% *(AJM 102(5A):34, 1997)*.
Skin papillomas	**Topical α-lactalbumin. Oleic acid** (from human milk) applied daily for 3 wks		↓ lesion size & recurrence vs placebo (p <0.001) *(NEJM 350:2663, 2004)*. Further studies warranted.
Parvo B19 Virus (Erythrovirus B19). See *NEJM 350:586, 2004*			
Uncomplicated or self-limited acute arthritis. May be chronic in children.	**No treatment recommended**		Bone marrow shows selective erythrocyte maturation arrest with giant pronormoblasts. IgM antibody available for diagnosis: Specialty Labs, Santa Monica, CA. Parvo B19 also associated with respiratory distress syndrome *(CID 27:900, 1998)* and myocarditis/myocardiopathy *(CID 28:1343, 1999)*.
Acute profound anemia: in utero, in hemolytic anemia, in HIV	**IVIG** 0.4 gm/kg IV qd x5 d in immune def. states with severe anemia		IVIG contains anti-parvo B19 antibody. In pts with pre-existing hemolytic anemia, parvo B19-induced bone marrow arrest can result in sudden severe anemia. See *Am J Hematol 61:16, 1999* for new suggestions on management.

NOTE: All dosage recommendations are for adults (unless otherwise indicated) and assume normal renal function.
* From 2004 DRUG TOPICS RED BOOK, Medical Economics. Price is average wholesale price (AWP). **NB** = name brand, **G** = generic

TABLE 14A (9)

VIRUS/DISEASE	DRUG/DOSAGE	SIDE EFFECTS/COMMENTS
Papovavirus/Polyomavirus		
Progressive multifocal leukoencephalopathy (PML)(JC virus) Usually in pts with advanced HIV disease & organ transplant (CID 35; 1061, 2002)	Cytarabine of no value in controlled trial (NEJM 338;1345, 1998). Camptothecin, a human topoisomerase I inhibitor, administered to a single pt with slowing of progression (Ln 349:1366, 1997). Use of cidofovir controversial (Clin Micro Rev 16:569, 2003).	Corticosteroids ↑ mortality rate and ↓ incubation in mice.
Polyomavirus-associated nephropathy — **Due to BK virus** post renal transplant	Possible rx role for **cidofovir** (LnID 3:611, 2003)	
Rabies (see Table 20C, pages 141–142, see Mayo Clin Proc 79:671, 2004) Rabid dogs account for 50,000 cases/yr worldwide. Most cases in the U.S. associated with bat contact in a rabid animal (CID 35; 738, 2003). 70% assoc. with 2 rare bat species; the eastern pipistrella in the southeast & the silver-hair bat in the northwest (EID 9:151, 2003). These viruses appear to exhibit ↑ infectivity.	**Mortality 100% with only survivors those who receive rabies vaccine before the onset of illness/symptoms** (CID 36:61, 2003). Therapies that have failed in human cases after symptoms develop include rabies vaccine, immunoglobulin, rabies virus neutralizing antibody, ribavirin, alfa interferon, & ketamine.	
Respiratory Syncytial Virus Major cause of morbidity in neonates/infants (IJID 180:41, 1999). ↑ recognition in adults; 2–9% of pts >65 yrs of age with pneumonia requiring hospitalization are due to RSV (JID 179:25, 1999). **Prevention** (1) Children <24 mos. old with bronchopulmonary dysplasia (BPD) requiring supplemental O₂. (2) Perhaps premature infant (<26 wks gestation) and <6 mos. old at start of RSV season	Rapid dx by antigen detection on nasopharyngeal wash. No rx proven to ↑ survival. Various combinations of ribavirin, RSV-IVIG & palivizumab have been used; see Comments (PIDJ 23:707, 2004; Pharmacother 24:932, 2004; Ped Drugs 6:177, 2004). **RSV immune globulin intravenous** (RSV-IVIG) 100 mg/kg IV once monthly Nov. through April (for northern hemisphere) 1st year of life for prematures. Perhaps up to 60 months of age for pts with BPD. **OR** **Palivizumab** 15 mg/kg IM q 1 month Nov–April as above (Scand J Int Dis 33:323, 2001)	Ribavirin reported to ↑ fever and other symptoms and signs. However, in controlled studies, **ribavirin had no beneficial effect** (J Ped 128: 422, 1996; AJRCCM 160:829, 1999). Still recommended by some authorities in immunocompromised children (PID 19:253, 2000) & still controversial (PIDJ 22:589, 2003). RSV-IVIG very expensive—estimated cost per infusion $1,175. See consensus opinion for details; Ped Inf Dis J 15:1059, 1996. See Ln 354:847, 1999 for updated review. Palivizumab reduced hospitalization rates for RSV in 1500 premature infants & children with chronic lung disease from 10.6% to 4.8% (Pediatrics 102:531, 1998). Cost: $3000–5000/yr
Rhinovirus (Colds) See Ln 361:51, 2003 Found in ½ of children with community-acquired pneumonia; role in pathogenesis unclear (CID 39:681, 2004).	No antiviral rx indicated. Symptomatic rx: • ipratropium bromide nasal (2 sprays) nostril tid • clemastine 1.34 mg 1–2 tab po bid-tid (OTC)	Six relief: ipratropium nasal spray ↓ rhinorrhea and sneezing, ↑ nose, mouth & throat dryness (an antihistamine) ↓ sneezing, rhinorrhea, but associated with dry nose, mouth & throat (J Fam Pract 125:89, 1996). Zinc lozenges were ineffective (CID 31:1202, 2000). Oral **pleconaril** given within 24 hrs of onset reduced duration (1 day) & severity of "cold symptoms" in DBPCT (p < 0.001 (JID 186:1523, 2003). A combination of intranasal interferon alfa-2b, oral chlorpheniramine & ibuprofen ↓ symptom score by 33–73% vs placebo when started 24 hrs after intranasal rhinovirus (JID 186:147, 2002). Rupintrivir inhibits rhinovirus 3C protease & ↓ symptom scores, nasal discharge weights, & viral titers in a DBPCT in 202 subjects with rhinovirus colds (AAC 47:3907, 2003). Echinacea didn't work (CID 39:759).
SARS-CoV See page 104		
Smallpox (NEJM 346:1300, 2002) See Ln 361:57, 2003 **Contact vaccinia** (JAMA 288:1901, 2002)	Smallpox vaccine (if within 4 days of exposure) + cidofovir (dosage uncertain; contact CDC: 770-488-7100) From vaccination: Progressive vaccinia—vaccinia immune globulin may be of benefit. To obtain immune globulin, contact CDC: 770-488-7100 (CID 39:759).	
West Nile virus See page 104		

---

¹ **DBPCT** = Double-blind placebo-controlled trial

NOTE: All dosage recommendations are for adults (unless otherwise indicated) and assume normal renal function.
* From 2004 DRUG TOPICS RED BOOK, Medical Economics. Price is average wholesale price (AWP). **NB** = name brand, **G** = generic

TABLE 14B: ANTIVIRAL DRUGS (Other Than Retroviral)

DRUG NAME(S) GENERIC (TRADE)	DOSAGE/ROUTE/COST*	COMMENTS/ADVERSE EFFECTS
CMV (See SANFORD GUIDE TO HIV/AIDS THERAPY)		
Cidofovir (Vistide)	5 mg/kg IV q week x2, then q2 weeks. (375 mg NB $888) Properly timed IV prehydration with normal saline and probenecid **must be used with each cidofovir infusion** (see pkg insert for details). Renal function (serum creatinine and urine protein) must be monitored prior to each dose (see pkg insert for details).	**Adverse effects: Nephrotoxicity**; dose-dependent proximal tubular injury (Fanconi-like syndrome): proteinuria, glycosuria, bicarbonaturia, phosphaturia, polyuria (nephrogenic diabetic insipidus may be noted), nausea, diarrhea. ↑ creatinine. Concomitant saline prehydration, probenecid, extended dosing intervals allowed use. 25% of pts dc IV cidofovir due to 31% nephrotoxicity. Other toxicities: fever 57%, asthenia 46%, alopecia 16%, myalgia 16%, ocular hypotensitivity 16%, neutropenia 29%. No effect on hematocrit, platelets, LFTs. **Comment**: Recommended dosage, frequency or duration of cidofovir must not be exceeded. Dose may be reduced or discontinued if changes in renal function occur during rx. For ↑ of 0.3–0.4 mg/dl in serum creatinine, cidofovir dose must be ↓ from 5 to 3 mg/kg; discontinue cidofovir if ↑ of 0.5 mg/dl above baseline or 3+ proteinuria develops (for 2+ proteinuria, observe pts carefully and consider discontinuation).
Fomivirsen (Vitravene)	330 mg by direct intravitreal injection q2 wks x2, then q 1 month (6.6 mg $4000)	This is an antisense oligonucleotide approved for treatment of CMV retinitis in AIDS pts who are intolerant of/have a contraindication to or were unresponsive to other treatments for CMV. It inhibits production of proteins responsible for regulation of viral gene expression essential for virulence. **Adverse effects:** ocular inflammation (uveitis), iritis and vitreitis, ↑ intraocular pressure, abnormal vision, anterior chamber inflammation and cataracts. Do not give if pt had received IV or intravitreal cidofovir (Vistide) within last 2–4 wks, may exaggerate ocular inflammation (Priority Pharmacy 3, J48, Oct. 30, 1998).
Foscarnet (Foscavir)	90 mg/kg q12h IV (induction) 90 mg/kg qd IV (maintenance) Dosage adjust. with renal dysfunction (see Table 17) (6 gm $95)	**Adverse effects: Major clinical toxicity is renal impairment (1/3 of patients)**—↑ creatinine, proteinuria, nephrogenic diabetes insipidus, ↓ K⁺, ↓ Ca⁺⁺, ↓ Mg⁺⁺. Toxicity ↑ with other nephrotoxic drugs (amphotericin B, aminoglycosides or pentamidine (especially severe ↓ Ca⁺⁺). Adequate hydration may ↓ toxicity. Other: headache, mild (100%); fatigue (100%); nausea (80%), fever (25%). CNS: seizures. Hematol.: ↓ WBC, ↓ Hgb. Hepatic: liver function tests ↑. Neuropathy. Penile ulcers.
Ganciclovir (Cytovene)	IV: 5 mg/kg q12h x14 days (induction) 5 mg/kg IV qd or 6 mg/kg 5x/wk (maintenance) Dosage adjust. with renal dysfunction (see Table 17) (500 mg IV $39) Oral: 1.0 gm tid with food (fatty meal) (500 mg cap $9)	**Adverse effects:** Absolute neutrophil count dropped below 500/mm³ in 15%, thrombocytopenia 21%, anemia 6%. Fever 48% GI 50%: nausea, vomiting, diarrhea, abdominal pain 19%, rash 10%. Retinal detachment 11% (relationship to ganciclovir?). Confusion, headache, psychiatric disturbances and seizures. Neutropenia may respond to hematopoietic growth factor (G-CSF or GM-CSF). Severe myelosuppression may be ↑ with coadministration of zidovudine or azathioprine. 32% dc/interrupted, primarily for neutropenia. Hematologic less frequent than with IV. Granulocytopenia 18%, anemia 12%, thrombocytopenia 6%. GI: skin same as with IV. Retinal detachment 8%
Ganciclovir (Vitrasert)	intraocular implant (~$5000/device + cost of surgery)	**Adverse effects:** Late retinal detachment (7/30 eyes). Does not prevent CMV retinitis in good eye or visceral dissemination. **Comment:** Replacement every 6 months recommended.
Valganciclovir (Valcyte)	900 mg (two 450 mg tabs) po bid x21 d for induction, followed by 900 mg po qd. Take with food. (450 mg cap $31.50, $1,890 for 60 caps)	A prodrug of ganciclovir with better bioavailability: 60% with food. **Adverse effects:** Similar to ganciclovir.
Herpesvirus (non-CMV)		
Acyclovir (Zovirax or generic)	Doses: see Table 14A 400 mg tab NB $2; G $0.70 IV 500 mg NB $46 Suspension 200 mg/5 ml: 1 gm $7 Ointment 5% 15 gm $107	**po**: Generally well-tolerated with occ. diarrhea, vertigo, arthralgia. Less frequent rash, fatigue, insomnia, fever, menstrual abnormalities, acne, sore throat, muscle cramps, lymphadenopathy. **IV**: Phlebitis, caustic with vesicular lesions with IV infiltration, CNS (1%): tremors, confusion, hallucinations, delirium, seizures, coma (CID 21:435, 1995). Improve ↑ 2 weeks after rx stopped. Renal (5%): ↑ creatinine, hematuria. With high doses may crystallize in renal tubules → obstructive uropathy (rapid infusion, dehydration, renal insufficiency and ↑ dose ↑ risk). Adequate pre-hydration may prevent such nephrotoxicity. Hepatic: ↑ ALT, AST. Uncommon: neutropenia (CID 20:1557, 1995), rash, diaphoresis, hypotension, headache, nausea
Famciclovir (Famvir)	250 mg tab $8 500 mg tab $8	Metabolized to penciclovir. **Adverse effects:** similar to acyclovir, included headache, nausea, diarrhea, and dizziness but incidence did not differ from placebo (JAMA 276:47, 1996). May be taken without regard to meals. Dose should be reduced if CrCl <60 ml/min (see package insert & Table 14, page 55).
Penciclovir (Denavir) Trifluridine (Viroptic)	Topical 1% cream 1.5 gm $26 (2 gm $55) (see Table 17, page 155)	Apply to area of recurrence of herpes labialis with start of sx, then q2h while awake x4 d. Well tolerated.
	Topical 1% solution q2h (max 9 drops/d) for	Mild burning (5%), palpebral edema (3%), punctata keratopathy, stromal edema

NOTE: All dosage recommendations are for adults (unless otherwise indicated) and assume normal renal function.
* From 2004 DRUG TOPICS RED BOOK, Medical Economics. Price is average wholesale price (AWP). **NB** = name brand, **G** = generic.

TABLE 14B (2)

DRUG NAME(S) GENERIC (TRADE)	DOSAGE/ROUTE/COST*	COMMENTS/ADVERSE EFFECTS
Herpesvirus (non-CMV) *(continued)*		
Valacyclovir (Valtrex)	500 mg cap $4.52	An ester pro-drug of acyclovir (prodrug of acyclovir). It is well-absorbed, bioavailability 3–5x greater than acyclovir. **Adverse effects** similar to acyclovir (see *JID 186:S40, 2002*). Thrombotic thrombocytopenic purpura/hemolytic uremic syndrome reported in pts with advanced HIV disease and transplant recipients participating in clinical trials at doses of 8 gm/day.
Hepatitis		
Adefovir dipivoxil (Hepsera)	10 mg po qd (with normal CrCl) / 20–49: 10 mg q48h / 10–19 CrCl: 10 mg q72h / Hemodialysis: 10 mg q7 days following dialysis. / Each tab contains 10 mg ($19)	Adefovir dipivoxil is a diester prodrug of the active moiety adefovir. It is an acyclic nucleotide analog with activity against hepatitis B (HBV) at 0.2–2.5 nM (CC_{50} at 1.2 mM). Peak plasma concentration after 10 mg po was 18.4 ± 6.26 ng/ml, 1–4 hrs after dose. Terminal elimination t½ was 7.48 ± 1.65 hrs. Primarily renal excretion—adjust dose. No food interactions. Remarkably few side effects. Nephrotoxicity found in early studies with 30 mg/d, not yet reported at 10 mg/d. Monitor renal function, esp. with pts with pre-existing or other risks for renal impairment. Lactic acidosis reported with nucleoside analogs, esp. in women. Pregnancy Category C. Hepatitis may exacerbate when rx dc. 6–25% of pts developed ALT ↑ 10x normal within 12 wks; usually responds to re-treatment or self-limited, but hepatic decompensation has occurred.
Interferon alfa is available as alfa-2a (Roferon-A), alfa-2b (Intron-A)	3 million units (Roferon $37, Intron $39; Intergen 9 µg $48)	**Adverse effects:** Flu-like reaction common, esp. during 1st week of rx: fever 98%, fatigue 89%, myalgia 73%, headache 71%, GI anorexia 46%, diarrhea 29%, CNS: dizziness 21%. Rash 18%, later profound fatigue & psychiatric symptoms in up to ⅓ of pts (*Ln Psych 64:708, 2003*) (depression, anxiety, emotional lability and agitation), alopecia, ↑ TSH, autoimmune thyroid disorders with hypo- or hyperthyroidism. Hematol.: ↓ WBC 49%, ↓ Hgb 27%, ↓ platelets 35%. Consider prophylactic antidepressant in pts with history. Acute reversible hearing loss and/or tinnitus in up to 1/3 (*Ln 343:1134, 1994*). Optic neuropathy (retinal hemorrhage, cotton wool spots, ↓ in color vision) reported (*AIDS 18:1805, 2004*). Side-effects ↑ with ↑ doses and dose reduction necessary in up to 46% receiving chronic rx for HBV.
PEG interferon alfa-2b (PEG-Intron)	0.5–1.5 µg/kg sc q wk (120 µg $391)	Attachment of INF to polyethylene glycol (PEG) prolongs half-life and allows weekly dosing. Better efficacy data with similar adverse effects profile compared to regular formulation.
Pegylated-40k interferon alfa-2a (Pegasys)	180 µg sc q wk x48 wks ($367)	
Lamivudine (3TC) (Epivir-HBV)	100 mg po qd x 1 yr for hepatitis B. NOTE: 100 mg q d tab $7	See *Table 14D, page 121.*
Ribavirin-Interferon alfa-2b combination pack (Rebetron)	Combination kit contains 2 wk supply of INF and 42, 70, or 84 caps of 200 mg ribavirin. **Dose:** INF 3 million U sc tiw AND ribavirin 400 mg po q a.m. + 600 mg po q p.m. (>75 kg) or 400 mg po bid (<75 kg) ($9552/24 wk course)	**Adverse effects:** Side-effects common with flu-like symptoms (>50%); see interferon alfa above. Hemolytic anemia common (mean reduction in Hgb 3 gm/dl) but usually ribavirin dosage (see package insert). Severe **psychiatric effects, esp. depression,** most common (23–36%) with rx. **Suicidal behavior reported.** Hyper- & hypothyroidism, alopecia (30%) & pulmonary disease reported (*Mayo Clin Proc 74:367, 1999*). **Since ribavirin is teratogenic, drug must not be used during pregnancy or within 6 months of pregnancy.** Also should not be used in pts with endstage renal failure, severe heart disease, or hemoglobinopathies. ARDS reported (*Chest 124:406, 2003*). **Dose changes:** <table><tr><td></td><td>Ribavirin</td><td>Interferon</td></tr><tr><td>Hgb: <10</td><td>↓ to 200 mg q a.m., 400 mg q p.m.</td><td>No change</td></tr><tr><td><8.5</td><td>DC</td><td>DC</td></tr><tr><td>WBC: <1500</td><td>↓ to 1.5 mIU sc 3x/wk</td><td>No change</td></tr><tr><td><1000</td><td>DC</td><td>DC</td></tr><tr><td>Abs. PMNs: <750</td><td>↓ to 1.5 mIU sc 3x/wk</td><td>No change</td></tr><tr><td><500</td><td>DC</td><td>DC</td></tr><tr><td>Platelets: <50,000</td><td>↓ to 1.5 mIU sc 3x/wk</td><td>No change</td></tr><tr><td><25,000</td><td>DC</td><td>DC</td></tr></table> Response of immune complex renal disease: *A/M 106:347, 1999.*

NOTE: All dosage recommendations are for adults (unless otherwise indicated) and assume normal renal function.
** From 2004 DRUG TOPICS RED BOOK, Medical Economics. Price is average wholesale price (AWP). **G** = generic*

TABLE 14B (3)

DRUG NAME(S) GENERIC (TRADE)	DOSAGE/ROUTE/COST*	COMMENTS/ADVERSE EFFECTS
Hepatitis (continued)		
Ribavirin (Rebetol)	For use with an interferon for hepatitis C & was unbundled from the combination Rebetron (see above) mostly for use with the pegylated interferons (alfa-2a & 2b). Available as 200 mg capsules. Dose <75 kg BW = 2 caps in a.m. & 3 caps in p.m., >75 kg BW 3 caps in a.m. & 3 caps in p.m. Cost 200 mg $10	Side-effects as above, esp. hemolytic anemia (during 1st 1–2 wks of rx) with hemoglobin ↓ of 3–4 gm. Should not be used with CrCl <50 ml/min & cautiously with cardiac disease.
Influenza A		
Amantadine (Symmetrel) or Rimantadine (Flumadine)	Amantadine and rimantadine doses are the same (rimantadine approved only for prophylaxis in children, not treatment). Amantadine 100 mg bid; >65 y.o., 100 mg qd. G: 100 mg cap $0.50, 100 mg/10 ml soln. $1.80. Rimantadine 100 mg tab/syrup $2	**Side-effects/toxicity:** CNS (nervousness, anxiety, difficulty concentrating, and lightheadedness). Symptoms occurred in 6% on rimantadine vs 14% on amantadine. They usually ↓ after 1st week and disappear when drug dc. GI (nausea, anorexia). Some serious side-effects—delirium, hallucinations, and seizures—are associated with high plasma drug levels resulting from renal insufficiency, esp. in older pts, with prior seizure disorders, or psychiatric disorders. In pts with normal renal function, dosage of both drugs should be reduced (amantadine: creatinine clearance <50 ml/min; rimantadine: CrCl <10 ml/min); see package inserts and Table 17, pages 135 & 136. Both drugs teratogenic in animals and contraindicated during pregnancy (Med Lett 39:72, 1997).
Influenza A and B—For both drugs, initiate within 48 hrs of symptom onset		
Zanamivir (Relenza) For pts ≥12 yrs of age	2 inhalations (2 x 5 mg) bid x5 d. Powder is inhaled using specially designed breath-activated device. Each medication-containing blister contains 5 mg of zanamivir. $57/course	Active by inhalation against neuraminidase of both influenza A and B and inhibits release of virus from epithelial cells of respiratory tract. Approx. 4–17% of inhaled dose absorbed into plasma. Excreted by kidney but with low absorption, dose reduction not necessary in renal impairment. Minimal side-effects: <3% cough, sinusitis, diarrhea, nausea and vomiting. **Reports of respiratory adverse events in pts with or without h/o airways disease, should be avoided in pts with respiratory disease.**
Oseltamivir (Tamiflu)	75 mg po bid for treatment [pediatric suspension (12 mg/ml) approved for treatment in children ≥1 yr at dose of 2 mg/kg (up to 75 mg total) bid x5 d. For prevention: 75 mg po qd for duration of peak of flu epidemic. $38/5 day course	Well absorbed (80% bioavailable) from GI tract as ethyl ester of active compound GS 4071. T½ 6–10 hrs; excreted unchanged by kidney. Adverse effects in 15% include diarrhea 1.6%, nausea 0.5%, vomiting, headache (J Am Ger Soc 50:608, 2002). Nausea with food. Also available as 12 mg/ml oral suspension.
Respiratory Syncytial Virus (RSV) and other		
Palivizumab (Synagis) (See Med Lett 41:1, 1999) Used only for prevention of RSV infection in high-risk children (Ped 102:1211, 1998)	15 mg/kg IM q month 100 mg vial (for 1 injection) $1312	A monoclonal antibody directed against the F glycoprotein on surface of virus; side-effects are nominal, occ. ↑ ALT (JID 176:1215, 1997).
Ribavirin (Virazole)	1.1 g/day (6 gm vial for inhalation $1374)	**Ribavirin side-effects:** Anemia, rash, conjunctivitis: Read package insert. Avoid procedures that lead to drug precipitation in ventilator tubing with subsequent dysfunction. Significant teratogenicity in animals. **Contraindicated in pregnant women and partners.** Pregnant health care workers should avoid direct care of pts receiving aerosolized ribavirin.
RSV-IV immunoglobulin (IG) (RespiGam)	100 mg/kg IV q month (50 ml) $1030	RespiGam side-effects rare but include fatal anaphylaxis, pruritus, rash, wheezing, fever, joint pain.
Warts (See CID 28:S37, 1999)		
Interferon alfa-2b or alfa-n3	Apply 1 million units into lesion	Interferon alfa-2b 3 million units/0.5 ml, interferon alfa-n3 5 mU/1 ml. Cost: $10.
Podofilox (Condylox)	3.5 ml for topical application, $130	Side-effects: Local reactions—pain, burning, inflammation in 50%. No systemic effects.
Imiquimod (Aldara)	Cream applied 3x/week to maximum of 16 wks. 250 mg packets $15	Mild erythema, erosions, itching and burning

NOTE: *All dosage recommendations are for adults (unless otherwise indicated) and assume normal renal function.*
* From 2004 Drug Topics Red Book, Medical Economics. Price is average wholesale price (AWP). **NB** = name brand, **G** = generic

TABLE 14C: ANTIRETROVIRAL THERAPY IN ADULTS

(See the 2004 SANFORD GUIDE TO HIV/AIDS THERAPY, Table 6, for additional information regarding treatment and complications of antiretroviral agents)

In 2004, several guidelines and recommendations for the treatment of individuals infected with HIV-1 were updated. Among these were DHHS guidelines for treatment of infected adults and adolescents, guidelines for the use of antiretroviral agents (ART) in pregnant women. New treatment recommendations by the International AIDS Society-USA Panel were published mid-year (JAMA 292:251, 2004), as were guidelines for primary care management of HIV-infected persons provided by the HIV Medicine Association of the IDSA (CID 39:609, 2004).

A. When to start therapy? (CD4 cells/µl www.aidsinfo.nih.gov)

HIV Symptoms	CD4 cells/µl	Start Treatment	Comment
Yes	Any	Yes	
No	<200	Yes	
No	>200–350	Offer (see Comment)	Risk for progression to AIDS also depends on viral load; consider on individual basis
No	>350	No (see Comment)	Maybe if CD4 decreasing rapidly and/or viral load > 100,000 copies/ml

• Acute retroviral syndrome—See page 117, section C.

B. Suggested Initial Therapy Regimens for Untreated Chronic HIV Infection (For pregnancy, see below and Table 8 of Sanford Guide to HIV/AIDS Therapy, 2004)

1. Preferred Regimens

Regimen	Capsule (pill size, mg)	Daily Regimen	No. pills/ day	Cost/month (AWP)	Comment
a. (Zidovudine + Lamivudine)+ Efavirenz	(300) + 150) + 600	(Combination—Combivir 1 tab po bid) + 1 tab po qd, hs, empty stomach[2]	3	$1090	Good efficacy, low pill burden, low AE profile. **If rx stopped, dc efavirenz 1–2 wks before Combivir** (for explanation, see footnote page 118.
b. (Tenofovir + Emtricitabine) + Efavirenz	(300) + 200) + 600	(Combination—Truvada 1 tab po qd) + 1 tab po qd	2	$1168	Tenofovir: emerging reports of renal toxicity. Do not use efavirenz 1st trimester of pregnancy
c. (Zidovudine + Lamivudine) + Lopinavir/ Ritonavir	(300) + 150) + 133.3/33.3 3	(Combination—Combivir 1 tab po bid) + 3 tabs bid po with food	8	$1362	Good virologic efficacy and durable effect. Tolerable AEs. Possible elevated triglycerides. → accumulation of resistance mutations than nelfinavir regimen (NEJM 346:2039, 2002)

2. Alternative Regimens

Regimen	Capsule (pill size, mg)	Daily Regimen	No. pills/ day	Cost/month (AWP)	Comment
a. Didanosine EC + Lamivudine[1] + Efavirenz	400 + 300 + 600	1 cap po daily hs, fasting + 1 tab po daily hs, empty stomach[2]	3	$1037	Low pill burden. Efficacy and durability under study. Potential didanosine AEs. **didanosine dosage shown for ≥60 kg**
b. Fosamprenavir + Ritonavir + (Zidovudine + Lamivudine)	700 + 100 + (300) + 150)	1 tab po bid fed or fasting + 1 tab po bid fed or fasting + (Combination—Combivir 1 tab po bid)	6	NA	Lower pill burden with fosamprenavir as compared to amprenavir
c. (Zidovudine + Lamivudine) + Nelfinavir	(300) + 150) + 625	(Combination—Combivir 1 tab po bid) + 2 tabs po bid, with food	6	$1065	Good efficacy. Nelfinavir-associated diarrhea in 20%. Nelfinavir contraindicated with drugs highly dependent on CYP3A4 elimination where ↑ levels may cause life-threatening toxicity.

3. Triple-nucleoside or nucleoside/nucleotide regimen: Due to inferior virologic activity, use only when preferred or alternative regimen not possible.

Regimen	Capsule (pill size, mg)	Daily Regimen	No. pills/ day	Cost/month (AWP)	Comment
(Zidovudine + Lamivudine) + Abacavir	(300) + 150 + 300)	(Combination—Trizivir 1 tab po bid) Avoid alcohol.	2	$1040	Reduced efficacy as compared to preferred & alternative regimens. Potential serious abacavir AEs.

4. During pregnancy: Expert consultation mandatory

Regimen	Capsule (pill size, mg)	Daily Regimen	No. pills/ day	Cost/month (AWP)	Comment
a. (Zidovudine + Lamivudine) + Nevirapine	(300) + 150) + 200	(Combination—Combivir 1 tab po bid) + 1 tab po fed or fasting [after 14-day lead-in period of 1 tab po daily]	4	$1040	Monitor hepatic-associated enzymes; 11% of women with CD4 >250/mm³ had symptomatic events. See Black box warnings (page 121). Timing of treatment initiation and choice of drugs must be individualized; certain drugs contraindicated. See www.aidsinfo.nih.gov for details, alternative NRTIs, and possible PI-based regimens. Resistance testing should be strongly considered. For regimens to prevent mother-child transmission, see www.aidsinfo.nih.gov

AWP = average wholesale price

[1] AWP = average wholesale price
[2] Food may ↑ serum concentration, which can lead to ↑ in the risk of adverse events.

TABLE 14C (2)

C. Suggested Regimen for Acute Primary HIV Infection (mono-like syndrome)

Regimen	Capsule (pill size, mg)	Daily Regimen	No. pills/day	Cost/month (AWP)	Comment
(Zidovudine + Lamivudine) + Efavirenz‡	Zidovudine 300 mg + Lamivudine 150 mg	(Combination—Combivir 1 tab po bid)	3	$1090	Adherence to rx is crucial. Check genotype. Treatment considered optional because benefits not yet defined. Duration of therapy is unknown (see *http://aidsinfo.nih.gov*).
	600 mg tab	1 tab po hs, empty stomach²			

* Can substitute emtricitabine (FTC) 200 mg po daily for lamivudine
‡ **Avoid efavirenz in pregnancy, in women who wish to conceive, or in women not using effective contraception**

D. Some Antiretroviral Therapies Should NOT Be Offered; see *2004 Sanford Guide to HIV/AIDS Therapy, Table 6,* for details

E. Selected Characteristics of Antiretroviral Drugs

1. Selected Characteristics of Nucleoside or Nucleotide Reverse Transcriptase Inhibitors (NRTIs)*

Generic/Trade Name	Pharmaceutical Prep. (AWP)	Usual Adult Dosage	% Absorbed, po	Serum T½, hrs	Intracellular T½, hrs	Elimination	Major Adverse Events/Comments
Abacavir (Ziagen)	300 mg tabs or 20 mg/ml oral solution ($408/month)	300 mg po bid or 600 mg po qd. Food OK	83	1.5	20	Liver metab., renal excretion of metabolites; 82%	Hypersensitivity reaction: fever, rash, N/V, diarrhea, abdominal pain, respiratory symptoms. (Severe reactions may be ↑ with 600 mg qd dose.) **Do not rechallenge!** Report to 800-270-0425. Lactic acidosis with hepatic steatosis
Didanosine (ddI, Videx or Videx EC)	25, 50, 100, 150, 200 mg chewable tabs; 100, 167, 250 mg powder for oral solution; 125, 200, 250, 400 delayed-coated caps ($313/month Videx EC)	≥60 kg. Usually 400 mg enteric-coated po qd ½ hr before or 2 hrs after meal. **Do not crush.** <60 kg 250 mg EC po qd. See Comment	30–40	1.6	25–40	Renal excretion, 50%	Pancreatitis, peripheral neuropathy, lactic acidosis & hepatic steatosis (rare but life-threatening). **Reduce dose to 250 mg EC qd if used with tenofovir.**
Emtricitabine (FTC, Emtriva)	200 mg caps ($290/month)	200 mg po qd. No significant effect of food	50–95% in animal studies	Approx. 10	>20	Renal excretion 86%, minor biotransformation; 14% excretion in feces	Well tolerated; headache 20%, nausea, vomiting & diarrhea occasionally, skin rash rarely. Skin hyperpigmentation. Potential for lactic acidosis with hepatic steatosis. Differs only slightly in structure from lamivudine (5-fluoro substitution). Also active vs hepatitis B; exacerbation of Hep B reported in pts after DC of FTC.
Emtricitabine/tenofovir disoproxil fumarate (Truvada)	Film-coated tabs: FTC 200 mg + TDF 300 mg	1 tab po qd for CrCl ≥50 ml/min. Food OK	92/25	10/17	—	Primarily renal/renal	See Comments for individual agents
Lamivudine (3TC, Epivir)	150, 300 mg tabs; 10 mg/ml oral solution ($303/month)	150 mg po bid or 300 mg po qd. Food OK	86	5–7	16	Renal excretion, minimal metabolism	Safest of NRTIs. Rare life-threatening lactic acidosis/hepatic steatosis. Potential exacerbation of Hep B after DC.
Lamivudine/abacavir (Epzicom)	Film-coated tabs: 3TC 300 mg + **abacavir 600 mg**	1 tab po qd for CrCl ≥50 ml/min. Food OK	86/86	5–7/1.5	16/20	Primarily renal/metabolism	See Comments for individual agents. **Note abacavir hypersensitivity Black Box warnings** (severe reactions may be ↑ with 600 mg/dose).

¹ AWP = average wholesale price
² Food may ↑ serum concentration, which can lead to ↑ in the risk of adverse events.

TABLE 14C (3)

1. Selected Characteristics of Nucleoside or Nucleotide Reverse Transcriptase Inhibitors (NRTIs)[1] (continued)

Generic/Trade Name	Pharmaceutical Prep. (AWP)[1]	Usual Adult Dosage	% Absorbed, po	Serum T½, hrs	Intracellular T½, hrs	Elimination	Major Adverse Events/Comments
							See Comments for individual agents
Lamivudine/zidovudine (Combivir)	Film-coated tabs: 3TC 150 mg + ZDV 300 mg	1 tab po bid for ClCr ≥50 ml/min. Food OK.	86/64	5–7/0.5–3	—	Primarily renal/ metabolism with renal elimination of glucuronide	
Stavudine (d4T, Zerit; Zerit XR)	15, 20, 30, 40 mg capsules or 75, 100 mg extended-release (XR) caps; 1 mg/ml oral solution ($347/month)	≥60 kg: 40 mg cap bid or 100 mg XR cap qd[a] <60 kg: 30 mg cap bid or 75 mg XR cap qd[a] Food OK.	86	1	3.5	Renal excretion, 50%.	**Highest incidence of lipotrophy, hyperlipidemia, & lactic acidosis of all NRTIs.** Pancreatitis. XR formulation FDA-approved, but not yet available (Oct. 2004).
Tenofovir disoproxil fumarate (Viread)—a nucleotide	300 mg tabs ($432/month)	ClCr ≥50 ml/min: 300 mg qd. Food OK; high-fat meal ↑ absorption	39	17	10–50	Renal excretion	Asthenia, headache. N/V. Potential lactic acidosis/hepatic steatosis (rare reports with combinations). Cases of renal dysfunction reported. If combined with didanosine, lower didanosine dose to 250 mg EC qd.
Zalcitabine (ddC; Hivid)	0.375, 0.75 tabs ($295/month)	0.75 mg po tid. Food OK.	85	1.2	3	Renal excretion, 70%.	Peripheral neuropathy, stomatitis, rarely life-threatening lactic acidosis, pancreatitis, rarely
Zidovudine (ZDV, AZT; Retrovir)	100, 300 mg tabs; 100 mg caps; 10 mg/ml IV solution; 10 mg/ml oral solution ($355/month)	300 mg po bid. Food OK.	60	1.1	3	Metabolized to glucuronide & excreted in urine	Bone marrow suppression, GI intolerance, headache, insomnia, weakness, rarely lactic acidosis

* All agents have Black Box warning: risk of lactic acidosis/hepatic steatosis. Also, labels note risk of fat redistribution/accumulation with ARV rx.

2. Selected Characteristics of Non-Nucleoside Reverse Transcriptase Inhibitors (NNRTIs)

Generic/Trade Name	Pharmaceutical Prep. (AWP)[1]	Usual Adult Dosage	% Absorbed, po	Serum T½, hrs	Elimination	Major Adverse Events/Comments
Delavirdine (Rescriptor)	100, 200 mg tabs ($316/month)	400 mg po tid. Food OK	85	5.8	Cytochrome P450 (3A inhibitor). 51% excreted in urine (<5% unchanged). 44% in feces	Rash severe enough to dc use of drug in 4.3%. ↑SGOT/SGPT, headaches
Efavirenz (Sustiva) See footnote[2]	50, 100, 200 mg capsules; 600 mg tablet ($432/month)	600 mg po hs, without food[3]	42	40–55 See footnote[2]	Cytochrome P450 (3A mixed inducer/inhibitor). 14–34% of dose excreted in urine as glucuronidated metabolites, 16–61% in feces	Rash severe enough to dc use of drug in 1.7%. High frequency of diverse CNS AEs: somnolence, dreams, confusion, agitation; false-positive cannabinoid test. Fetal malformations in monkeys.
Nevirapine (Viramune)	200 mg tabs, 50 mg/5 ml oral suspension ($382/month)	200 mg po qd x14 d & then 200 mg po bid. (see Comments) Food OK	>90	25–30	Cytochrome P450 (3A inducer). 80% of dose excreted in urine as glucuronidated metabolites, 10% in feces	Follow dose-escalation protocol. **Black Box warning** re: fatal hypersensitivity, skin reactions, & hepatotoxicity. Women with CD4 >250 esp. vulnerable, including pregnant women. Don't restart any suspension of such reactions. Rash severe enough to dc use of drug in 7%; severe or life-threatening in 2%.

---

[1] AWP = average wholesale price
[2] **Efavirenz:** Very long tissue half-life. If efavirenz to be discontinued, stop efavirenz 1–2 wks before stopping companion drugs. If all drugs stopped concomitantly, risk of developing efavirenz resistance, as after 1–2 days only efavirenz in blood and/or tissue.
[3] Food may ↑ serum concentration, which can lead to ↑ in the risk of adverse events.

TABLE 14C (4)

3. Selected Characteristics of Protease Inhibitors (PIs)*

Generic/Trade Name	Pharmaceutical Prep. (AWP)	Usual Adult Dosage	% Absorbed, po	Serum T½, hrs	Elimination	Major Adverse Events/Comments
Amprenavir (Agenerase)	50, 150 mg capsules (see Comment); 15 mg/ml oral solution. (For oral solution dosage, see package insert or PDR) ($736/month)	1200 mg (Eight 150 mg capsules) po bid OR With ritonavir (600 mg amprenavir (4 caps) + ritonavir 100 mg) po bid OR (1200 mg amprenavir caps + 200 mg ritonavir) po qd	No data Food OK, avoid high-fat meal	7.1–10.6	Cytochrome P450 (3A4 inhibitor)	Nausea/vomiting, diarrhea, rash, oral paresthesias, ↑ SGOT/ SGPT. Contains sulfa moiety. **Black Box warning:** Oral solution contains propylene glycol; do not use in pregnancy, children <4 y/o, renal/hepatic failure, with disulfiram or metronidazole. Use oral solution only when essential. **Sale of 150 mg caps in U.S. to be discontinued after 2004.**
Atazanavir (Reyataz)	100, 150, 200 mg capsules ($788/month)	400 mg qd with food (exception is atazanavir 300 mg qd + ritonavir 100 mg qd when combined with efavirenz 600 mg qd or TDF 300 mg qd). Take with food 2 hrs pre or 1 hr post buffered ddI. Dosage adjustment in hepatic insufficiency. Child-Pugh Class B—300 mg qd. Child-Pugh Class C—avoid. (See Comments)	Good oral bioavailability, food enhances bioavailability & ↓ pharmacokinetic variability	Approx. 7	Cytochrome P450 (3A4 inhibitor) & UGT1A1 inhibitor, 13% excreted in urine (7% unchanged), 79% excreted in feces (20% unchanged)	No ↑ lipids in available studies. Asymptomatic unconjugated hyperbilirubinemia common. Headache, rash, GI symptoms. **Prolongation of PR interval (1st degree AV block) reported.** Caution in pre-existing conduction system disease. **Efavirenz & tenofovir ↓ atazanavir exposure: use atazanavir/ritonavir regimen; also, atazanavir ↑ tenofovir concentrations—watch for adverse events** (see www.fda.gov/cder/drug/default.htm)
Fosamprenavir (Lexiva)	700 mg tablet	1400 mg (two 700 mg tabs) po bid OR With ritonavir: [1400 mg fosamprenavir (2 tabs) + ritonavir 200 mg] po qd OR [700 mg fosamprenavir (1 tab) + ritonavir 100 mg] po bid	Bioavailability not established. Food OK	7.7	Cytochrome P450 (3A4 substrate, inhibitor, inducer)	**Nephrolithiasis**, nausea, inconsequential ↑ of indirect bilirubin. ↑ SGOT/SGPT, headache, asthenia, blurred vision, metallic taste, hemolysis. ↑ urine WBC (>100/hpf) has been assoc. with nephritis/medullary calcification, cortical atrophy.
Indinavir (Crixivan)	100, 200, 333, 400 mg capsules ($546/month)	Two 400 mg caps (800 mg) po q8h. Without food or with light meal. Can take with enteric-coated Videx. [If taken with ritonavir (e.g., 800 mg indinavir + 100 mg ritonavir po bid), no food restrictions]	65	1.2–2	Cytochrome P450 (3A4 inhibitor)	
Lopinavir + ritonavir (Kaletra) Can be kept at room temperature x2 mos.	(133.3 mg lopinavir + 33.3 mg ritonavir) caps, 3 caps equal doses of 4 caps (533 mg lopinavir + 133 mg ritonavir)/ml. Refrigerate. ($703/month)	(400 mg lopinavir + 100 mg ritonavir, 3 caps po bid, with food. Higher dose of 4 caps (533 mg lopinavir + 133 mg ritonavir) po bid recommended when used with efavirenz, nevirapine, amprenavir, nelfinavir. [Dose adjustment in concomitant drugs may be necessary; see Table 22B & C, page 149]	Take with food for ↑ absorption	5–6	Cytochrome P450 (3A4 inhibitor)	Nausea/vomiting/diarrhea, asthenia, ↑ SGOT/SGPT. Oral solution 42% alcohol.

---

¹ **AWP** = average wholesale price

TABLE 14C (5)

3. Selected Characteristics of Protease Inhibitors (PIs)* (continued)

Generic/Trade Name	Pharmaceutical Prep. (AWP)	Usual Adult Dosage	% Absorbed, po	Serum T½, hrs	Elimination	Major Adverse Events/Comments
Nelfinavir (Viracept)	625, 250 mg tabs; 50 mg/gm oral powder ($757/month)	2 625 mg tabs (1250 mg) po bid, with food, or 5 250 mg tabs (1250 mg) po bid	20–80	3.5–5	Cytochrome P450 (3A4 inhibitor)	Diarrhea. Coadministration of drugs with life-threatening toxicities & which are cleared by CYP3A4 is contraindicated.
Ritonavir (Norvir) Room temperature x1 mo. OK. Many drug interactions—see Table 22A–C, pages 146 & 149	100 mg capsules; 600 mg/7.5 ml solution. Refrigerate caps but not solution. ($772/month)	Full dose: 6 caps (600 mg) po q12h with food. Escalate to full dose: 300 mg bid x2 d; 400 mg bid x3 d; 500 mg bid x7 d., then full dose. "Booster drug"—see Comment	Approx. 65	3–5	Cytochrome P450 3A4 inhibitor	Nausea,vomiting,diarrhea, extremity & circumoral paresthesias, hepatitis, pancreatitis, taste perversion, ↑ CPK & uric acid. Used to enhance pharmacokinetics of other PIs, using lower ritonavir doses.
Saquinavir (Invirase) hard gel caps + ritonavir	Saquinavir 200 mg caps; ritonavir 100 mg caps ($1,236/month)	5 caps saquinavir (1000 mg) + 1 cap ritonavir (100 mg) po bid with food	Erratic, 4 (saquinavir alone)	1–2	Cytochrome P450 (3A4 inhibitor)	Nausea, diarrhea, headache, ↑ SGOT/SGPT
Saquinavir (Fortovase) softgel caps	200 mg capsules. (can be kept at room temperature x3 mos.) ($720/month)	6 caps (1200 mg) po tid, with food OR 5 caps saquinavir (1000 mg) + 1 cap ritonavir (100 mg) po bid with food	Not known	1–2	Cytochrome P450 (3A4 inhibitor)	Nausea, diarrhea, abdominal pain, headache, ↑ SGOT/SGPT
Tipranavir[xxs] (Tex[x]pa)		500 mg with ritonavir 200 mg bid in Phase III studies	30% in animal studies. ↑ AUC & peak plasma conc. in presence of food & if combined with ritonavir			Cytochrome P450 (3A4 mixed inducer/inhibitor)	Nausea,vomiting, diarrhea, abdominal pain. Limited availability for compassionate use if CD4 count < 100; call 800-632-2464.

* All PIs: Glucose metabolism: new diabetes mellitus or deterioration of glucose control; fat redistribution; possible hemophilia bleeding; hypertriglyceridemia or hypercholesterolemia

4. Selected Characteristics of Fusion Inhibitors

Generic/Trade	Pharmaceutical Prep. (AWP)	Usual Adult Dosage	% Absorbed	Serum T½, hrs	Elimination	Major Adverse Events/Comments
Enfuvirtide (T20, Fuzeon)	Single-use vials of 90 mg/ml when reconstituted. Vials should be stored at room temperature. Reconstituted caps can be refrigerated for 24 hrs only. (~$20,000/year)	90 mg (1 ml) sc bid	84.3 ± 15.5	3.8 ± 0.6	Catabolism to its constituent amino acids with subsequent recycling of the amino acids in the body pool. Elimination pathway(s) have not been performed in humans. Does not alter the metabolism of CYP3A4, CYP2D6, CYP1A2, CYP2C19 or CYP2E1 substrates.	Local reaction site reactions 98%, <3% DC; erythema/induration – 80-90%; nodules/cysts – 80%. Hypersensitivity reactions reported—do not restart if occur, including background regimens, peripheral neuropathy 8.9%, insomnia 11.3%, ↓ appetite 6.3%, myalgia 5%, lymphadenopathy 2.3%, eosinophilia – 10%. ↑ incidence of bacterial pneumonias. Alone offers little benefit to a failing regimen (NEJM 348:2249, 2003).

¹ AWP = average wholesale price

TABLE 14D: ANTIRETROVIRAL DRUGS AND ADVERSE EFFECTS (www.aidsinfo.nih.gov—accessed Sept. 2004)

DRUG NAME(S); GENERIC (TRADE)	ADVERSE EFFECTS
Nucleoside Reverse Transcriptase Inhibitors (NRTI)[1]	
Abacavir (Ziagen)	**Most common:** Headache 7–13%, nausea 7–19%, diarrhea 7%, malaise **Most significant: Black Box warning—Hypersensitivity reaction** in 5% with malaise, fever, GI upset, rash, lethargy, & respiratory symptoms most commonly reported; myalgia, arthralgia, edema, paresthesia less commonly reported. **Rechallenge contraindicated; may be life-threatening.**
Didanosine (ddI) (Videx)	**Most common:** Diarrhea 28%, nausea 6%, rash 9%, headache 7%, fever 12%, hyperuricemia 2% **Most significant: Black Box warning—Cases of fatal and nonfatal pancreatitis** have occurred in pts receiving ddI, especially when used in combination with d4T or d4T + hydroxyurea. 12% required dose reduction. Peripheral neuropathy in 20%, 12% required dose reduction.
Emtricitabine (FTC, Emtriva)	**Most common:** Headache 20%, diarrhea, nausea, rash, skin hyperpigmentation **Most significant:** Potential for lactic acidosis (as with other NRTIs), exacerbation of hepatitis B on stopping drug
Lamivudine (3TC) (Epivir)	Well tolerated. Headache 35%, nausea 33%, diarrhea 18%, abdominal pain 9%, insomnia 11% (in combination with ZDV), Pancreatitis more common in pediatrics (15%) **Black Box warning.** Make sure to use HIV dosage, not Hep B dosage
Stavudine (d4T) (Zerit)	**Most common:** Diarrhea, nausea, vomiting, headache **Most significant: Peripheral neuropathy** 15–20%. Pancreatitis 1%. Appears to produce lactic acidosis more commonly than other NRTIs. **Black Box warning—Fatal & nonfatal pancreatitis with d4T + ddI ± hydroxyurea. Fatal lactic acidosis/hepatic steatosis in pregnant women receiving d4T + ddI.** Motor weakness in the setting of lactic acidosis mimicking the clinical presentation of Guillain-Barré syndrome (including respiratory failure) (rare)
Zalcitabine (ddC) (Hivid)	**Most common:** Oral ulcers 13%, rash 8% **Most significant: Black Box warning—Pancreatitis** <1%, **peripheral neuropathy** 22–35%. Severe continuous pain, slowly reversible when ddC is discontinued, ↑ risk with diabetes mellitus. **Hepatic failure in pts with Hep B.**
Zidovudine (ZDV, AZT) (Retrovir)	**Most common:** Nausea 50%, anorexia 20%, vomiting 17%, **headache 62%**, malaise 53%. Also reported: asthenia, insomnia, myalgias, nail pigmentation. Macrocytosis expected with all dosage regimens. **Most significant: Black Box warning—hematologic toxicity, myopathy. Anemia** (<8 gm/dL 1%), granulocytopenia (<750 1.8%). Anemia may respond to epoetin alfa if endogenous serum erythropoietin levels are <500 mU/mL
Nucleotide Reverse Transcriptase Inhibitor (NtRTI)	
Tenofovir (Viread)	**Most common:** Nausea 11%, diarrhea 9%, vomiting 5%, flatulence 4% (generally well tolerated) **Most significant: Black Box warning—Severe exacerbations of Hep B** in co-infected pts. **DC tenofovir. Not indicated for rx of chronic Hep B.** Reports of Fanconi syndrome & renal injury induced by tenofovir (Am J Kidney Dis 40:1331, 2002; CID 37:e174, 2003).
Non-Nucleoside Reverse Transcriptase Inhibitors (NNRTI)	
Delavirdine (Rescriptor)	**Most common:** Nausea, diarrhea, vomiting, headache **Most significant: Skin rash** has occurred in 18%, can continue or restart drug in most cases. Stevens-Johnson syndrome and erythema multiforme have been reported rarely, ↑ in liver enzymes in <5% of patients
Efavirenz (Sustiva)	**Most common: CNS side-effects 52%;** symptoms include dizziness, insomnia, somnolence, impaired concentration, psychiatric sx, and abnormal dreams; symptoms are worse after 1st or 2nd dose and improve over 2–4 weeks; discontinuation rate 2.6%. Rash 26%; improves with oral antihistamines; discontinuation rate 1.7%. Can cause false-positive urine test results for cannabinoid with CEDIA DAU multi-level THC assay. **Most significant:** Elevation in liver function tests. **Teratogenicity reported in pregnant women** (see Table 8 of the SANFORD GUIDE TO HIV/AIDS THERAPY).
Nevirapine (Viramune)	**Most common: Rash 37%;** occurs during 1st 6 wks of therapy. Women experience 7-fold ↑ in risk of severe rash (CID 32:124, 2001). 50% resolve within 2 wks of d/c drug and 80% by 1 month. 6.7% discontinuation rate. **Most significant: Black Box warning—Severe life-threatening skin reactions reported:** Stevens-Johnson syndrome, toxic epidermal necrolysis, and hypersensitivity reactions characterized by rash, constitutional findings, and organ dysfunction. **Severe, life-threatening, and in some cases fatal hepatotoxicity, including hepatic necrosis and hepatic failure, reported.** For symptomatic events, do not restart nevirapine after severe skin rash reactions. In a clinical trial, the use of prednisone ↑ the risk of rash. **Black Box warning—Life-threatening hepatotoxicity reported;** 2/3 during the first 12 wks of rx. Overall 1% develop hepatitis. Pts with pre-existing ↑ in ALT or AST and/or history of chronic Hep B or C susceptible (Hepatol 35:182, 2002). **Women with CD4 >250, including pregnant women, at ↑ risk.** Monitor pts monthly (clinical and LFTs), esp. during the first 12 wks of rx. If clinical hepatotoxicity occur, d/c drug and never rechallenge. A cohort study of nevirapine tolerance in French Aquitaine has been reported (CID 35:1231, 2002)

[1] **Black Box warning for all nucleoside/nucleotide RTIs: lactic acidosis/hepatic steatosis, potentially fatal**

TABLE 14D (2)

DRUG NAME(S); GENERIC (TRADE)	ADVERSE EFFECTS
Protease inhibitors (PI)	Abnormalities in glucose metabolism, dyslipidemias, fat redistribution syndromes are potential problems. Pts taking PI may be at increased risk for developing osteo-penia/osteoporosis. *(See Table 6C of the SANFORD GUIDE TO HIV/AIDS THERAPY.)* Spontaneous bleeding episodes have been reported in HIV+ pts with hemophilia being treated with PI. Rheumatoid complications have been reported with use of PIs *(An J Rheum Dis 61:82, 2002).* **Warnings for PIs:** Co-administration with drugs highly dependent on CYP3A (for elimination, where ↑ levels can cause serious/life-threatening toxicity, is contraindicated.
Amprenavir (Agenerase)	**Most common:** Nausea 43–74%, vomiting 24–34%, diarrhea 39–60%, paresthesias 26–31% **Most significant:** Skin rash 22%. Most maculopapular of mild–moderate intensity; some with pruritus. Severe or life-threatening rash, including Stevens-Johnson syndrome, in 1% of pts. **Black Box warning**—potential propylene glycol toxicity with oral solution.
Atazanavir (Reyataz)	**Most common:** Asymptomatic unconjugated hyperbilirubinemia in up to 60% of pts, grade 3 & 4 in 5–9% of pts, jaundice in 17%. Diarrhea 20–25%, nausea & abdominal pain 20%, headache 25%, rash 20%. **Most significant:** Prolongation of PR interval (1st degree AV block) reported.
Fosamprenavir (Lexiva)	**Most common:** Skin rash 19%, nausea 7%, diarrhea 5%, headache 7%. **Most significant:** Rarely Stevens-Johnson syndrome, hemolytic anemia.
Indinavir (Crixivan)	**Most common:** ↑ in indirect bilirubin 10–15% (≥2.5 mg/d), due to a drug-induced Gilbert's syndrome (of no clinical significance). Severe hepatitis reported in 3 cases *(Ln 349:924, 1997).* Nausea 12%, vomiting 4%, diarrhea 5%. Paronychia of big toe reported *(CID 32:140, 2001).* **Most significant: Kidney stones.** Due to indinavir crystals in collecting system (2–3% on 2.4 gm/d but higher in "hot climates" *(AIDS 14:296, 1997).* 12/174 (6.9%) developed nephrolithiasis within 4 months of starting indinavir. 5/8 who continued on had a 2nd episode *(ICAAC Abst. 183, 1997).* Prevent (minimize) by good hydration (at least 48 oz. water/day) *(AAC 42:332, 1998).* Tubulointerstitial nephritis/renal cortical atrophy reported in association with asymptomatic ↑ urine WBC.
Nelfinavir (Viracept)	**Most common:** Mild to moderate **diarrhea** 20%. Oat bran tabs, calcium, or oral anti-diarrheal agents (e.g. loperamide, diphenoxylate/atropine sulfate) can be used to manage diarrhea
Ritonavir (Norvir)	**Most common:** GI: bitter aftertaste ↓by taking with chocolate milk, Ensure, or Advera; nausea 23%, ↑ by initial dose escalation (titration) regimen; vomiting 13%, diarrhea 15%. Circumoral paresthesias 5–6%, ↑dose >100 mg/d assoc. with ↑ GI side-effects & ↑ in lipid abnormalities. **Most significant:** Hepatic failure *(AIM 129:670, 1998).* **Black Box warning** relates to many important drug-drug interactions—inhibits P450 CYP3A system—may be life-threatening (see *Table 22).*
Saquinavir (Invirase: hard cap) (Fortovase: softgel cap)	**Most common:** GI: **diarrhea** (6–20%, abdominal discomfort 9–13%, nausea 11–18%, Headache 5–9% **Black Box warning**—Invirase is not bioequivalent to Fortovase; use it only with ritonavir.
Tipranavir[AUS] (Texega)	**Most common:** Nausea & vomiting, diarrhea, abdominal pain
Lopinavir/Ritonavir (Kaletra)	**Most common: diarrhea** 14–24%, nausea 2–16%, lipid abnormalities in up to 30% **Most significant:** Pancreatitis, inflammatory edema of the legs *(AIDS 16:673, 2002)*
Fusion Inhibitor	
Enfuvirtide (T20, Fuzeon)	**Most common:** local injection site reactions (98% at least 1 local ISR, 3% dc because of ISR) (pain & discomfort, induration, erythema, nodules & cysts, pruritus, & ecchymosis). Diarrhea 27%, nausea 20%, fatigue 16% **Most significant:** ↑ rate of bacterial pneumonia (4.68 pneumonia events/100 pt yrs). hypersensitivity reactions <1% (rash, fever, nausea & vomiting, chills, rigors, hypotension, & ↑ serum liver transaminases)

TABLE 15A: ANTIMICROBIAL PROPHYLAXIS FOR SELECTED BACTERIAL INFECTIONS

CLASS OF ETIOLOGIC AGENT/DISEASE/CONDITION	PROPHYLAXIS: AGENT/DOSE/ROUTE/DURATION	COMMENTS
Group B streptococcal disease (GBS), neonatal: Approaches to management [CDC Guidelines, MMWR 51(RR-11):1, 2002]:		
Pregnant women—intrapartum antimicrobial prophylaxis procedures: 1. Screen all pregnant women with vaginal & rectal swab for GBS at 35-37 wks gestation (unless other indications for prophylaxis exist. GBS bacteriuria during this pregnancy or previously delivered infant with invasive GBS disease; even then cultures may be useful for susceptibility testing). Use transport medium; GBS survive at room temp. up to 96 hrs. **Rx during labor if swab positive.** 2. Rx during labor if previously delivered infant with invasive GBS infection, or if any GBS bacteriuria during this pregnancy (MMWR 53:506, 2004) 3. Rx if GBS status unknown but if any of the following are present: (a) delivery at <37 wks gestation [see MMWR 51(RR-11):1, 2002 algorithm for threatened preterm delivery], or (b) duration of ruptured membranes ≥18 hrs or (c) intrapartum temp. ≥100.4°F [≥38.0°C].	**Prophylactic regimens during labor:** **Pen** G 5 MU IV (load) then 2.5 MU IV q4h. Alternate rx: **Ampicillin** 2 gm IV (load) then give 1 gm IV q4h. **Pen-allergic: Not at high risk for anaphylaxis: Cefazolin** 2 gm IV initial dose, then 1 gm IV q8h. **Pts at high risk for anaphylaxis: GBS susceptible to** clinda & erythro: **Clindamycin** 900 mg IV q8h or **erythromycin** 500 mg IV q6h. Vancomycin for pts at high risk for anaphylaxis and alternative to clindamycin or erythromycin needed (e.g., GBS-resistant or unknown susceptibility). Continue treatment until delivery.	
Neonate of mother given prophylaxis	Careful observation of signs & symptoms. 95% of infants will show clinical signs of infection during the 1st 24 hrs whether mother received intrapartum antibiotics or not (Pediatrics 106:244, 2000). For gestational age <35 wks observation & ≥48 hr observation recommended. See algorithm. MMWR 51(RR-11):1, 2002.	
Preterm, premature rupture of the membranes in Group B strep-negative women	(IV **ampicillin** 2 gm q6h + IV **erythromycin** 250 mg q6h) for 48 hrs followed by po **amoxicillin** 250 mg q8h + po **erythromycin** base 333 mg q8h x5 d. Decreases infant morbidity. (JAMA 278:989, 1997)	Antibiotic rx reduced infant respiratory distress syndrome (50.6% vs 40.8%, p = 0.03), necrotizing enterocolitis (5.8% vs 2.3%, p = 0.03) and prolonged pregnancy (2.9 to 6.1 days, p < 0.001) vs placebo. In fancy study (4809 pts), amp-erythro rx improved neonatal outcomes (p = placebo 11.2% vs 14.4% poor outcomes, p=0.02 for single births) but not co-AM/CL or both drugs in combination (both assoc. with ↑ necrotizing enterocolitis) (Ln 357:979, 2001)
Post-splenectomy bacteremia. Likely agents: Pneumococci (90%), meningococci, H. influenzae type b (also at ↑ risk of fatal malaria, severe babesiosis) Ref. 2003 Red Book, 26th Ed., Amer Acad Pediatrics	**Immunizations:** Ensure admin. of protein conjugate pneumococcal vaccine, H. influenzae b, & quadrivalent meningococcal vaccines at recommended times. In addition, asplenic children with sickle cell anemia, thalassemia, & perhaps others, daily antimicrobial prophylaxis until at least age 5—see Comments	Antimicrobial prophylaxis: use age 5: Amox 20 mg/kg 1x/d or Pen V-K 125 mg bid. Over age 5: Consider Pen V-K 250 mg bid for all ages in children post-splenectomy. Maintain immunizations plus self-administer AM/CL with any febrile illness while seeking physician assistance. Pen. allergy: TMP/SMX or clarithro. May need to consider other alternatives if pen-resistant S. pneumo prevalence increases.
Sexual Exposure		
Sexual assault survivor [likely agents and risks, see NEJM 332:234, 1995; MMWR 51(RR-6):1, 2002]	(**Ceftriaxone** 125 mg IM) + (**metronidazole** 2 gm po single dose) + (**azithromycin** 1 gm po single dose) or **doxycycline** 100 mg po bid x7 d) [MMWR 51(RR-6):1, 2002]	Obtain expert advice re: forensic exam & specimens, pregnancy, physical trauma, psychological issues. At initial exam: Culture for gonococci & chlamydia (if available), wet mount for T. vaginalis (& culture vaginal swab). Serologic evaluation for syphilis, Hep B, HIV, others as appropriate. Initiate HIV post-exposure protocols &/or Hep B vaccine as appropriate (see Table 15D). Follow-up exam for STD at 1-2 wks. Retest syphilis & HIV serology at 6, 12, 24 wks if negative earlier.
Sexual contacts, likely agents: N. gonorrhoeae, C. trachomatis	(**Ceftriaxone** 125 mg IM) + (**doxycycline** 100 mg bid, po x7 d] or (**cefixime**[NUS] 400 mg po) + (**azithromycin** 1 gm po), each as single dose)	Be sure to check for syphilis since all regimens may not eradicate incubating syphilis. Identify & rx contacts as appropriate to suspected STD [see MMWR 51(RR-6):1, 2002 for other etiologies & rx options].
Syphilis exposure	Presumptive rx for exposure within 3 mos., as tests may be neg. See Table 1, page 15. Make effort to dx syphilis	
Sickle-cell disease. Likely agent: S. pneumoniae (see post-splenectomy, above) Ref. 2003 Red Book, 26th Ed., Amer Acad Pediatrics	Children <5 yrs: **Penicillin V** 125 mg po bid ≥5 yrs: **Penicillin V** 250 mg po bid (Alternative in children: Amoxicillin 20 mg/kg/d)	Start prophylaxis by age 2 mos. (Pediatrics 106:367, 2000; http://aappolicy.aappublications.org). Age-appropriate vaccines, including pneumococcal, Hib, influenza ± meningococcal. Treating infections, consider possibility of penicillin non-susceptible pneumococci.

TABLE 15B: SURGICAL ANTIBIOTIC PROPHYLAXIS (EID 7:220, 2001; CID 38:1706, 2004)

Surgical Procedures: To be optimally effective, **antibiotics must be started in the interval: 2 hrs before time of surgical incision** (NEJM 326:281, 1992). For most procedures the number of doses needed for optimal coverage is not defined. Most applications employ a single dose (Med Lett 43:92, 2001) although FDA-approved product labeling is often ≥ 3 times. If the surgical procedure lasts > 3 hrs, additional intraoperative doses should be given at approx. 3-hr intervals. A recent consensus statement from the National Surgical Infection Prevention Project (CID 38:1706, 2004) advises additional prophylaxis be started within 1 hr before incision (except vancomycin & quinolones), be supplemented intraoperatively if the procedure lasts more than 2 half-lives of the prophylactic agent, and in most cases not be extended beyond 24 hrs. (Note: The dose/route/durations listed below is what we use for adults not intolerant of these agents for the most part those approved in FDA product labeling for single dose regimens, are the same.)

TYPE OF SURGERY	PROPHYLAXIS	COMMENTS
Cardiovascular Surgery Antibacterial prophylaxis in cardiovascular surgery has been proven beneficial only in the following procedures: • Reconstruction of abdominal aorta • Procedures on the leg that involve a groin incision • Any vascular procedure that inserts prosthesis/foreign body • Lower extremity amputation for ischemia • Cardiac surgery • Perhaps permanent pacemakers (see Comment)	**Cefazolin** 1 gm IV as a single dose or q8h x1-2 d. or **cefuroxime** 1.5 gm IV as a single dose or q12h for total of 6 gm IV or **vancomycin** 1 gm IV as a single dose. Consider **intranasal mupirocin** evening before, day of surgery & bid x5 days post-op in pts with pos. nasal culture for S. aureus.	Single injection just before surgery probably as effective as multiple doses. Not recommended for cardiac catheterization. For prosthetic heart valves, customary to stop prophylaxis either after removal of retrosternal drainage catheters or just a 2nd dose after coming off bypass. Vancomycin may be preferable in hospitals with ↑ frequency of MRSA or in high-risk pts (CID 38:1555, 2004), or those colonized with MRSA (CID 38:1706, 2004); however, does not cover Gm-neg. bacilli, therefore would add cefazolin for gram incisions. Meta-analysis failed to demonstrate overall superiority of vancomycin over β-lactam prophylaxis for cardiac surgery (CID 38:1357, 2004). A meta-analysis of 7 placebo-controlled randomized studies of antimicrobial prophylaxis over implantation of permanent pacemakers, sig. ↓ in incidence of infection (Circ 97: 1796, 1998). Used historical controls (Ann Thoracic Surg 71:1572, 2001); in another trial, it reduced nosocomial S. aureus infections only in nasal carriers (NEJM 346:1871, 2002).
Gastric, Biliary & Colonic Surgery **Gastroduodenal/Biliary** Gastroduodenal, includes percutaneous endoscopic gastrostomy (high-risk only; see Comments)	**Cefazolin** or **cefoxitin** or **cefotetan** or **ceftizoxime** or **cefuroxime** 1 or 1.5 gm IV as a single dose (some give additional doses q12h q2-3 d).	Gastroduodenal: High-risk is marked obesity, obstruction, ↓ gastric acid or ↓ GI motility. Biliary: Cephalosporins do not active vs enterococci yet clinically effective as prophylaxis in biliary surgery. Without cholangitis, treat as infection, not prophylaxis: TcCl 3.1 gm q4-6h IV or (PIP/TZ 3.375 gm q6h or 4.5 gm q8h IV or AM/SB 3.0 gm q6h IV). Biliary high-risk: age > 70, acute cholecystitis, non-functioning gallbladder, obstructive jaundice or common duct stones. Meta-analysis supports use in percutaneous endoscopic gastrostomy (Am J Gastro 95:3133, 2000).
Biliary, includes laparoscopic cholecystectomy (high-risk only; see Comments)	In biliary surgery, cefazolin 1 gm & ceftizoxime 1 gm (± repeat dosing at 12 & 24 hrs) were equivalent (AAC 40:70, 1996).	
Endoscopic retrograde cholangiopancreatography	No rx without obstruction. If obstruction: **Ciprofloxacin** 500-750 mg po 2 hrs prior to procedure or	Most studies show that **achieving adequate drainage** will prevent postprocedural cholangitis or sepsis and the further benefit from prophylactic antibiotic is minimal. With inadequate drainage antibiotics may be of value. American Society for GI Endoscopy recommends use for known or suspected biliary obstruction.
Controversial: No benefit from single dose piperacillin in randomized placebo-controlled trial, AnIM 125:442, 1996 (see Comment)	**Ceftizoxime** 1.5 gm IV 1 hr prior to procedure or **Piperacillin** 4 gm IV 1 hr prior to procedure.	Oral CIP as effective as cephalosporins in 2 studies & less expensive (CID 23:360, 1996).
Colorectal, includes appendectomy Elective surgery	**Neomycin** + **erythromycin** po (see Comment for doses)	Elective colorectal prep: Pre-op day: (1) 10 am 4 L polyethylene glycol electrolyte solution (Colyte, GoLYTELY) po over 2 hr. (2) Clear liquid diet only. (3) 1 pm, 2 pm and 11 pm, neomycin 1 gm + erythro base 1 gm po. At OR time: if midnight. There are alternatives.
	Cefazolin 1-2 gm IV + **metronidazole** 0.5 gm IV (single dose) or **cefoxitin** or **cefotetan** 1-2 gm IV	Alternative regimens have been used. Metronidazole 2 gm po on day of surgery or po + neomycin 2 gm po at 7 pm and 11 pm. Oral regimen as effective as parenteral. parenteral in addition to oral is not required. For emergency colorectal surgery, use parenteral. (CID 15 Suppl.1:S313, 1992).
Emergency surgery		
Ruptured viscus: See Peritonitis/Peritoneum, page 31.		
Head and Neck Surgery (Ann Otol Rhinol Laryngol 101 Suppl:16, 1992) Antimicrobial prophylaxis in head & neck surgery appears effective only for procedures involving oral/pharyngeal mucosa (i.e. laryngeal or pharyngeal tumor) but even then with prophylaxis, wound infection rate high (41% in 1 center) (Head Neck 23:447, 2001). Uncontaminated head & neck surgery does not require prophylaxis.	**Cefazolin** 2 gm IV (single dose) or **clindamycin** 1.5 mg/kg IV (single dose)	**Cefazolin** 2 gm IV (single dose) or **clindamycin** 600–900 mg IV (single dose) + **gentamicin** 1.5 mg/kg IV (single dose)]

TABLE 15B (2)

TYPE OF SURGERY	PROPHYLAXIS	COMMENTS
Neurosurgical Procedures [Prophylaxis not effective in ↓ infection rate with intracranial pressure monitors in retrospective analysis of 215 pts (*J Neurol Neurosurg Psych* 69:381, 2000)]		
Clean, non-implant, e.g., craniotomy	**Cefazolin** 1 gm IV x1. Alternative: **vanco** 1 gm IV x1	Reference: *Ln 344:1547, 1994*
Clean, contaminated (cross sinuses, or naso/oropharynx)	**Clindamycin** 900 mg IV (single dose)	British recommend amoxicillin/clavulanate 1.2 gm IV[A&B] or (cefuroxime 1.5 gm IV + metronidazole 0.5 gm IV).
CSF shunt surgery controversial (Meta-analysis *CID 17:98, 1993*)	**Vancomycin** 10 mg into cerebral ventricles + **gentamicin** 3 mg into cerebral ventricles	Efficacy when infection rate >15%. Alternative: TMP (160 mg) + SMX (800 mg) IV pre-op and q12h x3 doses
Obstetric/Gynecologic Surgery		
Vaginal or abdominal hysterectomy	**Cefazolin** 1–2 gm or **cefoxitin** 1–2 gm or **cefotetan** 1–2 gm IV or **cefuroxime** 1.5 gm all IV x1 30 min. before surgery.	1 study found cefotetan superior to cefazolin (*CID 20:677, 1995*). For prolonged procedures, doses can be repeated q4–8h for duration of procedure.
Cesarean section for premature rupture of membranes or active labor	**Cefazolin** x1, administer IV as soon as umbilical cord clamped.	Not effective in elective C-section in a large prospective double-blind randomized trial (*BJOG 108:143, 2001*). However, meta-analysis of 7 trials suggested benefit (*Am J Ob Gyn 184:656, 2001*).
Abortion	1st trimester: high-risk only (see Comments) aqueous **pen G** 2 mU IV or **doxycycline** 300 mg po. 2nd trimester: **Cefazolin** 1 gm IV	High-risk: Pts with previous pelvic inflammatory disease, gonorrhea or multiple sexual partners (*Drugs 41:19, 1991*).
Orthopedic Surgery (Generally, pts with prosthetic joints do not need prophylaxis for dental procedures. Individual considerations prevail (*J Am Dental Assn 128:1004, 1997*). See Table 1, page 22		
Hip arthroplasty,[1] spinal fusion.	Same as cardiac:	Customarily stopped after "Hemovac" removed.
Total joint replacement (other than hip)	**Cefazolin** 1–2 gm IV pre-op (± 2nd dose) or **vancomycin** 1 gm IV on call to OR	Post-op: some would give no further rx (*Med Lett 39:98, 1997*)
Open reduction of closed fracture with internal fixation	**Ceftriaxone** 2 gm IV or IM x1 dose	3.6% vs 8.3% (for placebo) infection found in Dutch trauma trial (*Lancet 347:1133, 1996*).
Peritoneal Dialysis Catheter Placement	**Vancomycin** single 1000 mg dose 12 hrs prior to procedure	Effectively reduced peritonitis during 14 days post-placement in 221 pts: vanco 1%, cefazolin 7%, placebo 12% (p=0.02) (*Am J Kidney Dis 36:1014, 2000*).
Urologic Surgery/Procedures		
Antimicrobials not recommended in pts with sterile urine. Pts with pre-operative bacteriuria should be treated.	Recommended antibiotic to pts with pre-operative bacteriuria: **Cefazolin** 1 gm IV q8h x1–3 doses perioperatively, followed by oral antibiotics (**nitrofurantoin** or **TMP/SMX**) until catheter is removed or for 10 d. Modify based on susceptibility test results.	
Transrectal prostate biopsy	**Ciprofloxacin** 500 mg po 12 hrs prior to biopsy and repeated 12 hrs after 1st dose (levo, norflox should work)	CIP reduced bacteremia from 37% (in gentamicin-rx group) to 7% (*Urology 38:84, 1991*, and review in *JAC 39:115, 1997*).
Other		
Breast surgery, herniorrhaphy	**P Ceph 1,2**, dosage as *Gynecologic Surgery*, above	

[1] Gentamicin (12.5 mg/gm of acrylic bone cement) is released for at least 3 weeks. Usefulness not proven.

TABLE 15C: ANTIMICROBIAL PROPHYLAXIS FOR THE PREVENTION OF BACTERIAL ENDOCARDITIS IN PATIENTS WITH UNDERLYING CARDIAC CONDITIONS

[These are the recommendations of the American Heart Association (JAMA 277:1794, 1997). However, a population-based prospective case-controlled study brings into serious question whether dental procedures predispose to endocarditis and whether antibiotic prophylaxis is of any value (see AnIM 129:761, 1998; Br Dent J 189:610, 2000).]

ENDOCARDITIS PROPHYLAXIS RECOMMENDED	ENDOCARDITIS PROPHYLAXIS NOT RECOMMENDED
Cardiac conditions associated with endocarditis **High-risk conditions:** Prosthetic valves— bioprosthetic and homograft, as well as mechanical Previous bacterial endocarditis Complex cyanotic congenital heart disease, e.g., single ventricle, transposition, tetralogy of Fallot Surgically constructed systemic pulmonic shunts or conduits **Moderate-risk conditions:** Most other congenital heart abnormalities or acquired valvular disease; hypertrophic cardiac myopathy; mitral prolapse with regurgitation	**Negligible-risk** (same as general population): Atrial septal defect (secundum) or repaired ASD/VSD, or PDA (beyond 6 months) Previous CABG; mitral prolapse without MI (see discussion JAMA 277:1794, 1997) Physiologic, functional, or innocent heart murmurs Previous Kawasaki or rheumatic fever without valve dysfunction Cardiac pacemakers (all) and implanted defibrillators

ENDOCARDITIS PROPHYLAXIS RECOMMENDED	ENDOCARDITIS PROPHYLAXIS NOT RECOMMENDED
Dental and other procedures where prophylaxis is considered for patients with moderate- or high-risk cardiac conditions: Dental: Extractions, periodontal procedures[1] Implants, root canal, subgingival antibiotic fibers/strips Initial orthodontic bands (not brackets); intraligamentary local anesthetic Cleaning of implants if bleeding anticipated Respiratory: T&A, surgery on mucosa, rigid bronchoscopy GI: Sclerotherapy of esophageal varices; dilation of esophageal stricture; ERCP with biliary obstruction GU: Prostate surgery, cystoscopy/urethral dilatation	Dental: Filling cavities with local anesthetic Placement of rubber dams, suture removal, orthodontic removal Orthodontic adjustments, dental x-rays Shedding of primary teeth Respiratory: Intubation, flexible bronchoscopy[2] tympanostomy tube GI: Transesophageal cardiac echo[2]; EGD without biopsy[2] GU: Vaginal hysterectomy[2], vaginal delivery[2], C-section If uninfected: urethral cath, uterine D&C, therapeutic abortion, tubal ligation, insert/remove IUD Other: Cardiac cath, balloon angioplasty, implanted pacemaker, defibrillators, coronary stents Skin biopsy, circumcision

Abbreviations: T&A = tonsillectomy/adenoidectomy, **ERCP** = endoscopic retrograde cholangiopancreatography, **ASD/VSD** = atrial septal defect/ventricular septal defect, **PDA** = patent ductus arteriosus, **EGD** = esophagogastroduodenoscopy, **D&C** = dilation and curettage

PROPHYLACTIC REGIMENS FOR DENTAL, ORAL, RESPIRATORY TRACT, OR ESOPHAGEAL PROCEDURES

SITUATION	AGENT	REGIMEN[3]
Standard general prophylaxis	Amoxicillin	Adults 2 gm, children 50 mg/kg orally 1 hr before procedure
Unable to take oral medications	Ampicillin	Adults 2 gm IM or IV, children 50 mg/kg IM or IV within 30 min. before procedure
Allergic to penicillin	Clindamycin, OR	Adults 600 mg, children 20 mg/kg orally 1 hr before procedure
	(Cephalexin[4] or cefadroxil[4]), OR	Adults 2 gm, children 50 mg/kg orally 1 hr before procedure
	Azithromycin or clarithromycin	Adults 500 mg, children 15 mg/kg orally 1 hr before procedure
Allergic to penicillin and unable to take oral medications	Clindamycin, OR	Adults 600 mg, children 20 mg/kg IV within 30 min. before procedure
	Cefazolin[4]	Adults 1 gm, children 25 mg/kg IM or IV within 30 min. before procedure

[1] Some now recommend that for adults, prophylaxis prior to dental procedures should be used **only** for extractions and **gingival surgery** (including implant replacement) and **only** for patients with **prosthetic cardiac valves** or **previous endocarditis**. For high-risk patients [presumably those also] — prophylactic antibiotics according to American Heart Association are recommended.

[2] Prophylaxis optional for high-risk patients

[3] Total children's dose should not exceed adult dose

[4] Cephalosporins should not be used in individuals with immediate-type hypersensitivity reaction (urticaria, angioedema, or anaphylaxis) to penicillins.

TABLE 15C (2)
PROPHYLACTIC REGIMENS FOR GENITOURINARY/GASTROINTESTINAL (EXCLUDING ESOPHAGEAL) PROCEDURES

SITUATION	AGENT	REGIMEN
High-risk patients	Ampicillin + gentamicin	**Adults: ampicillin** 2 gm IM or IV + **gentamicin** 1.5 mg/kg (not to exceed 120 mg) within 30 min. of starting the procedure; 6 hr later, **ampicillin** 1 gm IM/IV or **amoxicillin** 1 gm orally. **Children: ampicillin** 50 mg/kg IM or IV (not to exceed 2.0 grn) + **gentamicin** 1.5 mg/kg within 30 min. of starting the procedure; 6 hrs later **ampicillin** 25 mg/kg IM/IV or **amoxicillin** 25 mg/kg orally
High-risk patients allergic to ampicillin/amoxicillin	Vancomycin + gentamicin	**Adults: vancomycin** 1 gm IV over 1-2 hrs + **gentamicin** 1.5 mg/kg IV/IM (not to exceed 120 mg); complete injection/infusion within 30 min. of starting the procedure **Children: vancomycin** 20 mg/kg IV over 1-2 hrs + **gentamicin** 1.5 mg/kg IV/IM, complete injection/infusion within 30 min. of starting the procedure
Moderate-risk patients	Amoxicillin or ampicillin	**Adults: amoxicillin** 2 gm orally 1 hr before procedure, or **ampicillin** 2 gm IM/IV within 30 min. of starting the procedure. **Children: amoxicillin** 50 mg/kg orally 1 hr before procedure, or **ampicillin** 50 mg/kg IM/IV within 30 min. of starting the procedure
Moderate-risk patients allergic to ampicillin/amoxicillin	Vancomycin	**Adults: vancomycin** 1 gm IV over 1-2 hrs, complete infusion, within 30 min. of starting the procedure. **Children: vancomycin** 20 mg/kg IV over 1-2 hrs; complete infusion within 30 min. of starting the procedure

1 Total children's dose should not exceed adult dose

TABLE 15D: MANAGEMENT OF EXPOSURE TO HIV-1 AND HEPATITIS

OCCUPATIONAL EXPOSURE TO BLOOD, PENILE/VAGINAL SECRETIONS WITH RISK OF TRANSMISSION OF HEPATITIS B/C AND/OR HIV-1 (E.G., NEEDLESTICK INJURY)

[Adapted from *MMWR* 50(RR-11):1, 2001 and *NEJM* 348:826, 2003.]
Free consultation for occupational exposures, call (PEPline) 1-888-HIV-4911.

General steps in management:
1. Wash clean wounds/flush mucous membranes immediately (use of caustic agents or squeezing the wound is discouraged; data lacking regarding antiseptics).
2. Assess risk by doing the following: (a) Characterize exposure; (b) Determine/evaluate source of exposure by medical history, risk behavior, & testing for hepatitis B/C, HIV; (c) Evaluate and test exposed individual for hepatitis B/C & HIV.

Hepatitis B Exposure *(See CDC recommendations: MMWR 50(RR-11), 2001)*

Exposed Person	Exposure Source		
	HBs Ag+	HBs Ag-	Status Unknown
Unvaccinated	Give HBIG 0.06 ml/kg IM & initiate HB vaccine	Initiate HB vaccine	Initiate HB vaccine and if possible, check HBs Ag of source person
Vaccinated (antibody status unknown)	Do anti-HBs on exposed person: If titer ≥10 MIU/ml, no rx If titer < 10 MIU/ml, give HBIG + 1 dose HB vaccine	No rx necessary	Do anti-HBs on exposed person: If titer ≥10 MIU/ml, no rx If titer < 10 MIU/ml, give 1 dose of HB vaccine (plus 1 dose HBIG if source high risk)

For known vaccine series responder (titer ≥10 MIU/ml), monitoring of levels or further doses not currently recommended. Known non-responder (< 10 MIU/ml) to 1° series HB vaccine & exposed to either HBsAg+ source—rx with HBIG & re-initiate vaccine series **or** 2 doses HBIG 1 month apart. For non-responders after a 2nd vaccine series, 2 doses HBIG 1 month apart is preferred approach to new exposure *[MMWR 40(RR-13):21, 2001].*

Hepatitis C Exposure
Determine antibody to hepatitis C for both exposed person and, if possible, exposure source. If source +, follow-up HCV testing advised. **No recommended prophylaxis;** immune serum globulin not effective. Monitor for early infection, as therapy may ↓ risk of progression to chronic hepatitis. *See Table 14 and discussion in Clin Micro Rev 16:546, 2003.*

TABLE 15D (2)

HIV: Occupational exposure management *(for non-occupational HIV exposures, see www.hivguidelines.org/public_html/center/clinical-guidelines/pep_guidelines/pep_guidelines.htm)*
- The decision to initiate post-exposure prophylaxis (PEP) for HIV is a clinical judgment that should be made in concert with the exposed healthcare worker (HCW). It is based on:
  1. Likelihood of the source patient having HIV infection: ↑ with history of high-risk activity—injection drug use, sexual activity with known HIV+ person, unprotected sex with multiple partners (either hetero- or homosexual), receipt of blood products 1978–1985, ↑ with clinical signs suggestive of advanced HIV (unexplained wasting, night sweats, thrush, seborrheic dermatitis, etc.).
     Remember, the vast majority of persons are **not** infected with HIV (1/200 women infected in larger U.S. cities) and likelihood of infection **extremely rare** if not in above risk groups.
  2. Type of exposure (approx. 1 in 300–400 needlesticks from infected source will transmit HIV).
  3. Limited data regarding efficacy of PEP (PEP with ZDV alone reduced transmission by >80% in 1 in 1 retrospective case-controlled study—*NEJM 337:1485, 1997*).
  4. Significant adverse effects of PEP drugs.

- If source person is **known positive for HIV or likely to be infected** and **status of exposure warrants PEP**, antiretroviral drugs should be started **immediately** (at least within 72 hrs). If source person ELISA for HIV is negative, drugs can be stopped unless source is suspected of having acute HIV infection. The HCW should be re-tested at **3–4 weeks, 3 & 6 months whether PEP is used or not** (the vast majority of seroconversions will occur by 3 months; delayed conversions after 6 months are exceedingly rare). Tests for HIV RNA should not be used for dx of HIV infection because of false-positives (esp. at low titers) & these tests are only approved for established HIV infection [a possible exception is if it develops signs of acute HIV (mononucleosis-like) syndrome within the 1st 4–6 wks of exposure when antibody tests might still be negative.]

- PEP for HIV is usually given for **4 weeks** and monitoring of adverse effects recommended: baseline **complete blood count, renal and hepatic panel** to be **repeated at 2 weeks** 50–75% of HCW on PEP demonstrate mild side-effects (nausea, diarrhea, myalgias, headache, etc.) but in up to ⅓ severe enough to discontinue PEP (*Antivir Ther 3:195, 2000*). Consultation with infectious diseases/HIV specialist valuable when questions regarding PEP arise. Seek expert help in special situations, such as pregnancy, renal impairment.

3 Steps to HIV Post-Exposure Prophylaxis (PEP) After Occupational Exposure: *(MMWR 50:RR-11, 2001)*

Step 1: Determine the exposure code (EC)

Is source material blood, bloody fluid, semen/vaginal fluid or other normally sterile fluid or tissue?
  → Yes → What type of exposure occurred?
  → No → No PEP

What type of exposure occurred?
- Mucous membrane or skin integrity compromised (e.g. dermatitis, open wound)
  → Volume
    - Small: Few drops → EC1
    - Large: Major splash and/or long duration → EC2
- Percutaneous exposure
  → Severity
    - Less severe: Solid needle, scratch → EC2
    - More severe: Large-bore hollow needle, deep puncture, visible blood, needle used in vein of source (risk 1:300/400) → EC3
- Intact skin → No PEP

Step 2: Determine the HIV Status Code (HIV SC)

What is the HIV status of the exposure source?
- HIV negative → No PEP
- HIV positive
  - Low titer exposure: asymptomatic & high CD4 count → HIV SC 1
  - High titer exposure: advanced AIDS, prim. HIV, high viral load or low CD4 count → HIV SC 2
- Status unknown → HIV SC unknown
- Source unknown → HIV SC unknown

TABLE 16D (3)

Step 3: Determine Post-Exposure Prophylaxis (PEP) Recommendation

EC	HIV SC	PEP
1	1	Consider basic regimen†
2	1	Recommend basic regimen†
1	2	Recommend basic regimen†
2	2	Recommend expanded regimen†
3	1 or 2	Recommend expanded regimen†
1, 2, 3	Unknown	If exposure setting suggests risks of HIV exposure, consider basic regimen†

Regimens: (Treat for 4 weeks)
Basic regimen: ZDV + 3TC, or d4T + 3TC. Best to avoid ddI + d4T (↑ side effects).
Expanded regimen: Basic regimen + one of the following: nelfinavir, lopinavir/ritonavir, indinavir (or indinavir/ritonavir), abacavir or efavirenz, could be used but generally avoided in this setting. [Do not use nevirapine: 22 HCWs receiving drug had serious adverse effects including 3 with hepatic necrosis (MMWR 49:1153, 2001).]
Other regimens can be designed. If possible, use 2 antiretroviral drugs that source pt (if known) is not currently taking or for which resistance is unlikely based on susceptibility data or treatment history. Seek expert consultation.

NOTE: Some authorities feel that an expanded regimen should be employed whenever PEP is indicated (NEJM 349:1091, 2003 & NY State AIDS Institute, 2004). For example, the latter recommends ZDV + 3TC + tenofovir (http://www.hivguidelines.org/public_html/center/clinical-guidelines/pep_guidelines/pep_guidelines.htm).

† **Around the clock, urgent expert consultation available from:**
National Clinicians' Post-Exposure Prophylaxis Hotline (PEPline) at 1-888-448-4911 (1-888-HIV-4911)

TABLE 15E: PREVENTION OF OPPORTUNISTIC INFECTION IN HUMAN STEM CELL TRANSPLANTATION (HSCT) OR SOLID ORGAN TRANSPLANTATION (SOT)

General comments: See Table 15F, page 130 for typical timing of infections post-transplant. References: MMWR 49/RR-10/:1, 2000; CID 33:S26, 2001; COID 17:353, 2004

OPPORTUNISTIC INFECTION (at risk)	TYPE OF TRANSPLANT	PROPHYLACTIC REGIMENS	COMMENTS/REFERENCES
Herpes simplex (seropositive)	HSCT	Acyclovir 200 mg po 3x/d, from conditioning to engraftment or resolution of mucositis	Do not add acyclovir if receiving CMV prophylaxis
	SOT	Acyclovir 200 mg po 3x/d. —start early post-transplant	
CMV (Recipient + OR Donor +, Recipient −)	HSCT	Universal (Recipient +): Ganciclovir 5 mg/kg IV q12h x5–7d., then 5–6 mg/kg 1x/d. 5 days/wk x100 days. Preemptive (Donor +, recipient neg.): 1–2 x/wk screen plasma for either (1) CMV antigen or (2) CMV-DNA by PCR—when positive, start ganciclovir as for Universal, above. For general review, see Clin Micro Rev 16:647, 2003.	
	SOT	Kidney, kidney/pancreas, heart: Valganciclovir 900 mg po 1x/d. by day 10 to day 100 post-transplant Liver: Ganciclovir 1000 mg po tid by day 10 to day 100 post-transplant Lung: (Ganciclovir 5 mg/kg IV q12h x5–7 d. + CMV-immune globulin 150 mg/kg within 72 hrs, then at 2, 4, 6 & 8 wks post-transplant; then 100 mg/kg at wks 12 & 16), then valganciclovir 900 mg po 1x/d. x6 months	
Hepatitis B-induced cirrhosis	Liver	Lamivudine 100–400 mg po 1x/d. 4 wks pre-transplant & 12 months post-transplant	Some have combined with HBIG (Hepatol 28:585, 1998)
Candida sp.	Liver	Fluconazole 200–400 mg IV/po 1x/d. starting before transplant & continuing up to 3 mos. in high-risk pts. Optimal duration unknown. Concerns for ↑ non-albicans candida with fluconazole prophylaxis (Transpl 75:2023, 2003).	
	HSCT	Fluconazole 400 mg po 1x/d. from day 0 to engraftment or ANC >1000	
Aspergillus sp.	Lung/Heart-lung	No controlled trials to determine optimal management. Randomized trial suggested ABLC better tolerated than Ampho B deoxycholate if nebulized route is used[AJ5] (Transpl 77:232, 2004).	
Coccidioides immitis	All	Reasonable: Fluconazole 400 mg po 1x/d. Duration 4 mos.–1 yr renal; ≥6 mos. for allogenic HSCT; ≥1 yr to lifetime for heart, lung, liver.	
Pneumocystis carinii (P. jiroveci) & Toxoplasma gondii	All	TMP/SMX-SS or –DS, 1 tab po 1x/d. Duration 4 mos.–1 yr renal; 2x/wk or daily atovaquone doses <1500 mg/d. (CID 38:e76, 2004). Breakthrough infections reported with atovaquone doses <1500 mg/d. (CID 38:e76, 2004).	
Trypanosoma cruzi	Heart	If known Chagas' disease in donor or recipient, contact CDC for nifurtimox	

TABLE 15F
TEMPORAL APPROACH TO DIFFERENTIAL DIAGNOSIS OF INFECTION AFTER ORGAN TRANSPLANTATION*

USUAL HOSPITAL-ACQUIRED INFECTIONS	OPPORTUNISTIC INFECTIONS	COMMUNITY-ACQUIRED OR CHRONIC INFECTIONS

VIRAL:
- HSV
- CMV
- Onset of Hepatitis B or C
- EBV, VZV, Influenza, RSV, Adenovirus ......▲[1]
- CMV retinitis or colitis... ‡
- Papillomavirus, PTLD[2]...‡

BACTERIAL:
- Pneumonia, IV line, UTI, Wound...
- Nocardia
- Listeria, Tuberculosis

FUNGAL:
- Candida
- Aspergillus
- Pneumocystis
- Cryptococcus
- Coccidioidomycosis, Histoplasmosis
- ‡

PARASITIC
- Leishmania
- Toxoplasma
- Strongyloides
- Trypanosoma cruzi

MONTHS AFTER TRANSPLANTATION
1 2 3 4 5 6

* Adapted from Fishman and Rubin. *NEJM* 338:1741, 1998. For hematopoietic stem cell transplant recipients, *see MMWR 49:RR-10*, 2000.
Solid lines indicate usual time period for onset of infection; dotted lines indicate risk at reduced level

[1] Symptomatic CMV antigenemia may be delayed in patients receiving 3-mo. ganciclovir prophylaxis *(Transpl Inf Dis 6:3, 2004)*.
[2] **PTLD** = Post-transplant lymphoproliferative disease.

TABLE 16: PEDIATRIC DOSAGES OF SELECTED ANTIBACTERIAL AGENTS
[Adapted from: (1) Nelson's Pocket Book of Pediatric Antimicrobial Therapy, 2002-2003, 15th Ed., J. Bradley & J. Nelson, eds., Lippincott Williams and Wilkins, and (2) 2003 Red Book, 26th Ed., American Academy of Pediatrics, pages 700–718]

| DRUG | BODY WEIGHT <2000 gm | | BODY WEIGHT >2000 gm | | >28 DAYS OLD |
	0-7 days old	8-28 days old	0-7 days old	8-28 days old	
Aminoglycosides, IV or IM (check levels; some dose by gestational age + wks of life; see Nelson's Pocket Book, page 19)					
Amikacin	7.5 q18-24h	7.5 q12h	10 q12h	10 q12h	10 q8h
Gent/tobra	2.5 q18-24h	2.5 q12h	2.5 q12h	2.5 q12h	2.5 q8h
Aztreonam, IV	30 q12h	30 q8h	30 q8h	30 q6h	30 q6h
Cephalosporins					
Cefaclor					20–40 div tid
Cefadroxil					30 div bid (max 2 g/d)
Cefazolin	20 q12h	20 q12h	20 q12h	20 q8h	20 q8h
Cefdinir					7 q12h or 14 qd
Cefepime					150 div q8h
Cefixime					8 as qd or div bid
Cefotaxime	50 q12h	50 q8h	50 q12h	50 q8h	50 q6h (75 q6h for meningitis)
Cefoxitin				20 q12h	80–160 div q8h
Cefpodoxime					10 div bid (max 400 mg/d)
Cefprozil					15–30 div bid (max 1 g/d)
Ceftazidime	50 q12h	50 q8h	50 q12h	50 q8h	50 q8h
Ceftibuten					4.5 bid
Ceftizoxime					33–66 q8h
Ceftriaxone	50 qd	50 qd	50 qd	75 qd	50–75 qd (meningitis 100)
Cefuroxime IV	50 q12h	50 q8h	50 q8h	50 q8h	50 q8h (80 q8h for meningitis)
po					10–15 div bid (max 1 g/d)
Cephalexin					25–50 div 4x/d (max 4 g/d)
Loracarbef					15–30 div bid (max 0.8 g/d)
Chloramphen. IV	25 q24h	25 q24h	25 q24h	15 q12h	12.5–25 q6h (max 2–4 g/d)
Clindamycin IV	5 q12h	5 q8h	5 q8h	5 q6h	7.5 q6h
po					5–6 q8h
Ciprofloxacin po[2]					20–30 div bid (max 1.5 g/d)
Imipenem[3] IV			25 q12h	25 q8h	15–25 q6h (max 2 g/d)
Linezolid	No data	10 q8h	No data	10 q8h	10 q8h to age 12
Macrolides					
Erythro IV & po	10 q12h	10 q8h	10 q12h	13 q8h	10 q6h
Azithro po					10–12 day 1, then 5/d[4]
Clarithro po					7.5 q12h (max. 1 g/d)
Meropenem IV	20 q12h	20 q8h	20 q12h	20 q8h	60–120 div q8h (120 for meningitis)
Metro IV & po	7.5 q24h	7.5 q12h	7.5 q12h	15 q12h	7.5 q6h
Penicillins					
Ampicillin	50 q12h	50 q8h	50 q8h	50 q6h	
Amp-sulbactam					100–300 div q6h
Amoxicillin po				30 div bid	25–50 div tid
Amox-Clav po	30 div bid	30 div bid	30 div bid	30 div bid	45 or 90 (AM/CL-HD) div bid if over 12 wks of age
Cloxacillin					50–100 div 4x/d
Dicloxacillin					12–25 div 4x/d
Mezlocillin	75 q12h	75 q8h	75 q12h	75 q8h	75 q6h
Nafcillin,oxacillin IV	25 q12h	25 q8h	25 q8h	37 q6h	37 q6h (to max. 8–12 gm/d)
Piperacillin, PIP/tazo IV	75 mg/kg q12h	75 mg/kg q12h	75 mg/kg q8h	75 mg/kg q8h	100–300 div q4–6h
Ticarcillin, T.clav IV	75 q12h	75 q8h	75 q8h	75 q8h	75 q6h
Penicillin G, U/kg IV	50,000 q12h	75,000 q8h	50,000 q8h	50,000 q6h	50,000 U/kg/d
Penicillin V					25–50 mg/kg/d div 3–4x/d
Rifampin po		10, single dose	20, single dose	20, single dose	20, single dose (max. 600 mg)
Sulfisoxazole po				120–150	120–150 mg/kg/d div q4–6h
TMP/SMX po,IV; UTI: 8–12 TMP component div bid; Pneumocystis: 20 TMP component div 4x/d					
Tetracycline po (age 8 or older)					25–50 div 4x/d
Doxycycline po,IV (age 8 or older)					2–4 div bid
Vancomycin IV	12.5 q12h	15 q12h	18 q12h	22 q12h	40–60 div q6h

Abbreviations: **Chloramphen** = chloramphenicol; **Clav** = clavulanate; **div** = divided; **Gent/tobra** = gentamicin/tobramycin; **Metro** = metronidazole; **Tazo** = tazobactam; **TMP** = trimethoprim; **TMP/SMX** = trimethoprim/sulfamethoxazole; **UTI** = urinary tract infection

1 May need higher doses in patients with meningitis: see CID 39:1267, 2004
2 With exception of cystic fibrosis, not approved for use under age 18.
3 Not recommended in children with CNS infections due to risk of seizures.
4 Dose for otitis; for pharyngitis, 12 mg/kg x5 d.

TABLE 17A: DOSAGE OF ANTIMICROBIAL DRUGS IN ADULT PATIENTS WITH RENAL IMPAIRMENT

Adapted from Drug PRESCRIBING IN RENAL FAILURE, 4th Ed., Aronoff et al (Eds.), American College of Physicians, 1999 and Bennett et al, Renal Aspects of Antimicrobial Therapy for HIV Infection. In: P. Kimmel & J. Berns, Eds., HIV INFECTION AND THE KIDNEY, Churchill-Livingstone, 1995, pp 195–236.

UNLESS STATED, ADJUSTED DOSES ARE % OF DOSE FOR NORMAL RENAL FUNCTION.
Drug adjustments are based on the patient's estimated endogenous creatinine clearance, which can be calculated as:

Ideal body weight for men: 50.0 kg + 2.3 kg per inch over 5 feet
Ideal body weight for women: 45.5 kg + 2.3 kg per inch over 5 feet

$$\frac{[140-age](Ideal\ body\ weight\ in\ kg)}{(72)(serum\ creatinine, mg/dL)} \text{ for men (x 0.85 for women)}$$

For alternative method to calculate estimated CrCl, see AnM 130-461, 1999.

NOTE: For summary of drugs requiring **no** dosage adjustment with renal insufficiency, see Table 17B, page 137.

ANTIMICROBIAL	HALF-LIFE (NORMAL/ESRD) hr	DOSE FOR NORMAL RENAL FUNCTION[1]	METHOD* (see footnote)	ADJUSTMENT FOR RENAL FAILURE Estimated creatinine clearance (CrCl), ml/min			SUPPLEMENT FOR HEMODIALYSIS, CAPD[1] (see footnote)	COMMENTS AND DOSAGE FOR CAVH[1]
				>50-90	10-50	<10		
ANTIBACTERIAL ANTIBIOTICS								
Aminoglycoside Antibiotics:		**Traditional multiple daily doses—adjustment for renal damage**						
Amikacin	1.4–2.3/17–150	7.5 mg/kg q12h	D&I	60–90% q12h	30–70% q12-18h **Same dose for CAVH**[1]	20–30% q24-48h	HEMO: Extra ½ of normal renal function dose AD*; CAPD: 15-20 mg lost/L dialysate/day[1] (see Comment)	High flux hemodialysis membranes lead to unpredictable aminoglycoside clearance, measure post-dialysis drug levels for efficacy and toxicity. With CAPD, pharmacokinetics highly variable— **check serum levels.** Usual method for CAPD: 2 liters of dialysis fluid placed qid or 8 liters/day (give 8, 20 mg lost/L per day)
Gentamicin, Tobramycin	2–3/20–60	1.7 mg/kg q8h	D&I	60–90% q8-12h	30–70% q12h **Same dose for CAVH**[1]	20–30% q24-48h	HEMO: Extra ½ of normal renal function dose AD*; CAPD: 3-4 mg lost/L dialysate/day	
Netilmicin[NUS]	2–3/35–72	2.0 mg/kg q8h	D&I	50–90% q8-12h	20–60% q12h **Same dose for CAVH**[1]	10–20% q24-48h	HEMO: Extra ½ of normal renal function dose AD*; CAPD: 3-4 mg lost/L dialysate/day	"Adjust dosing weight for obesity: ideal body weight + 0.4(actual body weight – ideal body weight)] CID 25:112, 1997. **Example: CrCl 0 on hemodialysis:** 60 mg/kg. Initial dose of 1.7 mg/kg = 102 mg. Then, 12-18 mg q48h with extra 51 mg AD*
Streptomycin	2–3/30–80	15 mg/kg (max. of 1.0 gm) q24h	I	50% q24h	q24-72h **Same dose for CAVH**[1]	q72-96h		= 160 mg of amikacin supplement IV per day)

ONCE-DAILY AMINOGLYCOSIDE THERAPY: ADJUSTMENT IN RENAL INSUFFICIENCY (see Table 10C for OD dosing/normal renal function)

Creatinine Clearance (ml/min):	>80	60–80	40–60	30–40	20–30	10–20	<10
Drug	Dose q24h (mg/kg)				Dose q48h and AD*		Dose q72h and AD*
Gentamicin/Tobramycin	5.1	4	3.5	2.5	4	3	2
Amikacin/kanamycin/streptomycin	15	12	7.5	4	7.5	4	8 q96h
Isepamicin[NUS]	8	8	8	8 q48h	8	8 q72h	8 q96h
Netilmicin[NUS]	6.5	5	4	3	4	3	2.0

Carbapenem Antibiotics								
Ertapenem	4/~4	1.0 gm q24h	D	1.0 gm q24h	0.5 gm q24h (CrCl <30)	0.5 gm q24h	HEMO: Dose as for CrCl <10, if dosed <6 hrs prior to HD, give 150 mg supplement AD*	
Imipenem (see Comment)	1/4	0.5 gm q8h	D&I	250–500 mg q6-8h	250 mg q6-12h **Same dose for CAVH**[1]	125–250 mg q12h	HEMO: Dose AD*; CAPD: Dose for CrCl <10	†potential for seizures if recommended doses exceeded in pts with CrCl <20 ml/min. See pkg insert, esp. for pts <70 kg
Meropenem	1/6–8	1.0 gm q8h	D&I	1.0 gm q8h **Same dose for CAVH**[1]	1.0 gm q12h	0.5 gm q24h	HEMO: Dose AD*; CAPD: Dose for CrCl <10	

* CAVH = continuous arteriovenous hemofiltration (NEJM 336:1303, 1997) usually results in CrCl of approx. 30 ml/min * **AD** = after dialysis. * **AD*** refers to timing of dose.
See page 136 for other footnotes and abbreviations. **Supplement is to replace drug lost via dialysis; extra drug beyond continuation of regimen used for CrCl <10 ml/min.**

TABLE 17A (2)

ANTIMICROBIAL	HALF-LIFE (NORMAL/ESRD) hr	DOSE FOR NORMAL RENAL FUNCTION*	METHOD* (see footnote)	ADJUSTMENT FOR RENAL FAILURE Estimated creatinine clearance (CrCl), ml/min			SUPPLEMENT FOR HEMODIALYSIS, CAPD (see footnote)	COMMENTS AND DOSAGE FOR CAVH†
				>50-90	10-50	<10		
Cephalosporin Antibiotics: DATA ON SELECTED PARENTERAL CEPHALOSPORINS		1.0-2.0 gm q8h						
Cefazolin	1.9/40-70	1.0-2.0 gm q8h	I	q8h	q8h	q12h	HEMO: Extra 0.5-1 gm AD* CAPD: 0.5 gm q12h	CAVH dose: As for CrCl 10-50
Cefepime	2.2/18	2.0 gm q8h (max. dose)	D&I	2 gm q8h	2 gm q12-24h **Same dose for CAVH†**	1 gm q24h	HEMO: Extra 1 gm AD* CAPD: 1-2 gm q48h	CAVH dose: Extra 1 gm AD* CAPD: 1-2 gm q48h
Cefotaxime, Ceftizoxime	1.7/15-35	2.0 gm q8h	I	q8-12h	q12-24h **Same dose for CAVH†**	q24h	HEMO: Extra 1 gm AD* CAPD: 0.5-1 gm qd	Active metabolite of cefotaxime in ESRD, ↓ dose further for hepatic & renal failure
Cefotetan	3.5/13-25	1-2 gm q12h	D	100%	50%	25%	HEMO: Extra 1 gm AD* CAPD: 1 gm qd	CAVH dose: 750 mg q12h
Cefoxitin	0.8/13-23	2.0 gm q8h	D	q8h	q8-12h **CAVH†** q24-48h	q24-48h	HEMO: Extra 1 gm AD* CAPD: 1 gm qd	May falsely increase serum creatinine by interference with assay
Ceftazidime	1.2/13-25	2 gm q8h	I	q8-12h **Same dose for CAVH†**	q24-48h	q48h	HEMO: Extra 1 gm AD* CAPD: 0.5 gm qd	Volume of distribution increases with infection.
Cefuroxime sodium	1.2/17	0.75-1.5 gm q8h	I	q8h	q8-12h	q24h	HEMO: Dose AD* CAPD: Dose for CrCl <10	CAVH dose: 1.5 gm, then 750 mg q24h
Fluoroquinolone Antibiotics								
Ciprofloxacin	4/6-9	500-750 mg po (or 400 mg IV) q12h	D	100%	50-75%	50%	HEMO: 250 mg po or 200 mg IV q12h CAPD: 250 mg po or 200 mg IV q8h	CAVH† dose: 200 mg IV q12h
Gatifloxacin	7-14/36	400 mg po/IV q24h	D	400 mg q24h	200 mg q24h **Same dose for CAVH†**	200 mg q24h AD*	HEMO: 200 mg q24h AD* CAPD: 200 mg q24h	CAVH dose: As for CrCl 10-50
Gemifloxacin	7/>7	320 mg po qd	D	320 mg qd	160 mg qd	160 mg qd	HEMO: 160 mg qd AD* CAPD: 160 mg qd	
Levofloxacin	4-8/76	500 mg qd IV, PO	D*	100%	500 mg x1, then 250 mg q24h	500 mg x1, then 250 mg q48h	HEMO/CAPD: Dose for CrCl <10	CAVH dose: As for CrCl 10-50
Ofloxacin	7.0/28-37	400 mg po/IV q12h	D&I	100%	200-400 mg q12h	200 mg q24h	HEMO: 100-200 mg AD* CAPD: Dose for CrCl <10	CAVH dose: 300 mg/d
Macrolide Antibiotics								
Clarithromycin	5-7/22	0.5-1.0 gm q12h	D	100%	75%	50-75%	HEMO: Dose AD* CAPD: None	CAVH dosing recommendations based on extrapolation
Erythromycin	1.4/5-6	250-500 mg q6h	D	100%	100%	50-75%	HEMO/CAPD/CAVH†: None	Ototoxicity with high doses in ESRD. Vol. of distribution increases in ESRD.
Miscellaneous Antibacterial Antibiotics								
Colistin	?	80-160 mg q8h	D	160-160 mg q12h	160 mg q36h	160 mg q36h	HEMO: 80 mg q12h	
Daptomycin	9.4/30	4 mg/kg/d	D	4 mg/kg/d	CrCl <30, 4 mg/kg q48h	4 mg/kg q48h	HEMO: 4 mg/kg q48h (after dialysis)	CAVH†: No data (after dialysis if possible)
Linezolid	6.4/7.1	600 mg po/IV q12h	None	600 mg q12h	600 mg q12h	600 mg q12h	HEMO: As for CrCl <10 CAPD: No data	CAVH†: No data. Accumulation of 2 metabolites—risk unknown.
Metronidazole	6-14/7-21	7.5 mg/kg q6h	D	100%	100%	50%	HEMO: Dose AD* CAPD: Dose for CrCl <10	Hemo clears metronidazole and its metabolites (AAC 29:235, 1986)
Nitrofurantoin	0.5/1	50-100 mg q6h	D	100% **Same dose for CAVH†**	Avoid	Avoid	Not applicable	
Sulfamethoxazole	10/20-50	1.0 gm q8h	D	q12h **Same dose for CAVH†**	q18h	q24h	HEMO: Extra 1 gm AD* CAPD: 1 gm qd	

* Regardless of CrCl, 1st dose is 500 mg, and then adjust dose and interval
† CAVH = continuous arteriovenous hemofiltration (NEJM 336:1303, 1997) usually results in CrCl of approx. 30 ml/min.
See page 136 for other footnotes and abbreviations. **Supplement is to replace drug lost via dialysis; extra drug beyond continuation of regimen used for CrCl <10 ml/min.**

* "Dose AD" refers to timing of dose. "Dose AD" = after dialysis.

TABLE 17A (3)

ANTIMICROBIAL	HALF-LIFE (NORMAL/ESRD) HRS	DOSE FOR NORMAL RENAL FUNCTION[1]	METHOD* (see footnote)	ADJUSTMENT FOR RENAL FAILURE Estimated creatinine clearance (CrCl), ml/min >50-90	10-50	<10	SUPPLEMENT FOR HEMODIALYSIS, CAPD* (see footnote)	COMMENTS AND DOSAGE FOR CAVH[1]
Miscellaneous Antibacterial Antibiotics (continued)								
Teicoplanin[AUS]	45/62-230	6 mg/kg/day	I	q24h	q48h	q72h	HEMO: Dose for CrCl <10; CAPD: Dose for CrCl <10	IV amoxicillin not available in the U.S.
Telithromycin	10/15	800 mg qd	D	800 mg qd	400 mg qd (<30 ml/min) **Same dose for CAVH[1]**	400 mg qd	HEMO: 800 mg AD*; CAPD: No data	
Trimethoprim	11/20-49	100-200 mg q12h	I	q12h	q18h	q24h	HEMO: Dose q18h; CAPD: q24h	CAVH dose: q18h
Vancomycin[1]	6/200-250	1 gm q12h	D&I	1 gm q12h	1 gm q24-96h	1 gm q4-7 d	HEMO/CAPD: Dose for CrCl <10	CAVH: 500 mg q24-48h. New hemodialysis membranes ↑ clear. of vanco, check levels
Penicillins								
Amoxicillin	1.0/5-20	250-500 mg q8h	I	q8h	q8-12h **Same dose for CAVH[1]**	q24h	HEMO: Dose AD*; CAPD: 250 mg q12h	
Ampicillin	1.0/7-20	250 mg-2 gm q6h	I	q6h	q6-12h **Same dose for CAVH[1]**	q12-24h	HEMO: Dose AD*; CAPD: 250 mg q12h	
Amoxicillin/ Clavulanate[3]	1.3 AM/1.0 ... 5-20/4.0 ...	500/125 mg q8h (see Comments)	D&I	500/125 mg q8h	250-500 mg AM component q12h	250-500 mg AM component q24h	HEMO: As for CrCl <10, extra dose after dialysis; CAPD: Dose for CrCl <10	If CrCl <30/ml, do not use 875/125 or 1000/62.5 AM/CL products
Ampicillin/ Sulbactam[SB]	1.0 (AM)/1.0 (SB) ... 9.0 (AM)/10.0 (SB)	2 gm AM + 1.0 gm SB q6h	I	q6h	q8-12h	q24h	HEMO: 2 gm AM/1 gm SB AD*; CAPD: Dose for CrCl <10	CAVH dose: 1.5 AM/0.75 SB q12h
Aztreonam	2.0/6-8	2 gm q8h	D	100%	50-75% **Same dose for CAVH[1]**	25%	HEMO: Extra 0.5 gm AD*; CAPD: Dose for CrCl <10	Technically a β-lactam antibiotic.
Penicillin G	0.5/6-20	0.5-4 million U q4h	D	100%	75% **Same dose for CAVH[1]**	20-50%	HEMO: Dose AD*; CAPD: Dose for CrCl <10	1.7 mEq potassium/mU. ↑ potential for seizures. 6 mU/d upper limit dose in ESRD.
Piperacillin	1.0/3.3-5.1	3-4 gm q4-6h	I	q4-6h	q6-8h **Same dose for CAVH[1]**	q8h	HEMO: Dose AD*; CAPD: Dose for CrCl <10	1.9 mEq sodium/gm
Pip (Pi)/tazo(T)	1.0 P/1.0 T ... 3.0 P/4.0 T	3.375 gm q6h	D&I	3.375 gm q6h	2.25 gm q6h	2.25 gm q8h	HEMO: Dose AD* + 0.75 gm; CAPD: Dose for CrCl <10	
Ticarcillin	1.2/13	3 gm q4h	D&I	1-2 gm q4h	1-2 gm q8h **Same dose for CAVH[1]**	1-2 gm q12h	HEMO: Extra 3.0 gm AD*; CAPD: Dose for CrCl <10	5.2 mEq sodium/gm
Ticarcillin/ Clavulanate[3]	1.0 (TC)/1.0 (CL) ... 13 (TC)/4.0 (CL)	3.1 gm q4h	D&I	3.1 gm q4-8h	2.0 gm q4-8h **Same dose for CAVH[1]**	2.0 gm q12h	HEMO: Extra 3.1 gm AD*; CAPD: 3.1 gm q12h	Avoid in ESRD
Tetracycline Antibiotics								
Tetracycline[2]	6-10/57-108	250-500 mg qid	I	q8-12h	q12-24h	q24h	HEMO/CAPD/CAVH[1]: None	Avoid in ESRD
ANTIFUNGAL ANTIBIOTICS								
Amphotericin B & ampho B lipid complex	24/unchanged	Non-lipid: 0.4-1.0 mg/kg/d; ABLC* 5 mg/kg/d; LAB* 3-5 mg/kg/d	I	q24h	q24h	q24-48h	HEMO: None; CAPD: Dose for CrCl <10	For ampho B, toxicity lessened by saline loading; risk amplified by concomitant cyclosporine A, aminoglycosides, or pentamidine
Fluconazole	37/100	200-400 mg q24h	D	100%	100-200 mg q24h	100-200 mg q24h	HEMO: 100% of recommended dose AD*; CAPD: Dose for CrCl <10	Goal is peak serum level >25 μg/ml and <100 μg/ml
Flucytosine	3-6/75-200	37.5 mg/kg/d	D&I	q12h	q12-24h **Same dose for CAVH[1]**	q24h	HEMO: Dose AD*; CAPD: 0.5-1.0 gm q24h	EMIT method OK

1 Vancomycin serum levels may be overestimated in renal failure if measured by either fluorescence polarization immunoassay or radioimmunoassay because vanco breakdown products interfere. "AD" = after dialysis. 30 ml/min.; "AD" = after dialysis. **Dose AD** refers to timing of dose.

2 Clavulanate cleared by liver, not kidney. Here use as dose of combination decreased if combination decreases; a deficiency of clavulanate may occur (JAMA 265:386, 2001).

3 ampho B = amphotericin B; **ABLC** = ampho B lipid complex; **LAB** = liposomal ampho B

CAVH = continuous arteriovenous hemofiltration (NEJM 336:1303, 1997) usually results in CrCl of approx. 30 ml/min.; "AD" = after dialysis; **Supplement is to replace drug lost via dialysis; extra drug beyond continuation of regimen used for CrCl <10 ml/min.**

See page 136 for other footnotes and abbreviations.

TABLE 17A (4)

ANTIMICROBIAL	HALF-LIFE (NORMAL/ESRD) hr	DOSE FOR NORMAL RENAL FUNCTION	METHOD* (see footnote)	ADJUSTMENT FOR RENAL FAILURE — Estimated creatinine clearance (CrCl), ml/min >50-90	10-50	<10	SUPPLEMENT FOR HEMODIALYSIS, CAPD (see footnote)	COMMENTS AND DOSAGE FOR CAVH
ANTIFUNGAL ANTIBIOTICS (continued)								
Itraconazole, po soln	35/–	100–200 mg q12h	–	100%	100%	100%	HEMO/CAPD/CAVH*: No adjustment	No adjustment with oral solution
Itraconazole, IV	35/–	200 mg IV q12h	–	200 mg IV q12h	Do not use IV if CrCl <30 due to accumulation of carrier: cyclodextrin			
Terbinafine	36–200/?	250 mg po/day	–	q24h	q24h	q24h	Use has not been studied. Recommend avoidance of drug.	
Voriconazole, IV	Non-linear kinetics	6 mg/kg IV q12h x2, then 4 mg/kg q12h	–	No change	No change	If CrCl <50 ml/min, accum. of IV vehicle (cyclodextrin). Switch to po or DC		
ANTIPARASITIC ANTIBIOTICS								
Pentamidine	29/118	4 mg/kg/d	I	q24h	q24h	q24–36h	HEMO/CAPD/CAVH*: None	Marked tissue accumulation
Quinine	5–16/5–16	650 mg q8h	I	650 mg q8h — Same dose for CAVH*	650 mg q8–12h — Same dose for CAVH*	650 mg q24h	HEMO: Dose AD* — CAPD: Dose for CrCl <10	
ANTITUBERCULOUS ANTIBIOTICS (Excellent review: Nephron 64:169, 1993)								
Ethambutol	4/7–15	15–25 mg/kg q24h	I	q24h — Same dose for CAVH*	q24–36h	q48h	HEMO: Dose AD* — CAPD: Dose for CrCl <10	25 mg/kg 4–6 hr prior to dialysis for usual 3x/wk dialysis. Streptomycin recommended in lieu of ethambutol in renal failure
Ethionamide	2.1/?	250–500 mg q12h	D	100%	100%	50%	HEMO/CAPD/CAVH*: None	
Isoniazid	0.7–4/8–17	5 mg/kg (max. 300 mg)	D	100%	100%	100%	HEMO: Dose AD* — CAPD/CAVH*: Dose for CrCl <10	
Pyrazinamide	9/26	25 mg/kg q24h (max. dose 2.5 gm qd)	D	25 mg/kg q24h	25 mg/kg q24h	12–25 mg/kg q24h	HEMO: 25–35 mg/kg after each dialysis. CAPD: No reduction; CAVH*: No data	
Rifampin	1.5–5/1.8–11	600 mg/d	D	600 mg q24h	300–600 mg q24h	300–600 mg q24h	HEMO/CAPD: Dose AD* — CAVH*: Dose for CrCl <10	Biologically active metabolite
ANTIVIRAL AGENTS								
Acyclovir, IV	2.5/20	5–12.4 mg/kg q8h	D&I	5–12.4 mg/kg q8h	5–12.4 mg/kg q12–24h	2.5–12.4 mg/kg q24h	HEMO: Dose AD* — CAPD: Dose for CrCl <10	Rapid IV infusion can cause renal failure. CAVH* dose: 3.5 mg/kg/d
Adefovir	12/600	10 mg po qd	I	10 mg qd	10 mg q48–72h	10 mg q7 days	HEMO: q7d AD*	
Amantadine	12/500	100 mg po bid	I	q24–48h	q48–72h	q7d	HEMO/CAPD/CAVH*: None	Major toxicity is renal. No efficacy, safety, or pharmacokinetic data in pts with moderate/severe renal disease.
Cidofovir: Complicated dosing—see package insert								
Induction	2.5/unknown	5 mg/kg 1x/wk for 2 wks	–	5 mg/kg 1x/wk	0.5–2 mg/kg 1x/wk	0.5 mg/kg 1x/wk	No data	
Maintenance	2.5/unknown	5 mg/kg q2wks	–	5 mg/kg q2wks	0.5–2 mg/kg q2wks	0.5 mg/kg q2wks	No data	
Didanosine tablets[1]	0.6–1.6/4.5	200 mg q12h buffered tabs	D	200 mg q12h	200 mg q24h	<60 kg: 150 mg q24h; >60 kg: 100 mg q24h — Do not use EC tabs	HEMO: Dose AD* — CAPD/CAVH*: Dose for CrCl <10	Based on incomplete data. Data are estimates. — If <60 kg & CrCl <10 ml/min, do not use EC tabs
Emtricitabine	10/>10	200 mg qd	I	200 mg q24h	200 mg q48–72h	200 mg q96h	HEMO: Dose for CrCl <10	

[1] Ref. for NRTIs and NNRTIs: Kidney International 60:821, 2001

CAVH = continuous arteriovenous hemofiltration (NEJM 336:1303, 1997) usually results in CrCl of approx. 30 ml/min. — **"Dose AD" refers to timing of dose.**

See page 136 for other footnotes and abbreviations. — **Supplement is to replace drug lost via dialysis; extra drug beyond continuation of regimen used for CrCl <10 ml/min.**

TABLE 17A (5)

ANTIMICROBIAL	HALF-LIFE (NORMAL/ESRD) hr	DOSE FOR NORMAL RENAL FUNCTION†	METHOD* (see footnote)	ADJUSTMENT FOR RENAL FAILURE Estimated creatinine clearance (CrCl), ml/min >50-90	10-50	<10	SUPPLEMENT FOR HEMODIALYSIS, CAPD§ (see footnote)	COMMENTS AND DOSAGE FOR CAVH‡
ANTIVIRAL AGENTS (continued)								
Famciclovir	2.3-3.0/10-22	500 mg q8h	D&I	500 mg q8h	500 mg q12-24h **Same dose for CAVH‡**	250 mg q24h	HEMO: Dose q24h* CAPD: No data	CAVH‡ dose: As for CrCl 10-50
Foscarnet (CMV dosage) Dosage adjustment based on est. CrCl (ml/min/kg by pt's kg)	Normal half-life (T½) 3 hrs with terminal T½ of 18-88 hrs. T½ very long with ESRD	Induction: 60 mg/kg q8h; ×2-3 wks IV Maintenance: 90-120 mg/kg/d IV		*(see CrCl ml/min/kg sub-table below)*				See package insert for further details

CrCl as ml/min/kg body weight—ONLY FOR FOSCARNET

	METHOD	>1.4	>1.0-1.4	>0.8-1.0	>0.6-0.8	>0.5-0.6	>0.4-0.5	<0.4
Induction 60 mg/kg IV		60 q8h	45 q8h	50 q12h	40 q12h	60 q24h	50 q24h	Do not use
Maintenance 90-120 mg/kg/d IV		120 q24h	90 q24h	65 q24h	105 q48h	80 q48h	65 q48h	Do not use

ANTIMICROBIAL	HALF-LIFE (NORMAL/ESRD) hr	DOSE FOR NORMAL RENAL FUNCTION†	METHOD*	>50-90	10-50	<10	SUPPLEMENT FOR HEMODIALYSIS, CAPD§	COMMENTS AND DOSAGE FOR CAVH‡
Ganciclovir	2.9/30	IV: Induction 5 mg/kg q12h IV Maintenance 5 mg/kg q24h IV po: 1.0 gm tid po	D&I	5 mg/kg q12h 2.5-5.0 mg/kg q24h 0.5-1 gm tid	1.25-2.5 mg/kg q24h 0.6-1.25 mg/kg q24h 0.5-1.0 gm qd	1.25 mg/kg 3x/wk 0.625 mg/kg 3x/week 0.5 gm 3x/week	HEMO: Dose AD* CAPD: Dose for CrCl <10 HEMO: Dose AD* CAPD: 0.6 mg/kg AD* Dose for CrCl <10 HEMO: Dose AD* CAPD: 0.5 gm AD*	
Indinavir/nelfinavir/nevirapine		No data on influence of renal insufficiency. Less than 20% excreted unchanged in urine. Probably no dose reduction.						
Lamivudine†	5-7/15-35	300 mg po qd	D&I	300 mg po qd	50-150 mg qd	25-50 mg qd	HEMO: Dose AD* CAPD/CAVH: No data	
Oseltamivir	1-3/no data	75 mg bid	I	75 mg bid	75 mg qd	No data	No data	
Ribavirin	Use with caution in patients with creatinine clearance <10 ml/min.							
Rimantadine	13-65/Prolonged	100 mg bid po	I	100 mg bid	100 mg qd-bid	100 mg qd recommended	HEMO/CAPD: No data	Use with caution, little data
Ritonavir & Saquinavir, SGC				Negligible renal clearance At present, no patient data				
Stavudine, po†	1-1.4/5.5-8	30-40 mg q12h	D&I	50% q12-24h **Same dose for CAVH‡**	≥60 kg 20 mg/d <60 kg 15 mg/d		HEMO: Dose as for CrCl <10 AD* CAPD: No data	CAVH‡ dose: As for CrCl 10-50
Tenofovir		300 mg q24h	D&I	300 mg po q24h	**DO NOT USE IF CrCl <60 ml/min.**		HEMO: Dose AD* CAPD: No data	
Valacyclovir	2.5-3.3/14	1.0 gm q8h	I	1.0 gm q8h	1.0 gm q12-24h	0.5 gm q24h	HEMO: Dose AD* CAPD: No data	CAVH‡ dose: As for CrCl 10-50
Valganciclovir	4/67	900 mg po bid	D&I	900 mg po bid	450 mg q12h to 450 mg qod	DO NOT USE	HEMO: Dose for CrCl <10 CAPD: No data	
Zalcitabine†	2.0/>8	0.75 mg q8h	D&I	0.75 mg q8h	0.75 mg q12h **Same dose for CAVH‡**	0.75 mg q24h	HEMO: Dose for CrCl <10 CAPD: Dose for CrCl <10	CAVH‡ dose: As for CrCl 10-50
Zidovudine†	1.1-1.4/1.4-3	300 mg q12h	D&I	300 mg q12h	300 mg q12h **Same dose for CAVH‡**	100 mg q6-8h; if hemo, AD*	HEMO: Dose for CrCl <10 CAPD: Dose for CrCl <10	CAVH‡ dose: 100 mg q8h

‡ **CAVH** = continuous arteriovenous hemofiltration (NEJM 336:1303, 1997); * **AD** = after dialysis.
Supplement to replace drug lost via dialysis; extra drug beyond continuation of regimen used for CrCl <10 ml/min. "**Dose AD**" refers to timing of dose.
§ Dosages are for life-threatening infections; * **D** = dosage reduction, **I** = interval extension; ** Per cent refers to % change from dose for normal renal function.
Abbreviations: HEMO = hemodialysis; **CAPD** = chronic ambulatory peritoneal dialysis; **ESRD** = endstage renal disease; **NUS** = not available in the U.S.
† Ref. for NRTIs and NNRTIs: Kidney International 60:821, 2001

TABLE 17B: NO DOSAGE ADJUSTMENT WITH RENAL INSUFFICIENCY, BY CATEGORY:

Antibacterials		Antifungals	Anti-TBc	Antivirals	
				Non-HIV	Anti-HIV Drugs
Azithromycin	Linezolid	Amphotericin B	Rifabutin	None	Abacavir
Ceftriaxone	Minocycline	Caspofungin	Rifapentine		Amprenavir;
Chloramphenicol	Moxifloxacin	Itraconazole oral solution			fosamprenavir
Ciprofloxacin XL	Nafcillin	Voriconazole, **po only**			Delavirdine
Clindamycin	Pyrimethamine				Efavirenz
Dirithromycin	Rifaximin				Lopinavir
Doxycycline					Nevirapine

TABLE 18: ANTIMICROBIALS AND HEPATIC DISEASE DOSAGE ADJUSTMENT

The following alphabetical list indicates antibacterials excreted/metabolized by the liver **wherein a dosage adjustment may be indicated** in the presence of hepatic disease. Space precludes details; consult the PDR or package inserts for details. List is **not** all-inclusive:

Amprenavir; fosamprenavir	Efavirenz	Rifabutin
Atazanavir	Indinavir	Rifampin
Caspofungin (Table 11B)	Isoniazid	Rimantadine
Ceftriaxone	Itraconazole solution	Tinidazole
Chloramphenicol	Metronidazole	Voriconazole
Clindamycin	Nafcillin	
Delavirdine	Nevirapine	

TABLE 19: TREATMENT OF CAPD PERITONITIS IN ADULTS[1]
(Periton Dial Intl 20:396, 2000)

EMPIRIC Intraperitoneal Therapy:[2] Culture Results Pending

Drug		Residual Urine Output	
		<100 ml/day	>100 ml/day
Cefazolin +	Can mix in same bag	1 gm/bag, qd	20 mg/kg BW/bag, qd
Ceftazidime		1 gm/bag, qd	20 mg/kg BW/bag, qd

Drug Doses for SPECIFIC Intraperitoneal Therapy—Culture Results Known. NOTE: Few po drugs indicated

Drug	Intermittent Dosing (once/day)		Continuous Dosing (per liter exchange)	
	Anuric	Non-Anuric	Anuric	Non-Anuric
Gentamicin	0.6 mg/kg	↑ dose 25%	MD 8 mg	↑ MD by 25%
Cefazolin	15 mg/kg	20 mg/kg	LD 500 mg, MD 125 mg	LD 500 mg, ↑ MD 25%
Ceftazidime	1000–1500 mg	ND	LD 250 mg, MD 125 mg	ND
Ampicillin	250–500 mg po bid	ND	250–500 mg po bid	ND
Ciprofloxacin	500 mg po bid	ND	LD 50 mg, MD 25 mg	ND
Vancomycin	15–30 mg/kg q5–7 d	↑ dose 25%	MD 30–50 mg/L	↑ MD 25%
Metronidazole	250 mg po bid	ND	250 mg po bid	ND
Amphotericin B	NA	NA	MD 1.5 mg	NA
Fluconazole	200 mg qd	ND	200 mg qd	ND
Itraconazole	100 mg q12h	100 mg q12h	100 mg q12h	100 mg q12h
Amp/sulbactam	2 gm q12h	ND	LD 1.0 gm, MD 100 mg	ND
TMP/SMX	320/1600 mg po q1–2 d	ND	LD 320/1600 mg po, MD 80/400 mg po qd	ND

[1] **All doses IP unless indicated otherwise.**
LD = loading dose, **MD** = maintenance dose, **ND** = no data; **NA** = not applicable—dose as normal renal function. **Anuric** = <100 ml/d, **non-anuric** = >100 ml/d.

[2] Does not provide treatment for MRSA. If Gram-positive cocci on Gram stain, include vancomycin.

TABLE 20A: RECOMMENDED CHILDHOOD AND ADOLESCENT IMMUNIZATION SCHEDULE[1]: UNITED STATES, 2004 *(MMWR 53:Q2, 2004) (For overall recommendations, see MMWR 51:RR-2, 2002)*

VACCINE		Range of recommended ages					Catch-up vaccination			Preadolescent assessment		
	Birth	1 mo	2 mos	4 mos	6 mos	12 mos	15 mos	18 mos	24 mos	4–6 yrs	11–12 yrs	13–18 yrs
Hepatitis B[2,9]	HepB #1 only if mother HBsAg(−)										HepB series	
		HepB #2			HepB #3							
Diphtheria,Tetanus, Pertussis[3,9]			DTaP	DTaP	DTaP		DTaP			DTaP	Td	Td
Haemophilus influenzae Type b			Hib	Hib	Hib	Hib						
Inactivated Polio[9]			IPV	IPV		IPV				IPV		
Measles, Mumps, Rubella[4]						MMR #1				MMR #2	MMR #2	
Varicella[5]						Varicella					Varicella	
Pneumococcal[6]			PCV	PCV	PCV	PCV			PCV		PPV	

————————Vaccines below this line are for selected populations————————

| Hepatitis A[7] | | | | | | | | | | | HepA series | |
| Influenza[8] | | | | | | Influenza (yearly) | | | | | | |

▓▓▓ Indicates age groups that warrant special effort to administer those vaccines not given previously.

[1] ▓▓▓ Indicates age groups that warrant special effort to administer those vaccines not given previously.

[2] **Hepatitis B vaccine (HepB).** *Infants born to HBsAg-positive mothers* should receive hepatitis B vaccine and 0.5 ml hepatitis B immune globulin (HBIG) within 12 hours of birth at separate sites. The 2nd dose is recommended at age 1–2 months. The last dose in the vaccination series should not be administered before age 6 months. These infants should be tested for HBsAg and anti-HBs at 9–15 months of age. *Infants born to mothers whose HBsAg status is unknown* should receive the 1st dose of the HepB vaccine series within 12 hours of birth. Maternal blood should be drawn as soon as possible to determine the mother's HBsAg status; if the HBsAg test is positive, the infant should receive HBIG as soon as possible (no later than age 1 week). The 2nd dose is recommended at age 1–2 months. The last dose in the vaccination series should not be administered before age 6 months.

[3] **Tetanus and diphtheria toxoids (Td).** Subsequent routine Td boosters are recommended every 10 years.

[4] **Measles, mumps, and rubella vaccine (MMR).** No evidence that MMR causes autism *(NEJM 347:1477, 2002).*

[5] **Varicella vaccine.** Primary vaccine failures may occur *(NEJM 347:1909, 2002).* Benefit outweighs risk *(JID 188:945, 2003).*

[6] **Pneumococcal vaccine. Pneumococcal polysaccharide vaccine (PPV)** is recommended in addition to PCV for certain high-risk groups. *See MMWR 49(RR-9):1, 2000.*

[7] **Hepatitis A vaccine.** Hepatitis A vaccine is recommended for children and adolescents and for certain high-risk groups *(MMWR 48(RR-12):1, 1999).*

[8] **Influenza vaccine** *[see MMWR 51(RR-3):1, 2002].* Children aged ≤12 years should receive vaccine in a dosage appropriate for their age (0.25 ml for 6–35 months or 0.5 ml if ≥3 years). Children aged ≤8 yrs who are receiving influenza vaccine for the first time should receive 2 doses separated by at least 4 weeks. A self-limited 48-hr oculorespiratory syndrome post-vaccine recognized *(CID 37:1059 & 1136, 2003).* Trivalent (types A & B) live, cold adapted, attenuated influenza virus vaccine (FluMist™) for intranasal application in subjects 5–49 yrs old approved by U.S. FDA 6/2003.

[9] **DTaP, HepB, IPV** available in combined vaccine (Pediarix™) which is given at 2, 4, and 6 months of age *(MMWR 52:203, 2003).*

Additional information about vaccines, including precautions and contraindications for vaccination and vaccine shortages, is available at www.cdc.gov/nip or at the National Immunization information hotline, 800-232-2522 (English) or 800-232-0233 (Spanish). Copies of the schedule can be obtained at www.cdc.gov/nip/recs/child-schedule.htm. Approved by the **Advisory Committee on Immunization Practices** (www.cdc.gov/nip/acip), the **American Academy of Pediatrics** (www.aap.org), the **American Academy of Family Physicians** (www.aafp.org), and the **Pan American Health Organization** (www.paho.org).

Catch-Up Schedule For Children Aged 4 Months–6 Years Who Start Late Or Are >1 Month Behind

Dose 1 (minimum age)	Minimum interval between doses			
	Dose 1 to dose 2	Dose 2 to dose 3	Dose 3 to dose 4	Dose 4 to dose 5
DTaP (6 wks)	4 wks	4 wks	6 mos.	6 mos.[1]
IPV (6 wks)	4 wks	4 wks	4 wks[2]	
HepB[3] (birth)	4 wks	8 wks (& 16 wks after 1st dose)		
MMR (12 mos.)	4 wks[4]			
Varicella (12 mos.)				
Hib[5] (6 wks)	**4 wks:** if 1st dose given at age <12 mos. **8 wks (as final dose):** if 1st dose given at age 12–24 mos. **No further doses needed:** if 1st dose given at age ≥15 mos.	**4 wks[6]:** if current age <12 mos. **8 wks (as final dose)[6]:** if current age ≥12 mos. & 2nd dose given at age <15 mos. **No further doses needed:** if previous dose given at age ≥15 mos.	**8 wks (as final dose):** this dose only necessary for children aged 12 mos.–5 yrs who received 3 doses before age 12 mos.	
PCV[7] (6 wks)	**4 wks:** if 1st dose given at age <12 mos. & current age <24 mos. **8 wks (as final dose):** if 1st dose given at age ≥12 mos. or current age 24–59 mos. **No further doses needed:** for healthy children if 1st dose given at age ≥24 mos.	**4 wks:** if current age <12 mos. **8 wks (as final dose):** if current age ≥12 mos. **No further doses needed:** for healthy children if previous dose given at age ≥24 mos.	**8 wks (as final dose):** this dose only necessary for children aged 12 mos.–5 yrs who received 3 doses before age 12 mos.	

TABLE 20A (2)

[1] **Diphtheria and tetanus toxoids and acellular pertussis vaccine (DTaP):** The 5th dose is not necessary if the 4th dose was given after the 4th birthday.

[2] **Inactivated polio (IPV):** For children who received an all-IPV or all-OPV series, a 4th dose is not necessary if 3rd dose was given at age ≥4 yrs. If both OPV and IPV were given as part of a series, a total of 4 doses should be given, regardless of the child's current age.

[3] **Hepatitis B vaccine (HepB):** All children and adolescents who have not been vaccinated against hepatitis B should begin the hepatitis B vaccination series during any visit. Providers should make special efforts to immunize children who were born in, or whose parents were born in, areas of the world where hepatitis B virus infection is moderately or highly endemic.

[4] **Measles, mumps, and rubella vaccine (MMR):** The 2nd dose of MMR is recommended routinely at age 4–6 yrs, but may be given earlier if desired.

[5] **Haemophilus influenzae type b (Hib):** Vaccine is not recommended generally for children aged ≥5 years.

[6] **Hib:** If current age is <12 months and the first 2 doses were PRP-OMP [PedVaxHIB® or ComVax (Merck)®], the 3rd (and final) dose should be given at age 12–15 months and at least 8 weeks after the 2nd dose.

[7] **Pneumococcal conjugate vaccine (PCV):** Vaccine is not recommended generally for children aged ≥5 years unless post-splenectomy.

Catch-Up Schedule for Children Aged 7–18 Years Who Start Late or Are >1 Month Behind

Vaccine	Dose 1 to dose 2	Dose 2 to dose 3	Dose 3 to booster dose
		Minimum interval between doses	
Td[1]	4 wks	6 mos.	**6 mos:** if 1st dose given at age <12 mos. & current age <11 yrs **5 yrs:** if 1st dose given at age ≥12 mos. & 3rd dose given at age <7 yrs & current age ≥11 yrs **10 yrs:** if 3rd dose given at age ≥7 yrs
IPV[2]	4 wks	4 wks	*See footnote 2 above*
HepB	4 wks	**8 wks** (& 16 wks after 1st dose)	
MMR	4 wks		
Varicella[3]	4 wks		

[1] **Tetanus toxoid:** For children aged 7–10 years, the interval between the 3rd & booster dose is determined by the age when the 1st dose was given. For adolescents aged 11–18 years, the interval is determined by the age when the 3rd dose was given.

[2] **Inactivated polio (IPV):** Vaccine is not recommended generally for persons aged ≥18 years.

[3] **Varicella:** Give 2-dose series to all susceptible adolescents aged ≥13 years.

Conjugate pneumococcal vaccine (PCV): For all infants <2 years old and high-risk children (e.g., HIV, asplenia, nephrotic syndrome, sickle cell anemia) between 2 and 5 years of age (*Med Lett* 42:25, 2000; *PIDJ* 19:181, 2000; *PIDJ* 19:371ff, 2000). Also approved for prevention of otitis media (*Med Letter* 45:27, 2003) and for cochlear implant recipients (*MMWR* 52:739, 2003). Use of vaccine associated with decline in invasive pneumococcal disease (*NEJM* 348:1737, 2003).

Immunization schedule: (see Schedule, page 138)

Age at first dose (0.5 ml)	Total number of doses	Timing
Infants	4	2, 4, 6, and 12–15 months
7–11 months	3	2 doses at least 4 wks apart; 3rd dose after 1 year birthday, separated from 2nd dose by at least 2 months
12–23 months	2	2 doses at least 2 months apart
≥24 months	1*	

* For children ≥24 months old who are chronically ill or immunosuppressed, ICIP recommends 2 doses of PCV admin. 2 mos. apart, followed by 1 dose of a 23-valent pneumococcal vaccine 2 or 3 mos. after 2nd PCV dose (*MMWR* 50:10, 2001).

TABLE 20B: ADULT IMMUNIZATION IN THE UNITED STATES (MMWR 52:966, 2003)
(Travelers: see Med Letter 38:17, 1996)

Recommended Adult Immunization Schedule—United States, 2003–2004

Vaccine	19–49	50–64	≥65
		Age group (years)	
Tetanus, diphtheria (Td)[1]	1 dose booster every 10 years		
Influenza	1 dose annually for persons with medical or occupational indications or household contacts of persons with indications	1 annual dose	
Pneumococcal (polysaccharide)	1 dose for persons with medical and other indications (1 dose revaccination for immunosuppressive conditions)[2]		1 dose for unvaccinated persons
			1 dose revaccination[2]
Hepatitis B[1]	3 doses (0, 1–2, 4–6 months) for persons with medical, behavioral, occupational, or other indications[3]		
Hepatitis A	2 doses (0, 6–12 months) for persons with medical, behavioral, occupational, or other indications[4]		
Measles, mumps, rubella (MMR)[1]	1 dose if MMR vaccination history is unavailable; 2 doses for persons with occupational, geographic, or other indications[5]		
Varicella[1]	2 doses (0, 4–8 weeks) for persons who are susceptible[6]		
Meningococcal (polysaccharide)	1 dose for persons with medical or other indications[7]		

☐ For all persons in this age group   ▨ For persons with medical/exposure indications   ▧ Catch-up on childhood vaccinations

[1] Covered by the Vaccine Injury Compensation Program.

TABLE 20B (2)

[2] Revaccination with pneumococcal polysaccharide vaccine: 1-time revaccination after 5 years for persons with chronic renal failure or nephrotic syndrome, functional or anatomic asplenia (e.g., sickle cell disease or splenectomy), immunosuppressive conditions (e.g., congenital immunodeficiency, HIV infection, leukemia, lymphoma, multiple myeloma, Hodgkin's disease, generalized malignancy, & organ or bone marrow transplantation), chemotherapy with alkylating agents, antimetabolites, or long-term systemic corticosteroids. For persons aged ≥65 yrs, 1-time revaccination if they were vaccinated ≥5 yrs previously & were aged <65 yrs at the time of primary vaccination [MMWR 46(RR-8), 1997].

[3] Medical indications: hemodialysis pts & pts who receive clotting-factor concentrates. Occupational indications: healthcare workers & public-safety workers who are exposed to blood in the workplace; persons in training in schools of medicine, dentistry, nursing, lab technology, & other allied health professions. Behavioral indications: injection-drug users; persons with more than 1 sex partner during the preceding 6 months, persons with a recently acquired STD, all clients in STD clinics, & men who have sex with men (MSM). Other indications: household contacts & sex partners of persons with chronic hepatitis B virus (HBV) infection, clients & staff of institutions for the developmentally disabled, international travelers who will be located for >6 months in countries with high or intermediate prevalence of chronic HBV infection, & inmates of correctional facilities [MMWR 40(RR-13), 1991].

[4] For the combined hepatitis A-hepatitis B vaccine, use 3 doses at 0, 1, & 6 months. Medical indications: persons with clotting-factor disorders or chronic liver disease. Behavioral indications: MSM & users of injection-drug & noninjecting illegal drugs. Occupational indications: persons working with hepatitis A virus (HAV)-infected primates or with HAV in a research lab setting. Other indications: persons traveling to or working in countries that have high or intermediate endemicity of hepatitis A [MMWR 48(RR-12), 1999].

[5] Measles component: Adults born before 1957 might be considered to be immune to measles. Administer 2 doses of MMR for adults with at least one of the following conditions & without vaccination history: • adults born after 1956; • persons vaccinated with killed-measles vaccine during 1963–1969; • students in post-secondary education institutions; • healthcare workers; • susceptible international travelers to countries in which measles is endemic. Mumps component: 1 dose of MMR should be adequate for protection. Rubella component: Administer 1 dose of MMR to women whose rubella vaccination history is unreliable & counsel women to avoid becoming pregnant for 4 weeks after vaccination. For women of childbearing age, regardless of birth year, determine rubella immunity & counsel women routinely regarding congenital rubella syndrome. Do not vaccinate pregnant women or those planning to become pregnant during the next 4 weeks. If pregnant & susceptible, vaccinate as early in postpartum period as possible [MMWR 47(RR-8), 1998].

[6] Recommended for all persons without evidence of prior varicella zoster virus (VZV) infection; healthcare workers & family contacts of immunocompromised persons; those who live or work in environments in which transmission is likely (e.g., teachers of young children, day care employees, & residents & staff members in institutional settings); persons who live or work in environments in which VZV transmission can occur (e.g., college students, inmates & staff members of correctional institutions, & military personnel); adolescents & adults living in households with children; women who are not pregnant but who might become pregnant in the future; & international travelers who are not immune to infection. Do not vaccinate pregnant women or those planning to become pregnant during the next 4 weeks. If pregnant & susceptible, vaccinate as early in postpartum period as possible [MMWR 45(RR-11), 1996; MMWR 48(RR-6), 1999].

[7] Meningococcal vaccine (quadrivalent polysaccharide for serogroups A, C, Y, & W-135). Medical indications: consider vaccination for adults with terminal complement-component deficiencies or anatomic or functional asplenia. Other indications: travelers to countries in which disease is hyperendemic or epidemic [e.g., the "meningitis belt" of sub-Saharan Africa & Mecca (Saudi Arabia) during Hajj]. Revaccination at 3–5 years might be indicated for persons at high risk for infection (e.g., persons residing in areas in which disease is epidemic). Counsel college freshmen, especially those who live in dormitories, about meningococcal disease & the vaccine so that they can make an educated decision about receiving the vaccination [MMWR 46(RR-5), 1997]. Healthcare providers need not initiate discussion of the meningococcal quadrivalent polysaccharide vaccine as part of routine medical care.

Recommended Immunizations for Adults with Medical Conditions—United States, 2003–2004

Medical condition	Vaccine					
	Tetanus-diphtheria (Td)[1]	Influenza	Pneumococcal (polysaccharide)	Hepatitis B[1]	Hepatitis A	Measles, mumps, rubella (MMR)[1]	Varicella[1]
Pregnancy		A				
Diabetes, heart disease, chronic pulmonary disease, & chronic liver disease, including chronic alcoholism		B	C		D	
Congenital immunodeficiency, leukemia, lymphoma, generalized malignancy, rx with alkylating agents, antimetabolites, radiation, or large amounts of corticosteroids			E				F
Renal failure/end-stage renal disease & recipients of hemodialysis or clotting factor concentrates			E	G		
Asplenia including elective splenectomy & terminal complement-component deficiencies			E,H,I			
HIV infection			E,J			K

☐ For all persons in this age group　▨ For persons with medical/exposure indications　▨ Catch-up on childhood vaccinations　▨ Contraindicated

[1] Covered by the Vaccine Injury Compensation Program

TABLE 20B (3)

A Vaccinate if pregnancy is at 2nd or 3rd trimester during influenza season
B Although chronic liver disease & alcoholism are not indicator conditions for influenza vaccination, administer 1 dose annually if the patient is aged ≥50.
C Asthma is an indicator condition for influenza but not for pneumococcal vaccination.
D For all persons with chronic liver disease
E Revaccinate once if ≥5 years have elapsed since initial vaccination.
F Persons with impaired humoral but not cellular immunity might be vaccinated [MMWR 48(RR-6), 1999].
G Hemodialysis patients: Use special formulation of vaccine (40 µg/ml) or two 1.0 ml 20 µg doses administered at one site. Vaccinate early in the course of renal disease. Assess antibody titers to hepatitis B surface antigen (anti-HBs) levels annually. Administer additional doses if anti-HBs levels decline to <10 mlU/ml.
H Also administer meningococcal vaccine; consider H. influenzae type b vaccine
I Elective splenectomy: Vaccinate ≥2 weeks before surgery.
J Vaccinate as close to diagnosis as possible when CD4 cell counts are highest.
K Withhold MMR or other measles-containing vaccines from HIV-infected persons with evidence of severe immuno-suppression (MMWR 45:603, 1996).

Administration schedule for vaccines: Review package insert for specific product being administered

TABLE 20C/1: ANTI-TETANUS PROPHYLAXIS, WOUND CLASSIFICATION, IMMUNIZATION

WOUND CLASSIFICATION			IMMUNIZATION SCHEDULE				
Clinical Features	Tetanus Prone	Non-Tetanus Prone	History of Tetanus Immunization	Dirty, Tetanus-Prone Wound		Clean, Non-Tetanus Prone Wound	
				Td[1,2]	TIG	Td	TIG
Age of wound	> 6 hours	≤ 6 hours	Unknown or < 3 doses	Yes	Yes	Yes	No
Configuration	Stellate, avulsion	Linear					
Depth	> 1 cm	≤ 1 cm	3 or more doses	No[3]	No	No[4]	No
Mechanism of injury	Missile, crush, burn, frostbite	Sharp wound (glass, knife)					
Devitalized tissue	Present	Absent					
Contaminants (dirt, saliva, etc.)	Present	Absent					

[1] Td = Tetanus & diphtheria toxoids adsorbed (adult)
   TIG = Tetanus immune globulin (human)
[2] Yes if wound >24 hours old.
   For children <7 years, DPT (DT if pertussis vaccine contraindicated);
   For persons ≥7 years, Td preferred to tetanus toxoid alone.
[3] Yes if >5 years since last booster
[4] Yes if >10 years since last booster

(From ACS Bull. 69:22,23, 1984, No. 10)   (From MMWR 39:37, 1990; MMWR 46(SS-2):15, 1997)

TABLE 20C/2: RABIES POST-EXPOSURE PROPHYLAXIS[1]. All wounds should be cleaned immediately and thoroughly with soap and water. This has been shown to protect 90% of experimental animals!
Post-Exposure Prophylaxis Guide, United States, 2000 (CID 30:4, 2000)

Animal Type	Evaluation and Disposition of Animal	Recommendations for Prophylaxis
Dogs, cats, ferrets	Healthy and available for 10-day observation	Don't start unless animal develops sx, then immediately begin HRIG + HDCV or RVA
	Rabid or suspected rabid	Immediate vaccination
	Unknown (escaped)	Consult public health officials
Skunks, raccoons, bats,* foxes, coyotes, most carnivores	Regard as rabid	Immediate vaccination
Livestock, rodents, rabbits; includes hares, squirrels,, hamsters, guinea pigs, gerbils, chipmunks, rats, mice, woodchucks		Almost never require anti-rabies rx. Consult public health officials.

* Most recent cases of human rabies in U.S. due to contact (not bites) with silver-haired bats or rarely big brown bats (MMWR 46:770, 1997; AIM 128:922, 1998). For more detail, see CID 30:4, 2000; JAVMA 219:1687, 2001; CID 37:96, 2003 (travel medicine advisory); Lancet 363:959, 2004.

**Post-Exposure Rabies Immunization Schedule
IF NOT PREVIOUSLY VACCINATED[2]**

Treatment	Regimen[2]
Local wound cleaning	All post-exposure treatment should begin with immediate, thorough cleaning of all wounds with soap and water.
Human rabies immune globulin (HRIG)	20 IU/kg body weight given once on day 0. If anatomically feasible, the full dose should be infiltrated around the wound(s), the rest should be administered IM in the gluteal area. HRIG should **not** be administered in the **same syringe, or** into the **same anatomical site** as vaccine, or more than 7 days after the initiation of vaccine. Because HRIG may partially suppress active production of antibody, no more than the recommended dose should be given.[3]
Vaccine	Human diploid cell vaccine (HDCV), rabies vaccine adsorbed (RVA), or purified chick embryo cell vaccine (PCEC) 1.0 ml **IM (deltoid area[4])**, one each on days 0, 3, 7, 14, & 28.

TABLE 20C (2)

IF PREVIOUSLY VACCINATED[5]	
Treatment	**Regimen[2]**
Local wound cleaning	All post-exposure treatment should begin with immediate, thorough cleaning of all wounds with soap and water.
HRIG	HRIG should **not** be administered
Vaccine	HDCV, RVA or PCEC, 1.0 ml **IM** (**deltoid area[4]**), one each on days 0 and 3

CORRECT VACCINE ADMINISTRATION SITES

Age Group	Administration Site
Children and adults	**DELTOID[4]** only (**NEVER** in gluteus)
Infants and young children	Outer aspect of thigh (anterolateral thigh) may be used (**NEVER** in gluteus)

[1] From *MMWR* 48:RR-1, 1999; *CID* 30:4, 2000; B.T. Matyas, Mass. Dept. of Public Health
[2] These regimens are applicable for all age groups, including children.
[3] In most reported post-exposure treatment failures, only identified deficiency was failure to infiltrate wound(s) with HRIG (*CID* 22:228, 1996). However, several failures reported from SE Asia in patients in whom WHO protocol followed (*CID* 28:143, 1999).
[4] The **deltoid** area is the **only** acceptable site of vaccination for adults and older children. For infants and young children, the outer aspect of the thigh (anterolateral thigh) may be used. Vaccine should **NEVER** be administered in the gluteal area.
[5] Any person with a history of pre-exposure vaccination with HDCV, RVA, PCEC; prior post-exposure prophylaxis with HDCV, RVA, PCEC; or previous vaccination with any other type of rabies vaccine and a documented history of antibody response to the prior vaccination

TABLE 21: SELECTED DIRECTORY OF RESOURCES

ORGANIZATION	PHONE/FAX	WEBSITE(S)
ANTIPARASITIC DRUGS and PARASITOLOGY INFORMATION (*CID* 37:694, 2003)		
CDC	Weekdays: 404-639-3670	www.cdc.gov/ncidod/srp/drugs/drug-service.html
	Evenings, weekends, holidays: 404-639-2888	
DPDx: Lab ID of parasites		www.dpd.cdc.gov/dpdx/default.htm
Gorgas Course Tropical Medicine		http://info.dom.uab.edu/gorgas
Panorama Compound. Pharm.	800-247-9767/818-787-7256	www.uniquerx.com
Parasites and Health		www.dpd.cdc.gov/dpdx/HTML/Para_Health.htm
BIOTERRORISM		
Centers for Disease Control & Prevention	770-488-7100	www.bt.cdc.gov
Infectious Diseases Society of America	703-299-0200/ 703-299-0204	www.idsociety.org
Johns Hopkins Center Civilian Biodefense		www.jhsph.edu
Center for Biosecurity of the Univ. of Pittsburgh Med. Center		www.upmc-biosecurity.org
US Army Medical Research Institute of Inf. Dis.		www.usamriid.army.mil
HEPATITIS C (*CID* 35:754, 2002)		
CDC		www.cdc.gov/ncidod/diseases/hepatitis/C
Individual		http://hepatitis-central.com
Medscape		www.medscape.com
HIV		
General		
HIV InSite		http://hivinsite.ucsf.edu
Johns Hopkins AIDS Service		www.hopkins-aids.edu
Drug Interactions		
Johns Hopkins AIDS Service		www.hopkins-aids.edu
Liverpool HIV Pharm. Group		www.hiv-druginteractions.org
Other		http://AIDS.medscape.com
Prophylaxis/Treatment of Opportunistic Infections; HIV Treatment		www.aidsinfo.nih.gov
IMMUNIZATIONS (*CID* 36:355, 2003)		
CDC, Natl. Immunization Program	404-639-8200	www.cdc.gov/nip
FDA, Vaccine Adverse Events	800-822-7967	www.fda.gov/cber/vaers/vaers.htm
National Network Immunization Info.	877-341-6644/ 703-299-0204	www.immunizationinfo.org
Influenza vaccine, CDC	404-639-8200	cdc.gov/nip/flu
Institute for Vaccine Safety		www.vaccinesafety.edu
OCCUPATIONAL EXPOSURE, BLOOD-BORNE PATHOGENS (HIV, HEPATITIS B & C)		
National Clinicians' Post-Exposure Hotline	888-448-4911	www.ucsf.edu/hivcntr
Q-T$_c$ INTERVAL PROLONGATION BY DRUGS		www.qtdrugs.org
SEXUALLY TRANSMITTED DISEASES		www.cdc.gov/std/treatment/TOC2002TG.htm
		Slides: www.hc-sc.gc.ca/pphb-dgspsp/std-mts
TRAVELERS' INFO: Immunizations, Malaria Prophylaxis, More		
Amer. Soc. Trop. Med. & Hyg.		www.astmh.org
CDC, general	877-394-8747/888-232-3299	www.cdc.gov/travel/index.htm
CDC, Malaria:		www.cdc.gov/ncidod/dpd/parasites/malaria/ default.htm
Prophylaxis	888-232-3228	www.cdc.gov/travel
Treatment	770-488-7788	www.who.int/health_topics/malaria
MD Travel Health		www.mdtravelhealth.com
Pan American Health Organization		www.paho.org
World Health Organization (WHO)	(41-22)-791-2122/ (00-41-22)-691-0746	www.who.int/home-page
VACCINE AND IMMUNIZATION RESOURCES (*CID* 36:355, 2003)		
American Academy of Pediatrics		www.cispimmunize.org
CDC, National Immunization Program		www.cdc.gov/nip
National Network for Immunization Information		www.immunizationinfo.org

TABLE 22: ANTI-INFECTIVE DRUG-DRUG INTERACTIONS

Significance/Certainty: ± = theory/anecdotal; + = of probable importance; ++ = of definite importance

ANTI-INFECTIVE AGENT (A)	OTHER DRUG (B)	EFFECT	SIGNIFICANCE/CERTAINTY
Amantadine (Symmetrel)	Alcohol	↑ CNS effects	+
	Anticholinergic and anti-Parkinson agents (ex. Artane, scopolamine)	↑ effect of B: dry mouth, ataxia, blurred vision, slurred speech, toxic psychosis	+
	Trimethoprim	↑ levels of A & B	+
	Digoxin	↑ levels of B	±
Aminoglycosides—parenteral (amikacin, gentamicin, kanamycin, netilmicin, sisomicin, streptomycin, tobramycin) *NOTE: Capreomycin is an aminoglycoside, used as alternative drug to treat mycobacterial infections.*	Amphotericin B	↑ nephrotoxicity	++
	Cis platinum (Platinol)	↑ nephro & ototoxicity	+
	Cyclosporine	↑ nephrotoxicity	+
	Neuromuscular blocking agents	↑ apnea or respiratory paralysis	+
	Loop diuretics (e.g., furosemide)	↑ ototoxicity	++
	NSAIDs	↑ nephrotoxicity	+
	Non-polarizing muscle relaxants	↑ apnea	+
	Radiographic contrast	↑ nephrotoxicity	+
	Vancomycin	↑ nephrotoxicity	+
Aminoglycosides—oral (kanamycin, neomycin)	Oral anticoagulants (dicumarol, phenindione, warfarin)	↑ prothrombin time	+
Amphotericin B and ampho B lipid formulations	Antineoplastic drugs	↑ nephrotoxicity risk	+
	Digitalis	↑ toxicity of B if K⁺ ↓	+
	Nephrotoxic drugs: aminoglycosides, cidofovir, cyclosporine, foscarnet, pentamidine	↑ nephrotoxicity of A	++
Ampicillin, amoxicillin	Allopurinol	↑ frequency of rash	++
Amprenavir and fosamprenavir	Antiretrovirals—see Table 22B & C		
	Contraceptives, oral	↓ levels of A; use other contraception	++
	Lovastatin/simvastatin	↑ **levels of B—avoid**	++
	Methadone	↓ levels of A & B	++
	Rifabutin	↑ levels of B (↓ dose by 50–75%)	++
	Rifampin	↓ **levels of A—avoid**	++
Atazanavir	See protease inhibitors and Table 22B & C		
Atovaquone	Rifampin (perhaps rifabutin)	↓ serum levels of A; ↑ levels of B	+
	Metoclopramide	↓ levels of A	+
	Tetracycline	↓ levels of A	++

Azole Antifungal Agents¹ [**Flu** = fluconazole, **Itr** = itraconazole, **Ket** = ketoconazole, **Vor** = voriconazole, + = occurs, **blank space** = either studied & no interaction OR no data found (may be in pharm. co. databases)]

Flu	Itr	Ket	Vor			
+	+			Amitriptyline	↑ levels of B	+
+	+	+	+	Calcium channel blockers	↑ levels of B	++
		+	+	Carbamazepine (vori contra-indicated)	↓ levels of A	++
+	+	+	+	Cyclosporine	↑ levels of B, ↑ risk of nephrotoxicity	+
	+	+		Didanosine	↓ absorption of A	+
	+	+		H₂ blockers, antacids, sucralfate	↓ absorption of A	+
+	+	+	+	Hydantoins (phenytoin, Dilantin)	↑ levels of B, ↓ levels of A	++
	+	+		Isoniazid	↓ levels of A	+
		+	+	Lovastatin/simvastatin	Rhabdomyolysis reported; ↑ levels of B	++
+	+	+	+	Midazolam/triazolam, po	↑ levels of B	++
+	+	+	+	Oral anticoagulants	↑ effect of B	++
+			+	Oral hypoglycemics	↑ levels of B	++
		+	+	Pimozide	↑ levels of B	++
	+	+	?	Protease inhibitors	↑ levels of B	++
	+	+	+	Proton pump inhibitors	↓ absorption of A, ↑ levels of B	+
+	+	+	+	Rifampin/rifabutin (vori contraindicated)	↑ levels of B, ↓ serum levels of A	++
			+	Sirolimus (vori contraindicated)	↑ levels of B	++
+		+		Tacrolimus	↑ levels of B with toxicity	++
+	+			Theophyllines	↑ levels of B	+
+	+		+	Trazodone	↑ levels of B	++
+				Zidovudine	↑ levels of B	+
Caspofungin				Cyclosporine	↑ levels of A	++
				Tacrolimus	↓ levels of A	++
				Carbamazepine, dexamethasone, efavirenz, nelfinavir, nevirapine, phenytoin, rifampin	↓ levels of A; ↑ dose of caspofungin to 70 mg/d	++
Cephalosporins with methyltetrathiozole-thiol side-chain				Oral anticoagulants (dicumarol, warfarin), heparin, thrombolytic agents, platelet aggregation inhibitors	↑ effects of B, bleeding	+
Chloramphenicol				Hydantoins	↑ toxicity of B, nystagmus, ataxia	++
				Iron salts, Vitamin B12	↓ response to B	++
				Protease inhibitors—HIV	↑ levels of A & B	++

¹ Major interactions given; unusual or minor interactions manifest as toxicity of non-azole drug due to ↑ serum levels: Caffeine (Flu), digoxin (Itr), felodipine (Itr), fluoxetine (Itr), indinavir (Ket), lovastatin/simvastatin (Ket), quinidine (Ket), tricyclics (Flu), vincristine (Itr), and ↓ effectiveness of oral contraceptives.

TABLE 22 (2)

ANTI-INFECTIVE AGENT (A)	OTHER DRUG (B)	EFFECT	SIGNIFICANCE/CERTAINTY
Clindamycin (Cleocin)	Kaolin	↓ absorption of A	+
	Muscle relaxants, e.g., atracurium, baclofen, diazepam	↑ frequency/duration of respiratory paralysis	+
Cycloserine	Ethanol	↑ frequency of seizures	+
	INH, ethionamide	↑ frequency of drowsiness/dizziness	+
Dapsone	Didanosine	↓ absorption of A	+
	Oral contraceptives	↓ effectiveness of B	+
	Pyrimethamine	↑ in marrow toxicity	+
	Rifampin/Rifabutin	↓ serum levels of A	+
	Trimethoprim	↑ levels of A & B (methemoglobinemia)	+
	Zidovudine	May ↑ marrow toxicity	+
Delavirdine (Rescriptor)	See non-nucleoside reverse transcriptase inhibitors (NNRTIs) and Table 22C		
Didanosine (ddI) (Videx)	Cisplatin, dapsone, INH, metronidazole, nitrofurantoin, stavudine, vincristine, zalcitabine	↑ risk of peripheral neuropathy	+
	Ethanol, lamivudine, pentamidine	↑ risk of pancreatitis	+
	Fluoroquinolones	↓ absorption 2° to chelation	+
	Drugs that need low pH for absorption: dapsone, indinavir, itra/ketoconazole, pyrimethamine, rifampin, trimethoprim	↓ absorption	+
	Methadone	↓ levels of A	++
	Ribavirin	↑ levels ddI metabolite—**avoid**	++
	Tenofovir	↑ levels of A **(reduce dose of A)**	++
Doxycycline	Aluminum, bismuth, iron, Mg⁺⁺	↓ absorption of A	+
	Barbiturates, hydantoins	↓ serum t/2 of A	+
	Carbamazepine (Tegretol)	↓ serum t/2 of A	+
	Digoxin	↑ serum levels of B	+
	Warfarin	↑ activity of B	++
Efavirenz (Sustiva)	See non-nucleoside reverse transcriptase inhibitors (NNRTIs) and Table 22C		
Ertapenem (Invanz)	Probenecid	↑ levels of A	++
Ethambutol (Myambutol)	Aluminum salts (includes didanosine buffer)	↓ absorption of A & B	+

Fluoroquinolones (*Cipro* = ciprofloxacin; *Gati* = gatifloxacin; *Gemi* = gemifloxacin; *Levo* = levofloxacin; *Lome* = lomefloxacin; *Moxi* = moxifloxacin; *Oflox* = ofloxacin)

NOTE: Blank space = either studied and no interaction OR no data found (pharm. co. may have data).

Cipro	Gati¹	Gemi¹	Levo	Lome	Moxi¹	Oflox	OTHER DRUG (B)	EFFECT	SIGNIFICANCE/CERTAINTY
	+		+		+	+	**Antiarrhythmics (procainamide, amiodarone)**	↑ Q-T interval (torsade)	++
+	+		+	+	+	+	Insulin, oral hypoglycemics	↑ & ↓ blood sugar	++
+							Caffeine	↑ levels of B	+
+			+				Cimetidine	↑ levels of A	+
+			+				Cyclosporine	↑ levels of B	±
+	+		+	+	+	+	Didanosine	↓ absorption of A	++
+	+	+	+	+	+	+	**Cations: Al⁺⁺⁺, Ca⁺⁺, Fe⁺⁺, Mg⁺⁺, Zn⁺⁺ (antacids, vitamins, dairy products), citrate/citric acid**	↓ absorption of A (some variability between drugs)	++
+							Foscarnet	↑ risk of seizures	+
+							Methadone	↑ levels of B	++
+			+			+	NSAIDs	↑ risk CNS stimulation/seizures	++
+							Phenytoin	↑ or ↓ levels of B	+
+			+			+	Probenecid	↓ renal clearance of A	+
+	+	+	+	+		+	Sucralfate	↓ absorption of A	++
+			+	+			Theophylline	↑ levels of B	++
+						+	Warfarin	↑ prothrombin time	+

ANTI-INFECTIVE AGENT (A)	OTHER DRUG (B)	EFFECT	SIGNIFICANCE/CERTAINTY
Foscarnet (Foscavir)	Ciprofloxacin	↑ risk of seizures	+
	Nephrotoxic drugs: aminoglycosides, ampho B, cis-platinum, cyclosporine	↑ risk of nephrotoxicity	+
	Pentamidine IV	↑ risk of severe hypocalcemia	++
Ganciclovir (Cytovene)	Imipenem	↑ risk of seizures reported	+
	Probenecid	↑ levels of A	+
	Zidovudine	↓ levels of A, ↑ levels of B	+
Gentamicin	See Aminoglycosides—parenteral		
Halofantrine	Mefloquine	Additive effect: prolong. Q-T interval	++ (avoid)
Indinavir	See protease inhibitors and Table 22B & C		
Isoniazid	**Alcohol, rifampin**	**↑ risk of hepatic injury**	++
	Aluminum salts	↓ absorption (take fasting)	++
	Carbamazepine, phenytoin	↑ levels of B with nausea, vomiting, nystagmus, ataxia	++
	Itraconazole, ketoconazole	↓ levels of B	+
	Oral hypoglycemics	↓ effects of B	+
Lamivudine	Zalcitabine	**Mutual interference—do not combine**	++

¹ Neither Gati, Gemi, nor Moxi interacts with Ca⁺⁺

TABLE 22 (3)

ANTI-INFECTIVE AGENT (A)	OTHER DRUG (B)	EFFECT	SIGNIFICANCE/CERTAINTY
Linezolid (Zyvox)	Adrenergic agents	Risk of hypertension	++
	Aged, fermented, pickled or smoked foods — ↑ tyramine	Risk of hypertension	+
	Serotonergic drugs (SSRIs)	Risk of serotonin syndrome	+
Lopinavir	See protease inhibitors		

Macrolides [**Ery** = erythromycin, **Azi** = azithromycin, **Clr** = clarithromycin; **Dir** = dirithromycin, + = occurs, **blank space** = either studied and no interaction OR no data (pharm. co. may have data)]

Ery	Dir	Azi	Clr	OTHER DRUG (B)	EFFECT	SIGNIFICANCE/CERTAINTY
+	+		+	Carbamazepine	↑ serum levels of B, nystagmus, nausea, vomiting, ataxia	++ (avoid with erythro)
+			+	Cimetidine, **ritonavir**	↑ levels of B	
+			+	Clozapine	↑ serum levels of B, CNS toxicity	+
+			+	Corticosteroids	↑ effects of B	+
+	+	+	+	Cyclosporine	↑ serum levels of B with toxicity	+
+	+	+	+	Digoxin, digitoxin	↑ serum levels of B (10% of cases)	+
			+	Efavirenz	↓ levels of A	++
+			+	Ergot alkaloids	↑ levels of B	++
+	+		+	Lovastatin/simvastatin	↑ levels of B; rhabdomyolysis	++
+			+	Midazolam, triazolam	↑ levels of B, ↑ sedative effects	+
+			+	Phenytoin	↑ levels of B	+
+	+	+	+	Pimozide	↑ Q-T interval	++
+			+	Rifampin, rifabutin	↓ levels of A	+
+			+	Tacrolimus	↑ levels of B	++
+			+	Theophyllines	↑ serum levels of B with nausea, vomiting, seizures, apnea	++
+	+		+	Valproic acid	↑ levels of B	+
+		+	+	Warfarin	May ↑ prothrombin time	+
+			+	Zidovudine	↓ levels of B	+
Mefloquine				ß-adrenergic blockers, calcium channel blockers, quinidine, quinine	↑ arrhythmias	+
				Divalproex, valproic acid	↓ level of B with seizures	++
				Halofantrine	Q-T prolongation	++ (avoid)
Methenamine mandelate or hippurate				Acetazolamide, sodium bicarbonate, thiazide diuretics	↓ antibacterial effect 2° to ↑ urine pH	++
Metronidazole				Alcohol	Disulfiram-like reaction	+
				Cyclosporin	↑ levels of B	++
				Disulfiram (Antabuse)	Acute toxic psychosis	+
				Lithium	↑ levels of B	++
				Oral anticoagulants	↑ anticoagulant effect	++
				Phenobarbital, hydantoins	↑ levels of B	++
Nelfinavir				See protease inhibitors and Table 22B & C		
Nevirapine (Viramune)				See non-nucleoside reverse transcriptase inhibitors (NNRTIs) and Table 22C		
Nitrofurantoin				Antacids	↓ absorption of A	+

Non-nucleoside reverse transcriptase inhibitors (NNRTIs): For interactions with protease inhibitors, see Table 22C.
Del = delavirdine, **Efa** = efavirenz, **Nev** = nevirapine

Del	Efa	Nev	Co-administration contraindicated:		SIGNIFICANCE/CERTAINTY
+			Anticonvulsants: carbamazepine, phenobarbital, phenytoin		++
+			Antimycobacterials: rifabutin, rifampin		++
+			Antipsychotics: pimozide		++
+	+		Benzodiazepines: alprazolam, midazolam, triazolam		++
+			Ergotamine		++
+	+		HMG-CoA inhibitors (statins): lovastatin, simvastatin		++
+			St. John's wort		++
			Dose change needed:		
+			Amphetamines	↑ levels of B—caution	++
+			Antiarrhythmics: amiodarone, lidocaine, others	↓ or ↑ levels of B—caution	++
+	+	+	Anticonvulsants: carbamazepine, phenobarbital, phenytoin	↓ levels of A and/or B	++
	±	+	Antifungals: itraconazole, ketoconazole	Potential ↓ levels of B	++
+			Antipsychotics: pimozide		++
+			Antirejection drugs: cyclosporine, rapamycin, sirolimus, tacrolimus	↑ levels of B	++
		+	Benzodiazepines: as above	↑ levels of B	++
+		+	Calcium channel blockers	↑ levels of B	++
+		+	Clarithromycin	↑ levels of B metabolite	++
+		+	Cyclosporine	↑ levels of B	++
+		+	Dexamethasone	↓ levels of A	++
+	+	+	Sildenafil, vardenafil, tadalafil	↑ levels of B	++
+		+	Fentanyl, methadone	↑ levels of B	++
+			Gastric acid suppression: antacids, H-2 blockers, proton pump inhibitors	↓ levels of A	++
+			HMG-CoA inhibitors (statins)		
	+	+	Methadone	↓ levels of B	++

TABLE 22 (4)

ANTI-INFECTIVE AGENT (A)	OTHER DRUG (B)	EFFECT	SIGNIFICANCE/ CERTAINTY

Non-nucleoside reverse transcriptase inhibitors (NNRTIs) *(continued)*: For interactions with protease inhibitors, see Table 22B. **Del** = delavirdine, **Efa** = efavirenz, **Nev** = nevirapine

Del	Efa	Nev	Co-administration contraindicated:		
+	+	+	Oral contraceptives	↑ or ↓ levels of B	++
+	+	+	Protease inhibitors—see Table 22C		
+	+	+	Rifabutin, rifampin	↑ or ↓ levels of rifabutin; ↓ levels of A—**caution**	++
+	+	+	St. John's wort	↓ levels of B	
+		+	Warfarin	↑ levels of B	++

Pentamidine, IV	Amphotericin B	↑ risk of nephrotoxicity	+
	Foscarnet	↑ risk of hypocalcemia	+
	Pancreatitis-associated drugs, e.g., alcohol, valproic acid	↑ risk of pancreatitis	+

Piperacillin	Cefoxitin	Antagonism vs pseudomonas	++

Primaquine	Chloroquine, dapsone, INH, probenecid, quinine, sulfonamides, TMP/SMX, others	↑ risk of hemolysis in G6PD-deficient patients	

Protease Inhibitors—Anti-HIV Drugs. (**Ampren** = amprenavir & fosamprenavir, **Atazan** = atazanavir, **Indin** = indinavir, **Lopin** = lopinavir, **Nelfin** = nelfinavir, **Riton** = ritonavir; **Saquin** = saquinavir). For interactions with antiretrovirals, see Table 22B & C

Only a partial list—check package insert
Also see http://aidsinfo.nih.gov

Atazan	Ampren	Indin	Lopin	Nelfin	Riton	Saquin		EFFECT	
							Analgesics:		
					+		1. Alfentanil, fentanyl, hydrocodone, tramadol	↑ levels of B	+
		+			+		2. Codeine, hydromorphone, morphine, methadone	↓ levels of B	+
+	+	+	+	+	+	+	**Anti-arrhythmics: amiodarone, lidocaine, mexiletine, flecainide**	↑ levels of B	+
+		+	+		+		**Anticonvulsants: carbamazepine, clonazepam, phenytoin, phenobarbital**	↓ levels of A, ↑ levels of B	++
+	+	+			+		Antidepressants, all tricyclic	↑ levels of B	+
+					+		Antidepressants, all other	↑ levels of B	+
					+		**Antihistamine: Loratadine**	↑ levels of B	++
		+					Atovaquone	↓ levels of B	+
+	+	+	+	+	+	+	**Benzodiazepines, e.g., diazepam**	↑ **levels of B—do not use**	++
					+		Beta blockers: Metoprolol, pindolol, propranolol, timolol	↑ levels of B	+
+	+	+	+	+	+	+	Calcium channel blockers (all)	↑ levels of B	++
					+	+	Clarithromycin, erythromycin	↑ levels of B if renal impairment	+
+		+		+	+		Contraceptives, oral	↓ levels of B	++
		+			+		Corticosteroids: prednisone, dexamethasone	↓ levels of A, ↑ levels of B	+
+	+	+	+	+	+	+	Cyclosporine	↑ levels of B, monitor levels	+
+	+	+	+	+	+	+	Ergot derivatives	↑ **levels of B—do not use**	++
					+		Erythromycin, clarithromycin	↑ levels of A & B	+
		+				+	Grapefruit juice (>200 ml/day)	↓ indinavir & ↑ saquinavir levels	++
+	+	+	+	+	+	+	H2 receptor antagonists	↓ levels of A, ↑ levels of B	++
+	+	+	+	+	+	+	HMG-CoA reductase inhibitors (statins): lovastatin, simvastatin	↑ **levels of B—do not use**	++
+							Irinotecan	↑ **levels of B—do not use**	++
	+	+	+	+			Ketoconazole, itraconazole, ? vori	↑ levels of A, ↑ levels of B	+
+		+		+	+		Metronidazole	Poss. disulfiram reaction, alcohol	+
+	+	+	+	+	+	+	Pimozide	↑ **levels of B—do not use**	++
+	+	+	+	+	+	+	Proton pump inhibitors	↓ levels of A	++
+	+	+	+	+	+	+	Rifampin, rifabutin	↑ levels of A, ↑ levels of B	++ (avoid)
+	+	+	+	+	+	+	Sildenafil (Viagra)	Varies, some ↑ & some ↓ levels of B	++
+							**St. John's wort**	↓ **levels of A—add ritonavir**	++
		+	+	+			Tenofovir	↓ levels of B—add ritonavir	++
		+		+	+		Theophylline	↓ levels of B	+
+	+		+		+		Warfarin	↑ levels of B	+

Pyrazinamide	INH, rifampin	May ↑ risk of hepatotoxicity	±

Pyrimethamine	Lorazepam	↑ risk of hepatotoxicity	+
	Sulfonamides, TMP/SMX	↑ risk of marrow suppression	+
	Zidovudine	↑ risk of marrow suppression	+

Quinine	Digoxin	↑ digoxin levels; ↑ toxicity	++
	Mefloquine	↑ arrhythmias	+
	Oral anticoagulants	↑ prothrombin time	++

TABLE 22 (5)

ANTI-INFECTIVE AGENT (A)	OTHER DRUG (B)	EFFECT	SIGNIFICANCE/ CERTAINTY
Quinupristin/ dalfopristin (Synercid)	Anti-HIV drugs: NNRTIs & PIs	↑ levels of B	+ +
	Antineoplastic: vincristine, docetaxel, paclitaxel	↑ levels of B	+ +
	Calcium channel blockers	↑ levels of B	+ +
	Carbamazepine	↑ levels of B	+ +
	Cyclosporine, tacrolimus	↑ levels of B	+ +
	Lidocaine	↑ levels of B	+ +
	Methylprednisolone	↑ levels of B	+ +
	Midazolam, diazepam	↑ levels of B	+ +
	Statins	↑ levels of B	+ +
Ribavirin	Didanosine	↑ levels of B → toxicity—avoid	+ +
	Stavudine	↓ levels of B	+ +
	Zidovudine	↓ levels of B	+ +
Rifamycins (rifampin, rifabutin) *See footnote for less severe or less common interactions*[1] Ref.: *ArIM* 162:985, 2002	Al OH, ketoconazole, PZA	↓ levels of A	+
	Atovaquone	↑ levels of A, ↓ levels of B	+
	Beta adrenergic blockers (metoprolol, propranolol)	↓ effect of B	+
	Clarithromycin	↑ levels of A, ↓ levels of B	+ +
	Corticosteroids	↑ replacement requirement of B	+ +
	Cyclosporine	↓ effect of B	+ +
	Delavirdine	**↑ levels of A, ↓ levels of B—avoid**	+ +
	Digoxin	↓ levels of B	+ +
	Disopyramide	↓ levels of B	+ +
	Fluconazole	↓ levels of A[1]	+
	Amprenavir, indinavir, nelfinavir, ritonavir	↑ levels of A (↓ dose of A), ↓ levels of B	+ +
	INH	Converts INH to toxic hydrazine	+ +
	Itraconazole[2], ketoconazole	↓ levels of B, ↑ levels of A[2]	+ +
	Methadone	↓ serum levels (withdrawal)	+
	Nevirapine	**↓ levels of B—avoid**	+ +
	Oral anticoagulants	Suboptimal anticoagulation	+ +
	Oral contraceptives	↓ effectiveness; spotting, pregnancy	+
	Phenytoin	↓ levels of B	+
	Protease inhibitors	**↑ levels of A, ↓ levels of B— CAUTION**	+ +
	Quinidine	↓ effect of B	+
	Sulfonylureas	↓ hypoglycemic effect	+
	Tacrolimus	↓ levels of B	+ +
	Theophylline	↓ levels of B	+
	TMP/SMX	↑ levels of A	+
	Tocainide	↓ effect of B	+
Rimantadine	*See Amantadine*		
Ritonavir	*See protease inhibitors and Table 22B & C*		
Saquinavir	*See protease inhibitors and Table 22B & C*		
Stavudine	Dapsone, INH	May ↑ risk of peripheral neuropathy	±
	Ribavirin	↓ levels of A—avoid	+ +
	Zidovudine	Mutual interference—do not combine	+ +
Sulfonamides	Cyclosporine	↓ cyclosporine levels	+
	Methotrexate	↑ antifolate activity	+
	Oral anticoagulants	↑ prothrombin time; bleeding	+
	Phenobarbital, rifampin	↓ levels of A	+
	Phenytoin	↑ levels of B; nystagmus, ataxia	+
	Sulfonylureas	↑ hypoglycemic effect	+
Telithromycin (Ketek)	Carbamazine	↓ levels of A	+ +
	Digoxin	↑ levels of B—do digoxin levels	+ +
	Ergot alkaloids	**↑ levels of B—avoid**	+ +
	Itraconazole; ketoconazole	↑ levels of A; no dose change	+
	Metoprolol	↑ levels of B	+ +
	Midazolam	↑ levels of B	+ +
	Phenobarb, phenytoin	↓ levels of A	+ +
	Pimozide	**↑ levels of B; QT prolongation— AVOID**	+ +
	Rifampin	**↓ levels of A—avoid**	+ +
	Simvastatin & other "statins"	↑ levels of B	+ +
	Sotalol	↓ levels of B	+ +
Tenofovir	Atazanavir	↓ levels of B—add ritonavir	+ +
	Didanosine (ddl)	**↑ levels of B (reduce dose)**	+ +
Terbinafine	Cimetidine	↑ levels of A	+
	Phenobarbital, rifampin	↓ levels of A	+

[1] The following is a partial list of drugs with rifampin-induced ↑ metabolism and hence lower than anticipated serum levels: ACE inhibitors, dapsone, diazepam, digoxin, diltiazem, doxycycline, fluconazole, fluvastatin, haloperidol, nifedipine, progestins, triazolam, tricyclics, voriconazole, zidovudine
[2] Up to 4 weeks may be required after RIF discontinued to achieve detectable serum itra levels; ↑ levels associated with uveitis or polymyolysis

TABLE 22 (6)

ANTI-INFECTIVE AGENT (A)	OTHER DRUG (B)	EFFECT	SIGNIFICANCE/ CERTAINTY
Tetracyclines	*See Doxycycline, plus:*		
	Atovaquone	↓ levels of B	+
	Digoxin	↑ toxicity of B (may persist several months—up to 10% pts)	++
	Methoxyflurane	↑ toxicity; polyuria, renal failure	+
	Sucralfate	↓ absorption of A (separate by ≥2 hrs)	+
Thiabendazole	Theophyllines	↑ serum theophylline, nausea	+
Tinidazole (Tindamax)	*See Metronidazole—similar entity, expect similar interactions*		
Tobramycin	*See Aminoglycosides*		
Trimethoprim	Amantadine, dapsone, digoxin, methotrexate, procainamide, zidovudine	↑ serum levels of B	++
	Potassium-sparing diuretics	↑ serum K⁺	++
	Thiazide diuretics	↓ serum Na⁺	+
Trimethoprim/Sulfa-methoxazole	Azathioprine	Reports of leukopenia	+
	Cyclosporine	↓ levels of B, ↑ serum creatinine	+
	Loperamide	↑ levels of B	+
	Methotrexate	Enhanced marrow suppression	++
	Oral contraceptives, pimozide, and 6-mercaptopurine	↓ effect of B	+
	Phenytoin	↑ levels of B	+
	Rifampin	↑ levels of B	+
	Warfarin	↑ activity of B	+
Vancomycin	Aminoglycosides	↑ frequency of nephrotoxicity	++
Zalcitabine (ddC) (HIVID)	Valproic acid, pentamidine (IV), alcohol, lamivudine	↑ pancreatitis risk	+
	Cisplatin, INH, metronidazole, vincristine, nitrofurantoin, d4T, dapsone	↑ risk of peripheral neuropathy	+
Zidovudine (ZDV) (Retrovir)	Atovaquone, fluconazole, metha-done	↑ levels of A	+
	Clarithromycin	↓ levels of A	±
	Indomethacin	↑ levels of ZDV toxic metabolite	+
	Nelfinavir	↓ levels of A	++
	Probenecid, TMP/SMX	↑ levels of A	+
	Ribavirin	↓ **levels of A—avoid**	++
	Rifampin/rifabutin	↓ levels of A	++

TABLE 22B: DRUG-DRUG INTERACTIONS BETWEEN PROTEASE INHIBITORS
(Adapted from Guidelines for the Use of Antiretroviral Agents in HIV-Infected Adults & Adolescents; see *www.aidsinfo.nih.gov*)

NAME (Abbreviation, Trade Name)	Amprenavir (APV, Agenerase)	Atazanavir (ATV, Reyataz)	Fosamprenavir (FOS-APV, Lexiva)	Indinavir (IDV, Crixivan)	Lopinavir/Ritonavir (LP/R, Kaletra)	Nelfinavir (NFV, Viracept)	Ritonavir (RTV, Norvir)	Saquinavir (SQV, Fortovase/Invirase)
Amprenavir (APV, Agenerase)		Do not co-administer; additive ↑ in bilirubin		Levels: APV AUC↑ 33%. Doses: standard	Dose: APV 750 mg bid, LP/R either standard or ↑ to 533/133 mg bid	Levels: APV AUC↑ ↑. Doses: inadequate data	Dose: 600/100 mg bid and or 1200/200 mg qd	Levels: APV AUC↓ 32%. Dose: Insufficient data
Atazanavir (ATV, Reyataz)	Do not co-administer; additive ↑ in bilirubin			Do not co-administer; risk of additive ↑ in indirect bilirubin			ATV/RTV 300/100 mg qd	SQV (Invirase) 1200 mg qd + ATV 400 mg qd. Insufficient data
Fosamprenavir (FOS-APV, Lexiva)						↓ serum conc. both drugs; do not co-administer	200 mg RTV qd + FOS-APV 1400 mg qd	
Indinavir (IDV, Crixivan)	Levels: APV AUC↑ 33%. Doses: not established	Do not co-administer; risk of additive ↑ in indirect bilirubin			IDV AUC↑; IDV dose 600 mg bid	↑ IDV & NFV levels. Dose: IDV 1200 mg bid; NFV 1250 mg bid	Dose: IDV/RTV bid as 800/100 or 800/200 mg	SQV levels ↑ 4–7 fold. Dose: Insufficient data
Lopinavir/Ritonavir (LP/R, Kaletra)	Dose: APV 750 mg either standard or ↑ to 533/133 mg bid			IDV AUC↑; IDV dose 600 mg bid		LP levels ↓; NFV levels ↑. Dose: No data	LP is co-formulated with RTV	SQV levels ↑ 4–7 fold. Dose: SQV (Fortovase) 1000 mg bid; LP/R standard
Nelfinavir (NFV, Viracept)	Levels: APV AUC↑ 1.5X. Doses: Inadequate data		↓ serum conc. both drugs; do not co-administer	↑ IDV & NFV levels. Dose: IDV 1200 mg bid; NFV 1250 mg bid	LP levels ↓; NFV levels ↑. Dose: No data		Dose: RTV 400 mg bid + NFV 500–750 mg bid	Dose: NFV 1000 mg bid + SQV softgel or Fortovase 1200 mg bid
Ritonavir (RTV, Norvir)	Dose: 600/100 mg APV/RTV bid or 1200/200 mg qd	ATV/RTV 300/100 mg qd	200 mg RTV qd + FOS-APV 1400 mg qd	Dose: IDV/RTV bid as 800/100 or 800/200 mg	LP is co-formulated with RTV	Dose: RTV 400 mg bid + NFV 500–750 mg bid		Dose: 1000 SQV softgel/100 RTV bid or 400/400 mg bid
Saquinavir (SQV, Fortovase/Invirase)	Levels: APV AUC↓ 32%. Doses: Insufficient data	SQV (Invirase) 1200 mg qd + ATV 400 mg qd. Insufficient data		SQV levels ↑ 4–7 fold. Dose: Insufficient data	SQV levels ↑ 4–7 fold. Dose: SQV (Fortovase) 1000 mg bid; LP/R standard	Dose: NFV 1000 mg bid + SQV softgel or Fortovase 1200 mg bid	Dose: 1000 SQV softgel/100 RTV bid or 400/400 mg bid	

TABLE 22C: DRUG-DRUG INTERACTIONS BETWEEN NON-NUCLEOSIDE REVERSE TRANSCRIPTASE INHIBITORS (NNRTIs) AND PROTEASE INHIBITORS
(Adapted from Guidelines for the Use of Antiretroviral Agents in HIV-Infected Adults & Adolescents; see *www.aidsinfo.nih.gov*)

NAME (Abbreviation, Trade Name)	Amprenavir (APV, Agenerase)	Atazanavir (ATV, Reyataz)	Fosamprenavir (FOS-APV, Lexiva)	Indinavir (IDV, Crixivan)	Lopinavir/Ritonavir (LP/R, Kaletra)	Nelfinavir (NFV, Viracept)	Ritonavir (RTV, Norvir)	Saquinavir—softgel (SQV, Fortovase)
Delavirdine (DLV, Rescriptor)	APV AUC↑ ↑30%, DLV AUC↓ 61%. Do not co-administer	No data	Co-administration not recommended	IDV levels↑ 40%. Dose: IDV 600 mg q8h; DLV standard	Expect LP levels to ↑. No dose data	NFV levels↑ 2X, DLV levels↓ 50%. Dose: No data	Levels of RTV↑ 70%. Dose: DLV standard; RTV no data	SQV levels ↑ 5X. Dose: SQV 800 mg tid; DLV standard
Efavirenz (EFZ, Sustiva)	APV AUC↓ 36%. Dose: ↑APV, add RTV 200 mg to standard APV	ATV AUC↓ 74%. Dose: EFZ standard; ATA/RTV 300/100 mg qd with food	FOS-APV levels↓. Dose: FOS-APV, EFZ standard; FOS-APV + RTV 300 mg qd or 700 mg FOS-APV + 100 mg RTV bid	IDV levels↓ 31%. Dose: IDV 1000 mg q8h; EFV standard	Level of LP↓ 40%. Dose: LP/R 533/133 mg bid; EFZ standard	NFV levels↑ 20%. Standard doses	Standard doses	SQV levels↓ 62%. Dose: SQV softgel 400 mg + RTV 400 mg both bid
Nevirapine (NVP, Viramune)	No data	No data	No data	IDV levels↓ 28%. Dose: IDV 1000 mg q8h or combine with RTV; NVP standard	LP levels↓ 53%. Dose: LP/R 533/133 mg bid; NVP standard	Standard doses	Standard doses	Dose: SQV softgel + RTV 400/400 mg both bid

¹ AUC = area under the curve

TABLE 23: LIST OF GENERIC AND COMMON TRADE NAMES

GENERIC NAME: TRADE NAMES	GENERIC NAME: TRADE NAMES	GENERIC NAME: TRADE NAMES
Abacavir: Ziagen	Drotrecogin alfa: Xigris	Nitazoxanide: Alinia
Acyclovir: Zovirax	Efavirenz: Sustiva	Nitrofurantoin: Macrobid, Macrodantin
Adefovir: Hepsera	Emtricitabine: Emtriva	Nystatin: Mycostatin
Albendazole: Albenza	Emtricitabine + tenofovir: Truvada	Ofloxacin: Floxin
Amantadine: Symmetrel	Enfuvirtide (T-20): Fuzeon	Oseltamivir: Tamiflu
Amikacin: Amikin	Ertapenem: Invanz	Oxacillin: Prostaphlin
Amoxicillin: Amoxil, Polymox	Erythromycin(s): Ilotycin	Palivizumab: Synagis
Amox./clav.: Augmentin, Augmentin ES-600, Augmentin XR	*Ethyl succinate:* Pediamycin *Glucoheptonate:* Erythrocin *Estolate:* Ilosone	Paromomycin: Humatin Pentamidine: NebuPent, Pentam 300
Amphotericin B: Fungizone	Erythro/sulfisoxazole: Pediazole	Piperacillin: Pipracil
Ampho B-liposomal: AmBisome	Ethambutol: Myambutol	Piperacillin/tazobactam: Zosyn
Ampho B-cholesteryl complex: Amphotec	Ethionamide: Trecator	Piperazine: Antepar
Ampho B-lipid complex: Abelcet	Famciclovir: Famvir	Podophyllotoxin: Condylox
Ampicillin: Omnipen, Polycillin	Fluconazole: Diflucan	Praziquantel: Biltricide
Ampicillin/sulbactam: Unasyn	Flucytosine: Ancobon	Primaquine: Primachine
Amprenavir: Agenerase	Fosamprenavir: Lexiva	Proguanil: Paludrine
Atazanavir: Reyataz	Foscarnet: Foscavir	Pyrantel pamoate: Antiminth
Atovaquone: Mepron	Fosfomycin: Monurol	Pyrimethamine: Daraprim
Atovaquone + proguanil: Malarone	Furazolidone: Furoxone	Pyrimethamine/sulfadoxine: Fansidar
Azithromycin: Zithromax	Ganciclovir: Cytovene	Quinupristin/dalfopristin: Synercid
Aztreonam: Azactam	Gatifloxacin: Tequin	Ribavirin: Virazole, Rebetol
Caspofungin: Cancidas	Gemifloxacin: Factive	Rifabutin: Mycobutin
Cefaclor: Ceclor, Ceclor CD	Gentamicin: Garamycin	Rifampin: Rifadin, Rimactane
Cefadroxil: Duricef	Griseofulvin: Fulvicin	Rifapentine: Priftin
Cefazolin: Ancef, Kefzol	Halofantrine: Halfan	Rifaximin: Xifaxan
Cefdinir: Omnicef	Idoxuridine: Dendrid, Stoxil	Rimantadine: Flumadine
Cefditoren pivoxil: Spectracef	INH + RIF: Rifamate	Ritonavir: Norvir
Cefepime: Maxipime	INH + RIF + PZA: Rifater	Saquinavir: Invirase, Fortovase
Cefixime^{NUS}: Suprax	Interferon alfa: Roferon-A, Intron A	Spectinomycin: Trobicin
Cefotaxime: Claforan	Interferon, pegylated: PEG-Intron, Pegasys	Stavudine: Zerit Stibogluconate: Pentostam
Cefotetan: Cefotan	Interferon + ribavirin: Rebetron	Silver sulfadiazine: Silvadene
Cefoxitin: Mefoxin	Imipenem + cilastatin: Primaxin	Sulfamethoxazole: Gantanol
Cefpodoxime proxetil: Vantin	Imiquimod: Aldara	Sulfasalazine: Azulfidine
Cefprozil: Cefzil	Indinavir: Crixivan	Sulfisoxazole: Gantrisin
Ceftazidime: Fortaz, Tazicef, Tazidime	Itraconazole: Sporanox	Telithromycin: Ketek
Ceftibuten: Cedax	Iodoquinol: Yodoxin	Tenofovir: Viread
Ceftizoxime: Cefizox	Ivermectin: Stromectol	Terbinafine: Lamisil
Ceftriaxone: Rocephin	Kanamycin: Kantrex	Thalidomide: Thalomid
Cefuroxime: Zinacef, Kefurox, Ceftin	Ketoconazole: Nizoral	Thiabendazole: Mintezol
Cephalexin: Keflex	Lamivudine: Epivir, Epivir-HBV	Ticarcillin: Ticar
Cephradine: Anspor, Velosef	Lamivudine + abacavir: Epzicom	Tinidazole: Tindamax
Chloroquine: Aralen	Levofloxacin: Levaquin	Tipranavir: Texega
Cidofovir: Vistide	Linezolid: Zyvox	Tobramycin: Nebcin
Ciprofloxacin: Cipro, Cipro XR	Lomefloxacin: Maxaquin	Tretinoin: Retin A
Clarithromycin: Biaxin, Biaxin XL	Lopinavir/ritonavir: Kaletra	Trifluridine: Viroptic
Clindamycin: Cleocin	Loracarbef: Lorabid	Trimethoprim: Proloprim, Trimpex
Clofazimine: Lamprene	Mafenide: Sulfamylon	Trimethoprim/sulfamethoxazole: Bactrim, Septra
Clotrimazole: Lotrimin, Mycelex	Mebendazole: Vermox	Valacyclovir: Valtrex
Cloxacillin: Tegopen	Mefloquine: Lariam	Valganciclovir: Valcyte
Colistimethate: Coly-Mycin M	Meropenem: Merrem	Vancomycin: Vancocin
Cycloserine: Seromycin	Mesalamine: Asacol, Pentasa	Voriconazole: Vfend
Daptomycin: Cubicin	Methenamine: Hiprex, Mandelamine	Zalcitabine: HIVID
Delavirdine: Rescriptor	Metronidazole: Flagyl	Zanamivir: Relenza
Dicloxacillin: Dynapen	Minocycline: Minocin	Zidovudine (ZDV): Retrovir
Didanosine: Videx	Moxifloxacin: Avelox	Zidovudine + 3TC: Combivir
Diethylcarbamazine: Hetrazan	Mupirocin: Bactroban	Zidovudine + 3TC + abacavir: Trizivir
Diloxanide furoate: Furamide	Nafcillin: Unipen	
Dirithromycin: Dynabac	Nelfinavir: Viracept	
Doxycycline: Vibramycin	Nevirapine: Viramune	

TABLE 23 (2)
LIST OF COMMON TRADE AND GENERIC NAMES

TRADE NAME: GENERIC NAME	TRADE NAME: GENERIC NAME	TRADE NAME: GENERIC NAME
Abelcet: Ampho B-lipid complex	Gantrisin: Sulfisoxazole	Retin A: Tretinoin
Agenerase: Amprenavir	Garamycin: Gentamicin	Retrovir: Zidovudine (ZDV)
Albenza: Albendazole	Halfan: Halofantrine	Reyataz: Atazanavir
Aldara: Imiquimod	Hepsera: Adefovir	Rifadin: Rifampin
Alinia: Nitazoxanide	Herplex: Idoxuridine	Rifamate: INH + RIF
AmBisome: Ampho B-liposomal	Hiprex: Methenamine hippurate	Rifater: INH + RIF + PZA
Amikin: Amikacin	HIVID: Zalcitabine	Rimactane: Rifampin
Amoxil: Amoxicillin	Humatin: Paromomycin	Rocephin: Ceftriaxone
Amphotec: Ampho B-cholesteryl complex	Ilosone: Erythromycin estolate	Roferon-A: Interferon alfa
	Ilotycin: Erythromycin	Septra: Trimethoprim/sulfa
Ancef: Cefazolin	Intron A: Interferon alfa	Seromycin: Cycloserine
Ancobon: Flucytosine	Invanz: Ertapenem	Silvadene: Silver sulfadiazine
Anspor: Cephradine	Invirase: Saquinavir	Spectracef: Cefditoren pivoxil
Antepar: Piperazine	Kantrex: Kanamycin	Sporanox: Itraconazole
Antiminth: Pyrantel pamoate	Kaletra: Lopinavir/ritonavir	Stoxil: Idoxuridine
Aralen: Chloroquine	Keflex: Cephalexin	Stromectol: Ivermectin
Asacol: Mesalamine	Kefurox: Cefuroxime	Sulfamylon: Mafenide
Augmentin, Augmentin ES-600	Ketek: Telithromycin	Suprax: Cefixime[NUS]
Augmentin XR: Amox./clav.	Lamisil: Terbinafine	Sustiva: Efavirenz
Avelox: Moxifloxacin	Lamprene: Clofazimine	Symmetrel: Amantadine
Azactam: Aztreonam	Lariam: Mefloquine	Synagis: Palivizumab
Azulfidine: Sulfasalazine	Levaquin: Levofloxacin	Synercid: Quinupristin/dalfopristin
Bactroban: Mupirocin	Lexiva: Fosamprenavir	Tamiflu: Oseltamivir
Bactrim: Trimethoprim/ sulfamethoxazole	Lorabid: Loracarbef	Tazicef: Ceftazidime
	Macrodantin, Macrobid: Nitrofurantoin	Tegopen: Cloxacillin
Biaxin, Biaxin XL: Clarithromycin	Malarone: Atovaquone + proguanil	Tequin: Gatifloxacin
Biltricide: Praziquantel	Mandelamine: Methenamine mandel.	Texega: Tipranavir
Cancidas: Caspofungin	Maxaquin: Lomefloxacin	Thalomid: Thalidomide
Ceclor, Ceclor CD: Cefaclor	Maxipime: Cefepime	Ticar: Ticarcillin
Cedax: Ceftibuten	Mefoxin: Cefoxitin	Timentin: Ticarcillin-clavulanic acid
Cefizox: Ceftizoxime	Mepron: Atovaquone	Tinactin: Tolnaftate
Cefotan: Cefotetan	Merrem: Meropenem	Tindamax: Tinidazole
Ceftin: Cefuroxime axetil	Minocin: Minocycline	Trecator SC: Ethionamide
Cefzil: Cefprozil	Mintezol: Thiabendazole	Trizivir: Abacavir + ZDV + 3TC
Cipro, Cipro XR: Ciprofloxacin & extended release	Monocid: Cefonicid	Trobicin: Spectinomycin
	Monurol: Fosfomycin	Truvada: Emtricitabine + tenofovir
Claforan: Cefotaxime	Myambutol: Ethambutol	Unasyn: Ampicillin/sulbactam
Coly-Mycin M: Colistimethate	Mycobutin: Rifabutin	Unipen: Nafcillin
Combivir: ZDV + 3TC	Mycostatin: Nystatin	Valcyte: Valganciclovir
Crixivan: Indinavir	Nafcil: Nafcillin	Valtrex: Valacyclovir
Cubicin: Daptomycin	Nebcin: Tobramycin	Vancocin: Vancomycin
Cytovene: Ganciclovir	NebuPent: Pentamidine	Vantin: Cefpodoxime proxetil
Daraprim: Pyrimethamine	Nizoral: Ketoconazole	Velosef: Cephradine
Diflucan: Fluconazole	Norvir: Ritonavir	Vermox: Mebendazole
Duricef: Cefadroxil	Omnicef: Cefdinir	Vfend: Voriconazole
Dynapen: Dicloxacillin	Omnipen: Ampicillin	Vibramycin: Doxycycline
Emtriva: Emtricitabine	Pediamycin: Erythro. ethyl succinate	Videx: Didanosine
Epivir, Epivir-HBV: Lamivudine	Pediazole: Erythro. ethyl succinate + sulfisoxazole	Viracept: Nelfinavir
Epzicom: Lamivudine + abacavir		Viramune: Nevirapine
Factive: Gemifloxacin	Pegasys, PEG-Intron: Interferon, pegylated	Virazole: Ribavirin
Famvir: Famciclovir		Viread: Tenofovir
Fansidar: Pyrimethamine + sulfadoxine	Pentam 300: Pentamidine	Vistide: Cidofovir
	Pentasa: Mesalamine	Xifaxan: Rifaximin
Flagyl: Metronidazole	Pipracil: Piperacillin	Xigris: Drotrecogin alfa
Floxin: Ofloxacin	Polycillin: Ampicillin	Yodoxin: Iodoquinol
Flumadine: Rimantadine	Polymox: Amoxicillin	Zerit: Stavudine
Fortaz: Ceftazidime	Priftin: Rifapentine	Ziagen: Abacavir
Fortovase: Saquinavir	Primaxin: Imipenem + cilastatin	Zinacef: Cefuroxime
Fulvicin: Griseofulvin	Proloprim: Trimethoprim	Zithromax: Azithromycin
Fungizone: Amphotericin B	Prostaphlin: Oxacillin	Zovirax: Acyclovir
Furadantin: Nitrofurantoin	Rebetol: Ribavirin	Zosyn: Piperacillin/tazobactam
Furoxone: Furazolidone	Rebetron: Interferon + ribavirin	Zyvox: Linezolid
Fuzeon: Enfuvirtide (T-20)	Relenza: Zanamivir	
Gantanol: Sulfamethoxazole	Rescriptor: Delavirdine	

INDEX TO MAJOR ENTITIES